Wilbur Smith was born in Central Africa in 1933. He was educated at Michaelhouse and Rhodes University. He became a full-time writer in 1964 after the successful publication of *When the Lion Feeds*, and has since written over thirty novels, all meticulously researched on his numerous expeditions worldwide. His books are now translated into twenty-six languages. *Warlock* is the third of his four Egyptian novels.

Find out more about Wilbur Smith by
looking at his own author website,
www.wilbursmithbooks.com

'This is a stirring tale, full of chariot battles . . . Smith has whipped up a heady brew'
Evening Standard

'Smith brings to life every colourful detail in the world of Egypt so much so you can almost feel the heat and taste the dust as the narrative builds to a cracking pace . . . [*Warlock*] is a ripping yarn and a classic adventure story'
Irish News

THE NOVELS OF WILBUR SMITH

The Courtneys

When the Lion Feeds The Sound of Thunder

A Sparrow Falls Birds of Prey Monsoon

Blue Horizon The Triumph of the Sun

The Courtneys of Africa

The Burning Shore Power of the Sword Rage

A Time to Die Golden Fox Assegai

The Ballantyne Novels

A Falcon Flies Men of Men The Angels Weep

The Leopard Hunts in Darkness

The Egyptian Novels

River God The Seventh Scroll Warlock

The Quest

Also

The Dark of the Sun Shout at the Devil

Gold Mine The Diamond Hunters

The Sunbird Eagle in the Sky

The Eye of the Tiger Cry Wolf

Hungry as the Sea Wild Justice

Elephant Song Those in Peril

WILBUR SMITH

WARLOCK

PAN BOOKS

First published 2001 by Macmillan

This edition published 2011 by Pan Books
an imprint of Pan Macmillan, a division of Macmillan Publishers Limited
Pan Macmillan, 20 New Wharf Road, London N1 9RR
Basingstoke and Oxford
Associated companies throughout the world
www.panmacmillan.com

ISBN 978-1-447-20160-1

1 3 5 7 9 8 6 4 2

A CIP catalogue record for this book is available from
the British Library.

Typeset by SetSystems Ltd, Saffron Walden, Essex
Printed in the UK by CPI Mackays, Chatham ME5 8TD

For my new love

MOKHINISO

Spirits of Genghis Khan and Omar Khayyam

reincarnated in a moon as lucent as

a perfect pearl

Like an uncoiling serpent, a line of fighting chariots wound swiftly down the gut of the valley. From where he clung to the dashboard of the leading chariot the boy looked up at the cliffs that hemmed them in. The sheer rock was pierced by the openings to the tombs of the old people that honeycombed the cliff. The dark pits stared down at him like the implacable eyes of a legion of *djinn*. Prince Nefer Memnon shuddered and looked away, furtively making the sign to avert evil with his left hand.

Over his shoulder he glanced back down the column and saw that from the following chariot Taita was watching him through the swirling clouds of dust. The dust had coated the old man and his vehicle with a pale film, and a single shaft of sunlight that penetrated to the depths of this deep valley glittered on the mica particles so that he seemed to glow like the incarnation of one of the gods. Nefer ducked his head guiltily, ashamed that the old man had witnessed his fleeting superstitious dread. No royal prince of the House of Tamose should show such weakness, not now when he stood at the gateway to manhood. But, then, Taita knew him as no other did, for he had been Nefer's tutor since infancy, closer to him than his own parents or siblings. Taita's expression never changed but even at that distance his ancient eyes seemed to bore into the core of Nefer's being. Seeing all, understanding all.

Nefer turned back and drew himself up to his full height beside his father, who flipped the reins and urged the horses on with a crack of the long whip. Ahead of them the valley opened abruptly into the great amphitheatre that contained the stark and tumbled ruins of the city of Gallala. Nefer thrilled to his first sight of this famous battlefield. As a young man Taita himself had fought on this site when the demigod Tanus, Lord Harrab, had destroyed the dark forces that were threatening this very Egypt. That had been over sixty years ago but Taita had related to him every detail of the fight, and so vivid was his storytelling that Nefer felt as if he had been there on that fateful day.

Nefer's father, the god and Pharaoh Tamose, wheeled the chariot up to the tumbled stones of the ruined gateway, and reined in the horses. Behind them a hundred chariots in succession neatly executed the same manoeuvre, and the charioteers swarmed down from the footplates to begin watering the horses. When Pharaoh opened his mouth to speak the coated dust crumbled from his cheeks and dribbled down his chest.

'My lord!' Pharaoh hailed the Great Lion of Egypt, Lord Naja, his army commander and beloved companion. 'We must be away again before the sun touches the hilltops. I wish to make a night run through the dunes to El Gabar.'

The blue war crown on Tamose's head gleamed with mica dust, and his eyes were bloodshot with tiny lumps of tear-wet mud in the corners as he glanced down at Nefer. 'This is where I will leave you to go on with Taita.'

Although he knew that it was futile to protest, Nefer opened his mouth to do so. The squadron was going in against the enemy. Pharaoh Tamose's battle plan was to circle south through the Great Dunes and weave a way between the bitter natron lakes to take the enemy in his rear and rip an opening in his centre through which the Egyptian legions, massed and waiting on the Nile bank before Abnub, could pour. Tamose would combine the two forces and before the enemy could rally, drive on past Tell el-Daba and seize the enemy citadel of Avaris.

It was a bold and brilliant plan which, if it succeeded, would bring to a close, at one stroke, the war with the Hyksos that had already raged through two lifetimes. Nefer had been taught that battle and glory were the reasons for his existence on this earth. But, even at the advanced age of fourteen years, they had so far eluded him. He longed with all his soul to ride to victory and immortality at his father's side.

Before his protest could pass his lips, Pharaoh forestalled him. 'What is the first duty of a warrior?' he demanded of the boy.

Nefer dropped his eyes. 'It is obedience, Majesty,' he replied softly, reluctantly.

'Never forget it.' Pharaoh nodded and turned away.

Nefer felt himself spurned and discarded. His eyes smarted and his upper lip quivered, but Taita's gaze stiffened him. He blinked to clear his vision of tears, and took a pull from the waterskin that hung on the side rail of the chariot before turning to the old Magus with a jaunty toss of his thick dust-caked curls. 'Show me the monument, Tata,' he commanded.

The ill-assorted pair made their way through the concourse of chariots, men and horses that choked the narrow street of the ruined city. Stripped naked in the heat, twenty troopers had climbed down the deep shafts to the ancient wells, and formed a bucket chain to bring the sparse, bitter water to the surface. Once those wells had been bountiful enough to support a rich and populous city that sat full upon the trade route between the Nile and the Red Sea. Then, centuries ago, an earthquake had shattered the water-bearing stratum and blocked the subterranean flow. The city of Gallala had died of thirst. Now there was scarcely sufficient water to slake the thirst of two hundred horses and top up the waterskins before the wells were dry.

Taita led Nefer through the narrow lanes, past temples and palaces now inhabited only by the lizard and the scorpion, until they reached the deserted central square. In its centre stood the monument to Lord Tanus and his triumph over the armies of bandits who had almost choked the life out of the richest and most powerful nation on earth. The monument was a bizarre pyramid of human skulls, cemented together and protected by a shrine made of red rock slabs. A thousand and more skulls grinned down upon the boy as he read aloud the inscription on the stone portico: 'Our severed heads bear witness to the battle at this place in which we died beneath the sword of Tanus Lord Harrab. May all the generations that follow learn from that mighty lord's deeds the glory of the gods and the power of righteous men. Thus decreed in the fourteenth year of the reign of the God Pharaoh Mamose.'

Squatting in the monument's shadow Taita watched the Prince as he walked around the monument, pausing every few paces with hands on hips to study it from every angle. Although Taita's expression was remote his eyes were fond. His love for the lad had its origins in two other lives. The first of these was Lostris, Queen of Egypt. Taita was a eunuch, but he had been gelded after puberty and had once loved a woman. Because of his physical mutilation Taita's love was pure, and he had lavished it all on Queen Lostris, Nefer's grandmother. It was a love so encompassing that even now, twenty years after her death, it stood at the centre of his existence.

The other person from whom his love for Nefer sprang was Tanus, Lord Harrab, to whom this monument had been erected. He had been dearer than a brother to Taita. They were both gone now, Lostris and Tanus, but their blood mingled strongly in this child's veins. From their illicit union so long ago had sprung the child who had grown up to become the Pharaoh Tamose, who now led the squadron of chariots that had brought them here; the father of Prince Nefer.

'Tata, show me where it was that you captured the leader of the robber barons.' Nefer's voice cracked with excitement and the onset of puberty. 'Was it here?' He ran to the broken-down wall at the south side of the square. 'Tell me the story again.'

'No, it was here. This side,' Taita told him, stood up and strode on those long, stork-thin legs to the eastern wall. He looked up to the crumbling summit. 'The ruffian's name was Shufti, and he was one-eyed and ugly as the god Seth. He was trying to escape from the battle by climbing over the wall up there.' Taita stooped and picked up half of a baked-mud brick from the rubble and suddenly hurled it upwards. It sailed over the top of the high wall. 'I cracked his skull and brought him down with a single throw.'

Even though Nefer knew, at first hand, the old man's strength, and that his powers of endurance were legend, he was astonished by that throw. He is old as the mountains, older than my grandmother, for he nursed her as he has done me, Nefer marvelled. Men say he has witnessed two hundred inundations of the Nile and that he built the pyramids with his own hands. Then aloud he asked, 'Did you hack off his head, Tata, and place it on that pile there?' He pointed at the grisly monument.

'You know the story well enough, for I have told it to you a hundred times.' Taita feigned modest reluctance to extol his own deeds.

'Tell me again!' Nefer ordered.

Taita sat down on a stone block while Nefer settled at his feet in happy anticipation and listened avidly, until the rams' horns of the squadron sounded the recall with a blast that shattered into diminishing echoes along the black cliffs. 'Pharaoh summons us,' Taita said, and stood up to lead the way back through the gate.

There was a great bustle and scurry outside the walls, as the squadron made ready to go on into the dune lands. The waterskins were bulging again and the troopers were checking and tightening the harness of their teams before mounting up.

Pharaoh Tamose looked over the heads of his staff as the pair came through the gateway, and summoned Taita to his side with an inclination of his head. Together they walked out of earshot of the squadron officers. Lord Naja made as if to join them. Taita whispered a word to Pharaoh, then Tamose turned and sent Naja back with a curt word. The injured lord, flushed with mortification, shot a look at Taita that was fierce and sharp as a war arrow.

'You have offended Naja. Some day I might not be at hand to protect you,' Pharaoh warned.

'We dare trust no man,' Taita demurred. 'Not until we crush the head of the serpent of treachery that tightens its coils around the pillars of your palace. Until you return from this campaign in the north only the two of us must know where I am taking the Prince.'

'But Naja!' Pharaoh laughed dismissively. Naja was like a brother. They had run the Red Road together.

'Even Naja.' Taita said no more. His suspicions were at last hardening into certainty, but he had not yet gathered all the evidence he would need to convince Pharaoh.

'Does the Prince know why you are going into the fastness of the desert?' Pharaoh asked.

'He knows only that we are going to further his instruction in the mysteries, and to capture his godbird.'

'Good, Taita.' Pharaoh nodded. 'You were ever secretive but true. There is nothing more to say, for we have said it all. Now go, and may Horus spread his wings over you and Nefer.'

'Look to your own back, Majesty, for in these days enemies are standing behind you as well as to your front.'

Pharaoh grasped the Magus' upper arm and squeezed hard. Under his fingers the arm was thin but hard as a dried acacia branch. Then he went back to where Nefer waited beside the wheel of the royal chariot, with the injured air of a puppy ordered back to its kennel.

'Divine Majesty, there are younger men than me in the

squadron.' The Prince made one last despairing effort to persuade his father that he should ride with the chariots. Pharaoh knew that the boy was right, of course. Meren, the grandson of the illustrious General Kratas, was his junior by three days and today was riding with his father as lance-bearer in one of the rear chariots. 'When will you allow me to ride into battle with you, Father?'

'Perhaps when you have run the Red Road. Then not even I will gainsay you.'

It was a hollow promise, and they both knew it. Running the Red Road was the onerous test of horsemanship and weapons that few warriors attempted. It was an ordeal that drained, exhausted and often killed even a strong man in his prime and trained to near perfection. Nefer was a long way from that day.

Then Pharaoh's forbidding expression softened and he gripped his son's arm in the only show of affection he would allow himself before his troops. 'Now it is my command that you go with Taita into the desert to capture your god-bird, and thus to prove your royal blood and your right one day to wear the double crown.'

Nefer and the old man stood together beside the shattered walls of Gallala and watched the column fly past. Pharaoh led it, the reins wrapped around his wrists, leaning back against the pull of the horses, his chest bare, linen skirts whipping around his muscular legs, the blue war crown on his head rendering him tall and godlike.

Next came Lord Naja, almost as tall, almost as handsome. His mien was haughty and proud, the great recurved bow slung over his shoulder. Naja was one of the mightiest warriors of this very Egypt and his name had been given to him as a title of honour: Naja was the sacred cobra in the

royal *uraeus* crown. Pharaoh Tamose had bestowed it upon him on the day that, together, they had won through the ordeal of the Red Road.

Naja did not deign to glance in Nefer's direction. Pharaoh's chariot had plunged into the mouth of the dark gorge before the last vehicle in the column went racing past where Nefer stood. Meren, his friend and companion of many illicit boyhood adventures, laughed in his face and made an obscene gesture, then raised his voice mockingly above the whine and rattle of the wheels. 'I will bring you the head of Apepi as a toy,' he promised, and Nefer hated him as he sped away. Apepi was the King of the Hyksos, and Nefer needed no toys: he was a man now, even if his father refused to recognize it.

The two were silent for long after Meren's chariot had disappeared, and the dust had settled. Then Taita turned without a word and went to where their horses were tethered. He tightened the surcingle around his mount's chest, hiked up his kilts and swung up with the limber movement of a much younger man. Once astride the animal's bare back he seemed to become one with it. Nefer remembered that legend related he had been the very first Egyptian to master the equestrian arts. He still bore the title Master of Ten Thousand Chariots, bestowed upon him with the Gold of Praise by two pharaohs in their separate reigns.

Certain it was that he was one of the few men who dared to ride astride. Most Egyptians abhorred this practice, considering it somehow obscene and undignified, not to mention risky. Nefer had no such qualms and as he vaulted up on to the back of his favourite colt, Stargazer, his black mood started to evaporate. By the time they had reached the crest of the hills above the ruined city he was almost his usual ebullient self. He cast one last longing glance at the feather of distant dust left on the northern horizon by the squadron then firmly turned his back upon it. 'Where

are we going, Tata?' he demanded. 'You promised to tell me once we were on the road.'

Taita was always reticent and secretive, but seldom to the degree that he had been over the matter of their ultimate destination on this journey. 'We are going to Gebel Nagara,' Taita told him.

Nefer had never heard the name before, but he repeated it softly. It had a romantic, evocative ring. Excitement and anticipation made the back of his neck prickle, and he looked ahead into the great desert. An infinity of jagged and bitter hills stretched away to a horizon blue with heat-haze and distance. The colours of the raw rocks astounded the eye: they were the sullen blue of stormclouds, yellow as a weaver bird's plumage, or red as wounded flesh, and bright as crystal. The heat made them dance and quiver.

Taita looked down on this terrible place with a sense of nostalgia and homecoming. It was into this wilderness that he had retired after the death of his beloved Queen Lostris, at first creeping away like a wounded animal. Then, as the years passed and some of the pain with them, he had found himself drawn once more to the mysteries and the way of the great god Horus. He had gone into the wilderness as a physician and a surgeon, as a master of the known sciences. Alone in the fastness of the desert he had discovered the key to gates and doorways of the mind and the spirit beyond which few men ever journey. He had gone in a man but had emerged as a familiar of the great god Horus and an adept of strange and arcane mysteries that few men even imagined.

Taita had only returned to the world of men when his Queen Lostris had visited him in a dream as he slept in his hermit's cave at Gebel Nagara. Once more she had been a fifteen-year-old maiden, fresh and nubile, a desert rose in its first bloom with the dew upon its petals. Even as he slept his heart had swollen with love and threatened to burst his chest asunder.

'Darling Taita,' Lostris had whispered, as she touched his cheek and stirred him awake, 'you were one of the only two men I have ever loved. Tanus is with me now, but before you can come to me also there is one more charge that I lay upon you. You never once failed me. I know that you will not fail me now, will you, Taita?'

'I am yours to command, mistress.' His voice echoed strangely in his ears.

'In Thebes, my city of a hundred gates, this night is born a child. He is the son of my own son. They will name this child Nefer, which means pure and perfect in body and spirit. My longing is that he carry my blood and the blood of Tanus to the throne of Upper Egypt. But great and diverse perils already gather around the babe. He cannot succeed without your help. Only you can protect and guide him. These years you have spent alone in the wilderness, the skills and knowledge you have acquired here were to that purpose alone. Go to Nefer. Go now swiftly and stay with him until your task is completed. Then come to me, darling Taita. I will be waiting for you and your poor mutilated manhood shall be restored to you. You will be whole and entire when next you stand by my side, your hand in my hand. Do not fail me, Taita.'

'Never!' Taita had cried in the dream. 'In your life I never failed you. I will not fail you now in death.'

'I know you will not.' Lostris smiled a sweet, haunting smile, and her image faded into the desert night. He woke, with his face wet with tears, and gathered up his few possessions. He paused at the cave entrance only to check his direction by the stars. Instinctively, he looked for the bright particular star of the goddess. On the seventieth day after the Queen's death, on the night that the long ritual of her embalmment had been completed, that star had appeared suddenly in the heavens, a great red star that glowed where none had been before. Taita picked it out and made obeisance to it. Then he strode away into the western desert, back towards the Nile and the city of Thebes, beautiful Thebes of a hundred gates.

That had been over fourteen years ago, and now he hungered for the silent places, for only here could his powers grow back to their full strength, so that he could carry through the charge that Lostris had laid upon him. Only here could he pass some of that strength on to the Prince. For he knew that the dark powers of which she had warned him were gathering around them.

'Come!' he said to the boy. 'Let us go down and take your godbird.'

On the third night after leaving Gallala, when the constellation of the Wild Asses made its zenith in the northern night sky, Pharaoh halted the squadron to water the horses and to eat a hasty meal of sun-dried meat, dates and cold *dhurra* millet cakes. Then he ordered the mount-up. There was no sounding of the ram's horn trumpet now for they were into the territory where often the patrolling Hyksosian chariots ranged.

The column started forward again at the trot. As they went on the landscape changed dramatically. They were out of the bad lands at last, back into the foothills above the river valley. Below them they could make out the strip of dense vegetation, distant and dark in the moonlight, that marked the course of great Mother Nile. They had completed the wide circuit around Abnub and were in the rear of the main Hyksosian army on the river. Although they were a tiny force to go in against such an enemy as Apepi, they were the best charioteers in the armies of Tamose, which made them the finest in the world. Moreover, they held the element of surprise.

When Pharaoh had first proposed this strategy and told them he would lead the expedition in person, his war council had opposed him with all the vehemence they could muster against the word of a god. Even old Kratas, once the most reckless and savage warrior in all the armies of Egypt, had torn at his thick white beard and bellowed, 'By Seth's ragged and festering foreskin, I did not change your shit-smeared swaddling sheet so that I could send you straight into the loving arms of Apepi.' He was perhaps the one man who might dare to speak to a god-king in this fashion. 'Send another to do such menial work. Lead the breakthrough column yourself if it amuses you, but do not disappear into the desert to be devoured by ghouls and *djinn*. You are Egypt. If Apepi takes you he takes us all.'

Of all the council only Naja had supported him, but Naja was always loyal and true. Now they had won through the desert, and were into the enemy rear. In tomorrow's dawn they would make the one desperate charge that would split Apepi's army, and allow five more of Pharaoh's squadrons, a thousand chariots, to come boiling through to join him. Already he had the melliferous taste of victory on his tongue. Before the next full moon he would dine in the halls of Apepi's palace in Avaris.

It was almost two centuries since the Upper and Lower Kingdoms of Egypt had been split apart. Since then either an Egyptian usurper or a foreigner invader had ruled in the northern kingdom. It was Tamose's destiny to drive out the Hyksos and unite the two lands once more. Only then could he wear the double crown with justification and the approval of all the ancient gods.

The night air blew in his face, cool enough to numb his cheeks, and his lance-bearer crouched low behind the dashboard to shield himself. The only sound was the crunch of the chariot wheels over the coarse gravel, the lances rattling softly in their scabbards, and the occasional low warning cry of 'Beware! Hole!' passed on down the column.

Suddenly the wide wadi of Gebel Wadun opened ahead

of him and Pharaoh Tamose reined down the team. The wadi was the smooth roadway that would lead them down on to the flat alluvial plain of the river. Pharaoh tossed the reins to his lance-bearer and vaulted down to earth. He stretched his stiff, aching limbs and, without turning, heard the sound of Naja's chariot come up behind him. A low command and the wheels crunched into silence, then Naja's light, firm footsteps came to his side. 'From here the danger of discovery will be stronger,' Naja said. 'Look down there.' He pointed with a long, muscular arm over Pharaoh's shoulder. Where the wadi debouched on to the plain below them a single light showed, the soft yellow glow of an oil lamp. 'That is the village of El Wadun. That is where our spies will be waiting to lead us through the Hyksosian pickets. I will go ahead to the rendezvous to make safe the way. Do you wait here, Majesty, and I will return directly.'

'I will go with you.'

'I beg you. There may be treachery, Mem.' He used the King's childhood name. 'You are Egypt. You are too precious to risk.'

Pharaoh turned to look into the beloved face, lean and handsome. Naja's teeth gleamed white in the starlight as he smiled, and Pharaoh touched his shoulder lightly but with trust and affection. 'Go swiftly, and return as swiftly,' he acceded.

Naja touched his own heart, and ran back to his chariot. He saluted again as he wheeled past where the King stood, and Tamose smiled as he returned the salute then watched him go down the side of the wadi. When he reached the flat hard sand of the dry riverbed, Naja whipped up the horses, and they sped down towards the village of El Wadun. The chariot left black-shaded wheel-tracks behind it on the silvery sands, before it disappeared beyond the first bend of the wadi. When it had gone Pharaoh walked back down the waiting column, speaking quietly to the troopers, calling many by name, laughing softly with them, encouraging and cheering them. Small wonder they loved him, and followed him so gladly wherever he led them.

Lord Naja drove warily, hugging the south bank of the dry riverbed. Every now and then he glanced upwards at the crest of the hills, until at last he recognized the tower of wind-blasted rock that leaned slightly askew against the skyline, and grunted with satisfaction. A little further on he reached the point where a faint footpath left the wadi bottom and wound up the steep slope to the foot of the ancient watchtower.

With a curt word to his lance-bearer he jumped down from the footplate, and adjusted the cavalry bow over his shoulder. Then he unslung the clay fire-pot from the rail of the chariot, and started up the pathway. It was so well disguised that if he had not memorized every turn and twist he would have lost his way a dozen times before he reached the top.

At last he stepped out on to the upper rampart of the tower. It had been built many centuries ago and was in ruinous condition. He did not approach the edge for there was a precipitous drop into the valley below. Instead he found the bundle of dry faggots hidden in the niche of the wall where he had left it and dragged it into the open. Quickly he built up a tiny pyramid of the kindling, then blew on the charcoal nuggets in the fire-pot, and when they glowed he crumbled a handful of dried grass on to them. They burst into flame and he lit the small signal beacon. He made no attempt to hide himself but stood out where a watcher below would see him illuminated on the height of the tower. The flames died away as the kindling was consumed. Naja sat down to wait in the darkness.

A short while later he heard a pebble rattle on the stony

path below the walls and he whistled sharply. His signal was returned, and he stood up. He loosened the bronze blade of his sickle sword in its scabbard and nocked an arrow in the bow, standing ready for an instant draw. Moments later a harsh voice called to him in the Hyksosian language. He replied fluently and naturally in the same tongue, and the footsteps of at least two men sounded on the stone ramp.

Not even Pharaoh knew that Naja's mother had been Hyksosian. In the decades of their occupation the invaders had adopted many of the Egyptian ways. With a dearth of their own women to choose from, many of the Hyksos had taken Egyptian wives, and over the generations the blood-lines had become blurred.

A tall man stepped out on to the rampart. He wore a skull-hugging basinet of bronze, and multicoloured ribbons were tied in his full beard. The Hyksos dearly loved bright colours.

He opened his arms. 'The blessing of Seueth on you, cousin,' he growled, as Naja stepped into his embrace.

'And may he smile on you also, Cousin Trok, but we have little time,' Naja warned him, and indicated the first light fingers of the dawn stroking the eastern heavens with a lover's touch.

'You are right, coz.' The Hyksosian general broke the embrace, and turned to take a linen-wrapped bundle from his lieutenant, who stood close behind him. He handed it to Naja, who unwrapped it as he kicked life back into the beacon fire. In the light of the flames he inspected the arrow quiver it contained. It was carved from a light tough wood and covered with finely tooled and stitched leather. The workmanship was superb. This was the accoutrement of a high-ranking officer. Naja twisted free the stopper and drew one of the arrows from the container. He examined it briefly, spinning the shaft between his fingers to check its balance and symmetry

The Hyksosian arrows were unmistakable. The fletching feathers were dyed with the bright colours of the archer's regiment and the shaft was branded with his personal signet. Even if the initial strike was not fatal, the flint arrowhead was barbed and bound to the shaft in such a way that if a surgeon attempted to draw the arrow from a victim's flesh, the head would detach from the shaft and remain deep in the wound channel, there to putrefy and cause a lingering, painful death. Flint was much harder than bronze, and would not bend nor flatten if it struck bone.

Naja slipped the arrow back into the quiver and replaced the stopper. He had not taken the chance of bringing such distinctive missiles with him in his chariot. If discovered in his kit by his groom or lance-bearer, its presence would be remembered, and difficult to explain away.

'There is much that we still should discuss.' Naja squatted down and gestured for Trok to do the same. They talked quietly until at last Naja rose. 'Enough! Now we both know what must be done. The time for action has at last arrived.'

'Let the gods smile upon our enterprise.' Trok and Naja embraced again, and then, without another word, Naja left him, ran lightly down the rampart of the tower and took the narrow path down the hill.

Before he reached the bottom he found a place to cache the quiver. It was a niche where the rock had been split open by the roots of a thorn tree. Over the quiver he placed a rock the size and roughly the shape of a horse's head. The twisted upper branches of the tree formed a distinctive cross against the night sky. He would recognize the place again without difficulty.

Then he went on down the path to where his chariot stood in the wadi bottom.

Pharaoh Tamose saw the chariot returning, and knew by the impetuous manner in which Naja drove that something untoward was afoot. Quietly he ordered the squadron to mount up and stand with drawn weapons, ready to meet any eventuality.

Naja's chariot rattled up the pathway from the wadi bottom. The moment it drew level with where Pharaoh waited he sprang down.

'What's amiss?' Tamose demanded.

'A blessing from the gods,' Naja told him, unable to stop his voice shaking with excitement. 'They have delivered Apepi defenceless into our power.'

'How is that possible?'

'My spies have led me to where the enemy king is encamped but a short distance from where we now stand. His tents are set up just beyond the first line of hills, yonder.' He pointed back with his drawn sword.

'Can you be certain it is Apepi?' Tamose could barely control his own excitement.

'I saw him clearly in the light of his campfire. Every detail of his features. His great beaked nose and beard shot with silver shining in the firelight. There is no mistaking such stature. He towers above all those around him, and wears the vulture crown on his head.'

'What is his strength?' Pharaoh demanded.

'With his usual arrogance he has a bodyguard of less than fifty. I have counted them, and half of them are asleep, their lances stacked. He suspects nothing and his watchfires burn bright. A swift charge out of the darkness and we will have him in our grasp.'

'Take me to where Apepi lies,' Pharaoh commanded, and leaped to the footplate.

Naja led them, and the soft silvery sands of the wadi

muffled the sounds of the wheels, so that in a ghostly silence the squadron swept around the last bend and Naja raised his clenched fist high to order the halt. Pharaoh drew up alongside him and leaned across.

'Where lies Apepi's camp?'

'Beyond the ridge. I left my spies overlooking it.' Naja pointed up the pathway towards the watchtower on the crest. 'On the far side is a hidden oasis. A sweet-water well and date palms. His tents are set among the trees.'

'We will take a small patrol with us to scout the camp. Only then can we plan our attack.'

Naja had anticipated the order, and with a few terse orders selected a scouting party of five troopers. Each one was bound to him by blood oath. They were his men, hand and heart.

'Muffle your scabbards,' Naja ordered. 'Make not a sound.' Then, with his recurved bow in his left hand, he stepped on to the pathway. Pharaoh came close behind him. They went upwards swiftly, until Naja saw the crossed branches of the thorn tree silhouetted against the dawn sky. He stopped abruptly, and held up his right hand for silence. He listened.

'What is it?' Pharaoh whispered close behind him.

'I thought I heard voices on the crest,' Naja answered, 'speaking the Hyksosian tongue. Wait here, Majesty, while I clear the path ahead.' Pharaoh and the five troopers sank down and squatted beside the path, while Naja went on stealthily. He stepped around a large boulder and his dim figure disappeared from view. The minutes passed slowly and Pharaoh began to fret. The dawn was coming on swiftly. The Hyksosian king would soon be breaking his camp, and moving on, out of their grasp. As a soft whistle came down to him he sprang to his feet eagerly. It was a skilful imitation of a nightingale's dawn call.

Pharaoh hefted his fabled blue sword. 'The way is clear,' he murmured, 'Come, follow me.'

They went on upwards, and Pharaoh reached the tall rock that blocked the pathway. He stepped round it then stopped abruptly. Lord Naja faced him at a distance of twenty paces. They were alone, hidden by the rock from the men who followed. Naja's bow was at full draw and the arrow was aimed at Pharaoh's naked chest. Even before he could move, the full realization of what confronted him blazed in Pharaoh's mind. This was the foul and loathsome thing that Taita, with his clairvoyant powers, had smelt in the air.

The light was strong enough for him to make out every detail of the enemy he had loved as a friend. The bowstring was pulled hard against Naja's lips, twisting them into a dreadful smile, and his eyes were honey gold and fierce as those of the hunting leopard as he glared at Pharaoh. The fletching of the arrow was crimson and yellow and green, and in the Hyksosian fashion the arrowhead was made from razor-sharp flint, designed to tear through the bronze of an enemy's helmet and cuirass.

'May you live for ever!' Silently Naja mouthed the words as though they were a curse, and he loosed the arrow. It flew from the bowstring with a twang and a hum. It seemed to come quite slowly, like some poisonous flying insect. The feathers spun the shaft, and it made one full revolution as it covered the twenty paces. Though Pharaoh's eyesight was sharpened and his other senses were heightened by the mortal danger in which he found himself, he could move only with the slowness of nightmare, too slowly to avoid the missile. The arrow took him high in the centre of his chest, where his royal heart pounded in its cage of ribs. It struck with the sound of a boulder dropped from a height into a bed of thick Nile mud, and half the length of the shaft was driven through his chest. He was spun round by the force of the impact, and thrown against the red rock of the boulder. For a moment he clung to the rough surface with his hooked fingers. The flint arrowhead had pierced him through and through. The blood-clotted barb stood out of the knotted muscles that ran down the right side of his spine.

The blue sword dropped from his fist, and a low cry burst from his open mouth, the sound muffled by a gout of his own bright lung blood. He began to slide down to his knees, his legs buckling under him, his fingernails leaving shallow scratches on the red rock.

Naja sprang forward with a wild cry, 'Ambush! Beware!' and he slipped one arm around Pharaoh's chest below the protruding arrow.

Supporting the dying king he bellowed again, 'On me, the guards!' and two stout troopers appeared almost instantly from around the rock wall, responding to his rallying cry. They saw at a glance how Pharaoh was struck and the bright bunch of feathers on the base of the arrow.

'Hyksos!' one yelled, as they snatched Pharaoh from Naja's grasp and dragged him back behind the shelter of the rock.

'Carry Pharaoh back to his chariot while I hold off the enemy,' Naja ordered, and whirled around, pulling another arrow from his quiver and loosing it up the path towards the deserted summit, bellowing a challenge, then answering himself with a muffled counter-challenge in the Hyksosian language.

He snatched up the blue sword from where Tamose had dropped it, bounded back down the path and caught up with the small party of charioteers who were carrying the king away, down to where the chariots were waiting in the wadi.

'It was a trap,' Naja told them urgently. 'The hilltop is alive with the enemy. We must get Pharaoh away to safety.' But he could see by the way the king's head rolled weakly on his shoulders that he was past any help, and Naja's chest swelled with triumph. The blue war crown toppled from Pharaoh's brow and bumped down the path. Naja gathered it up as he ran past, fighting down the temptation to place it on his own head.

'Patience. The time is not yet ripe for that,' he chided himself silently, 'but already Egypt is mine, and all her crowns and pomp and power. I am become this very Egypt. I am become part of the godhead.'

He held the heavy crown protectively under his arm, and aloud he cried, 'Hurry, the enemy is on the path hard behind us. Hurry! The king must not fall into their hands.'

The troops below had heard the wild cries in the dawn, and the regimental surgeon was waiting for them beside the wheel of Pharaoh's chariot. He had been trained by Taita, and though lacking the old man's special magic he was a skilled doctor and might be capable of staunching even such a terrible wound as had pierced Pharaoh's chest. But Lord Naja would not risk having his victim returned to him from the underworld. He ordered the surgeon away brusquely. 'The enemy is hard upon us. There is no time for your quackery now. We must get him back to the safety of our own lines before we are overrun.'

Tenderly he lifted the king from the arms of the men who carried him and laid him on the footplate of his own chariot. He snapped off the shaft of the arrow that protruded from the king's chest and held it aloft so that all his men could see it clearly. 'This bloody instrument has struck down our Pharaoh. Our god and our king. May Seth damn the Hyksosian pig-swine who fired it, and may he burn in eternal flame for a thousand years.' His men growled in warlike agreement. Carefully Naja wrapped the arrow in a linen cloth, and placed it in the bin on the side wall of the chariot. He would deliver it to the council in Thebes to substantiate his report on Pharaoh's death.

'A good man here to hold Pharaoh,' Naja ordered. 'Treat him gently.'

While the king's own lance-bearer came forward, Naja unbuckled the sword-belt from around Pharaoh's waist, sheathed the blue sword and carefully stowed it in his own weapons bin.

The lance-bearer jumped on to the footplate and cradled Tamose's head. Fresh bright blood bubbled from the corners of his mouth as the chariot wheeled in a circle then sped back up the dry wadi with the rest of the squadron driving hard to keep up with it. Even though he was supported by the strong arms of his lance-bearer Pharaoh's limp body was jolted cruelly.

Facing forward so that none could see his expression, Naja laughed softly. The sound was covered by the grinding wheels and the crash of the chassis over the small boulders he made no attempt to avoid. They left the wadi and raced on towards the dunes and the natron lakes.

It was mid-morning and the blinding white sun was halfway up the sky before Naja allowed the column to halt and the surgeon to come forward again to examine the king. It did not need his special skills to tell that Pharaoh's spirit had long before left his body and started on its journey to the underworld.

'Pharaoh is dead,' the surgeon said quietly, as he stood up with the royal blood coating his hands to the wrists. A terrible cry of mourning started at the head of the column and ran down its entire length. Naja let them play out their grief then sent for his troop captains.

'The state is without a head,' he told them. 'Egypt is in dire peril. Ten of the fastest chariots must take Pharaoh's body back to Thebes with all haste. I shall lead them for it may be that the council will wish me to take up the duties of regent to Prince Nefer.'

He had planted the first seeds and saw by their awed expressions that they had taken root almost immediately. He went on, with a grim, businesslike air that suited the tragic circumstances which had overtaken them, 'The surgeon must wrap the royal corpse before I take it home to the funeral temple. But in the meantime we must find

Prince Nefer. He must be informed of his father's death and of his own succession. This is the single most urgent matter of state, and of my regency.' He had assumed that title smoothly, and no man questioned him or even looked askance. He unrolled a papyrus scroll, a map of the territory from Thebes down to Memphis, and spread it on the dashboard of his chariot. He pored over it. 'You must split up into your troops and scour the countryside for the prince. I believe that Pharaoh sent him into the desert with the eunuch to undertake the rituals of manhood, so we will concentrate our search here, from Gallala where we last saw him towards the south and east.' With the eye for ground of a commander of armies Naja picked out the search area, and ordered a net of chariots to be spread out across the land to bring in the prince.

The squadron returned to Gallala with Lord Naja in the van. Next in line came the vehicle carrying the partially embalmed body of Pharaoh. On the shore of the natron lake Waifra, the surgeon, had laid out the royal corpse and made the traditional incision in his left side. Through this he had removed the viscera and internal organs. The contents of the stomach and intestines had been washed in the viscous salt water of the lake. Then all the organs were packed with the white crystals of evaporated natron from the lake edge and stored in pottery wine jars. The king's body cavity was packed with natron salts, then wrapped in linen bindings soaked with the harsh salt. When they reached Thebes he would be taken to his own funerary temple and handed over to the priests and embalmers for the ritual seventy days of preparation for burial. Naja grudged every minute spent upon the road, for he was in desperate haste to return to Thebes before the news of the King's death preceded him. Yet at the gates of the ruined city he took more precious time to instruct the troop captains who were to undertake the search for the prince.

'Sweep all the roads to the east. The eunuch is a wily old bird and will have covered his tracks, but smell him out,' he ordered them. 'There are villages at the oases of Satam and Lakara. Question the people. You may use the whip and the hot iron to make certain they hide nothing. Search all the secret places of the wilderness. Find the prince and the eunuch. Fail me not, at your peril.'

When at last the captains had refilled their waterskins and were ready to take their divisions out into the desert, he held them with a final order, and they knew from his voice and his ferocious yellow eyes that this was the most fateful order of all, and that to disobey would mean death. 'When you find Prince Nefer, bring him to me. Give him into no other hand but mine.'

There were Nubian scouts with the divisions, black slaves from the wild southlands highly skilled in the art of tracking down men and beasts. They trotted ahead of the chariots as they fanned out into the wilderness, and Lord Naja spent another few precious minutes watching them go. His jubilation was tempered with unease. He knew that the ancient eunuch, Taita, was an adept; that he possessed strange and wonderful powers. If there is one single man who can stop me now, it is he. I wish that I could run them down myself, the eunuch and the brat, rather than send underlings to pit themselves against the Warlock's wiles. But my destiny calls to me from Thebes and I dare not linger.

He ran back to his chariot and seized the reins. 'Onwards!' He gave the command to advance with a clenched fist. 'Onwards to Thebes!'

They drove the horses hard, so that when they raced down the escarpment of the eastern hills on to the wide alluvial plain of the river, the lather had dried white on their heaving flanks and their eyes were red and wild.

Naja had withdrawn a full legion of the Phat Guards from the army encamped before Abnub. He had explained to Pharaoh that these were the strategic reserves to throw into the gap and prevent a Hyksosian break-out should the offensive fail. However, the Phat Guard was his own special regiment. The commanders were oath-bound to him. Following his secret orders they had pulled back from Abnub, and were waiting for him now at the oasis of Boss, only two leagues from Thebes.

The guards' pickets saw the dust of the approaching chariots and stood to arms. The colonel, Asmor, and his officers were turned out in full armour to meet Lord Naja. The legion, under arms, was drawn up behind them.

'Lord Asmor!' Naja hailed him from the chariot. 'I have dreadful news to take to the council at Thebes. Pharaoh is killed by a Hyksosian arrow.'

'Lord Naja, I stand ready to carry out your orders.'

'Egypt is a child without a father.' Naja halted his chariot in front of the ranks of plumed and glittering warriors. Now he raised his voice so it carried clearly to the rear ranks. 'Prince Nefer is a child still, and not yet ready to rule. Egypt stands in desperate need of a regent to lead her, lest the Hyksos take advantage of our disarray.' He paused and stared significantly at Colonel Asmor. Asmor lifted his chin slightly in acknowledgement of the trust that Naja had placed in him. He had been promised rewards greater than any he had ever dreamed of.

Naja raised his voice to a bellow: 'If Pharaoh falls in battle, the army has the right by acclamation to appoint a regent in the field.' He fell silent and stood with one fist clenched on his breast and the lance in his other hand.

Asmor took a pace forward and turned to face the ranks of heavily armed guards. With a theatrical gesture he removed his helmet. His face was dark and hard. A pale scar from a sword slash twisted his nose to one side, and his shaven pate was covered by a plaited horsehair wig. He pointed his drawn sword to the sky, and he shouted, in a voice that had been trained to carry over the din of battle, 'Lord Naja! Hail to the Regent of Egypt! Hail to Lord Naja!'

There was a long moment of stunned silence before the legion erupted in a roar, like a pride of hunting lions, 'Hail to Lord Naja, Regent of Egypt.'

The cheering and the uproar lasted until Lord Naja raised his fist again, and in the silence that followed he spoke clearly: 'You do me great honour! I accept the charge you place upon me.'

'*Bak-her!*' they shouted, and beat upon their shields with sword and lance until the echoes broke like distant thunder on the hills of the escarpment.

In the uproar Naja summoned Asmor to him. 'Place pickets on all the roads. No man leaves this place until I do. No word of this must reach Thebes ahead of me.'

The journey from Gallala had taken three days of hard riding. The horses were worn out, and even Naja was exhausted. Yet he allowed himself only an hour to rest, bathe away the dust of the journey and change his apparel. Then, with his jaw shaven, his hair oiled and combed, he mounted the ceremonial chariot that Asmor had ready and waiting at the entrance to the tent. The gold leaf that decorated the dashboard shone in the sunlight.

Naja wore a white linen skirt, with a pectoral plate of gold and semi-precious stones covering his bare muscled chest. On his hip he carried the fabulous blue sword in its golden scabbard that he had taken from Pharaoh's dead body. The blade was beaten from some marvellous metal, heavier, harder and sharper than any bronze. There was none other like it in all Egypt. It had once belonged to Tanus, Lord Harrab, and had come to Pharaoh by his bequest.

The most significant of all his accoutrements, however, was the least eye-catching. On his right arm, held in place by a plain band of gold above the elbow, was the blue hawk seal. Like the sword Naja had taken it from Tamose's royal corpse. As Regent of Egypt, Naja was now entitled to wear this potent badge of imperial power.

His bodyguard formed up around him, and the full legion fell in behind him. With five thousand men at his back the new Regent of Egypt began his march on Thebes.

Asmor rode as his lance-bearer. He was young for the command of a full legion, but he had proved himself in battle against the Hyksos, and he was Naja's close companion. He, too, had Hyksosian blood in his veins. Once, Asmor had thought the command of a legion was the summit of his ambition, but now he had scaled the foothills and suddenly before him rose the glorious alps of exalted office, of power unfettered, and – dare he even think it? – elevation to the highest ranks of the nobility. There was nothing he would not do, no act so reckless or base that he would not undertake it willingly to hasten his patron Lord Naja's ascension to the throne of Egypt.

'What stands before us now, my old comrade?' It seemed that Naja had read his thought, for the question was so appropriate.

'The Yellow Flowers have cleared all but one of the princes of the House of Tamose from your path,' Asmor answered, and pointed with his lance across the grey silt-laden waters of the Nile to the far hills in the west. 'They lie there in their tombs in the Valley of the Nobles.'

Three years previously the plague of the Yellow Flowers had swept through the two kingdoms. The disease was named for the dreadful yellow lesions that covered the faces and bodies of the stricken before they succumbed to the pox's burning fevers. It was no respecter of persons, choosing its victims from every station and level of society, sparing neither Egyptian nor Hyksos, man nor woman nor child, neither peasant nor prince, it had mown them down like fields of *dhurra* millet before the sickle.

Eight princesses and six princes of the House of Tamose had died. Of all Pharaoh's children, only two girls and Prince Nefer Memnon had survived. It was as though the gods had set out deliberately to clear the path to the throne of Egypt for Lord Naja.

There were those who vowed that Nefer and his sisters would have died also, had not the ancient Magus Taita wrought his magic to save them. The three children still bore the tiny scars on their left upper arms where he had cut them and placed in their blood his magical charm against the Yellow Flowers.

Naja frowned. Even in this moment of his triumph he could still give thought to the strange powers possessed by the Magus. No man could deny that he had found the secret of life. He had already lived so long that no one knew his age; some said a hundred years and others two hundred. Yet he still walked and ran and drove a chariot like a man in his prime. No man could better him in debate, none could surpass him in learning. Surely the gods loved him, and had bestowed upon him the secret of life eternal.

Once he was Pharaoh, that would be the only thing that Naja lacked. Could he wring the secret out of Taita the Warlock? First, he must be captured and brought in along with Prince Nefer, but he must not be harmed. He was far too valuable. The chariots Naja had sent to scour the eastern deserts would bring him back a throne in the form of Prince Nefer, and life eternal in the human guise of the eunuch, Taita.

Asmor interrupted his thoughts: 'We of the loyal Phat

Guard are the only troops south of Abnub. The rest of the army is deployed against the Hyksos in the north. Thebes is defended by a handful of boys, cripples and old men. Nothing stands in your way, Regent.'

Any fears that the legion under arms would be denied entrance to the city proved baseless. The main gates were thrown open as soon as the sentries recognized the blue standard, and the citizens ran out to meet them. They carried palm fronds and garlands of water-lilies, for a rumour had swept through the city that Lord Naja brought tidings of a mighty victory over Apepi of the Hyksos.

But the welcoming cries and laughter soon gave way to wild ululations of mourning when they saw the swaddled royal corpse on the floorboards of the second chariot and heard the cries of the leading charioteers: 'Pharaoh is dead! He has been slain by the Hyksos. May he live for ever.'

The wailing crowds followed the chariot that carried the royal corpse to the funerary temple, clogging the streets, and in the confusion no one seemed to notice that divisions of Asmor's men had taken over from the guards at the main gates, and had swiftly set up pickets at every corner and in every square.

The chariot bearing Tamose's corpse had drawn the crowds along with it. The rest of the usually swarming city was almost deserted, and Naja galloped his chariot team swiftly through the narrow crooked streets to the river palace. He knew that every member of the council would hurry to the assembly chamber as soon as they heard the dreadful news. They left the chariots at the entrance to the gardens, and Asmor and fifty men of the bodyguard formed up around Naja. They marched in close order through the inner courtyard, past the ponds of the water garden filled with hyacinth and fish from the river, which shone like jewels below the surface of the limpid pools.

The arrival of such a band of armed men took the council unawares. The doors to the chamber were unguarded, and only four members were already assembled. Naja paused in the doorway and looked them over swiftly. Menset and Talla were old and past their once formidable powers; Cinka had always been weak and vacillating. There was only one man of force in the chamber with whom he had to reckon.

Kratas was older than any of them, but in the way that a volcano is old. His robes were in disarray – clearly he had come directly from his pallet, but not from sleep. They said that he was still able to keep his two young wives and all of his five concubines in play, which Naja did not doubt, for the tales of his feats with arms and amours were legion. The fresh, damp stains on his white linen kilt and the sweet natural perfume of female concupiscence that enveloped him were apparent even from where Naja stood. The scars on his arms and bare chest were testimony to a hundred battles fought and won over the years. The old man no longer deigned to wear the numerous chains of the Gold of Valour and the Gold of Praise to which he was entitled – in any case, such a mass of the precious metal would have weighed down an ox.

'Noble lords!' Naja greeted the members of the council. 'I come to bring you dire tidings.' He strode down into the chamber and Menset and Talla shrank away, staring at him like two rabbits watching the sinuous approach of the cobra. 'Pharaoh is dead. He was cut down by a Hyksosian arrow while storming the enemy stronghold above El Wadun.'

The council members gawked at him in silence, all except Kratas. He was the first to recover from the shock of that news. His sorrow was matched only by his anger. He rose ponderously to his feet, and glowered at Naja and his bodyguard, like an old bull buffalo surprised in his wallow by a pride of half-grown lion cubs. 'By what excess of treasonable impudence do you wear the hawk seal upon your arm? Naja, son of Timlat out of the belly of a Hyksosian slut, you are not fit to grovel in the dirt under the feet of the man from whom you looted that talisman. That sword at your waist has been wielded by hands more noble by far than your soft paws.' The dome of Kratas' bald head turned purple and his craggy features quivered with outrage.

For a moment Naja was taken aback. How did the old monster know that his mother had been of Hyksosian blood? That was a close secret. He was forcefully reminded that this was the only man, besides Taita, who might have the strength and the power to wrest the double crown from his grasp.

Despite himself he took a step backwards. 'I am the Regent of the royal Prince Nefer. I wear the blue hawk seal by right,' he answered.

'No!' Kratas thundered. 'You do not have the right. Only great and noble men have the right to wear the hawk seal. Pharaoh Tamose had the right, Tanus, Lord Harrab had the right, and a line of mighty kings before them. You, you slinking cur, have no such right.'

'I was acclaimed by my legions in the field. I am the Regent of Prince Nefer.'

Kratas strode towards him across the chamber floor. 'You are no soldier. You were thrashed at Lastra and Siva by your Hyksos jackal kin. You are no statesman, no philosopher. You have gained some small distinction only by Pharaoh's lapse in judgement. I warned him against you a hundred times.'

'Back, you old fool!' Naja warned him. 'I stand in the place of Pharaoh. If you handle me, you give offence to the crown and dignity of Egypt.'

'I am going to strip the seal and that sword off you.' Kratas did not check his step. 'And afterwards I might give myself the pleasure of whipping your buttocks.'

At Naja's right hand Asmor whispered, 'The penalty for *lèse-majesté* is death.'

Instantly Naja realized his opportunity. He lifted his

chin and looked into the old man's still bright eyes. 'You are an ancient bag of wind and dung,' he challenged. 'Your day has passed, Kratas, you doddering old idiot. You dare not lay a finger on the Regent of Egypt.'

As he had intended, the insult was too great for Kratas to bear. He let out a bellow and rushed the last few paces. He was surprisingly quick for a man of his age and bulk, and he seized Naja, lifted him off his feet and tried to rip the hawk seal from his arm.

'You are not fit—'

Without looking round, Naja spoke to Asmor, who stood only a pace behind his shoulder with his drawn sickle sword in his right hand.

'Strike!' said Naja softly. 'And strike deep!'

Asmor stepped to the side, opening Kratas' flank above the waistband of the kilt for the thrust low in the back, into the kidneys. In his trained hand the blow was true and powerful. The bronze blade slipped in silently, easily as a needle into a sheet of silk, right in to the hilt, then Asmor twisted it in the flesh to enlarge the wound channel.

Kratas' whole body stiffened and his eyes opened wide. He loosed his grip and let Naja drop back to his feet. Asmor pulled out the blade. It came away reluctantly against the suck of clinging flesh. The bright bronze was smeared with dark blood, and a sluggish trickle ran down to soak into Kratas' white linen kilt. Asmor stabbed again, this time higher, angling the blade upwards under the lowest rib. Kratas frowned and shook his great leonine head, as though annoyed at some childish nonsense. He turned away and began to walk towards the door of the chamber. Asmor ran after him and stabbed him again in the back. Kratas kept walking.

'My lord, help me kill the dog,' Asmor panted, and Naja drew the blue sword and ran to join him. The blade bit deeper than any bronze as Naja hacked and stabbed. Kratas reeled out through the doors of the chamber into the courtyard, blood spurting and pulsing from a dozen wounds. Behind him the other members of the council shouted, 'Murder! Spare the noble Kratas.'

Asmor shouted just as loudly, 'Traitor! He has laid hands on the Regent of Egypt!' And he thrust again, aiming for the heart, but Kratas staggered against the surrounding wall of the fish pond, and tried to steady himself. However, his hands were red and slick with his own blood and found no grip on the polished marble. He collapsed over the low coping and, with a heavy splash, disappeared under the surface.

The two swordsmen paused, hanging over the wall to catch their breath as the waters were stained pink by the old man's blood. Suddenly his bald head thrust out of the pool and Kratas drew a noisy breath.

'In the name of all the gods, will not the old bastard die?' Asmor's voice was filled with astonishment and frustration.

Naja vaulted over the wall into the pond and stood waist-deep over the huge, floundering body. He placed one foot on Kratas' throat and forced his head beneath the surface. Kratas struggled and heaved beneath him, and the waters were stained with blood and churned river mud. Naja trod down with all his weight and kept him under. ''Tis like riding a hippopotamus.' He laughed breathlessly, and immediately Asmor and the soldiers joined in with him, crowding the edge of the pool. They roared with laughter and jeered, 'Have your last drink, Kratas, you old sot.'

'You will go to Seth bathed and sweet smelling as a babe. Even the god will not recognize you.'

The old man's struggles grew weaker, until a vast exhalation of breath bubbled to the surface and at last he was still. Naja waded to the side of the pool and stepped out. Kratas' body rose slowly to the surface and floated there face down.

'Fish him out!' Naja ordered. 'Do not have him embalmed, but hack him into pieces and bury him with the other bandits, rapists and traitors in the Valley of the Jackal. Do not mark his grave.' Kratas was thus denied the chance to reach Paradise. He would be doomed eternally to wander in darkness.

Dripping wet to the waist Naja strode back into the council chamber. By this time all the other members of the council had arrived. They had been witness to Kratas' fate and huddled, pale and shaken, on their benches. They stared at Naja aghast as he stood before them with the reeking blue blade in his hand. 'My noble lords, death has always been the penalty for treason. Is there any man among you who would question the justice of this execution?' He looked at each in turn and they dropped their eyes: the Phat Guards stood shoulder to shoulder around the wall of the chamber and, with Kratas gone, there was no man to give them direction.

'My lord Menset,' Naja singled out the president of the council, 'do you endorse my action in executing the traitor Kratas?'

For a long moment it seemed that Menset might defy him, but then he sighed and looked at his hands in his lap. 'The punishment was just,' he whispered. 'The council endorses the actions of the Lord Naja.'

'Does the council also ratify the appointment of Lord Naja as the Regent of Egypt?' Naja asked softly but his voice carried clearly in the fraught and silent chamber.

Menset raised his eyes and looked around at his fellow members, but not one would catch his eye. 'The President and all the councillors of this assembly acknowledge the new Regent of Egypt.' At last Menset looked directly at Naja, but such a dark, scornful expression blighted his usually jovial features that before the full of this moon he would be found dead in his bed. For the time being Naja merely nodded.

'I accept the duty and heavy responsibility you have placed upon me.' He sheathed his sword and mounted the dais to the throne. 'As my first official pronouncement in my capacity of Regent in Council I wish to describe to you the gallant death of the divine Pharaoh Tamose.' He paused significantly, then for the next hour he related in detail his version of the fatal campaign and the attack on the heights of El Wadun. 'Thus died one of Egypt's most gallant kings. His last words to me as I carried him down the hill were, "Care for my only remaining son. Guard my son Nefer until he is man enough to wear the double crown. Take my two small daughters under your wings, and see that no harm befalls them."'

Lord Naja made little attempt to hide his terrible grief and it took him some moments to bring his emotions under control. Then he went on firmly, 'I will not fail the god who was my friend and my pharaoh. Already I have sent my chariots into the wilderness to search for Prince Nefer and bring him back to Thebes. As soon as he arrives we will set him on the throne, and place the scourge and the sceptre in his hands.'

There was the first murmur of approval among the councillors, and Naja continued, 'Now send for the princesses. Have them brought to the chamber immediately.'

When they came hesitantly through the main doors, Heseret the elder was leading her little sister, Merykara, by the hand. Merykara had been playing pitch and toss with her friends. She was flushed from her exertions and her slim body was dewed with sweat. She was still several years from womanhood so her legs were long and coltish and her bare chest was as flat as a boy's. She wore her long black hair in a side-lock that hung over her left shoulder, and her linen breech clout was so diminutive that it left the lower half of her little round buttocks exposed. She smiled shyly around this formidable gathering of famous men, and clung harder to her elder sister's hand.

Heseret had seen her first red moon and was dressed in the linen skirts and wig of a marriageable woman. Even the old men looked at her avidly for she had inherited in full measure her grandmother Queen Lostris' celebrated beauty. Her skin was milky. Her limbs were smooth and shapely, and her naked breasts were like celestial moons. Her expression was serene but the corners of her mouth lifted in a secret, mischievous smile, and there were intriguing lights in her huge dark green eyes.

'Come forward, my pretty darlings,' Naja called to them, and only then they recognized the man who was the close and beloved friend of their father. They smiled and came towards him trustingly. He rose from the throne, went down to meet them and placed his hands on their shoulders. His voice and his expression were tragic. 'You must be brave now, and remember that you are princesses of the royal house, because I have bitter news for you. Pharaoh your father is dead.' For a minute they did not seem to understand, then Heseret let out the high keening wail of mourning, followed immediately by Merykara.

Gently Naja put his arms around them, and led them to sit at the foot of the throne, where they sank to their knees and clung to each other, weeping inconsolably.

'The distress of the royal princesses is plain for all the world to see,' Naja told the assembly. 'The trust and the duty that Pharaoh placed upon me is equally plain. As I have taken Prince Nefer Memnon into my care, so now I take the two princesses, Heseret and Merykara, under my protection.'

'Now he has all the royal brood in his hands. But no matter where he is in the wilderness, and how hale and strong the Prince Nefer may seem,' Talla whispered to his neighbour, 'methinks he is already sickening unto death. The new Regent of Egypt has made abundantly clear his style of government.'

Nefer sat in the shadow of the cliff that towered above Gebel Nagara. He had not moved since the sun had first shown its upper rim above the mountains across the valley. At first the effort of remaining still had burned along his nerve endings and made his skin itch as though poisonous insects were crawling upon it. But he knew that Taita was watching him so he had forced his wayward body slowly to his will and risen above its petty dictates. Now at last he sat in a state of exalted awareness, his every sense tuned to the wilderness about him.

He could smell the water that rose from its secret spring in the cleft in the cliff. It came up a slow drop at a time and dripped into the basin in the rock that was not much larger than the cup of his two hands, then overflowed and dribbled down into the next basin, green-lined with slippery algae. From there it ran down to disappear for ever into the ruddy sands of the valley bottom. Yet much life was supported by this trickle of water: butterfly and beetle, serpent and lizard, the graceful little gazelle that danced like whiffs of saffron dust on the heat-quivering plains, the speckled pigeons with their ruffs of wine-coloured feathers that nested on high ledges all drank here. It was because of these precious pools that Taita had brought him to this place to wait for his godbird.

They had begun to make the net on the day of their arrival at Gebel Nagara. Taita had bought the silk from a merchant in Thebes. The hank of thread had cost the price of a fine stallion, for it had been brought from a land far to the east of the Indus river on a journey that had taken years to complete. Taita had shown Nefer how to weave the net out of the fine threads. The mesh was stronger than thick strands of linen or thongs of leather but almost invisible to the eye.

When the net was ready Taita had insisted that the boy catch the decoys himself. 'It is your godbird. You must take it yourself,' he had explained. 'That way your claim will be more secure in the sight of the great god Horus.'

So, in the baking daylight out on the valley floor, Nefer and Taita had studied the route up the cliff. When darkness fell Taita had sat beside the small fire at the base of the cliff and softly chanted his incantations, at intervals throwing a handful of herbs on to the fire. When the crescent moon rose to illuminate the darkness of midnight Nefer had started the precarious climb to the ledge where the pigeons roosted. He had seized two of the big, fluttering birds while they were still disorientated and confused by the darkness and the spell that Taita had cast over them. He brought them down in the leather saddlebag slung on his back.

Under Taita's instruction Nefer had plucked the feathers from one wing of each bird, so that they were no longer able to fly. Then they had selected a spot close to the base of the cliff and the spring, but exposed enough to make the birds clearly visible from the sky above. They tethered the pigeons by the leg with a thread of horsetail hair and a wooden peg driven into the hard earth. Then they had spread the gossamer net above them, and supported it on stalks of dried elephant grass, which would snap and collapse under the stoop of the godbird.

'Stretch the net gently,' Taita had shown him, 'not too tight, nor again too slack. It must catch in the bird's beak and his talons and tangle him so that he cannot struggle and damage himself before we can free him.'

When all was set up to Taita's satisfaction, they began the long wait. Soon the pigeons had become accustomed to their captivity, and pecked greedily at the handfuls of *dhurra* millet that Nefer scattered for them. Then they sunned and dusted themselves contentedly under the silken net. One day succeeded the next hot, sun-riven day, and still they waited.

In the cool of the evening they brought in the pigeons, furled the net, and then they hunted for food. Taita climbed to the top of the cliff where he sat cross-legged on the edge, overlooking the long valley. Nefer waited in ambush below, never in the same place so that the game were always surprised when they came to drink at the spring. From his vantage-point Taita wove his spell of enticement, which seldom failed to seduce the dainty gazelle within fair shot of where Nefer lay with his arrow nocked and bow held at draw. Every evening they grilled gazelle steaks over the fire at the entrance to the cave.

The cave had been Taita's retreat during all the years after the death of Queen Lostris when he had lived here as a hermit. It was his place of power. Although Nefer was a novice, and had no deep understanding of the old man's mystical skills, he could not doubt them, for every day they were demonstrated to him.

They had been at Gebel Nagara for many days before Nefer began to understand that they had not come here to find the godbird alone: this interlude was an extension of the training and instruction Taita had lavished upon him from as far back as Nefer's young memory stretched. Even the long hours of waiting beside the decoys was a lesson in itself. Taita was teaching him control over his body and being, teaching him to open doors within his mind, teaching him to look inward, to listen to the silence and hear whispers to which others were deaf.

Once he had been conditioned to the silence, Nefer was more amenable to the deeper wisdom and learning that Taita had to impart. They sat together in the desert night, under the swirling patterns of the stars that were eternal but ephemeral as the winds and the currents of the oceans, and Taita described to him wonders that seemed to have no explanation but could only be perceived by an opening and extension of the mind. He sensed that he stood merely on the shadowy periphery of this mystical knowledge, but he felt growing inside him a great hunger for more.

One morning when Nefer left the cave in the grey light before dawn, he saw a huddle of dark, silent figures sitting out in the desert beyond the spring of Gebel Nagara. He went to tell Taita, and the old man nodded. 'They have been waiting all night.' He spread a woollen cloak over his shoulders and went out to them.

When they recognized Taita's gaunt figure in the half-light they burst into wails of supplication. They were people of the desert tribes and they had brought children to him, children stricken by the Yellow Flowers, hot with fever and covered with the terrible sores of the disease.

Taita ministered to them, while they remained camped beyond the spring. None of the children died, and after ten days the tribe brought gifts of millet, salt and tanned hides, which they left at the entrance to the cave. Then they were gone into the wilderness. After that there came others, suffering from disease and wounds inflicted by men and beasts. Taita went out to all of them, and turned none away. Nefer worked beside him and learned much from what he saw and heard.

No matter if there were the sick and ailing Bedouin to care for, or food to be gathered, or instruction or learning to be imparted, each morning they set out the decoys under the silken net and waited beside them.

Perhaps they had fallen under the calming influence of Taita, for the once-wild pigeons became docile and quiescent as chickens. They allowed themselves to be handled without any sign of fear, and uttered soft throaty coos as their legs were secured to the pegs. Then they settled and fluffed up their feathers.

On the twentieth morning of their stay, Nefer took up his position over the decoys. As always, even without looking directly at Taita, Nefer was deeply aware of his presence. The old man's eyes were closed and he, like the pigeons, seemed to be dozing in the sunlight. His skin was criss-crossed with innumerable fine wrinkles and dappled with age spots. It seemed so delicate that it might tear as easily as the finest papyrus parchment. His face was hairless, no trace of beard or eyebrows; only fine lashes, colourless as glass, surrounded his eyes. Nefer had heard his father say that neutering had left Taita's face beardless and little marked by the passage of time, but he was certain that there were more esoteric reasons for his longevity and the persistence of his strength and life-force. In vivid contrast to his other features, Taita's hair was dense and strong as that of a healthy young woman, but bright burnished silver in colour. Taita was proud of it and kept it washed and groomed in a thick plait down his back. Despite his learning and age, the old Magus was not inured to vanity.

This little touch of humanity heightened Nefer's love for him to the point where it stabbed his chest with a strength that was almost painful. He wished that there was some way in which he could express it, but he knew that Taita already understood, for Taita knew everything.

He reached out surreptitiously to touch the old man's arm as he slept, but suddenly Taita's eyes opened, focused and aware. Nefer knew that he had not been asleep at all, but that all his powers had been concentrated on bringing in the godbird to the decoys. He knew that, in some way, his wandering thoughts and his movement had affected the outcome of the old man's efforts, for he sensed Taita's disapproval as clearly as if it had been spoken.

Chastened, he composed himself, and brought his mind and body under control again in the manner that Taita had taught him. It was like passing through a secret doorway into the place of power. The time passed swiftly, without being counted or grudged. The sun climbed to its zenith and seemed to hang there for a long while. Suddenly Nefer was blessed with a marvellous sense of prescience. It was almost as if he, too, hung above the world and saw everything happening below him. He saw Taita and himself sitting beside the well of Gebel Nagara, and the desert stretching away around them. He saw the river that contained the desert like a mighty barrier and marked out the boundaries of this very Egypt. He saw the cities and the kingdoms, the lands divided under the double crown, great armies in array, the machinations of evil men, and the striving and sacrifice of the just and good. In that moment he was aware of his destiny with an intensity that almost overwhelmed and crushed his courage.

In that same moment he knew that his godbird would come on this day, for he was ready to receive it at last.

'The bird is here!'

The words were so clear that, for an instant, Nefer thought Taita had spoken, but then he realized his lips had not moved. Taita had placed the thought in Nefer's mind in the mysterious manner that Nefer could neither fathom nor explain. He did not doubt that it was so, but in the next instant it was confirmed by the wild fluttering of the decoy pigeons who had sensed the menace in the air above them.

Nefer made no move to show that he had heard and understood. He did not turn his head or lift his eyes to the sky. He dared not look upwards lest he alarm the bird, or incur the wrath of Taita. But he was aware with every fibre of his being.

The royal falcon was such a rare creature that few men had ever seen it in the wild. For the previous thousand years the huntsmen of every pharaoh had sought out the birds, had trapped and netted them, and to fill the royal mews had even lifted their young from the nest before they were fledged. Possession of the birds was proof that Pharaoh had the divine approval of the god Horus to reign in this very Egypt.

The falcon was the *alter ego* of the god: statues and depictions of him showed him with the falcon head. Pharaoh was a god himself so might capture, own and hunt the bird, but any other man did so on pain of death.

Now the bird was here. His very own bird. Taita seemed to have conjured it out of heaven itself. Nefer felt his heart held in a suffocating grip of excitement and the breath in his lungs seized up so that he thought his chest might burst. But still he dared not turn his head to the sky.

Then he heard the falcon. Its cry was a faint lament, almost lost in the immensity of sky and desert, but it thrilled Nefer to the core, as though the god had spoken directly to him. Seconds later the falcon called again, directly overhead, its voice shriller and more savage.

Now the pigeons were wild with terror, leaping against the thongs that secured them to the pegs, beating their wings with such violence that they shed feathers, and the downdraught of air raised a pale cloud of dust around them.

High overhead Nefer heard the falcon begin its stoop on the decoys, with the wind singing over its wings in a rising note. He knew that at last it was safe to raise his head, for all the falcon's attention would be focused on its prey.

He looked up and saw the bird drop against the aching blue of the desert sky. It was a thing of divine beauty. Its wings were folded back, like half-sheathed blades, and its head was thrust forward. The strength and power of the creature made Nefer gasp aloud. He had seen other falcons of this breed in his father's mews, but never before like this in all its wild grace and majesty. Miraculously the falcon seemed to swell in size, and its colours grew more intense as it fell towards where he sat.

The curved beak was a lovely deep yellow with a tip sharp and black as obsidian. The eyes were fiercest gold with tear-like markings in the inner corners, the throat was creamy and dappled like ermine, the wings were russet and black, and the whole creature was so exquisite in every detail that he never doubted it was an incarnation of the god. He wanted to possess it with a longing he had never imagined possible.

He braced himself for the moment of impact when the falcon would strike the silken net and ensnare itself in the voluminous folds. Beside him he felt Taita do the same. They would rush forward together.

Then something happened that he could not believe was possible. The falcon was fully committed to its stoop, the velocity of its dive was such that nothing could have stopped it but the impact of the strike into the pigeons' soft-feathered bodies. But, against all probability, the falcon flared out. Its wings changed their profile and for an instant the wind-force threatened to rip away the pinions at their juncture with its body. The air shrieked over the spread feathers and the falcon had changed direction, was hurtling aloft once more, using its own momentum to arc up into the sky until in seconds it was only a black speck against the blue. Its cry sounded once more in the air, plaintive and remote, and then it was gone.

'He refused!' Nefer whispered. 'Why, Taita, why?'

'The ways of the gods are not for us to fathom.' Although he had been still for all those hours, Taita stood up with the lithe movement of a trained athlete.

'Will he not return?' Nefer asked. 'He was my bird. I felt it in my heart. He was my bird. He must return.'

'He is part of the godhead,' Taita said softly. 'He is not part of the natural order of things.'

'But why did he refuse? There must be some reason,' Nefer insisted.

Taita did not reply immediately, but went to release the pigeons. After all this time their wing feathers had grown again, but as he freed their legs from the horsehair fetters they made no attempt to escape. One fluttered up and perched on his shoulder. Gently Taita took it in both hands and threw it aloft. Only then did it fly up the cliff face to its roost on the high ledge.

He watched it go then turned and walked back to the entrance of the cave. Nefer followed him slowly, his heart and legs leaden with disappointment. In the gloom of the cave Taita seated himself on the stone ledge below the back wall, and leaned forward to build up the smoky fire of thorn branches and horse dung until it burst into flames. Heavily, filled with foreboding, Nefer took up his accustomed place opposite him.

They were both silent for a long while, Nefer containing himself, although his disappointment at the loss of the falcon was a torment as intense as if he had thrust his hand into flames. He knew that Taita would only speak again when he was ready. At last Taita sighed, and said softly, almost sadly, 'I must work the Mazes of Ammon Ra.'

Nefer was startled. He had not expected that. In all their time together Nefer had only seen him work the Mazes twice before. He knew that the self-induced trance of divination was a little death that drained and exhausted the old man. He would only undertake the dreaded journey into the supernatural when no other course was open to him.

Nefer kept silent, and watched in awe as Taita went through the ritual of preparing the Mazes. First he crushed the herbs with a pestle in a mortar of carved alabaster, and measured them into a clay pot. Then he poured boiling water from the copper kettle over them. The steam that rose in a cloud was so pungent it made Nefer's eyes water.

While the mixture cooled, Taita brought the tanned leather bag that contained the Mazes from its hiding-place at the back of the cave. Sitting over the fire, he poured the ivory discs into one hand and rubbed them gently between his fingers as he began to chant the incantation to Ammon Ra.

The Mazes comprised ten ivory discs, which Taita had carved. Ten was the mystical number of the greatest potency. Each carving depicted one of the ten symbols of power, and was a miniature work of art. As he sang he fondled the discs so that they clicked between his fingers. Between each verse of the invocation, he blew on the discs to endow them with his life force. When they had taken on the warmth of his own body he passed them to Nefer.

'Hold them and breathe upon them,' he urged, and while Nefer obeyed these instructions, Taita began to sway in rhythm to the magical verses he was reciting. Slowly his eyes seemed to glaze over as he retreated into the secret places in his mind. He was already in the trance when Nefer stacked the Mazes in two piles in front of him.

Then with one finger Nefer tested the temperature of the infusion in the clay pot as Taita had taught him. When it was cool enough not to scald the mouth, he knelt before the old man and with both hands offered it to him.

Taita drank it to the last drop, and in the firelight his face turned white as building chalk from the quarry at Aswan. For a while longer he kept up the chant, but slowly his voice dropped to a whisper, then descended into silence. The only sound was his hoarse breathing as he succumbed to the drug and the trance. He subsided on to the floor of the cave, and lay curled like a sleeping cat beside the fire.

Nefer covered him with his woollen shawl, and stayed beside him until he started to twitch and groan, and the sweat streamed down his face. His eyes opened and rolled back in their sockets until only the whites glared blindly into the dark shadows of the cave.

Nefer knew there was nothing he could do for the old man now. He had journeyed far into the shadowy places where Nefer could not reach him, and he could no longer bear the terrible distress and suffering that the Mazes inflicted upon the Magus. Quietly he stood up, fetched his bow and quiver from the back of the cave and stooped to see out through the entrance. Across the hills the sun was low and yellow in the dust haze. He climbed the western dunes, and when he reached the top and looked out across the valleys he felt so strongly his disappointment at the lost bird, his concern for Taita in his agony of divination, and his sense of foreboding at what Taita would discover in his trance, that he was seized by the urge to run, to escape as though from some dreadful predator. He bounded away down the face of the dune, the sand cascading and hissing beneath his feet. He felt tears of terror brim in his eyes and stream down his cheeks in the wind, and he ran until the sweat poured down his flanks, his chest heaved and the sun was on the horizon. Then at last he turned back towards Gebel Nagara and covered the last mile in darkness.

Taita was still curled under the shawl beside the fire, but he was sleeping more easily now. Nefer lay down beside him, and after a while he, too, fell into a sleep that was restless with dreams and haunted by nightmares.

When he awoke dawn was glimmering at the entrance to the cave. Taita was sitting at the fire, grilling gazelle cutlets on the coals. He still looked pale and sick, but he skewered one on the point of his bronze dagger and offered it to Nefer. The boy was suddenly ravenous, and he sat up and gnawed on the bone. When he had devoured the third portion of sweet tender meat he spoke for the first time. 'What did you see, Tata?' he asked. 'Why did the godbird refuse?'

'It was obscured,' Taita told him, and Nefer knew that the omen had been unpropitious, that Taita was protecting him from it.

They ate in silence for a while, but now Nefer hardly tasted the food and at last he said softly, 'You have freed the decoys. How can we set the net tomorrow?'

'The godbird will not come to Gebel Nagara again,' said Taita simply.

'Then am I never to be Pharaoh in my father's place?' Nefer asked.

There was deep anguish in his voice, so Taita softened his answer. 'We will have to take your bird from the nest.'

'We do not know where to find the godbird.' Nefer had stopped eating. He stared at Taita with pitiful appeal.

The old man inclined his head in affirmation. 'I know where the nest is. It was revealed in the Mazes. But you must eat to keep up your strength. We will leave before first light tomorrow. It is a long journey to the site.'

'Will there be fledglings in the nest?'

'Yes,' said Taita. 'The falcons have bred. The young are almost ready for flight. We will find your bird there.' Silently he told himself, *Or the god will reveal other mysteries to us.*

In the darkness before dawn they loaded the waterskins and the saddlebags on to the horses then swung up bareback behind them. Taita led the way, skirting the cliff face and taking the easy route up the hills. By the time the sun was above the horizon they had left Gebel Nagara far below them. When Nefer looked ahead he started with surprise: there ahead of them was the faint outline of the mountain, blue against the blue of the horizon, still so far off that it seemed insubstantial and ethereal, a thing of mist and air rather than of earth and rock. The sensation that he had seen it before overcame Nefer, and for a while he was at a loss to explain it to himself. Then it came rushing back and he said, 'That mountain.' He pointed it out. 'That is where we are going, is it not, Tata?' He spoke with such assurance that Taita looked back at him.

'How do you know?'

'I dreamed it last night,' Nefer replied.

Taita turned away so that the boy would not see his

expression. At last the eyes of his mind are opening like a desert bloom in the dawn. He is learning to peer through the dark curtain that hides the future from us. He felt a deep sense of achievement. Praise the hundred names of Horus, it has not been in vain.

'That is where we are going, I know it is,' Nefer repeated, with utmost certainty.

'Yes,' Taita agreed at last. 'We are going to Bir Umm Masara.'

Before the hottest part of the day, Taita led them to where a clump of ragged acacia thorn trees grew in a deep ravine, their roots drawing up water from some deep source far below the surface. When they had unloaded the horses and watered them, Nefer cast around the grove and within minutes had discovered sign of others who had passed this way. Excitedly, he called Taita over and showed him the wheel-marks left by a small division of chariots, ten vehicles by his reckoning, the ashes of the cooking fire, and the flattened earth where men had lain down to sleep with the horses tethered to the acacia trunks nearby.

'Hyksos?' he hazarded anxiously, for the dung of the horses in their lines was very fresh, not more than a few days old – it was dry on the outside, but still damp when he broke open a lump.

'Ours.' Taita had recognized the tracks of the chariots. After all, he had made the first designs of these spoked wheels many decades before. He stooped suddenly and picked up a tiny bronze rosette ornament that had fallen from a dashboard and was half buried in the loose earth. 'One of our light cavalry divisions, probably from the Phat regiment. Part of Lord Naja's command.'

'What are they doing out here, so far from the lines?' Nefer asked, puzzled, but Taita shrugged and turned away to cover his unease.

The old man cut short their period of rest and they went on while the sun was still high. Slowly the outline of Bir

Umm Masara hardened and seemed to fill half of the sky ahead of them. Gradually they could make out the etching and scarification of gorge, bluff and cliff. As they reached the crest of the first line of foothills, Taita checked his horse and looked back. Distant movement caught his attention, and he held up his hand to shade his eyes. He could see a tiny feather of pale dust many leagues out in the desert below. He watched it for a while and saw that it was moving eastwards, towards the Red Sea. It might have been thrown up by a herd of moving oryx, or by a column of fighting chariots. He did not remark on it to Nefer, who was so intent on the hunt for the royal falcon that he could not tear his eyes from the silhouette of the mountain ahead. Taita thumped his heels into the flanks of his horse and moved up beside the boy.

That night, when they camped halfway up the slope of Bir Umm Masara, Taita said quietly, 'We will make no fire this night.'

'But it's so cold,' Nefer protested.

'And we are so exposed here that a fire could be seen for ten leagues across the desert.'

'Are there enemies out there?' Nefer's expression changed, and he gazed down over the darkening landscape with trepidation. 'Bandits? Raiding Bedouin?'

'There are always enemies,' Taita told him. 'Better cold than dead.'

After midnight when the icy wind woke Nefer, and his colt, Stargazer, stamped and whinnied, he rolled out of his sheepskin blanket and went to calm him. He found Taita already awake, sitting a little apart.

'Look!' he ordered, and pointed down on to the lowland. There was a distant glimmer and flicker of light. 'A campfire,' Taita said.

'They might be one of our own divisions. Those who made the tracks we saw yesterday.'

'They might indeed,' agreed Taita, 'But then again, they might be somebody else.'

After a long, thoughtful pause Nefer said, 'I have slept enough. It's too cold, anyway. We should mount again and move on. We don't want the dawn to catch us here on the bare shoulder of the mountain.'

They loaded the horses and in the moonlight found a rough path made by wild goats that led them round the eastern shoulder of Bir Umm Masara, so that when the light began to strengthen they were already out of sight of any watchers in the distant encampment.

The chariot of Ammon Ra, the sun god, burst furiously out of the east, and the mountain was suffused with golden light. The gorges were dark with shadow, made more sombre by the contrast, and far below the wilderness was vast and grand.

Nefer threw back his head, shouted with joy, 'Look! Oh, look!' and pointed up past the rock peak. Taita followed his gaze and saw the two dark specks, turning in a wide circle against the heavens. The sunlight caught one, so that it glowed for a second like a shooting star.

'Royal falcons.' Taita smiled. 'A mating pair.'

They unloaded the horses and found a vantage-point from which they were able to watch the circling birds. Even at this distance they were regal and beautiful beyond Nefer's ability to express it. Then suddenly one of the birds, the smaller male, the tiercel, broke the pattern of flight, and angled up against the wind, his leisurely wingbeats taking on a sudden ferocity.

'He has discovered,' Nefer shouted, with the excitement and joy of the true falconer. 'Watch him now.'

When it began the stoop was so swift that to have taken the eye off it for even a moment would have meant missing the kill. The tiercel dropped down the sky like a thrown javelin. A single pigeon was coasting unsuspectingly near the base of the cliff. Nefer recognized the moment when the plump bird became suddenly aware of the danger, and tried to avoid the falcon. It turned so violently towards the safety of the rock face that it rolled over on to its back in full and frantic flight. For an instant its belly was exposed. The tiercel tore into it with both sets of talons, and the big bird seemed to dissolve in a burst of puce and blue smoke. The feathers drifted away in a long cloud on the morning wind and the falcon bound on, locking its talons deep into its prey's belly, and plunged with it into the gorge. The killer and its victim hit the rocky scree slope only a short distance from where Nefer stood. The heavy thud of their fall echoed off the cliff and resounded down the gorge.

By this time Nefer was dancing with excitement, and even Taita, who had always been a lover of the hunting hawks, gave voice to his pleasure.

'*Bak-her!*' he cried, as the falcon completed the ritual of the kill with the mantling: it spread its magnificently patterned wings over the dead pigeon, covering it and proclaiming the kill as its own.

The female falcon came down to join him in a series of graceful spirals and landed on the rock beside her mate. He folded away his wings to let her share the kill, and between them they dismembered and devoured the carcass of the pigeon, ripping into it with their razor-sharp beaks, and pausing between each stroke to lift their heads and glare at Nefer, with those ferocious yellow eyes, while they gulped down the bloody fragments of flesh and bone and feathers. They were fully aware of the presence of the men and horses, but tolerated them as long as they kept their distance.

Then, when all that was left of the pigeon were a blood spot on the rock and a few drifting feathers, and the usually sleek bellies of the falcons were crammed with food, the pair launched into flight again. Wings flogging now to carry them, they rose up the sheer cliff face.

'Follow them!' Taita hitched up his kilt and scampered over the treacherous footing of the scree slope. 'Don't lose them.'

Nefer was faster and more agile, and he kept the rising birds in sight as he raced along the shoulder of the mountain beneath them. Below the peak the mountain was split into twin needles, mighty pinnacles of dark stone, terrifying even from below. They watched the falcons rise up this mighty natural monument, until Nefer realized where they were headed. Where the rock overhung, halfway up the eastern tower, there was a V-shaped cleft in the stone face. Stuffed into it was a platform of dried branches and twigs.

'The nest!' Nefer shrieked. 'There is the nest!'

They stood together, heads thrown back, watching the falcons alight, one after the other, on the edge of the nest, and begin to heave and strain to regurgitate the pigeon flesh from their crops. Another faint sound came to Nefer on the wind that soughed along the cliff-face: a chorus of importunate cries from the young birds demanding to be fed. From this angle he and Taita could not glimpse the falcon chicks, and Nefer was hopping with frustration. 'If we climb the western peak, there,' he pointed, 'we should be able to look down into the nest.'

'Help me with the horses first,' Taita ordered, and they hobbled them, and left them to graze on sparse clumps of mountain grass nurtured by the dews carried by the breeze from the distant Red Sea.

The climb up the western peak took the rest of the morning, but even though Taita had unerringly picked out the easiest route around the far side of the peak, in places the drop beneath them made Nefer draw in his breath sharply, and look away. They came out at last on to a narrow ledge just below the summit. They crouched there for a while to compose themselves, and to stare out at the grandeur of land and distant sea. It seemed that the whole of creation was spread beneath them, and the wind moaned around them, tugging at the folds of Nefer's kilt and ruffling his curls.

'Where is the nest?' he asked. Even in this lofty and precarious place, high above the world, his mind was fixed on one thing only.

'Come!' Taita rose and shuffled sideways along the ledge with the toes of his sandals overhanging the drop. They made their way round the angle and slowly the eastern peak came into view. They looked across to the vertical rock face only a hundred cubits away, but separated from them by such an abyss that Nefer swayed with vertigo.

On this side of the gulf they were slightly higher than the nest, and could look down upon it. The female falcon was perched on the edge, obscuring its contents. She turned her head and stared implacably at them as they rounded the shoulder of the peak. She raised the feathers along her back, as an angry lion lifts its mane in threat. Then she let out a wild cry and launched herself out over the drop, to hang almost motionless on the wind, watching them intently. She was so close that every feather in her wings was clearly revealed.

Her movement had exposed the interior of the cleft that contained the nest. A pair of young birds was crouched in the cup of twigs and branches lined with feathers and the wool of wild goats. They were fully fledged already, and almost as large as their mother. As Nefer stared across at them in awe, one raised itself and spread its wings wide, then beat them fiercely.

'He is beautiful.' Nefer groaned with longing. 'The most beautiful thing I have ever seen.'

'He practises for the moment of flight,' Taita warned him softly. 'See how strong he has grown. Within days he will be gone.'

'I will climb for them this very day,' Nefer vowed, and made as if to go back along the ledge, but Taita stopped him with a hand on his shoulder.

'It is not something to enter into lightly. We must spend a little precious time in planning it carefully. Come, sit beside me.'

As Nefer leaned against his shoulder Taita pointed out the features of the rock opposite them. 'Below the nest the rock is smooth as glass. For fifty cubits sheer there is no handhold, no ledge on which to place a foot.'

Nefer tore his eyes from the young bird and peered down. His stomach churned, but he forced himself to ignore it. It was as Taita had said: not even one of the rock hyrax, those furry, sure-footed rabbit-like creatures that made these lofty places their home, could have found a footing on that pitch of vertical rock. 'How can I get to the nest, Tata? I want those chicks – I want them so.'

'Look above the nest.' Taita pointed across. 'See how the cleft continues upwards, to the very top of the cliff.'

Nefer nodded – he could not speak as he stared at the perilous road Taita was showing him.

'We will find a way to reach the summit above the nest. We will take up the harness ropes with us. From the top I will lower you down the crack. If you wedge your bare feet and bunched fists sideways into the opening they will hold you, and I will steady you with the rope.'

Still Nefer could not speak. He felt nauseated by what Taita had suggested. Surely no living person could make that climb and survive. Taita understood what he was feeling and did not insist on a reply.

'I think . . .' Hesitantly Nefer started to refuse, then fell silent and stared at the pair of young birds in the nest. He knew that this was his destiny. One of them was his godbird, and this was the only way to achieve the crown of his fathers. To turn away now was to deny everything for which the gods had chosen him. He must go.

Taita sensed the moment when the boy beside him accepted the task and thus became a man. He rejoiced deep in his heart, for this also was his destiny.

'I will make the attempt,' Nefer said simply, and rose to his feet. 'Let us go down and prepare ourselves.'

The next morning they left their rudimentary camp and started upwards while it was still dark. Somehow Taita was able to place his feet on a path that even Nefer's young eyes could not discern. Each of them carried a heavy coil of rope, plaited from linen and horsehair and used to tether the horses. They had also brought one of the small waterskins: Taita had warned that it would be hot on the pinnacle once the sun reached its height.

By the time they had worked their way round to the far side of the eastern pinnacle the light had strengthened and they could see the face above them. Taita spent an hour surveying the route up it. At last he was satisfied. 'In the name of great Horus, the all-powerful, let us begin,' he said, and made the sign of the god's wounded eye. Then he led Nefer back to the point he had chosen from which to begin the ascent.

'I will lead the way,' he told the boy, as he knotted one end of the rope around his waist. 'Pay out the rope as I go. Watch what I do, and when I call you, tie it to yourself and follow me. If you slip I will hold you.'

At first Nefer climbed cautiously, following the route that Taita had taken, his expression set and his knuckles white with tension as he fastened on each hold. Taita murmured encouragement from above, and the boy's confidence grew with each move upwards. He reached Taita's side and grinned at him. 'That was easy.'

'It will grow harder,' Taita assured him drily, and led up the next pitch of rock. This time Nefer was scampering behind him like a monkey, chattering with excitement and enjoyment. They stood below a chimney in the rock face that tapered near the top into a narrow crack.

'This is like the climb you will have to make down to the nest when we reach the top. Watch how I wedge my hands and feet into the crack.' Taita stepped up into the chimney and went up slowly but without pause. When the chimney narrowed he kept on steadily, like a man climbing a ladder. His kilts flapped about his skinny old legs, and Nefer could see up under the linen to the grotesque scar where his manhood had been cut away. Nefer had seen it before, and grown so accustomed to it that the terrible mutilation no longer appalled him.

Taita called to him from above, and this time Nefer danced up the rock, falling naturally into the rhythm of the ascent.

Why should it not be so? Taita tried to keep his pride within reasonable bounds. In his veins runs the blood of warriors and great athletes. Then he smiled and his eyes sparkled as though he were young again. And he has had me to teach him – of course he excels.

The sun was only halfway up the sky when at last they stood together on the summit of the eastern peak. 'We will rest awhile here.' Taita took the waterskin from his shoulder and sank down.

'I am not tired, Tata.'

'Nevertheless, we will rest.' Taita passed him the skin and watched as he gulped down a dozen mouthfuls. 'The descent to the nest will be more difficult,' he said, when Nefer stopped for breath. 'There will be nobody to show you the way, and there is one place where you cannot see your feet when the rock leans away from you.'

'I will be all right, Tata.'

'If the gods allow,' Taita agreed, and turned away his head as if to admire the glory of mountain, sea and desert spread below them but in fact so that the boy would not see his lips move as he prayed. 'Spread your wings over him, mighty Horus, for this is the one you have chosen. Cherish him, my mistress Lostris, who has become a goddess, for this is the fruit of your womb and the blood of your blood. Turn your hand from him, foul Seth, and touch him not, for you cannot prevail against those who protect this child.' He sighed as he reconsidered the wisdom of challenging the god of darkness and chaos, then softened his admonition with a small bribe: 'Pass him by, good Seth, and I will sacrifice an ox to you in your temple at Abydos when next I pass that way.'

He stood up. 'It is time to make the attempt.'

He led the way across the summit and stood on the far lip, looking down at the campsite and the grazing horses, which were rendered tiny as new-born mice by the drop. The female falcon was in flight, circling out over the gorge. He thought there was something unusual in her behaviour, particularly when she uttered a strange, forlorn cry, such as he had never before heard from a royal falcon. There was no sign of her mate, though he searched the heavens for him.

Then he lowered his eyes and looked across the abyss at the main peak of the mountain and the ledge on which they had stood the previous day. This enabled him to orientate himself, for the bulge of the rock face under him hid the nest from sight. He moved slowly along the lip until he found the beginning of the crack, which he recognized as the one that ran down and opened into the cleft in which the falcons had built their nest.

He picked up a loose pebble and dropped it over the edge. It clattered as it dropped down the wall and out of sight. He hoped that it might alarm the tiercel off the nest and so confirm its exact position, but there was still no sign of it. Only the female bird continued her aimless circles and uttered her strange, lonely cries.

Taita called Nefer to him and tied the end of the rope around his waist. He checked the knot carefully and then, an inch at a time, drew the full length of the rope through his fingers, checking for any frayed or weakened spot. 'You have the saddlebag to carry the fledgling.' He checked the knot with which Nefer had secured it over his shoulder so that it would not hamper his movements on the climb.

'Stop fussing so, Tata. My father says that sometimes you are like an old woman.'

'Your father should show more respect. I wiped his arse when he was a mewling infant, just as I wiped yours.' Taita sniffed, and again checked the knot at the boy's waist, delaying the fateful moment. But Nefer walked to the edge and stood straight-backed above the drop without any sign of hesitation.

'Are you ready?' He looked over his shoulder, and smiled with a flash of white teeth and a sparkle of his dark green eyes. Those eyes reminded Taita so vividly of Queen Lostris. With a pang he thought Nefer even more comely than his father had been at the same age.

'We cannot dally here all day.' Nefer uttered one of his father's favourite expressions in lordly tones, aping the royal manner faithfully.

Taita sat down and wriggled into a position in which he could anchor his heels in the crack and lean back to brace himself against the rope over his shoulder. He nodded at Nefer, and saw the cocky grin leave the boy's face as he edged down over the drop. He paid out the rope as Nefer worked his way down.

Nefer reached the bulge in the wall and, hanging on grimly with both hands, let his legs down to grope for a foothold beneath the overhang. He found the crack with his toes and thrust his bare foot into it, twisting his ankle to lock the hold, then slithered down. He glanced up one last time at Taita, tried to smile, but made a sickly grimace, then swung round the overhang. Before he could find another hold he felt his foot slip in the crack and he started to swivel on the rope. If he lost his footing he would pivot and swing out helplessly over the drop. He doubted that the old man above would have the strength to haul him back.

He snatched desperately at the crack, and his fingers hooked on, steadying him. He lunged with his other hand and grabbed the next hold. He was round the bulge, but his heart was hammering and his breath hissed in his throat.

'Are you all right?' Taita's voice came down to him.

'All right!' he gasped. He looked down between his knees and saw the crack in the rock widen into the top of the cleft above the nest. His arms were tiring and beginning to shake. He stretched his right leg down, and found another foothold.

Taita was right: it was more difficult to descend than to climb upwards. When he moved his right hand down he saw that already his knuckle was raw and he left a small bloody smear on the rock. Inching down, he reached the point where the crack opened into the main cleft. Again he was forced to reach round the lip and find a hidden hold.

Yesterday, when he and Taita had discussed it, sitting together on the other side of the gulf, this transition point had looked so easy, but now both his feet were swinging out freely over the lip of the cleft, and the abyss seemed to suck at him like some monstrous mouth. He moaned and hung on with both hands, freezing to the rock face. He was afraid now, the last vestige of courage blown away on the gusts of hot wind that tugged at him, threatening to tear him from the cliff. He looked down and tears mingled with the sweat on his cheeks. The drop beckoned, pulled at him with claws of terror, sickening him to the guts.

'Move!' Taita's voice drifted down to him, faint but filled with urgency. 'You must keep moving.'

With a huge effort Nefer rallied himself for another effort. His bare toes groped under him and he found a ledge that seemed wide enough to give him purchase. He lowered himself on aching, juddering arms. Abruptly his foot slipped from the ledge, and his arms were too tired to support his weight any longer. He fell and screamed as he went.

He dropped only the span of his two arms, and then the rope bit cruelly into his flesh, binding up under his ribs and choking the breath out of him. He came up short and dangled out into space, held only by the rope and the old man above him.

'Nefer, can you hear me?' Taita's voice was rough with the strain of holding him. The boy whimpered like a puppy. 'You must catch a hold. You cannot hang there.' Taita's voice calmed him. He blinked the tears out of his eyes, and saw the rock only an arm's length from his face.

'Latch on!' Taita goaded him, and Nefer saw that he was hanging opposite the cleft. The opening was deep enough to accommodate him, the sloping ledge wide enough for him to stand on, if only he could reach it. He stretched out a shaking hand and touched the wall with his fingertips. He started to swing himself back towards it.

It seemed an eternity of struggle and heartbreaking effort, but at last he swung into the opening and managed to place both bare feet on the ledge, and to crouch doubled over in the opening. He wedged himself there, panting and gasping for air.

Above him Taita felt his weight go off the rope, and called down encouragement. '*Bak-her*, Nefer, *Bak-her*! Where are you?'

'I am in the cleft, above the nest.'

'What can you see?' Taita wanted to keep the boy's mind fixed on other things, so that he would not dwell on the void beneath his feet.

Nefer wiped the sweat from his eyes with the back of his hand and peered down. 'I can see the edge of the nest.'

'How far?'

'Close.'

'Can you reach it?'

'I will try.' Nefer braced his bowed back against the roof of the narrow cleft, and shuffled slowly down the sloping floor. Below him he could just make out the dried twigs that protruded from the nest site. As he went down further, his view into the nest opened slowly an inch at a time.

The next time he called out his voice was stronger and excited. 'I can see the tiercel. He is still on the nest.'

'What is he doing?' Taita shouted back.

'He is crouched down. It seems as though he is sleeping.' Nefer's voice was puzzled. 'I can only see his back.'

The male bird was motionless, lying on the high side of the untidy nest. But how could he be sleeping and unaware during the commotion above him, Nefer wondered. His own fear was forgotten now in the excitement of having the falcon so close and the nest almost within touching distance.

He moved faster, more confidently, as the floor of the cleft levelled out under his feet, and there was more headroom for him to stand erect.

'I can see his head.' The tiercel was stretched out with his wings spread as though he was mantling a kill. He is beautiful, Nefer thought, and I am almost close enough to touch him, yet he still shows no fear.

Suddenly he realized he could seize the sleeping bird. He braced himself for the effort, wedging his shoulder into the cleft, his bare feet in a secure stance under him. Slowly he leaned out towards the tiercel, then stopped with his hand poised above it.

There were tiny droplets of blood on the russet back feathers. Bright as polished rubies, they twinkled in the sunlight, and with a sudden, swooping sensation in the pit of his stomach, Nefer realized that the tiercel was dead. He was overcome with a dreadful sense of loss, as though something of great value to him had been taken away for ever. It seemed more than just the death of the falcon. The royal bird represented something more: it was the symbol of a god and a king. As he stared at it, the carcass of the tiercel seemed to be transformed into the dead body of Pharaoh himself. A sob choked Nefer and he jerked away his hand.

He had moved only just in time, for then he heard a dry, rasping sound and an explosive hiss of air. Something huge and glittering black whipped out at where his hand had been the moment before, and slammed into the mattress of dried twigs with such force that the whole nest shook.

Nefer recoiled as far as the cramped space in the cleft would allow, and stared at the grotesque creature that now swayed and wove before his face. His vision seemed sharpened and magnified, time moved with the slow horror of nightmare. He saw the dead fledglings huddled in the cup of the nest beyond the carcass of the tiercel, the thick, glittering coils of a gigantic black cobra twisted around them. The snake's head was raised, its hood, marked with a bold pattern of black and white, was spread.

The slippery black tongue flickered out between the thin, grinning lips. Its eyes were fathomless black, each with a star of reflected light in the centre as they held Nefer in a mesmeric stare.

Nefer tried to scream a warning to Taita, but no sound came from his throat. He could not tear away his gaze from the cobra's dreadful stare. It's head swayed gently, but the massive coils that filled the falcon's nest to overflowing pulsed and clenched. Every polished scale was burnished like a jewel as they rasped against the twigs of the nest. Each coil was as thick as Nefer's arm, and slowly they revolved upon themselves.

The head swayed back, the mouth gaped, and Nefer could see the pale lining of the throat. The almost transparent fangs came erect in the folds of soft membrane: there was a tiny bead of colourless venom on the tip of each bony needle.

Then the wicked head flashed forward, as the cobra struck at Nefer's face.

Nefer screamed and hurled himself sideways, lost his balance and tumbled backwards from the cleft.

Even though Taita was braced to take any sudden weight on the rope, he was almost jerked from his stance on top of the cliff as Nefer's weight hit the line. A coil of the horsehair rope slid through his fingers, scorching the flesh, but he held hard. He could hear the boy screaming incoherently below him, and feel him swinging at the end of the rope.

Nefer pendulumed out from the cleft then swung straight back towards the falcon's nest. The cobra had recovered swiftly from its abortive strike, and was once more poised and erect. It fixed its gaze on the boy and swivelled its head to face him. At the same time a harsh hiss erupted from its throat.

Nefer screamed again and kicked out wildly at the snake as he flew straight towards it. Taita heard the terror in that scream and lay back on the rope, hauling until he felt his old muscles crack under the strain.

The cobra struck instinctively at Nefer's eyes as he came within range, but at that instant Taita's heave on the rope end jerked Nefer off-line. The snake's gaping jaws passed a finger's width from his ear and then, like the lash of a chariot whip, the heavy body flogged across his shoulder. Nefer screamed again, knowing he was fatally bitten.

As he swung out once more over the open drop he glanced down at the spot on his shoulder into which the serpent had sunk its fangs, and saw the pale yellow venom splashed across the thick leather fold of the saddlebag. With a wild lift of relief he tore the bag free and as he started to swing back towards where the cobra still stood menacingly, he held the bag like a shield in front of him.

The instant he was within range the cobra struck again, but Nefer caught the blow on the thick leather folds of the bag. The beast's fangs snagged in the leather and held fast. As Nefer swung back the snake was dragged with him. It was hauled cleanly out of the nest, a writhing, seething ball of coils and polished scales. It thrashed against Nefer's legs, the heavy tail lashing him, hissing fearsomely, clouds of venom spraying from its gaping jaws and dribbling down the leather bag. So great was its weight that Nefer's whole body was shaken violently.

Almost without thought, Nefer hurled the leather bag away from him, the cobra's fangs still hooked into the leather. The bag and the snake dropped away together, the sinuous body still curling, coiling and whipping furiously. The penetrating hisses grew fainter as it plunged away down the cliff. It seemed to fall for ever until at last it struck the rocks far below. The impact did not kill or stun it, and it whipped about as it rolled down the scree slope, bouncing over the rocks like a huge black ball until Nefer lost sight of it among the grey boulders.

Through the mists of terror that clouded his mind, Taita's voice reached him. It was hoarse with effort and concern. 'Speak to me. Can you hear me?'

'I am here, Tata.' Nefer's voice was weak and shaky.

'I will pull you up.'

Slowly, one heave at a time, Nefer was drawn upwards. Even in his distress Nefer marvelled at the old man's strength. When the rock came within reach, he was able to take some of his weight off the rope and it went quicker. At last he clawed his way round the overhang, and saw, with vast relief, Taita looking down at him from the summit, the ancient features, like those of a sphinx, riven into deep lines by his exertions on the rope.

With one last heave Nefer tumbled over the top and fell into the old man's arms. He lay there gasping and sobbing, unable to speak coherently. Taita hugged him. He too was shaking with emotion and exhaustion. Slowly they calmed and regained their breath. Taita held the waterskin to

Nefer's lips and he gulped, choked and gulped again. Then he looked into Taita's face so abjectly that the old man hugged him closer.

'It was horrible.' Nefer's words were barely intelligible. 'It was in the nest. It had killed the falcons, all of them. Oh, Tata, it was terrible.'

'What was it, Nefer?' Taita asked gently.

'It killed my godbird, and the tiercel.'

'Gently, lad. Drink some more.' He offered the water-skin.

Nefer choked again and was seized with a paroxysm of coughing. The moment he could speak again he wheezed, 'It tried to kill me also. It was huge, and so black.'

'What was it, boy? Tell me clearly.'

'A cobra, a huge black cobra. In the nest, waiting for me. It had bitten the chicks and the falcon to death, and it went for me as soon as it saw me. I never imagined a cobra could grow so large.'

'Are you stricken?' Taita demanded, with dread, and hauled Nefer to his feet to examine him.

'No, Tata. I used the bag as a shield. It never touched me,' Nefer protested, but Taita stripped off his kilt and made him stand naked while he went over his body looking for puncture wounds. One of his knuckles and both his knees were grazed but otherwise the strong young body was marked only by the pharaonic cartouche on the smooth skin of his inner thigh. Taita had tattooed the design himself, and it was a miniature masterpiece that would for ever endorse Nefer's claim to the double crown.

'Thanks be to the great god who protected you,' Taita murmured. 'With this cobra apparition, Horus has sent you a portent of terrible events and dangers.' His face was grave, and touched with the marks of grief and mourning. 'That was no natural serpent.'

'Yes, Tata. I saw it close. It was enormous, but it was a real snake.'

'Then how did it reach the nest site? Cobras cannot fly, and there is no other way to scale the cliff.'

Nefer stared at him aghast, 'It killed my godbird,' he whispered aloud.

'And it killed the royal tiercel, Pharaoh's other self.' Taita agreed grimly, sorrow still in his eyes. 'There are mysteries here revealed. I saw their shadows in my vision, but they are confirmed by what has happened to you this day. This is a thing beyond the natural order.'

'Explain it to me, Tata,' Nefer insisted.

Taita handed him his kilt. 'First we must get down off this mountain, and fly from the great dangers that beset us before I can consider the omens.'

He paused and looked to the sky, as if in deep thought. Then he lowered his eyes and looked into Nefer's face. 'Put on your clothes,' was all he said.

As soon as Nefer was ready, Taita led him back to the far side of the summit and they began the descent. It went swiftly, for they had opened the route, and the urgency in every move Taita made was infectious. The horses were where they had left them, but before they mounted Nefer said, 'The place where the cobra struck the rocks is but a short way from here.' He pointed to the head of the scree slope below the cliff on which the falcons' nest was still visible. 'Let us search for the carcass. Perhaps if we find its remains you could work some charm to destroy its powers.'

'It would be precious time wasted. There will be no carcass.' Taita swung up on to the mare's back. 'Mount, Nefer. The cobra has returned to the shadow places from which it sprang.'

Nefer shivered with superstitious awe, then scrambled up on to the back of his colt.

Neither of them spoke again until they were off the upper slopes and into the broken eastern foothills. Nefer knew well that when Taita was in this mood it was wasted effort to speak to him, but he urged his horse alongside and pointed out respectfully, 'Tata, this is not the way to Gebel Nagara.'

'We are not going back there.'

'Why not?'

'The Bedouin know that we were at the spring. They will tell those who search for us,' Taita explained.

Nefer was puzzled. 'Who searches for us?'

Taita turned his head and looked at the boy with such pity that he was silenced. 'I will explain when we are off this cursed mountain and in a safe place.'

Taita avoided the crests of the hills, where they might be silhouetted on the skyline, and wove a path through the gorges and valleys. Always he headed east, away from Egypt and the Nile, towards the sea.

The sun was setting before he reined in his mare again, and spoke: 'The main caravan road lies just beyond the next line of hills. We must cross it, but enemies may be watching for us there.'

They left the horses tethered in a hidden wadi, with a few handfuls of crushed *dhurra* millet in their leather nosebags to keep them contented, then climbed cautiously to the crest of the hills and found a vantage-point behind a bank of purple shale from which they could look down on to the caravan road below.

'We will lie here until dark,' Taita explained. 'Then we will cross.'

'I don't understand what you are doing, Tata. Why are we travelling east? Why don't we return to Thebes, and the protection of Pharaoh, my father?'

Taita sighed softly and closed his eyes. How do I tell him? I cannot hide it much longer. Yet he is a child still, and I should shield him.

It was almost as if Nefer had read his thoughts, for he laid his hand on Taita's arm and said quietly, 'Today, on the mountain, I proved that I am a man. Treat me as one.'

Taita nodded. 'Indeed, you proved it.' Before he went on

he swept another look along the well-beaten road below them, and immediately ducked his head, 'Someone coming!' he warned.

Nefer flattened himself behind the shale bank and they watched the column of dust coming swiftly down the caravan road from the west. By this time the valley was in deep shadow and the sky was filled with all the glorious shades of the sunset.

'They are moving fast. Those are not merchants, they are fighting chariots,' Nefer said. 'Yes, I can see them now.' His bright young eyes had picked out the shape of the leading chariot, with the teamed horses trotting ahead of the charioteer on his high carriage. 'They are not Hyksos,' he went on, as the shapes hardened and drew closer, 'they are ours. A troop of ten chariots. Yes! See the pennant on the leading vehicle.' The fluttering pennant on the long, limber bamboo rod rode high above the rolling dustcloud. 'A cohort of the Phat Guards! We are safe, Tata!'

Nefer sprang to his feet and waved both hands over his head, 'Here!' he yelled. 'Here, the Blues. Here I am. I am Prince Nefer!'

Taita reached up a bony hand and hauled him down violently. 'Get down, you little fool. Those are the minions of the cobra.'

He shot another quick glance over the bank, and saw that the leading charioteer must have spotted Nefer on the skyline, for he had whipped his team into a canter and was tearing up the road towards them.

'Come!' he told Nefer. 'Hurry! They must not catch us.'

He dragged the boy off the ridge and started down the slope. After his initial reluctance, Nefer was spurred on by Taita's haste. He began to run in earnest, jumping from rock to rock, but he could not catch the old man. Taita's long skinny legs flew and the silver mane of his hair streamed out behind him. He reached the horses first, and was on the mare's bare back in a single leap.

'I don't understand why we are running from our own people,' Nefer panted. 'What is happening, Tata?'

'Mount! No time now to talk. We must get clear.'

As they galloped out of the mouth of the wadi and into the open, Nefer shot a longing look back over his shoulder. The leading chariot came soaring over the top of the ridge, and the driver let out a shout, but the distance and the rumble of the wheels muffled his voice.

Earlier, Taita had led them through an area of broken volcanic rock through which no chariot would find a way. Now they rode for it, the horses running shoulder to shoulder, and stride for stride.

'If we can get among the rocks, we can lose them during the night. There is only a whisper of daylight left.' Taita looked up at the last glow of the sun that had already sunk behind the western hills.

'A single horseman can always hold off a chariot,' Nefer declared, with a confidence he did not truly feel. But when he looked back over his shoulder he saw it was true. They were pulling away from the troop of bouncing, jolting vehicles.

Before Nefer and Taita reached the broken ground the chariots had dropped so far behind that they were almost obscured by their own dustcloud and by the gathering blue dusk. As soon as they reached the fringe of rocks they were forced to bring the horses down to a cautious trot, but the footing was so dangerous and the light so bad that they were quickly reduced to a walk. In the last glimmer of the light Taita looked back and saw the dark shape of the leading chariot of the squadron halt at the edge of the bad ground. He recognized the voice of the driver who shouted after them, even though his words were faint.

'Prince Nefer, why do you flee? You need not fear us. We are the Phat Guards, come to escort you home to Thebes.'

Nefer made as if to turn his horse's head. 'That is Hilto.

I know his voice so well. He is a good man. He is calling my name.'

Hilto was a famous warrior, who wore the Gold of Valour, but Taita ordered Nefer onwards sternly.

'Don't be deceived. Trust nobody.'

Obediently Nefer rode on into the wilderness of broken rock. The faint shouts behind them dwindled and were snuffed out by the eternal silence of the desert. Before they had gone much further the darkness forced them to dismount and walk through the difficult places where the twisting path narrowed, and sharp pillars of black stone might maim a careless horse or shatter the wheels of any vehicle that tried to follow them through. At last they had to stop to water and rest the horses. They sat close together and, with his dagger, Taita sliced a loaf of *dhurra* bread, and they munched it as they talked softly.

'Tell me of your vision, Tata. What did you truly see when you worked the Mazes of Ammon Ra?'

'I told you. They were obscured.'

'I know that is not true.' Nefer shook his head. 'You said that to protect me.' He shivered from the chill of the night, and from the sense of dread that had been his constant companion ever since that visitation of evil at the falcons' nest. 'You saw something of terrible portent, I know you did. That is why we are fleeing now. You must tell me all your vision. I must understand what is happening to us.'

'Yes, you are right.' Taita agreed at last. 'It is time for you to know.' He put out one thin arm and drew Nefer close under his shawl – the boy was surprised by the warmth of the old man's skinny frame. Taita seemed to be collecting his thoughts, and then at last he spoke.

'In my vision I saw a great tree growing on the banks of Mother Nile. It was a mighty tree and its blooms were blue as hyacinth and over it hung the double crown of the Upper and Lower Kingdoms. In its shade were all the multitudes of this very Egypt, men and women, children and greybeards, merchants and farmers and scribes, priests and warriors. The tree gave them all protection, and they prospered mightily and were content.'

'That was a good vision.' Eagerly Nefer translated it, the way Taita had taught him: 'The tree must have been Pharaoh, my father. The colour of the House of Tamose is blue, and my father wears the double crown.'

'That is the meaning as I read it.'

'Then what did you see, Tata?'

'I saw a serpent in the muddy waters of the river, swimming towards where the tree stood. It was a mighty serpent.'

'A cobra?' Nefer guessed, and his voice was small and fearful.

'Yes,' Taita affirmed, 'it was a great cobra. And it crawled from the waters of the Nile and climbed into the tree, twisting itself around the trunk and the branches until it seemed part of the tree, supporting it and giving it strength.'

'That I do not understand,' Nefer whispered.

'Then the cobra reared up above the uppermost branches of the tree, struck down and buried its fangs in the trunk.'

'Sweet Horus.' Nefer shuddered. 'Was it the same snake that tried to bite me, do you think?' He did not wait for an answer, but went on quickly, 'What did you see then, Tata?'

'I saw the tree wither, fall and shatter. I saw the cobra still reared triumphantly on high, but now it wore on its evil brow the double crown. The dead tree began to throw out green shoots but as they appeared the serpent struck at them, and they, too, were poisoned and died.'

Nefer was silent. Although the meaning seemed evident, he was unable to voice his interpretation of the vision.

'Were all the green shoots of the tree destroyed?' he asked eventually.

'There was one that grew in secret, beneath the surface of the earth, until it was strong. Then it burst out like a mighty vine and locked itself in conflict with the cobra. Although the cobra attacked it with all its strength and venom, still it survived and had a life of its own.'

'What was the end of the conflict, Tata? Which of them triumphed? Which one wore the double crown at the end?'

'I did not see the end of the conflict, because it was obscured in the smoke and dust of war.'

Nefer was silent for so long that Taita thought he had fallen asleep, but then the boy began to shake and he realized he was weeping. At last Nefer spoke, with a dreadful finality and certainty. 'Pharaoh is dead. My father is dead. That was the message of your vision. The poisoned tree was Pharaoh. That was the same message at the falcons' nest. The dead tiercel was Pharaoh. My father is dead, killed by the cobra.'

Taita could not answer him. All he could do was tighten his grip around Nefer's shoulders, and try to impart strength and comfort to him.

'And I am the green shoot of the tree,' Nefer went on. 'You saw this. You know that the cobra is waiting to destroy me as he did my father. That is why you would not let the soldiers take me back to Thebes. You know that the cobra waits for me there.'

'You are right, Nefer. We cannot return to Thebes until you are strong enough to defend yourself. We must fly from this very Egypt. There are lands and mighty kings to the east. It is my purpose to go to them and seek an ally to help us destroy the cobra.'

'But who is the cobra? Did you not see his face in the vision?'

'We know that he stands close to your father's throne. For in the vision he was entwined with the tree and gave it support.' He paused, and then, as if making a decision, went on, 'Naja is the name of the cobra.'

Nefer stared at him. 'Naja!' he whispered. 'Naja! Now I

understand why we cannot return to Thebes.' He paused for a while, then said, 'Wandering in the eastern lands we will become two outcasts, beggars.'

'The vision showed that you will grow strong. We must put our trust in the Mazes of Ammon Ra.'

Despite his grief for his father, Nefer slept at last, but Taita roused him in the darkness before dawn. They mounted again and rode eastwards until the bad ground fell away behind them and Nefer thought he smelt the salt of the sea on the dawn wind.

'At the port of Seged we will find a ship to take us across to the land of the Hurrians.' Taita seemed to read what was in his mind. 'King Sargon of Babylon and Assyria, those mighty kingdoms between the Tigris and the Euphrates, is your father's satrap. He is bound in treaty to your father against the Hyksos, and all our mutual enemies. I think that Sargon will hold to that treaty, for he is an honourable man. We must trust that he will take us in and foster your claim to the throne of united Egypt.'

Ahead of them the sun came up in a furnace glow, and when they topped the next rise they saw the sea below them blazing like a freshly forged bronze war shield. Taita judged the distance. 'We will reach the coast before the sun sets this evening.' Then, with narrowed eyes, he turned to look back over his mount's rump. He stiffened as he made out not one but four separate plumes of yellow dust rising on the plain behind them. 'Hilto, again,' he exclaimed. 'I should have known better than to think that old rogue had given up the chase so readily.' He jumped up and stood erect on his horse's back for a better field of view, an old cavalryman's trick. 'He must have detoured around the rocky ground in the night. Now he has thrown out a ring of chariots in an extended line to sweep for our tracks. He did not need a necromancer to tell him we must be heading east for the coast.'

Swiftly he looked in every direction for cover. Although

the open stony plain over which they were travelling seemed devoid of any feature, he picked out an insignificant fold of ground that might offer concealment if they could reach it in time.

'Dismount!' he ordered Nefer. 'We must keep as low as possible and raise no dust for them to spot us.' Silently he rebuked himself for not having taken more care to cover their tracks during the night. Now as they turned aside and led the horses towards the concealing fold of ground, he took care to avoid the patches of soft earth and keep to a natural rock pavement, which would leave no tracks. When they reached the hidden ground they found it was too shallow to cover a standing horse.

Nefer looked back anxiously. The nearest column of moving dust was less than half a league behind them, and coming on fast. The others were spread out in a wide semicircle.

'There is no place to hide here, and it's too late to run now. Already they have us surrounded.' Taita slipped down from the back of his mare, spoke to her softly and stooped to caress her front legs. The mare stamped and snorted, but when he insisted, she lowered herself reluctantly and lay flat on her side still snorting in mild protest. Taita took off his kilt and used it to blindfold her, so that she would not attempt to stand up again.

Then he came quickly to Nefer's colt and performed the same trick. When both horses were down he told Nefer sharply, 'Lie at Stargazer's head and hold him down if he tries to stand.'

Nefer laughed for the first time since he had learned of his father's death. Taita's way with animals never failed to enchant him. 'How did you make them do that, Tata?'

'If you speak to them so that they understand, they will do whatever you tell them. Now, lie beside him and keep him quiet.'

They lay behind the horses and watched the encircling

columns of dust sweep across the plain around them. 'They won't be able to pick out our tracks on the stony ground, will they, Tata?' Nefer asked hopefully.

Taita grunted. He was watching the approach of the nearest chariot. In the dancing mirage it seemed insubstantial, wavering and distorted as an image seen through water. It was moving quite slowly, weaving from side to side as it cast for spoor. Suddenly it moved forward with more determination and purpose, and Taita could see that the charioteer had picked up their tracks and was following them.

The chariot came on until they could make out the men on the footplate more clearly. They were leaning out over the dashboard, examining the earth as they passed over it. Suddenly Taita muttered unhappily, 'By Seth's stinking breath, they have a Nubian scout with them.'

The tall black man was made even taller by the headdress of heron's feathers he wore. Five hundred cubits from where they lay concealed, the Nubian jumped down from the moving vehicle and ran ahead of the horses.

'They are at the spot where we turned aside,' Taita whispered. 'Horus conceal our spoor from that black savage.' It was said that Nubian scouts could follow the track left by a swallow flying through the air.

The Nubian brought the chariot to a halt with a peremptory hand signal. He had lost the tracks where they turned on to the stony ground. Bent almost double, he circled out over the bare earth. At that distance he looked like a secretary bird hunting for serpents and rodents.

'Can you not weave a spell of concealment for us, Tata?' Nefer whispered uneasily. Taita had worked the spell for them often when they were hunting gazelle out on the open plains, and most times had enticed the dainty little animals within easy bow-shot without them becoming aware of the hunters. Taita did not reply, but when Nefer glanced across to where he lay he saw that the old man already had his most potent charm in his hand, a golden five-pointed star of exquisite workmanship, the Periapt of Lostris. Nefer knew that sealed within it was a lock of hair Taita had snipped from the head of Queen Lostris as she lay on the embalmer's table before her deification. Taita touched it to his lips as he silently recited the canticle for Concealment from the Eyes of an Enemy.

Out on the plain the Nubian straightened with a fresh air of purpose, and gazed straight in their direction.

'He has found the twist in our tracks,' Nefer said, and they watched the chariot pull in behind him as the Nubian started towards them over the rocky ground.

Taita said softly, 'I know that devil well. His name is Bay and he is a shaman of the Usbak tribe.'

Nefer watched in trepidation as the chariot and its outrider came on steadily. The charioteer was standing high on the footplate. Surely he could look down on them from there. But he made no sign of having spotted them.

Closer still they came and Nefer recognized Hilto as the charioteer, even down to the white battle scar on his right cheek. For a moment it seemed he stared straight at Nefer with those hawk-sharp eyes, then his gaze slid away.

'Do not move.' Taita's voice was soft as the light breeze over the bright plain.

Now Bay, the Nubian, was so close that Nefer could see every charm in the necklace that dangled on his broad bare chest. Bay stopped abruptly and his scarified features creased into a frown, as he turned his head, slowly questing all around, like a hunting dog with the scent of game in his nostrils.

'Still!' Taita whispered. 'He senses us.'

Bay came on a few slow paces then stopped again and held up his hand. The chariot pulled up behind him. The horses were restless and fidgeting. Hilto touched the dash-board with the shaft of the lance in his hand. The small rasping sound was magnified in the silence.

Now Bay was staring directly into Nefer's face. Nefer

tried to hold that dark implacable stare without blinking, but his eyes watered with the strain. Bay reached up and clasped one of the charms on his necklace. Nefer realized it was the floating bone from the chest of a man-eating lion. Taita had one in his armoury of talismans and magical charms.

Bay began to chant softly in his deep melodious African bass. Then he stamped one bare foot on the hard earth, and spat in Nefer's direction.

'He is piercing my curtain,' Taita said flatly. Suddenly Bay grinned and pointed directly at them with the lion charm in his fist. Behind him Hilto shouted with astonishment, and gaped at where Taita and Nefer were suddenly revealed, lying on the open ground only a hundred cubits away.

'Prince Nefer! We have searched for you these thirty days past. Thank great Horus and Osiris, we have found you at last.'

Nefer sighed and scrambled to his feet, and Hilto drove up, leaped out of the chariot and went down on one knee before him. He lifted the bronze skull helmet from his head, and cried, in a voice pitched to giving commands on the battlefield, 'Pharaoh Tamose is dead! Hail, Pharaoh Nefer Seti. May you live for ever.'

Seti was the Prince's divine name, one of the five names of power that had been given him at birth, long before his accession to the throne was assured. No one had been allowed to use the divine name until this moment when he was first hailed as Pharaoh.

'Pharaoh! Mighty bull! We have come to bear you to the Holy City that you may be risen in Thebes in your own divine image as Horus of Gold.'

'What if I should choose not to go with you, Colonel Hilto?' Nefer asked.

Hilto looked distressed. 'With all love and loyalty, Pharaoh, it is the strictest order of the Regent of Egypt that you be brought to Thebes. I must obey that order, even at the risk of your displeasure.'

Nefer glanced sideways at Taita, and spoke from the side of his mouth: 'What must I do?'

'We must go with them.'

They began the return to Thebes with an escort of fifty fighting chariots led by Hilto. Under strict orders the column rode first to the oasis of Boss. Fast horsemen had been sent ahead to Thebes and Lord Naja, the Regent of Egypt, had come out from the city to the oasis to meet the young Pharaoh Nefer Seti.

On the fifth day the squadron of chariots, dusty and battered from months in the wilderness, trotted into the oasis. As they entered the shade of the canopy of the palm groves a full regiment of the Phat Guards formed up in parade order to welcome them. The troopers had sheathed their weapons and instead carried palm fronds, which they waved as they chanted the anthem to their monarch.

'Seti, mighty bull.
Beloved of truth.
He of the two ladies, Nekhbet and Wadjet.
Fiery serpent, great of strength.
Horus of Gold, who makes hearts live.
He of the sedge and the bee.
Seti, son of Ra, god of the sun, living for ever and eternity.'

Nefer stood between Hilto and Taita on the footplate of the leading chariot. His clothing was ragged and dusty, and his thick locks were matted with dust. The sun had burnt his face and arms to the colour of ripe almonds. Hilto drove the chariot down the long alley formed by the soldiers, and Nefer smiled shyly at those men in the ranks whom he recognized and they cheered him spontaneously. They had loved his father, and now they loved him.

In the centre of the oasis an assembly of multicoloured tents had been set up beside the well. In front of the royal tent Lord Naja, surrounded by a concourse of courtiers, nobles and priests, waited to receive the king. He was mighty in the power and grace of regency, glistening and beautiful in gold and precious stones, redolent of sweet unguents and fragrant lotions.

On his either hand stood Heseret and Merykara, the princesses of the royal House of Tamose. Their faces were pearly white with makeup, eyes huge and dark with kohl. Even the nipples of their bare breasts had been rouged red as ripe cherries. The horsehair wigs were too large for their pretty heads, and their skirts were so heavy with pearls and gold thread that they stood as stiffly as carved dolls.

As Hilto brought the chariot to a halt in front of him, Lord Naja stepped forward and lifted down the dirty boy. Nefer had not had an opportunity to bathe since leaving Gebel Nagara, and he smelt like a billy-goat.

'As your regent I salute you, Pharaoh. I am your foot servant and your loyal companion. May you live a thousand years,' he intoned, so that all those in the closest ranks could hear every word. Lord Naja led Nefer by the hand to the dais of council, carved from precious black woods from the interior of the African continent and inlaid with ivory and mother-of-pearl. He placed him upon it, then went down on his knees and kissed Nefer's grazed and grubby feet without any sign of repugnance. The toenails were torn and caked with black dirt.

He stood up and lifted Nefer to his feet, stripped away the torn kilt so the pharaonic tattoo on his thigh was revealed. He turned the boy slowly so that everyone in the audience could see it clearly.

'Hail, Pharaoh Seti, god and son of the gods. Behold thy sign. Look upon this mark, all the nations of the earth, and tremble at the power of the king. Bow down before the might of Pharaoh.'

A great shout went up from the soldiers and the courtiers packed around the dais. 'Hail, Pharaoh! In his might and majesty may he live for ever.'

Naja led the princesses forward, and they knelt before their brother to take their oaths of allegiance. Their voices were inaudible until Merykara, the younger, could contain herself no longer and sprang up on to the dais in a flurry of jewelled skirts. She rushed to her brother. 'Nefer,' she squealed, 'I have missed you so very much. I thought you were dead.' Nefer returned her embrace awkwardly, until she pulled away and whispered, 'You smell terribly,' and giggled.

Lord Naja signalled for one of the royal nursemaids to take the child away, and then, one by one, the mighty lords of Egypt, headed by the members of the council, came forward to take the loyal oath. There was one uncomfortable moment when Pharaoh surveyed the gathering and asked, in a clear, penetrating voice, 'Where is my good uncle Kratas? He of all my people should have been here to greet me.'

Talla mumbled a placatory explanation. 'Lord Kratas is unable to attend. It shall be explained later to Your Majesty.' Talla, old and feeble, was now president of the council of state. He had become Naja's creature.

The ceremony ended when Lord Naja clapped his hands. 'Pharaoh has come on a long journey. He must rest before leading the procession into the city.'

He took Nefer's hand in a proprietary manner and led him into the royal tent whose spacious galleries and saloons could have accommodated a full regiment of the guards. There the master of the wardrobe, the perfumers and hairdressers, the keeper of the royal jewels, the valets, manicurists, masseurs and the maids of the bath were waiting to receive him.

Taita had determined to stay at the boy's side where he could protect him. He tried unobtrusively to include himself among this entourage, but his lanky frame and head of silver hair marked him out, while his fame and reputation were such that he could never have passed inconspicuously anywhere in the land. Almost immediately a serjeant-at-arms confronted him. 'Greetings, Lord Taita. May the gods always smile upon you.' Although Pharaoh Tamose had elevated him to the nobility on the day that he had sealed the deed of his manumission, Taita still felt awkward at being addressed by his title.

'The Regent of Egypt has sent for you.' He looked down at the Magus' filthy clothing and dusty old sandals. 'It would be as well not to attend him in your present state of dress. Lord Naja detests uncouth odours and unwashed apparel.'

Lord Naja's tent was larger and more luxuriously appointed than Pharaoh's. He sat on a throne of carved ebony and ivory decorated in gold and the even rarer and more precious silver with representations of all the principal gods of Egypt. The sandy floor was covered with woollen rugs from Hurria, woven in wonderful colours, including the bright green that signified the verdant fields that covered both banks of the Nile. Since his elevation to the stature of regent, Naja had adopted that green as the colour of his house.

He believed that pleasing aromas encouraged the gods to draw nigh, and incense burned in the silver pots suspended on chains from the ridge-pole of the tent. There were open glass vases filled with perfume on the low table in front of the throne. The Regent had discarded his wig, and a slave held a cone of perfumed beeswax on his shaven pate. As the wax melted it ran down his cheeks and neck, cooling and soothing him.

The interior of the tent smelt like a garden. Even the ranks of courtiers, ambassadors and supplicants who sat facing the throne had been induced to bathe and perfume their bodies before entering the presence of the Regent. Likewise, Taita had followed the advice of the serjeant-at-arms. His hair was washed and combed into a silver cascade over his shoulders, and his linen was freshly laundered and bleached to purest white. At the entrance to the tent, he knelt to make obeisance to the throne. There was a hum of comment and speculation as he rose to his feet. The foreign ambassadors stared at him curiously, and he heard his name whispered. Even the warriors and priests nodded and leaned close together as they told each other, 'It is the Magus.'

'The holy Taita, adept of the Mazes.'

'Taita, the Wounded Eye of Horus.'

Lord Naja looked up from the papyrus he was scanning and smiled down the length of the tent. He was truly a handsome man, with sculpted features and sensitive lips. His nose was straight and narrow, and his eyes were the colour of golden agate, lively and intelligent. His naked chest was devoid of fat, and his arms were lean and covered with hard muscle.

Swiftly Taita surveyed the ranks of men who now sat closest to the throne. In the short time since the death of Pharaoh Tamose there had been a redistribution of power and favour among the courtiers and nobles. Many familiar faces were missing, and many others had emerged from obscurity into the sunshine of the Regent's goodwill. Not least of these was Asmor of the Phat Guards.

'Come forward, Lord Taita.' Naja's voice was pleasant and low. Taita moved towards the throne, and the ranks of courtiers opened to let him pass. The Regent smiled down at him. 'Know you that you stand high in our favour. You have discharged the duty that Pharaoh Tamose placed upon you with distinction. You have given the Prince Nefer Memnon invaluable instruction and training.' Taita was astonished by the warmth of this greeting, but he did not let it show. 'Now that the prince has become Pharaoh Seti, he will stand in even greater need of your guiding hand.'

'May he live for ever,' Taita responded, and the gathering echoed his words.

'May he live for ever.'

Lord Naja gestured. 'Take your seat here, in the shadow of my throne. Even I will have much need of your experience and wisdom when it comes to ordering the affairs of Pharaoh.'

'The royal Regent does me more honour than I deserve.' Taita turned a gentle face to Lord Naja. It was prudent never to let your hidden enemy recognize your animosity. He took the seat that was offered him, but declined the silken cushion, and sat on the woollen rug. His back was straight, and his shoulders square.

The business of the Regency proceeded. They were dividing up the estate of General Kratas: as a declared traitor everything Kratas owned was forfeited to the Crown. 'From the traitor Kratas, unto the temple of Hapi and the priests of the mysteries,' Naja read from the papyrus, 'all his lands and the buildings on the east bank of the river between Dendera and Abnub.'

As Taita listened he mourned his oldest friend, but he let no shadow of grief show on his face. During the long journey back from the desert, Hilto had related the manner of Kratas' death, then gone on to tell him, 'All men, even the noble and the good, walk softly in the presence of the new Regent of Egypt. Menset is dead, he who was president of the council of state. He died in his sleep, but there are those who say he had a little help to start him on the journey. Cinka is dead, executed for treason, though he had no longer the wits to cheat on his ancient wife. His estates are confiscated by the Regency. Fifty more have gone in company with the good Kratas to the underworld. And the council members are all Naja's dogs.'

Kratas had been Taita's last link with the golden days when Tanus, Lostris and he had been young. Taita had loved him well.

'From the traitor Kratas, unto the Regent of Egypt, all the store of millet held in his name in the granaries of Athribis,' Lord Naja read from the papyrus.

That was fifty bargeloads, Taita calculated, for Kratas had been a shrewd investor in the millet exchanges. Lord Naja had paid himself generously for the onerous work of assassination.

'These stores to be used for the common good.' The expropriation was qualified, and Taita wondered expressionlessly who would determine the public good.

The priests and the scribes were busily recording the division on their clay tablets. These would be stored in the archives of the temple. While Taita watched and listened, he kept his anger and his sorrow locked away in his heart.

'We will move on now to another important royal matter,' Lord Naja said, when Kratas' heirs had been deprived of all their inheritance, and he was richer by three lakhs of gold. 'I come to the consideration of the well-being and status of the princesses royal, Heseret and Merykara. I have consulted earnestly with the members of the council of state. All are agreed that, for their own good, I should take both the Princess Heseret and the Princess Merykara in marriage. As my wives, they will come under my full protection. The goddess Isis is the patron of both the royal maidens. I have ordered the priestesses of the goddess to consult the auguries, and they have determined that these marriages are pleasing to the goddess. Therefore, the ceremony will take place in the temple of Isis at Luxor on the day of the next full moon after the burial of Pharaoh Tamose, and the coronation of his heir, Prince Nefer Seti.'

Taita remained unmoving, his face blank, but all around him there was a rustle and murmur at this pronouncement. The political considerations of such a double marriage were monumental. All of those present knew that Lord Naja was intent on making himself a member through marriage of the royal House of Tamose, and thus the next in line of succession.

Taita felt chilled to his bones, as though he had just heard the death sentence of Pharaoh Nefer Seti cried aloud from the White Tower in the centre of Thebes. There remained only twelve more days of the required seventy for the Royal embalming of the dead pharaoh. Immediately after the interment of Tamose in his tomb in the Valley of the Kings on the west bank of the Nile, the coronation of his successor and the weddings of his surviving daughters would take place.

Then the cobra will strike again. Taita felt the certainty of it. He was roused from his preoccupation with the dangers that surrounded the prince by a general stir in the gathering around him, and he realized that, without him hearing it, the Regent had just declared the levee closed, and was rising and retiring through the tent flap behind the throne. He rose with the others to leave the tent.

Colonel Asmor stepped forward to stop him, with a smile and a courteous bow. 'Lord Naja, the Regent of Egypt, asks you not to leave. He invites you to a private audience.'

Asmor was now colonel of the Regent's bodyguard, with the rank of Best of Ten Thousand. In a short time he had become a man of power and influence. There was no point in or possibility of refusing the summons, and Taita nodded. 'I am the servant of Pharaoh and of his regent. May they both live a thousand years.'

Asmor led him to the back of the tent, and held open the curtaining for him to pass through. Taita found himself out in the open palm groves, and Asmor led him through the trees to where a smaller, single-roomed tent was pitched on its own. A dozen guards were posted in a ring around this pavilion, for this was a place of secret council which no person was permitted to approach without the Regent's summons. At a command from Asmor, the guards stood aside and the colonel ushered Taita into the shaded interior.

Naja looked up from the bronze bowl in which he was washing his hands. 'You are welcome, Magus.' He smiled warmly, and waved to the pile of cushions in the centre of the rug-covered floor. While Taita seated himself, Naja nodded to Asmor, who went to take up a guard position at the tent opening, his sickle sword drawn. There were only the three of them in the tent, and their conversation would not be overheard.

Naja had discarded his jewellery, and insignia of office. He was affable and friendly as he came to take a seat on one of the cushions facing Taita. He indicated the tray of sweetmeats and sherbet in golden bowls that stood between them. 'Please refresh yourself.'

Taita's instinct was to decline, but he knew that to refuse the Regent's hospitality would advertise his own hostility, and alert Naja to his deadly opposition.

As yet, Lord Naja had no reason to know that Taita was aware of his intentions towards the new Pharaoh, or of Naja's crimes and his further ambitions. He inclined his head in thanks and selected the golden bowl furthest from his hand. He waited for Naja to pick up the other bowl of sherbet. The Regent took it, raised it, drank and swallowed without hesitation.

Taita lifted the bowl to his lips, and sipped the cordial. He held it on his tongue. There were those who boasted of possessing poisons that were tasteless and undetectable, but Taita had studied all the corrosive elements, and even the tart fruit could not mask their flavours from him. The drink was uncontaminated, and he swallowed it with pleasure.

'Thank you for your trust,' said Naja gravely, and Taita

knew that he referred to more than his acceptance of the refreshment.

'I am the servant of the King, and therefore of his regent.'

'You are a person of inestimable value to the Crown,' Naja countered. 'You have faithfully served three pharaohs and all of them have relied on your advice without question.'

'You overestimate my worth, my lord Regent. I am an old man and feeble.'

Naja smiled. 'Old? Yes, you are old. I have heard it said that you are more than two hundred years old.' Taita inclined his head, neither confirming nor denying it. 'But feeble, no! You are old and as monumental as a mountain. All men know that your wisdom is boundless. Even the secrets of eternal life are yours.'

The flattery was blatant and unashamed, and Taita searched behind it for the hidden reason and meaning. Naja was silent, watching him expectantly. What was he waiting to hear? Taita looked into his eyes, and tuned his mind to catch the other man's thoughts. They were as fleeting and evanescent as the darting shapes of cave bats against the darkling sky at sunset.

He captured one thought entire, and suddenly understood what Naja wanted from him. The knowledge gave him power, and the way ahead opened before him like the gates of a captured city.

'For a thousand years, every king and every learned man has searched for the secret of eternal life,' he said softly.

'Perhaps one man alone has found it.' Naja leaned forward eagerly, with his elbows on his knees.

'My lord, your questions are too profound for an old man like me. Two hundred years is not life eternal.' Taita spread his hands deprecatingly, but dropped his eyes, allowing Naja to read what he wanted to hear in the half-hearted denial. The double crown of Egypt, and eternal life, he thought, and smiled inwardly, keeping his expression solemn. This regent's wants are few and simple.

Naja straightened. 'We will speak of these deep matters another time.' There was a triumphant light in his yellow eyes. 'But now there is something else I would ask of you. It would be a way for you to prove that my good opinion of you is fully justified. You would find my gratitude without bounds.'

He twists and turns like an eel, Taita thought, and I once believed him to be a dull clod of a soldier. He has been able to hide the light of his lantern from all of us. Aloud he said simply, 'If it is within my power, I would deny Pharaoh's regent nothing.'

'You are an adept of the Mazes of Ammon Ra,' Naja said, with a finality that brooked no denial.

Once more Taita glimpsed the shadowy depths of this man's ambition. Not only the crown and eternal life! He wishes also to have the future revealed to him, Taita marvelled, but nodded humbly and replied, 'My lord Naja, all my life I have studied the mysteries, and perhaps I have learned a little.'

'All your very long life.' Naja placed his own emphasis on the phrase. 'And you have learned a very great deal.'

Taita bowed his head and remained silent. Why did I ever dream that he would have me killed? he asked himself. He will protect me with his own life, for that is what he believes I hold in my hands – the key to his immortality.

'Taita, beloved of kings and gods, I wish you to work the Mazes of Ammon Ra for me.'

'My lord, I have never worked the Mazes for anyone who was not a queen or a pharaoh, or one who was not destined to sit upon the throne of this very Egypt.'

'It may well be that one such person asks you now,' said Lord Naja, with deep significance in his tone.

Great Horus has delivered him to me. I have him in my hands, Taita thought, and said, 'I bow to the wishes of Pharaoh's regent.'

'Will you work the Mazes for me this very day? I am most anxious to know the wishes of the gods.' Naja's handsome features were alive with excitement and avarice.

'No man should enter the Mazes lightly,' Taita demurred. 'There are great dangers, not only for me but also for the patron who requests the divination. It will take time to prepare for the journey into the future.'

'How long?' Naja's disappointment was evident.

Taita clasped his forehead in a pantomime of deep thought. Let him sniff the bait for a while, he thought. It will make him more eager to swallow the hook. At last he looked up. 'On the first day of the festival of the Bull of Apis.'

The next morning, when he emerged from the great tent, Pharaoh Seti was transformed from the dusty and odorous little rapscallion who had entered the oasis of Boss the previous day.

With a regal fury and fire that had dismayed his entourage, he had resisted the attempts of the barbers to shave his head. Instead, his dark curls had been shampooed and combed until they shone in the early sunlight with russet lights. On top of them he wore the *uraeus*, the circlet of gold depicting Nekhbet, the vulture goddess, and Naja, the cobra. Their images were entwined on his forehead, with eyes of red- and blue-coloured glass. On his chin was the false beard of kingship. His makeup was skilfully created so that his beauty was enhanced, and the packed crowds who waited before the tent sighed with admiration and awe as they sank to the ground in adoration. His false fingernails were of beaten gold, and there were gold sandals on his feet. On his chest was one of the most precious of the Crown Jewels of Egypt: the pectoral medallion of Tamose, a jewelled portrait of the god Horus the Falcon. He walked with a stately tread for one so young, carrying the flail and the sceptre crossed over his heart. He stared solemnly ahead until, from the corner of his eye, he glimpsed Taita in the front rank of the crowd: he rolled his eyes at the old man then made an impish moue of resignation.

In a cloud of perfume, Lord Naja walked a pace behind him, splendid with jewels and awesome with authority. On his hip hung the blue sword, and on his right arm he wore the hawk seal.

Next came the princesses, with the golden feathers of the goddess Isis on their heads, and golden rings on their fingers and toes. They were no longer in the stiff, encrusted robes of yesterday: from throat to ankles they were encased in long dresses, but the linen was so fine and transparent that the sunlight struck through it, as though through the river mist at dawn. Merykara's limbs were slim, and her chest boyish. The outline of Heseret's body was moulded into voluptuous curves, her breasts were rosy-tipped through the diaphanous folds, and at the base of her belly, in the fork of her thighs, nestled the shadowy triangle of womanhood.

Pharaoh mounted the processional carriage and took his seat on the elevated throne. Lord Naja stood at his right hand, and the princesses sat at his feet.

The companies of priests from every one of the fifty temples of Thebes fell in ahead, strumming the lyre, beating drum and shaking sistrum, sounding the horns, chanting and wailing praises and supplications to the gods.

Then Asmor's bodyguard took up their positions in the procession, and after them came Hilto's squadron of chariots, all freshly burnished and decked with pennants and flowers. The horses were curried until their hides glowed like precious metal, and ribbons were plaited into their manes. The bullocks in the traces of the royal carriage were all of unblemished white, their massive humps decorated with bouquets of lilies and water-hyacinth. Their wide-spread horns and even their hoofs were covered with gold leaf.

The drivers were stark naked Nubian slaves. Every hair had been plucked from their heads and bodies which greatly emphasized the size of their genitals. They had been anointed from head to foot with rich oils so that they glistened in the sunlight, black as the eye of Seth, in magnificent contrast to the snowy hides of their bullocks. They goaded the team forward, and the bullocks plodded through the dust. A thousand warriors of the Phat Guards fell in behind them and burst with one voice into the anthem of praise. The populace of Thebes had opened the main gates of the city in welcome and were lining the tops of the walls. From a mile outside it they had covered the dusty surface of the road with palm fronds, straw and flowers.

The walls, towers and buildings of Thebes were all built of sun-baked mud bricks – stone blocks were reserved for the construction of tombs and temples. It hardly rained in the Nile valley so these constructions never deteriorated; they had all been freshly whitewashed and hung with banners in the sky blue of the House of Tamose. The procession passed through the gates, with the crowds dancing, singing and weeping with joy, filling the narrow streets so that the pace of the royal carriage was that of a giant tortoise. At every temple along the way the royal carriage came to a ponderous halt, and Pharaoh dismounted in solemn dignity to sacrifice to the god who dwelt within.

It was late afternoon before they reached the docks at the riverside where the royal barge waited to ferry Pharaoh's party across to the palace of Memnon on the west bank. Once they had gone on board, two hundred rowers in massed banks plied their paddles. To the beat of the drum they rose and fell in unison, wet and shining like the wings of a gigantic egret.

Surrounded by a fleet of galleys, feluccas and other small craft they made the crossing in the late sunlight. Even when they reached the west bank the King's duties for his first day were not completed. Another royal carriage bore him through the crowds to the funerary temple of his father, Pharaoh Tamose.

It was dark before they rode up the causeway, lit on both sides by bonfires, and the populace had indulged themselves all that day on beer and wine provided by the royal treasury. The uproar was deafening as Pharaoh dismounted at Tamose's temple, and climbed the stairway between ranks of granite statues of his father and of his patron god Horus in all his hundred divine guises – Horus as the child Harpocrates, with side-lock and a finger in his mouth, suckling at the breast of Isis, or squatting on a lotus blossom, or falcon-headed, or as the winged sun disc. It seemed that king and god had become one.

Lord Naja and the priests led the boy Pharaoh through the tall wooden gates into the Hall of Sorrow, that holy place where Tamose's mummy lay on its embalming slab of black diorite. In a separate shrine in the side wall, guarded by a black statue of Anubis, the god of cemeteries, stood the pearly alabaster canopic jars that held the king's heart, lungs and viscera.

In a second shrine against the opposite wall the gold-covered sarcophagus stood ready to receive the royal corpse. The lid of the coffin bore a portrait of Pharaoh in gold so lifelike that Nefer's heart twisted, impaled with grief, and tears started in his eyes. He blinked them away, and followed the priests to where his father's body lay in the centre of the hall.

Lord Naja took up his position opposite him on the far side of the diorite slab, facing Nefer, and the high priest stood at the head of the dead king. When all was in readiness for the ceremony of Opening the Mouth of the dead king, two priests drew aside the linen sheet that covered the corpse, and Nefer recoiled involuntarily as he looked down on his father.

For all the weeks after his death, while Nefer and Taita had been in the desert, the embalmers had been at work on the King's body. First they had probed a long-handled silver spoon up his nostril and, without marking his head, scooped out the soft custard of the brains. They removed the eyeballs, which would putrefy swiftly, and filled the eye sockets and the cavity of the skull with natron salts and aromatic herbs. Then they had lowered the corpse into a bath of highly concentrated salts, with the head exposed, and let it soak for thirty days, daily changing the harsh alkali fluids. The fats were leached out of the corpse and the skin peeled away. Only the hair and skin of the head were unaffected.

When at last the corpse was removed from the natron bath it was laid on the diorite slab and wiped down with oils and herbal tinctures. The empty stomach cavity was stuffed with linen pads soaked in resins and waxes. The arrow wound in the chest was sewn closed, and amulets of gold and precious stones placed over it. The barbed and broken shaft that had killed the king had been removed from Pharaoh's body by the embalmers. After it had been examined by the council of state, the missile had been sealed in a golden casket and would go into his tomb with him, a powerful charm against any further evil that might befall him on his journey through the netherworld.

Then, during the remaining forty days of the embalming, the corpse was allowed to dry thoroughly with the hot desert wind through the open doorways streaming over it.

Once it was as desiccated as firewood, it could be bound up. The linen bandages were laid on it in an intricate design, as incantations to the gods were chanted by choirs of priests. Under them were placed more precious talismans and amulets, and each layer was painted with resins that dried to a metallic hardness and sheen. Only the head was left uncovered, and then for the week before Opening the Mouth, four of the most skilful makeup artists of the guild of embalmers, using wax and cosmetics, had restored the King's features to lifelike beauty.

They replaced the missing eyes with perfect replicas of rock-crystal and obsidian. The whites were translucent, the iris and pupils an exact match of the king's natural colour. The glass orbs seemed endowed with life and intelligence, so that now Nefer gazed into them with awe, expecting to see the lids blink and his father's pupils widen in recognition. The lips were shaped and rouged so that at any moment they might smile, and his painted skin looked silken and warm, as though bright blood still ran beneath it. His hair had been washed and set in the familiar dark ringlets that Nefer remembered so well.

Lord Naja, the high priest and the choir began to chant the incantation against dying for the second time, but Nefer could not tear his gaze away from his father's face.

'He is the reflection and not the mirror,
He is the music and not the lyre,
He is the stone and not the chisel,
He will live for ever.'

The high priest came to Nefer's side and placed the golden spoon in his hand. Nefer had been coached in the ritual, but his hand trembled as he placed the spoon on his father's lips and recited, 'I open thy lips that thou might have the power of speech once more.' He touched his father's nose with the spoon. 'I open thy nostrils that thou might breathe once more.' He touched each of the magnificent eyes. 'I open thine eyes that thou might behold the glory of this world once more, and the glory of the world to come.'

When at last it was done, the royal party waited as the embalmers wrapped the head and painted it with aromatic resins. Then they laid the golden mask over the blind face, and once more it glowed with splendid life. Contrary to custom and usage, there was only one death mask and one golden sarcophagus for Pharaoh Tamose. His father had gone before him to his tomb covered by seven masks and seven sarcophagi, one within the other, each larger and more ornate than the next.

For the rest of that night Nefer stayed beside the golden sarcophagus, praying and burning incense, entreating the gods to take his father among them and seat him in the midst of the pantheon. In the dawn he went out with the priests on to the terrace of the temple where his father's head falconer waited. He carried a royal falcon on his gloved fist.

'Nefertem!' Nefer whispered the bird's name. 'Lotus Flower.' He took the magnificent bird from the falconer and held it high upon his own fist, so that the populace gathered below the terrace might see it clearly. Around its right leg the falcon wore a tiny goldtag on a golden chain. On it was engraved his father's royal cartouche. 'This is the godbird of Pharaoh Tamose Mamose. It is the spirit of my father.' He paused to regain his composure, for he was near to tears. Then he went on, 'I set my father's godbird free.' He slipped the leather rufterhood from the falcon's head. Fierce eyes blinked at the light of the dawn and the bird ruffled its feathers. Nefer unknotted the jesses from its leg, and the bird spread its wings. 'Fly, divine spirit!' Nefer cried. 'Fly high for me and my father!'

He threw the bird up, it caught the dawn wind and soared on high. Twice it circled overhead, and then, with a wild and haunting cry, it sped away across the Nile.

'The godbird flies to the west!' the high priest called out.

Every member of the congregation upon the steps of the temple knew that that was a most unpropitious omen.

Nefer was so physically and emotionally exhausted that as he watched the bird fly away he swayed on his feet. Taita steadied him before he fell and led him away.

Back in Nefer's bedchamber in the palace of Memnon, Taita mixed a draught at his bedside and knelt beside him to offer it. Nefer took one long swallow then lowered the cup and asked, 'Why does my father have only one small coffin when you tell me my grandfather was entombed in seven heavy golden sarcophagi and that it took twenty strong oxen to draw his funeral wagon?'

'Your grandfather was given the richest funeral in all the history of our land, and he took a great store of grave goods to the underworld with him, Nefer,' Taita agreed. 'But those seven coffins consumed thirty lakhs of pure gold, and almost beggared the nation.'

Nefer looked thoughtfully into the cup, then drained the last few drops of the draught. 'My father deserved such a rich funeral, for he was a mighty man.'

'Your grandfather thought much of his afterlife,' Taita explained patiently. 'Your father thought much of his people and the welfare of this very Egypt.'

Nefer thought about this for a while, then sighed, settled down on the sheepskin mattress and closed his eyes. He opened them again. 'I am proud of my father,' he said simply.

Taita laid his hand upon his forehead in blessing and whispered, 'And I know that one day your father will have reason to be proud of you.'

It did not need the ill omen of the flight of the falcon Nefertem to warn Taita that they had reached the most dire and fateful period in all the long history of this very Egypt. When he left Nefer's bedchamber and started out into the desert, it was as though the stars stood frozen in their courses and all the ancient gods had drawn back and deserted them, abandoning them in this their most dangerous hour.

'Great Horus, we need your guidance now. You hold this *Ta-meri*, this precious land, in the cup of your hands. Do not let it slip through your fingers and shatter like crystal. Do not turn your back upon us now that we are in our agony. Help me, mighty falcon. Instruct me. Make your wishes clear to me, so that I may follow your will.'

Praying as he went, he climbed the hills at the periphery of the great desert. The clicking of his long staff against the rocks alarmed a yellow jackal and sent it scampering away up the moonlit slope. When he was certain that he was not observed he turned parallel to the river, and quickened his stride. 'Horus, well you know that we are balanced on the sword edge of war and defeat. Pharaoh Tamose has been struck down and there is no warrior to lead us. Apepi and his Hyksos in the north are grown so mighty as to have become almost invincible. They gather against us, and we cannot stand against them. The double crown of the two kingdoms is rotten with the worm of treachery, and cannot survive against the new tyranny. Open my eyes, mighty god, and show me the way, that we might triumph against the invading Hyksosian hordes from the north and against the destroying poison in our blood.'

For the rest of that day Taita journeyed through the stony hills and the silent places, praying and searching to discover the way forward. In the late evening he turned back towards the river, and came at last to his ultimate destination. He could have chosen to come here by the direct means of a felucca, but too many eyes would have remarked his passing, and he had needed that time alone in the desert.

In the deep darkness when most men slept he approached the temple of Bes on the riverbank. A guttering torch burned in its niche above the gate. It lit the carved figure of the god Bes, which guarded the entrance. Bes was the deformed dwarf god of drunkenness and joviality. His tongue lolled out between his leering lips. In the wavering light of the torch he gave Taita an inebriated grin as he passed.

One of the temple acolytes was waiting to receive the Magus. He led him to a stone cell in the depths of the temple where a jug of goat's milk stood on the table beside a platter of *dhurra* bread and honey in the comb. They knew that one of the Magus' weaknesses was honey from the pollen of the mimosa blossom.

'There are three men already waiting your arrival, my lord,' the young priest told him.

'Bring Bastet to me first,' Taita instructed.

Bastet was the chief scribe of the Nomarch of Memphis. He was one of Taita's most valued sources of information. Not a rich man, he was burdened with two pretty but expensive wives and a brood of brats. Taita had saved his children when the Yellow Flowers devastated the land. Although of little consequence in the scheme of things, he sat close to the seat of power, using his ears and phenomenal memory to good effect. He had much to tell Taita of what had transpired in the nome since the accession of the new Regent, and received his payment with genuine gratitude. 'Your blessing would have been sufficient payment, mighty Magus.'

'Babes don't grow fat on blessings.' Taita dismissed him.

Next came Obos, the high priest of the great Horus

temple at Thebes. He owed his appointment to Taita, who had interceded for him with Pharaoh Tamose. Most of the nobles came to the temple of Horus to worship and make sacrifice, and they all confided in the high priest. The third man to report to Taita was Nolro, the secretary of the army of the north. He also was a eunuch, and there was a bond between those who had suffered such mutilation.

From the days of his youth, when Taita had first found himself directing affairs of state from the shadows behind the throne, he had been aware of the absolute necessity of having impeccable intelligence on which to base decisions. All the rest of that night and most of the following day he listened to these men and questioned them narrowly, so that when he was ready to return to the palace of Memnon he was informed of all the important events that had transpired, and the significant undercurrents and political whirlpools that had developed while he had been away in the wilderness of Gebel Nagara.

In the evening he started back towards the palace, taking the direct route along the bank of the river. The peasants returning from their labours in the fields recognized him, made the sign for good luck and long life, and called to him, 'Pray to Horus for us, Magus,' for they all knew he was a Horus man. Many pressed small gifts upon him, and a ploughman called to him to share his dinner of millet cakes and crisply roasted locusts and goat's milk warm from the udder.

As night fell Taita thanked the friendly ploughman, bade him farewell, and left him sitting beside his fire. He hurried on through the night, anxious not to miss the ceremony of the royal rising. It was dawn before he reached the palace, and he had barely time to bathe and change his raiment before he hurried to the royal bedchamber. At the door his way was barred by the two guards, who crossed their spears across the entrance.

Taita was astonished. This had never happened before. He was the royal tutor, appointed thirteen years ago by Pharaoh Tamose. He glared at the sergeant of the guard. The man dropped his eyes but remained steadfast in his denial of entry. 'I mean no offence, mighty Magus. It is on the specific orders of the commander of the bodyguard, Colonel Asmor, and the palace chamberlain. No person not approved by the Regent is allowed in the royal presence.'

The sergeant was adamant, so Taita left him and strode down the terrace to where Naja was at breakfast with a small circle of his particular favourites and toadies. 'My lord Naja, you are fully aware that I was appointed by Pharaoh's own father as his tutor and mentor. I was given the right of access at any time of day and night.'

'That was many years ago, good Magus,' Naja replied smoothly, as he accepted a peeled grape from the slave who stood behind his stool and popped it into his mouth. 'It was right for that time, but Pharaoh Seti is a child no more. He no longer needs a nursemaid.' The insult was casual, but that did not make it less cutting. 'I am his regent. In future he looks to me for advice and guidance.'

'I acknowledge your right and duty to the King, but to keep me from Nefer's side is unnecessary and cruel,' Taita protested, but Naja waved a lordly hand to silence him.

'The safety of the King is paramount,' he said, and stood up from the breakfast board, to indicate that the meal and the interview were over. His bodyguard closed in around him so that Taita was forced to fall back.

He watched Naja's entourage set off down the cloister towards the council chamber. He did not follow immediately but turned aside and sat down on the coping of one of the fish pools to ponder this development.

Naja had isolated Nefer. He was a prisoner in his own palace. When the time came he would be alone, surrounded by his enemies. Taita searched for some means to protect him. Once again he considered the idea of flight from Egypt, to spirit Nefer away across the desert to the protection of a foreign power until he had grown old and strong enough to return to claim his birthright. However, he could be certain that Naja had not only barred the door to the royal quarters but that every escape route from Thebes and Egypt would have already been closed.

There seemed no easy solution, and after an hour of deep thought, Taita rose to his feet. The guards at the door to the council chamber stood aside for him, and Taita went down the aisle and took his accustomed seat on the front bench.

Nefer was seated on the dais beside his regent. He wore the lighter *hedjet* crown of Upper Egypt, and he looked pale and peaky. Taita felt a flare of concern that he might already be the victim of slow poison, but he could detect no deadly aura surrounding the boy. He concentrated on sending a current of strength and courage to him, but Nefer gave him a cold, accusing stare to punish him for missing the royal rising ceremony.

Taita turned his attention to the council business. They were considering the latest reports from the northern front, where King Apepi had recaptured Abnub after a siege that had lasted the previous three years. That unfortunate city had changed hands eight times since the first Hyksosian invasion in the reign of Pharaoh Mamose, Tamose's father.

If Pharaoh Tamose had not been struck down by the Hyksosian arrow, his bold strategy might have averted this tragic reversal of arms. Instead of now being forced to prepare for the next Hyksosian strike towards Thebes, the armies of Egypt might have been surging towards the enemy capital of Avaris.

Taita found that the council was bitterly divided in every consideration of the crisis. They were seeking to place the blame for this most recent defeat, when it was plain for any fool to see that Pharaoh's untimely death had been the main cause. He had left his army without a head and a heart. Apepi had taken immediate advantage of his death.

Listening to them argue Taita felt more strongly than ever that this war was a running abscess in the body of this very Egypt. Exasperated, he rose quietly and left the council chamber. There was nothing further he could accomplish here, for they were still wrangling over who should be given command of the northern armies to replace the dead Pharaoh Tamose. 'Now that he has gone, there is not one of our commanders who can match Apepi, not Asmor or Teron or Naja himself,' Taita muttered, as he stalked away. 'The land and our armies are bled white by sixty years of warfare. We must have time to build up our strength again, and for a great military leader to emerge from our ranks.' He thought of Nefer, but it would be years before the lad could take over the role that Taita knew, from his study of the Mazes of Ammon Ra, destiny had devised for him.

I have to win him that time and keep him safe until he is ready.

Next he went to the women's quarters of the palace. Because he was a eunuch he could pass through the gates, which were barred to other men. It was three days since the princesses had learned that they were soon to become brides, and Taita knew he should have visited them before. They would be confused and distressed, and sorely in need of his comfort and advice.

Merykara was the first to see him when he entered the courtyard. She sprang up from where a priestess of Isis had been instructing her with writing tablet and brush, and flew to him on those long legs, her side-lock bouncing on her shoulder. She flung her arms around his waist and hugged him with all her strength. 'Oh, Taita, where have you been? I have searched for you these last days.'

When she looked up at him, Taita saw that she had been weeping for her eyes were red-rimmed and heavily underscored with dark bruises. Now she started again, her shoulders shaking with her sobs. Taita picked her up and held her in his arms until she had quieted a little. 'What is it, my little monkey? What has made you so unhappy?'

'Lord Naja is going to take me to a secret place and do terrible things to me. He is going to put something huge and sharp inside me that will hurt me and make me bleed.'

'Who told you that?' Taita controlled his anger with difficulty.

'Magara and Saak.' Merykara sobbed. 'Oh, Taita, can't you stop him doing these things to me? Please, oh, please.'

Taita should have known that the two Nubian slave girls had been responsible for her terror. Usually their tales were of African hobgoblins and ghouls, but now they had something else with which to torment their charge. Grimly Taita swore retribution on both little hussies, and set about calming the princess's fears. It needed all his tact and gentleness, for Merykara was terrified.

He led her to an arbour in a quiet corner of the garden, sat down and she scrambled up on to his lap and pressed her cheek to his chest.

Of course, her fears were unfounded. Even after marriage, it was beyond nature, law and custom that Naja would take her to the marriage bed before Merykara had seen her first red moon, and that event was still years away. He succeeded at last in calming her then took her down to the royal stables to admire and fondle the colt that had been born that morning.

When she was smiling and chattering again, Taita led her back to the *zenana*, and performed a few minor miracles for her amusement. He transformed a jug of Nile water into delicious sherbet by dipping his finger into it, and they drank this together. Then he threw a pebble into the air, which turned into a live canary and flew to the top branches of a fig tree. There it hopped and trilled while the child danced and squealed with glee beneath it.

He left her, went to find the two slave girls, Magara and Saak, and gave them such a verbal lambasting that soon they were clinging together and wailing dolefully. He knew that Magara was always the ringleader in any such unpleasantness, so he produced a live scorpion from her ear and held it inches in front of her face, which reduced her to such paroxysms of terror that she urinated in little squirts down her legs.

Satisfied, he went to look for Heseret. As he had anticipated, she was down on the bank of the river with her lyre. She looked up at him with a sad little smile but went on strumming. He sat down beside her, on the grassy verge under the trailing branches of the willow. The tune she was playing had been her grandmother's favourite. Taita had taught it to her, and now she began to sing the words.

> 'My *heart flutters up like a wounded quail*
> *when I see my beloved's face.*
> *And my cheeks bloom like the dawn sky*
> *to the sunshine of his smile.*'

Her voice was sweet and true, and Taita felt his own tears brimming. It was as though he were listening to Lostris once again. He joined in with the chorus, his voice still clear and steady, without the quavering of age. Out on the river the rowers on a passing galley rested on their oars while they listened with rapt expressions as the current carried the vessel past where the pair sat together.

When the song ended Heseret laid aside the lyre, and turned to him. 'Darling Taita, I am so glad you have come.'

'I am sorry to have kept you waiting, moon of all my nights.' She smiled faintly at the pet name, for she had always had a romantic side to her nature. 'What service do you wish of me?'

'You must go to Lord Naja, and present him with my sincere apologies, but I cannot marry him.'

She was so much like her grandmother had been at the same age. Lostris, too, had saddled him with an impossible task, with the same assurance and confidence in his ability to accomplish it. Heseret now turned those enormous green eyes on him. 'You see, I have already promised Meren that I will be his wife.' Meren was the grandson of Kratas, and the boon companion of Prince Nefer.

Taita had noticed him looking at Heseret with calf's eyes, but had never suspected that she returned his feelings. Fleetingly he wondered how far they had gone towards the consummation of their passions, but put aside the thought. 'Heseret, I have explained to you many times that you are not like other girls. You are a princess royal. Your marriage cannot be undertaken in the light fancy of youth. It is something of dire political consequence.'

'You don't understand, Taita,' Heseret said softly, but with the sweet obstinacy he dreaded. 'I love Meren, I have loved him since I was a little girl. I want to marry him, not Lord Naja.'

'I cannot overrule the decree of the Regent of Egypt,' he tried to explain, but she shook her head and smiled at him.

'You are so wise, Taita. You will think of something. You always do,' she told him, and he felt as though his heart would break.

'Lord Taita, I refuse to discuss your access to Pharaoh or my impending marriage to the royal princesses. In both these matters my mind is set.' To emphasize that he had closed the subject, Naja returned his full attention to the scroll spread on the writing table in front of him. Enough time passed for a flock of wild geese to rise from the swampland on the east bank, cross the wide grey Nile waters on heavy wingbeats and pass over the palace gardens where they sat. At last Taita brought his eyes down from the sky, and rose to leave. As he bowed to the Regent and began to back away, Naja looked up at him. 'I have not given you leave to go.'

'My lord, I thought you had no further need of me.'

'On the contrary, I have the most urgent need.' He glared at Taita and gestured for him to sit again. 'You are testing my good temper and favour. I know that you were wont to work the Mazes for Pharaoh Tamose whenever he called upon you to do so. Why do you procrastinate with me? As the Regent of this land, I will brook no further delay. I ask this not for my own profit, but for the very survival of our nation in this war with the north. I need the guidance of the pantheon of the gods. You are the only one who can provide that for me.'

Naja stood up so suddenly that the table in front of him overturned, spilling scrolls of papyrus, brushes and ink on to the terracotta tiles. He paid it no attention, but his voice rose to a shout: 'I command you, with all the authority of the hawk seal . . .' he touched the amulet on his right arm '. . . I command you to work the Mazes of Ammon Ra on my behalf.'

Taita bowed his head in theatrical resignation. For weeks past he had been prepared for this ultimatum, and had delayed only to extend to the limit that period of grace during which Nefer would be relatively safe from the ambitions of the Regent. He was still convinced that Lord Naja would make no fatal move towards Nefer until he had been given the sanction of the Mazes.

'The full of the moon is the most propitious period for the Mazes,' Taita told him. 'I have already made the preparations.'

Naja sank back on his stool. 'You will you do it here, in my quarters,' he said.

'Nay, Lord Regent, that would not be ideal.' Taita knew that if he were to gain ascendancy over Naja, he must keep him off-balance. 'The closer we can be to the influence of the gods, the more accurate will be the predictions. I have arranged with the priests at the temple of Osiris at Busiris. That is where I will work the Mazes at midnight in the full of the moon. I will conduct the mystery in the inner sanctum of the temple. The backbone of the god, the *djed*-pillar, dismembered by his brother, Seth, is held there. This holy relic will magnify the force of our deliberations.' Taita's voice was heavy with arcane meaning. 'Only you and I will be present in the sanctuary. No other mortal must overhear what the gods have to tell you. One of Asmor's regiments will guard the approaches to the sanctuary.'

Naja was an Osiris man, and his expression was solemn. Taita had known that he would be impressed by the time and place he had chosen.

'As you say, so let it be,' Naja agreed.

The journey to Busiris in the royal barge took two days, with Asmor's regiment following in four naval galleys. They landed on the yellow beach under the walls of the temple, and the priests were waiting to welcome the Regent with psalms and offerings of gum arabic and myrrh. The Regent's delight in sweet-smelling substances was already known throughout the land.

They were shown to the quarters that had been prepared for them. While Naja bathed, perfumed and refreshed himself with fruit and sherbet, Taita visited the sanctuary in company with the high priest and made sacrifice to the great god Osiris. Afterwards, at Taita's subtle suggestion, the high priest withdrew and left him alone to make his preparations for the evening. Lord Naja had never been present at the working of the Mazes – there were few living persons who had. Taita would put on an impressive show for him, but he had no intention of subjecting himself to the exhausting and harrowing ordeal of the authentic ritual.

After sunset the high priest entertained the Regent at a banquet. In his honour he served the famous wine from the vineyards that surrounded the temple. It had been at Busiris that the great god Osiris had first introduced the grape to Egypt. When the luscious vintage had mellowed the Regent and the rest of the company, the priests presented a series of theatrical acts representing the life-history of the great god. In each of these Osiris was depicted with different skin colorations, white as the wrappings of a mummy, black for the realm of the dead, red for the god of retribution. Always he held the crook and the flail, the insignia of the ruler, and his feet were held together like those of a corpse. In the final act his face was painted green to symbolize his vegetable aspect. As with the *dhurra* millet, which signified life and sustenance, Osiris was buried in the earth, which signified death. In the darkness of the netherworld he germinated like the millet seed, then emerged into the glorious cycle of life eternal.

While the tableaux were enacted, the high priest recited the god's names of power: 'Eye of the Night', 'The Eternally Good Being', 'Son of Geb' and 'Wennefer, Perfect in Majesty'.

Then, surrounded by the smoke of the incense pots, to the beat of gong and drum, the priests chanted the epic poem of the struggle between good and evil. The legend related how Seth, envious of his virtuous brother, locked Osiris in a chest and threw him into the Nile to drown. When his dead body washed up on the riverbank, Seth hacked it to pieces and hid the various parts. Here at Busiris he hid the *djed*-pillar, the backbone. Isis, their sister, searched for and found all the parts of the corpse and reassembled them. Then she copulated with Osiris. While they were locked in union her wings fanned the breath of life back into him.

Long before midnight the Regent of Egypt had consumed a flagon of the rich and heady wine, and was in a nervous, susceptible condition, his religious superstitions titillated by the priests. As the silver beam of the full moon entered through the precisely aligned aperture in the roof of the temple and moved softly across the flags of the nave towards the closed door of the sanctuary, the high priest gave a signal and all the other priests rose and moved out in procession leaving Lord Naja and Taita alone.

When the chanting of the departing priests had dwindled with distance into a heavy silence, Taita took the Regent by the hand and led him down the moonlit nave to the doors of the sanctuary. As they approached the great bronze-covered doors swung open of their own accord. Lord Naja started and his hand trembled in Taita's. He might have drawn back, but the Magus led him forward.

The sanctuary was lit by four braziers, one in each corner

of the small chamber. There was a low stool in the centre of the tiled floor. Taita led Naja to it and gestured for him to be seated. As he did so, the doors swung closed behind them, and Naja looked round at them fearfully. He would have started up again, but Taita placed a hand on his shoulder to restrain him. 'No matter what you see and what you hear, do not move. Do not speak. As you value your life, do nothing. Say nothing.'

Taita left him sitting and, with stately tread, approached the statue of the god. He raised his hands, and suddenly he was holding a golden chalice by its stem. He lifted it on high and called on Osiris to bless the contents, then brought it back to Naja and urged him to drink. The honey-viscous liquid tasted of crushed almonds, rose petals and mushrooms. Taita clapped his hands and the chalice was gone.

He held out his empty hands and made a mystical pass back and forth before Naja's face, and in the blink of an eye the Mazes of Ammon Ra filled his cupped hands. These ivory counters Naja recognized from the fanciful accounts he had heard of the ritual. Taita invited him to cover them with his own hands, while he recited an invocation to Ammon Ra and the host of the pantheon. 'Greatness in light and fire, furious in divine majesty, approach and hearken to our pleas.'

Naja squirmed on his stool as the Mazes grew hot to the touch, and it was with relief that he passed them back to Taita. He was sweating heavily as he watched the old man carry them across the sanctuary and place them at the feet of the gigantic statue of Osiris. The Magus knelt there, bowed over them. For a while there was no sound within the chamber except the hiss of the flames, no movement except the shadows, cast by the lambent light of the braziers, dancing on the stone walls.

Then, abruptly, a terrible disembodied shriek rang through the sanctuary. It sounded as though once again the god's vitals were being ripped from his body by his evil brother. Naja moaned softly and covered his head with his shawl.

Again there was silence until suddenly the flames of the braziers flared as high as the roof, and turned from yellow to fierce shades of green and violet, crimson and blue. Great clouds of smoke boiled from them and filled the chamber. Naja choked and coughed. He felt as though he were suffocating, and his senses reeled. He could hear his own breath reverberating in his head.

Taita turned slowly to face him, and Naja shuddered in horror, for the Magus was transformed. His face glowed with green light, like the face of the resurrected god. Green foam frothed from his gaping mouth and poured down his chest, and his eyes were blind orbs that flashed silver rays in the light of the braziers. Without moving his feet he glided towards where Naja sat, and from his gaping frothing mouth issued the voices of a wild horde of demons and *djinns*, a terrible chorus of screams and moans, hisses and grunting, retching and insane laughter.

Lord Naja tried to rise, but the sounds and the smoke seemed to fill his skull, and blackness overwhelmed him. His legs gave way beneath him and he slumped forward off the stool on to the tiles in a dead faint.

When the Regent of Egypt regained consciousness the sun was high, sparkling on the waters of the river. He found himself lying on the silken mattress on the poop deck of the royal barge under the yellow awning.

He looked around him blearily, and saw the sails of the escort galleys white as egret wings against the lush green of the riverbanks. The sunlight was dazzling, and he closed his eyes again. He had a consuming thirst, his throat felt as though he had swallowed a handful of sharp gravel chips, and there was a pounding in his skull as though all the demons of his vision were trapped within it. He moaned, shuddered and vomited copiously into the bucket that a slave held for him.

Taita came to his side, raised his head and gave him a cool draught of some miraculous brew that soon eased the pounding in his head, and loosened the gases trapped in his swollen belly, allowing them to erupt from his nether orifice in spluttering gusts of foul-smelling wind. When he had recovered enough to speak again, he whispered, 'Tell it all to me, Taita. I remember nothing. What did the Mazes reveal?'

Before he would reply Taita sent all the crew and slaves out of earshot. Then he knelt beside the mattress. Naja laid a trembling hand on his arm and whispered pitifully, 'I remember nothing after . . .' He hesitated as the terrors of the previous night came back to him, and shuddered.

'We have almost reached Sebennytos, Majesty,' Taita told him. 'We will be back at Thebes before nightfall.'

'What happened, Taita?' He shook Taita's arm. 'What did the Mazes reveal?'

'Great wonders, Majesty.' Taita's voice trembled with emotion.

'Wonders?' Naja's interest quickened, and he struggled to sit up. 'Why do you call me "Majesty"? I am not Pharaoh.'

'It is part of what was revealed.'

'Tell it to me! Tell it all to me!'

'Do you not remember how the roof of the temple opened like the petals of the lotus, and the great causeway descended to us from the night sky?'

Naja shook his head, and then nodded uncertainly. 'Yes, I think so. The causeway was a ladder of gold?'

'You do remember,' Taita commended him.

'We ascended the golden ladder.' Naja looked at him for confirmation.

'We were borne upwards on the backs of the two winged lions.' Taita nodded.

'Yes, I remember the lions, but after that it is all shadowy and vague.'

'These mysteries numb the mind and dim eyes unaccustomed to them. Even I, an adept of the seventh and final degree, was amazed by what we endured,' Taita explained kindly. 'But do not despair, for the gods have commanded me to explain them to you.'

'Speak, good Magus, and spare no detail.'

'On the backs of the flying lions we crossed high above the dark ocean and over the peaks of the white mountains, with all the kingdoms of earth and heaven spread below us.'

Naja nodded avidly. 'Go on!'

'We came at last to the citadel in which the gods dwell. The foundations reached to the depths of the netherworld, and the pillars supported the sky and all the stars. Ammon Ra rode above us in fiery splendour, and all the other gods of the pantheon were seated on thrones of silver and gold, of fire, crystal and sapphire.'

Naja blinked at him, focusing with difficulty. 'Yes. Now that you tell me, I remember it. The thrones of sapphire and diamonds.' The desperate need to believe was like a fire within him. 'Then the god spoke?' he hazarded. 'He spoke to me, did he not?'

'Yes, In a voice loud as the fall of a mountain the great god Osiris spoke thus: "Beloved Naja, you have always been faithful in your devotion to me. In this you shall be rewarded."'

'What was his meaning? Did he make it clear, Taita?'

Taita nodded solemnly. 'Yes, Majesty.'

'You use that title again. Tell me why.'

'As you command, Majesty. I shall tell you every word. Great Osiris rose up in all his terrible glory, and lifted you off the back of the winged lion and placed you beside him on the throne of fire and gold. He touched your mouth and your heart, and he greeted you with the title Brother Divine.'

'He called me Brother Divine? What did he mean by that?'

Taita suppressed a twinge of irritation. Naja had always been a clever man, sharp and perceptive. He did not usually need to have every detail spelt out so laboriously. The effects of the essence of the magical mushroom, which Taita had administered to him the night before, and the drugged smoke of the braziers had not yet worn off. It might be days before he was thinking clearly again. I shall have to ply a heavy paintbrush, he decided, and went on, 'I too was puzzled by his words. The meaning was not clear to me, but then the great god spoke again: "I welcome you to the pantheon of heaven, Brother Divine."'

Naja's face cleared, and his expression became proud and triumphant. 'Was he not deifying me, Taita? Surely there can be no meaning other than that.'

'If there had been any doubt it was immediately dispelled, for Osiris took up the double crown of Upper and Lower Egypt, placed it upon your head and spoke again. "Hail, Brother Divine! Hail, Pharaoh who shall be."' Naja was silent now, but he stared at Taita with glittering eyes. After a long silence Taita went on, 'With the crown upon your brow, your holiness was manifest. I knelt before you and worshipped you with the other gods.'

Naja made no effort to hide his emotions. He was in transport. He was as vulnerable as if he had been in orgasm. Taita seized the moment. 'Then Osiris spoke again, "In these wondrous things, your guide shall be the Magus Taita, for he is an adept of all the mysteries, and the master of the Mazes. Follow his instruction faithfully, and all the rewards I have promised will be yours."'

He watched Naja's reaction. Had he made it too pointed, he wondered, but the Regent seemed to accept the stricture without resistance.

'What else, Taita? What more did the great god have to say to me?'

'Nothing more to you, my lord, but now he spoke directly to me. His words struck through to the depths of my soul, for he laid a heavy charge upon me. These are his exact words, each one branded in fire upon my heart. "Taita, master of the Mazes, from henceforth you have no other love, loyalty or duty. You are the servant of my royal and divine brother, Naja. Your only concern is to help him fulfil his destiny. You will not cease until you see the double crown of Upper and Lower Egypt placed upon his head."'

'"No other loyalty or love,"' Naja repeated softly. He seemed now to have thrown off most of the ill-effects of his ordeal. His strength was flooding back, and the familiar light of cunning grew stronger in his yellow eyes. 'And did you then accept the charge that great Osiris placed upon you, Magus? Say fair and true, are you my man now, or would you deny the word of the great father?'

'How could I deny the great god?' Taita asked simply. He lowered his head and pressed his forehead to the planking of the deck. With both hands he took Naja's bare right foot and placed it on his own head. 'I accept the charge that the gods have placed upon me. I am your man, divine Majesty. Heart and head and soul, I belong to you.'

'What of your other duties? What of the oath of allegiance you swore to Pharaoh Nefer Seti at his birth, and even more recently at his coronation?'

'Majesty, the great god Osiris has absolved me from anything that came before. No oath counts for me other than the one I now make to you.'

Naja raised him up and stared into his eyes, searching for any trace of deceit or guile. Taita looked back at him serenely. He could sense the Regent's doubts, hopes and suspicions swarming together like a basket of live rats waiting to be fed to the falcons in the royal mews. The wish is father to the deed, Taita thought. He will allow himself to believe, because he longs for it to be so.

He watched the doubts clear in those yellow eyes and Naja embraced him. 'I believe you. When I wear the double crown you will have rewards beyond your expectation or imagination.'

Over the days that followed Naja kept Taita close to his side, and the old man used this new position of trust to change some of the Regent's undeclared intentions. At Naja's urging, Taita made another examination of the auguries. He slaughtered a sheep and examined its entrails, he released a falcon from the royal mews and watched its flight pattern. From these he was able to determine that the god would sanction no marriage of Naja to the princesses until at least the beginning of the next inundation of the Nile waters or the flooding would certainly fail. This would be a disaster that even Naja could not risk. The life of this very Egypt depended upon the inundations of the great river. With this prophecy Taita had delayed the danger to Nefer, and the agony of the two princesses.

Naja protested and argued, but since that terrible night at Busiris he had found it almost impossible to resist Taita's predictions. In this he was made more amenable by the ominous news from the northern war front. On Naja's orders, and against Taita's counsel, the Egyptians had launched a desperate counter-attack to try to retake Abnub. They had failed, losing three hundred chariots and almost a regiment of foot in the dreadful fighting around the city. Now Apepi seemed poised to deliver a crushing stroke through the demoralized and weakened Egyptian regiments, and come storming on to Thebes. It was not the time for a wedding, which even Naja conceded, and Nefer's safety was ensured for a while longer.

Already a constant stream of refugees fled from Thebes by road and river towards the south. The volume of trade caravans from the east fell alarmingly, as the merchants waited to see the outcome of the imminent Hyksosian offensive. All commodities were in short supply and prices shot up.

'The only way in which you can stave off an annihilating defeat at the hands of Apepi is to negotiate a truce,' Taita advised the Regent.

He was about to qualify this by adding that the truce would in no circumstances be a surrender, that they would merely use the respite to strengthen their military position, but Naja did not allow him the chance to elaborate. 'This I believe also, Magus,' he agreed eagerly. 'Oft-times I tried to convince my beloved companion, Pharaoh Tamose, of the wisdom of this course. He would never listen to me.'

'We need time,' Taita explained, but Naja waved a hand to silence him.

'Of course you are right.' Naja was excited by this unexpected support. He had tried without success to convince the individual members of the council to agree to a peace with the Hyksos, but none, not even Cinka, had supported him. Even the loyal Asmor had risked his wrath by vowing to fall on his own sword rather than surrender to Apepi. It had been a sobering revelation to find honour flowering in such unlikely ground, and to learn that even as regent there were limits to what he could force through the council.

Peace with the Hyksos was the cornerstone of Naja's vision, a vision of the two kingdoms reunited and a single pharaoh ruling both. Only a pharaoh who was part Egyptian and part Hyksosian could hope to achieve that, and he knew, without any doubt, that this was what the gods had promised him through the Mazes.

He went on earnestly, 'I should have known that you, Taita, were the one person who would not let yourself be blinded by prejudice. All the others cry, "No surrender," and "Death rather than dishonour".' He shook his head. 'You and I can see that what we could not achieve by force of arms, we can bring about perhaps in a more gentle fashion. After sixty years in the Nile valley, the Hyksos are becoming more Egyptian than Asian. They have been seduced by our gods, our philosophy and our women. Their savage blood has been softened and sweetened by ours. Their wild ways have been tempered by our noble manners.'

The Regent's response to his tentative suggestion was so overpowering that Taita was taken aback. There was much more here than he had suspected. To gain time to think it out, and garner some inkling of Naja's true intentions, he murmured, 'Those are words of wisdom. How could we hope to bring about this truce, Lord Regent?'

Naja was eager to explain. 'I know there are many among the Hyksos who agree with these sentiments. It would take little for them to join us. Then we can bring peace and unity to the two kingdoms.'

The veils began to part. Taita was reminded suddenly of a suspicion he had once heard expressed but had rejected at the time.

'Who are these Hyksos sympathizers?' he asked. 'Are they highly placed? Close to Apepi?'

'Noblemen, indeed. One sits on Apepi's war council.' Naja seemed about to enlarge on this, but he stopped himself with an obvious effort.

It was enough for Taita. That faint rumour of Hyksosian connections in Naja's background must have had substance, and if it was true the rest fell neatly into place. Once again, he was amazed at the width and breadth of Naja's ambitions.

'Would it be possible to meet these noblemen and speak to them?' Taita asked carefully.

'Yes,' Naja confirmed. 'We could reach them within days.'

For Taita the implications of that simple statement were enormous. The Regent of Egypt had covert allies in the ranks of the traditional enemy. What else about him was hidden? Where else had his avaricious fingers reached? A chill ran down Taita's spine, and the silver hairs on the back of his neck came erect.

This is the loving friend who was at Pharaoh's side when he was struck down. Here is the only witness to the manner of Pharaoh's death. This creature of boundless ambition and cruel purpose admits to being an intimate and confidant of Hyksosian noblemen, and it was a Hyksosian arrow that killed Pharaoh. How deep does the plot run?

He let nothing of this show on his face, but nodded thoughtfully, and Naja went on quickly, 'I am certain that we can reach agreement with the Hyksos, and I envisage a co-regency between Apepi and myself with a joint council of state. Then your influence would be needed to persuade our own councillors to ratify it. Perhaps you could consult the Mazes again, and make the wishes of the gods known.'

Naja was suggesting that he make a fraudulent divination. Did he suspect that that was what had happened at Busiris? Taita did not think so, but he must quash the idea at once. His expression became stern. 'In any matter to do with the Mazes, to take the word or name of the god Ammon Ra in vain or to misrepresent his oracle would be to court terrible retribution.'

Quickly Naja retracted. 'I suggested no such impiety, but through the Mazes the gods have already given sanction to me.'

Taita grunted. 'First we must determine if this treaty is

feasible. Apepi might believe his military position is unassailable and refuse to meet us. Despite any approaches from us for peace, he might decide to prosecute this war to the bitter end.'

'I do not think that will happen. I will give you the names of our allies on the other side. You must go to them secretly, Taita. You are well known and respected even among the Hyksos, and I will give you a talisman that will prove you come from me. You are the best emissary for our cause. They will listen to you.'

Taita sat a while longer in thought. He tried to see if he could wring any further advantage to Nefer and the princesses from the situation, but at this stage he could find none. Whatever happened, Nefer would still be in mortal danger.

There was only one certain course open to Taita if he were to ensure Nefer's survival and that was to get him out of Egypt while Naja was still in power. Was there an opportunity to do that now? Naja was offering him a safe conduct to the frontier. Could he use that to take Nefer with him? Within seconds he realized he could not. His contacts with the boy Pharaoh were still severely circumscribed by Naja. He was never allowed to be alone with him. He was not even allowed to sit close to him at sessions of the council, or to exchange even the most innocent messages with him. The only time in the last few weeks that he had been allowed close to him was when Nefer had developed an agonizing septic throat. Then Taita had been allowed into the royal bedchamber to tend him, but both Naja and Asmor had been present, watching everything that transpired, listening to every word that was spoken. Because of his affliction Nefer had not been able to speak above a whisper, but his eyes never left Taita's face and he clung to his hand when the time came for them to part. That had been almost ten days ago.

Taita learned that Naja had chosen tutors to replace

him, and Asmor had provided instructors from the Blue Guards to continue Nefer's exercises in horsemanship and chariot handling, swordsmanship and archery. None of his old friends were allowed to visit him. Even his crony Meren had been ordered out of Pharaoh's quarters.

If he made an attempt to get Nefer away and failed, not only would he have sacrificed Naja's confidence, he would have placed Nefer in terrible peril. No, he could use this sortie across the lines into the Hyksosian territory only to make more careful and secure arrangements for the young Pharaoh's safety.

'It is my duty, a duty placed upon me by the gods, to help you in every way. I will undertake this mission,' Taita said. 'What is the safest way for me to pass through the Hyksosian lines? You say I am well known among them, and that I will be recognized.'

Naja had foreseen this query. 'You must use the old chariot road through the dunes and down the wadi at Gebel Wadun. My friends on the other side keep the road under surveillance.'

Taita nodded. 'That is the road along which Pharaoh Tamose met his death. I have never travelled beyond Gallala. I will need a guide to show me the rest of the way.'

'I will send my own lance-bearer and a squadron of the Blues to take you through,' Naja promised. 'But the road is long and hard. You must leave at once. Every day, every hour might make the difference.'

Taita had driven the chariot all the way from the ruined city of Gallala with only four halts. They had made the run in half a day less than it had taken Naja and Tamose to cover the same route, and at less cost to the condition of the animals.

The troopers in the nine vehicles that followed him were in awe of the Magus' reputation. They knew him as the father of the corps of cavalry, for he had been the first Egyptian ever to build a chariot and harness a team to it. His celebrated ride from Thebes to Elephantine to carry the news of the victory of Pharaoh Tamose over the Hyksos was the stuff of legend. Now, as they followed his chariot through the dunes, they learned that the legend was well founded. The old man's stamina was amazing, and his concentration never wavered. His gentle but firm hands on the reins never tired, as hour after hour he coaxed the horses into giving their best. He had impressed every man in the squadron, not least the one riding beside him in the cockpit.

Gil was Naja's lance-bearer. He had a rugged, sun-darkened face and was lightly built, which was desirable for a charioteer, but he possessed also a wiry strength and cheerful disposition. He had to have been one of the best to be selected to ride in the commander's chariot.

With the moon waxing and the weather at its hottest they had driven through the cool of the night. Now, in the dawn, they halted to rest. When he had watered the horses, Gil came to where Taita sat on a boulder overlooking the wadi of Gebel Wadun and handed him a ceramic water jug. Taita took a long swig from the spout and swallowed the bitter water they had carried with them from Gallala with no sign of repugnance. It was the first drink he had taken since their last stop at midnight.

The old devil-rouser is tough as a Bedouin raider, Gil thought, with admiration, and squatted at a respectful distance to await any order that Taita might issue.

'Where is the place at which Pharaoh was struck down?' Taita asked at last.

Gil shaded his eyes against the glare of the rising sun and pointed down the wadi towards where the dry riverbed debouched on to the plains. 'Down there, my lord. Near that distant line of hills.'

The first time Taita had questioned Gil had been before the council when the lance-bearer had given evidence on the circumstances of Pharaoh's death. The council had called every person who might have any knowledge of it to testify at the inquiry. Taita remembered that Gil's evidence had been coherent and credible. He had not been overawed by the pomp of the council and its illustrious members, but had spoken out like the honest, simple soldier he was. When it was shown to him, he had recognized the Hyksosian arrow as the one that had struck down Pharaoh Tamose. The shaft had been snapped in two. Lord Naja had broken it off to ease the pain of the wound.

That had been the first occasion of their meeting. They had spoken briefly once or twice since leaving Thebes, but until now there had not been the opportunity for any long conversation.

'Are any other men here who were with you on that day?' Taita asked now.

'Only Samos, but he was waiting with the chariots in the wadi when we were attacked,' Gil replied.

'I want you to point out the exact place to me, and I want you to take me over the battleground,' Taita told him.

Gil shrugged. 'It was no battle, just a skirmish. There will be precious little to see. 'Tis a barren place. However, it shall be as the mighty Magus commands.'

The troop mounted and descended the steep side of the wadi in single file. There had been no rain here in a hundred years and even the desert wind had not wiped away the tracks of Pharaoh's chariots, which were still deeply scored and plain to read. When they reached the floor of the wadi Taita continued to follow them, his own wheels riding in the deep grooves that they had left.

They were alert for a Hyksos ambush and watched both banks of the wadi, but although the raw rock danced in the heat mirage, there was no sign of an enemy.

'There is the watchtower.' Gil pointed ahead, and Taita saw its gnarled silhouette leaning drunkenly against the unblemished pale blue of the sky.

They swept around another bend in the riverbed, and even from two hundred paces Taita could make out the area of confused wheel-tracks where the chariots of Pharaoh's squadron had halted and circled, and where many men had dismounted and remounted in the soft sand of the wadi bottom. Taita signalled his small force to slow down and they moved forward at a walk.

'This is where Pharaoh dismounted and we went forward with Lord Naja to scout the camp of Apepi.' Gil pointed over the side of the dashboard.

Taita halted the chariot and signalled the others to do the same. 'Wait for me here,' he ordered the sergeant of the following vehicle, then turned to Gil. 'Come with me. Show me the battleground.'

Gil led the way up the rude pathway. At first he went slowly, in deference to the old man, but soon realized that Taita was matching him step for step and speeded up. The gradient increased and the surface became more uneven as they went on. Even Gil was breathing hard when at last they reached the tumble of large boulders halfway up the hill that almost blocked the pathway.

'This is as far as I went,' Gil explained.

'So where did Pharaoh fall?' Taita looked around him at the steep but open hillside. 'Where were the Hyksosian troops hidden? From where was the fatal arrow fired?'

'I cannot tell you, lord.' Gil shook his head. 'I and the rest of the men were ordered to wait here, while Lord Naja went forward beyond that outcrop of boulders.'

'Where was Pharaoh? Did he go forward with Naja?'

'No. Not at first. The King waited with us. Lord Naja heard something up ahead, went to scout and disappeared from our view.'

'I do not understand. At what point were you attacked?'

'We waited here. I could see that Pharaoh was becoming impatient. After a while Lord Naja whistled from beyond the rocks. Pharaoh sprang up. "Come on, lads!" he told us, and went up the path.'

'Were you close behind him?'

'No, I was near the rear of the file.'

'Did you see what happened next?'

'Pharaoh disappeared behind the boulders. Then there was shouting and the sound of fighting. I heard Hyksos voices and arrows and spears striking the rocks. I ran forward but the path was crowded with our men who were trying to get round the boulders here to reach the fight.'

Gil ran forward to show him how the path narrowed and wove around the tallest boulder. 'This was as far as I got to. Then Lord Naja was shouting that Pharaoh had been struck down. The men ahead of me were milling around, and suddenly they dragged the King down to where I was standing. I think he was dead even then.'

'How close were the Hyksos? How many were they? Were they cavalry or infantry? Did you recognize their regiments?' Taita demanded. All the Hyksos wore distinctive regalia, which the Egyptian troops had come to know well.

'They were very close,' Gil told him, 'and there were a lot of them. At least a squadron.'

'What regiment?' Taita insisted. 'Did you pick out their plumes?'

For the first time Gil looked uncertain and a little shame-faced. 'My lord, I did not actually set eyes on the enemy. You see, they were behind the rocks up there.'

'Then how do you know their strength and numbers?' Taita frowned at him.

'Lord Naja was shouting—' Gil broke off and dropped his eyes.

'Did any of the others, apart from Naja, see the enemy?'

'I do not know, honourable Magus. You see, Lord Naja ordered us back down the pathway to the chariots. We could see that the King was mortally wounded, probably already dead. We had all lost heart.'

'You must have discussed it later with your companions. Did any of them tell you he had engaged an enemy? That he had hit one of the Hyksos with arrow or lance?'

Gil shook his head doubtfully. 'I don't remember. No, I don't think so.'

'Apart from the King, were any others wounded?'

'None.'

'Why did you not tell this to the council? Why did you not tell them that you had not seen an enemy?' Taita was angry now.

'Lord Naja told us to answer the questions simply and not to waste the council's time with idle boasting and long tales of our part in the fighting.' Gil hunched his shoulders with embarrassment. 'I suppose that none of us wanted to admit that we ran without a fight.'

'Do not feel ashamed, Gil. You carried out your orders,' Taita told him, in a kinder tone. 'Now, climb up on the rocks there, and keep your eyes open. We are still deep in Hyksosian territory. I shall not be long.'

Taita went forward slowly and stepped round the boulder that blocked the path. He paused and surveyed the ground ahead. From this angle he could just make out the top of the ruined watchtower. The path went up towards it in a series of dog-legs. Then it disappeared over the crest of a slope, which was fairly open, with little cover for a Hyksosian ambush, just a few clumps of rock and scattered sun-blasted thorn trees. Then he remembered that it had happened at night. But something disturbed him. Taita felt a vague sense of evil, as though he was being watched by a powerful malignant force.

This feeling grew so strong that he stood motionless in the sunlight and closed his eyes. He opened his mind and his soul, becoming a dry sponge to soak up any influence from the air around him. Almost at once the feeling grew stronger still: there were terrible things here, but the focus of evil emanated from somewhere not far ahead of him. He opened his eyes and walked slowly towards it. There was nothing to be seen, other than heat-blasted rock and thorn, but now he could even smell evil in the hot air, a faint but rank odour like the breath of a carrion-eating wild beast.

He stopped and sniffed, like a hunting dog, and immediately the air smelt dusty and dry, but clean. This proved to him that the elusive stench was something outside natural law. He was catching the faint echo of an evil that had been perpetrated in this place, but when he tried to pinpoint it, it disappeared. He took a pace forward then another, and once more the nauseating stench wafted around him. Another pace, and now the smell was accompanied by a feeling of great sorrow, as though he had lost something of inestimable value, something that could never be replaced.

He had to force himself to take the next step up the rocky pathway, and at that instant something struck him with a force that drove the air from his lungs. He cried out in agony and dropped to his knees, clutching his chest, unable to breathe. It was extreme pain, the pain of death, and he struggled with it as though with a serpent that had wound its coils about him. He managed to throw himself back down the path, and immediately the pain fell away.

Gil had heard him cry out and came bounding up the

path. He seized Taita, and helped him to his feet. 'What is it? What ails you, my lord?'

Taita thrust him away. 'Go! Leave me! You are in danger here. This is a thing not of men but of gods and demons. Go! Wait for me at the bottom of the hill.'

Gil hesitated, but then he saw the look in those glittering eyes and recoiled as if from a ghost.

'Go!' Taita said, in a voice Gil wanted never to hear again, and he fled.

For a long time after he had gone Taita struggled to bring his body and mind back under his own control, to enable him to counter the forces arrayed against him. He reached into the pouch on his belt and brought out the Periapt of Lostris. He held it in his right hand and stepped forward again.

As he came to the exact spot on the pathway the pain struck once more with even more savage intensity, like a flint-tipped arrow through the chest, and he could barely prevent himself screaming as he reeled backwards and the pain fell away as it had before.

Panting, he stared down at the stony ground. At first it seemed unmarked and no different from any other point on the rugged pathway he had traversed. Then, a small ethereal shadow appeared on the earth. As he watched, it changed, became a shimmering dark scarlet pool. Slowly he sank to his knees. 'The heart blood of a king and a god,' he whispered. 'Here, on this very spot, died Pharaoh Tamose.'

He rallied himself and in a quiet yet firm voice spoke the invocation to Horus, so potent that only an adept of the seventh degree dared voice it. On the seventh repetition he heard the rustle of unseen wings, which stirred the desert air around him. 'The god is here,' he whispered, and he began to pray. He prayed for his Pharaoh and his friend, entreating Horus to relieve his suffering and lift his torture.

'Allow him to escape from this dread place,' he beseeched the god. 'It must have been murder for his soul to have been trapped here.'

As he prayed he made the signs for the exorcism of evil. Before his eyes the pool of blood began to shrink, as though it were soaking away into the dry earth. As the last drop disappeared Taita heard a soft, formless sound, like the cry of a sleepy child, and the terrible weight of loss and sorrow that had burdened him fell from his shoulders. As he stood up he felt a great sense of release. He stepped forward on to the spot where the pool of blood had been. Even when his sandalled feet were firmly planted upon it he felt no pain and his sense of well-being remained intact.

'Go in peace, my friend and my king, and may you live for all eternity,' he said aloud, and made the sign for long life and happiness.

He turned away, and would have started back down the hill to where the chariots waited but something stopped him in his tracks. He lifted his head and tested the air again. There was still a faint whiff of that evil smell, just an elusive trace of it. Warily he turned back up the slope, passing the place where Pharaoh had died, and went on. With each pace the stench of evil grew stronger, until it caught in his throat and made his gorge rise. Once again, he realized that this was something from beyond the natural order. He went on, until after twenty measured paces the odour began to fade. He stopped and retraced his steps. Immediately the stench grew stronger. He quested back and forth until it was at its zenith. Then he stepped off the path and found it stronger still, almost suffocating.

He was standing under the twisted branches of a thorn tree that grew next to the path. He looked up and saw that the branches were strangely shaped, as though they had been fashioned by a human hand into a distinctive cross that stood out against the blue of the sky. He looked down and a rock the size and shape of a horse's head caught his attention. It had recently been dislodged then replaced in its original position. Taita lifted it out of the depression in which it sat, and saw that it had covered a niche between the roots of the thorn tree. He laid it aside and peered into the niche. There was something in it and he reached in gingerly – it was the kind of shelter that might hide a snake or scorpion.

He brought out a magnificently carved and tooled object. He stared at it for a moment before he realized that it was an arrow quiver. There was no doubting its origin, for the design was in the Hyksosian heraldic style, and the image tooled into the leather cover was Seueth, the crocodile god of war revered by Hyksosian warriors.

Taita twisted off the stopper cover and found that the quiver contained five war arrows, fletched in green and red. He drew out one of the shafts and his heart beat fiercely as he recognized it. There could be no mistake. He had minutely examined the broken, blood-caked one that Naja had brought before the council. This was identical to the arrow that had killed Pharaoh.

He held it to the light and peered closely at the signet etched into the painted shaft. It was a stylized head of a leopard, holding the hieratic letter T in its jaws. This was the device he had seen on the fatal arrow. This was its identical twin. Taita turned it over and over in his hands, as though trying to draw from it the last grain of information. He held it to his nose and sniffed it. There was just the smell of wood, paint and feathers. The foul odour that had guided him to the cache had disappeared.

Why should the assassin of Pharaoh hide his quiver? After the fight the Hyksos had been left in possession of the field. They would have had all the time they needed to recover their weapons. This is a beautiful and valuable object. No warrior would abandon it, unless he were forced to, Taita thought.

For another hour he searched the hillside, but found no

other item of interest, nor did he detect again the supernatural odour of putrefaction and evil. When he went down to where the chariots waited in the sand of the wadi he carried the quiver concealed under his apron.

They waited hidden in the wadi until after nightfall. Then, the wheel-hubs freshly greased with mutton fat to stop them squealing, the horses' hoofs covered with leather boots, and all the loose weapons and tack carefully muffled, they went on deep into Hyksosian territory, with Gil guiding them.

The lance-bearer knew the area well, and although Taita made no comment, he wondered how often the man had travelled this way with his master, and what other rendezvous they had kept with the enemy.

By now they were down on the alluvial plain of the Nile. Twice they had to turn off the road and wait while parties of armed men, anonymous in the darkness, rode past their hiding-place. After midnight they came to an abandoned temple of some forgotten god that had been hollowed out of the side of a low clay hill. The cave was large enough to shelter the entire squadron, vehicle, horses and men. It was immediately apparent that it had been used before for this purpose: lamps and an oil amphora were hidden behind the ruined altar, and bales of horse fodder were stacked in the sanctum.

As soon as they had removed the horses' harness and fed them, the troopers ate their own meal then settled down on mattresses of dried straw and were soon snoring. In the meantime Gil had changed from his cavalry uniform to the nondescript attire of a peasant. 'I cannot use a horse,' he explained to Taita. 'It would attract too much interest. On foot it will take me half a day to reach the camp at Bubasti.

Do not expect me back before tomorrow evening.' He slipped out of the cave and disappeared into the night.

Honest Gil is not such a simple bluff soldier as he seems, Taita thought, as he settled down to wait for Lord Naja's allies to answer the message that Gil was taking to them.

As soon as it was light he posted a sentry at the top of the hill, where the air shaft from the subterranean temple emerged. Just before noon a low whistle down the shaft warned them of danger and Taita climbed up to join the sentry. From the east a caravan of heavily laden donkeys was heading directly for the temple entrance, and Taita guessed that it was these merchants who used the temple as a makeshift caravanserai. It was almost certainly they who had left the store of fodder in the sanctum. He scrambled down the hillside, keeping out of sight of the approaching caravan. In the middle of the roadway he arranged a pattern of white quartz stones while he recited three verses from the Assyrian Book of the Evil Mountain. Then he retired to await the arrival of the caravan.

The leading donkey was fifty cubits or so ahead of the rest of the column. It was clear that the animal knew of the temple and the delights it contained, for he needed no encouragement from his driver to come on at a trot. As he reached the pile of white quartz stones in the path the little animal shied so violently that the pack slid over and hung under his belly. He started to buck and gallop at the same time, heading out across the plain away from the temple, hoofs flying in every direction. His hoarse honking and braying affected the rest of the animals in the column, and soon they were rearing and throwing their heads against the lead reins, kicking out at their drivers and running in circles as though attacked by a swarm of bees.

It took the caravan drivers half of the rest of the afternoon to catch and reassemble the runaways, to pacify the terrified animals and to set off again on the road towards the temple. This time the portly and richly robed figure of the head driver marched in the van, dragging the reluctant donkey behind him on a long rein. He saw the stones in the middle of the road and stopped. The column crowded up behind him, and the other drivers came forward. They held an impromptu conference with raised voices and arms waving. Their voices carried to where Taita sat hidden among the olive trees on the hillside.

At last the head driver left the others and came on alone. At first his step was bold and assured, but soon it slowed and became timid until at last he stood ill-at-ease and, from a distance, studied the pattern of quartz stones. Then he spat towards the stones and jumped back, as if he expected them to return the insult. Finally he made the sign against the evil eye, turned and trotted back with alacrity to join his fellows, shouting and waving them back. The others needed little convincing. Soon the entire caravan was in full retreat along the road it had come. Taita went down the hill and scattered the stones, allowing the influences they contained to disperse, and opening the way for the other visitors he was expecting.

They came in the short summer dusk, twenty armed men riding hard, Gil leading them on a borrowed steed. They swept down past the scattered stones and up to the entrance of the temple, where they dismounted with a clatter of weapons. The leader was a tall man, wide across the shoulders with a heavy beetling brow and a fleshy hooked nose. His heavy black moustaches were trained to droop down on to his chest, and coloured ribbons were plaited into his beard.

'You are the warlock. Yes?' he said, in a thick accent.

Taita did not think it opportune to let them know he spoke Hyksos like one of them, so he replied modestly in Egyptian, neither claiming nor denying magical powers. 'My name is Taita, a servant of the great god Horus. I call his blessing down upon you. I see that you are a man of might, but I do not know your name.'

'My name is Trok, Paramount Chief of the Clan of the Leopard, and commander of the north in the army of King Apepi. You have a token for me, Warlock?'

Taita opened his right hand and showed him the broken shard of blue glazed porcelain, the upper half of a tiny votive statue of the god Seueth. Trok examined it briefly, then took another fragment of porcelain from the pouch on his sword-belt and fitted the two pieces together. The broken edges matched perfectly, and he grunted with satisfaction. 'Come with me, Warlock.'

Trok strode out into the gathering night with Taita beside him. They climbed the hill in silence, and squatted down facing each other in the starlight. Trok kept his scabbard between his knees and his hand on the hilt of his heavy sickle sword. From habit more than distrust, Taita thought, but nevertheless the war chief was a man to reckon with.

'You bring me news of the south,' Trok said, in a statement, not a question.

'My lord, you have heard of the death of Pharaoh Tamose?'

'We know of the death of the Theban pretender from prisoners captured when we took the city of Abnub.' Trok was careful not to acknowledge by word or inference the authority of the Egyptian Pharaoh. To the Hyksos, the only ruler in either of the two kingdoms was Apepi. 'We heard also that a child now pretends to the throne of Upper Egypt.'

'Pharaoh Nefer Seti is only fourteen years of age,' Taita confirmed, equally careful to insist on the title of Pharaoh when he spoke of him. 'He will not attain his majority for some years. Until then Lord Naja acts as his regent.'

Trok leaned forward with sudden intense interest. Taita

smiled inwardly. The Hyksosian intelligence was poor indeed if they did not know at least that much about the affairs of the Upper Kingdom. Then he recalled the campaign that, just before the King's death, he and Pharaoh Tamose had waged against Hyksosian spies and informers in Thebes. They had winkled out and arrested over fifty. After interrogation by torture, they had executed every one. Taita felt a smug satisfaction at this confirmation that they had cut off the flow of information to the enemy.

'So, then, you come to us with the authority of the Regent of the south.' Taita detected a strange air of triumph about Trok, as he demanded, 'What message do you bring from Naja?'

'Lord Naja wants me to carry his proposal directly to Apepi,' Taita hedged. He did not want to give Trok any more information than was strictly necessary.

Trok took immediate umbrage at this. 'Naja is my cousin,' he said coldly. 'He would wish me to hear every word he has sent.' Taita had such control over his emotions that he showed no surprise, although it was a grave indiscretion on Trok's part. His suspicions as to the Regent's antecedents were confirmed, but his voice was measured as he answered, 'Yes, my lord, this much I know. However, what I have for Apepi is of such moment . . .'

'You underestimate me, Warlock. I have the complete confidence of your regent.' Trok's voice was rough with exasperation. 'I know full well that you have come to offer Apepi a truce, and to negotiate a lasting peace with him.'

'I can tell you nothing more, my lord.' This Trok might be a warrior, but he is no conspirator, Taita thought, but his voice and manner did not change as he said, 'I can give my message only to the Shepherd Chieftain, Apepi.' This was how the Hyksosian ruler was referred to in Upper Egypt. 'Can you take me to him?'

'As you wish, Warlock. Keep your mouth shut, if you will, though there is no purpose in it.' Trok stood up angrily. 'King Apepi is at Bubasti. We will go there immediately.'

In stilted silence they returned to the subterranean temple, where Taita called Gil and the sergeant of the bodyguard to him. 'You have done your work well,' he told them, 'but now you must return to Thebes as secretly as you have come.'

'You will return with us?' Gil asked anxiously. Clearly he felt responsible for the old man.

'No.' Taita shook his head. 'I will remain here. When you report to the Regent tell him that I am on my way to meet Apepi.'

By the dim light of the oil lamps the horses were harnessed to the chariots, and within a short time they were ready to leave. Gil brought Taita's leather saddlebag from the chariot and handed it to him. Then he saluted respectfully. 'It has been a great honour to ride with you, my lord. When I was a child my father told me many tales of your adventures. He rode with your regiment at Asyut. He was captain of the left wing.'

'What was his name?' Taita asked.

'Lasro, my lord.'

'Yes.' Taita nodded. 'I remember him well. He lost his left eye in the battle.'

Gil gazed at him with awe and wonder. 'That was forty years ago, and still you remember.'

'Thirty-seven,' Taita corrected him. 'Go well, young Gil. I cast your horoscope last night. You will have a long life, and attain much distinction.'

The lance-bearer took up the reins and rode out into the night, speechless with pride and gratification.

By this time Lord Trok's troop was also mounted and ready to leave. They had given Taita the horse on which Gil had returned to the temple. Taita threw the saddlebags over its withers then swung up behind them. The Hyksos did not have the same scruples about riding astride as the

Egyptians, and they clattered out of the cave entrance and turned west, in the opposite direction to that taken by the column of chariots.

Taita rode in the centre of the party of heavily armed Hyksos. Trok led them and he did not invite Taita to ride alongside him. He had been distant and aloof since Taita had refused to give Naja's message to him directly. Taita was content to be ignored, for he had much to think about. In particular the revelation of Naja's confused blood-lines opened a host of fascinating possibilities.

They rode on through the night, heading west towards the river and the main enemy base at Bubasti. Even though it was still night-time, they encountered more and more traffic on the road. There were long lines of wagons and carts, all heavily laden with military supplies, moving in the same direction as they were. Returning towards Avaris and Memphis were equal numbers of empty vehicles that had discharged their cargo.

As they came closer to the river, Taita saw the fires of the Hyksosian troops encamped around Bubasti. It was a field of flickering light that stretched many miles in both directions along the riverbank, a huge agglomeration of men and animals unseen in the darkness.

There was nothing on earth like the smell of an army encamped. It grew stronger as they approached until it was almost overpowering. It was a mixture of many odours, the smell of the cavalry lines, manure and the smoke of dung fires, of leather and mouldy grain. On top of this was the smell of unwashed men and their festering wounds, cooking food and fermenting beer, unburied rubbish, and filth, the ammoniacal reek of the latrine pits and the dung heaps, and the even more biting stench of unburied corpses.

Underlying this stifling blend of odours Taita picked out another sickly taint. He thought he recognized it, but it was only when one of the sufferers staggered drunkenly in front of his horse, forcing him to rein in sharply, that he saw the rose-coloured blotches on the pale face and he was certain. He knew now why Apepi had failed so far to follow up his victory at Abnub, why he had not yet sent his chariots tearing southwards towards Thebes where the Egyptian army was in disarray, and at his mercy. Taita pushed his horse up alongside Trok's mount, and asked him quietly, 'My lord, when did the plague first strike your troops?'

Trok reined in so roughly that his mount danced and circled under him, 'Who told you that, Warlock?' he demanded. 'Is this cursed disease one of your spells? Is it you who have laid this pestilence upon us?' He spurred away angrily without waiting for a denial. Taita followed at a discreet distance, but his eyes were busy taking in every detail of what was happening around him.

By this time the light was strengthening, and a weak, hazy sun barely showed through the heavy bank of mist and woodsmoke that blanketed the land and blotted out the dawn sky. It gave the scene a weird, unearthly aspect, like a vision of the underworld. Men and animals were transformed by it into dark and demoniacal figures, and under the hoofs of their horses the mud of the recent inundation was black and glutinous.

They passed the first of the burial carts, and the men around Taita used their cloaks to cover their mouths and noses against the stink and the evil humours that hung over the heap of naked, bloated corpses piled high in the back of the cart. Trok spurred his horse to overtake it quickly, but ahead there were many more similarly laden vehicles almost blocking the roadway.

Further on they passed one of the cremation fields, on which more carts were unloading their grisly burden. Firewood was a scarce commodity in this land, and the flames were not fierce enough to consume the heaps of corpses. They spluttered and flickered as the fats oozed out of the decaying flesh, and sent up clouds of oily black smoke that coated the mouths and throats of the living men who breathed it.

How many of the dead are victims of the plague? Taita wondered. And how many from the fighting with our army?

The plague was like some grim spectre that marched in step with any army. Apepi had been here at Bubasti for many years in camps that swarmed with rats, vultures and the carrion-eating marabou storks. His men were crowded together in their own filth, their bodies crawling with fleas and lice, eating rotten food and drinking the water from the irrigation canals into which the effluent from the graves and dung heaps drained. These were the conditions in which the plague flourished.

Closer to Bubasti the encampments became more numerous, tents, huts and hovels crowded right up to the walls and ditches that surrounded the garrison town. The more fortunate among the plague victims lay under tattered roofs of palm fronds, scant protection from the hot morning sunlight. Others lay out in the trampled mud of the fields, abandoned to thirst and the elements. The dead were mixed with the dying, those wounded in the fighting lying side by side with those ravaged by streaming dysentery.

Although his instincts were those of a healer, Taita would do nothing to succour them. They were condemned by their own multitudes, for what could one man do to help so many? What was more, they were the enemies of this very Egypt, and it was clear to him that the pestilence was a visitation from the gods. Should he heal a single Hyksos, it would mean that there was one more to march on Thebes and put his beloved city to flame and rapine.

They entered the fortress and found that conditions were not much better within its walls. Plague victims lay where they had been struck down by the disease, and the rats and pariah dogs gnawed at their corpses, and even at those still alive but too far gone to defend themselves.

Apepi's headquarters was the principal building in Bubasti, a massive sprawling mud-brick and thatch palace in the centre of the town. Grooms took their horses at the gates, but one carried Taita's saddle-bags. Lord Trok led Taita through courtyards and the dark shuttered halls where incense and sandalwood burned in bronze braziers to cloak the plague stench that wafted up from the town and the surrounding encampments, but whose guttering flames made the heated air scarcely bearable. Even here in the main headquarters the groans of plague victims rang eerily through the rooms, and huddled figures lay in dark corners.

Sentries stopped them outside a barred bronze door in the deepest recesses of the building, but as soon as they recognized Trok's hulking figure they stood aside and allowed them to pass through. This area was Apepi's private quarters. The walls were hung with magnificent carpets and the furniture was of precious wood, ivory and mother-of-pearl, much of it plundered from the palaces and temples of Egypt.

Trok ushered Taita into a small but luxuriously furnished antechamber, and left him there. Female slaves brought him a jug of sherbet and a platter of ripe dates and pomegranates. Taita sipped the drink but ate only a little of the fruit. He was always abstemious.

It was a long wait. A sunbeam through the single high window moved sedately along the opposite wall measuring the passage of time. Lying on one of the carpets, he used his saddlebags as a pillow, dozing, never sinking into deep sleep, and coming instantly awake at every noise. At intervals he heard the distant sound of women weeping, and the keening wail of mourning somewhere behind the massive walls.

At last there came the tramp of heavy footsteps down the passage outside, and the curtains over the doorway were thrown open. A burly figure stood in the doorway. He wore only a crimson linen kilt belted below his great belly with a gold chain. His chest was covered with grizzled wiry curls, coarse as the pelt of a bear. There were heavy sandals on his feet and greaves of hard polished leather covered his shins. But he carried no sword or other weapon. His arms and legs seemed massive as the pillars of a temple, and were covered with battle scars, some white and silky, long-ago healed; others, more recent, were purple and angry-looking. His beard and dense bush of hair were grizzled also, but lacking the usual ribbons or plaits. They had not been oiled or combed and were in careless disarray. His dark eyes were wild and distracted, and his thick lips under the great beaked nose were twisted as if with pain.

'You are Taita, the physician,' he said. His voice was powerful, but without accent for he had been born in Avaris and had adopted much of the Egyptian culture and way of life.

Taita knew him well: to him Apepi was the invader, the bloody barbarian, mortal enemy of his country and his Pharaoh. It took the exercise of all his self-control to keep his expression neutral and his voice calm as he replied, 'I am Taita.'

'I have heard of your skills,' said Apepi. 'I have need of them now. Come with me.'

Taita slung the saddlebags over his shoulder and followed him out into the cloister. Lord Trok was waiting there with an escort of armed men. They fell in around Taita as he followed the Hyksosian king deeper into the palace. Ahead the sound of weeping became louder, until Apepi threw aside the heavy curtains that covered another doorway, and took Taita's arm to push him through.

Dominating the crowded chamber was a large contingent of priests from the temple of Isis in Avaris. Taita's lip curled as he recognized them by their headdress of egret feathers. They were chanting and shaking sistrums over the brazier in one corner in which cauterizing tongs glowed red hot.

Taita's professional feud with these quacks went back two generations.

Apart from the healers, twenty others were gathered around the sickbed in the centre of the floor, courtiers and army officers, scribes and other officials, all looking solemn and funereal. Most of the women were kneeling on the floor, wailing and keening. Only one was making any attempt to nurse the young boy who lay on the couch. She seemed not much older than her patient, probably thirteen or fourteen years of age, and she was sponging him down with heated, perfumed water from a copper bowl.

With a single glance Taita saw that she was a striking-looking girl, with a determined, intelligent face. Her concern for her patient was evident, her expression loving and her hands quick and competent.

Taita switched his attention to the boy. His naked body was also well formed, but wasted by disease. His skin was blotched with the characteristic stigmata of the plague, and dewed with perspiration. On his chest were the raw and inflamed wounds where he had been bled and cauterized by the priests of Isis. Taita saw that he was in the final stages of the disease. His thick dark hair was sodden with sweat, it hung over his eyes, which were sunk into plum-coloured cavities, open and bright with fever but unseeing.

'This is Khyan, my youngest son,' Apepi said, as he went to the bedside, and looked down at the child helplessly. 'The plague will take him, unless you can save him, Magus.'

Khyan groaned and rolled on to his side with his knees drawn up in agony to his lacerated chest. With an explosive spluttering sound a mixture of liquid faeces and bright blood spurted from between his shrunken buttocks on to the soiled bed linen. The girl who was nursing him at once cleaned his backside with the cloth, then wiped up the mess on the sheets without any sign of distaste. In the corner the healers renewed their chants, and the high priest took up a pair of hot tongs from the charcoal brazier and came towards the bed.

Taita stepped forward, barring the man's way with his long staff. 'Get out!' he said softly. 'You and your butchers have done enough damage here.'

'I must burn the fever out of his body,' the man protested.

'Out!' Taita repeated grimly, then to the others who crowded the chamber, 'Out, all of you.'

'I know you well, Taita. You are a blasphemer, and a familiar of demons and evil spirits.' The priest stood his ground, and brandished the glowing bronze instrument menacingly. 'I do not fear your magic. You have no authority here. The prince is in my charge.'

Taita stepped back and dropped his staff at the feet of the priest, who shrieked and sprang back as the rod of tambootie wood began to writhe, hiss and snake towards him over the tiles. Suddenly it reared up head-high, its forked tongue darting between thin grinning lips and its beady black eyes glittering.

Instantly there was a yelling stampede for the door. Courtiers and priests, soldiers and servants panicked, clawing and elbowing their way through the press to be the first out. In his haste to escape, the high priest knocked over the brazier, then screamed as he danced barefoot on the scattered coals.

Within seconds the chamber was deserted except for Apepi, who had not moved, and the girl at the sickbed. Taita stooped and picked up the writhing serpent by the tail. Instantly it was straight, rigid and wooden in his grasp. He pointed the restored staff at the girl at the bedside. 'Who are you?' he demanded.

'I am Mintaka. This is my brother.' She laid her hand protectively on the boy's sweat-damp curls, and lifted her chin with a defiant air. 'Do your worst, Magus, but I will not leave him.' Her lips trembled and her dark eyes were huge with terror. She was clearly overawed by his reputation and by the serpent staff that Taita was pointing at her. 'I am not afraid of you,' she told him, then moved around the bed until it was between them.

'Good,' said Taita briskly. 'Then you will be of more use to me. When did the boy last drink?'

It took a moment for her to gather herself. 'Not since this morning.'

'Can't those quacks see that he is dying of thirst as much as of the disease? He has sweated and voided most of the water from his body,' Taita grunted, and picked up the copper jug from beside the bed to sniff the contents.

'This is foul with priest poison and plague humours.' He hurled it against the wall. 'Go to the kitchens and find another jug. Make sure it is clean. Fill it from the well, not with river water. Hurry, girl.' She fled and Taita opened his bag.

Mintaka returned almost immediately with a brimming jug of clean water. Taita prepared a potion of herbs, and heated it on the brazier.

'Help me give it to him,' he ordered the girl when it had brewed. He showed her how to position her brother's head and to stroke his throat as he dribbled the water into his mouth. Soon Khyan was swallowing freely.

'What can I do to help you?' the king asked.

'My lord, there is nothing for you here. You are better at destroying than at healing.' Taita dismissed him without looking up from his patient. There was a long silence, then the tramp of Apepi's bronze-studded sandals as he left the chamber.

Mintaka soon lost her terror of the Magus, and as a helper she was quick and willing. She seemed able to anticipate Taita's wishes. She forced her brother to drink while Taita brewed up another cup of medicine from his bag on the brazier. Between them they were able to get this down his throat without losing a drop. She helped him smear a soothing ointment on the burns that covered his chest. Then between them they wrapped Khyan in linen sheets and soaked them with well water to cool his burning body.

When she came to sit beside him to rest for a moment Taita took her hand and turned it palm up. He examined the red lumps on the inside of her wrist, but Mintaka tried to pull her hand away. 'Those are not plague spots.' She flushed with embarrassment. 'They are only flea-bites. The palace is crawling with fleas.'

'Where the flea bites, the plague follows,' Taita told her. 'Take off your shift.'

She stood up without hesitation and let it drop around her ankles. Her naked body, though slim and nubile, was also athletic and strong. Her breasts were in first bud, the perky nipples pricking out like ripening mulberries. A triangle of soft fluff nestled between her long shapely legs.

A flea hopped from her pale belly. Deftly Taita picked it out of the air and crunched it between his fingernails. The insect had left a chain of pink spots around her neatly puckered belly button.

'Turn round,' he ordered, and she obeyed. Another of the loathsome insects ran down her back towards the deep cleft between her hard round buttocks. Taita pinched it between his fingers and crushed its shiny black carapace. It popped in a spot of blood. 'You will be the next patient if we don't get rid of these little pets of yours,' he told her, and sent her to fetch a bowl of water from the kitchens. On the brazier he boiled up the dried purple flowers of the pyrethrum plant and washed her down from head to toe in the brew. He snapped four or five more fleas that tried to escape the pungent douche by leaping off her drenched skin.

Afterwards Mintaka sat beside him while her naked body dried, and chatted unselfconsciously as they picked over her clothes companionably, removing the last fleas and their eggs from the seams and pleats. They were fast becoming good friends.

Before nightfall Khyan's bowels voided once more, but sparingly, and there was no blood in the stool. Taita sniffed the faeces, and the stench of the plague humours was milder. He administered a stronger distillation of the herbs, and between them they forced Khyan to drink another jugful of well water. By next morning the fever had broken and Khyan was resting more comfortably. He urinated at last, which Taita declared to be beneficial, even though his water was dark yellow and acrid. An hour later he passed more water, lighter in colour and not so evil-smelling.

'Look, my lord,' Mintaka exclaimed, stroking her brother's cheek, 'the red blotches are fading, and his skin feels cooler.'

'You have the healing touch of a nymph of paradise,' Taita told her, 'but do not forget the water jug. It is empty.'

She raced away to the kitchens, and came back almost immediately with a brimming jug. While she gave it to him, she began to sing a Hyksosian lullaby, and Taita was delighted by the sweetness and clarity of her voice:

'Listen to the wind in the grass, little darling,
Sleep, sleep, sleep.
Hear the sound of the river, my little baby,
Dream, dream, dream.'

Taita studied her face. In the Hyksosian way, it was a little too broad, and her cheekbones too prominent. Her mouth was large, her lips full, her nose strongly bridged. Not one of these features was perfect in itself, but each was finely balanced with and matched to all the others, and her neck was long and graceful. Her almond-shaped eyes were truly magnificent under arched black brows. Her expression was alert and bright. Hers was a different kind of beauty, he thought, but beauty none the less.

'Look!' She broke off the song and laughed. 'He is awake.'

Khyan's eyes were open and he was looking up at her.

'You have come back to us, you horrid little beast.' When she laughed her teeth were square and very white in the lamplight. 'We were so worried. You must not do that again, ever.' She hugged him to hide the tears of joy and relief that suddenly sparkled in her eyes.

Taita looked beyond the pair on the bed and saw the bulky figure of Apepi in the doorway. Taita did not know how long he had been there, but now he nodded at Taita without smiling, then turned and disappeared.

By that evening Khyan was able to sit up with a little help from his sister, and to drink from the soup bowl she held to his lips. Two days later his rash had disappeared.

Three or four times a day Apepi visited the chamber. Khyan was still too weak to rise, but as soon as his father appeared, he touched his heart and his lips in a gesture of respect.

On the fifth day he tottered from the couch and tried to prostrate himself before the King, but Apepi stopped him and lifted him back on to the pillows. Even though his feelings for the boy were clear, Apepi had little to say and left again almost immediately, but in the doorway he looked back at Taita and ordered him to follow with a curt inclination of his head.

They stood alone on the summit of the highest tower of the palace. They had climbed two hundred steps to reach this height, and from here they had a view upriver over the captured citadel of Abnub, which lay ten miles upstream. Thebes was less than a hundred miles beyond that.

Apepi had ordered the sentries to go down and leave

them alone in this lofty place, so that they would not be spied upon or overheard. He stood staring out over the great grey river towards the south. He was in full war costume, hard leather greaves and breastplate, sword-belt studded with gold rosettes, and his beard was plaited with crimson ribbons to match his ceremonial apron. Incongruously he wore the golden *uraeus*, the vulture and cobra crown, over his dense silver-shot curls. It infuriated Taita that this invader and despoiler considered himself Pharaoh of all Egypt, and wore the sacred regalia, but his expression was serene. Instead he tuned his mind to catch Apepi's thoughts. They were a tangled web, so deep and devious that even Taita could not discern them clearly, but he could sense the force within that made Apepi such a dreadful adversary.

'At least something they say of you is true, Magus.' Apepi broke the long silence. 'You are a physician of great skill.' Taita remained silent.

'Can you work a charm to heal the plague in my army as you have in my son?' Apepi asked. 'I would pay you a lakh of gold. As much gold as ten strong horses can carry.'

Taita smiled bleakly. 'My lord, if I could work such a charm I could as well conjure a hundred lakhs out of the thin air without the effort of curing your ruffians.'

Apepi turned his head and returned his smile, but it lacked any humour or goodwill. 'How old are you, Warlock? Trok says you are over two hundred years old. Is that true?'

Taita gave no indication of having heard him, and Apepi went on, 'What is your price, Warlock? If not gold then what can I offer you?' The question was rhetorical and he did not wait for an answer, but stamped away to the northern parapet of the tower, and stood with his fists on his hips. He looked down over the encampments of his army, and the cremation fields beyond. The fires were still burning and the smoke drifted low across the green waters of the river and out into the desert beyond.

'You have won a victory, my lord,' Taita said softly, 'but you do well to contemplate the pyres of your dead. Pharaoh will have reinforced and regrouped his forces before the plague burns itself out and your men are ready to fight again.'

Apepi shook himself with annoyance, like a lion shaking off flies. 'Your persistence irks me, Warlock.'

'Nay, lord, it is not me but the truth and the logic that irk you.'

'Nefer Seti is a child. I have defeated him once, I will do it again.'

'What is more crucial to you, there is no plague in his army. Your spies will have told you that Pharaoh has five more legions at Aswan, and another two at Asyut. They are already on the river coming north with the current. They will be here before the new moon.'

Apepi growled softly, but made no response. Taita went on relentlessly, 'Sixty years of war have bled both kingdoms white. Would you pass on the legacy of Salitis, your own father, sixty years of bloodshed? Is that what your sons will inherit from you?'

Apepi rounded on him, scowling, 'Do not press me too hard, old man. Do not insult my father, the divine god Salitis.' After an interval long enough to express his disapproval, Apepi spoke again. 'How long will it take you to arrange a parley with this so-called Regent of the Upper Kingdom, this Naja?'

'If you give me safe conduct through your lines, and a fast galley to carry me, I can be in Thebes in three days. The return with the current will be even swifter.'

'I will send Trok with you to see you safely through. Tell Naja I will meet him at the temple of Hathor on the west bank at Perra beyond Abnub. Do you know it?'

'I know it well, my lord,' Taita said.

'We can talk there,' Apepi said. 'But tell him not to

expect too many concessions from me. I am the victor, and he the vanquished. You can go now.'

Taita stood his ground.

'You may go, Warlock.' Apepi dismissed him a second time.

'Pharaoh Nefer Seti is almost of an age with your daughter, Mintaka,' Taita said stubbornly. 'You might wish to bring her with you to Perra.'

'To what purpose?' Apepi stared at him suspiciously.

'An alliance between your dynasty and that of the Tamosian pharaohs might seal a lasting peace in the two kingdoms.'

Apepi stroked the ribbons in his beard to hide his smile. 'By Seueth, you intrigue as cunningly as you mix a potion, Warlock. Now, get you gone before you irk me past forbearance.'

The temple of Hathor had been excavated out of the rocky hillside above the river in the reign of Pharaoh Sehertawy hundreds of years previously, but had been added to by every pharaoh since then. The priestesses were a rich, influential sisterhood who had contrived somehow to survive during the long civil wars between the kingdoms and even to prosper in difficult times.

Dressed in their yellow robes they were gathered in the courtyard of the temple, between the two massive statues of the goddess. One of these depicted Hathor as the piebald cow with golden horns, and the other was her human manifestation, the tall, beautiful lady wearing the crown of horns and the golden sun disc on her head.

The priestesses chanted and rattled the sistrum as the suite of Pharaoh Nefer Seti filed into the courtyard from the eastern wing, while King Apepi's courtiers entered through the western colonnade. The order of arrival at the conference had been a matter of such heated debate that the negotiations had almost broken down before they had begun. The first arrival would have the prestige of the incumbent in the position of power, while the second arrival would appear as the supplicant begging for peace. Neither side had been willing to forgo the advantage.

It was Taita who had suggested the expedient of a simultaneous arrival. He had also tactfully settled the equally vexing question of the regalia to be worn by the two protagonists. Both would eschew the double crown. Apepi would wear the red *deshret* crown of Lower Egypt, while Nefer Seti would confine himself to the white *hedjet* crown of Upper Egypt.

The entourages of both rulers packed the spacious courtyard, their ranks facing each other unsmiling and grim. Only a few paces separated them physically, but the bitterness and hatred of sixty years' strife formed a mighty barrier between them.

The hostile silence was shattered by a rolling fanfare of rams' horns, and the thunder of bronze gongs. This was the signal for the royal parties to emerge from the opposite wings of the temple.

Lord Naja and Pharaoh Nefer Seti paced out solemnly and took their places on the high-backed thrones, while the two princesses, Heseret and Merykara, followed them meekly and took their seats at the foot of Naja's throne, for they were his betrothed. Both girls were so heavily made-up that their faces were as expressionless as that of the statue of Hathor in whose shadow they sat.

At the same time the Hyksosian royal family emerged from the opposing wing of the temple. Apepi led them, an impressive, warlike figure in full battle armour. He glared across the courtyard at the boy pharaoh. Eight of his sons followed him; only Khyan, the youngest, had not recovered sufficiently from the plague to make the journey upriver.

Like their father they were armed and armoured, and strutted and posed with the same bravado.

A formidable coterie of bloodthirsty ruffians, Taita thought, as he surveyed them from where he stood close to Nefer's throne.

Apepi had brought only one of his many daughters with him. Like a desert rose in a thicket of spiny cactus, the contrast to her brothers made Mintaka's beauty shine out. She picked out Taita's tall lank figure and silver hair in the crowd opposite and her face lit in a smile so radiant that it seemed for a moment that the sun had burst through the awnings stretched over the courtyard. None of the Egyptians had ever laid eyes on her before, and there was a subdued rustle and murmur through their ranks. They had been unprepared for her. The myth was that all Hyksosian women were as heavily built as their menfolk and twice as ugly.

Pharaoh Nefer Seti leaned forward slightly and despite the solemnity of the occasion tugged at his earlobe under the bottle-shaped white crown. It was a habit Taita had tried to break, and Nefer only did it when he was intensely interested in something, or when he was distracted. Taita had not seen Nefer for over two months – Naja had kept them separated since his return from Apepi's headquarters at Bubasti – yet he was so familiar with the boy, so attuned to his mind, that he could still read his thoughts with ease. He sensed that Nefer was in a ferment of elation and excitement, as intense as if he had just spotted a gazelle moving within arrow range, or was about to mount an unbroken colt, or had launched a hawk at a heron and was watching it begin its stoop.

Taita had never known him react like this to the presence of a member of the opposite sex. Nefer had always looked upon all females, including his sisters, with a regal disdain. However, it was less than a year since he had been launched on to the troubled waters of puberty, and most of that time he had been sequestered with Taita in the wilderness of Gebel Nagara where there had been nothing to rivet his attention in the way that Mintaka was now doing.

Taita felt smug at what he had achieved with so little effort. It would have complicated all his plans and enhanced the danger in which they found themselves if Nefer had taken a violent dislike to the Hyksosian girl. If the two married, Nefer would be the son-in-law of Apepi and come under his protection. Even Naja must pause before giving offence to someone so powerful and dangerous. Mintaka might unwittingly save Nefer from the Regent's machinations and ambitions. That at least was Taita's intention in fostering the union.

During the short time they had nursed and cared for her brother Taita and Mintaka had formed a firm friendship. Now Taita nodded almost imperceptibly and returned her smile. Then Mintaka's gaze moved past him. She looked with interest at the noble Egyptian women opposite her. She had heard much about them, but these were the first she had seen. Swiftly she singled out Heseret. With sure feminine instinct she recognized someone as attractive as herself, and a possible future rival. Heseret reacted to her in exactly the same way, and they exchanged a brief but haughty and mutually hostile glance. Then Mintaka raised her eyes to the impressive figure of Lord Naja and stared at him with fascination.

He was such a splendid sight, so different from her own father and brothers. He shone with gold and precious stones, and his linen was dazzling in its purity. She could smell his perfume across the distance that separated them, like a field of wild flowers. His face was a mask of makeup, his skin almost luminous and his eyes outlined and enhanced with kohl. Yet she thought that his was the fatal beauty of a snake or a poisonous insect. She shivered and turned her eyes to the figure on the throne beside the Regent.

Pharaoh Nefer Seti was staring at her with such intensity that she caught her breath. His eyes were so green – that was the first thing that struck her and she wanted to look away but found she could not. Instead she started to blush.

Pharaoh Nefer Seti looked so dignified and divine under the white crown and with the false goatee beard on his chin that she felt flustered. Then, suddenly, Pharaoh gave her a warm and conspiratorial smile. Instantly his face was boyish and appealing, and unaccountably her breath came faster and she blushed deeper. With an effort she tore away her eyes, and studied the cow statue of the goddess Hathor with great attention.

It took her some time to bring herself under control, and by that time Lord Naja, the Regent of Upper Egypt, was speaking. In measured tones he greeted Apepi, diplomatically referring to him as King of the Hyksos but avoiding any reference to his claims to Egyptian territory. Mintaka watched his lips intently, but she was aware of Nefer's eyes on her, and determined not to look at him.

Lord Naja's voice was sonorous and boring, and at last she could hold out no longer. She sneaked a quick sideways glance at Nefer, intending to look away again immediately, but his eyes were still fastened on her. They glinted with silent laughter and fascinated her. Hers was not a timid nature, but this time her smile was shy and hesitant, and she felt her colour rise again. She dropped her eyes and looked at her hands in her lap, twisting her fingers together until she realized that she was fidgeting and stopped herself. She kept her hands still, but now she was irritated with Nefer for having ruffled her calm. He is only a precious Egyptian fop. Any one of my brothers is more of a man and twice as handsome. He is only trying to make me look a fool by staring at me in that boorish way. I will not look at him again. I will ignore him completely, she decided, and her resolve lasted until Lord Naja stopped speaking, and her father rose to answer him.

She shot Nefer another quick look from under her thick dark lashes. He was gazing at her father, but the moment her glance touched his face his eyes swivelled to her. She tried to make her expression severe and forbidding, but as soon as he smiled her lips twitched in sympathy. He really is as handsome as some of my brothers, she conceded, then took another quick peek. Or perhaps as any of them. She looked back at her lap and thought about it. Then she took another peep just to make certain. Perhaps even more handsome than any of them, even Ruga. Immediately she felt that she had betrayed her eldest brother and qualified her opinion: but in a different kind of way, of course.

She glanced sideways at Ruga: with his beribboned beard and dark brow, he was all warrior. Ruga is a fine-looking man, she thought loyally.

In the ranks opposite, Taita did not seem to be watching her but he missed not a single nuance of the surreptitious exchanges between Nefer and Mintaka. He saw more than that. Lord Trok, Naja's cousin, was standing close behind Apepi's throne, almost within arm's reach of Mintaka. His arms were folded over his chest, and he wore embossed wristlets of solid gold. Over one shoulder was slung a heavy recurved bow, over the other an arrow quiver covered with gold leaf. Around his neck were the gold chains of valour and praise. The Hyksos had adopted Egyptian military honours and decorations as well as their beliefs and customs. Trok was watching the Hyksosian princess with an unfathomable expression.

There was another brief exchange of glances between Mintaka and Nefer, which Trok followed with his dark, brooding gaze. Taita could sense his anger and jealousy. It was as though the hot and oppressive cloud of the *khamsin*, the terrible Saharan sandstorm, was building up on the desert horizon. I had not foreseen this. Is Trok's interest in Mintaka romantic or political? he wondered. Does he lust for her, or see her merely as a staircase to power? In either case it is dangerous, and something else we must take into account.

The speeches of greeting were coming to an end and nothing of significance had been said: negotiation of the truce would begin in secret session the next day. Both sides were rising from their thrones and exchanging bows and salutations, and the gongs began to beat and the ram's horns to sound again as they withdrew.

Taita took one last look at the Hyksosian ranks. Apepi and his sons disappeared through a gateway guarded by tall granite pillars, topped with the twin cow heads of the goddess. With a final backward look Mintaka followed her father and brothers. Lord Trok followed her closely, and also shot a last glance at Pharaoh Nefer Seti over his shoulder. Then he, too, strode out between the pillars. As he did so the arrows in his quiver rattled softly, and their coloured fletchings caught Taita's eye. Unlike the workaday leather war quiver with its stopper to prevent the arrows spilling out, this ceremonial one was covered in gold leaf, and the barrel end was open so that the fletched tips of the arrows protruded above his shoulder. The feathers were red and green, and something evil stirred in Taita's memory. Trok marched away through the gateway, leaving Taita gazing after him.

Taita returned to the stone cell in the temple annexe that had been allocated to him for the duration of the peace conference. He drank a little sherbet, for it had been hot in the courtyard, then went to the window in the thick stone wall. A flock of bright-coloured weavers and tits hopped and twittered on the sill, and on the flagged terrace below. While he fed them with crushed *dhurra* millet, and they sat on his shoulders or pecked from his cupped hands, Taita thought about the events of the morning and began to piece together all the disparate perceptions he had garnered during the opening ceremony.

His amusement and pleasure at what had transpired between Mintaka and Nefer were forgotten as he went on to think of Trok. He considered the man's relationship to the Hyksosian princess, and the complications that might ensue when he tried to force through his plans for the young couple.

His train of thought was interrupted as he noticed a stealthy shadow creeping along the edge of the terrace outside the window. It was one of the temple cats, gaunt, scarred and flayed in patches with mange. It was stalking the birds that hopped on the flags outside the window, picking up the spilled grains of *dhurra* millet.

Taita's pale eyes slitted as he concentrated on the cat. The old tom stopped and peered around suspiciously. Suddenly its back arched and every hair on its body stood erect as it stared at an empty spot on the stone flags in front of it. It uttered a spitting shriek, spun round and raced away down the terrace until it came to a palm tree. It flew up the tall trunk until it reached the crowning top fronds where it clung pathetically. Taita threw another handful of grain to the birds and picked up his thoughts.

Even during their long ride together, Trok had kept his

war quiver firmly stoppered and it had not occurred to Taita to compare one of the arrows it contained to those he had found at the site of Pharaoh's murder. How many other Hyksosian officers had red and green fletchings he could only guess, but it was probably a great number, though each would have his unique signet. There was only one way to connect Trok to the death of Pharaoh Tamose, and through him to implicate his cousin Naja. That was to study one of his arrows. How to do this without arousing his suspicions, he wondered.

Once again he was distracted from his thoughts. There were voices in the passage outside the door of his cell. One was young and clear, and he recognized it at once. The others were gruff, pleading and protesting.

'Lord Asmor has given specific orders—'

'Am I not Pharaoh? Are you not bound to obey me? I wish to visit the Magus, and you dare not prevent me. Stand aside, both of you.' Nefer's voice was strong and commanding. The uncertain timbre of puberty was gone, and he spoke with the tones of a man.

The young falcon is spreading his wings and showing his talons, Taita thought, and turned from the window, dusting the millet powder from his hands, to greet his king.

Nefer jerked aside the curtain that covered the doorway, and stepped through. Two armed bodyguards followed him helplessly, crowding into the doorway behind him. Nefer ignored them and faced Taita with his hands on his hips.

'Taita, I am much displeased with you,' Nefer said.

'I am distraught.' Taita made a deep obeisance. 'In what way have I given you offence?'

'You have been avoiding me. Whenever I send for you they tell me that you are gone on a secret mission to the Hyksos, or that you have returned to the desert, or some other such moonlit tale.' Nefer scowled to mask his delight at being with the old man again. 'Then suddenly you pop up from nowhere, as though you had never left, but still you ignore me. You did not even look in my direction during the ceremony. Where have you been?'

'Majesty, there are long ears about.' Taita glanced at the hovering guards.

Immediately Nefer turned upon them wrathfully. 'I have ordered you more than once to be gone. If you do not go this instant I will have you both strangled.'

They withdrew unhappily, but not too far. Taita could still hear their murmurs and the clink of their weapons as they waited in the passage beyond the curtain. He jerked his head at the window and whispered, 'I have a skiff at the jetty. Would Your Majesty like to go fishing?' Without waiting for his reply, Taita hitched up the skirts of his *chiton* and hopped on to the window-sill. He glanced over his shoulder. Nefer had forgotten his anger and was grinning delightedly as he ran across the cell to join him. Taita jumped down on to the terrace outside and Nefer followed him nimbly. Like truants from the classroom, they sneaked across the terrace and down through the date palms to the river.

There were guards at the jetty, but they had received no orders to restrain their young Pharaoh. They saluted and stood aside respectfully as the pair scrambled into the small fishing skiff. Each took up a paddle and shoved off. Taita steered into one of the narrow passages in the banks of waving papyrus, and within minutes they were alone on the swamp waters, hidden from the banks in the maze of secret waterways.

'Where have you been, Taita?' Nefer dropped the regal air. 'I have missed you so.'

'I will tell you everything,' Taita assured him, 'but first you should tell me all that has happened to you.'

They found a quiet mooring in a tiny papyrus-enclosed lagoon, and Nefer related everything that had happened to him since they had last been able to talk in private. He had been held on Naja's orders in a gilded prison, without being able to see any of his old friends, not even Meren or his own sisters. His only distractions had been his studies of the scrolls from the palace library, his chariot drills and arms practice under the coaching of the old warrior, Hilto.

'Naja will not even let me go out hawking or fishing without Asmor to wet-nurse me,' he complained bitterly.

He had not known that Taita was to be at the welcoming ceremony in the temple courtyard until he had seen him there. He had believed him to be at Gebel Nagara. At his first opportunity, when Naja and Asmor were locked in the truce conclave with Apepi, Trok and the other Hyksosian warlords, he had browbeaten his guards and blustered his way out of the quarters to which he had been confined to come to Taita.

'Life is so dull without you, Taita. I think I might die of boredom. Naja must let us be together again. You should cast a spell on him.'

'It is something we can consider,' Taita avoided the suggestion adroitly, 'but now we have little time. Naja will send the whole army out to search for us once he finds that we are missing from the temple. I must tell you my own news.' Rapidly, in simple outline, he told Nefer what had happened to him since their last meeting. He explained the relationship between Naja and Trok, and described how he had visited the scene of Pharaoh Tamose's death and the discovery he had made there.

Nefer listened without interruption, but when Taita spoke of the death of his father his eyes filled with tears. He looked away, coughed and wiped his eyes on the back of his hand.

'Now you can appreciate the danger you are in,' Taita told him. 'I am certain that Naja had much to do with Pharaoh's murder, and the closer we come to the proof of it, the greater that danger becomes.'

'One day I will avenge my father,' Nefer vowed, and his voice was cold and hard.

'And I will help you do it,' Taita promised, 'but now we must protect you from Naja's malice.'

'How do you plan to do that, Taita? Can we escape from Egypt as we planned before?'

'No.' Taita shook his head. 'Naturally I have considered that course, but Naja has us too securely imprisoned here. If we tried to run for the frontier again we would have a thousand chariots hot behind us.'

'What can we do, then? You are in danger also.'

'No. I have convinced Naja that he cannot succeed without my help.' He described the false divination ceremony at the temple of Osiris, and how Naja believed that Taita could share with him the secret of eternal life.

Nefer grinned at the Magus' cunning. 'So what do you plan?'

'We must wait until the right time either to escape or rid the world of Naja's evil presence. In the meantime I will protect you as best I can.'

'How will you do that?'

'Naja sent me to Apepi to arrange this peace conference.'

'Yes, I know that you went to Avaris. They told me that when I demanded to see you.'

'Not to Avaris, but to Apepi's battle headquarters at Bubasti. Once Apepi had agreed to the meeting with Naja, I was able to convince him that they should seal the treaty by a marriage between you and Apepi's daughter. Once you are under the protection of the Hyksosian king, Naja's knife will be blunted. He could not risk plunging the land back into civil war by voiding the treaty.'

'Apepi is going to give me his daughter as a wife?' Nefer stared at him in wonder. 'The one in the red dress whom I saw at the ceremony this morning?'

'Yes,' Taita agreed. 'Mintaka is her name.'

'I know her name,' Nefer assured him vehemently. 'She is named after the tiny star in the belt of the Hunter constellation.'

'Yes, that's her.' Taita nodded. 'Mintaka, the ugly one with the big nose and funny mouth.'

'She is not ugly!' Nefer flared at him, springing to his feet so that he almost overturned the skiff and dumped them in the mud of the lagoon. 'She is the most beautiful . . .' When he saw the expression on Taita's face, he subsided. 'I mean, she is quite pleasing to look at.' He grinned ruefully. 'You always catch me out. But you must admit to me that she's beautiful, Taita.'

'If you like big noses, and funny mouths.'

Nefer picked up a dead fish from the bilges and threw it at his head. Taita ducked. 'When can I speak to her?' he asked, trying to sound as though it was a request of no real importance to him. 'She does speak Egyptian, doesn't she?'

'She speaks it as well as you do,' Taita assured him.

'Then when can I meet her? You can arrange it for me.'

Taita had anticipated this request. 'You could invite the princess and her suite to a hunt here in the swamps, and perhaps a picnic afterwards.'

'I will send Asmor to invite her this very afternoon,' Nefer decided, but Taita shook his head.

'He would go to the Regent first, and Naja would immediately see the danger. He would never allow it, and once he was alerted he would do everything in his power to prevent you coming together.'

'What shall we do, then?' Nefer looked agitated.

'I will go to her myself,' Taita promised, and at that moment there were faint shouts from different directions in the papyrus swamps around them, and the splash of paddles. 'Asmor has found out that you are missing, and has sent his hounds to bring you in,' Taita said. 'It proves how difficult it will be to elude him. Now, listen carefully for we have little time before we will be separated again.'

They spoke quickly, making arrangements to exchange messages in any emergency and to put other plans into place, but all the time the shouting and splashing was growing louder, drawing nearer. Within minutes a light fighting galley packed with armed men burst through the screen of papyrus, thrust onward by twenty oars. A shout went up from the command deck: 'There is Pharaoh! Steer for the skiff!'

The Hyksos had set up a practice field on the alluvial plain abutting the papyrus swamp of the river. When Taita came down from the temple, two battalions of Apepi's guards were exercising at arms under a cloudless sky from which the morning sun blazed down. Two hundred fully armed men were running relay races through the swamp, toiling waist deep through the mud, while squadrons of chariots performed complicated evolutions out on the plain, from columns of four forming a single line ahead, then fanning out into line abreast. Dust swirled out behind the racing wheels, the lance tips shot beams of sunlight and the brightly coloured pennants danced in the wind.

Taita stopped by the butts to watch for a while as the line of fifty archers shot at a hundred cubits, each man loosing five rapid arrows. Then they raced forward to the straw man-shaped targets, retrieved their arrows and shot again at the next line of targets two hundred cubits further on. The flail of the instructor fell heavily on the back of any man who was slow to cross the open ground or who missed the mark when he shot. The bronze studs on the leather thongs left spots of bright blood where they bit through the linen tunics.

Taita walked on unchallenged. As he passed, the matched pairs of lancers who were practising the standard thrusts and blocks with warlike shouts, broke off their bouts and fell silent. They followed him with a respectful gaze.

His was a fearsome reputation. Only after he had passed did they engage each other again.

At the far end of the field, on the short green grass beside the swamp, a single chariot was speeding through a course of markers and targets. It was one of the scout chariots, with spoked wheels and bodywork of woven bamboo, very fast, and light enough for two men to lift and carry over an obstacle.

It was drawn by a pair of magnificent bay mares from the personal string of King Apepi. Their hoofs threw up lumps of turf as they spun round the markers at the end of the course and came back at full gallop with the light chariot bouncing and swerving behind them.

Lord Trok was driving, leaning forward with the reins wrapped around his wrists. His beard fluttered in the wind, his moustaches and the coloured ribbons were blown back over his shoulders as he urged the horses on with wild shouts. Taita had to acknowledge his skill: even at such speed he had the pair under perfect control, running a tight line between the markers, giving the archer on the footplate beside him the best chance at the targets as they sped past.

Taita leaned on his staff as he watched the chariot come on at full gallop. There was no mistaking the slim straight figure and royal bearing. Mintaka was dressed in a pleated crimson skirt that left her knees bare. The cross-straps of her sandals were wound high around her shapely calves. She wore a leather guard on her left wrist, and a hard leather cuirass moulded to the shape of her small round breasts. The leather would protect her tender nipples from the whip of the bowstring as she loosed her arrows at the targets as they sped by.

Mintaka recognized Taita, called a greeting and waved her bow over her head. Her dark hair was covered by a fine-woven net and it bounced on her shoulders at each jolt of the chariot. She wore no makeup but the wind and exertion had rouged her cheeks and put a sparkle in her eyes. Taita could not imagine Heseret riding as lance-bearer in a war chariot, but Hyksosian attitudes towards women were different.

'Hathor smile upon you, Magus!' She laughed as Trok brought the chariot to a broadsiding halt in front of him. He knew that Mintaka had adopted the gentle goddess as her patron, rather than one of the monstrous Hyksosian deities.

'May Horus love you for ever, Princess Mintaka.' Taita returned her blessing. It was a mark of his affection that he accorded her the royal title when he would not acknowledge her father as king.

She jumped down in the dust cloud and ran to embrace him, reaching up to throw her arms around his neck so that the hard edge of her cuirass dug into his ribs. She felt him wince and stepped back. 'I have just shot five heads straight,' she boasted.

'Your warlike skills are exceeded only by your beauty.' He smiled.

'You do not believe me,' she challenged. 'You think that just because I am a girl I cannot draw a bow.' She did not wait for his disclaimer but ran back to the chariot and leaped up on to the footplate. 'Drive on, Lord Trok,' she commanded. 'Another circuit. At your best speed.'

Trok shook out the reins and turned the chariot so sharply that the inside wheel stood still. Then, as he lined up, he shouted, 'Ha! Ha!' and they sped away down the course.

Each target was set on top of a short pole, at the level of the eye of the archer. They were in the shape of human heads, each carved from a block of wood. There was no mistaking their nationality. Each dummy head was a caricature of an Egyptian warrior, complete with helmet and regimental insignia, and the painted features were as grotesque as ogres.

Little doubt of the artist's opinion of us, Taita thought wryly.

Mintaka plucked an arrow from the bin on the dashboard, nocked and drew. She held her aim, the bright yellow fletchings touching her pursed lips as though in a kiss. Trok brought the chariot in towards the first target, trying to give her a fair shot, but the ground was rough. Even though she flexed from the knees to ride the bumps, she swayed with the motion of the carriage.

As the target flashed by Mintaka loosed, and Taita found he was holding his breath for her. He need not have worried for she handled the light bow with perfect aplomb. The arrow slapped into the left eye of the dummy and quivered there, the yellow fletching bright in the sunlight.

'*Bak-her!*' He applauded, and she laughed with delight as the chariot raced on. Twice more she shot. One arrow lodged deep in the forehead, the next in the mouth of the target. It was excellent shooting even for a veteran charioteer, let alone a slip of a girl.

Trok spun the chariot around the far marker and they came back again. The horses' ears were laid back, their manes flying. Mintaka shot again, scoring another hit right on the tip of the dummy's oversized nose.

'By Horus!' Taita said, with surprise. 'She shoots like a *djinn*!'

The last target came up fast and Mintaka was balancing gracefully, cheeks flushed and white teeth gleaming as she bit her lip in concentration. She shot and the arrow flew high and right missing the head by the breadth of a hand.

'Trok, you clumsy oaf! You drove straight into that hole just as I was loosing!' she yelled at him.

She jumped down from the chariot while it was still moving and blazed up at Trok, 'You did that on purpose to make a fool of me in the sight of the Magus!'

'Your Highness, I am mortified by my own incompetence.' The mighty Trok was as awkward as a small boy in the face of her anger. Taita saw that his feelings for her were every bit as ardent as he had suspected.

'You are not forgiven. I shall not allow you the privilege of driving me again. Not ever.'

Taita had not seen her show such spirit before, and this, together with her recent exhibition of marksmanship, sent his good opinion of her to an even higher level. This is a fitting wife for any man, even a pharaoh of the Tamosian dynasty, he decided, but he was careful not to show any sign of levity, lest Mintaka switch her wrath to him. He need not have worried, though, for as soon as she turned to face him her smile bloomed again.

'Four out of five is good enough for a warrior of the Red Road, Your Highness,' Taita assured her, 'and it was indeed a treacherous hole that you hit.'

'You must be thirsty, Taita. I know I am.' She took his hand artlessly and led him to where her maids had spread a woven woollen rug at the edge of the river, and laid out platters of sweetmeats and jugs of sherbet.

'There is so much I have to ask you, Taita,' she told him, as she settled on the sheepskin rug beside him. 'I have not seen you since you left Bubasti.'

'How is your brother, Khyan?' He forestalled her question.

'He is his usual self,' she laughed, 'if not even naughtier than before. My father has ordered that he join us here as soon as he has fully recovered. He wants all his family around him when the truce is signed.' They chatted of trivialities for a while longer, but Mintaka was distracted. He waited for her to broach the subject uppermost in her mind. She surprised him by turning suddenly to Trok, who was standing nearby with a hang-dog air.

'You may leave us now, my lord,' she said to him coolly.

'Will you ride with me again tomorrow morning, Princess?' Trok was close to pleading.

'Tomorrow I shall probably be otherwise occupied.'

'Then the day after?' Even his moustache seemed to droop pitifully.

'Fetch me my bow and my quiver before you go,' she ordered, ignoring his question. He brought them to her like a lackey, and placed them close to her hand.

'Farewell, my lord.' She turned back to Taita. Trok hovered for a few minutes longer, then stumped off to his chariot.

As he drove off Taita murmured, 'How long has Trok been in love with you?'

She looked startled then laughed delightedly. 'Trok in love with me? Why, that's ridiculous! Trok is as ancient as the Pyramids at Giza – he must be almost thirty years old! And he has three wives and Hathor only knows how many concubines!'

Taita drew one of her arrows from the magnificently decorated quiver and inspected it casually. The fletchings were blue and yellow, and he touched the tiny carved signet on the shaft.

'The three stars of the Hunter's belt,' he remarked, 'with Mintaka the brightest.'

'Blue and yellow are my favourite colours.' She nodded. 'My arrows are all made for me by Grippa. He is the most famous fletcher in Avaris. Each of the arrows he makes is perfectly straight and balanced to fly true. His decorations and signets are works of art. Look how he has carved and painted my star.' Taita turned the arrow between his fingers and admired it at length, before returning it to the quiver.

'What is Trok's arrow signet?' he asked casually.

She made a gesture of annoyance. 'I do not know. For all I care it is probably a wild hog, or an ox. I have had enough of Trok for this day and many days to come.' She poured sherbet into Taita's bowl. 'I know how you like honey.' Ostentatiously she changed the subject, and Taita waited for her to choose the next.

'Now, I have certain delicate things to discuss with you,'

she admitted shyly. She picked a wild flower from the grass on which they sat and began to twist it into the beginning of a garland, still not looking at him, but her cheeks, which had lost the flush of exertion, turned rosy once more.

'Pharaoh Nefer Seti is fourteen years and five months old, almost a year older than you. He was born under the sign of the Ibex, which makes a fine match for your Cat.'

Taita had anticipated her, and she looked up at him in astonishment. 'How did you know what I was going to ask you?' Then she clapped her hands. 'Of course you knew. You are the Magus.'

'Speaking of Pharaoh, I have come to deliver a message from His Majesty,' Taita told her.

Immediately all her attention was fixed on him. 'A message? Does he even know I exist?'

'He is very much aware of that fact.' Taita sipped his sherbet. 'This needs a little more honey.' He poured some into the bowl, and stirred.

'Do not tease me, Warlock,' she snapped at him. 'Give me my message at once.'

'Pharaoh invites you and your suite to a duck hunt in the swamps tomorrow at dawn, and afterwards to a picnic breakfast on the Isle of the Little Dove.'

The dawn sky was the glowing shade of a sword-blade fresh from the coals of the forge. The top of the papyrus formed a stark black frieze below it. In this time before the sunrise there was no breath of air to set them nodding, or any sound to break the stillness.

The two hunting skiffs were moored at opposite ends of a small lagoon, hard against the wall of reeds that surrounded the open water. Less than fifty cubits separated them. The royal huntsmen had bent the tall papyrus stems over to form a screening roof over the hunters.

The surface of the lagoon was still and unruffled, reflecting the sky like a polished bronze mirror. It was just light enough for Nefer to make out the graceful form of Mintaka in the other boat. She had her bow across her lap, and she sat as motionless as a statuette of the goddess Hathor. Any other girl he could think of, particularly his own sisters Heseret and Merykara, would have been hopping around like a canary on a perch and twittering twice as loudly.

In his mind he ran lingeringly over their brief meeting this morning. It had been dark, not the faintest glow of dawn to dim the glory of the star panoply that hung over the world, each star so plump and bright that it seemed he could reach up and pluck them like ripe figs from the tree. Mintaka had come down the pathway from the temple, her way lit for her by torch-bearers, and her maids following close behind her. She wore a woollen hood over her head to ward off the river chill, and no matter how hard he stared her face remained in darkness.

'May Pharaoh live a thousand years.'

These were the first words he had ever heard her speak. Her voice was sweeter than the music of any lute. It was as though ghostly fingers were stroking the back of his neck. It took him some moments to find his own voice. 'May Hathor love you through all eternity.' He had consulted Taita on the form of greeting he should employ, and he had rehearsed it until he had it off pat. He thought he saw the flash of her teeth as she smiled under the hood, and he was encouraged to add something else that Taita had not suggested. It came to him in a flash of inspiration. He pointed up at the star-bright sky. 'Look! There is your own star.' She raised her head to look up at the constellation of the Hunter. The starlight fell on her face, so that he saw it for the first time since she had come down the pathway. He caught his breath sharply. Her expression was solemn, but he thought that he had never seen anything more enchanting. 'The gods placed it there especially for you.' The compliment tripped off his tongue.

Immediately her face lit up, and she was even more beautiful. 'Pharaoh is as gallant as he is gracious.' She made a small, slightly mocking obeisance. Then she stepped into the waiting skiff. She did not look back as the royal huntsmen rowed her out into the swamp.

Now he repeated her words to himself as though they were a prayer: 'Pharaoh is as gallant as he is gracious.'

Out in the swamp a heron boomed. As though this was a signal, the air was filled suddenly with the sound of wings. Nefer had almost forgotten the reason they were out on the water, which was a measure of his distraction for he loved the hunt with a singular passion. He tore his eyes off the dainty figure in the boat across the water, and reached for his throwing sticks.

He had decided to use the sticks rather than the bow, because he was certain that she did not have the brawn or skill to handle the heavier weapons. This would give him a distinct advantage. When skilfully thrown the spinning stick cut a wider swathe than the arrow. Its bludgeoning weight was more likely to knock down a bird than the blunt-tipped arrow, which might be deflected by the dense plumage of the waterfowl. Nefer was determined to impress Mintaka with his hunting skills.

The first flight of ducks came sweeping in low out of the dawn. They were glossy black and white, and each had a distinctive knob on top of its beak. The lead bird shied away, leading the others out of range. At that moment the traitor ducks began to call seductively. They were captured and tamed birds that the huntsmen had placed out on the open waters of the lagoon, held there by a line around the leg that was anchored to a stone on the muddy bottom.

The wild ducks turned back in a wide circle then started to drop and line up to settle on the open water alongside the traitors. They set their wings and streamed in, losing height swiftly, passing directly over Nefer's skiff. Pharaoh judged his moment neatly, and rose to his feet with the stick cocked and ready to throw. He waited for the lead bird to flare out and then let fly, sending the stick cartwheeling up. The duck saw the missile coming and dropped a wing to avoid it. For an instant it seemed it might have succeeded, but then there was a thud, a burst of feathers and the duck dropped into an uncontrolled dive, trailing a broken wing. It hit the water with a heavy splash but almost instantly recovered and dived under the surface.

'Quickly! Go after him!' Nefer shouted. Four naked slave boys were hanging in the water alongside, only their heads showing. They clutched at the side of the skiff with numb fingers. Already their teeth were chattering with cold.

Two swam to retrieve the fallen bird, but Nefer knew that it would be in vain. With no injury other than a broken wing the duck could outdive and outswim the retrievers indefinitely.

Lost bird, he thought bitterly, and before he could throw the second stick the flight of duck had angled across the lagoon, directly towards Mintaka's boat. They were still keeping low, unlike teal who would have rocketed almost straight up. However, they were going very fast, their blade-shaped wings whistling through the air.

Nefer had almost discounted the hunter in the other boat. At that height and speed the targets were too difficult for all but the most expert archer. In quick succession two arrows rose to meet the straggle of ducks. The sound of the double impact carried clearly across the lagoon. Then two birds were falling with that peculiar inert look, wings loose and head flopping, killed cleanly, stone dead in the air at the same time. They plopped on to the water and floated there, motionless. The swimmers picked them up easily and swam back to Mintaka's skiff, carrying the carcasses gripped in their teeth.

'Two lucky arrows,' Nefer voiced his opinion.

In the bows of the skiff, Taita added, without a smile, 'Two unlucky ducks.'

Now the sky was filled with birds, which rose in dark clouds as the first rays of the sun struck the waters. So dense were the flocks that from a distance it looked as though the reed beds were smouldering and spewing up clouds of dark smoke.

Nefer had ordered twenty light galleys and as many smaller boats to patrol all the open waters within three miles of the temple of Hathor, and to chase up any waterbirds that settled. The winged multitudes never thinned. Not only a dozen varieties of duck and geese, but ibis and herons, egrets, spoonbills and openbills were in flight. At every level, from high overhead to low down over the waving tops of the papyrus, they wheeled in dark cohorts or raced low in V-formations with rapid wingbeats. They squawked and honked and quacked and bleated and wailed.

At intervals through the avian cacophony sounded a peal of sweet laughter and squeals of girlish glee as Mintaka's slave girls urged her to greater efforts.

Her light bow was well suited to the task. It was quick to align and draw without taxing her strength unduly. She was not firing the traditional blunt-tipped arrows but using instead sharp metal heads that had been especially forged for her by Grippa, the famous armourer. The needle-points drove through the dense layer of plumage and went straight to the bone. She had realized, without a word being exchanged, that Nefer intended to make a contest of the hunt, and she was proving that her competitive instincts were every bit as fierce as his.

Nefer had been badly rattled both by his first failure and by Mintaka's unexpected skill with the bow. Instead of concentrating on his own task, he was distracted by what was happening in the other skiff. Every time he glanced in that direction it seemed to him that dead birds were falling from the sky. This flustered him further. His sense of judgement deserted him, and he began to hurl the sticks too soon or too late. To try to compensate he strained and started to jerk his arm into the stroke instead of using his whole body to launch the club. His right arm tired quickly, so instinctively he shortened the arc of his throwing arm and bent his elbow, almost spraining his wrist as a result.

Usually he could count on hitting with six out of ten throws, now he was missing more than half. His frustration increased. Many of the birds he brought down were only stunned or crippled, and eluded his slave boys by diving under the surface and swimming into the thick papyrus beds, staying submerged beneath the mat of roots and stems. The number of dead birds piled on the floorboards of the skiff grew pitifully slowly. In contrast the happy cries from the other skiff continued almost without a break.

In desperation Nefer discarded his curved sticks and snatched up the heavy war bow, but it was too late. His right arm was almost exhausted by his efforts with the sticks. His draw was laboured and he shot behind the faster birds and in front of the slower ones. Taita watched him flounder ever deeper into the trap he had set for himself. A little humiliation will do him no real harm, he told himself.

With a few words of advice he could have corrected Nefer's mistakes: almost fifty years ago Taita had written the standard texts, not only on chariot handling and tactics but also on archery. For once his sympathy was not wholeheartedly with the boy, and he smiled secretly as he watched Nefer miss again and Mintaka take down two birds from the same flight as they passed over her head.

However, he felt pity for his king when one of Mintaka's slaves swam across the lagoon, and hung on to the side of Nefer's skiff. 'Her Royal Highness Princess Mintaka hopes that mighty Pharaoh might enjoy jasmine-scented days and starry nights filled with the song of the nightingale. However, her boat begins to sink under the weight of her bag, and she is hungry for her breakfast, which she says was promised her these hours past.'

An untimely sally! Taita thought, as Nefer scowled furiously at this impertinence.

'You can give thanks to whatever god of apes and cur-dogs you worship, slave, that I am a man of compassion. Otherwise I would myself hack off your ugly head and send it back to your mistress to answer that jest.'

It was time for Taita to intervene smoothly: 'Pharaoh apologizes for his thoughtlessness, but he was enjoying the sport so much that he forgot the passage of time. Please tell your mistress that we shall all go in to breakfast immediately.'

Nefer glowered at him but put up his bow and made no effort to revoke Taita's decision. The two small boats paddled back towards the island in close formation, so that the piles of duck on the floorboards of each could be readily compared. Not a word was said by the crew of either skiff, but everyone was conscious of the results of the morning's hunt.

'Your Majesty,' Mintaka called across to Nefer, 'I must thank you for a truly diverting morning. I cannot remember when last I enjoyed myself so much.' Her voice was lilting and her smile angelic.

'You are too kind and forgiving.' Unsmilingly Nefer made a regal gesture of dismissal. 'I thought it was rather poor sport.'

He turned half away from her and stared broodingly out at the horizon of reeds and water. Mintaka showed not the least distress at the pointed snub, but turned to her slave girls. 'Come, let us give Pharaoh a few verses of "The Monkey and the Donkey".' One of her maids handed her the lute, and she strummed the opening bar then launched into the first verse of the silly children's song. The maids joined in with the chorus, which involved raucous animal imitations and uncontrolled hilarity.

Nefer's lips twitched with amusement but he had taken up a position of frosty dignity from which he could not retreat. Taita could see that he longed to join in the fun, but once again he had trapped himself.

First love is such unmitigated joy, Taita thought, with sympathetic irony, and to the delight of all the girls in the other boat he improvised a new version of what the monkey said to the donkey, which was much funnier than any that had preceded it. They squealed anew and clapped their hands with delight. Nefer felt himself further excluded and sulked ostentatiously.

They came in to the landing on the island still singing. The bank was cut away steeply, and the mud below it black and glutinous. The boatmen jumped over the side into the knee-deep ooze and held the first skiff steady while the slaves handed the princess and her maids across the gap onto the firm dry ground at the top of the bank.

As soon as they were safely ashore the royal skiff came in and the slaves made ready to hand Nefer across to join Mintaka on the high bank. He waved them aside imperiously. He had suffered enough humiliation for one morning, and he was not about to lower his dignity further by clinging to a pair of half-naked wet slaves for support. He balanced easily on the transom and the entire company watched respectfully for he was a splendid sight. Mintaka tried not to let her emotions show, but she thought he was the most beautiful creature she had ever seen, slim and sleek with his boyish body just starting to take on the hard contours of manhood. Even his haughty, sullen expression enthralled her.

He is of the stuff from which heroes and great pharaohs are moulded, she thought, in a surfeit of romantic ardour. I wish I had not angered him so. It was unkind, and before this day is ended I shall make him laugh again, as Hathor is my witness.

Nefer launched himself across the gap between skiff and

land like a young leopard springing from the branch of an acacia tree. He landed gracefully on the high bank almost within arm's length of where she stood. He paused there conscious of every eye upon him.

Then the bank collapsed beneath him. A chunk of the friable dry clay on which he was standing broke off under his feet. For an aching moment he windmilled his arms, trying to keep his balance, then toppled backwards into the swamp.

Everyone stared down at him in horror, appalled by the spectacle of Royal Egypt sitting waist deep in sticky black Nile mud with a startled expression on his face.

For long moments nobody moved or spoke. Then Mintaka laughed. She had not meant to do so, but it was too much for her self-control and once it began she could not stop herself. It was a delightful, infectious laugh, that none of her maids could resist. They burst into merry squeals and giggles that set the huntsmen and boatmen off. Even Taita joined in, cackling unrestrainedly.

For a moment Nefer looked as though he might burst into tears, but then his anger, kept so long on a tight rein, exploded. He snatched up a handful of thick black mud and hurled it up at the laughing princess. His humiliation gave strength to his arm and improved his aim while Mintaka was so helpless with mirth that she could neither duck nor dodge and it hit her full in the face. Her laughter died and she stared at Nefer with huge eyes in a running black mask.

It was Nefer's turn to laugh. Still sitting in the swamp he threw back his head and gave vent to all his frustration and humiliation with a howl of mocking laughter. When Pharaoh laughs all the world laughs with him. The slaves, boatmen and huntsmen redoubled their shouts of merriment.

Mintaka recovered swiftly from her shock, and then, without any warning, launched herself over the bank into the attack. She dropped on top of Nefer with all her weight. He was taken so completely by surprise that he could not even draw a full breath before he was driven clean under with her sitting on his head.

He floundered about beneath the surface, trying to get purchase on the muddy bottom but her weight kept him pinned. She had both arms locked around his neck. He tried to throw her off, but she was nimble and slippery as an eel with the coating of mud. With a huge effort he lifted her just long enough to allow him to stick his head out and catch a quick breath, then she plunged him under again. He managed to get on top of her but it took a mighty effort to hold her. She wriggled and kicked with surprising strength. Her tunic had rucked up round her waist and her legs were bare and smooth. She hooked her one leg through his and hung on. Now they were face to face, and he could feel her body warmth through the slippery mud.

Their filthy faces were only inches apart, her hair was streaming down into her eyes, and he was startled to realize that she was grinning at him through the slimy coating. He grinned back, and then they were both laughing. But neither would concede defeat, and they kept up the struggle.

His chest was bare, and her shift so wet and flimsy that it might not have existed. Her bare legs were still hooked around his. He reached down with one hand to prise himself free of their tenacious grip. Unintentionally his right hand came upon a hard round buttock that was wriggling around with great energy.

Nefer became aware of a strange and pleasurable sensation that seemed to suffuse his entire body, and the urgency went out of his efforts to subdue her. He was content to hold her and let her struggle against him while he enjoyed this new and extraordinary feeling.

Abruptly she stopped laughing as she in her turn made a momentous discovery. Between their lower bodies had grown up a protuberance that, only moments before, had not existed. It was so rubbery and large that she could not previously have overlooked it. She pushed her hips out to test its nature, but every time she did that it grew harder and larger. This was something beyond her experience, and in a spirit of discovery she repeated the movement.

She hardly noticed that he had stopped his violent efforts to dislodge her, and that his left arm was wrapped around her upper body. His right hand was cupped around her posterior and when next she pushed out her hips to examine the lump, he imitated her movement thrusting out to meet her and his cupped hand drew her closer still. The lump prodded against her as though it were some small animal with a life of its own.

She had never anticipated the sensation that overcame her. Suddenly that mysterious creature took on an importance far beyond anything she had dreamed of up to that time. Her entire being was filled with a dreamy, pleasurable warmth. Without conscious intent she reached down with one hand to catch hold of it, to capture it as though it were a kitten or a puppy.

Then, with a shock like a blow to her stomach, she remembered the wild tales her slave girls had told her about that thing, and what men did with it. On more than one occasion they had described it to her in startling detail. Up to that time she had discounted these descriptions as pure invention, for they bore no resemblance to the small dangling appendages that her younger brothers carried in that area of their anatomy.

She particularly remembered what Saak, the Numidian slave girl, had told her: 'You won't waste any more prayers on Hathor once you have seen the one-eyed god when he is angry.'

Mintaka threw herself backwards out of Nefer's embrace and sat in the mud staring at him in consternation. Nefer struggled into a sitting position and returned her stare with a bemused air. Both were panting as though they had run a gruelling race.

The guffaws and shrieks of laughter from the high bank slowly petered out as the spectators became aware that something untoward had taken place, and the silence became uncomfortable. Taita covered it up smoothly: 'Your Majesty, if you extend your swim much longer you will offer a fine breakfast to any passing crocodile.'

Nefer jumped up and sloshed across to where Mintaka sat. He lifted her to her feet as gently as if she were made of the most delicate Hurrian glass.

Dripping slime and Nile water, with her hair dangling in a muddy tangle over her face and shoulders, her maids led the princess away to find a clean pool well screened by reeds. When she reappeared some time later she was washed clean of the last traces of slime and ooze. The maids had brought with them a change of apparel, so Mintaka was resplendent in a clean dry apron embroidered with silk and seed pearls and there were golden bracelets on her arms and a necklace of turquoise and coloured glass at her throat. Her hair, though damp, was combed and plaited neatly.

Nefer hurried to meet her and led her to a giant kigelia tree under whose spreading branches a breakfast feast was laid out in the shade. At first the young couple were restrained and shy, still overawed by the momentous awakening that they had shared, but soon their natural high spirits reasserted themselves, and they joined in the banter and the chatter, although their eyes kept meeting and almost every word they uttered was aimed at the other.

Mintaka loved to riddle and she challenged him to an exchange. She made it more difficult for Nefer by couching her clues in the Hyksosian language.

'I have one eye and a sharp nose. I run my victim through and through, but I draw no blood. What am I?'

'That's easy!' Nefer laughed triumphantly. 'You are a sewing needle.' And Mintaka threw up her hands in surrender.

'Forfeit!' cried the slave girls. 'Pharaoh is right. Forfeit!'

'A song!' Nefer demanded. 'But not the monkey. We have had enough of him for one day.'

'I shall give you "The Song of the Nile",' she agreed, and when she finished Nefer demanded another. 'Only if you help me, Majesty.'

His voice was a robust tenor but whenever he slipped off-key she covered his mistake and made him sound much better than he was.

Of course Nefer had brought his bao board and stones. Taita had taught him to love it, and he had become expert. When he tired of the singing he inveigled Mintaka into a game.

'You will have to be patient with me. I am a novice,' she warned him, as he set out the board. Bao was an Egyptian game, and this time he expected confidently to outmatch her.

'Don't feel bad about it,' Nefer encouraged her. 'I will coach you.'

Taita smiled because he and Mintaka had wiled away a few hours at bao in the palace of Bubasti when they were nursing her little brother. Within eighteen moves her red stones dominated the west castle and were menacing his centre.

'Have I done the right thing?' she asked sweetly.

Nefer was saved by a hail from the riverbank and looked up to see a galley flying the Regent's pennant coming swiftly down the channel. 'What a pity. Just when the game was getting interesting.' He began to pack up the board with alacrity.

'Can't we hide from them?' Mintaka asked, but Nefer shook his head.

'They have seen us already.' He had been expecting this

visitation all morning. Sooner or later the Regent must hear about this illicit outing and send Asmor to bring in his errant charge.

The galley nosed into the bank below where they sat and Asmor sprang ashore. He strode up to the picnic party. 'The Regent is much displeased by your absence. He bids you return at once to the temple, where matters of state await your attention.'

'And I, Lord Asmor, am much displeased by your ill manners.' Nefer tried to retrieve some of his hurt dignity. 'I am not a groom or a house servant to be addressed in that manner, and neither have you shown respect for the Princess Mintaka.' But there was no escaping that he was being treated like a child.

Still, he tried to put a good face on it and invited Mintaka to sail back with him in the skiff while her maids followed in the second vessel. Taita kept tactfully to the bows as this was their first opportunity to hold a private conversation. Not quite certain what to expect of her Nefer was startled when, rather than bothering with polite niceties, she launched immediately into a discussion of the chances of success or failure of the peace conference between their opposing sides. She soon impressed him with her political acumen and her strong views. 'If only we women were allowed to run this world, there would never have been a stupid war in the first place,' she summed up, but he could not let that go unchallenged. They argued animatedly all the way back to the temple. The journey was far too short for Nefer's liking, and as they came into the landing he took her hand. 'I should like to see you again.'

'I should like that well enough,' she replied, without withdrawing her hand.

'Soon,' he insisted.

'Soon enough.' She smiled and gently took back her hand. He felt strangely bereft as he watched her walk away towards the temple.

'My lord, you were present at the divination of the Mazes of Ammon Ra. You know of the dire charge placed upon me by the gods. You know that I can never flout their express wishes and that therefore I am committed to your interest. I had good reason to assist the boy in what was only, after all, a harmless escapade.'

Naja was not so easily placated. He was still furious that Nefer had given Asmor the slip and managed to spend the morning out in the swamps with the Hyksosian princess.

'How can I believe that when you aided Nefer? Nay! You instigated this piece of folly.'

'My lord Regent, you must realize how crucial to our enterprise it is that I retain the young Pharaoh's complete trust. If I appear to flout your orders and authority, then this will make the boy believe that I am still his man. It will make the difficult task laid upon me by the Mazes easier to accomplish.'

Diplomatically Taita turned aside each of the Regent's accusations, until he was no longer ranting but merely grumbling bitterly. 'It must not happen again, Magus. Of course I trust your loyalty. You would be a fool indeed to fly against the express strictures of the gods. However, in future whenever Nefer leaves his quarters he must be accompanied by Asmor and a full escort of his men. I cannot take the chance that he will disappear.'

'My lord, how goes the negotiation with the Shepherd Chieftain? Is there aught that I can do to help you ensure a successful outcome in this matter?' Adroitly Taita set the hounds on a different scent, and Naja followed them.

'Apepi is indisposed. This morning he had a coughing fit so intense he brought up blood and had to leave the conference chamber. Even though he cannot attend himself, he will not let any other speak on his behalf, not even Lord Trok who usually has his confidence. Only the gods know how long it will be before the great bear returns to the conference. We may be forced to waste days or even weeks.'

'What is Apepi's ailment?' Taita asked.

'I do not know—' Naja broke off as an idea occurred to him. 'Why did I not think of it before? With your skills, you will be able to cure whatever ails him. Go to him at once, Magus, and do your utmost.'

As he approached the king's apartments, Taita could hear Apepi from across the courtyard. He sounded like a black-maned lion caught in a trap, and the roars grew louder as Taita entered the chamber. As he stepped over the threshold he was almost knocked over by three priests of Osiris fleeing the royal presence in terror, and a heavy bronze bowl crashed into the doorsill. It had been thrown across the room by the Hyksosian king, who sat naked on a muddle of furs and tangled bedsheets in the middle of the chamber.

'Where have you been, Warlock?' he roared, as soon as he saw Taita. 'I sent Trok to find you before dawn. Why do you come only in the middle of the afternoon to save me from those infernal priests with their stinking poisons and hot tongs?'

'I have not seen Trok,' Taita explained, 'but I came as soon as Lord Naja told me you were indisposed.'

'Indisposed? I am not indisposed, Warlock. I am at the point of death.'

'Let us see what can be done to save you.'

Apepi rolled over on to his hairy belly and Taita saw the grotesque purple swelling on his back. It was the size of both the king's bunched fists. When he touched it lightly with a fingertip Apepi bellowed again and broke out in a running sweat. 'Gently, Taita. You are as bad as all the priests in Egypt together.'

'How did this come about?' Taita stepped back. 'What were your symptoms?'

'It started with a bitter pain in my chest.' Apepi touched it. 'Then I started coughing, and the pain became sharper. I felt something move in here, and then the pain seemed to move to my back, and there was this lump.' He reached over his shoulder with one hand to touch the swelling, and groaned again.

Before going further, Taita administered a draught of the Red Shepenn, the sleeping flower. It was a draught that would have knocked a baby elephant off its feet, but though Apepi's eyes crossed and his voice was slurred he was still lucid. Taita palpated the swelling again, and the king groaned but made no other protest.

'There is some foreign object lodged deep in your flesh, my lord,' he stated at last.

'This comes as no great surprise to me, Warlock. Evil men, most of them Egyptians, have been sticking foreign objects into my flesh since I last sucked on my wet-nurse's paps.'

'I would have thought it was an arrowhead or a blade, but there is no entry wound,' Taita mused.

'Use your eyes, fellow. I am covered with them.' The king's hairy carcass was indeed laced and blotched with old battle scars.

'I am going to cut for it,' Taita warned him.

Apepi snarled, 'Do it, Warlock, and stop yapping about it.'

While Taita selected a bronze scalpel from his chest, Apepi picked up his thick leather belt from the floor and doubled a length of it. He bit down on it, and composed himself to the knife.

'Come here!' Taita called to the guards at the door. 'Come and hold the king.'

'Get out, you idiots!' Apepi countermanded the order. 'I need no man to hold me still.'

Taita stood over him, calculated the angle and depth of the cut, then made one swift, deep incision. Apepi let out a muffled bellow from between clamped teeth, but did not move. Taita stood back as a fountain of dark blood and thick yellow pus erupted from the wound. A gut-wrenching stench filled the chamber. Taita laid aside the scalpel and ran his forefinger deep into the opening. Blood bubbled up around it but he felt something hard and sharp in the bottom of the incision. He picked up the ivory forceps that he had placed ready to hand, and probed the opening until he felt the tip strike something solid.

Apepi had stopped yelling, and he lay without movement, except the involuntary shuddering of his back muscles. He breathed with loud porcine snuffles through his nose. At the third attempt Taita gripped the object with the jaws of the forceps, and tugged at it until he felt it give and start to rise towards the surface. It came out – the last inch with a rush of pus and detritus – and Taita held it up so that the light from the window fell upon it.

'An arrowhead,' he announced, 'and it's been in there for a long time. I am amazed it did not mortify years ago.'

Apepi spat out the belt and sat up, chuckling shakily. 'By the hairy testicles of Seueth, I recognize that pretty little bauble. One of your ruffians shot that into me at Abnub ten years ago. At the time, my surgeons said it lay so close to my heart that they could not reach it, so they left it in and I have been gestating it ever since.'

He took the triangle of shaped flint from Taita's bloody fingers and beamed at it with proprietary pride. 'I feel like a mother with her first-born. I will have it made into a charm to wear around my neck on a gold chain. You can weave a spell over it. That should ward off any other missiles. What do you think, Warlock?'

'I am sure it will prove highly efficacious, my lord.' Taita filled his mouth with hot wine and honey from the bowl he had prepared and used a hollow brass tube to syringe out the pus and blood, squirting it deep into the wound.

'What a waste of good wine,' Apepi said, lifted the bowl with both hands and drained the remainder of the contents to the dregs. He hurled it against the far wall and belched. 'Now, as a reward for your services, I have an amusing tale for you, Warlock, that harks back to our last conversation on the tower top at Bubasti.'

'I am listening with fixed attention to your lordship's every word.' Taita bent over him and began to bandage the open wound with linen strips, murmuring the incantation for the binding up of wounds as he did so:

'I bind thee up, thing of Seth.
I stop thy red mouth, thing of great evil.'

Apepi interrupted harshly, 'Trok has offered a lakh of gold as a bride price for Mintaka.'

Taita's hands stopped moving. He stood with the bandage wound half around Apepi's barrel chest. 'What did you answer him, Majesty?'

He was so distressed that the royal title slipped out before he could check himself. This was a dangerous and unforeseen development. 'I told him the bride-price was five lakhs.' Apepi grinned. 'The dog is so hot for my little bitch that his prong is standing up between his eyes and blinding him, but despite the booty he has stolen from me over the years, even he can never find five lakhs.' He belched again. 'Do not worry, Warlock, Mintaka is too valuable to waste on someone like Trok, when I can use her to chain your little pharaoh into my realm.'

He stood up and lifted one thickly muscled arm, trying to peer under it at his bandaged back, like an old rooster with its head under its wing. 'You have made me into a mummy before my time,' he laughed, 'but it's a neat job. Go and tell your regent that I am ready to risk another whiff of his perfume, and I will meet him in the conference chamber again in an hour's time.'

Naja was mollified by Taita's success, and the message from Apepi. Any inkling he might have had of Taita's disloyalty was expunged. 'I have that old rogue Apepi at the brink,' Naja gloated. 'He is about to make even more concessions than he realizes, which is why I was so angry when he broke off the conference and went to his couch.' He was so delighted with himself that he could not remain seated. He jumped up and paced the stone floor. 'How is he, Magus? Did you give him any potion that might cloud his mind?'

'I sent a dose down his gullet that would have stunned a bull buffalo,' Taita assured him. Naja crossed to his cosmetics chest and sprinkled perfume from a green glass vial into the cup of his hand and stroked it down the back of his neck. 'Well, I shall take full advantage.' He started towards the door, then looked back over his shoulder. 'Come with me,' he ordered. 'I might have use of your powers before I am done with Apepi.'

Binding Apepi to the treaty was not the easy task that Naja had suggested it would be. He showed no ill effect from either his wound or from the medication, and he was still ranting, shouting and banging his clenched fist on the table long after the watchman on the temple walls had called the midnight hour. No compromise Naja offered seemed enough for him, and at last even Taita was exhausted by his intransigence. Naja adjourned the conference and, to the crowing of the roosters in the courtyard, staggered off to bed.

The next day, when they met again at noon, Apepi was no more amenable to reason, and if anything the negotiations were even more stormy. Taita used his best influences to calm him, but Apepi allowed himself to be wooed only very slowly. So it was only on the fifth day that the scribes could begin to write down the terms of the treaty on the clay tablets in both the hieratic script and in hieroglyphics, translated into Hyksosian and Egyptian. They laboured late into the night.

Up to this time Naja had excluded Pharaoh Nefer Seti from the conclave. He had kept him occupied with trivial tasks, lessons with his tutors, and practice at arms, meetings with ambassadors and delegations of merchants and priests, all of whom sought concessions or donations. In the end Nefer had rebelled so Naja sent him out hawking and hunting with Apepi's younger sons. These outings were not the most amiable of events, and the first day had ended in a loud dispute over the bag, which had almost led to an exchange of blows.

On the second day, at Taita's suggestion, Princess Mintaka joined the hawking party to act as peace-maker between the two factions. Even her older brothers held her in considerable awe, and deferred to her when at any other time they might have drawn their weapons and rushed to wreak havoc on the Egyptian party. In like manner, when Mintaka was riding beside him in his hunting chariot, Nefer's warlike instincts were lulled. He took little notice of the threatening, boastful behaviour of her loutish siblings and enjoyed her wit and erudition, to say nothing of her close physical presence. In the confined cockpit of the chariot they were often thrown together as they bounced over the rough ground in pursuit of the fleeing gazelle herds. Then Mintaka would grab and hold him, even when the immediate danger was past.

When Nefer returned to the temple after the first outing, he sent for Taita, ostensibly to describe the day's sport to him but he was vague and distracted. Even when Taita questioned him on the performance of his favourite falcon, Nefer showed no great enthusiasm. Until he suddenly remarked dreamily, 'Does it not amaze you, Taita, just how soft and warm girls are?'

By the morning of the sixth day the scribes had completed their work and the fifty tablets of the treaty were ready to be ratified. Now Naja sent for Pharaoh to take part in the proceedings. Likewise, all Apepi's offspring, including Mintaka, were to be present at the ceremony.

Once again the courtyard of the temple was filled with a glittering congregation of royalty and nobility as, in stentorian tones, the Herald Royal began to read out the text of the treaty. Immediately Nefer was absorbed by what it contained. He and Mintaka had discussed it in detail during the days they had spent together, and exchanged significant glances whenever they thought they had detected a flaw or an oversight in the terms. However, these were few, and Nefer was certain that he detected Taita's shadowy influence in many areas of the long document.

At last it was time to affix the seals. To a series of blasts on the rams' horns Nefer pressed his cartouche on to the damp clay and Apepi did the same. It annoyed Nefer to see that the Hyksosian king had usurped the pharaonic prerogative by adopting the sacred cartouche.

While Naja watched, with an enigmatic expression behind his heavy makeup, the new co-rulers of the two kingdoms embraced. Apepi folded Nefer's slim form in his bearlike embrace and the congregation exploded in loud shouts of '*Bak-her! Bak-her!*' Men rattled their weapons against their shields, or hammered the butts of their spears and lances on the stone flags.

Nefer found himself almost overcome by Apepi's powerful bodily odours. One of the Egyptian mores that the Hyksos had not adopted was their concept of personal hygiene. Nefer consoled himself with the thought that if he found the odour repugnant, then Naja was in for a shock when the king bestowed his affection upon him. Gently he eased himself out of the arms of his co-pharaoh, but Apepi beamed down on him in avuncular fashion and placed one hairy paw on his shoulder. Then he turned to face the crowded courtyard. 'Citizens of this mighty land, which is once again united, I pledge you my duty and my patriotic love. In token of these, I offer the hand of my daughter, Princess Mintaka, in marriage to the Pharaoh Nefer Seti who is my co-ruler of this very Egypt. Pharaoh Nefer Seti, who shares with me the double crown of the Upper and Lower Kingdoms, and who shall be my son and whose sons shall be my grandsons!'

There was a long moment of utter stillness in the courtyard as the assembly came to terms with this startling announcement. Then they burst out in even more enthusiastic cries of approval while the drumming of weapons and the stamp of armoured sandals became deafening.

Pharaoh Nefer Seti had an expression on his face that in any lesser mortal would have been described as an idiotic grin. He was gazing across the courtyard at Mintaka. She was frozen, with one hand covering her mouth, as though to stop herself shrieking or squealing, and her eyes were wide open with astonishment as she gazed at her father. Slowly a dark blush suffused her face and shyly she turned her eyes to meet Nefer's. The two gazed at each other as if no other person was in the crowded courtyard.

Taita watched from the foot of Pharaoh's throne. He realized that Apepi's timing of the announcement had been masterly. Now there was no possible way in which anybody – Naja, Trok or any other – could stand in the way of the marriage.

Taita stood close to Naja's throne. Under his makeup the Regent was plainly in a state of deep consternation, especially aware of his own predicament. If Nefer married the princess he was beyond Naja's reach. He saw the double crown slipping from his grasp. Naja must have sensed Taita's eyes upon him, for he glanced in his direction. For a moment only Taita looked into his soul, and it was as though he had looked into a dry well filled with the live cobras for which the Regent was named. Then Naja veiled his fierce yellow eyes, smiled coolly and nodded in agreement and approval, but Taita knew that he was thinking furiously. However, those thoughts were so swift and complex that even he could not follow them.

Taita turned his head and sought out the burly figure of Lord Trok in the Hyksosian ranks opposite. Unlike the Regent, Trok was making no attempt to disguise his feelings. He was in a black rage. His beard seemed to bristle and his face was swollen with dark blood. He opened his mouth as if to shout an insult or a protest, then closed it, and placed one hand on the hilt of his sword. His knuckles glazed white with the pressure of his grip, and briefly Taita thought that he was about to draw his blade and rush across the courtyard to Nefer's slim figure. With a huge effort he regained control of himself, smoothed down his beard then turned abruptly and pushed his way out of the courtyard. The commotion was such that almost no one noticed him go. Only Apepi watched him with a cynical smile.

As Trok disappeared between the tall granite Hathor pillars, Apepi dropped his hand from Nefer's shoulder and crossed to Naja's throne. He lifted the Regent easily off his cushions and embraced him with even more vigour than he had Pharaoh. His lips were pressed to Naja's ear when he whispered softly, 'No more Egyptian tricks now, my sweet-smelling flower, or I shall ram them as far up your arse as my arm can reach.'

He dropped Naja back on his cushions, then took the throne that had been placed alongside for him. Naja blanched and held a linen pad soaked in perfume to his nose while he gathered his wits. Wave after wave of applause swept over the courtyard. As it died away Apepi slammed his huge paws on the arms of his throne to encourage them to fresh efforts, and the cheering began all over again. He was enjoying himself hugely and he kept them at it until they were almost exhausted.

With the *deshret* crown of lower Egypt on his head, his was the dominant figure. Beside him Nefer, even under the authority of the tall *hedjet* crown, was a mere stripling. At last, after a final burst of applause, Naja rose to his feet and held up both arms. A grateful silence at last descended.

'Let the holy virgin come forward!' Led out in procession by her acolytes from behind the carved screen of the chancel, the high priestess of the temple advanced to the double throne. Before her, two priestesses carried the *pshent* crowns of the double kingdom. While the temple choir sang praises to the goddess the venerable old woman removed the single crowns from the heads of the co-rulers and replaced them with the double crowns, signifying the reunification of Egypt. Then she pronounced her quavering blessing on the two pharaohs and the new land, and retired into the depths of the temple. There was a short pause of indecision, for this was the first time in the long history of Egypt that a ceremony of reunification had been held and there were no established protocols to follow.

Adroitly Naja seized his opportunity. Once again he rose and stepped in front of Apepi. 'On this auspicious and joyous day, we rejoice not only in the joining of the two kingdoms, but also in the betrothal of Pharaoh Nefer Seti and the beautiful Princess Mintaka. Therefore, be it known throughout the two kingdoms that the marriage will take place in this temple on the day that Pharaoh Nefer Seti celebrates his majority, or fulfils one of the conditions to ratify his claim to the crown and rules in his own right without a regent to protect and advise him.'

Apepi frowned and Nefer made a small gesture of dismay, but it was too late. It had been announced in full session and, as regent, Naja spoke with the authority of both crowned heads. Unless Nefer captured his own godbird, or succeeded in running the Red Road, thereby ratifying his claim to the throne, Naja had effectively prevented the marriage taking place for a number of years.

That was a masterly stroke, Taita thought bitterly, but he admired the political acumen behind it. Naja had averted disaster for himself by his quick thinking and timely intervention. Now, while his opposition was off-balance, he went even further. 'On an equally happy note, I invite Pharaoh Apepi and Pharaoh Nefer Seti to celebrate my own marriage to the princesses Heseret and Merykara. This joyous ceremony will take place ten days from now, on the first day of the festival of Isis Ascending at the temple of Isis in the city of Thebes.'

So, in ten days' time Lord Naja will be a member of the Tamosian royal family, and will stand next in succession to Pharaoh Nefer Seti, Taita thought grimly. Now we know, past all doubt, who was the cobra in the nest of the royal falcon on the cliffs of Bir Umm Masara.

By the terms of the treaty of Hathor, Apepi's seat would remain at Avaris and Nefer Seti's at Thebes. Each would govern his former kingdom, but in the name of the biumvirate. Twice every year, at the beginning and the end of the inundation of the Nile, the two kings would hold a combined royal assize at Memphis where all matters concerning the two kingdoms would be dealt with, new laws enacted and legal appeals considered.

However, before the two pharaohs parted, each to take up his seat in his respective capital, Apepi and his train would sail upriver in company with Nefer Seti's fleet to Thebes. There they would attend Lord Naja's double wedding.

The simultaneous embarkation of both trains from the wharf below the temple was a chaotic affair that took up most of the morning. Taita mingled with the throng of boatmen and dockers, slaves and important passengers. Even he was amazed by the mountains of luggage and equipment piled upon the beach, waiting to be loaded on the lighters, feluccas and galleys. Rather than drive the long, rough road back down-river, the regiments of both Thebes and Avaris had broken down their chariots and were loading them and the horses on to the lighters. This contributed greatly to the confusion on the riverbank.

For once Taita was not the centre of attraction: there was work to keep everyone fully occupied. Occasionally a man would look up from what he was doing, recognize him and ask for his blessing, or a woman would bring him a sick child to tend. However, he was able to work his way gradually along the beach, casually looking out for the chariots and equipment of Lord Trok's regiment. He recognized them by their green and red pennants, and as he approached he made out the unmistakable figure of Trok among his men. Taita edged closer and saw him standing over a pile of equipment and weapons, haranguing his lance-bearer: 'You brainless baboon, how have you packed my kit? That is my favourite bow lying there unprotected. Some oaf is sure to drive the horses over it.' His mood of the previous day had not improved, and he stamped away down the wharf, lashing out with his chariot whip at any unfortunate who stood in his way. Taita watched him pause to talk to another of his sergeants, then take the path up to the temple.

As soon as he had disappeared Taita approached the lance-bearer. The trooper was stripped to breech-clout and sandals, and as he stooped over one of the chests of Trok's equipment and staggered with it to the waiting lighter, Taita saw the distinctive circular rash of the ring-worm on his naked back. The lance-bearer handed up the chest to a boatman on the deck of the galley then came back. For the first time he noticed Taita standing nearby and touched his own breast with a clenched fist, saluting respectfully. 'Come here, soldier.' Taita called him across. 'How long have you had the itch on your back?'

Instinctively the fellow twisted up one arm between his shoulder-blades, and scratched himself so vigorously that he drew blood. 'Cursed thing has been bothering me ever since we captured Abnub. I think it's a gift from one of those dirty Egyptian whores—' He broke off guiltily. Taita knew that he was speaking about a woman he had raped during the capture of the city. 'Forgive me, Warlock, we are allies and fellow countrymen now.'

'That is why I will attend to your affliction, soldier. Go up to the temple, ask at the kitchens for a jar of lard and bring it to me. I will mix an ointment for you.' Taita sat down on the pile of Trok's luggage and equipment, and the lance-bearer hurried away down the beach. Among the luggage were three war bows – Trok had been unfair in his accusations for each of the bows was unstrung and carefully wrapped in its leather cover.

Taita's seat was a stack of wooden chests. This was not by chance for he had seen that the top chest bore the seal of Grippa, the Avaris fletcher who made arrows for all the high-ranking Hyksosian officers. Taita remembered that he had discussed Grippa's work with Mintaka. He slipped the little dagger from the sheath under his *chiton*, cut the cord that secured the lid, and lifted it. A layer of dry straw protected the arrows, and under it they were packed alternately, flint head to gaudy red and green feathers. Taita picked one out and turned it in his fingers.

The carved signet leaped out at him, the stylized head of the leopard with the hieratic letter T held in its snarling jaws. The arrow was identical to the ones he had found in the quiver at the scene of Pharaoh's murder. It was the last thread in the fabric of treason and treachery. Naja and Trok were linked inextricably in the bloody plot, whose whole shape as yet he could only guess at.

Taita slipped the incriminating arrow under the folds of his *chiton* and closed the lid of the chest. Deftly he retied the cord, and waited for the lance-bearer to return.

The old soldier was volubly grateful for Taita's ministrations, then went on to plead for a further favour: 'A friend of mine has the Egyptian pox, Magus. What should he do about it?' It always amused Taita how the Hyksos called it the Egyptian pox, and the Egyptians returned the compliment. It seemed that no man ever contracted it himself but always had a friend suffering from the disease.

The wedding ceremony and feast to celebrate the marriage of Lord Naja to the two Tamosian princesses was the most lavish ever recorded. Taita recalled that it far exceeded in splendour any of those of either Pharaoh Tamose or his father Pharaoh Mamose, both divine sons of Ra, may they live for ever.

To the common citizens of Thebes, Lord Naja gave five hundred head of prime oxen, two lighters of millet from the state granaries, and five thousand large clay pots of the best beer. The feasting continued for a week but even the hungry mouths of Thebes could not devour such quantities of food in so short a time. The remains of the millet and the meat, which they smoked to preserve it, fed the city for months thereafter. However, the beer was another matter: they drank it in the first week.

The wedding was celebrated in the temple of Isis before both pharaohs, six hundred priests and four thousand invited guests. As they entered the temple each guest was presented with a commemorative carved jewel, ivory, amethyst, coral or some other precious gemstone, with the guest's own name engraved upon it between the names of the Regent and his brides.

The two brides came to meet their groom on one of the

state carriages drawn by the sacred white hump-backed oxen, driven by naked Nubian coachmen. The road was strewn with palm fronds and flowers, and a chariot drove ahead of the wedding coach throwing rings of silver and copper to the deliriously happy crowds that lined the way. Their enthusiasm was due in no small measure to Lord Naja's largesse of beer.

The girls were clad in cloud-white linen of gossamer quality, and little Merykara was almost weighed down by the gold and jewels that covered her small body. Her tears had cut runnels through the kohl and antimony makeup. Heseret squeezed her hand tightly to try to console her.

When they reached the temple they were met by the two pharaohs as they disembarked from the great state coach. Nefer whispered to Merykara, as he led her into the nave of the temple, 'Don't cry, little kitten. Nobody is going to hurt you. You will be back in the nursery before your bedtime.'

To register his protest at the marriage of his sisters, Nefer had tried to avoid the duty of leading his little sister into the sanctuary, but Taita had reasoned with him. 'We cannot prevent it happening, although you know how we have tried. Naja is determined. It would be cruel of you not to be there to comfort her in this the most dread episode of her short life.' Reluctantly Nefer had acquiesced.

Close behind them Apepi led Heseret. She was as lovely as a nymph of paradise in her snowy robes and glittering jewellery. Months ago she had come to terms with the fate the gods had apportioned her and her initial dismay and horror had slowly given way to curiosity and a sneaking anticipation. Lord Naja was a magnificent-looking man, and her nurses, handmaidens and playmates had discussed him in avid detail, endlessly pointing out his more obvious virtues and, with breathless giggles, speculating in salacious detail on his hidden attributes.

Perhaps as a consequence of these discussions Heseret

had recently been experiencing intriguing dreams. In one she had run naked through a lush garden on the bank of the river pursued by the Regent. When she looked back at him over her shoulder she saw that he also was naked, but that he was human only as far as his waist. From there down he was a horse, exactly like Nefer's favourite stallion, Stargazer. When he was with the mares, she had often seen Stargazer in the same amazing condition as the Regent now exhibited, and she had always found herself strangely moved by the sight. However, just as the Regent caught up with her and reached out a bejewelled hand to seize her the dream ended abruptly and she found herself sitting bolt upright on her mattress. Without realizing what she was doing she reached down and touched herself. Her fingers came away wet and slippery. She was so disturbed that she could not sleep again and pick up the dream where it had broken off, although she tried hard to do so. She wanted to know the outcome of this enthralling experience. The next morning she felt restless and irritable, and took out her bad temper on all those around her. From that time onwards her girlish interest in Meren began to fade. She saw him seldom, these days, anyway: since the death of his grandfather at Lord Naja's hands his fortune had been forfeit, and the family had fallen into disgrace. She came to realize that he was an impecunious boy, a common soldier without favour or prospects. Lord Naja's social rank almost matched hers, and his fortune far exceeded her own.

Now she kept a demure and chaste demeanour as Apepi led her down the long hypostyle gallery of the temple to the sanctuary. Lord Naja was waiting there for the bridal party, and although he was surrounded by courtiers and officers in fine costumes and magnificent uniforms, Heseret had eyes for him alone.

He wore a plumed headdress of ostrich feathers to emulate the god Osiris and stood tall above even Asmor and Lord Trok, who flanked him. As Heseret approached him she became aware of his perfume. It was a blend of essences of blooms from a land beyond the Indus and also contained the precious ambergris, found only rarely on the seashore, a bounty from the gods of the ocean depths. The aroma stirred her, and she took the hand that Naja offered her without hesitation, and looked up into those fascinating yellow eyes.

When Naja offered his other hand to Merykara she burst into loud sobs, and it was all Nefer could do to comfort her. She sobbed softly at intervals during the long ceremony that followed.

When at last Lord Naja broke the jars of Nile water to mark the culmination of the ceremony, the crowds gasped with amazement: the waters of the great river, on whose bank the temple stood, turned a brilliant blue. Around the first bend Naja had caused a line of barges to be anchored from bank to bank, and at a signal relayed from the temple roof they had released jars of dye into the waters. The effect was breathtaking, for blue was the colour of the Tamosian dynasty. Naja was declaring to the world his new pharaonic connections.

Watching from the roof of the western enclosure, Taita saw the river change colour and shuddered with a sense of foreboding. It seemed that for a moment the sun darkened in the tall Egyptian sky while the blue waters took on the colour of blood. But when he looked up there was no cloud, no passing flock of birds to dull its rays, and when he looked down the waters were once more cerulean blue.

Now Naja is of the blood royal, and Nefer is stripped of even that protection. I am the only shield he has, and I am one man and old. Will my powers be enough to turn away the cobra from the fledgling falcon? Give me your strength, divine Horus. You have been my buckler and my lance down all the years. Do not forsake me now, mighty god.

Lord Naja and his two new wives rode back in splendour down the sacred avenue guarded by the ranks of granite lions to the palace gates. There they dismounted and went in procession through the gardens to the banquet hall. Most of the guests had arrived ahead of them, and had been sampling the wine from the vineyards of the temple of Osiris. The commotion as the wedding party entered was deafening. Naja led a new young wife on each hand. The trio processed with dignity through the throng and briefly inspected the heaps of gifts stacked in the centre of the banquet hall, which were fitting to such a momentous occasion. Apepi had sent a chariot covered in gold leaf. It was so brilliant that even in the dimly lit hall it was difficult to look at it directly. From Babylon King Sargon had sent a hundred slaves, each bearing a sandalwood chest filled with jewellery, precious stones or golden vessels. They knelt before the Regent and offered their burdens. Naja touched each as a sign of acceptance. Pharaoh Nefer Seti, at the suggestion of Lord Naja, had deeded to his new brother-in-law five expansive estates on the riverbank. The scribes had calculated that all these treasures were worth upward of three lakhs of pure gold. The Regent had become almost as rich as his pharaoh.

When the connubial trio took their seats at the head of the wedding board, the palace cooks laid a feast before them and their guests that consisted of forty different dishes served by a thousand slaves. There were trunks of elephants, tongues of the buffalo and fillets of Nubian mountain goat, the flesh of wild boar and warthog, gazelle and Nubian ibex, of monitor lizard and python, of crocodile and hippopotamus, oxen and sheep. Every type of Nile fish was served, from barbelled catfish, whose flesh ran with rich yellow fat, to white-fleshed perch and bream. From the northern sea there was tuna, shark, grouper, crayfish and crab, sent up by fast river galley from the delta. The birds of the air, including mute swans, three types of goose, numerous varieties of duck, and lark, bustard, partridge and quail, were roasted, baked or grilled, marinated in wine or wild honey, or stuffed with herbs and spices from the Orient. The aromatic smoke from the fires and the smell of cooking was savoured by the crowds of beggars and commoners at the palace gates, and by those who lined the far bank of the river, or filled the feluccas in mid-stream all vying for a closer view of the festivities.

To entertain the guests there were musicians and jugglers, acrobats and animal trainers. Maddened by the uproar, one of the huge brown bears broke its chain and escaped. A party of Hyksosian nobles, led by Lord Trok, pursued it through the gardens with drunken shouts and slew the cringing animal on the riverbank.

King Apepi was titillated by the suppleness and athleticism of two of the Assyrian female acrobats: so he picked up one under each arm and carried them, kicking and squealing, from the dance floor into the private quarters of the palace. When he returned he confided to Taita, 'One of them, the pretty one with long curls, was a boy. I was so surprised when I discovered what he had between his legs that I almost let him escape.' He roared with laughter. 'Luckily I did not, for he was by far the most succulent of the two.'

By nightfall most of the guests were drunk or so stuffed with food that few could stand when Lord Naja and his brides retired. As soon as they were in the private apartments Naja called for the nursemaids to take Merykara to her own quarters. 'Treat her gently,' he warned them. 'The poor child is asleep on her feet.'

Then he took Heseret by the hand and led her to his

own sumptuous apartments, which overlooked the river. The Nile's dark waters were spangled with the reflection of the golden stars.

As soon as they entered the chamber, Heseret's handmaidens took her behind the screen of bamboo to remove her wedding dress and jewellery.

Covering the marriage bed was a sheepskin that had been bleached shining white. Lord Naja inspected it carefully, and when he was assured of its perfection he went out on to the terrace and inhaled deeply the cool river air. A slave brought him a bowl of spiced wine, and he sipped appreciatively. It was the first he had allowed himself all evening. Naja knew that one of the most vital secrets of survival was to keep his wits clear in the presence of his enemies. He had watched all the other guests drink themselves into a pitiful state. Even Trok, in whom he placed so much trust and confidence, had succumbed to his animal nature – Naja had last seen him puking copiously into a bowl held for him by a pretty Libyan slave girl. When he had finished Trok had wiped his mouth on the girl's skirts then lifted them over her head, pushed her down on the grassy sward and mounted her from behind. Naja's fastidious nature had been offended by this display.

He returned to the chamber as two slaves staggered in, bearing between them a cauldron of hot water, in which floated lotus petals. Naja set aside the wine bowl and went to bathe. One of the slaves dried and braided his hair, while the other brought him a clean white robe. He dismissed them and returned to the marriage bed. He lay upon it, stretched out his long, elegant limbs and rested his braided head on the gold-inlaid ivory headrest.

From the far end of the chamber came the rustle of clothing and feminine whispers. Once he recognized Heseret's giggle and the sound aroused him. He propped himself up on one elbow and looked across at the bamboo screen.

The gaps in it were just large enough to afford him tantalizing glimpses of pale smooth skin.

Power and political aspiration were the main reasons for this marriage, but they were not the only ones. Although he was a warrior by trade and an adventurer by disposition, Naja had a voluptuous and sensual nature. For years he had watched Heseret surreptitiously, and his interest had increased at each stage in her journey towards womanhood; from infancy through gawky girlhood, and then that tantalizing period when her breast buds had bloomed and the puppy fat had melted away, to leave her body delicate and graceful. The smell of her had changed too: whenever she was close he had detected the faint sweet musk of womanhood, which enthralled him.

Once when out hawking Naja had come across Heseret and two of her friends collecting lotus blooms to plait into garlands. She had looked up at him as he stood above her on the riverbank, and her wet skirts had clung to her legs so the skin shone through the fine linen. She had brushed the hair off her cheeks with an innocent gesture that was nevertheless intensely erotic. Even though her expression had remained serious and chaste, the slanted eyes had hinted at a sly, lascivious streak in her that had fascinated him. This revelation had lasted only a moment before she had called to her friends and splashed to the bank then raced away across the grassy field towards the palace. He had watched her long wet legs glinting, the round buttocks oscillating and changing shape beneath the linen skirt, and suddenly his breath had come short and fast.

At the memory his loins stirred and quickened. He longed for her to come out from behind the screen, but perversely he wanted to delay the moment so that he could savour the anticipation to the full. It happened at last. Two of the handmaidens led her out, then slipped away quietly leaving her standing alone in the middle of the floor.

Her nightrobe fell from her throat to her ankles. It was of a rare and precious silk from the eastern lands, creamy in colour and so fine that it seemed to float around her like river mist, stirring with every breath she took. There was an oil lamp on a tripod in the corner behind her, and the soft yellow light shone through the silk, highlighting the curves of her hips and shoulders so they shone softly as polished ivory. Her bare feet and her hands were dyed with henna. Her face had been washed clean of makeup so the young blood beneath the flawless skin delicately rouged her cheeks, and her lips trembled as though she were on the point of tears. She hung her head in an appealingly girlish manner and looked up at him from under lowered lashes. Her eyes were green, and his blood thrilled again as he detected that same wicked glint in them that had originally intrigued him.

'Turn round,' he said gently, but his throat was as dry as if he had sucked the juice from a green persimmon. She obeyed him, but with a dream-slow movement, rolling her hips, her belly gleaming softly through the silk. Her buttocks undulated, round and lustrous as ostrich eggs, and the shining tresses of her hair swayed.

'You are beautiful.' His voice caught. Now a hint of a smile lifted the corners of her lips, and she wet them with the tip of a tongue that was as pink as that of a kitten. 'I am glad that my lord regent finds me so.'

He rose from the bed and went to her. He took her hand, which was warm and soft in his. He led her to the bed, and she followed him without hesitation. She knelt upon the white sheepskin and hung her head so that her hair veiled her face. He stood over her and leaned forward until his lips touched it. She exuded the elusive fragrance of a healthy young woman in the first flush of physical arousal. He stroked her hair and she looked up at him through the dark curtain. Then he parted the tresses and cupped her chin with one hand. Slowly, teasing himself, he lifted her face.

'You have eyes like Ikona,' she whispered. Ikona was his tame leopard: the beast had always frightened and fascinated her. She felt those same emotions now for he was as sleek and feline as the great cat, his eyes yellow and implacable. With a woman's instinct she sensed the cruelty and ruthlessness in them, which evoked in her emotions that she had never before experienced. 'You also are beautiful,' she whispered, and it was true. In this moment she realized that he was the most beautiful creature she had ever known.

He kissed her and his mouth startled her. It tasted of some ripe fruit she had never eaten before, and quite naturally she opened her own mouth to savour it. His tongue was as flickeringly quick as a snake's, but it did not revolt her. She closed her eyes and touched it with her own. Then he placed one of his hands behind her head and pressed his mouth harder against hers. She was so lost in his kiss that when his hand closed over her breast she was unprepared. Her eyes flew open and she gasped. She tried to pull away but he held her, and now he caressed her with a gentle but skilful touch that stilled her fears. He teased out her nipple, and the sensation flowed through her body, rippling down her arms to her fingertips. She felt a sharp disappointment when he took away his hand. He lifted her to her feet so she stood on the sheepskin above him with her breasts at the level of his face.

With a single movement he swept off her silken robe and let it fall to the floor. Then, as he sucked her engorged nipple deep into his mouth, she cried aloud. At the same time one of his hands came up between her thighs and cupped the soft nest of dark fluff.

She had not the slightest inclination to resist what he was doing to her. Instead she surrendered herself to it. From what her slave girls had told her she had been terrified that he might hurt her, but his hands, though swift and strong, were gentle. He seemed to know her body better than she did herself, and he played upon it with such skill that she found herself drawn deeper and deeper, faster and faster beneath the surface, sinking away and drowning in this sea of new sensations.

She surfaced only once more when suddenly she opened her eyes and found that his own robe was gone, and that he stood over her naked. She remembered the dream in which he had had the same thing down there as Stargazer, the stallion. She looked down in trepidation, but it was nothing like the dream: it was smooth and rosy, yet hard as bone, perfect and clean in form as a temple column. Her fears evaporated and once again she surrendered herself to his hands and his mouth. There was only one sharp moment of stinging pain, but that was much later, and it was fleeting, replaced almost as swiftly by an unaccustomed but wonderful feeling of fullness. Then later still she heard him cry out above her. The sound triggered something in her own body, turning almost unbearable pleasure into its own kind of pain, and she held him with all the strength of her encircling arms and legs and cried out with him.

Twice more during that too-short enchanted night he forced her to cry out in that same frenzy of pleasure, and when the dawn suffused the chamber with its rose and silver light she lay still in his arms. She felt as though the life force had been drawn out of her, as though her bones had turned soft and malleable as river clay, and there was a soft ache deep in her belly that she savoured.

He slipped out of her arms and she just had the strength left to protest, 'Don't go. Oh! Please don't go, my lord. My beautiful lord.'

'Not for long,' he whispered and gently drew out the sheepskin from under her. She saw the stains upon the snowy fleece, the blood bright as the petals of a rose. She had experienced only that brief pain at the piercing of her womanhood.

He carried the fleece to the terrace and she watched him through the doorway as he hung it over the parapet wall. From far below there came the faint sound of cheering as the citizens waiting below saw this proof of her virginity displayed. She cared nothing for the approbation of the peasant hordes, but watched the naked back of her new husband and felt her chest and her aching womb swell with love for him. As he came back to her she held out both arms to him.

'You are magnificent,' she whispered, and fell asleep in his arms. Much later she came gradually awake and found that her whole being was filled with a lightness and a feeling of joy that she had never known before. At first she was not certain of the source of her well-being. Then she felt his hard muscular warmth stir in her arms.

When she opened her eyes he was watching her with his strange yellow ones, and he smiled gently. 'What a splendid queen you would make,' he said softly. This he meant sincerely. During the night he had discovered in her qualities that he had not before suspected. He sensed that he had found in her someone whose desires and instincts were in perfect harmony with his own.

'And what a splendid pharaoh you would make for this very Egypt.' She smiled back at him and stretched voluptuously. Then she laughed softly, reached up and touched his cheek, 'But that could never happen.' She stopped smiling abruptly and asked softly, seriously, 'Could it?'

'There is only one thing that stands in our way,' he answered. He did not have to say anything more, for he saw a sly acquisitive expression bloom in her eyes. She was entirely in step with him.

'You are the dagger, and I shall be the scabbard. No matter what you ask of me, I shall never fail you, my beautiful lord.'

He laid one finger on her lips, which were inflamed and swollen with his kisses. 'I see clearly that there is little need of words between us, for our hearts beat in unison.'

King Apepi's entourage remained in Thebes for almost a month after the wedding. They were the guests of Pharaoh Nefer Seti and of his regent, and were entertained in royal fashion. Taita encouraged this delay. He felt certain that Naja would take no action against Nefer while Apepi and his daughter were in Thebes.

The royal visitors spent their days hunting or hawking, visiting the numerous temples on both banks of the river dedicated to all the gods of Egypt, or in tournaments between the regiments of the northern and southern kingdom. There were chariot races, archery contests, and foot races. There were even swimming races, in which the chosen champions swam the full width of the Nile for a prize of a golden statue of Horus.

Out in the desert they hunted gazelle and oryx from speeding chariots, or hawked for the great bustards with the swift Sakers. No royal falcons remained in the palace mews, for they had been released into the wild during the funeral rites of Nefer's father. Along the riverbank the guests hawked for herons and duck, and speared the huge whiskered catfish in the shallows. They hunted the river horse, the mighty hippopotamus, from the fleet war galleys, with Nefer at the tiller of his own galley named the *Eye of Horus*. Princess Mintaka stood beside him and shrieked with excitement as the great beasts broke the surface, their backs studded with spears, and the waters turned pink with their blood.

During these days Mintaka was often at Nefer's side. She rode in his chariot when they hunted and handed him the lance when they drove up alongside a galloping oryx. She carried her own falcon on her arm as they quartered the reed beds for heron. At the hunting picnics in the desert, she sat beside him and prepared little treats for him. She selected the sweetest grapes for him and peeled them with her long, tapered fingers and then popped them into his mouth.

Every evening there were banquets in the palace and there also she sat at his left side, the traditional place for a woman so that she never blocked her man's sword arm. She made him laugh with her wry wit and she was a marvellous mimic: she imitated Heseret to perfection, simpering and rolling her eyes, and speaking of 'my husband, the Regent of Egypt' in the portentous tones as Heseret now employed.

Though they tried, they could never be completely alone. Naja and Apepi saw to that. When Nefer appealed to Taita for assistance, not even he could manoeuvre a secret meeting for them. It never occurred to Nefer that Taita did not exert himself to do so, or that he was as set on keeping them innocent as the others were. Long ago Taita had engineered a tryst for Tanus and his beloved Lostris, and the consequences still echoed like thunder down the years. When Nefer and Mintaka played bao there was always an audience of slave girls, while courtiers and the ubiquitous Lord Asmor hovered nearby. Nefer had learned his lesson well, and no longer underrated Mintaka's skill on the board. He played against her as if he were matched against Taita. He came to learn her strengths, and to recognize her few weaknesses: she was always overprotective of her home castle, and if he pressed her hard in that quadrant she might sometimes offer an opening in her flanks. Twice he exploited this and broke up her defence, but the third time he discovered too late that she had anticipated his tactic and had laid a trap. When he had exposed his west castle she rammed a phalanx through the gap, and laughed so deliciously when he was forced to capitulate that he almost, but not quite, forgave her. Their bouts became ever more keenly contested and in the end were of epic proportions, so that even Taita spent hours watching them and occasionally nodding in approval or smiling his thin, ancient smile.

Their love was so apparent that it cast a glow upon all those around them, and wherever they went together there were smiles and laughter. As Nefer's chariot sped through the streets of Thebes with Mintaka on the footplate as his lance-bearer, her dark hair flowing in the wind like a banner, the goodwives ran out of their houses and the men paused from their labours to shout greetings and good wishes. Even Naja smiled benignly upon them, and none would have believed that he fiercely resented the attention of the populace having been diverted from his own nuptials and brides.

Lord Trok was the only sombre presence at the hunting parties, the picnics in the countryside and the banquets in the palace.

Their time together sped by too fast.

'There are always so many people around us,' Nefer whispered over the bao board. 'I long to be alone with you even for just a few minutes. There are only three more days before you have to return to Avaris with your father. It might be months, even years, before we meet again, and there is so much I want to tell you, but not with all these eyes and ears pointed at us like nocked arrows.'

She nodded, then reached across and moved a stone that in his preoccupation he had overlooked. He glanced down and almost discounted it, until he realized that his west castle was now under a forked attack. Three moves later she had broken his front. He kept up the losing battle for a while longer, but his forces were in disarray and the outcome was inevitable. 'You caught me when I was distracted by other things,' he groused. 'So much like a woman.'

'Your Majesty, I make no claims to being anything else than a woman.' She used his title with an irony that bit like the jewelled dagger she wore on her belt. Then she leaned close and whispered, 'If I were alone with you, would you promise to respect my chastity?'

'I swear by the wounded eye of the great god Horus that I will never, as long as I live, cause you shame,' he told her earnestly.

She smiled at him. 'My brothers will not be overpleased to hear that. They would welcome an excuse to slit your throat.' She slanted those magnificent dark eyes at him. 'Or, failing your throat, some other part of you might satisfy them.'

Their chance came the next day. One of the royal huntsmen came in from the hills above the village of Dabba to report that a lion had come out of the eastern wilderness and raided the cattle pens during the night. It had jumped the stockade and killed eight of the terrified beasts. In the dawn a horde of villagers, brandishing burning torches, blowing horns, beating drums and screaming wildly, had driven it off.

'When did this happen?' asked Naja.

'Three nights ago, Your Grace.' The man was prostrate before the throne. 'I came upriver as soon as I could, but the current runs strongly and the winds were flukey.'

'What has happened to the beast?' King Apepi interrupted eagerly.

'It has gone back into the hills, but I have sent two of my best Nubian trackers to follow it.'

'Did any man see it? What size is it? Lion or lioness?'

'The villagers say that it is a large male, with a full mane, thick and black.'

Up until the last sixty years lions had been almost unheard-of in the lands along the river. They were royal game, and had been hunted ruthlessly by successive pharaohs, not only because of the damage they inflicted on the livestock of the peasant farmers but also because they were the most sought-after trophy of the royal hunt.

During the long, bitter struggle of the Hyksos wars the pharaohs of both kingdoms had been preoccupied and the lions had been hunted seldom. In addition the human corpses left on the battlefields had provided an easy source of food for the lion prides. In the last few decades they had flourished, their numbers had increased many-fold and so had their boldness.

'I will have the chariots loaded on to the boats at once,' Apepi decided. 'With the state of the river we can be at Dabba early tomorrow morning.' He grinned and punched his fist into the horny palm of his sword hand. 'By Seueth, I would like a chance at this old black-mane. Since I have had to give up killing Egyptians, I am starved for real sport.'

Naja frowned at the sally. 'Majesty, you are expected to sail back to Avaris the day after tomorrow morning.'

'You are right, Regent. However, most of our baggage is already loaded and the fleet lies ready to depart. Moreover, Dabba lies on my way homewards. I can afford a day or two to join in the hunt.'

Naja hesitated. He was not so addicted to the hunt that he wished to neglect the numerous affairs of state that awaited his attention. He had looked forward to the departure of Apepi, whose boisterous, uncouth presence in Thebes had long since palled. Also he had other plans afoot, which could only be furthered once Apepi had left Thebes. Yet he could not allow the Hyksosian Pharaoh to hunt alone in the Upper Kingdom. Not only would it be churlish to do so, but it would be impolitic to let Apepi behave in the southern kingdom as though he had sole right to it.

'Your Majesty,' Nefer intervened, before Naja could compose a suitable refusal, 'we will join in the hunt with the greatest of pleasure.' He saw an opportunity for magnificent sport, for he had never had the chance to run down a lion in his chariot and test his own courage by standing down the charge. But, a hundred times more important, the hunt might also delay Mintaka's dreaded departure. This happy circumstance might even provide the opportunity that had so far eluded them of spending a short time alone. Before Naja could prevent him Nefer had turned to the huntsman, who still lay with his forehead pressed to the tiled floor. 'Well done, my good fellow. The chamberlain will give you a gold ring for your trouble. Return to Dabba at once in the fastest felucca in our fleet. Make ready for our arrival. We will go after this beast in full array.'

Nefer's only cause for regret was that Taita would not be with him during his first lion hunt to offer counsel and advice. The old man had disappeared into the wilderness on another of his periodic and mysterious forays, and no one knew when he would return.

In the early morning of the next day the hunting party disembarked on the bank of the river below the village of Dabba. Then all the horses and twenty chariots were off-loaded from the small convoy of lighters and galleys. While this was being done, the lance-bearers sharpened the spear blades, restrung the hunting bows and checked the arrows for balance and straightness. While the horses were watered, fed and groomed, the hunters ate a hearty breakfast that the villagers had provided.

The mood was ebullient, and Apepi sent for the tracker who had returned from the hills to report. 'It is a very big lion. The biggest I have ever seen east of the river,' the man told them, increasing their excitement.

'You actually saw him?' Nefer demanded. 'Or did you only read his sign?'

'I saw him clearly but only at a distance. He stands as tall as a horse and he walks with the dignified tread of a monarch. His mane waves like a sheaf of *dhurra* millet stalks in the wind.'

'By Seth, the fellow is a poet,' Naja sneered. 'Stick to the facts and eschew the fine words, knave.'

The huntsman touched his heart with his fist to show his contrition, and went on with his report in a subdued tone. 'He lay up yesterday in a wooded wadi two leagues from here, but he left at the fall of night to prowl. It is four days since he last fed and he is hungry and hunting again. During the night he tried to drag down an oryx, but it kicked him off and ran free.'

'Where do you hope to find him today?' Nefer asked, in a kinder voice than Naja had used. 'If he hunted he will be thirsty as well as hungry. Where will he drink?'

The huntsman looked at him with respect, not only for his royal eminence but also for the knowledge of the wild he displayed. 'After his attempt to bring down the oryx, he went into stony ground where we could no longer read his tracks.' Apepi made a gesture of annoyance, and the huntsman hurried on, 'But I expect him to have drunk this morning at a small oasis. A hidden place little known to any except the Bedouin.'

'How long to reach this place?' Nefer asked, and the man swept his arm through part of an arc, indicating the sun's progress over the passage of three hours.

'Then we have little time to waste.' Nefer smiled at him, and turned away to shout at the troop captain of the chariots, 'How much longer, soldier?'

'All is ready, Majesty.'

'Sound the mount up,' Nefer ordered, and the ram's horns blared as the hunters scattered to the waiting chariots. Mintaka walked at Nefer's side. In these informal circumstances all royal dignity was forgotten, and they were simply boy and girl on an exciting outing. Lord Trok spoiled the illusion: just as he leaped into his own chariot and gathered up the reins, he called across to King Apepi, 'Your Majesty, it is not wise to let the Princess ride with an untried boy. This is not a gazelle we are hunting now.'

Nefer froze and stared at Trok with outrage. Mintaka laid a small hand on his bare arm. 'Do not provoke him. He is a formidable fighter with a terrible temper, and if you challenge him even your rank will not protect you.'

Nefer shrugged off her hand furiously. 'My honour will not allow me to ignore such an insult.'

'Please, my heart, for my sake, let it pass.' It was the first time she had used such an endearment. She did it deliberately, knowing the effect it must have on him: she was already learning to manage his volatile moods and tempers with a loving woman's instinct far beyond her years and experience. In the instant Nefer forgot Trok and the slur to his honour.

'What did you call me?' he asked huskily.

'You are not deaf, my darling.' He blinked at this second endearment. 'You heard quite clearly.' And she smiled into his face.

Apepi bawled into the silence, 'Do not worry, Trok. I am sending my daughter to take care of Pharaoh. He will be quite safe.' He gave a snort of laughter and shook the reins. As his team jumped forward he shouted again, 'We have wasted half the morning here. Huntsmen, take up the chase!'

Nefer steered his chariot behind Apepi, cutting steeply past the noses of Lord Trok's team. As he went by he gave Trok a cold glare, and told him, 'You are impudent. Rest assured that this is not the end of it. We will speak further on this matter, Lord Trok.'

'I fear he is now your enemy, Nefer,' Mintaka murmured. 'Trok has an evil reputation and an even more evil temper.'

Led by the royal huntsman, who rode bareback astride a scrubby but tough little pony, the hunting column climbed into the bare, stony hills. They went at the trot, saving the horses, letting them blow after every steep gradient. Within the hour they found one of the Nubian trackers waiting for them on a hilltop, and he ran down to report to the huntsman. They spoke to each other earnestly, then the huntsman trotted back to report to the royal party. 'The Nubians have cast the hills but without finding the spoor again. They are sure that he will drink at the waterhole, but not wanting to disturb him they have waited for us to catch up.'

'Lead us to the water,' Apepi ordered, and they went on.

Before midday they came down into a shallow valley. They were not far from the river, but this seemed like the deep desert, waterless and forbidding. The huntsman trotted alongside Apepi's chariot and said, 'The waterhole is at the head of this valley. The beast will probably be lying up nearby.'

Naturally Apepi, the old warrior, took command, and Nefer did not dispute his right to do so. 'We will split into three squadrons, and surround the oasis. If the chase breaks cover we will have him surrounded. My lord Regent, do you take the left wing. Pharaoh Nefer Seti, take the centre. I will cover the right flank.' He brandished his heavy war bow over his head. 'Whoever draws first blood will win the trophy.'

They were all expert charioteers and the new formation evolved swiftly and without check. They threw out a wide net to encircle the waterhole. Nefer had his bow over his shoulder and the reins unwrapped from his wrists, ready to drop them in an instant to leave both hands free to draw. Mintaka pressed close to his side. She held the long lance ready to hand to him. They had perfected this change of weapons over the past weeks, and he knew he could rely upon her to slap the grip of the lance into his palm at the very moment he needed it.

They approached the oasis at a walk, closing in steadily. The horses sensed the tension in their drivers, and perhaps they had picked up the lion scent. They flung up their heads, and rolled their eyes and blew through their nostrils, stepping high and nervously.

The line of vehicles closed slowly around the patch of low scrub and rank grass that concealed the waterhole. When the encirclement was complete, Apepi raised his hand above his head to signal the halt. The royal huntsman dismounted and went forward on foot, leading his pony. He approached the sparse brown cover cautiously.

'If the lion was here, surely we would have seen such a large animal by now.' Mintaka's voice shook, and Nefer loved her all the more for this little show of fear.

'A lion can flatten himself until he becomes part of the earth, and you could walk close enough to touch him without ever suspecting his presence,' he told her.

The huntsman went forward a few paces at a time, stopping to listen and search every bush and clump of rank grass in his path. At the edge of the scrub he stooped and picked up a handful of small stones, and began to lob them systematically at each possible hiding place.

'What is he doing?' Mintaka whispered.

'The lion will growl before it charges. He is trying to provoke it and make it reveal itself.'

The silence was broken only by the plop of the pebbles, the snorting of the horses and the restless stamping of their hoofs. Every one of the hunters had nocked an arrow and was poised to draw at an instant. Suddenly there was a squawk and clatter in the grass. Every bow went up at once and the lance-bearers hefted their weapons. They all relaxed and looked sheepish as a chocolate brown hammerhead stork launched itself into the air and flapped away down the valley in the direction of the river.

The huntsman took a minute to recover his nerve, then began to work his way, a pace at a time, deeper into the cover until he reached the seep. The brackish water came up a sluggish drop at a time, and filled a shallow basin in the rocky ground, hardly enough to quench the thirst of a great predator. The huntsman went down on one knee to search the rim of the basin for sign, then shook his head and stood up. More quickly he worked back through the scrub, and at last mounted the pony and trotted back to Apepi's chariot. The other hunters drove across to hear his report, but the huntsman was crestfallen. 'Majesty, I was mistaken in my judgement,' he told Apepi. 'The lion has not come this way.'

'What now, fellow?' Apepi was making no effort to hide his disappointment and irritation.

'This was the most promising place to look, but there are others. From where we last saw him, he could have crossed the valley, or he may be lying up close to here and waiting for darkness before drinking. There is cover further down.' He pointed back to the stony slopes.

'Where else?' Apepi demanded.

'There is another waterhole in the next valley, but there are Bedouin encamped there. They might have scared off the beast. There is another small water seep below those hills to the west.' He pointed out a low line of purple peaks on the horizon. 'The lion could be at any of those places, or at none,' the man admitted. 'Also he might have doubled back and be on the edge of the plain where there is an abundance of water. Perhaps he has been drawn by the smell of cattle and goats as well as by thirst.'

'You have not the least idea where he is hiding, have you?' Lord Naja demanded. 'We should call off the hunt and get back to the boats.'

'No!' Nefer cut in. 'We have barely begun. How can we give up so soon?'

'The boy is right,' Apepi agreed. 'We must go on, but there is much ground to cover.' He paused for a moment, then reached a decision. 'We will have to split up and search each area separately.' He looked across at Naja. 'My lord Regent, you take your squadron to the Bedouin encampment. If they have seen the chase they will direct you. I will ride to the seep below the hills.' He turned to Trok. 'Take three chariots down the valley. One of the trackers will go with you to search for sign.' To Asmor he said, 'Take three chariots and cast back along the edge of the plain to Dabba, in case he has returned to where he last killed.' Then he looked at Nefer. 'Pharaoh, you cast in the opposite direction, north towards Achmim.'

Nefer realized that he was being given the least promising ground to cover, but he had no complaint. This new plan meant that for the first time he and Mintaka would be away from the direct surveillance of his guardians. Naja, Asmor and Trok were being sent in different directions. He waited for someone to point this out, but they were all so wrapped up in the hunt that no one seemed to realize the significance of this move. Except Naja.

He looked hard at Nefer. Perhaps he was weighing the advisability of countermanding Apepi's orders, but in the end he must have realized that this would be unwise and concluded that Nefer was guarded by the desert as effectively as he would have been by Asmor: there was no place for him to run to, and if he took Mintaka with him on some wild adventure he would have the entire armies of both kingdoms upon him like swarms of wild bees.

Naja looked away from him as Apepi went on to nominate an assembly point, and to give his final orders. At last the ram's horns sounded the mount-up and the advance, and the five columns drove out of the valley. On the level ground they split into their separate squadrons and headed out in diverging directions.

As the last of the other squadrons disappeared among the stark hills, Mintaka leaned even closer to Nefer and murmured, 'At last Hathor has shown mercy to us.'

'I believe it is Horus who has granted us his favour,' Nefer grinned down at her, 'but I will accept this benevolence from whomsoever it comes.'

There were two other chariots in Nefer's squadron, commanded by Colonel Hilto, the old soldier who had discovered him and Taita when they had tried to escape from Egypt. He had served under Nefer's father and was loyal unto death: Nefer knew he could trust him without reservation.

Nefer led them fast, wanting to make the most of the remaining daylight, and within an hour's ride the vast vista of the river plain opened beneath them. He reined in to admire it for a few minutes. The river was an emerald mounted in the luscious green of fields and plantations that enclosed it.

'How beautiful it is, Nefer.' Mintaka spoke almost dreamily. 'Even when we are married, we must always remember that this land owns us, and that we do not own it.'

Sometimes he forgot that she had been born in Avaris and had as strong claim to the land as he had. He felt his heart swell with pride that she loved it as he did, and felt the same patriotic duty.

'I will never forget it, not with you at my side.' She lifted her face to him and her lips were parted slightly. He could smell her sweet breath, and the temptation to reach down for those lips with his own mouth was almost irresistible. Then he felt the gaze of Hilto and the other men on them, and from the corner of his eye saw one smile knowingly. He drew back and looked at Hilto coolly. He had been rehearsing his next order since they had left the rest of the hunting party. 'Colonel, if the lion is here it will probably be lying up somewhere on the slope of the hills down below us.' He indicated the area with a sweep of his arm. 'I want to extend in line abreast. The left flank must be on the edge of the plain and our right up here on the crest of the hills. We will sweep northwards.' He made a wide gesture, but Hilto looked dubious and scratched the scar on his cheek.

'That is a broad front, Your Majesty. It's almost half a league to the valley bottom. At times we will be out of sight of each other.'

Nefer could see that it went against all his military instincts to spread his front too thin, and he went on swiftly to mollify him. 'If we do become separated we will reassemble on the third ridge ahead of us, under that small hillock over there. It will give us a good landmark.' He pointed out a distinctive rock pile four miles ahead. 'If any of us is late to the rendezvous the others must wait until the sun is at that angle before coming back to look for the missing vehicle.'

He had given himself a few hours before they would begin to search for him and Mintaka. Still Hilto hesitated. 'I beg Your Majesty's indulgence, but the Lord Naja charged me most strictly—'

Nefer cut in with a sharp tone and cold expression: 'Do you presume to argue with your pharaoh?'

'Never, Majesty!' Hilto was shocked at the accusation.

'Then do your duty, fellow.'

Hilto saluted with deep respect and hurried back to his own chariot shouting urgent orders to his men as he ran. As the squadron wheeled out down the slope, Mintaka nudged Nefer and smiled. 'Do your duty, fellow!' She mimicked his haughty tone then laughed. 'Please never look at me like that or use that tone to me, Your Majesty. I am sure I would die of fright.'

'We have only a little time,' he replied. 'We must make the most of it, and find a place where we can be alone.'

He swung the chariot back over the skyline so that they could no longer be seen from the river valley or by the chariots lower down the slope, and as they trotted forward they were both craning eagerly ahead.

'Look, over there.' Mintaka pointed to the right. A small grove of thorn trees was almost hidden by a fold in the ground, only the dull green tops showing. Nefer turned towards it, and they found a narrow ravine that had been cut, over millennia, into the hillside by wind and weather, and rare thunderstorms. There must have been subterranean water for the thorn trees were robust. Their thick foliage offered shade and privacy in this hot midday. Nefer drove down the bank and into the shade. As soon as he stopped Mintaka hopped down from the footplate.

'Loosen the harness, and give the horses a rest,' she suggested.

Nefer hesitated, then shook his head. It was against his training: in a detached and unsupported position such as this, he must have the vehicle ready for any sudden alarm or excursion. He jumped down and went to fill the bucket from the waterskin to water the horses. Mintaka came to help him. They worked side by side in silence.

Now that the moment they had both longed for had arrived, they were shy and tongue-tied. Suddenly they turned to each other simultaneously, and spoke in unison.

Nefer said, 'I wanted to tell you—'

Mintaka said, 'I think that we should—'

They stopped and laughed shyly, standing close together in the shade. Mintaka blushed and looked down at her feet, and Nefer stroked the head of his stallion.

'What were you going to say?'

'It was nothing. Nothing important.' She shook her head and he saw that she was blushing. He so loved to watch the colour bloom in her cheeks. She was still not looking at him, and her voice was so soft as to be barely audible as she asked in her turn, 'What were you going to say?'

'When I think that you will be gone in just a few more days' time, I feel as though my right arm has been cut off, and I want to die.'

'Oh, Nefer.' She looked up at him and her eyes were huge and liquid with the turmoil and rapture of first love. 'I love you. I do truly love you.'

In the same instant they both lunged for each other, and their teeth came together with a click. His lower lip was caught between them and a drop of blood oozed from the nick, so their kiss was salt flavoured. Their embrace was unpractised and unrehearsed, clumsy and frenzied. It evoked wild and uncontrolled feelings in both of them. They clung together, moaning with the strength of these new sensations. Even though her body was flattened against his, he tried to pull her closer still, while she clung harder as though to weld their separate flesh into one entity, like potter's clay. She reached up and twisted her fingers into his thick dusty curls and said, 'Oh! Oh!' but her voice was blurred.

'I don't want to lose you.' He broke the kiss. 'I never want to lose you.'

'I don't want to leave you ever – ever!' she gasped, and they kissed again, if possible even more furiously than before. From here onwards they were in unexplored realms of mind and body. They rode together on a chariot that was out of their control drawn by the runaway horses of love and desire.

Still clinging together they sank down on the soft white sand of the wadi bottom, and clawed at each other's bodies as though they were enemies. Their eyes were wild and unseeing, their breathing ragged and broken. The linen of her skirt tore like papyrus parchment in his hands, and he reached through the opening. She moaned as though in mortal agony but her thighs fell apart and she went limp and pliable. Neither had any inkling of where this was leading. All Nefer wanted was to feel his bare skin against her smoothness. It was a deep need on which his very life seemed to depend. He ripped away his own apron and they pressed their bodies together, both absorbed in the ecstatic sensation of her warm young flesh against his hardness. Then without any conscious thought he began to move against her, rocking rhythmically, and she rode his movements as though she were flying in a chariot over rough ground.

Then abruptly she felt something hard pressing imperiously at the very portals of her womanhood, and she experienced the almost undeniable urge to meet thrust with thrust, to help him break through, to welcome him into her soft, secret places.

Then reality rushed back upon her. She kicked out wildly, arching her back and struggling with renewed strength like a gazelle in the jaws of a hunting cheetah. She tore her mouth from his and screamed, 'No, Nefer! You promised! By Horus' wounded eye, you promised!'

He sprang away from her, recoiling as though from a slash with a chariot whip. He stared at her with wide and terrified eyes. His voice was hoarse and panting, as though he had run far and fast. 'Mintaka, my love, my darling. I don't know what happened to me. It was a madness. I did not intend it.' He made a despairing gesture. 'I would rather die than break my oath, and bring dishonour upon you.'

Her breathing was so laboured that she could not answer him at once. She averted her eyes from his naked body, and he went on piteously, 'Please don't hate me. I did not know what was happening.'

'I don't hate you, Nefer. I could never hate you.' His distress was too much to bear, she wanted to throw herself back into his arms and to comfort him. But she knew how dangerous that would be. She used the wheel of the chariot to pull herself to her feet. 'I am as much at fault as you are. I should never have let that happen.' Her legs trembled under her, and she tried to push her hair back off her face with both hands.

He stood up guiltily, took one step towards her but when she recoiled he stopped at once. 'I have torn your skirt,' he said. 'I did not mean to.'

She looked down, and saw how blatantly she was exposed – she was almost as naked as he was. Hastily she pulled the ripped ends together and stepped further from him. 'You must dress yourself,' she whispered, and despite herself she looked down at him. He was so lovely, and she felt desire rise again. She forced herself to look away. He stooped quickly, gathered up the discarded *chiton* and fastened it around his waist.

They stood in guilty, awkward silence. Desperately Mintaka searched for words to distract them both from this terrible moment. Her own body came to her aid. She became aware of a real and pressing fullness in her bladder. 'I must go!'

'No,' he pleaded. 'I did not mean it. Forgive me. It won't happen again. Stay with me. Don't leave me.'

She smiled shakily. 'No. You don't understand. I will be gone for a short while only.' She made an unmistakable gesture with the hands holding her torn skirt together. 'I won't be long.'

His relief was almost pathetic. 'Oh, I understand. I will make the chariot ready.' He turned to the horses, and she left him and picked her way deeper into the grove of thorn trees.

The lion watched her come through the trees towards where he lay. He flattened his ears against his skull, and pressed his body closer to the stony earth.

He was an old beast, past his prime. There were grey hairs in the dark, shaggy bush of his mane. His back had once had a bluish sheen, but now it was lightly frosted with age. His teeth were worn and stained, and one of the long fangs was broken off close to the gum. Although he could still pull down a full-grown bullock and kill it with a single blow of one of his huge paws, his claws were worn and blunted so that it was difficult for him to cling to more agile prey. The previous night he had missed an oryx, and his hunger was a dull, insistent pain in his gut.

He watched the human creature with yellow eyes, and his upper lip lifted in a silent snarl. As a cub his dam had taught him to feed on the dead flesh that they scavenged from the battlefields. He did not have the natural repugnance that most other carnivorous animals feel for the taste of human flesh. Over the years he had killed and feasted upon this meat whenever the opportunity presented itself. He saw this creature come towards him through the low scrub as natural prey.

Mintaka stopped fifty paces short of where he lay, and looked around her. The instinct of the lion during the stalk was to avoid the direct gaze of its prey. He kept his head low to the ground and hooded his eyes to slits. This was not the moment for the attack, and his tail was held stiff and low.

Mintaka stepped behind the trunk of one of the trees, crouched down and voided her bladder. The lion's snout creased into deep wrinkles as he picked up the sharp scent of her urine. It quickened his interest. Mintaka stood again and let her torn skirt drop back around her thighs. She turned away from the lion, and started back towards where Nefer waited.

The lion slashed its tail back and forth, the prelude to the charge. He lifted his head, and the black tufted tail whipped against his flanks.

Mintaka heard the rhythmic swish and thud of the tail, stopped and looked back, puzzled. She looked straight into the yellow gaze of the beast. She screamed, a high-pitched sound that struck Nefer to the heart. He whirled round and in an instant took in the situation: the girl and the crouching beast facing her.

'Don't run!' he shouted. He knew that if she ran it would trigger the feline reflex of the lion to chase. 'I am coming!'

He snatched his bow and quiver from the rack on the dashboard, and raced towards her, nocking an arrow as he ran.

'Don't run!' he repeated desperately, but at that moment the lion growled. It was a terrible sound that seemed to vibrate in Mintaka's bones and make the ground tremble under her feet. She could not control the terror that overwhelmed her. She whirled and ran back blindly towards Nefer, sobbing with each stride.

Instantly the lion's mane rose like a dark aura around his head and he launched himself into his charge, coming straight after her, a dark, tawny streak through the trees. He overtook her as though she were still rooted to the earth.

Nefer stopped dead and dropped the quiver to free both hands, and he threw up the bow. He drew the fletching to his lips and set his aim on the massive heaving chest. Even though the range was short, it was a difficult shot. The beast was coming at an angle, so the deflection was critical, and Mintaka was in the direct line of his fire. On top of that, he knew that a wounding would not save Mintaka. He must drive an arrowhead through the beast's vital organs to pin it down, and give her the chance to get clear. Yet there was no time for precise calculation, the lion was almost on top of her.

It came grunting at each bound, clods and pebbles spurting up under the drive of its great paws. The yellow eyes were terrible. Nefer swung just a touch ahead, allowing a hand's breadth for the drop of the arrow in flight and he yelled, with all the urgency he could muster, 'Down, Mintaka! Clear my shot!'

They had developed a close accord over the weeks in which they had hunted together, and she had learned to trust him implicitly. Even in her transport of terror he could still reach her. She did not hesitate but from full run she threw herself flat upon the stony earth almost under the jaws of the onrushing lion.

In the same instant that she went down, Nefer let fly. The arrow sprang from his bowstring. To Nefer's fear-crazed eyes it seemed to move across the gap that separated them with the leisurely flight of some overburdened bird of prey. It passed over where Mintaka lay, already beginning to drop, seeming tiny, slow and ineffectual against such a massive animal.

Then it struck soundlessly and Nefer half expected the flimsy shaft to snap, be thrown aside contemptuously by the grunting, bounding animal.

Just as the lion's mouth gaped wide, showing the full array of ragged stained fangs, the flint arrowhead disappeared into the thick coating of dark hair that covered its chest. There was no sound of the impact but the slim straight shaft of the arrow slid in after it, until only a hand's span of shaft and the bright feathers of the fletching protruded.

Nefer thought that he had struck the heart. The lion leaped high in a monumental convulsion and its grunting changed to a barrage of continuous roars that shook a cloud of dried leaves from the thorn branches over its head. Then the beast spun in a circle snapping at its own chest, chewing the projecting end of the shaft of the arrow to splinters. Mintaka lay almost under his flying, slashing paws.

'Get away from him!' Nefer screamed. 'Run!'

He stooped and grabbed a second arrow from the quiver at his feet, and ran forward, nocking the arrow as he closed in. Mintaka sprang up. She had recovered enough of her wits not to impede his aim by racing to him for protection, and dodged behind the trunk of the nearest thorn tree.

The movement was enough to draw the wounded lion's attention back to her. Now in pain and fury, rather than in hunger, it lashed out at her. The hooked yellow claws tore a slab of wet bark from the tree trunk behind which Mintaka crouched.

'Come! Here I am! Come to me!' Nefer yelled wildly, trying to pull the lion off her. It swung its huge, mane-shaggy head towards him, and Nefer drew and shot the next shaft with one desperate movement. His arms were shaking and his aim was hurried and wild. The arrowhead took the beast too far back, lancing deep into its belly, and it coughed at its sting. It left Mintaka and hurled itself towards Nefer.

Though it was mortally wounded and already slowing, there was no chance for Nefer to evade this fresh charge. He had shot his last arrow and the quiver lay on the hard ground well out of his reach. He reached down and drew his dagger from the sheath on his belt.

It was a flimsy weapon against this furious beast. The thin bronze blade was not long enough to stab through to the heart, but he had heard the royal huntsman tell tales of miraculous escapes from just such a deadly predicament. As the lion launched itself into the death spring, Nefer fell backwards, not even attempting to resist the beast's weight and impetus. He lay between its forepaws, and the lion opened its jaws to full stretch and thrust its head down to crush Nefer's skull with those terrible fangs. Its breath was so foul, with the stench of rotten meat and open graves, that Nefer felt hot vomit rise in his throat. He steeled himself for the moment and thrust his right hand, with the dagger, deep into the open jaws. The lion bit down instinctively.

Nefer had the dagger held firmly in his fist, with the blade aligned upright, and as the lion's jaws closed the bronze point was driven up through the roof of its mouth. Nefer snatched away his hand before the fangs could crush the bones of his wrist, but the lion's jaws were fixed open by the dagger held between them, and it could not bite down.

It was ripping at him with both its forepaws, the claws fully extended. He wriggled and writhed beneath the heavy body, evading some of the claw strokes, but his apron was ripped from him, and he felt the bony hooks tearing into his flesh. He knew he could not hold out much longer. Involuntarily he screamed at the lion above him, 'Leave me, you filthy creature! Get off me!'

The lion was still roaring and the blood from its skewered palate blew out in a crimson cloud, mingled with its stinking breath and hot saliva, into Nefer's face.

His shouts galvanized Mintaka, and when she peered out from behind the bole of the thorn tree Nefer was a blood-soaked spectacle beneath the lion's bulk. He was being mauled to death, and her own fear was forgotten.

Nefer's bow was trapped under his body, and without it the quiver full of arrows was useless to her. She sprang out from behind the tree and raced towards the chariot. The screams and roars behind her goaded her on and she ran until her heart seemed on the point of bursting.

Ahead of her the horses were terrified by the scent of the beast and its roaring. They reared and threw their heads, kicking out at the traces. They would have bolted long ago had not Nefer secured the locking brake on one wheel so they could only turn in a tight, right-handed circle. Mintaka ran in under their flying hoofs, and jumped up on to the footplate. She seized the loose reins and called to the team, 'Ho there, Stargazer! Hold hard, Hammer!'

On many of their previous outings, Nefer had let her drive, so the horses knew her voice and recognized her touch on the traces. Swiftly she brought them under control, but it seemed to her an eternity for she could hear Nefer's screams and the lion's deafening bellows. The moment she had the pair in hand she leaned over the side and knocked off the brake. She brought the horses round in a hard left-hand turn then drove them forward straight at the lion and its victim.

Hammer balked, but Stargazer held true. She snatched up the whip that Nefer had never used on them, and laid a stroke across Hammer's glossy haunches that raised a welt as thick as her thumb.

'Ha!' she yelled. 'Pull, curse you, Hammer!'

Startled, Hammer leaped forward, and they pounded down on the lion. All its attention was on the shrieking, writhing victim between its front paws, and it did not look up at the chariot bearing down on it.

Mintaka dropped the whip, and instead snatched the long lance from its rack. She had carried it for Nefer during hours of hunting, and now it felt light and familiar in her right hand. Guiding the racing team with the reins in her left hand, she leaned far out over the side panel and raised the lance high. As they ran past the crouching lion, its head was lowered and the back of its neck was fully exposed. The exact juncture of spine and skull in the back of its neck was covered by the dense black bush of its mane, but she guessed at the spot and thrust down with all the strength of her fear and her love for Nefer.

Her lance hand had the impetus of the flying chariot behind it. To her amazement the blade slid in readily, full length through the taut hide, and deep into the back of the animal's neck. She felt the slight tick in her hand as the point found the joint between the vertebrae of the spine and went on to sever the spinal column.

As the chariot raced past, the haft of the lance was plucked from her grip. But the lion collapsed in a loose, inert heap on top of Nefer. It did not twitch again, killed on the instant.

It took her fifty cubits to bring the crazed horses to a halt, wheel them round and force them back to where Nefer lay beneath the huge carcass. She had the presence of mind to throw on the wheel brake before she jumped down from the footplate.

It was obvious how badly Nefer was hurt. From the sheets of blood that covered him she thought he might even be dead. She fell to her knees beside him. 'Nefer, speak to me. Can you hear me?'

To her immense relief he rolled his head towards her and his eyes were open and focused. 'You came back,' he breathed. '*Bak-her*, Mintaka, *bak-her*!'

'I will get this off you.'

She could see that the enormous weight of the dead beast was crushing the wind from his lungs. She jumped up and tugged at its head.

'The tail,' Nefer whispered painfully through a running mask of blood. 'Roll him over by the tail.'

She was quick to obey him, and seized the long tufted tail then heaved with all her strength. Slowly the hindquarters began to swing, the whole carcass flopped over and he was free.

Mintaka knelt beside him and helped him into a sitting position, but he swayed drunkenly and reached out to her for support.

'Hathor help me,' she pleaded. 'You are desperately wounded. There is so much blood.'

'Not all of it is mine,' he blurted, but from his right thigh rose a feathery crimson fountain where the claws had ripped open a blood vessel. Taita had instructed him long and earnestly in the treatment of war wounds, and he thrust his thumb down into the torn flesh and pressed until the jet of blood shrivelled.

'Get the waterskin,' he said, and Mintaka ran to the chariot and brought it back to him. She held it for him while he drank thirstily, and then, tenderly, she washed the blood and filth from his face, relieved to find it unmarked. However, when she inspected his other injuries she had difficulty in hiding her shock at how grievous they were.

'My bedroll is in the chariot.' His voice was weaker. When she brought it to him he asked her to undo the bundle, where she found his housewife roll. She selected a needle and silk thread. He showed her how to tie off the spurting blood vessel. It was work that came easily to her, and she did not hesitate or flinch from it. Her hands were bloody to the wrists as, with nimble fingers, she pulled a thread around the open artery then closed the deeper rents in his flesh. Still under his instruction she used strips torn from his tattered *chiton* to bind up the wounds. It was rough, rudimentary surgery, but sufficient to stem the worst of the bleeding.

'That is all we can do now. I must help you into the chariot and get you to where a surgeon can do the rest. Oh, if only Taita were here.'

She ran to Stargazer's head and led the pair back to where he lay. Nefer was up on one elbow staring longingly at the carcass of the lion that lay beside him.

'My first lion,' he whispered ruefully. 'Unless we skin it, the trophy will spoil. The hair will slip and slough off.'

In the heat of emotion and her terrible concern for him, she lost her temper. 'That is the most stupid piece of man's nonsense I have ever heard uttered. Would you risk your very life for a stinking bit of fur?' Angrily she came to help him to his feet. It took the extreme efforts of both of them to raise him up. He leaned on her with all his weight as he hobbled to the chariot and collapsed weakly on to the footplate.

Mintaka used the sheepskin from the bedroll to make him as comfortable as she could, then climbed up and stood over him with the reins in her hands.

'Which way?' she asked.

'The rest of the squadron will be far up the valley by now, and they will be driving too fast for us to catch them. Also they are heading in the wrong direction,' he told her. 'The other hunters are scattered across the desert. We could search for them all day without finding them.'

'We must return to where the fleet is lying at Dabba. There is a surgeon with the ships.' She had reached the only feasible conclusion, and he nodded. She urged the horses into a walk, and they left the grove and climbed to the high ground heading south once again.

'It's three hours or more to reach Dabba,' she said.

'Not if we cut across the loop of the river,' he answered. 'We can shorten the return by at least four leagues.'

Mintaka hesitated and looked eastwards into the bleak desert, which he wanted her to attempt. 'I might lose the way,' she murmured fearfully.

'I will guide you,' he answered, confident in the instruction that Taita had given him in desert travel. 'It's our best chance.'

She swung the team to the left, marking a blue shale hillock in the direction Nefer had pointed out to her.

When they were strong and well they both delighted in the motion of a chariot running hard over broken ground, and they rode the pitch and roll with young legs. But now, even though she kept the horses down to a walk or a trot, the collision with every stone or hump, the drop into every hole, was transmitted through the rigid chassis into Nefer's torn body. He winced and sweated, but tried to hide his pain and discomfort from her. Yet as the hours wore on, his wounds stiffened, and the pain became unbearable. He groaned aloud at a particularly nasty impact, and slumped into unconsciousness.

Immediately Mintaka reined the pair to a halt, and tried to revive him. She soaked a pad of linen with water and squeezed a few drops between his lips. Then she sponged his pale, sweating face. But when she tried to rebandage his wounds she found that the gash in his thigh was bleeding again. She worked to staunch it, but succeeded only in reducing it to a slow leak. 'You are going to be all right, my darling,' she told him, with a confidence she did not feel. She embraced him gently, kissed the top of his dusty blood-caked head, and took up the reins again.

An hour later she gave the last of the water to Nefer and the horses, not drinking herself. Then she stood as high as she could on the dashboard of the chariot and looked about her at the gravel and shale hills that danced and wavered in the heat mirage. She knew she was lost. Have I drifted too far eastwards? she wondered, glancing up at the sun and trying to calculate its angle. At her feet Nefer stirred and moaned, and she looked down with a brave face and smiled. 'Not much further now, my heart. We should see the river over the next crest.'

She rearranged the sheepskin from the bedroll under his head, then stood up, gathered the reins and braced herself. Suddenly she realized how exhausted she was: every muscle in her body ached and her eyes were sore and red from the sun's glare and the dust. She forced herself and the team onwards.

Soon the horses were showing signs of distress. They had stopped sweating and the salt rime dried white across their backs. She tried to urge them into a trot but they could not respond, so she climbed down, took the stallion's head and led them on. Now she was staggering herself, but at last she found the tracks of a chariot in a sandy valley bottom, and her spirits lifted.

'They are heading west,' she whispered, through lips that were beginning to swell and crack. 'They will lead us back to the river.' She kept moving along the wheel ruts for some time, until she stopped in confusion as she found her own footprints in front of her. It took her some time to realize that she must have walked in a circle and was following her own tracks.

At last despair overtook her. She sank down to her knees, helpless and lost, and whispered to Nefer as he lay, still unconscious, 'I am sorry, my darling. I have failed you.' She stroked the matted hair from his face. Then she looked up at the low hilltop to the east, and blinked. She shook her head to clear her vision, glanced away to rest her burning eyes, then looked back. She felt her spirits surge upwards once again, but still she could not be sure that what she was seeing was illusion or reality.

On the crest of the hills above them, a gaunt figure stood on the skyline, leaning on his long staff. His silver hair shone like a cloud, and the hot light breeze off the desert flapped his skirts against his heron-thin legs. He was staring down at them.

'Oh, Hathor and all the goddesses, it can't be so,' she whispered.

Beside her, Nefer opened his eyes. 'Taita is near,' he murmured. 'I feel him close.'

'Yes. Taita is here.' Her voice was faint, and she held her own throat in shock. 'But how did he know where to find us?'

'He knows. Taita knows,' Nefer replied, closed his eyes and slumped back into unconsciousness.

The old man was striding down the rugged slope towards them now, and Mintaka pulled herself to her feet and tottered to meet him. Swiftly her fatigue fell away and she waved and screamed greetings at him, almost delirious with joy.

Taita drove down the escarpment towards the river and the village of Dabba. The horses responded to his touch, moving to an easy motion that cosseted the wounded boy on the footplate. Taita seemed to have known with some deep instinct just what medicines and dressings Nefer would need, and he had carried these with him. After he had re-dressed the wounds he had led the horses to a hidden water seep nearby, where the bitter water had revived them. He had taken Mintaka up on the footplate and turned the horses' heads unerringly in the direction of Dabba and the river.

Beside him, Mintaka had pleaded with him, almost tearfully, to explain to her how he had known that they needed him, and where to find them. Taita had smiled gently, and called to the horses, 'Gently now, Hammer! Steady, Stargazer!'

On the floorboards Nefer was deep in the drugged sleep of the Red Shepenn, but his wounds were staunched, cleaned and bound with linen bandages.

A red and angry sunset was fading over the Nile like a dying bush-fire. The boats of the fleet were still anchored in the stream, like children's toys in the fading light.

Apepi and Naja rode out to meet them from the village of Dabba. Lord Naja was highly agitated, and Apepi bellowed at his daughter as soon as they were in range of his bull voice, 'Where have you been, you stupid child? Half the army is out looking for you.'

Lord Naja's agitation abated as soon as he came close enough to see Nefer bandaged and unconscious in the bottom of the chariot cockpit. He became almost sanguine when Taita explained to him the extent of Pharaoh's injury.

Barely conscious, Nefer was carried down to the riverbank on a litter and lifted gently aboard one of the galleys by a party of boatmen. 'I want Pharaoh taken up to Thebes with all possible speed,' Taita told Naja, 'even if it means a night journey. There is a very real danger that the wounds will putrefy. This happens with injuries received from one of the great cats. It is almost as though their fangs and claws are steeped in some virulent poison.'

'You can order the galley to sail at once,' Naja said, in front of the company, but then took Taita's arm and led him a short way along the riverbank to where they could not be overheard. 'Bear in mind, Magus, the charge laid on you by the gods. Clearly I discern their divine intervention in these extraordinary circumstances. If Pharaoh were to die from his wounds no person in either kingdom would take it as unnatural.' He said no more but gazed into Taita's face with those piercing yellow eyes.

'The will of the gods will prevail against all else,' Taita agreed quietly, but enigmatically.

Naja read in his reply what he wanted to hear. 'We are in accord, Taita. I place my trust in you. Go in peace. I will follow you back to Thebes after Apepi has been taken care of.' The phrasing of this last remark struck Taita as unusual, but he was too distracted to ponder it. Naja smiled mysteriously and went on, 'Who knows? We may have momentous news for each other when we meet again.'

When Taita hurried back on board the galley, and went to the small deck cabin in which Nefer lay, he found Mintaka kneeling beside the litter in tears.

'What is it, my darling?' he asked her gently. 'You have been as brave as a lioness. You have fought like a warrior of the guards. How can you dissolve into despair now?'

'My father is taking me back to Avaris in the morning, but I should be with Nefer. I am his betrothed. He needs me. We need each other.' She looked up at him piteously, and he could see that she was both physically and emotionally exhausted.

She seized his hand. 'Oh, Magus! Will you not go to my father and ask him to let me go back to Thebes to help you to take care of Nefer? My father will listen to you.'

But Apepi snorted with laughter when Taita attempted to persuade him. 'Place my lamb in Naja's pen?' He shook his head with amusement. 'I trust Naja as I would a scorpion. Who knows what tricks he would try if I gave him that coin to bargain with? As for that young puppy, Nefer, he would be up her skirts as quick as a hawk on a bustard, if he hasn't travelled that road already.' He laughed again. 'I don't want to debase the currency of her virginity. No, Warlock, Mintaka comes back under my wing to Avaris until her wedding day. And none of your magic spells will change my mind on that.'

Sadly Mintaka went to take her leave of Nefer. He was on the edge of consciousness, weak from the blood he had lost and the drug. But when she kissed him he opened his eyes. She spoke quietly, pledging her love, and he watched her eyes as she spoke. Before she rose to leave him, she took the golden locket that hung at her throat. 'This contains a lock of my hair. It is my soul, and I give it to you.' She placed it in his hand and he folded his fingers tightly around it.

So Mintaka stood alone on the bank of the Nile as the swift galley bearing Nefer and Taita breasted the current. With twenty oarsmen a side and a white curl under her prow she headed upstream towards Thebes. Mintaka did not wave at Taita's tall silhouette on the stern, but watched him forlornly.

The next morning there was a final meeting between Apepi and the Regent, Lord Naja, on board the Hyksosian royal barge. All Apepi's nine sons were present and Mintaka was seated beside her father. Apepi had kept her on a tight rein since the previous evening when the ship bearing Pharaoh Nefer Seti had left. From long experience, he knew his headstrong daughter well enough to trust neither her judgement nor her sense of filial duty and obedience when she had set her heart on a course of action.

The farewell ceremony took place on the deck of Apepi's galley, with protestations of mutual trust and devotion to the peace.

'May it last a thousand years!' Naja intoned, as he bestowed upon Apepi the Gold of Eternity, an honour he had created for this auspicious occasion.

'A thousand times a thousand,' Apepi replied, with equal gravity, as the chain of the order, encrusted with precious and semi-precious gems, was placed around his shoulders. The Regent and the king embraced with the affection of brothers, then Naja was rowed across to his own galley. As the two fleets diverged, one to return to Thebes the other to run down with the current hundreds of leagues to Memphis and Avaris, the crews cheered each other out of sight. Garlands and wreaths of palm fronds and blossoms tossed from one vessel towards the other bestrewed the surface of the wide river.

The urgency of King Apepi's voyage did not dictate that his fleet should sail on in the darkness of this moonless night, so that evening they anchored at Balasfura, opposite the temple of Hapi, the half hippopotamus hermaphroditic god of the Nile. The king and his family went ashore and made sacrifice of a pure white ox at the altar in the sanctuary. The high priest disembowelled the bellowing beast, and while it still lived he drew and inspected the entrails to read the auspice for the king. He was appalled to find that the animal's guts were infested with stinking white worms, which spilled on to the temple floor in a seething mass. He tried to hide this hideous phenomenon from the king by spreading his cloak and beginning to make up some mendacious nonsense, but Apepi shouldered him aside and stared at the horrible sight. Even he was visibly shaken, and for once he was subdued as they left the temple and went down to the riverbank where Trok and the officers under his command had arranged a banquet and entertainment for him.

Even the sacred black cockerels of the temple refused to peck at the contaminated entrails of the sacrifice. The priests threw the grisly mess on the temple fire, but rather than consume the entrails the fire, which had burned since antiquity, was extinguished by them. The signs could not have been more inauspicious, but the high priest ordered the entrails to be buried and the fire to be relit. 'I have never seen such an unhappy omen,' he told his acolytes. 'Such a sign from the god Hapi can only presage some terrible event, such as war or the death of Pharaoh. We must pray through all this night for the recovery of Pharaoh Nefer Seti from his wounds.'

On the riverbank Lord Trok had set up pavilions hung

with vivid red, yellow and green curtains to receive the royal family. Whole oxen were grilling over the pits of glowing ash, and amphorae of the choicest wines were cooling in the river waters. Slaves staggered up the bank under the weight of them as one after the other they were drained by the company and Apepi bellowed for fresh jars to be brought.

The king's sombre mood lightened with each bowl he lowered, and soon he encouraged his sons to join him in singing the ribald marching songs of his army. Some were so scurrilous that Mintaka pleaded exhaustion and a sick headache, and she and her slave girls rose to retire to the royal barge anchored offshore. She tried to take her youngest brother, Khyan, with her, but Apepi intervened. The good wine had helped him to throw off the misgivings brought upon him by the divination in the temple. 'Leave the boy where he is, you little vixen. He should be taught to appreciate good music.' He hugged the boy to him in an excess of affection, and held the wine bowl to his lips. 'Take a sup. It will make you sing all the sweeter, my princeling.'

Khyan adored his father, and such public comradeship reduced him to a transport of pride and hero-worship. At last his father was treating him like a man and a warrior. Even though he gagged upon it, he managed to drain the bowl and the company, led by Lord Trok, cheered him as though he had killed his first enemy in battle.

Mintaka hesitated. She felt an almost maternal sense of protection for her little brother, but she realized that her father was beyond reason. With all dignity she led her maids down to the riverbank and, to the ironic and inebriated cheers of the company, they went aboard the barge.

Mintaka lay on her mattress and listened to the sounds of revelry. She tried to compose herself to sleep, but Nefer was in the forefront of her mind. The sense of loss that she had held at bay all day, and her concern for Nefer's injuries, flooded back, and though she tried to prevent them, tears welled up. She smothered her sobs in her pillows.

At last she sank into a black, dreamless sleep, from which she woke with difficulty. She had sipped only a little of the wine, but she felt drugged and her head ached. She wondered what had roused her. Then she heard raucous voices through the side of the hull, and the barge rocked under her as a weight of men clambered aboard. There was drunken laughter and voices, and heavy footfalls from the deck over her head. From their comments it seemed that her father and her brothers were being carried on board. It was not unusual for the men in her family to drink themselves into this condition, but she was worried about little Khyan.

She dragged herself from her bed and began to dress, but she felt strangely listless and confused. She staggered as she climbed up on deck.

The first person she met was Lord Trok. He was directing the men who were carrying her father. It took six of them to handle his huge inert bulk. Her elder brothers were in no better case. She felt angry and ashamed of them.

Then she saw Khyan being carried by a boatman, and she ran to him. Now they have done it to Khyan also, she thought bitterly. They will not rest until they have turned him into a drunkard too.

She directed the boatman to carry Khyan down to the mattress in her father's cabin where she undressed him and forced a distillation of herbs between his lips to revive him. The potion was a cure-all that Taita had mixed for her, and it seemed to be efficacious. At last Khyan murmured and opened his eyes, then fell back immediately into a deep but natural sleep. 'I hope he learns from this,' she told herself. There was nothing more she could do other than leave him to sleep it off. Besides, she still felt lethargic and her headache was unbearable. She went back to her own cabin and, without bothering to undress, she dropped on to the mattress, and almost immediately succumbed to sleep again.

The next time she woke she believed that she was in nightmare for she could hear screams and she was choking on clouds of thick smoke that scalded the back of her throat. Before she was fully conscious she found herself bundled out of her bed, swaddled in a blanket of furs and carried on deck. She struggled, but she was as helpless as an infant in a powerful grip.

On deck the moonless night was lit by leaping flames. They were roaring out of the open forward hatch of the royal barge, climbing the masts and rigging in a hellish orange torrent. She had never seen a wooden hull burn before and the speed and ferocity of the flames appalled her.

She could not stare at it for long, for she found herself carried swiftly across the deck and down the side into a waiting felucca. Her senses returned to her in a rush, and she began again to struggle and scream. 'My father! My brothers! Khyan! Where are they?'

The felucca pushed off into the stream and now she fought with all her strength to free herself, but the arms that pinioned her were remorseless. She managed to twist her head and see the face of the man who held her.

'Trok!' She was angered by his presumption, at the way he was handling her, and ignoring her cries. 'Let me go! I command you!'

He did not respond. He held her easily but he was watching the burning galley with a calm, detached expression.

'Go back!' she shrieked at him. 'My family! Go back and fetch them!'

His only response was to snap an order to the oarsmen. 'Hold the stroke!' They shipped their paddles and the felucca rocked on the current. The crew watched the burning hulk with fascination. There were agonizing screams from those trapped below the decks.

Abruptly part of the after-deck collapsed in a tower of flame and sparks. The mooring cables burned through and the galley swung round slowly on the current and drifted downstream.

'Please!' Mintaka changed her tone. 'Please, Lord Trok, my family! You cannot let them burn.'

Now the screams from inside the hull died away and were replaced by the low thunder of the flames. Tears poured down Mintaka's cheeks and dripped from her chin, but still she was helpless in his grasp.

Suddenly the main hatch on the burning deck was thrown open, and the crew of the felucca gasped with horror as a figure emerged. Lord Trok's arms tightened around Mintaka until it seemed that he would crush in her ribs. 'It cannot be!' he grated.

Seen through the smoke and flames it seemed like an apparition from the shades of the underworld. Naked and covered with hair, great belly bulging, Apepi staggered towards the side of the barge. He carried the body of his youngest son in his arms, and his mouth was wide open, gasping for air in the holocaust of flame.

'The monster is hard to kill.' Trok's anger was tinged with fear. Even in her own distress Mintaka read the meaning of his words.

'You, Trok!' she whispered. 'You have done this to them.' Trok ignored the accusation.

The hair on Apepi's body singed and in a puff of heat was gone, for a moment leaving him naked and blackened. Then his skin began to blister and fall away in tatters. His bush of beard and the hair upon his head burst into flame like a pitch-soaked torch. He was no longer moving forward, but he stood with legs astraddle and lifted Khyan high above his head. The boy was as scorched as he was, and the raw flesh showed red and wet where his skin had been burned away. Perhaps Apepi was attempting to throw him over the ship's side into the river to escape the flames, but his strength failed him at last and he stood like a colossus with his head in flames, unable to summon the last reserves to hurl his son to safety in the cool Nile waters.

Mintaka could not move and she was silenced by the horror of the spectacle. To her it seemed to last an eternity, until suddenly the deck under Apepi's feet burst open. He and his son dropped through, and in a tall fountain of flame, sparks and smoke were gone into the guts of the hull.

'It's over.' Trok's voice was dispassionate and detached. He released Mintaka so suddenly that she fell into the bilges of the felucca. He looked at his horrified crew. 'Row to my galley,' he ordered.

'You did this to my family,' Mintaka repeated, as she lay at his feet. 'You will pay for it. I swear it to you. I will make you pay.'

But she felt numbed and bruised as though she had been beaten with the knotted leather lashes of a flail. Her father was gone, that monumental figure in her life whom she had hated a little and loved a great deal. Her family was gone, all of her brothers, even little Khyan, who had been more a son than a sibling to her. She had watched him burn and she knew that the horror of it would stay with her all her days.

The felucca drew alongside Lord Trok's galley and she made no protest as he picked her up as though she were a doll and carried her on board, then down to the main cabin. He laid her on the mattress with uncharacteristic gentleness. 'Your slave girls are safe. I will send them to you,' he said, and went out. She heard the locking bar placed across the door then the sound of him climbing the companion ladder, and crossing the deck above her head.

'Am I a prisoner, then?' she whispered, but that seemed of little importance in the light of what she had just witnessed. She hid her face in pillows that smelt of Trok's stale sweat, and wept until her tears were exhausted. Then she slept.

The burning hull of Apepi's royal barge drifted up on to the riverbank opposite the temple of Hapi. In the dawn the smoke rose high into the still air. It was tainted by the stench of burned flesh. When Mintaka awoke the smell had penetrated into the cabin and sickened her. The smoke seemed to act like a beacon, for the sun had hardly risen above the eastern hills before the fleet of Lord Naja came sweeping around the bend of the river.

The slave girls brought the news to Mintaka. 'Lord Naja has come in full array,' they told her excitedly. 'Yesterday he left us to return to Thebes. Is it not strange that he could reach here so soon when he should be twenty leagues upriver?'

'Surpassing strange,' Mintaka agreed grimly. 'I must dress and be ready for whatever new atrocity awaits me now.'

Her baggage had all gone up in flames in the royal barge, but her maids borrowed clothing from the other noble ladies in the fleet. They washed and curled her hair, then dressed her in a simple linen shift, gold girdle and sandals.

Before noon an armed escort came aboard the galley, and she followed them on deck. Her eyes went first to the blackened timbers of the royal barge that lay on the far bank, burned down to the waterline. No effort was being made to recover any bodies from the wreck. It was her family's funeral pyre. The Hyksosian tradition called for cremation, not embalmment and elaborate funeral procedures and ceremonials.

Mintaka knew that her father would have approved of the manner of his own going, and this gave her some small comfort. Then she thought of Khyan and averted her eyes.

It was with an effort that she held back further tears as she went down into the waiting felucca and was taken to the bank below the temple of Hapi.

Lord Naja was waiting with all his company assembled to meet her. She remained aloof and pale when he embraced her. 'This is a bitter time for all of us, Princess,' he said. 'Your father, King Apepi, was a mighty warrior and statesman. In view of the recent treaty between the two kingdoms, and the combining of this very Egypt into one sacred and historical whole, he leaves a dangerous gap. For the good of all, this must be filled immediately.'

He took her hand and led her to the pavilion, which had last evening been the scene of feasting and festivity, but where now were assembled in solemn conclave most of the nobility and officialdom of both the kingdoms.

She saw Trok in the forefront of this throng. He was a striking figure in full regimentals. He wore his sword on a gold-studded belt and carried his war bow over his shoulder. Behind him in packed ranks were all his officers, grim, cold-eyed and menacing despite the gay ribbons plaited in their beards. They stared at her, unsmilingly, and she was bitterly aware that she was the last of the Apepi line, abandoned and unprotected.

She wondered to whom she could appeal, and whose loyalty she still commanded. She searched for friendly familiar faces in the multitude. They were all there, her father's councillors and advisers, his generals and comrades of the battlefield. Then she saw their eyes slide away from her face. None smiled at her or returned her scrutiny. She had never felt so alone in her life.

Naja led her to a cushioned stool at one side of the pavilion. When she sat down Naja and his staff formed a screen around her, hiding her from view. She was certain that this had been deliberately arranged.

Lord Naja opened the conclave with a lamentation for the tragic death of King Apepi and his sons. Then he launched into a eulogy of the dead pharaoh. He recounted his numerous military triumphs and his feats of statesmanship, culminating with his participation in the treaty of Hathor, which had brought peace to the two kingdoms torn by decades of internecine warfare and strife.

'Without King Apepi, or a strong pharaoh to guide the affairs of the Lower Kingdom and to rule in conjunction with Pharaoh Nefer Seti and his regent in Thebes, the treaty of Hathor is in jeopardy. A return to the horrors and warfare of the last sixty years prior to the treaty is unthinkable.'

Lord Trok beat his sword scabbard against his bronze buckler, and shouted, '*Bak-her*! *Bak-her*!' Immediately the applause was taken up by all the military commanders behind him, and spread slowly through the entire assembly until it was a deafening thunder.

Naja let it continue for a while, then held up both arms. When silence fell he continued, 'In the tragic circumstances of his death, King Apepi leaves no male heir to the Crown.' Smoothly he passed over any mention of Mintaka. 'As a matter of urgency I have consulted the senior councillors and nome governors of both kingdoms. Their choice for the new Pharaoh has been unanimous. With one voice they have asked Lord Trok of Memphis to pick up the reins of power, to take the double crown upon himself and steer the nation forward in the noble tradition set by King Apepi.'

The silence that followed this announcement was profound and drawn-out. Men looked at each other in blank astonishment, and only then became aware that while they had been absorbed in Lord Naja's address two regiments of the northern army commanded by, and loyal to, Trok had come silently out of the palm groves and surrounded the assembly. Their swords were sheathed, but every gloved hand was on the hilt. It would take a moment only to draw the bronze blades. An air of dismay and consternation fell upon them all. Mintaka seized the moment. She sprang off the stool where she had been hidden and cried, 'My lords and loyal citizens of this very Egypt . . .'

She got no further. Four of the tallest Hyksosian warriors crowded around her, hiding her. They rattled their drawn swords against their shields and shouted in unison, 'Long live Pharaoh Trok Uruk.' The shout was taken up by the rest of the army. In the joyous uproar that followed strong hands took Mintaka and spirited her away through the cheering press. She struggled ineffectually, her movements smothered and her voice unheard in the storm of cheering. On the riverbank she twisted in the arms of her captors and glanced back. Over the heads of the crowd she glimpsed Lord Naja raising the double crown over the head of the new Pharaoh.

Then she was hustled down the bank to the waiting felucca, and back to her locked and guarded cabin on board Lord Trok's galley.

Mintaka sat with her slave girls in the crowded little cabin and waited to learn what was to be her fate when the new Pharaoh returned on board. Her girls were terrified and as confused as she was. However, she tried to comfort them. When they had calmed a little she started them playing their favourite games. These soon palled so she called for a lute. Her own had been lost on her father's barge, but they borrowed one from a guard.

Mintaka held a competition, making each girl dance in turn in the confined space of the little cabin. They were laughing and clapping when they heard the new Pharaoh returning on board. The girls fell silent but she urged them to continue, and soon they were as rowdy as before.

Mintaka did not join in the merriment. Previously she

had carefully explored her surroundings. Attached to her main cabin was a much smaller one, little more than a cupboard, which served as a latrine. It contained a large pottery toilet bowl with a lid and, beside it, a pitcher of water for washing. The bulkhead dividing it from the next cabin was thin and flimsy. The boat-builders had been concerned to save weight. Mintaka had been on board this galley in happier times, when she and her father had been guests of Lord Trok. She knew that the main cabin lay on the other side of this bulkhead.

Mintaka slipped into the latrine. Even above the noise her girls were making, she heard men's voices from beyond the partition. She recognized Naja's clear, commanding tones, and Trok's gruff replies. Carefully she laid her ear against the planking of the bulkhead and immediately the voices were clearer, the words intelligible.

Naja was dismissing the guards who had accompanied them on board. She heard them stump away, and there was a long silence. So long that she thought Naja might be alone in the saloon. She heard the gurgle of wine being poured into a drinking bowl, and Naja's voice, heavy with sarcasm. 'Your Majesty, have you not over-refreshed yourself already?'

Then Trok's unmistakable laugh, and Mintaka could hear from the impediment to his speech that he was indeed already in his cups as he replied to Naja's jibe, 'Come, cousin, be not so severe. Take a bowl with me. Let us drink to the successful outcome of all our endeavours. Drink to the crown on my head, and the one that will soon bless yours.'

Naja's tone mellowed a little. 'A year ago, when we first began to plan, it all seemed so impossible, so remote. Then we were disparaged and overlooked, as far from the throne as the moon is from the sun, and yet here we are, two pharaohs holding between us the whole of Egypt.'

'And two pharaohs gone on ahead of us,' Trok joined in,

'Tamose with your arrow through his heart and Apepi, the great hog, fried in his own lard along with all his piglets.' He shouted with triumphant laughter.

'Pray, not so loud. You are indiscreet, even if we are alone,' Naja rebuked him gently. 'It would be best if we never repeated those things. Let our little secrets go with Tamose to his tomb in the Valley of the Kings, and with Apepi to the bottom of the river.'

'Come!' Trok insisted. 'Drink with me to all that we have achieved.'

'To what we have achieved,' Naja agreed. 'And to all that is to follow.'

'Today Egypt, and tomorrow the treasures and riches of Assyria, Babylon and the rest of the world! Nothing can stand in our way.'

Mintaka heard Trok gulp noisily. Then there was a crash against the bulkhead at the level of her ear. It startled her and she jumped back, then realized that Trok had hurled the empty wine bowl against the panel smashing it to shards. He belched loudly, and went on, 'Yet there is one detail that remains. Tamose's puppy has your crown upon his head still.'

As she listened Mintaka was in a whirlpool of emotion that tugged her one way then the other, and spun her until her senses reeled. She had listened in horror as, dispassionately, they discussed the murders of her father, her brothers and Pharaoh Tamose, but she was ill-prepared for what they had to say about Nefer.

'Not for much longer,' Naja said. 'That will be taken care of as soon as I return to Thebes. It is all arranged.'

Mintaka clamped her hands across her mouth to prevent herself crying out. They were going to murder Nefer as coldly as they had all the others. Her heart seemed to shrivel within her, and she felt helpless. She was a prisoner and without friends. She tried to think of some way in which she could send a warning to Nefer, for only in that moment did she know the full extent of her love for him: she would do anything in her power to save him.

''Tis a pity the lion did not do your work for you,' said Trok, 'instead of only scratching him a little.'

'The beast set the stage nicely. Nefer needs just a little push, and I will give him a funeral even more splendid than I gave his father.'

'You were always a generous man.' Trok chuckled drunkenly.

'While we speak of Tamose's brat, let us also speak of what remains of Apepi's brood,' Naja suggested silkily. 'The little princess was meant to burn with the rest of them, was that not what we agreed?'

'I decided to change that.' Trok's tone had become sulky. She heard him fill another wine bowl.

'It is dangerous to leave any seed of Apepi unreaped,' Naja warned him. 'Mintaka might easily become a figurehead in the years ahead, a rallying point for rebellion and insurrection. Get rid of her, cousin, and that soon.'

'Why did you not do the same with Tamose's girls? Why do they still live?' Trok challenged him defensively.

'I married them,' Naja pointed out, 'and Heseret dotes on me already. She would do anything I ask of her. We share the same ambitions. She is as hot to see her brother Nefer buried as I am. She lusts for the crown almost as much as for my royal sceptre.'

'Once she has felt my honey bee in her little pink lotus flower, Mintaka will be the same,' Trok declared.

Mintaka's flesh crawled. Once again she was thrown into the maelstrom. She was so appalled at the picture that Trok's boast conjured up that she almost missed Naja's next remark.

'So she has you by the testicles, cousin,' Naja said, but his tone was unamused. 'She is too bold and unruly for my taste, but I wish you joy of her. Be careful of her, Trok, there is a wildness in her. She may take more managing than you think.'

'I will marry her immediately and breed her as swiftly,' Trok assured him. 'With a bundle in her belly she will be more tractable. But for these many years past she has lighted a fire in my loins that cannot be extinguished except by her sweet young juices.'

'You should use your head more, cousin, and your prong less.' Naja's voice was resigned. 'Let us hope that we do not live to regret this passion of yours.' Mintaka heard the deck creak under his feet as Naja stood up. 'So, then, may the gods love and protect you, cousin.' Naja took his leave. 'We both have grave matters to attend. We must part on the morrow, but let us meet as already planned in Memphis at the end of the inundation of the Nile.'

During the rest of the voyage downriver from Balasfura, Mintaka was confined to Trok's galley. While they were under way she had the freedom of the deck, but at anchor or at moorings she was locked in her cabin, and there was a guard at the door.

That happened often, for at every temple along the way Trok went ashore to sacrifice and give thanks to the resident god or goddess for his elevation to the throne of Egypt. Though no others knew it as yet, Trok was also giving notice to those gods that he would soon be joining them in the pantheon as their equal.

Apart from these restrictions, Trok's attempts to ingratiate himself with Mintaka made up in perseverance for what they lacked in subtlety. Each day he presented her with at least one marvellous gift. Once it was a pair of white stallions, which she gave to the captain of the galley. The next day it was a gilt and jewelled chariot that had been captured from the king of Libya by her father. She gave it to the colonel of the palace guard, who had been a stalwart of Apepi. Another time it was a roll of gorgeous silk from the Orient, and on another a silver casket of gemstones, which she distributed among her slave girls. When they were decked in their finery Mintaka paraded them in front of Trok. 'These tawdry pieces look well enough on slaves,' she remarked dismissively, 'but not on any lady of quality.'

The new Pharaoh was undeterred and as soon as they sailed past Asyut into the Lower Kingdom he pointed out a lush and fertile estate that extended for almost a league along the east bank. 'That is yours now, Your Highness, my gift to you. Here is the deed of ownership.' Trok handed it to her with a flourish and a smirk.

She sent for the scribes that same day and had them draw up a charter of manumission, freeing all the slaves who were owned by the estate, and a second deed transferring the entire estate to the priestesses of the temple of Hathor in Memphis.

When Mintaka tried to throw off her sorrow and mourning by relaxing with her girls on the after-deck, dancing and singing, playing bao and setting riddles, Trok tried to join in the sport. He made two of the girls dance the Flight of the Three Swallows with him, then turned to Mintaka. 'Set me a riddle, Princess,' he pleaded.

'What smells like a buffalo bull, looks like a buffalo bull, and when it cavorts with the gazelles does so with all the grace of a buffalo bull?' she asked sweetly. The girls giggled while Trok scowled and flushed. 'Forgive me, Your Highness, that is too obscure for me,' he replied, and stalked away to join his officers.

The next day he had forgiven, but not forgotten, the insult. When they anchored at the village of Samalut, he ordered a troupe of itinerant entertainers, acrobats and musicians to come aboard the galley to entertain Mintaka. One of the magicians was a handsome fellow, with an amusing patter. However, his repertoire of tricks was stale and his execution lacking in finesse. Yet as soon as Mintaka learned that the troupe was taking advantage of the peace that had come with the treaty of Hathor and was on its way upriver to Thebes, where they hoped to play before the court of the southern Pharaoh, Mintaka became enthralled with their performances, particularly that of the magician whose name was Laso. After the performance she invited them to join her for refreshments of sherbet and honeyed dates. She gestured at the magician to sit on the cushions at her feet. He soon overcame his awe of her and regaled her with a few stories at which she laughed merrily.

Under the cover of the chatter and giggling of her girls she asked Laso to deliver a message to the famous Magus, Taita, when he reached Thebes. Almost overcome with her condescension Laso agreed readily. First she impressed upon him the secrecy and the delicacy of the task, then slipped into his hand a small roll of parchment, which he hid under his *chiton*.

She felt a great lift of relief as she watched the troubadours go ashore. She had been desperately seeking some means to convey a warning to Taita and Nefer. The parchment contained protestations of her love for Nefer as well as a warning of Naja's murderous intentions, and that his sister Heseret could no longer be trusted as she had joined their enemies. She went on to tell of the true circumstances surrounding the death of her father and brothers. Finally she told of how Trok planned to take her to wife, despite her betrothal to Nefer, and asked Nefer to intervene with all his authority to prevent this happening.

She estimated that it might take the troupe ten days or more to reach Thebes and prostrated herself on the deck to pray to Hathor that her warning would not arrive too late. That night she slept better than she had since the terrible events at Balasfura. In the morning she was almost gay, and her girls remarked on how beautiful she looked.

Trok insisted that she joined him for breakfast on the foredeck. His cooks had provided a lavish banquet. There were twenty other guests and Trok seated himself next to Mintaka. She determined that she would not allow even this imposition to dampen her spirits. Pointedly she ignored Trok and directed all her charm and wit to the officers of his army who made up most of the rest of the company.

At the end of the meal Trok clapped his hands for attention, and was rewarded with an obsequious silence. 'I have a gift for the Princess Mintaka.'

'Oh, no!' Mintaka shrugged. 'And what shall I do with this one?'

'I believe Your Highness will find it more to her taste than my other poor offerings.' Trok was looking so pleased with himself that she began to feel uneasy.

'Your generosity is misplaced, my lord.' She would not address him by any of his numerous new royal titles. 'Thousands of your subjects, victims of war and plague, are starving and stand in greater need than I.'

'This is something special, which will have value to you alone,' he assured her.

She threw up her hands in resignation. 'I am only one of your loyal subjects.' She made no effort to hide her sarcasm. 'If you insist, far be it from me to deny you anything.'

Trok clapped his hands again and two of his guardsmen came down the deck from the bows, carrying between them a large bag of untanned leather. The smell it gave off was strong and unpleasant. Some of the girls exclaimed with disgust, but Mintaka remained expressionless as the two soldiers stopped in front of her.

Trok nodded at them and they loosened the drawstring at the mouth of the bag, then tipped out the contents on to the deck. The girls shrieked with horror, and even some of the men started and exclaimed with disgust.

The severed human head rolled across the planking to

Mintaka's feet, and lay there, staring up at her with a wide and startled gaze. The long dark locks were stiff with dried black blood.

'Laso!' Mintaka whispered the name of the inept magician whom she had entrusted with her message to Thebes.

'Ah! You recall his name.' Trok smiled. 'His tricks must have impressed you as much as they did me.'

In the summer heat the head had begun to decompose, and the smell was strong. The flies came swiftly and crawled on the open eyeballs. Mintaka's gorge rose, and she swallowed hard. She saw that a scrap of papyrus parchment protruded from between Laso's purple lips.

'Alas, it seems that his last trick was his most amusing.' Trok leaned over and retrieved the blood-smeared parchment. He held it so that Mintaka could be certain it was her own cartouche that sealed the message, then dropped the papyrus into the charcoal brazier on which the lamb kebabs were roasting. It burned quickly and the ashes curled into grey powder.

Trok gestured for the head to be removed. One of the soldiers picked it up by the hair, dropped it back into the bag and took it away. The company sat for a long minute in shocked silence, except that one of the girls was sobbing softly.

'Your Royal Highness, your divine father of illustrious memory must have had some premonition of the fate that awaited him,' Trok addressed her gravely. Mintaka was too disturbed to reply. 'Before his tragic death he spoke to me. He placed you under my protection. I gave him my oath, and I accepted this as a sacred charge. You need never appeal to any other for protection. I, Pharaoh Trok Uruk, am your oath man.' He placed his right hand upon her bowed head, and in the other hand he raised another scroll of parchment.

'This is my royal proclamation setting aside the betrothal

of Princess Mintaka of the House of Apepi to Pharaoh Nefer Seti of the House of Tamose. Furthermore, it contains a proclamation of the marriage of the Princess Mintaka to Pharaoh Trok Uruk. The proclamation has been ratified by the cartouche of Lord Naja, accepting and confirming it in the name of Pharaoh Nefer Seti.' He handed the scroll to his chamberlain with a terse instruction. 'Have one hundred copies made of this proclamation and cause them to be publicly displayed in every city in every nome of this very Egypt.'

Then, with both hands, he lifted Mintaka to her feet. 'You will not be alone for much longer. You and I will be husband and wife before the rise of the Moon of Osiris.'

Three days later Pharaoh Trok Uruk arrived at Avaris, his military capital in the Lower Kingdom, and immediately plunged with indefatigable energy into securing to his own hand all the affairs of state, and the trappings of power.

The populace was delirious with joy at the news of the treaty of Hathor, and at the promise of peace and prosperity in the years ahead. However, there was some puzzlement and dismay when one of the first acts of the new Pharaoh was to put in hand another massive enforced draft of men for the army. It soon became clear that he was intent on doubling the size of his infantry regiments and building two thousand more fighting chariots.

The question was asked, but not to Trok's face, where he expected to find a new enemy now that Egypt was once more united and at peace. The loss of working men from the millet fields and pastures to the army resulted in a shortage of food and a sharp increase in the prices in the markets. The expenditure on new chariots, weapons and military equipment necessitated an increase in taxation. There were mutters now that Apepi, despite his warmongering, taxation and contempt of the gods, had not been as bad a ruler as they had believed him to be.

Within weeks Trok ordered work to commence on the extensive enlargements and refurbishment to the palace in Avaris into which he intended to move with his bride, Princess Mintaka. The architects estimated that these works would cost over two lakhs of gold. The muttering grew louder.

Well aware of the rising discontent, Trok met it with the proclamation of his own divinity and elevation to the pantheon. Work was to begin within the week on the construction of his temple on a choice site alongside the magnificent temple of Seueth in Avaris. Trok was determined that his temple would exceed that of his brother god in splendour. The architects estimated that the completion of the temple would require at the very least five thousand labourers, five years and another two lakhs of gold.

The revolt started in the delta where a regiment of foot, who had been unpaid for over a year, murdered their officers and marched on Avaris, calling on the population to rise and join them against the tyrant. Trok met them with three hundred chariots near Manashi and cut them to pieces with his first charge.

He emasculated and impaled five hundred mutineers on stakes. Like a macabre forest, they decorated both sides of the road for half a league beyond the village of Manashi. The ringleaders of the revolt were roped to the back of chariots and dragged to Avaris to state their grievances. Unfortunately none of the prisoners survived the journey: by the time they arrived they were barely recognizable as human – their skin and much of their flesh had been ripped away as they were dragged over the rough ground. Ragged pieces of flesh and splinters of bone were scattered over twenty leagues of the roadway, to the delight of the pi-dogs, jackals and carrion crows.

A few hundred mutineers escaped the massacre and disappeared into the desert. Trok did not bother to pursue them beyond the eastern borders, for this petty matter had already occupied too much of his attention and delayed his wedding by months. He hurried back to Avaris, using up three pairs of horses in his furious impatience.

While Trok was away, Mintaka had tried twice more to send a message to Taita in Thebes. The first of her messengers had been one of the eunuchs of the harem, a fat, kindly black man she had known all her life. There was a special bond between the eunuchs in both kingdoms that transcended race or country. Even during the years when the two kingdoms were split asunder, Soth, for that was the eunuch's name, had honoured this special tie to Taita, and had been his friend and confidant.

However, Trok's spies were ubiquitous and unsleeping. Soth never reached Assyut but was brought back in a leather bag barely alive. He died when his head was plunged into a cauldron of boiling water. His skull, with the flesh boiled away, the bone bleached and polished, the eye-sockets filled with orbs of lapis lazuli, was presented to Mintaka as a special gift from Pharaoh Trok.

After that Mintaka could not bring herself to recruit another messenger, and thus condemn him or her to a gruesome death. Nevertheless, one of her Libyan slave girls, Thana, who knew the depth of her mistress's love volunteered to carry her message. She was not the prettiest of the girls, for she had a cast in one eye and a large nose, but she was loyal, loving and true. At her suggestion Mintaka sold her to a merchant who was travelling to Thebes the following day. He took Thana with him, but three days later she was back in Avaris, bound by wrists and ankles to the side frame of a chariot of the border guards.

Trok dealt with Thana on his return from Manashi: he condemned her to death by love and she was given to the regiment that had led the charge at Manashi. Over four hundred men took their pleasure with her until, at sunset on the third day, she bled to death.

For three days Mintaka wept for her without cease.

The wedding of Pharaoh Trok Uruk and Princess Mintaka Apepi was played out in the ancient Hyksosian tradition that had its origins a thousand years earlier, and a thousand leagues to the east, on the vast treeless steppe beyond the mountains of Assyria from which their ancestors had ridden to the conquest of Egypt.

At dawn on the day of the wedding, a party of two hundred of the relatives and members of the tribe of Princess Mintaka burst into the royal apartments where she had been kept captive ever since her return to Avaris. There was no resistance from the guards who had been expecting this incursion. The members of her faction carried Mintaka away, and rode towards the east in a tight formation with the princess in their midst, shouting defiance and brandishing clubs and staves. Edged weapons of any sort were banned from the festivities.

When the bridal party had been given a head-start the bridegroom led a party of his own tribe, the leopards, in pursuit. The fugitives had shown no urgency to escape, and as soon as the pursuers came into view they turned back and gleefully launched themselves into the fray. Even though swords and daggers were not allowed, two men suffered fractured limbs, and there were a few cracked skulls. Not even the bridegroom escaped without cuts and bruises.

In the end Trok claimed his prize. He snatched up Mintaka with an arm around her waist and lifted her into his chariot.

Mintaka's resistance was not in the least play-acting, and with her fingernails she inflicted a deep scratch down the right side of Trok's face, which narrowly missed his eye, and the dripping blood spoiled the colourful splendour of his costume.

'She will give you many warlike sons!' his supporters shouted in admiration for the ferocity of Mintaka's resistance.

Grinning delightedly at the belligerent spirit of his bride Trok drove her triumphantly back to his temple where the newly appointed priests of his order waited to perform the final rituals.

The temple was as yet only open foundation trenches and tall heaps of stone building blocks, but this did not detract from the pleasure of the wedding guests or the enthusiasm of the bridegroom as they stood under the canopy of woven reeds while the high priest bound Mintaka to him with a halter rope.

At the culmination of the ceremony, Trok cut the throat of his favourite war horse, a beautiful chestnut stallion, as a sign that he placed a higher value on his bride than on this other precious possession. As the animal fell kicking and spurting blood from the open carotid artery the company shouted their acclamation and lifted the couple into the flower-bedecked chariot.

Trok drove back to the palace with one arm still firmly around his bride, taking no chances on a second escape. The army lined the way, swarming around the vehicle, and showered gifts of amulets and good-luck charms into the cockpit. Others held up bowls of wine to Trok as he drove past, and he gulped them, spilling much of it down his tunic where it mingled with the blood from his torn cheek.

By the time they reached the palace Trok was soaked with blood and red wine, sweating and dusty from the ride and the fight to claim his bride, reckless with wine and wild-eyed with lust.

He carried Mintaka through the crowd into their new apartments, and the guards at the door turned back the wedding guests with drawn swords. However, they did not disperse but surrounded the palace, chanting encouragement to the bridegroom and ribald advice to the bride.

In the bedchamber Trok threw Mintaka on to the white sheepskin that covered the mattress and used both hands to struggle with his sword-belt, trying to loosen the clasp and cursing it lustily when it would not yield. Mintaka hit the bed and bounced off it like a rabbit startled from her burrow by a ferret.

She raced to the terrace door and tried to wrest it open. The locking bars on the outside had been put in place by Trok's orders. Desperately she tried to tear open the panel with her fingernails, but the doors were solid and thick and did not even tremble to her onslaught.

Behind her Trok had at last rid himself of the sword-belt and the scabbard clattered on the mosaic tiles. He came lumbering unsteadily after her. 'Fight as much as you wish, prettyling,' he slurred. 'It sets my prong on fire when you kick and scream.'

He placed one arm around her waist, and reached around with the other hand to seize one of her breasts. 'By Seueth, what ripe, juicy fruit is this?' He squeezed hard with fingers callused by the hilt of sword and by the reins of his chariot. The pain shot through her chest, and she screamed and twisted in his arms, raking for his eyes again. He caught her wrist. 'You'll not play that little trick twice.' He swung her off her feet and carried her back to the bed.

'Baboon!' she cried. 'You smelly hairy ape. You foul animal.'

'You sing a sweet love song, little one. My heart and my prong swell when I hear how much you desire me.'

He threw her down again and this time pinned her with

one huge muscular arm across her chest. His face was inches from hers. His beard prickled her cheeks, and his breath smelt of sour wine. She twisted her face away. He laughed and hooked one finger in the neck of her shift and ripped the silk to below her waist.

He prised out her breasts and one after the other squeezed them hard enough to leave red fingermarks on the tender flesh. He pinched her nipples and pulled them out until they darkened in colour, then ran his right hand over her belly. Playfully he prodded one thick finger into her belly button, then tried to force his hand between her thighs. She locked her legs, one over the other, to deny him.

Suddenly he reared up, straddled her, sitting across her lower body with all his weight so that she could not struggle, and ripped off his tunic. Under it he was naked. His body was trained by war, hunting and rough games, and although her vision was distorted by pain, tears and terror, she had an impression of wide shoulders and bulging muscle, limbs thick and thewy as the branches of a cedar of Lebanon.

Still pinning her under him, he twisted round until his belly pressed against hers, and the coarse hair that covered his chest rasped against her breasts. With mounting terror she felt his massive penis prodding against her.

She fought not only for her dignity and modesty, but as if for her very life. She tried to bite his face but her small sharp teeth were smothered in his beard. She clawed at his back and the skin peeled away to jam under her nails, but he did not seem to feel it.

He was trying to force a knee between her thighs, but she kept them locked together, hooking one of her legs over the other. Every muscle in her lower body was frozen in a rigor of fear and revulsion, hard and as impenetrable as a granite statue of the goddess.

Both of them were sweating, he more heavily. It poured from his body, greasing their skin so that his huge member slithered over her belly and pounded at the junction of her thighs.

Suddenly he heaved his upper body free, and swung a heavy blow, flat-handed, across her face. It jarred her clenched jaws, crushing her lips and nose. She felt blood flood into her mouth and darkness fill her head.

'Open up, bitch!' he panted above her. 'Open that hot little slit and let me in.' He was thrusting hard with his hips, and she felt the loathsome thing slithering over her. Even in the pain and darkness of the blow she managed to deny him entry, but she knew she could not last out much longer. He was too heavy and powerful.

'Hathor, help me!' She closed her eyes and prayed. 'Sweet goddess, do not let it happen!'

She heard him groan above her, and her eyes flew open. His face was swollen and dark with congested blood. She felt him arch his back, and he moaned as though in pain. His eyes were wide, sightless and shot with blood. His mouth opened in a terrible rictus.

Mintaka did not understand what was happening. For a moment she thought that the goddess must have heard her plea and struck him through the heart with a divine dart. Then she felt hot liquid spray over her stomach, so hot it seemed to scald her skin. She tried to twist away to avoid it, but he was too heavy and strong. At last the loathsome stream shrivelled and dried up. Suddenly he groaned again and collapsed on top of her. He lay quiescent, and she dared not move lest it incite him to further efforts. They lay for a long time, until in the quiet chamber they both became aware of the lewd cries of the crowd waiting outside the palace walls. Trok roused himself and looked down at her. 'You have shamed me, you little slut. You have made me spill my seed in vain.'

Before she knew what he was about, he grabbed her by the back of her neck and forced her face into the white sheepskin.

'Never fear, I shall use the blood from your nose if I can't have it from your honeypot.'

He rolled her aside and inspected the crimson stain from her bleeding face on the pure white wool with grim satisfaction. Then he jumped to his feet, strode, stark naked, to the shutters and kicked them open with a crash of shattering timber. He disappeared out into the bright daylight.

With a fold of the bed linen Mintaka wiped away the loathsome slime that was clotting on her ivory smooth belly. There were angry red marks on her breasts and on her limbs. Her fear turned to fury.

His sword-belt lay where he had dropped it. Quietly she slipped from the bed and drew the burnished bronze blade from its scabbard. She crept to the door that led on to the terrace and flattened herself against the jamb.

Outside, Trok was acknowledging the applause of the crowd and flapping the stained sheepskin for all to see. 'She loved it!' he answered some shouted comment. 'When I finished with her, she was wide and wet as the delta swamps, as hot as the Sahara.'

Mintaka tightened her grip on the haft of the heavy sword and gathered herself.

'Farewell, my friends,' Trok shouted. 'I am going back for another bite at that sweet fig.'

She heard his bare feet swish on the tiles as he returned and then his shadow fell across the entrance. She drew back the sword with both hands, and held the point at belly height.

As he stepped into the chamber she braced herself and then with all her strength thrust at him, aiming halfway between the pit of his navel and the dense black bush from which dangled the heavy excrescence of his genitals.

Once, long ago, while hunting with her father, she had

watched him aim at a monster male leopard that was unaware of their presence. The cat had been alerted by the twang and hum of her father's bowstring, and instantly leaped aside before the arrow reached its mark. Trok possessed the same feral instinct for danger and survival.

Her thrust was still in the air, when he twisted away from the sharp bronze point. It flew the width of a finger past his hairy stomach, without cutting skin or drawing a drop of blood. Then he clamped both her wrists in one of his huge paws. He squeezed until she felt the bones in her wrist crushing and she had to let the weapon drop and clatter on the floor.

He was laughing as he dragged her across the room, but it was an ugly sound. He threw her back on to the rumpled and sweat-sour bed. 'You are my wife now,' he said, as he stood over her. 'You belong to me, like a brood mare or a bitch-dog. You must learn to obey and respect me.'

She lay face down, pressing her face into the soiled linen, refusing to look at him. He picked up the sword scabbard from where it lay beside the bed. 'This lesson in obedience is for your own good. A little pain now will save us both a great deal of unhappiness and suffering later.'

He weighed the scabbard in his right hand. It was of polished leather, bound with gold and electrum bands, studded with metal rosettes. He swung it down across the back of her naked legs. It slapped across the white flesh and left a welt with the raised pattern of rosettes in brighter scarlet. She was so taken by surprise that despite herself she shrieked aloud.

He laughed at her pain, and lifted the scabbard again. She tried to roll away from him but the next blow caught her across her raised right arm, and the next across her shoulder. She stopped herself crying out again, and tried to hide her distress by forcing a wicked smile and spitting at him like a lynx. This infuriated him, and he struck with more venom.

He knocked her off the bed and followed her as she crawled across the floor. He beat her across the back, and when she rolled herself into a ball he lashed her across her back, shoulders and buttocks. He spoke to her while he kept the blows falling to a steady rhythm, punctuating his words with the exhalation of effort as he struck. 'You will never lift a hand to me again, hah! Next time I come to you, hah! You will behave as a loving wife, hah! Or I will have four of my men hold you down, hah! While I mount you, hah! Then when I have finished, hah! I will beat you again, hah! Like this, hah!'

She clenched her jaws as the blows rained down upon her until at last she could no longer fight back, but mercifully he stepped away, breathing heavily.

He pulled on his stained and dust-streaked tunic, belted the scabbard around his waist and thrust his sword into the scabbard that was smeared with her blood, and stalked to the door of the chamber. There he paused and looked back at her. 'Remember one thing, wife, either I break my mares,' he said, 'or, by Seueth, they die under me.' He turned and was gone.

Mintaka lifted her head slowly and stared after him. She could not speak. Instead she filled her mouth with spittle and spat it after him. It splattered on the tiles streaked with blood from her swollen mouth.

It was long after the waning of the Moon of Isis before the scabs fell off Mintaka's injuries and the bruises faded to greenish-yellow stains on her smooth, creamy skin. Either by design or luck, Trok had not knocked out any of her teeth, broken any bones or left her face scarred.

Since their calamitous wedding day he had left her alone. Most of that time he was campaigning in the south. Even when he returned for brief periods to Avaris he avoided her. Perhaps he was repelled by her unsightly injuries, or perhaps he was shamed by his inability to consummate their marriage. Mintaka did not ponder the reason too deeply, but she rejoiced in being free for a while of his brutish attentions.

There had been further serious rebellion in the south of the kingdom. Trok had responded savagely. He had fallen on the insurgents and had slaughtered those who opposed him, seized their property and sold their families into slavery. Lord Naja had sent two regiments to assist in these operations against the rebels, supporting his cousin and pharaoh, and at the same time sharing in the spoils.

Mintaka knew that Trok had returned triumphantly to Avaris three days ago, but she had still not seen him. She thanked the goddess for that, but it was premature. The summons came from him on the fourth day. Mintaka was to attend an extraordinary session of the state council. So urgent was the matter that she was allowed only an hour to prepare herself. His message warned her that should she choose to ignore his summons he would send his bodyguards to drag her to the conclave. She had no option, and her girls dressed her.

This was the first occasion on which Mintaka had appeared in public since her wedding. With her makeup carefully applied she was as lovely as ever as she took her seat on the queen's throne, below that of Pharaoh, in the lavishly redecorated assembly hall of the palace. She tried to make her expression remote, and to keep aloof from the proceedings, but her reserve slipped as she recognized the royal herald who came in and prostrated himself before the twin thrones. She leaned forward attentively.

Trok acknowledged the herald then called upon him to rise and state his news to the council. When he rose to his feet Mintaka saw that he was in the grip of deep emotion. He had to clear his throat several times before he could utter a word, and then at last he spoke, in a voice so shaken that at first Mintaka did not understand what he was saying. She heard the words but could not bring herself to accept them.

'Your Sacred Majesty Pharaoh Trok Uruk, Queen Mintaka Apepi Uruk, distinguished members of the state council, citizens of Avaris, brothers and fellow countrymen of this reunited Egypt, I bring tragic tidings from the south. I would rather die outnumbered a hundred to one in battle than have to tell you this.' He paused and coughed again. Then his voice rose stronger and clearer.

'I have made the voyage by fast galley downriver from Thebes. Travelling day and night, stopping only to change rowers, I have taken twelve days to reach Avaris.'

He paused again and spread his arms in a gesture of despair. 'Last month, on the eve of the festival of Hapi, the young Pharaoh Nefer Seti whom we all loved, and in whom we placed so much trust and hope, died of the grievous wounds that he received at Dabba while hunting a cattle-raiding lion.' There was concerted sigh of despair. One of the councillors covered his eyes and began to weep silently.

The herald spoke into the silence: 'The Regent of the Upper Kingdom, Lord Naja, who is of the royal family of Tamose by marriage, and who is next in the line of succession, has been raised to the throne in the place of the departed Pharaoh. He purifies the land in his name of Kiafan, he endures unto eternity in his name of Naja, the fear of him through all the world is great in his name of Pharaoh Naja Kiafan.'

The cries of mourning for the dead Pharaoh, and the clamour of acclamation for his successor filled the hall.

In the uproar, Mintaka stared at the herald. Under the makeup she had turned chalky pale and her eyes needed no kohl to make them huge and tragic. The world seemed to turn dark around her, and she swayed on her stool. Although she had heard Nefer's death being planned and plotted, she had convinced herself that it would not happen. She had made herself believe that, even without her warnings, Nefer, with Taita to help him, would somehow avoid the malignant web spun by Naja and Trok.

Trok was watching her with a sly, gloating smile, and she knew he was revelling in her pain. She did not care any longer. Nefer was gone and with him her will and her reason to resist and to go on living herself. She stood up from the throne and, like a sleep-walker, left the hall. She expected her husband to order her back, but he did not. In the general consternation and lamentation few of the other guests noticed her leave. Those who did were aware of her terrible sorrow. They recalled that she had once been betrothed to the dead Pharaoh, and they forgave her this breach of decorum and protocol.

Mintaka stayed in her own chamber for three days and nights without eating. She drank only a little wine mixed with water. She ordered everyone to leave her, even her girls. She would see nobody, not even the physicians Trok sent to her.

On the fourth day she asked for the chief priestess of the temple of Hathor. They were alone together for the entire morning, and when the old woman left the palace she had covered her shaven head with her white shawl as a sign of mourning.

The next morning the priestess returned with two of her acolytes, who carried a large basket of woven palm fronds. They placed the basket in front of Mintaka, then covered their heads and withdrew.

The priestess knelt beside Mintaka and asked her quietly, 'Are you certain that you wish to take the way of the goddess, my daughter?'

'There is nothing further for me to live for,' Mintaka said simply.

The priestess had tried for hours the previous day to dissuade her, but now she made one last attempt. 'You are young still . . .'

Mintaka held up one slim hand. 'Mother, I may not have lived many years, but in that short time I have experienced more pain than most encounter in all their long lives.'

The priestess bowed her head and said, 'Let us pray to the goddess.' Mintaka closed her eyes as she went on, 'Blessed lady, mighty cow of the sky, mistress of music and love, all-seeing, all-powerful, hear the prayers of your daughters who love you.'

Something in the basket in front of them moved and there was a faint susurration like the river breeze in the papyrus beds. Mintaka felt the coldness in her stomach, and knew that it was the first chill of death. She listened to the prayer, but her thoughts were with Nefer. She recalled vividly so much that they had shared together, and in her mind a picture of him appeared as though he still lived. She saw again his smile and the way he held his head so perfectly balanced on his strong, straight neck. She wondered what point he had reached on his dread journey through the netherworld, and she prayed for his safety. She prayed for him to reach the green hills of paradise, and that she should soon be reunited with him there. I shall follow you soon, my heart, she promised him.

'Your beloved daughter, Mintaka, the wife of the divine Pharaoh Trok Uruk, begs from you the favour you have promised to those who have suffered too much in this world. Allow her to meet your dark messenger, and through him to find peace in your bosom, mighty Hathor.'

The priestess ended her prayer and waited. The next step must be taken by Mintaka alone. Mintaka opened her eyes, and studied the basket as though seeing it for the first time. Slowly she reached out with both hands and lifted the lid. The interior of the basket was dark, but there was movement within, a heavy, languid coiling and uncoiling, a glinting of black upon black like oil spilled on water in a deep well.

Mintaka leaned forward to peer within, and slowly a scaled head rose to meet her. As it emerged into the light the hood distended until it was wide as a woman's fan, patterned in black and ivory. The eyes were as shiny as glass beads. The thin lips were curved in a sardonic grin, and the feathery black tongue flickered out between them, tasting the air, and the scent of the girl who sat in front of it.

They stared at each other, the girl and the cobra, for a hundred slow beats of her heart. Once the serpent swayed back as though to strike, then came gently upright once more like some fatal flower on a long stem.

'Why will it not do its work?' Mintaka asked, with her lips close enough to those of the cobra to exchange a kiss. She reached out her hand and the serpent turned his head to watch her fingers come towards him. Mintaka showed no fear. Gently she stroked the back of the cobra's widely distended hood. Instead of attacking the cobra turned half away from her, almost like a cat offering its head to be caressed.

'Make it do what has to be done,' Mintaka begged the priestess, but the old woman shook her head in puzzlement.

'This I have never seen before,' she whispered. 'You must strike the messenger with your hand. That will surely make him deliver the gift of the goddess.'

Mintaka drew back her hand, with open palm and fingers spread. She aimed at the ophidian head of the serpent and was on the point of striking, when she started with surprise and lowered her hand. Puzzled, she glanced around the darkened chamber, into the shadowed corners, then looked directly at the priestess.

'Did you speak again?' she asked.

'I said nothing.'

Mintaka raised her hand again, but this time the voice was closer and clearer. She recognized it with a rush of superstitious fear, and felt the hairs rise upon the back of her neck.

'Taita?' she whispered, looking around. She expected him to be standing at her shoulder, but the chamber was still empty except for the two of them kneeling in front of the basket. 'Yes!' Mintaka said, as though replying to a question or an instruction. She listened to the silence and twice nodded, then softly, 'Oh, yes!'

The priestess heard nothing, but she knew and understood that there had been some mystical intervention in their proceedings. She was unsurprised when the cobra sank back slowly into the depths of the basket. She replaced the lid, and stood up.

'Forgive me, Mother,' Mintaka said softly, 'I will not take the way of the goddess. There is still much for me to do in this world.'

The priestess picked up the basket, and said to the girl, 'May the goddess bless you and grant you eternal life hereafter.' She backed away to the door of the chamber, and left Mintaka sitting in the gloom. She seemed to be listening still to a voice that the old woman could not hear.

Taita brought Nefer back to Thebes from Dabba in the deep sleep of the Red Shepenn. As soon as the galley carrying them moored at the stone jetty below the palace, Taita had him carried ashore on a litter, curtained from the gaze of the common people. It would have been unwise for Pharaoh's critical condition to become widely known in the city. There had been previous occasions when the death of a king had plunged the city and the entire state into wild despair, and caused devastating speculation in the millet exchange, riots, looting and a breakdown of all the mores and conventions of society.

Once Nefer was safely ensconced in his royal quarters at

the palace, Taita was able to work on him in safety and seclusion. His first concern was to examine again the terrible lacerations down the front of the boy's legs and lower abdomen and assess if there had been any morbid changes.

His greatest fear was that the entrails had been punctured and that their contents had leaked into the stomach cavity. If this had happened then his skills would be to little avail. He unwrapped the bandages, probed the openings gently, sniffed the effluent for the stink of faeces, and was greatly relieved to find no taint of that contamination. He syringed the deepest wounds with a mixture of vinegar and Oriental spices. Then he stitched them closed with cat-gut and bandaged them with all his skill, touching them with the golden Periapt of Lostris, commending her grandson to the goddess with each wrap of the linen strip.

Over the days that followed Taita gradually reduced the dosage of the Red Shepenn and was rewarded when Nefer recovered consciousness, and smiled at him. 'Taita, I knew you were with me.' Then he looked around him, still drowsy with the drug. 'Where is Mintaka?'

When Taita explained her absence, Nefer's disappointment was almost palpable, and he was too weak to conceal it. Taita tried to console him by telling him that the parting was only temporary, and that he would soon be well enough to make the voyage northwards to visit Avaris. 'We will find a fine excuse for Naja to allow you to make the journey,' Taita assured him.

For a while Nefer's recovery was encouraging. The following day he was sitting up, and ate a hearty meal of *dhurra* bread and chick-pea soup. The next day he took a few steps on the crutches Taita had carved for him, and asked for meat with his meal. In order not to heat his blood, Taita forbade red meat, but allowed him fish and poultry.

The next day Merykara came to visit her brother, and

spent most of the day with him. Her merry laughter and her childlike prattle cheered him. Nefer asked after Heseret, and wanted to know why she had not come also. Merykara answered evasively and invited him to play another game of bao. This time he deliberately opened his centre castle to let her win.

The next day the terrible news of the tragedy at Balasfura reached Thebes. The first reports were that Apepi and his entire family, including Mintaka, had perished in the flames. Nefer was stricken down again, this time by grief. Taita had to mix him another potion of the Red Shepenn, but within hours the wounds in his leg had turned. Over the next few days his condition worsened, and soon he was at the very frontiers of death. Taita sat with him and watched him tossing and raving in delirium while the livid scarlet lines of morbidity ran like rivers of fire up his limbs and his belly.

Then news came from the Lower Kingdom that Mintaka had survived the tragedy that had engulfed the rest of her family. When Taita whispered these wonderful tidings in his ear Nefer seemed to understand and respond. The next day he was weak but lucid, and he tried to convince Taita that he was strong enough to make the long journey to be with Mintaka in her bereavement. Gently Taita dissuaded him, but promised that as soon as Nefer was strong enough he would use all his influence to convince Lord Naja to allow him to go. With this goal to strive towards, Nefer rallied strongly once again. Taita could see him subduing the fevers and evil humours in his blood by sheer strength of will.

Lord Naja returned from the north, and within hours Heseret came to visit Nefer for the first time since his mauling by the lion. She brought him gifts of sweetmeats, a pot of wild honey in the comb, and a magnificent bao board made of coloured agate, with stones of carved ivory and black coral. She was sweet, infinitely gentle and concerned with his suffering, excusing herself for having neglected him.

'My dear husband, the Regent of the Upper Kingdom, the illustrious Lord Naja, has been away all these weeks,' she explained, 'and I have pined so much for his return that I was not fit company for anyone as ill as you have been. I was afraid that my unhappiness might affect you badly, my poor darling Nefer.' She stayed an hour, sang to him, and related some of the doings of the court, much of it scandalous. At last she excused herself: 'My husband, the Regent of the Upper Kingdom, does not like me to leave his side for long. We are so much in love, Nefer. He is a wonderful man, so kind and dedicated to you and Egypt. You must learn to trust him completely, as I do.' She rose to her feet and then, as though as an afterthought, she remarked lightly, 'You must have been relieved to hear that Pharaoh Trok Uruk and my dear husband, the Regent of Upper Egypt, have agreed for reasons of state to cancel your betrothal to that little Hyksosian barbarian, Mintaka. I was so sorry for you when I heard that such a disgraceful marriage was thrust upon you. My husband, the Regent of Upper Egypt, was against it from the very beginning, as I was.'

After she had gone Nefer sank back weakly on the pillow and closed his eyes. When Taita came to him a little later he was puzzled by the way in which he had relapsed. He removed the bandages and found that the infection in his injuries had flared up again, and that the malodorous pus streaming from the deepest wound was thick and yellow. He stayed with him through that night, exerting all his skill and his powers to ward off the shadows of evil that surrounded the young Pharaoh.

At dawn Nefer was in a coma. Taita was truly alarmed by his condition. It could not be explained entirely by the boy's grief. Suddenly he was startled and angered by a commotion at the door. He was about to call for silence when he heard Lord Naja's commanding voice ordering the guards to stand aside. The Regent strode into the chamber and, without greeting Taita, stooped over Nefer's still form and peered into his pale, drawn face. After a long moment he straightened up and signed to Taita to follow him on to the terrace.

When Taita came out behind him he was gazing across the river. On the far bank a squadron of chariots was practising its evolutions, changing formations at full gallop. Strangely, there had been much warlike preparation since the treaty of Hathor. 'You wished to speak to me, my lord?' Taita asked.

Naja turned to him. His expression was grim. 'You have disappointed me, old man,' he said, and Taita bowed his head but made no reply. 'I had hoped that my way forward, my destiny as predicted by the gods, would be cleared by now of impediment.' He stared hard at Taita. 'Yet it seems that, far from allowing this to come to pass, you have done all in your power to prevent it.'

'This has been pretence. I have made a show of caring for my patient, while in reality I have been fostering your interests. As you can see for yourself, Pharaoh hangs over the great abyss.' Taita made a gesture towards the sick chamber where Nefer lay. 'Surely you can sense the shades drawing in more closely around him. My lord, we have almost obtained our object. Within days the way ahead will be cleared for you.'

Naja was not convinced. 'I am reaching the limit of my patience,' he warned, and strode from the terrace. He passed through the chamber without another glance at the still form upon the bed.

During that day Nefer's condition fluctuated between deep coma and bouts of restless sweating and delirious ravings. When it became clear that the leg was giving him intense agony, Taita removed the linen bandages and found the whole of his thigh grotesquely swollen. The stitches holding the wound closed were strained and cutting deeply into the hot, purple flesh. Taita knew that he dared not move the boy while his life hung on such a slender thread. The plans that he had laid so carefully over the past weeks could not go forward unless he took drastic action. To interfere further with the wound in this condition was to risk a fatal poisoning of the blood, but there was no other course open to him. He laid out his instruments and bathed the entire leg in a solution of vinegar. Then he forced another heavy dose of the Red Shepenn between Nefer's lips, and while he waited for the drug to take effect he prayed to Horus and to the goddess Lostris for their protection. Then he took up the scalpel and cut one of the stitches that held the lips of the wound together.

He was taken aback by the way in which the flesh burst open and at the gagging flood of yellow corruption that poured out. He used a gold spoon to scrape it clean, and when he felt the metal strike some hard obstruction in the depths of the wound, he probed with ivory forceps and gripped the object in the jaws. At last he prised it free. He took it to the light from the doorway and found that it was a ragged splinter of the lion's claw, half as long as his little finger, which must have broken off as the beast was savaging Nefer.

He placed a gold tube in the wound to allow it to drain, then rebandaged it. By evening Nefer's recovery was miraculous. In the morning he was weak but the fever in his blood had abated. Taita gave him a tonic to fortify him, and placed the Periapt of Lostris on his leg. While he sat beside him in the noonday, gathering his resolve, there was a soft scratching at the shutters. When he opened them a crack, Merykara slipped into the chamber. She was distraught and had been weeping. She flung herself against Taita and hugged his legs.

'They have forbidden me to come here,' she whispered and she did not have to explain who 'they' were, 'but I know the guards on the terrace and they let me pass.'

'Gently, my child.' Taita stroked her hair. 'Do not distress yourself so.'

'Taita, they are going to kill him.'

'Who are they?'

'The two of them.' Merykara started sobbing again and her explanation was barely coherent. 'They thought I was asleep or that I would not understand what they were discussing. They never said his name, but I knew they were talking about Nefer.'

'What did they say?'

'They will send for you. When you leave Nefer alone, they say that it won't take long.' She broke off and gulped, 'It's so horrible, Taita! Our own sister, and that awful man – that monster.'

'When?' Taita shook her gently to brace her.

'Soon. Very soon.' Her voice steadied.

'Did they say how, Princess?'

'Noom, the surgeon from Babylon. Naja says that he will push a thin needle up through Nefer's nostril and into his brain. There will be no bleeding or any other sign.' Taita knew Noom well: they had debated against each other at the library of Thebes, arguing the correct treatment for fractured limbs. Noom had come away smarting from the lash of Taita's eloquence and knowledge. He was deeply jealous of Taita's reputation and his powers. He was a rival and a bitter enemy.

'The gods will reward you, Merykara, for daring to come and warn us. But you must go now, before they find out that you have been here. If they suspect you, they will treat you as they plan to do Nefer.'

When she had gone Taita sat for a while collecting his thoughts, reviewing his plans. He could not do it alone, and he would have to rely on others, but he had chosen the best and most reliable. They were ready to act, and they had been waiting for his word. He could delay no longer.

At his bidding the slaves brought kettles of hot water and Taita washed Nefer carefully from head to foot and rebandaged his wounds, placing a dressing of lambswool over the gaping opening in his thigh that was still draining.

When he had finished, he warned the guards not to let anybody pass, and barred all the entrances to the chamber. He prayed for a while and then threw incense on the brazier and in the blue and aromatic smoke made an ancient, potent incantation to Anubis, the god of death and cemeteries.

Only then did he prepare the elixir of Anubis in a new and unused oil lamp. He warmed the mixture on the brazier until it was the temperature of blood, and took it to the bed where Nefer was sleeping quietly. Gently he turned his head to one side and placed the spout of the lamp in his ear. He poured the elixir into the eardrum, a heavy viscid drop at a time. Carefully he wiped away the excess, taking care that it should not touch his own skin. Then he plugged Nefer's ear with a small ball of wool and pushed it deeply into the passage until it could not be detected by any but a detailed examination.

He emptied what remained of the elixir on to the coals of the brazier, and it flared in a puff of acrid steam. Then he filled the lamp with oils and lit the wick. He placed it with the other lamps in the corner of the chamber.

He went back to the bed and squatted beside it. He watched Nefer's chest rise and fall to his breathing. Each breath was slower and the intervals between them longer. At last they ceased altogether. He placed two fingers on Nefer's throat beneath his ear, and felt the slow deliberate pulsing of the life force within him. Gradually that also faded away until it was only a flutter like the wing of tiny insect that took all his skill and experience to detect. With the fingers of his left hand he counted the beating of the life force in his own neck, and compared the two.

At last his own beat was three hundred to a single barely detectable flutter in Nefer's neck. Gently he closed the boy's eyes, placed an amulet on the lids in the traditional preparation of the corpse. Next he bound a strip of linen over them, and another strip under his jaw to keep his mouth from gaping open. He worked quickly for there was danger in every minute that Nefer remained under the influence of the elixir. At last he went to the door and removed the locking bar.

'Send word to the Regent of the Upper Kingdom. He should come immediately to hear terrible tidings of Pharaoh.'

Lord Naja arrived with surprising alacrity. Princess Heseret was with him, and they were followed by a crowd of their intimates, which included Lord Asmor, the Assyrian doctor Noom, and most of the members of the council.

Naja ordered the others to wait in the corridor outside the royal apartments, while he and Heseret came into the chamber. Taita rose from beside the bed to greet them.

Heseret was weeping ostentatiously and covering her eyes with an embroidered linen shawl. Naja glanced at the bandaged body laid out stiffly on the couch, then glanced at Taita with a question in his eyes. In reply Taita nodded slightly. Naja masked the gleam of triumph in his eyes, then knelt beside the bed. He laid one hand on Nefer's chest and felt the warmth slowly ebbing to be replaced by a spreading coolness. Naja prayed aloud to Horus, who was the patron god of the dead pharaoh. When he rose to his feet again he took Taita's upper arm in a firm grip.

'Console yourself, Magus, you did all that we could require of you. You will not lack reward.' He clapped his hands, and when the guard hurried through the door he ordered, 'Summon the members of the council to assemble.'

They filed into the room in solemn procession and formed up around the bed three deep.

'Let the good doctor Noom come forward,' Naja ordered. 'Let him confirm the Magus' pronouncement of Pharaoh's death.'

The ranks opened for the Assyrian to reach the couch. His long locks had been curled with hot tongs and dangled to his shoulders. His beard had also been curled in the fashion of Babylon. His robe swept the floor and was decorated with embroidered symbols of strange gods and magical patterns. He knelt beside the deathbed and began an examination of the corpse. He sniffed at Nefer's lips with a huge hooked nose from whose nostrils protruded clumps of black hair. Then he placed his ear against Nefer's chest and listened, during a hundred beats of Taita's anxious heart. He had placed much store in the Assyrian's ineptitude.

Then Noom took a long silver pin from the hem of his robe and opened Nefer's limp hand. He pricked the point deeply up under the fingernail and watched for a muscular reaction or for a drop of blood to form.

At last he stood up slowly, and Taita thought that there was evidence of deep disappointment in his curled lip and lugubrious expression as he shook his head. Taita reflected that he had certainly been offered untold rewards to use the silver pin to other effect. 'Pharaoh is dead,' he announced, and those around the bed made the sign against the evil eye and the wrath of the gods.

Lord Naja threw back his head and gave the first cry of lamentation, and Heseret, standing behind him, took up the wailing cry in her lovely soaring voice.

Taita hid his impatience while he waited for the mourners to file past the couch, and one by one to leave the chamber. When only Naja and Heseret, Noom and the viziers of the nomes of the Upper Kingdom remained, Taita stepped forward again. 'Lord Naja, I beg your indulgence. You are aware that I have been Pharaoh Nefer Seti's tutor and servant since his birth. I owe him respect and duty, even now in death. I beg you to grant me a boon. Will you allow me to be the one to convey his corpse to the Hall of Sorrow, and there to make the incision to remove his heart and viscera? I would take that as the greatest honour you could bestow on me.'

Lord Naja thought for a while, then nodded. 'You have earned that honour. I charge you with the duty of conveying Pharaoh's sacred body to the funeral temple, and of beginning the process of embalming by making the incision.'

The old warrior, Hilto, came swiftly to Taita's summons. He had been waiting in the guardroom at the palace gates. With him he brought the Nubian shaman, Bay, and four of his most trusted men. One of these was Meren, the friend and companion of Nefer's childhood. He was now a handsome ensign of the guards, tall of stature and clear of eye. Taita had asked for him particularly to take part in these duties.

Between them they carried the long woven basket that the embalmers used to transport their cadavers to the funerary temple. The empty basket appeared heavier than one might have expected.

Taita let them into the death chamber and whispered to Hilto, 'Swiftly now! Every second is precious.'

He had already wrapped Nefer in a long white winding sheet, with a loose fold of linen covering his face. The pallbearers laid the basket beside the couch and lifted Nefer reverently into it. Taita packed bolsters around the body to cushion it during the move, then closed the lid, and nodded. 'To the temple,' he said. 'All is in readiness.'

Taita trusted his bag to Meren, and they moved quickly through the passages and courtyards of the palace. The sounds of mourning and lamentation followed them. The guards lowered the points of their weapons and knelt as the dead Pharaoh passed. The women covered their faces, and wailed. All the lamps had been extinguished, and the fires in the kitchens had been drawn so that no smoke rose from the chimneys.

In the entrance courtyard a squadron of Hilto's chariots was drawn up with the horses in the traces. The bearers laid the long basket on the footplate of the leading chariot and secured it with leather straps. Meren placed Taita's leather instrument bag in the cockpit, and Taita mounted and took the reins. The ram's horns of the regiment sounded a dirge, and the column moved out through the gates at a walk.

The news of Pharaoh's death had spread through the city like the plague. The citizens crowded around the gates, wailing and ululating as the column passed. Crowds lined the route along the river. Women, howling their grief, ran forward and threw the sacred lotus blossoms on to the basket.

Taita pushed the horses into a trot, then into a canter. He was desperate to get the basket into the sanctuary of the funerary temple. The temple of Nefer's father had not yet been demolished even though Pharaoh Tamose had been taken months ago to his tomb in the bleak hills to the west. No temple had yet been built for Nefer: he was so young that the expectation of his life stretched far ahead of him. His death now was untimely and left them no alternative but to use the building prepared for his father.

The tall, rose-coloured granite walls and portico of the temple were set upon a low prominence overlooking the green river. The priests, hastily assembled, were waiting to greet the column. Their heads were freshly shaven and anointed with oil. The drums and sistrum beat a slow tempo as Taita drove up the wide causeway and halted the chariot at the foot of the staircase that mounted to the Hall of Sorrow.

Hilto and his warriors lifted the basket and climbed the staircase with it balanced on their shoulders. The priests fell in behind them, singing mournfully. Before the open wooden doors of the Hall of Sorrow the pall-bearers paused, and Taita looked back at the priests,

'By the grace and authority of the Regent of Egypt, I, Taita, have been charged with lifting Pharaoh's viscera.' He fixed the high priest with a mesmeric gaze. 'All others will wait without while I perform this sacred charge.'

There was a hum of consternation among the brotherhood of Anubis. This was a solecism, against tradition and their own authority. But Taita held the priest's eye sternly, then slowly lifted his right hand holding the Periapt of Lostris. The priest knew, by fearful repute, the power of that relic. 'As the Regent of Egypt has decreed,' he capitulated. 'We will pray without while the Magus performs his duty.'

Taita led Hilto and the bearers through the doorway and they solemnly laid the basket on the floor beside the black diorite slab in the centre of the Hall of Sorrow. Taita glanced at Hilto, and the grizzled old commander marched to the doors with great dignity and shut them in the faces of the assembled priests. Then he hurried back to Taita's side. Between them they opened the basket and lifted out Nefer's wrapped body. They laid it on the black slab.

Taita turned back the fold of cloth that covered Nefer's face. He looked pale and lovely as an ivory carving of the young god Horus. Gently Taita turned his head to one side, and nodded at Bay who placed the leather instrument bag close to his right hand and opened it. Taita selected the ivory forceps, slipped the points into Nefer's ear and drew out the woollen plug. He filled his own mouth with dark ruby-coloured liquid from a glass jar, and through a gold tube carefully sluiced the dregs of the elixir of Anubis from Nefer's eardrums. When he looked deep into the ear passages he was relieved to see that there was no inflammation. Next he introduced a soothing ointment into the ear orifices and replugged them. Bay had the antidote to the elixir ready in another phial. When he opened the stopper it released a sharp odour of camphor and sulphur. Hilto helped them to lift Nefer into a sitting position and Taita administered the entire contents of the phial.

Meren and the others had been watching this with blank incomprehension. Suddenly Nefer coughed harshly and, with superstitious dread, they sprang back from the slab and made the sign against evil. Taita massaged Nefer's bare back and he coughed again, vomiting a little yellow bile. While Taita kept working steadily at reviving him, Hilto ordered his men to their knees and made them swear a dreadful oath of secrecy as to all that they were witnessing. Shaken and pale they swore their lives into jeopardy.

Taita placed his ear to Nefer's back, listened for a while then nodded. He massaged him again, and listened once more. He signed to Bay, who took a twist of dried herbs from the bag and lit the end at one of the temple lamps. He held it under Nefer's nose. The boy sneezed and tried to turn his head away. Satisfied at last Taita rewrapped him in the linen sheet, and made another sign to Bay and Hilto.

The three turned back to the basket. The others gaped as Taita lifted out the false bottom and revealed another corpse laid in the compartment beneath. This body also was wrapped in a white linen winding-sheet.

'Come!' Hilto ordered. 'Lift it out!'

Under Taita's sharp eye and Hilto's stern instruction they exchanged the two bodies. They laid Nefer in the hidden compartment in the bottom of the basket, but did not yet replace the false bottom. Bay squatted beside the basket to watch Nefer and to check his condition. The others laid the strange corpse on the diorite slab.

Taita swept away the winding sheet and revealed the body of a youth of about the same age and bodily shape of Nefer. He had the same thick dark hair. It had been Hilto's responsibility to procure this corpse. In the present climate in the land this had not been difficult. The plague was still flourishing in the poorer outlying areas of the nome. In addition, there were the nightly gleanings from the streets and alleys of the city, the victims of brawling, outright murder, or footpads.

Hilto had considered all these sources. However, in the end he had found, in circumstances so perfect to the quest that they could not have been coincidental, the ideal substitute for the young Pharaoh. The city bailiffs had arrested this lad in the very act of slitting the purse of one of the most influential millet merchants in Thebes, and the magistrates had not hesitated to sentence him to death by strangulation. The condemned lad was so like in body and general complexion to Nefer as to be able to pass as his brother. In addition he was well set-up and healthy, not like the starvelings and plague victims. Hilto had spoken to the commander of the city guards who had been charged with carrying out the execution, and during this friendly exchange three heavy gold rings had found their way into that worthy's purse. It was agreed that the strangulation be delayed until Hilto gave him the word, and that it would be carried out with as little apparent damage to the victim as the executioner's skill could encompass. The prisoner had been given justice that very morning and his body was not yet cold.

The canopic jars were arranged in the small shrine at the end of the hall. Taita ordered Meren to fetch them and open the stoppers ready for filling. While he was doing this, Taita rolled the corpse over and made a sweeping incision down his left side. There was little time for surgical finesse. He thrust his hand into the opening and drew forth the viscera then, using both hands, he worked the scalpel deep into the interior of the corpse. First he cut through the diaphragm to gain access to the chest cavity, then reached deeper, past the lungs, liver and spleen, until he could sever the windpipe above its juncture with the lungs. Finally he rolled the corpse over, ordered Meren to hold the buttocks apart and with sure strokes freed the sphincter muscles of the anus. Now all the contents of the interior of the chest and abdomen were unanchored.

He brought them out on to the diorite slab in a single mass. Meren blanched, swayed on his feet and clapped his hand over his mouth.

'Not on the floor, in the sink,' Taita ordered brusquely. Meren had fought against Apepi's regiments in the north. He had killed a man and been unaffected by the carnage of the battlefield, but now he fled to the stone basin in the corner and puked noisily into it.

Bloodied to the elbows, Taita began to separate the liver, lungs, stomach and entrails into piles. As soon as this was done he took the entrails and stomach to the sink, wherein already reposed Meren's contribution. He flushed out the contents of the dismembered stomach and entrails and packed them into their jars. He filled every jar with the pickling natron salts, and sealed the stoppers. Then he washed his hands and arms in the bronze basins filled with water expressly for that purpose.

He glanced enquiringly at Bay, and the Nubian nodded his bald, scarified head, reassuring Taita as to Nefer's condition. Working with controlled haste Taita stitched the abdominal incision closed. Then he bandaged the head until its features were hidden. When that was done, he and Hilto carried the corpse to the large natron bath and lowered it into the harsh alkali mixture, until only the bandaged head was not immersed. It would remain in the bath, with the head covered, for the next sixty days. At the end of that time the priests would remove the bandage, and discover the substitution. By that time, however, Taita and Nefer would be far away.

It took only a little longer to sluice down the slab with leather buckets of water, and to pack Taita's instruments, before they were ready to leave. Taita knelt beside the basket in which Nefer lay, and laid a hand on his naked chest to feel the warmth of his skin and to check his breathing. It was slow and even. He drew down one eyelid and watched the pupil react to the light. Satisfied, he stood up and gestured for Hilto and Bay to cover the hidden compartment. When this was done and they began to replace the basket lid, Taita stopped them. 'Leave it open,' he ordered. 'Let the priests see that it is empty.'

The bearers lifted the basket by its handles and Taita led them to the doors. As they approached Hilto threw them open, and the assembly of priests craned forward. They gave the empty basket only a cursory glance as it was carried out, then rushed into the Hall of Sorrow with almost indecent haste to take over the duties that had been usurped from them.

Ignored by the crowds that had gathered outside the temple, Taita's men loaded the basket on to the leading chariot and drove in column back to the city.

When they entered the main gates they found the narrow streets almost deserted. The populace had either flocked to the funerary temple to pray for the young pharaoh, or they had hurried to the palace to await the announcement of his successor, although there was little doubt in anyone's mind as to who would be the next pharaoh of the upper kingdom.

Hilto drove the chariot to the guards' barracks near the east gate, and the basket was carried through the back entrance of his private quarters. Here, everything was in readiness to receive Nefer. They lifted him out of the bottom compartment and Taita, with Bay assisting him, went to work to revive Nefer fully. Within hours he was well enough to eat a little millet bread and drink a bowl of warm mare's milk and honey.

At last Taita judged it safe to leave him for a while in Bay's charge, and drove through the narrow empty streets. Ahead of him he heard the sudden din of wild cheering. When he reached the environs of the palace he found himself enveloped in a dense crowd of citizens celebrating the ascension of the new pharaoh. 'Eternal life to His Sacred Majesty Pharaoh Naja Kiafan!' they howled, with loyal fervour, and passed the wine jugs from hand to hand.

So thick were the crowds that Taita was forced to leave the chariot with Meren to go the rest of the way on foot. At the palace gate the guards recognized him, and used the butts of their spears to clear the way for him to pass. Once he was in the grounds he hurried to the great hall, and there he found another press of obsequious humanity. All the military officers, courtiers and state dignitaries were waiting to swear loyalty and fealty to the new pharaoh, but Taita's reputation and his unnerving gaze ensured that the crowd made way for him to pass to the front ranks.

Pharaoh Naja Kiafan and his queen were in the private cabinet beyond the doors at the end of the hall, but Taita had to wait only a short while before he was granted access to the royal presence.

To his astonishment he found that Naja was already wearing the double crown, and holding the flail and the crook crossed over his chest. Beside him Queen Heseret seemed to have blossomed like the desert rose under the caress of rain. She was as lovely as Taita had ever known her, pale and serene under her makeup, her eyes made enormous by skilfully applied kohl.

When Taita entered Naja dismissed those around him and soon the three were alone. This, in itself, was a sign of high favour. Then Naja laid aside the flail and the crook and came to embrace Taita. 'Magus, I should never have doubted you,' he said, his voice even more sonorous and commanding than before. 'You have earned my gratitude.' He took from his right hand a magnificent ring of gold and ruby, and placed it on Taita's right index finger. 'This is but a small token of my favour.' Taita wondered that he had placed such a powerful talisman in his hands: only a lock of Naja's hair or the clippings of his nails would have been more potent.

Heseret came forward and kissed him. 'Dearest Taita, you have always been faithful to my family. You shall have gold, land and influence beyond anything you have ever coveted.'

After all these years she knew so little of him. 'Your generosity is exceeded only by your beauty,' he said, and she simpered. Then he turned back to Naja. 'I have done what the gods required of me, Your Grace. But it has cost me dear. It is not a light or easy matter to go against my sense of duty and the dictates of my own heart. You know that I loved Nefer. Now I owe you that same duty and love. But for a space I must mourn Nefer, and make my peace with his shade.'

'It would be strange indeed if you did not feel for the dead Pharaoh,' Naja agreed. 'What do you wish of me, Magus? You have only to speak the words.'

'Your Grace, I ask your dispensation to go out into the desert to be alone for a time.'

'How long?' Naja asked, and Taita could see he was alarmed by the thought of losing the key to eternal life, which he truly believed Taita held in his hands.

'Not too long, Majesty,' Taita assured him.

Naja thought about it for a while. He was never a man for hasty decisions. At last he sighed and went to the low table upon which stood stylus and papyrus. Swiftly he wrote out a safe pass and sealed it with his royal cartouche. It was clear that the seal had been carved long ago in anticipation of his succession. While Naja waited for the ink to dry he said, 'You may absent yourself until the next inundation of the Nile begins, but then you must return to me. This safe-conduct will allow you to travel at large and to avail yourself of whatever food and equipment you may need from my royal storehouses anywhere in my domains.'

Taita prostrated himself in gratitude, but Naja lifted him to his feet in another extraordinary act of condescension. 'Go, Magus! But return to us on the appointed day to receive the rewards you so richly deserve.'

Clutching the roll of papyrus Taita backed towards the door, making the signs of blessing and benediction.

They left Thebes in the early hours of the next morning while most of the city still slept and even the guards at the east gate were yawning and heavy-eyed.

Nefer was laid in the back of the wagon drawn by a team of four horses. These draught animals had been chosen carefully by Hilto. They were strong and healthy, but not exceptional in any way that might excite envy or comment. The wagon was loaded with essential supplies and the equipment they might need once they had left the river valley. Hilto was dressed as a wealthy farmer, Meren as his son and Bay as their slave.

Nefer was laid on a straw mattress in the bed of the wagon, under a screen of tanned leather. He was now fully conscious and able to understand all that Taita had to tell him. Despite the royal safe-conduct the sergeant of the guard was officious. He did not recognize Taita under his hood, so he climbed into the back of the wagon to inspect the contents. When he pulled back the screen and Nefer peered out at him with his gaunt, pale features spotted with the unmistakable scarlet stigmata of the plague that Taita had applied, the sergeant of the guard swore with horror and leaped down from the wagon signing so vehemently against evil that he dropped his lamp, which shattered at his feet.

'Get you gone!' he shouted frantically at Hilto on the reins. 'Take that filthy poxy wretch out of the city.'

Twice more during the days that it took them to cross the littoral plain of the river and to reach the hills that marked the frontiers of the cultivated lands and the desert they were stopped by military patrols. Each time the royal scroll and the plague victim were enough to send them on their way again with only the briefest delay.

It was clear from the attitude of the patrols that in Thebes the substitution of corpses had not been discovered, and that no alarm had been raised. All the same Taita was relieved when they climbed the hills into the desert and followed the old trade route eastwards towards the Red Sea.

Now Nefer was able to climb down from his bed in the wagon, and for short periods limp along beside it. At first it was clear that, despite his denials, the leg was painful, but soon he was walking more easily and for longer periods.

They rested for three days at the ancient ruined city of Gallala. They refilled the waterskins at the meagre and bitter well and let the horses recover from the rigours of the hard, stony road. Bay and Taita tended their hocks and hoofs. When they were fit to resume the journey, they turned aside from the known way: travelling in the cool of the night, they took the path known only to Taita that led to Gebel Nagara. Bay and Hilto swept their back-trail and covered all signs of their passage.

They arrived at the cave in the middle of a night lit by bright stars. There was not enough water in the tiny seep to supply so many men and horses, so once the wagon was unloaded Hilto and Bay started back, leaving only Meren to serve Taita and Nefer. Hilto had resigned from his regiment on the pretext of ill-health, so he was free, with

Bay, to return with every full moon to bring supplies, medicine and news from Thebes.

The first month at Gebel Nagara passed swiftly. In the clean, dry desert air Nefer's wounds closed without further reverses, and soon he was limping out into the desert to hunt with Meren. They startled the desert hares and bowled them over with their throwing sticks, or Taita sat on the crags of the hills above the spring and worked his charm of concealment to entice the herds of gazelle within arrow shot.

At the end of that month Hilto returned from Thebes with Bay. They brought the news that Taita's subterfuge had not yet been discovered and Pharaoh Naja Kiafan, along with all the populace, still believed that Nefer's corpse was pickling in the natron bath in the Hall of Sorrow.

They also brought news of insurrections in the Lower Kingdom, and the terrible reprisals by Pharaoh Trok at Manashi. Unrest had also flared in the Upper Kingdom where Naja, like Trok, had increased taxation and ordered an enlistment of men into the army. 'The people are angry that there should be such an enlargement of the armed forces when there is peace throughout the land,' Hilto reported. 'I think that the armed insurrection will soon spread to the Upper Kingdom, where Naja will deal with it as kindly as Trok has in the north. Those who cheered the ascension of these two pharaohs will soon have reason to regret it.'

'What other news have you from the Lower Kingdom?' Nefer asked eagerly. Hilto launched into a long recitation of trade news and millet prices, of the visit of the Assyrian special envoy to the court of Pharaoh Trok. Nefer listened impatiently, and when Hilto had finished he asked, 'What news is there of Princess Mintaka?'

Hilto looked puzzled. 'None that I know of. I should think she is in Avaris, but I cannot be certain.'

On the incoming leg of his journey Hilto had crossed the spoor of a large herd of oryx, and asked Taita's permission to follow them up and hunt them. Dried venison would eke out their supplies, so Taita agreed readily. But he decreed that Nefer was not yet strong enough to join the hunting party. Strangely, this did not seem to make Nefer unhappy: instead, he suggested that Taita go out with the hunting party to use his powers to find the game, and to conceal the hunters when they closed in.

As soon as he was alone in the cave, Nefer unpacked the small cedarwood chest of fresh papyrus scrolls and writing material that Hilto had brought him, and began to compose a letter to Mintaka. He knew with all certainty that by now the reports of his death would have been received in Avaris. He remembered his own terrible suffering when he had heard the false reports of Mintaka's death with her family at Balasfura, and he wanted to spare her the same kind of agony. He wanted also to explain that it was Naja and Trok who had annulled their betrothal, but that as far as he, Nefer, was concerned he still loved her beyond his own hope of eternal life, and would never rest until she was his wife.

All this had to be couched in language that, should the scroll fall into the wrong hands, would be meaningless to any person other than Mintaka.

He saluted her in his opening as 'The First Star'. She would remember how, when they had discussed the derivation of her name, she had told him, 'I am called after the third star in the belt of the celestial Hunter.'

He had replied, 'No, not the third. The very first in all the firmament.'

He drew the symbols of the hieratic with great care – he had always excelled at penmanship. He signed himself as the 'Fool from Dabba', sure that she would recognize the reference to his solecism when they had been alone in the desert.

That evening when the hunters had returned and they were feasting on fresh oryx steaks, Nefer waited his opportunity to speak to Hilto in private. This came when Taita left the circle around the camp fire to stalk out into the desert night for a while. Hilto had brought several large jars of beer among the load of supplies from Thebes, and Taita had enjoyed a bowl or two, but one of the few signs he showed of his age was the rate at which the brew passed through him.

As soon as he was out of earshot, Nefer leaned closer to Hilto and whispered, 'I have a special duty for you to perform for me.'

'I shall be greatly honoured, Your Majesty.'

Nefer passed him the tiny roll of papyrus. 'Guard this with your very life,' he ordered, and when Hilto had hidden it in his shawl Nefer gave him the orders for its delivery to the princess in Avaris. He ended with a further caution: 'Tell nobody of this. Not even the Magus. On your sacred oath!'

The following evening Hilto and Bay left Gebel Nagara at the setting of the sun, when the air had started to cool. They made their loyal obeisance to Nefer, asked Taita for his blessing and a charm of protection, then struck out into the starlit wilderness. The horses toiled up the first slope of the dune hills and into the jumble of moon silver rocks that crackled as they cooled in the night.

Walking ahead of the horses, Bay suddenly recoiled, gave a startled exclamation in his savage tongue and reached for the lion-bone charm on his necklace. He pointed it at the strange shape that had emerged from the shadows of the rocks.

Hilto was even more agitated, 'Stand aside, evil shade,' he shouted, cracked his whip, and made the sign against evil then gabbled an incantation to turn aside all ghosts and hobgoblins.

'Peace, Hilto!' The apparition spoke at last. The moon

was so bright that it threw a long shadow along the shale-hard earth and made the head of the creature glow like molten silver in the crucible. 'It is I, Taita the Magus.'

'It cannot be you!' Hilto shouted. 'I left Taita at Gebel Nagara at sunset. I know you. You are some dreadful shade from the netherworld, pretending to be the Magus.'

Taita strode forward and seized Hilto's whip hand. 'Feel the warmth of my flesh,' he said, then lifted Hilto's hand to his face. 'Feel my face, and listen to my voice.'

However, it was only when Bay had touched Taita's breast with the lion bone, smelt his breath for the stench of the tomb and declared him to be who he claimed he was that the old warrior was reluctantly convinced. 'But how did you reach this place ahead of us?' he demanded plaintively.

'These are the ways of the adept,' Bay told him mysteriously. 'It is best never to ask that question.'

'Hilto, you have something on your person that places all of us in mortal danger.' Taita cut through the trivialities. 'It exudes the smell of death and confusion.'

'I cannot think what that might be,' Hilto said uneasily.

'It is something that was entrusted to you by the very Egypt,' Taita insisted, 'and you know it well enough.'

'By the very Egypt.' Hilto scratched his beard, and shook his head.

Taita held out his hand, and Hilto sighed and capitulated without further resistance. He reached into the leather purse on his belt and brought out the roll of parchment. Taita took it from him. 'Say nothing of this,' Taita warned him, 'not to anybody, not to Pharaoh himself. Do you hear me, Hilto?'

'I hear you, Magus.'

Taita held the papyrus in his right hand and stared hard at it. After a few seconds a tiny glowing spot appeared on the scroll, a wisp of smoke curled up into the night air, then abruptly it burst into flame.

Taita let it burn out between his fingers without flinching at the heat, then crumbled the ashes to dust.

''Tis magic,' Hilto gasped.

'A simple feat,' Bay muttered, 'one that even an apprentice could perform.'

Taita raised his right hand in benediction. 'May the gods keep you safe during your journey,' he said, and watched the wagon roll away and merge with the gloom.

When Taita stood once again beside the small hearth fire in the cave of Gebel Nagara, warming his old bones from the desert chill, he studied Nefer's sleeping form covered by a sheepskin, against the back wall.

He felt no anger at the boy's pathetic attempt to outwit him. Age had not withered his humanity, or dimmed his memories of the torments of passion, and he empathized with Nefer's wish to allay Mintaka's fears and her suffering. Added to which was the deep affection, verging on love, that he had conceived for Mintaka.

He would never confront Nefer with what might have been the consequences of this deed of compassion. He would allow him the opiate of believing that Mintaka would soon know that he still lived.

He squatted down beside Nefer and, without touching him, gently worked his way into the boy's inner being. From long exercise of this power over his patient, he achieved it readily. Nefer stirred, groaned and gabbled something that made no sense. Even in deep sleep Taita's power, cast like a web over him, had touched him and brought him almost awake.

His body has journeyed well along the road to full recovery. Taita delved deeper. His spirit is strong, and he has lost nothing by the ordeal through which he has passed.

It will not be long now before we can move on to our next endeavour.

He went back to the fire, and placed a few more acacia sticks upon it. Then he settled back, not to sleep, for at his age he needed only a few hours each night, but to open his mind to the currents generated by events, some distant and others much closer. He let them eddy around him as though he were a rock in the stream of existence.

The next moon passed more swiftly than the last, as Nefer grew stronger and more restless. Each day his limp became less noticeable until at last it disappeared. Soon he was racing Meren from the valley floor to the crest of the hills. These contests became a regular part of their lives at the oasis. At first Meren won easily, but soon that changed.

At dawn on the twentieth day after the departure of Hilto, they started at the mouth of the cave and flew across the stony valley bottom shoulder to shoulder, but when they started the climb up the dune face Nefer edged ahead. Halfway up he unleashed a sudden, powerful rush and left Meren struggling after him. On the crest of the hill he turned back and laughed down at Meren, placing his hands on his hips in a triumphant gesture. In the dawn wind his long dense tresses floated on his shoulders. The early sun was rising behind him and the golden rays cast a nimbus of light around his head.

Taita had watched it all from below, and was about to turn back into the cave when an eerie sound in the desert silence stopped him. He lifted his face to the sky to see a dark speck describing a high circle against the blue, and felt the divine presence of the god close at hand. The cry sounded again, small and faint, but it pierced to the heart: the unforgettable cry of a royal falcon.

On the crest of the dune Nefer heard it also, and turned his head to search for the source. He picked out the tiny shape and lifted both hands towards it. As though the gesture was a command the falcon dropped into a stoop, seeming to swell in size. The wind across its cocked wings sighed as it dived straight at Nefer. If it struck at that speed it would rip flesh and break bone, but Nefer did not flinch as it came straight for his upturned face.

At the last possible second the falcon flared out of the stoop, and hovered above the boy's head. Nefer reached up and could almost touch the sleek, beautiful plumage of its breast. For a moment Taita thought that the bird might allow itself to be captured, but then it changed its wingbeats and rose on high. Once again it uttered that forlorn and lovely cry, then sped away towards the sun and seemed to disappear into the flaming orb.

On his last visit to Gebel Nagara Hilto had brought with him a full-weight war bow. Under Taita's instruction Nefer practised with it every day, building up the muscles in his back and shoulders until he had the strength to throw up the weapon, draw to full stretch and hold his aim without his arms beginning to tire and shake. Then, at Taita's word of command, he would send an arrow arcing high to drop on to the target two hundred cubits distant.

Nefer cut himself a heavy acacia-wood staff from a hidden grove in the foothills and shaped, scraped and polished it until it had perfect balance and length in his hands. In the cool of the dawn, he and Taita fought in the traditional fashion. At first Nefer held back in deference to Taita's age, but the Magus bloodied his shins and raised a lump on his scalp. Furious and humiliated, Nefer attacked in earnest, but the old man was quick and nimble. He hopped just out of reach of Nefer's slashing staff, then darted in to impart a painful rap on an unprotected elbow or knee.

Taita had lost little of his skill with the blade. Hilto had brought them a rack of heavy sickle swords, and when Taita decided that they had had sufficient practice with the fighting staffs, he brought out the swords and led Nefer and Meren through the entire repertoire of cuts, thrusts and parries. He made them repeat every manoeuvre fifty times, then start again. By the time he called a halt for supper both Nefer and Meren were flushed and running with sweat as though they had plunged into a pool of the Nile. Taita's skin, though, was dry and cool. When Meren remarked ruefully on this, he chuckled. 'I sweated my last drop of juice before you were ever born.'

On other evenings Nefer and Meren stripped naked, oiled their bodies and wrestled, while Taita umpired their bouts and called advice and instruction. Although Meren was taller by a hand and heavier in the shoulders and limbs, Nefer had natural balance and Taita had taught him how to use his opponent's weight against him. They matched each other throw for throw.

In the evenings and late into the night Taita and Nefer sat by the fire and debated every subject from medicine and politics to war and religion. Often Taita would outline a theory, then require Nefer to discover any flaws in his postulates and arguments. He placed hidden traps and illogicalities in these lessons, and more often now, and with greater alacrity, Nefer would uncover and question them. Then there was always the bao board to puzzle over in the attempt to unravel the laws and infinite possibilities inherent in the movements and patterns of the stones.

'If you could understand all there is to know of the bao stones, you would know all there is to know of life itself,' Taita told him. 'The subtleties and nuances of the game tune and sharpen the mind to the greater mysteries.'

The month passed so swiftly that it was with a small shock of surprise that Nefer, while running hard through the desert in pursuit of a mortally wounded gazelle, suddenly descried on the horizon, distorted by the mirage, a tiny cloud of yellow dust, and beneath it the distant shape of the wagon returning from the river valley. On the instant, he forgot the gazelle he was chasing and raced to meet Hilto. Even though Hilto was accustomed to feats of physical prowess from his men, he was impressed with the speed at which Nefer covered the ground through the shimmering heat.

'Hilto!' Nefer yelled, still at a distance, and without any sign of laboured breathing. 'May the gods love you and grant you eternal life! What news? What news?'

Hilto pretended to misunderstand the significance of the question, and as Nefer walked at his side he began a long-winded recital of political and social events in the kingdoms. 'There has been another rebellion in the north. This time Trok found it harder to put down. He lost four hundred men in three days of hard fighting, and half the rebels escaped his wrath.'

'Hilto, you know that is not what I wanted to hear from you.'

Hilto indicated Bay with a jerk of his head. 'Perhaps this is not the time to touch on certain matters,' he suggested tactfully. 'Your Majesty, should we not speak later and in private?'

Nefer was forced to contain his impatience.

As they sat that evening around the campfire in the cave, it was agony for Nefer to have to listen to Hilto making another long, detailed report to Taita, the most important part of which was that the substitution of bodies had been discovered when the priests of Anubis had unwrapped the head of the corpse in the Hall of Sorrow. Pharaoh Naja Kiafan had done his best to suppress the news and to prevent it becoming public knowledge for the foundations of his throne would be undermined if the populace suspected that Nefer was still alive. However, it was impossible to keep such an extraordinary event secret when many people, priests and courtiers were privy to it. Hilto reported that rumours were rife in the streets and market-places of the city of Thebes and the outlying towns and villages.

Partly as a result of these rumours, the unrest in both kingdoms had become more widespread and concerted. The rebels were calling themselves the Blue Faction. Blue was the colour of the Tamosian dynasty; Naja had selected green as his own royal colour, and Trok's was red.

Added to this, trouble was brewing in the east. The Egyptian pharaohs had sent the Hurrian ambassador back to his master, King Sargon of Babylon, that mighty kingdom between the Tigris and Euphrates, demanding that Sargon's annual tribute be increased to twenty lakhs of gold. It was a crippling amount to which Sargon could never agree.

'So, this accounts for the build-up of the armies in both kingdoms,' Taita said, as Hilto paused in his report. 'It is clear at last that the two pharaohs are greedy for the riches of Mesopotamia. They are intent on conquest. After Babylon, they will turn on Libya and Chaldea. They will not rest until the entire world comes under their sway.'

Hilto looked amazed. 'I had not considered that, but you must be right.'

'They are as cunning as two old baboons raiding the farmers' fields along the riverbank. They know that war is a uniting factor. If they march on Mesopotamia the populace will rally behind them in a patriotic frenzy. The army loves the prospect of booty and glory. The merchants love the prospect of increased trade and profit. It is a marvellous way to take the minds of the people off their grievances.'

'Yes.' Hilto nodded. 'I see it now.'

'Of course, this is to our advantage,' Taita mused. 'I have

been seeking a haven for us. If he is at war with Trok and Naja, then Sargon will welcome us to his side.'

'We are leaving Egypt?' Hilto interjected.

Taita explained, 'Now that Naja and Trok know that Nefer still lives, they will come after us. The road to the east is the only one open to us. It will not be for long, just until we have built up our strength and support throughout the two kingdoms and have made ourselves powerful allies. Then we will return to reclaim Pharaoh Nefer's birthright.'

They all stared at him silently as they recovered from the shock of this prospect. They had not thought so far ahead, and it had never occurred to them that they would be forced to leave their native land.

It was Nefer who broke the silence. 'We can't do that,' he said. 'I cannot leave Egypt.'

Taita glanced at the others, and jerked his head in dismissal. Obediently Hilto, Bay and Meren stood up and filed out of the cave.

Taita had been anticipating this situation. He knew it would take all his cunning to resolve it, for Nefer wore his set expression and had made his declaration in a stubborn tone that Taita recognized. He knew it was going to be difficult to move Nefer from this position. The boy was staring into the fire, and Taita realized he must force him to break his silence. When he did so, Taita's position would be strengthened.

'You should have discussed this plan with me,' Nefer said at last. 'I am no longer a child, Taita. I am man and Pharaoh.'

'I told you my intentions,' Taita said quietly.

They sat in silence again, staring into the flames of the fire, and Taita could sense the cracks appearing in Nefer's resolve.

At last Nefer spoke again. 'You see, there is Mintaka.'

Still Taita said nothing. Intuitively he understood that

they were approaching a crisis in their relationship. It had had to come at some time, so he made no effort to avoid it.

'I sent Mintaka a message,' Nefer said. 'I told her I loved her, and I gave her an oath on my life and eternal spirit that I would not desert her.'

Now Taita broke his silence. 'Are you certain that Mintaka received this foolhardy oath of yours that placed you, her and all around you in mortal danger?'

'Yes, of course. Hilto—' Nefer stopped and his expression changed as he stared at Taita across the flames of the campfire. Suddenly he sprang up and strode to the cave entrance. He moved not like a boy but like a man, an angry man. In these last few short months he had changed completely. Taita experienced a deep satisfaction. The way ahead would be hard, and Nefer would need all this new-found strength and determination.

'Hilto!' Nefer called into the darkness. 'Come to me.' Perhaps Hilto heard the new authority in his tone because he came swiftly and dropped to one knee before Nefer.

'Majesty?' he asked.

'Did you deliver the message I entrusted to you?' Nefer demanded.

Hilto glanced at Taita beside the fire.

'Don't look to him,' Nefer snapped. 'I am asking you the question. Answer me.'

'I did not deliver the message,' Hilto answered. 'Do you wish to know the reason why I did not?'

'I know the reason well enough,' Nefer said ominously. 'But hear this. If ever you wilfully disobey me at any time in the future you will pay the full penalty.'

'I understand,' Hilto said stolidly.

'If there is ever again a choice between Pharaoh and an interfering old man, you will choose Pharaoh. Is that clear to you?'

'It is clear as the midday sun.' Hilto hung his head penitently, but smiled into his beard.

'You have been evading my questions, Hilto. Now, what news do you have of the princess?'

Hilto stopped smiling, and opened and closed his mouth, trying to find the courage to tell him the dire news.

'Speak!' Nefer ordered. 'Have you so soon forgotten your duty?'

'Gracious Majesty, the news will not please you. Six weeks ago the Princess Mintaka was married in Avaris to Pharaoh Trok Uruk.'

Nefer stood as still as if he had been turned into a granite statue. For a long time the only sound in the cave was the crackle of the acacia logs in the fire. Then, without another word, Nefer walked past Hilto, out into the desert night.

When he returned the dawn was a faint red promise in the eastern sky. Hilto and Meren were wrapped in their sheepskins at the back of the cave, but Taita sat in exactly the same position as Nefer had left him. For a moment he thought that the old man was asleep also. Then Taita raised his head and looked at him with eyes that were bright and alert in the firelight.

'I was wrong, and you were right. I need you now, more than ever, old friend,' said Nefer. 'You will not desert me?'

'You need not ask,' Taita said softly.

'I cannot leave her with Trok,' Nefer said.

'No.'

Nefer came back to his seat opposite Taita, who took a slow, deep breath. The storm had passed. They were still together.

Nefer picked up a charred stump of firewood and pushed it deeper into the flames. Then he looked up at Taita again. 'You have tried to teach me to overlook at a distance,' he said. 'I have never acquired the gift. Not until this last night. Out there in the darkness and the great silence, I tried again to overlook Mintaka. This time I saw something, Taita, but only dimly and I did not understand it.'

'Your love for her has made you sensitive to her aura,' Taita explained. 'What did you see?'

'I saw only shadows, but I felt devastating sorrow and grief. I sensed despair so insupportable that it made me wish for death myself. I knew that these were Mintaka's emotions and not my own.'

Taita stared expressionlessly into the fire, and Nefer went on, 'You must overlook her for me. There is something terribly wrong. Only you can help her now, Taita.'

'Do you have anything of Mintaka's?' he asked. 'Any gift or token that she gave you?'

Nefer's hand went to the necklace at his throat. He touched the tiny golden locket that hung in the centre of the chain. 'It is my most precious possession.'

Taita held out his hand across the fire. 'Give it to me.' Nefer hesitated, then opened the clasp and held the amulet in his closed fist.

'Other than my own, hers were the last fingers to touch it. It contains a lock of her hair.'

'Then it is highly potent. It contains her essence. Give it to me, if you wish me to help her.' Nefer passed it to him.

'Wait here,' Taita said, and stood up. Although he had squatted cross-legged through all the hours of darkness, there was no stiffness in his movements, which were those of a young, virile man. He went out into the dawn and climbed to the crest of the dunes, then gathered the skirts of his *chiton* around his skinny shanks and squatted in the sand, facing the dawn.

He pressed Mintaka's amulet to his forehead and closed his eyes. He began to rock slightly from side to side. The sun cleared the horizon and struck fully into his face.

The amulet in his right hand seemed to take on some

strange life of its own. Taita felt it pulse softly in rhythm to his own heartbeats. He opened his mind and let the currents of existence enter freely, swirling around him like a great river. His own spirit broke free of his body and he soared aloft. As though he was borne on the wings of some gigantic bird, he saw fleeting, confused images of lands and cities, forests, plains and deserts far below him. He saw armies on the march, the squadrons throwing up thunderclouds of yellow dust in which spearheads glinted. He saw ships on high seas battered by wave and wind. He saw cities burning as they were sacked, and he heard strange voices in his head, and knew they were from the past and the future. He saw the faces of those long dead, and those not yet born.

He moved on, his spirit ranging wide, always with the amulet his lodestone. In his mind he called for her, Mintaka! and felt the amulet grow warm then burning hot in his hand.

Slowly the images cleared away, and he heard her sweet voice reply, 'I am here. Who is it that calls?'

'Mintaka, it is Taita,' he replied, but he was aware that something evil had intervened and broken the stream between them. Mintaka had gone and instead there was a fateful presence. He focused all his powers upon it, trying to disperse the dark clouds. They seemed to coalesce, and took the shape of a rearing cobra, the same baleful influence that he and Nefer had encountered in the nest of the royal falcon on the cliffs of Bir Umm Masara.

In his mind he wrestled with the cobra, extending his powers to drive it back, but rather than succumbing, the image of the serpent became clearer and more menacing. Suddenly he knew that this was not a psychic manifestation, but a direct and mortal threat exerted against Mintaka. He redoubled his efforts to break through the curtains of evil and to reach her, but so much pain and grief was interposed between them that it was an impenetrable barrier.

Then, suddenly, he saw a hand, slim and graceful, reach out towards the sinister scaly head. He knew it was Mintaka's hand, for the blue lapis lazuli ring on the index finger was engraved with her cartouche. He held the venomous serpent in check with all his life force, and prevented it striking at Mintaka's hand as she stroked the back of its extended hood. The cobra turned half away from her, almost like a cat offering its head to be caressed.

'Make it do what has to be done.' Taita heard Mintaka's voice, and another voice he recognized replied, 'This I have never seen before. You must strike the messenger with your hand. That will surely make him deliver the gift of the goddess.' It was the voice of the high priestess of the temple of Hathor in Avaris, and Taita understood. Mintaka, overwhelmed with grief, was about to take the way of the goddess.

'Mintaka!' He exerted himself to reach her, and was rewarded at last.

'Taita?' she whispered, and because Mintaka was at last aware of him, Taita's view expanded so that he could see it all clearly.

Mintaka was in a stone-walled bedchamber. She was kneeling in front of a basket. The holy priestess was at her side, and in front of her reared the deadly snake.

'You must not take this road,' Taita ordered her. 'It is not for you. The gods have prepared a different destiny for you. Do you hear me?'

'Yes!' Mintaka turned her head towards him, as though she could see his face.

'Nefer is alive. Nefer lives. Do you hear me?'

'Yes! Oh, yes.'

'Be strong, Mintaka. We will come for you. Nefer and I will come for you.'

So fierce was his concentration that he dug his fingernails deeply into the palms of his hands until the blood welled, but he could hold her no longer. She began to slip away from him, her image blurred and faded, but before she was gone he saw her smile, a beautiful thing, full of love and renewed hope.

'Be strong!' he urged her. 'Be strong, Mintaka!' The echo of his voice came back to him as though from a great distance.

Nefer was waiting for him at the foot of the dunes. When Taita was only halfway down the boy realized that something momentous had taken place. 'You saw her!' he shouted, and it was not a question. 'What has happened to her?' and he ran forward to meet Taita.

'She needs us,' Taita said, and laid a hand on Nefer's shoulder. He could never tell him of the extremes of sorrow and despair in which he had found Mintaka, nor of the fate she had prepared for herself. Nefer could never bear that. It might easily drive him to some wild endeavour that would destroy both the lovers. 'You were right,' Taita went on. 'All my plans to leave this land and find sanctuary in the east must be set aside. We have to go to Mintaka. I have promised her that.'

'Yes!' Nefer agreed. 'When can we leave for Avaris?'

Taita replied, 'There is great urgency. We will leave at once.'

It took them fifteen days of hard travel to reach the tiny garrison and remount station of Thane a day's travel south of Avaris. They had changed horses four times on the road – Taita used the royal requisition order that Naja had given him to replace the worn-out animals and to replenish their supplies at the military garrisons and camps they had passed along the way.

Since leaving Gebel Nagara they had discussed their plans endlessly, knowing that they were pitted against the might of Pharaoh Trok Uruk. The officers they spoke to at the garrisons estimated that Trok now had twenty-seven fully trained and equipped regiments at his disposal, and almost three thousand chariots. To oppose this multitude they had a wagon showing the effects of long, hard service with a back wheel that showed a marked propensity to fall off at the most inappropriate times and bodywork held together with twine and leather strips. There were only the four of them: Nefer and Meren, Hilto and Bay. But the fifth was Taita.

'The Magus is worth twenty seven regiments at least,' Hilto pointed out, 'so we are evenly matched against Trok.'

Hilto knew the captain in charge of the encampment at Thane, a scarred and grizzled old warrior named Socco. Long ago they had run the Red Road together. They had fought, roistered and whored together. After they had reminisced for an hour and shared a pot of sour beer, Hilto handed him the requisition scroll. Socco held it upside down at arm's length and looked wise.

'See the cartouche of Pharaoh.' Hilto touched the seal.

'If I know you at all, Hilto, and by Horus I do, you probably drew that pretty picture yourself.' Socco handed the scroll back to Hilto. 'What do you need, you old rogue?'

They selected fresh horses from the herd of several hundred in the remount herd, then Taita went over the ranks of parked chariots in the garrison pool that had just been sent out from the makers in Avaris. He selected three vehicles, and they harnessed the fresh horses.

When they left Thane, Taita was driving the old wagon. Meren, Hilto and Nefer each drove a chariot, while Bay brought up the rear herding twenty spare horses. They did not head directly for Avaris but made a detour to the east of the city.

On the edge of the desert there was a small oasis used by

the Bedouin and by merchant caravans heading out to and returning from the Orient.

While the others unloaded the fodder they had carried from Thane in the wagon, hobbled the horses and greased the wheel hubs of the new chariots, Taita went to barter with the Assyrian master of the caravan that was encamped nearby. He bought an armful of dirty, tattered clothing, and twenty woollen rugs woven in the land along the Further Sea. They were of inferior workmanship and material, but he was forced to pay an extortionate price for them. 'That Assyrian ape is a cut-throat and a robber,' he muttered, as they loaded the carpets on to the wagon.

'Why do we need them?' Nefer wanted to know, but Taita pretended not to hear the question.

That night Taita dyed his mane of silver hair with an extract of mimosa bark, which altered his appearance dramatically. In the darkness of early morning they left Bay in charge of the herd of horses and the chariots, climbed into the dilapidated wagon and, sitting high on the pile of dusty carpets, headed west towards Avaris. They were dressed in the rags and cast-offs that Taita had procured. Taita wore a long robe and sash, and the lower half of his face was veiled in the fashion of a citizen of Ur of the Chaldeas. With his dyed dark hair he was unrecognizable as the Magus.

It was evening when they reached the royal city of the north. There was a permanent encampment of several thousand souls outside the walls, mostly beggars, itinerant players, foreign traders and other riff-raff. They set up camp among them, and early the next morning they left Meren to watch the wagon and went to join the throng waiting outside the city for the gates to open at sunrise.

Once they were past the city guard, Hilto went to tour the taverns and brothels in the narrow streets of the old quarter where he hoped to find some of his cronies and former comrades-in-arms and gather the latest news from them. Taita took Nefer with him and they made their way through the crowded streets of the awakening city to the palace gates. Here they joined the beggars, tradesmen and supplicants. Taita made no effort to gain entry to the palace, rather they spent the morning listening to the chatter of those around them, and gossiping with the other idlers.

At last Taita struck up a conversation with a merchant from Babylon, dressed in similar style to himself, who introduced himself as Nintura. Taita spoke the Akkadian language like a native of Mesopotamia, which was why he had chosen this particular disguise. The two shared a pot of coffee brewed with rare and expensive beans imported from Ethiopia, and Taita exerted all his wiles to charm Nintura, who had been loitering outside the palace for the last ten days, waiting for his turn to display his wares to Trok's new bride. He had already paid the exorbitant *baksheesh* demanded by the palace vizier to be allowed to enter the presence of the young consort, but many others were ahead of him.

'They say that Trok has been cruelly treated by his young wife. She will not allow him into her bed.' Nintura chuckled. 'He is wild for her, like a stag in rut, but she keeps her legs crossed and the door to her chamber locked. Trok is trying to win her favours with expensive gifts. They say he will refuse her nothing. Also she buys everything that is offered to her and then, to spite him, she immediately resells it for a fraction of what he was forced to pay and distributes the proceeds to the poor of the city.' He slapped his knee and roared with laughter. 'They say she buys the same things over and over, and Trok keeps paying.'

'Where is Trok?' Taita asked.

'He is campaigning in the south,' Nintura replied. 'He is stamping out the flames of rebellion, but no sooner does he turn his back than they flare up again behind him.'

'Whom should I approach to enter the presence of this Queen Mintaka?'

'The palace vizier. Soleth, is his name, the fat, gelded freak.' Nintura had not realized Taita's own physical status.

Taita knew Soleth only by reputation and that he was one of the secret brotherhood of eunuchs. 'Where can I find him?' Taita asked.

'It will cost you a gold ring just to enter his presence,' Nintura warned him.

Soleth was sitting beside the lotus pond in his own walled garden. He did not rise when one of the harem-keepers brought Taita to him.

The Hyksos had so forsaken their ancient customs, and taken to Egyptian ways, that they no longer kept their wives sequestered in the *zenana*. The eunuchs still exercised much of their former power over the royal women, but when suitably chaperoned their charges were allowed much freedom. They could walk abroad, sail on their pleasure barges on the river, have merchants visit them to display their wares or dine, sing, dance and play games with their friends.

Taita made a dignified salutation as he introduced himself to Soleth under an assumed name. He followed that with the recognition sign of the brotherhood, crooking both his little fingers and touching them together. Soleth blinked with surprise and ran his eyes down Taita's lean frame: he did not have the shape or the look of a eunuch. Nevertheless he waved to Taita to seat himself on the cushions opposite him. Taita accepted the bowl of sherbet a slave offered, and they talked for a while of seemingly trivial matters, but swiftly they established Taita's credentials and common acquaintances within the brotherhood. Without seeming to do so, Soleth was studying Taita's features thoughtfully, looking beyond the veil and the dyed hair. Slowly recognition bloomed in his eyes and at last he asked softly, 'In your travels you might have met the famous

Magus, known through both kingdoms, and beyond, as Taita?'

'I know Taita well,' Taita agreed.

'Perhaps as well as you know yourself?' Soleth asked.

'At least as well as I know myself,' Taita affirmed, and Soleth's chubby face creased in a smile.

'Say no more. What service can I perform for you? You need only ask.'

That evening Nefer, Meren and Hilto were on the carpet load when Taita drove the creaking wagon, its incorrigible back wheel wobbling lopsidedly, up to one of the side gates of the palace where a gang of ragged urchins skulked in the mean, narrow lane. Taita gave one a copper ring to guard the wagon, then banged on the gate with the butt of his staff. It swung open at once, but they were confronted by a file of levelled spears. The entrance to the *zenana* was heavily guarded: Trok was taking good care of his little hind.

Soleth was not there to greet him – obviously, he was keeping his nose clean – but he had sent one of his underlings, an old black slave, to usher Taita past the guards and to act as a guide. Although Taita was armed with the papyrus scroll that Soleth had given him, the captain of the guard insisted on searching them before he would allow them to pass. He ordered Hilto to unroll the carpets and prodded every fold with his spear point. At last he was satisfied, and waved them through.

The ancient slave hobbled ahead of them, guiding them through a labyrinth of narrow passages. As they progressed the surroundings became grander, until they stopped before an elaborately carved sandalwood door guarded by two huge eunuchs. There was a whispered exchange between them and the old slave, then the sentries stood aside and Taita led the others through into a large airy room redolent of flowers, perfume and the tantalizing aroma of young womanhood. Beyond there was a wide terrace, from which floated the sounds of a lute and feminine voices.

The old slave went out on to the terrace. 'Your Majesty,' he quavered, 'there is a merchant with fine silk carpets from Samarkand to wait upon Your Grace.'

'I have seen enough rubbish for one day,' a woman's voice replied, and Nefer thrilled to those familiar well-beloved tones so that his breathing came short. 'Send them away.'

The guide looked back at Taita and pulled a face, spreading his hands helplessly. Nefer dropped the rolled carpet off his shoulder on to the stone floor tiles with a weighty thump, and strode to the entrance on to the terrace where he paused. He was dressed in tatters and a grubby cloth was wrapped around his head, covering the lower half of his face. Only his eyes were visible.

Mintaka was sitting on the parapet wall with two of her slave girls at her feet. She did not look in his direction but started singing again. It was the monkey and donkey song, and Nefer felt every word twist his heart as he studied the sweet curve of the cheek turned half away from him and the tresses of thick dark hair that hung down her back.

Abruptly she broke off and looked at him with annoyance. 'Don't stand there gawking at me, you insolent oaf,' she snapped. 'Take your wares and go.'

'Forgive me, Majesty.' He spread his arms in supplication, 'I am but a poor fool from Dabba.'

Mintaka screamed and dropped her lute, then covered her mouth with both hands. Patches of bright crimson rouged her cheeks and she stared into his green eyes. The black slave drew his dagger and tottered forward feebly to attack Nefer, but Mintaka recovered herself at once. 'No, leave him.' She raised her right hand to reinforce the command. 'Leave us. I will speak with the stupid fellow.'

The slave looked dubious and hesitated, the naked dagger still aimed uncertainly at Nefer's belly.

'Do as I tell you,' Mintaka snarled, like a leopardess. 'Go, fool. Go!'

Confused, the old fellow sheathed his blade and backed away. Mintaka was still staring at Nefer, her eyes huge and dark. Her girls could not fathom what ailed her. They knew only that something strange was afoot. The curtains over the entrance fell back into place as the slave withdrew. Nefer whipped off the cloth that covered his head and his curls fell to his shoulders.

Mintaka screamed again. 'Oh, by the grace of Hathor, it is you. It is really you! I thought you would never come.' She flew to him and he ran to meet her, enfolding her in his embrace. They clung to each other, both talking at the same time, incoherently trying to tell each other of their love and how much they had missed each other. The slave girls recovered from their astonishment and danced around them, clapping their hands and weeping with joy and excitement until Taita silenced them with a few well-directed prods of his staff.

'Stop that mindless squealing. You will have all the sentries here in a minute.' Once he had them under control, he turned back to Hilto and Meren. At his direction they spread the largest carpet out on the tiles.

'Mintaka, listen to me! There will be time for that later.'

She turned her face to him, but kept her hands locked around Nefer's neck. 'It was you who called to me, wasn't it, Taita? I heard your voice so clearly. If you hadn't stopped me I would have—'

'I thought you more sensible than to stand here chattering when so much is at stake,' Taita cut across her. 'We are going to hide you in the carpet to get you out of the palace. Hurry now.'

'Do I have time to fetch my—'

'No,' Taita said. 'You have time for nothing other than to obey me.'

She kissed Nefer once more, a lingering embrace, then ran into the chamber and threw herself full length on the carpet. She looked up at her girls, who stood amazed in the doorway. 'Do whatever Taita tells you.'

'You cannot leave us, mistress,' her favourite, Tinia, wailed. 'Without you we are nothing.'

'It will not be for long,' Mintaka said. 'I promise I will send for you, Tinia, but until then be brave, and do not fail me.'

Nefer helped Hilto and Meren roll Mintaka in the patterned red carpet, and placed one end of a long hollow reed between her lips. The other end, protruding a few inches from the heavy folds, would enable her to breathe.

In the meantime Taita instructed the weeping slave girls: 'Tinia, you are to go into the bedchamber and bar the door. Cover yourself with bed linen, as though you were your mistress. The rest of you will stay here in the vestibule. You must not open the door to any demands. Tell anyone who asks that your mistress is laid low by her moon sickness and can see no one. Do you understand that?' Tinia nodded, broken-hearted, not trusting herself to speak. 'Delay them as long as you are able, but when you are discovered and can no longer dissemble, tell them what they want to know. Do not try to hold out under torture. Your death or crippling will serve little purpose, except to prey upon the conscience of your mistress.'

'Can I not go with the Queen?' Tinia blurted. 'I cannot live without her.'

'You heard your mistress's promise. Once she is safe she will send for you. Now, bar the door behind us when we leave.'

The old slave was waiting in the passage when they carried out the rolled carpet on their shoulders.

'I am sorry. I did my best for you, as Soleth ordered me. Queen Mintaka was once a kind and happy girl,' he told them, 'but no longer. Since her marriage she has become sad and angry.' He beckoned them to follow and led them back through the warren of the *zenana* until at last they reached the small side gate, where the sergeant of the guards confronted them once more.

'Unroll those carpets!' he ordered brusquely.

Taita stepped closer to him and stared into his eyes. The sergeant's hostile expression faded. He looked mildly confused. 'I can see that you are feeling contented and happy,' Taita said softly, and a slow grin spread over the man's ugly, wrinkled features. 'Very happy,' Taita said, and laid his hand gently on the man's shoulder.

'Very happy,' the sergeant repeated.

'You have already searched the carpets. Surely you do not want to waste your valuable time. Do you?'

'I don't want to waste my time,' the sergeant declared, as though it was his own idea.

'You want us to pass.'

'Pass!' said the sergeant. 'I want you to pass.' And he stood aside. One of his men raised the locking bar and let them out into the lane. The last glimpse they had of the sergeant as the door closed showed them that he was grinning benignly after them.

The wagon stood where they had left it with the urchins guarding it. Gently they loaded the carpet into the wagon bed and Nefer called quietly into the mouth of the roll, 'Mintaka, my heart, are you all right?'

'It is hot and stuffy, but that is a small price to pay to know that you are near.' Her voice was muffled and he reached down the tube formed by the roll and touched the top of her head.

'You are as brave as a lioness,' he said, and scrambled up behind Taita on the wagon box as he urged the horses forward.

Taita whipped up the horses. 'The city gates will soon be closed for the night. When Mintaka's escape is discovered the first thing they will do is seal off the city, search every building and vehicle, and question every stranger within the walls.'

They galloped down the wide avenue leading to the eastern gate. As they approached they saw that the way was blocked with other wagons and chariots lined up in front of the gate. There had been a religious festival and procession earlier in the day, and these were worshippers and revellers returning to the outlying villages around Avaris. Their forward progress was tantalizingly slow.

The sun had already sunk behind the walls and the light was fading, but there were still two vehicles ahead of them when the captain of the guard came out of the gate house and yelled at his men, 'That is enough! The sun has set. Close the gates!'

There were yells of protest from all the travellers still trying to pass out.

'I have a sick child. I must take her home.'

'I have paid my toll, let me pass. My load of fish will spoil.'

One of the smaller wagons drove forward deliberately and blocked the efforts of the guards to force the gates shut. A small riot broke out, with shouting guards swinging clubs, outraged citizens screaming back at them and frightened horses rearing and whinnying. Suddenly there was a further commotion from without the walls. Louder voices drowned the protests of travellers and guards alike.

'Make way for Pharaoh! Clear the road for Pharaoh Trok Uruk!'

The boom of a war-drum enforced the order. The guards ceased their efforts to shut the gates and instead fell over each other in their haste to throw them wide open again to reveal on the roadway outside a squadron of fighting chariots. Over the leading vehicle waved the red leopard pennant. Standing tall on the footplate, his bronze helmet gleaming and his beribboned beard thrown over one shoulder, stood Pharaoh Trok Uruk, whip and reins in his gauntleted hands.

As soon as the gates were wide open he drove his four-horse team straight into the mass of people and wagons in the roadway, lashing out indiscriminately with his whip at any who stood in his way. His men ran ahead of him, overturning any vehicle that blocked the road, and dragging it aside, spilling loads of wet slippery fish and vegetables into the gutters.

'Make way for Pharaoh!' they roared, above the screams of those caught up in the confusion. The troopers reached Taita's vehicle and began to tip it over to clear the path for Trok. Taita stood up and lashed at them with the whip, but his blows fell on their helmets and their bronze epaulettes. They laughed at him and heaved together. The wagon went over. The rolled carpet slid across the wagon bed and might have been crushed under the capsizing vehicle.

'Help me!' shouted Nefer, and jumped back to hold the carpet roll and cushion its fall. Hilto caught one end and Bay the other. As the wagon crashed on its side with a crackle of breaking timber they dragged Mintaka, still cocooned in the roll, to safety against the wall of the nearest building.

Pharaoh Trok forced his chariot through the wreckage and spilled loads, cracking his whip over the heads of his team, roaring commands at his warhorses.

'Strike! Strike!' The horses were battle-trained, and at his urging they reared and struck out at anyone in their way with their bronze-shod hoofs. Nefer saw one old woman scurry straight under the flying hoofs. One caught her full in the face. Her head split open, and her teeth flew from her mouth like a burst of white hailstones. They rattled on the cobbles and she sprawled in front of Trok's chariot.

The bronze wheel rims bumped over her body as he

drove on, passing so close to where Nefer crouched protectively over Mintaka's carpet roll that for an instant they looked into each other's eyes. Trok did not recognize him in his rags with the headcloth wound around his head, but with casual cruelty he snapped the whip over Nefer's shoulder. The metal tips of the lash cut through the cloth and raised a line of bright blood spots. 'Out of my way, peasant!' Trok snarled, and Nefer gathered himself to leap on to the footplate and drag Trok out of the chariot by his beard. This was the beast who had defiled Mintaka, and Nefer's rage was a red veil over his vision.

Taita grabbed his arm to restrain him. 'Let it pass. Get the carpet out of the gates, you fool. We will be trapped here.' Nefer strained to be free of his grip, and Taita shook him. 'Do you want to lose her again so soon?'

Nefer regained control of his temper. He stooped to seize the end of the roll and the others helped him. They ran with it to the gates, but the squadron of chariots was through and once more the guards were swinging the heavy wooden doors to. Taita ran ahead and scattered the guards with his staff. When one of the sentries raised a club over his head, Taita turned on him and stared into his face with those mesmeric eyes. The man recoiled as though confronted by a man-eater.

Carrying the rolled carpet between them they squeezed through the narrow gap between the closing gates, then ran into the encampment below the city walls. Although angry shouts followed them, they disappeared from the guards' view into the gathering darkness among the leather tents and shacks. Behind the walls of a goat pen they lowered their burden to the ground and unrolled it. Dishevelled and hot, Mintaka sat up and smiled to see Nefer kneeling in front of her. They reached for each other and embraced as the others looked on.

Taita brought them back to reality. 'Trok has returned unexpectedly,' he told Mintaka. 'It will not be long before he discovers that you are missing.' He pulled Mintaka to her feet. 'We have lost the wagon. Ahead of us we have a long journey on foot. Unless we set out now it will be after daylight tomorrow before we reach the oasis where we left the chariots.'

Mintaka sobered immediately. 'I am ready,' she said.

Taita glanced down at her flimsy gold sandals decorated with turquoise studs, and strode away among the huts. He returned in a few minutes with a slatternly old woman following close behind him. He was carrying a pair of hard-worn but sturdy peasant's sandals. 'I have exchanged these for yours,' he said.

Mintaka did not demur but slipped off the lovely sandals and handed them to the old woman, who scuttled away before anyone could take them back from her. Then Mintaka stood up. 'I am ready,' she said. 'Which way, Magus?'

Nefer took her hand and they fell in behind Taita as he strode out into the desert.

Trok drove through the palace gates and reined in his dusty, lathered horses in the front courtyard before his own magnificent quarters. Two colonels of his cavalry, both members of the leopard clan and his particular cronies, stumped after him into the banquet hall with weapons and bucklers clattering. The house slaves had laid out a feast to welcome Pharaoh home. Trok drained a bowl of sweet red wine, and seized the boiled haunch of a wild boar.

'There is something I need more than food or drink.' He winked at his companions, who guffawed and nudged each other. Trok was aware that his marital reverses were common gossip in the army, and that the manner in which his new wife treated him was weakening his reputation. Despite his victories over the rebels in the south, and the harsh retribution he had imposed upon them, his prestige as a man was suffering. He was determined to change that this very night.

'There is more food than even you two oxen can eat, and enough wine in which to drown a hippopotamus.' Trok waved at the groaning board. 'Do your worst, but don't expect me to join you before morning. I have a field to plough, and an incorrigible filly to break to my will.'

He strode from the hall gnawing at the bone in his hand, and gulping down mouthfuls of the fat pork as he went. Two slaves with burning torches ran ahead of him to light his way down the gloomy passages to the *zenana*. In front of the doors to Mintaka's quarters the eunuch sentries had heard him coming. They flourished their weapons and crossed them over their fat chests in salute.

'Open up!' Trok ordered. He tossed aside the pork bone and wiped his greasy hands on the skirts of his tunic.

'Your Majesty,' one of the sentries saluted again nervously, 'the doors are barred.'

'By whose orders?' Trok demanded furiously.

'By orders of Her Majesty Queen Mintaka.'

'By Seueth, I'll have none of that! The arrogant hussy knows I am here,' Trok stormed, drew his sword and pounded on the door with the bronze pommel. There was no reply, so he tried again. The sound of the blows echoed down the silent passages, but still there was no sign of life beyond the doors. He backed away then charged the door with his shoulder. It shook but did not yield. He snatched the pike from the hands of the nearest sentry and hacked at the panel.

Splinters of timber flew under the blade and with a few more blows he had chopped a hole wide enough for him to reach through and dislodge the locking bar on the far side. He kicked open the door and marched into the room beyond. The slave girls were against the far wall in a terrified huddle. 'Where is your mistress?'

They gabbled and cackled incoherently, but could not prevent their collective eyes from turning towards the door of the bedchamber. Trok went to it, and there was an immediate outcry from the girls.

'She is sick.'

'She cannot see you.'

'Her moon has come.'

Trok laughed. 'She has used that excuse too often.' He hammered on the door. 'If there is blood, then there had better be a river of it – more than I spilled on the field of Manashi. By Seueth, I will wade through it to reach the happy portals.'

He kicked at the bedchamber door. 'Open up, you little witch! Your husband has come to show you his duty and respect.'

At his next kick the door flew open, torn off its leather hinges, and Trok swaggered through. The couch was carved from African ebony, and inlaid with silver and mother-of-pearl. The feminine form upon it was hidden under a pile of linen bedclothes but one small foot protruded. Trok let his sword-belt drop to the floor and called, 'Have you missed me, my little lily? Have you been pining for my loving arms?'

He grabbed the bare foot and hauled the girl out from under the bedclothes. 'Come my, sweet ewe lamb. I have another gift for you, so long and hard, that you will not be able to sell it or give it away—' He broke off and gawked at the terrified, snivelling girl. 'Tinia, you dirty little harlot, what are you doing in your mistress's bed?' He did not wait for her reply, but threw her on to the floor, and rampaged through the room, ripping down the curtains and wall hangings. 'Where are you?' He kicked in the doors to her closet. 'Come out! This childishness will serve you little.'

It took him only a minute to make certain that Mintaka was not hiding. Then he rushed back to Tinia and seized her by the hair. He dragged her across the floor. 'Where is she?' He kicked her in the belly. She screamed and tried to roll away from his metal-shod foot. 'I will beat it out of you, I will flay every inch of skin from your miserable body.'

'She is not here!' Tinia screamed. 'She has gone!'

'Where?' Trok kicked her again. His war sandals were studded with bronze nails. They cut her tender flesh like knives. 'Where?'

'I know not,' she howled. 'Men came and took her away.'

'What men?' He kicked her again, and she rolled into a ball, sobbing and shivering.

'I don't know.' Despite Taita's instruction, she would not betray her beloved mistress. 'Strange men. I had never seen them before. They covered her with a carpet and carried her away.' Trok gave her a last brutal kick, then strode to the door. He shouted at the eunuch sentries, 'Find Soleth. Bring the fat slug here immediately.'

Soleth came cringing and wringing his smooth, plump hands. 'Divine Pharaoh! Greatest of the gods! Might of this very Egypt!' He threw himself at Trok's feet.

Trok kicked him with a full swing of his armoured sandal. 'Who were these men you allowed to enter the *zenana*?'

'On your orders, gracious Pharaoh, I allowed any vendor of fine merchandise to display it before the Queen.'

'Who was the carpet-seller? The last one to enter these quarters.'

'Carpet-seller?' Soleth seemed to ponder the question.

Trok kicked him again. 'Yes, Soleth, carpets! What was his name?'

'I remember now. The carpet-merchant from Ur. I forget his name.'

'I will help your memory.' Trok called the eunuch sentries to him. 'Hold him over the bed.'

They dragged Soleth to the rumpled couch and pinned him face down. Trok picked up his discarded sword-belt and drew the weapon. 'Lift his robes.' One of them hoisted

Soleth's skirts and exposed his chubby buttocks. 'I know that half the palace guard have passed this way,' Trok touched his anus with the point of the sword, 'but none of them were as hard or as sharp as this one will be. Now, tell me, who was the carpet merchant?'

'I swear on bread and Nile water that I never saw him before.'

'For you that is a great pity,' Trok said, and ran the point of the sword the length of a forefinger up Soleth's rectum. Soleth shrieked on a high, quavering note of agony.

'That was only the tip,' Trok warned him. 'If you are enjoying it so much, I can give you another cubit of bronze right up to your gullet.'

'It was Taita,' Soleth screamed, with the blood spraying out of him. 'Taita took her away.'

'Taita!' Trok exclaimed with astonishment and jerked the blade free. 'Taita, the Magus.' There was superstitious dread in his tone. Then he was silent for a long pause. At last he ordered the eunuchs who still held Soleth. 'Release him.'

Soleth sat up moaning. At the movement the gas from his bowels rushed out through the slack opening in a long, bubbling fart.

'Where has he taken her?' Trok ignored the sound and the sickening faecal odour that filled the chamber.

'He did not tell me.' Painfully Soleth bundled the linen bed-sheet and thrust it in between his legs to staunch the bleeding. Trok lifted the point of the sword and touched one of his naked pendulous breasts.

Soleth whimpered and farted again. 'He did not tell me, but we spoke of the land between the two rivers, the Tigris and the Euphrates. Maybe that is where he intends taking the Queen.'

Trok thought about it only briefly. It was logical. By now Taita would know of the strained relationships between Egypt and the eastern kingdoms. He would know that he might find sanctuary and protection there, if he could run that far.

But what was his reason for abducting Mintaka? Surely it could not be for ransom. Taita was famous for his scorn of gold and riches. It could not be for some salacious desire. As an ancient eunuch, Taita was not capable of physical lust. Was it the friendship that had grown up between the old man and the girl? Had she appealed to him to help her escape from Avaris and the marriage that was so insufferable to her? Certainly, she must have gone with him willingly and probably gladly. The manner in which her slave girls had tried to cover her escape proved that, and clearly she had made no outcry, for if she had the sentries would have heard it.

He put aside those considerations for the moment. The main concern now was to get the pursuit in hand and to recapture her and the Warlock before they reached the shores of the Red Sea and crossed into the territories loyal to Sargon of Babylon. He smiled down at Soleth. 'I hope that your paramours will find the alterations I have made to your joy passage to their liking. I will deal with you further when I return. There are hungry hyenas and vultures to be fed.'

The two colonels were still in the banquet chamber, hogging the food and wine, although they had not been at it long enough to drink themselves stupid.

'How many chariots can we have manned and running eastward before midnight?' Trok demanded. They looked startled, but they were warriors and responded swiftly to his angry mood.

Colonel Tolma spat out the mouthful of wine he was about to swallow and leaped to his feet, only slightly unsteadily. 'I can have fifty on the road within two hours,' he blurted.

'I want that to be a hundred,' Trok demanded.

'I will have a hundred under command before midnight.'

Colonel Zander sprang up, eager not to be outdone. 'And another hundred running east before dawn.'

Taita led them through the night under a moon only days from full. The tip of his staff clicked on the stony path, and his shadow flitted ahead of him like a monstrous black bat. The others had to stretch their legs to keep him in sight.

After midnight Mintaka began to fail. She was limping heavily and falling back steadily. Nefer shortened his stride to stay with her. He had not expected this from her: usually she was as strong as any boy he knew, and could outrun most of them. He murmured encouragement to her, not loud enough to reach the ears of Taita. He did not want the Magus to realize Mintaka's weakness, and to shame her in the sight of the others.

'It is not far now,' he told her, and took her hand to lead her faster. 'Bay will have the horses ready for us. We will ride the rest of the way to Babylon in royal style.' She laughed but it was a strained, painful sound. It was only then that he realized something was wrong with her.

'What is it that ails you?' he demanded.

'Nothing,' she said, 'I have been locked up in the palace too long. My legs have gone soft.'

He would not accept it. He took her arm and forced her to sit on a rock beside the path, lifted one of her small feet and unlaced the strap of the sandal. He pulled it off and gasped, 'Sweet Horus, how did you manage a single step on this?' The rough ill-fitting sandal had galled her grievously. The blood was black and shining in the moonlight. He lifted the other foot and gently eased off its sandal. Slabs of skin and flesh peeled away with it.

'I am sorry,' she whispered, 'but don't worry, I can go on barefoot.'

Furiously he hurled the bloodied footwear out among the rocks. 'You should have warned me of this earlier.' He stood up, lifted her to her feet, turned his back to her and braced himself to receive her weight. 'Put your arms around my neck and jump up'. Then he set off after the others who, by this time, were merely a dark moving shadow on the moonlit desert far ahead.

Her mouth was close to his ear, and she whispered to him as he toiled on, trying to distract him, and to encourage him. She told him how she had missed him, and how when she had heard of his reputed death she had not wanted to live without him. 'I wanted to die, so that I could be with you again.' Then she told him about the priestess of Hathor and how she had brought the serpent to her. Nefer was so appalled that he lowered her to the earth and scolded her angrily.

'That was stupid.' In his agitation he shook her roughly. 'Don't ever think like that again, whatever happens in the future.'

'You cannot know how much I love you, my darling. You cannot imagine the devastation I felt when I thought you were gone.'

'We must make a pact. We must live for each other from this day onwards. We must never think of death again until it comes to us uninvited. Swear it to me!'

'I swear it to you. From now onwards I will live only for you,' she said, and kissed him to seal their bargain. He lifted her on to his shoulders again and they went on.

Her weight seemed to increase with every pace he took. Where the road was soft and sandy he lowered her and she leaned upon him, hobbling along beside him on her raw and bleeding feet. When the ground became rough and stony he lifted her again and trudged onwards. She told him of how Taita had overlooked her and saved her from her resolve to die. 'It was the most extraordinary feeling,' she said, 'As though he stood at my side and spoke to me in a strong clear voice. He told me that you were still alive. How far away were you when he overlooked me?'

'We were at Gebel Nagara in the south, fifteen days' travel from Avaris.'

'He could reach so far?' she asked incredulously. 'Is there no end to his powers?'

Once more they stopped to rest in the darkness and she leaned against his shoulder and whispered to him, 'There is something I want to tell you, about my wedding night with Trok . . .'

'No!' he said vehemently. 'I don't want to hear. Do you think I have not tortured myself each day with the thought of it?'

'You must listen to me, my heart. I was never wife to him. Though he tried to force me, I was able to resist him. My love for you gave me the strength to deny him.'

'I have heard that he displayed the red-stained sheepskin on the palace walls.' The words were painful to him and he turned away his face.

'Yes, it was my blood,' she said, and he tried to pull away from her embrace but she held him. 'It was not my virgin blood. It was the blood from my nose and mouth where he had beaten me to force me to submit. I swear to you on the love I have for the goddess, and on my hope to bear your sons, that I am virgin still and will be until you accept my maidenhead from me as a proof of my love.'

He took her in his arms and kissed her and wept with relief and joy, and she wept with him.

After a time he stood up again and he lifted her on to his back. It was as though her vow had given him new strength and they went on more strongly.

It was after midnight before the others realized that something had befallen them, and came back to search for them. Taita bound up Mintaka's feet and after that Hilto and Meren took their turns at carrying her. They went on faster, but the stars were fading and the dawn light growing stronger when they finally reached the oasis where Bay waited for them with the horses.

All of them were exhausted by that time, but Taita would not allow them to rest. They watered the horses for the last time and refilled the waterskins until they were tight and shiny, with drops of moisture oozing from them.

While they were doing this Taita half filled a bucket with water from the well, and, using some foaming unguent, washed the dye from his hair until once more it shone silver.

'Why does he wash his hair at a time like this?' Meren wondered.

'Perhaps it restores some of his force that he lost when he dyed it,' Mintaka suggested, and no one questioned this.

When they were ready to leave Taita forced them to drink again from the well, to fill their bellies with all the water they could swallow without vomiting. While they were doing so Taita spoke quietly to Bay. 'Can you feel it?'

Bay scowled and nodded. 'It is in the air and I can feel it reverberating through the soles of my feet. They are coming.'

Despite the urgency of the moment and the menace of an enemy close at hand, Taita took one last opportunity to treat Mintaka's feet. He smeared the raw and bruised places with salve and rebandaged them. Then at last he ordered them to mount.

Taita took Meren in the leading chariot as his lance-bearer. Nefer followed with Mintaka clinging to the dash-board to take the weight off her feet. Hilto and Bay brought up the rearguard in the last chariot.

The Assyrian merchant who had sold them the carpets was supervising his servants and slaves as they loaded up his wagons and draught animals. He turned to watch them as they passed, and he called a farewell to Taita. But his interest quickened as he saw the girl in the second chariot. Not even her dusty clothing and dishevelled hair could hide her striking looks. He was still staring after them as they topped the last rise and disappeared into the wilderness, heading east along the caravan road that would lead eventually to the shores of the Red Sea.

While Trok was waiting impatiently for his squadrons to assemble before the city gates he ordered Colonel Tolma to send his men to search the encampment of beggars and foreigners outside the walls of Avaris. 'Turn out every hovel. Make certain that Queen Mintaka is not hiding in any of them. Search for Taita the Warlock. Bring me any tall, thin old man you find. I will question him myself.'

There were screams and cries among the huts, the sounds of doors being broken down and flimsy walls smashed in as Tolma's men carried out his orders. Within a short time two of the troopers returned, dragging a filthy old Bedouin harridan to where Trok stood beside his chariot. The woman was screaming hysterical abuse at her captors as she kicked and struggled in their grip.

'What is it, soldier?' Trok demanded, as they threw the woman down at his feet. The trooper held up a pair of delicate golden sandals, decorated with turquoise studs that glittered in the torchlight.

'Your Majesty, we found these in her hut.'

Trok's face darkened with fury as he recognized them and he kicked the woman in the belly. 'Where did you steal them, you foul old she-baboon?'

'I never stole nothing, divine Pharaoh,' she whined. 'He gave them to me.'

'Who was he? Answer me straight or I will push your head up your cunt until you drown in your own stinking juices.'

'The old man, he gave them to me.'

'Describe him to me.'

'Tall, he was, and skinny.'

'How old?'

'Old as the rocks of the desert. He gave them to me.'

'Was there a girl with him?'

'Three other men and a pretty little harlot dressed in fine stuff with paint on her face and ribbons in her hair.'

Trok jerked her to her feet and shouted into her startled face, 'Where did they go. Which way?'

With a shaking finger the woman pointed along the road that led into the hills and the desert beyond.

'When?' Trok demanded.

'That much of the moon's journey,' she said, indicating an arc of the sky that corresponded to four or five hours of the lunar orbit.

'How many horses did they have?' Trok snarled. 'Chariots? Wagons? How were they travelling?'

'No horses,' she answered. 'They went on foot, but in great haste.'

Trok pushed her away. He grinned at Tolma who stood beside him. 'They will not get far on foot. We will have them just as soon as you can get your idle ruffians out of their sleeping rugs and mounted.'

The sun was hot and halfway up the sky when Trok topped the hills above the oasis at the threshold of the wilderness. Two hundred chariots followed him in a column of fours. Five miles further back, their dust-cloud clearly visible in the bright sunlight, came Zander with another two hundred. Each vehicle carried two heavily armed troopers, and was loaded with waterskins and sheaths of spare javelins and arrows.

Below them they saw the Assyrian trader coming up the slope from the well at the head of his caravan. Trok rode forward to meet him, and hailed him from a distance. 'Well met, stranger. Whence come you, and what is your business?'

The trader looked up at this warlike host in trepidation, not certain what to expect. Trok's friendly greeting meant little. On the long road from Mesopotamia he had met robbers, bandits and warlords.

Trok reined in his chariot in front of him. 'I am His Divine Majesty Pharaoh Trok Uruk. Welcome to the Lower Kingdom. Fear not. You are under my protection.'

The trader fell to his knees and made his obeisance. For once Trok was impatient of the honours being paid to him, and he cut the man short. 'Stand and speak up, my brave fellow. If you are honest with me and tell me what I need to know, I shall give you a licence to trade throughout my kingdom free of any tax, and send ten chariots to escort you to the gates of Avaris.'

The merchant scrambled to his feet, and began to express his deep gratitude, although he knew from long experience that such royal condescension was usually costly. Trok cut him short. 'I am in pursuit of a band of criminal fugitives. Have you seen them?'

'I have met a number of travellers along the way,' the Assyrian replied cautiously. 'Would Your Divine Majesty deign to describe these villains to me, and I will do my best to place you upon their tracks?'

'Probably five or six in number. They will be heading towards the east. One young woman with them, and the rest of them men. Their leader is an ancient rogue. Tall and thin. He may have dyed his hair black or brown.'

Trok got no further with his description, before the Assyrian broke in excitedly. 'Your Majesty, I know them well. Some days ago the old man with dyed hair purchased carpets and old clothing from me. At that time the woman was not with him. He left horses and three chariots at the oasis down yonder, in the charge of an ugly black ruffian.

With the others in an old wagon loaded with the carpets I had sold him, he took this high road we are standing on towards Avaris.'

Trok grinned triumphantly. 'That is the one I want. Have you seen him since? Did he return to pick up the chariots?'

'He and the other three came back early this morning, on foot from the direction of Avaris. With them was the young woman you asked after. She seemed to be injured in some way, for they carried her.'

'Where have they gone, fellow? Which way?' Trok demanded eagerly, but the Assyrian would not be hurried.

'The woman was young. Though she was injured and could only walk with difficulty, she wore fine cloth. She was clearly of high rank and beautiful, with long dark hair.'

'Enough of that. I know the woman well enough without your description. After they left the oasis, which way did they go?'

'They harnessed the horses to the three chariots and left immediately.'

'Which way, man? Which direction did they take?'

'East along the caravan road.' He pointed out the winding track that climbed the low hills into the dune country. 'But the old man's hair was no longer dyed. When last I saw him, it shone like a cloud in the summer sky.'

'When did they leave?'

'An hour after sunrise, Majesty.'

'What was the condition of their horses?'

'Well watered and rested. They had been lying up at the oasis for three days and they had brought a load of fodder with them when they arrived. When they left this morning their waterskins were filled at the well and they seemed to be provisioned for the long journey to the sea.'

'Then they are only hours ahead of us.' Trok exulted. 'Well done, fellow. You have earned my gratitude. My scribes will issue you with the licence to trade, and Colonel

Tolma will assign you an escort to Avaris. You will be further rewarded when I return to the city with the fugitives in bonds. You shall have a fine seat in the front row of spectators at their execution. Until then I wish you a good journey and much profit in my kingdom.'

He turned from him and began issuing orders to Colonel Tolma who followed him closely in the second chariot of the column. 'Give this fellow a trade licence and an escort to Avaris. Top up the waterskins at the well, and let the horses drink their fill. But swiftly, Tolma. Be ready to leave again before noon. In the meantime send your wizards and the regimental priests to me.'

The troopers took the horses down to the well in batches of twenty at a time to drink. The men who were not busy with this work stretched out in the shade thrown by their own vehicles to rest and eat a frugal meal of millet bread and dried meat, the staple diet of the cavalry.

Trok found a patch of shade under a gnarled tamarind near the well. The wizards and holy men came in response to his summons and squatted in a circle around him. There were four of them, two shaven priests of Seueth in their black robes, a Nubian shaman hung with necklaces and bracelets of charms and bones, and a sorcerer from the east known as Ishtar the Mede. Ishtar had one wall eye and his face was tattooed with purple and red whorls and circles.

'The man we are pursuing is an adept of the occult arts,' Trok warned them. 'He will exert all his powers to frustrate us. It is said that he can weave a spell of concealment, and that he can conjure up images that might dismay our legions. You will have to work your own spells to turn aside his powers.'

'Who is this charlatan?' asked Ishtar the Mede. 'You can be certain that he will not prevail against our combined force.'

'His name is Taita,' Trok replied, and only Ishtar showed no dismay at the identity of their adversary.

'I know Taita only by reputation,' he said, 'but I have long looked for an opportunity to match him.'

'Weave your magic,' Trok ordered them.

The priests of Seueth went aside a short distance and laid out their accoutrements and mystical trappings on the sand. They began to chant softly and shake their rattles over them.

The Nubian searched among the rocks around the well, until he found a venomous horned adder under one of them. He lopped off its head and dribbled the blood over his own head. With it running down his cheeks and dripping off the tip of his nose, he hopped in circles like a great black toad. As he completed each turn he spat copiously towards the east where Taita lay.

Ishtar built a small fire near the well and squatted over it, rocking on his heels and muttering incantations to Marduk, the most powerful of all the two thousand and ten gods of Mesopotamia.

Once he had given his orders to Tolma, Trok went across to watch him at work. 'What magic are you making here?' he asked at last, as Ishtar opened a vein in his wrist and let a few drops of his own blood drip and sizzle in the flames of the fire.

'This is the hex of fire and blood. I am placing obstacles and hardships in Taita's path.' Ishtar did not look up. 'I am confusing and confounding the minds of his followers.'

Trok grunted sceptically, but secretly he was impressed. He had seen Ishtar work before. He walked a short way along the road and glared at the line of eastern hills. He was hot for the pursuit and grudged this stay. On the other hand he was enough of a general to realize the absolute necessity of resting and watering the horses after the long night ride.

He knew well the nature of the ground ahead. As a young captain of chariots he had patrolled there on many occasions. He had crossed the shale beds that cut hoofs and hocks like flint knives, and had endured the terrible heat and thirst of the dunes.

He walked back to where he had left his chariot, but he had to pause and turn his back as a sudden dust devil came swirling across the yellow plain, spinning upon itself and rising several hundred cubits into the sultry air. The vortex encompassed him. The air was as hot as the breath from a bronze furnace, and he had to cover his nose and eyes with his headcloth and breathe through the material to strain out the flying sand. It swept past and spun away across the hot earth with the grace of a harem dancer, leaving him coughing and wiping his eyes.

It was a little before noon and they had just finished the watering when the second column under Colonel Zander caught up with them and came down the slope to the well. They were as much in need of water as the first column and now there was danger of congestion at the oasis. Already the water was depleted and muddied. They would be forced to fall back on the precious waterskins to eke out the supply.

Trok held a brief conference with Zander and Tolma, explaining his plan of action, and the formation he wanted to employ to prevent Taita from twisting and turning out of the net they were spreading for him. 'Warn the regimental commanders to be on the alert for any magical snares that Taita puts out to confuse us,' he ended. 'Ishtar the Mede has worked a potent spell. I have much faith in him. He has never failed me before. If we are fully aware of the wiles of the Warlock we will succeed. After all, how can he prevail against such an array?' With a sweep of his arm he indicated the huge gathering of chariots and horses and élite troops. 'No! By the breath of Seueth, this time tomorrow I will be dragging Taita and Mintaka behind my chariot on the way back to Avaris.'

He ordered the leading column to mount. Four chariots abreast and in a column half a league long they headed out into the wilderness. On the soft sandy earth ahead the wheel tracks of their quarry were clearly etched.

Taita signalled the two vehicles that followed him to halt. They stopped in the purple shade thrown across the sands by a tall slip-faced dune shaped like the elegant curve of a gigantic seashell.

The horses were already showing signs of distress. They hung their heads and their chests heaved as they breathed. The sweat had dried in salt white rime on their dust-dulled hides.

Carefully they measured out a water ration from the waterskins into the leather buckets and the horses drank eagerly. Taita treated Mintaka's feet and was relieved to find no evidence that the injuries were mortifying. When he had retied the bandages he led Bay out of earshot of the others.

'We are being overlooked,' he said flatly. 'There is a baleful influence slowly enveloping us.'

'I have felt it also,' Bay agreed, 'and I have begun to resist it. But it is powerful.'

'We can best frustrate it if we combine our powers against it.'

'We must be careful of the others. They are more vulnerable.'

'I will warn them to be on their guard.'

Taita walked back to where the others were just finishing the watering. 'Be ready to go on,' he told Nefer. 'Bay and I are going to scout the ground ahead. We will return in a short while.'

The two adepts went forward on foot and disappeared around the curved sand wall of the slip-face. Out of sight of the chariots they halted. 'Do you know who Trok has with him who can work such a potent spell?'

'He has priests and sorcerers with all his regiments, but the most powerful of them is Ishtar the Mede.'

'I know of him.' Taita nodded. 'He works in fire and blood. We must try to turn his influence back on him.'

Bay started a small fire of dried horse dung, and when it was burning steadily they pricked the end of their thumbs and squeezed out a few red drops into the flames. With the whiff of burnt blood in the air they faced the enemy, for they could feel that the influence was in the western segment, from the direction that they had come. They exerted their combined powers and after a while they felt it begin to diminish, and disperse like the smoke of the dying fire.

When they had completed the ritual, and were smothering the fire with sand, Bay said softly, 'It is still there.'

'Yes,' Taita said. 'We have weakened it, but it is still dangerous, especially to those who have not learned how to resist it.'

'The youngest will be more susceptible,' Bay suggested. 'The two boys, Pharaoh and Meren, and the girl.'

They went back to where the chariots waited. Before they mounted again Taita spoke to the others. He knew that they would be frightened if he mentioned the true reason for his concern, so he said, 'We are entering the most inhospitable and dangerous area of the dune-lands. I know you are all tired and thirsty, drained by the rigours of the journey, but it could be fatal for any of you to become careless. Watch the horses and the ground ahead. Do not allow yourselves to be distracted by any strange sound or by an unusual sight, a bird or an animal.' He paused and looked directly at Nefer. 'That applies to you particularly, Your Majesty. Be on your guard at all times.'

Nefer nodded and for once did not argue. The rest of them also looked grave, realizing that Taita had some reason of his own to give them this warning.

As they went forward again, following the valleys between the high dunes the heat seemed to increase with every turn of the chariot wheels. The loose sand walls that rose on either hand took on a motley of vivid colours, lemon yellow and gold, plum, purple and heron blue, fox-red and tawny lion-brown. In places the dunes were streaked with frosty talc, or etched with patterns of black sand like the soot of an oil lamp.

Overhead the sky turned brazen and ferocious. The quality of light changed: it became yellow and ethereal. Distances were rendered confusing and distorted. Nefer slitted his eyes against the shimmering glare of the brassy sky. It seemed close enough to touch with the end of his whip. At the same time the shape of Taita's vehicle only fifty cubits ahead seemed to recede to a blurred and distant horizon.

The heat scorched any exposed skin on face or body. Nefer felt a formless dread take hold of him. There was no reason for it, but he could not shake it off.

When Mintaka shuddered against him and gripped his whip arm he knew that she had sensed it too. Great evil hung in the air. He wanted to call out to Taita, to ask him for guidance and reassurance, but his throat was closed by dust and heat. No sound issued from it.

Suddenly at his side he felt Mintaka stiffen and her fingers dug painfully into the biceps of his whip arm. He looked down at her face and saw that she was terrified. With her free hand she pointed frantically to the crest of the dune that seemed to hang suspended above them.

Something colossal and dark detached itself from the heights and began to tumble down towards them. He had never seen anything like it. It had the same weighty amorphous shape as a monstrous waterskin, but was so large that it covered the entire side of the dune, large enough to engulf and squash not only the three chariots below it but an entire regiment. As it rolled down the almost sheer slope it gathered speed, undulating, wobbling and bouncing silently, coming down on them so swiftly that it blotted out the yellow desert sky. In the heat it exuded a sudden cold that squeezed the breath from their lungs as if they had plunged into an icy pool in a high mountain stream.

The horses had seen it also: they plunged wildly and swung off the sandy track and bolted across the valley bottom, trying to outrun the terrifying apparition. There was a field of ragged black lava rocks directly ahead of them and they were racing straight into it. Nefer realized the danger and tried to turn their heads but they were out of control. As he wrestled with the reins Mintaka was screaming beside him.

Certain that they were about to be overwhelmed by the dark monstrosity, Nefer glanced over his shoulder. He expected it to be looming over them, for he could feel the cold emanation on the back of his neck, but there was nothing. The side of the dune was bare, smooth and silent. The yellow sky above was empty and bright. The other two chariots were halted under the slope, the horses calm and under control. Taita and the others were staring at them, astonished.

'Whoa!' Nefer yelled at the runaway team, and threw his full weight on the reins, but the horses never checked. At full gallop they flew into the field of lava rock with the chariot bounding and swerving behind them. 'Whoa!' he screamed again. 'Stop, curse you, stop!'

The horses were mad with terror, far beyond restraint. They arched their necks to fight the reins, striding out at full stretch, grunting with every stride.

'Hold hard, Mintaka!' Nefer shouted, and threw one arm around her shoulders to protect her. 'We are going to strike!'

The black rocks were worn and carved by windblown sand into strange shapes. Some were the size of a man's head and others as big as the chariot under them. Nefer managed to steer the crazed horses clear of the first, but they ran on into a gap between two of the largest rocks. It was too narrow for them to pass through: the off-wheel struck with a rending crash, and disintegrated. Shattered spokes and sections of the rim were hurled into the air. The carriage dropped on to its axle, dragging down the off horse, which was thrown into the next rock. Nefer heard its front legs snap like kindling, even as he and Mintaka were hurled clear of it.

They hit the soft sand, narrowly avoiding being thrown into the rock that had maimed the horse. When they came to a standstill, Nefer was still holding Mintaka in his arms. He had cushioned her fall, and now he demanded breathlessly, 'Are you all right? Are you hurt?'

'No,' she answered at once. 'Are you?'

Nefer came to his knees, and stared in horror at the wreckage of the chariot and the crippled horses.

'Sweet Horus!' he cried. 'We are finished.' The chariot was smashed beyond any hope of repair. One horse was down for ever, both front legs shattered. The other was standing, still in its traces and harnessed to the single shaft of the chariot, but one leg was swinging loosely from its dislocated shoulder.

Unsteadily he came to his feet, and pulled Mintaka up after him. They clung to each other as Taita drove his chariot to the edge of the lava field, tossed the reins to Meren and jumped down from the footplate. He came to them with long strides. 'What happened? What caused the horses to bolt?'

'Did you not see it?' Nefer asked, still shaken and bewildered.

'What was it?' Taita insisted.

'A thing. Dark and huge as a mountain. It rolled down the dune on top of us.' Nefer groped for words to describe what they had seen.

'It was big as the temple of Hathor.' Mintaka supported him. 'It was terrifying. You must have seen it also.'

'No,' Taita replied. 'It was an aberration of your mind and vision. Something placed there by our enemies.'

'Witchcraft?' Nefer was bemused. 'But the horses saw it also.'

Taita turned away from them and called to Hilto as he drove up, 'Destroy those poor beasts.' He pointed to the maimed horses. 'Help him, Nefer.' Taita wanted to distract him from the disaster and its consequences.

With a heavy heart Nefer held the head of the downed horse. He stroked its forehead and covered its eyes with his headcloth so that it would not see death coming.

Hilto was an old trooper and had done this sad work on many far-flung battlefields. He placed the point of the dagger behind the animal's ear and with a single thrust drove it into the brain. The horse stiffened, shivered and then relaxed. They went to the second animal. It dropped instantly to Hilto's thrust and lay without moving again.

Taita and Bay stood together, watching this harrowing act of mercy, and Bay said softly, 'The Mede is stronger than I thought him to be. He has singled out the most vulnerable among us and directed his powers at them.'

'He has Trok's other sorcerers to reinforce his influence. From now onwards we will have to watch over Hilto and Meren also,' Taita agreed. 'Until I can gather my own force to oppose Ishtar we are in great danger.'

He left Bay's side. It would trouble the others if they saw the two of them conferring secretly together. It was of the utmost importance to keep up their spirits.

'Bring the waterskins,' Taita ordered. One had burst in the crash and the other two were only half full, but they strapped them on to the remaining chariots.

'From here onwards, Meren will ride with Hilto and Bay. I will take Their Majesties with me.'

With the waterskins and the weight of the extra passengers the chariots were now overloaded. The horses were straining as they went forward into the glaring heat, with the lurid sun almost obscured by the strange yellow overcast.

Taita held the golden Periapt of Lostris in his right hand, and chanted softly to himself, warding off the evil that was thickening everywhere around them. In the following chariot Bay was singing also, a monotonous repetitive refrain.

They came to a section of the road where the wind had wiped away the tracks of other caravans and travellers. There were no signs to follow except for the small cairns of stones that had been placed at intervals. Eventually even these petered out, and they went on into the trackless sands. They relied now on Taita's experience, his knowledge of the desert, and his deep instincts.

At last they came out into flat ground between two ranges of high dunes. The sand here was smooth and level, but Taita stopped at the edge of it and considered it carefully. He climbed down from the footplate and beckoned to Bay. The black man came to his side and together they examined the innocuous surface.

'I like it not at all,' Taita said. 'We must look for a detour around this plain. There is something here.'

Bay walked a short way out on to the firm level sand and sniffed the hot air. He spat twice and studied the pattern of his own spittle. Then he came back to Taita. 'I can find nothing troublesome here. If we look for a way round it may cost us hours, even days. The pursuit is not far behind. We must decide which is the greatest risk.'

'There is something,' Taita repeated. 'Like you, I also feel an impulse to cross here. That feeling is too strong and illogical. The idea has been placed in our minds by the Mede.'

'Mighty Magus.' Bay shook his head. 'In this case I do not agree with you. We must take the risk and cross this valley. Otherwise Trok will catch up with us before nightfall.'

Taita took him by the shoulders and stared into his black eyes. He saw that they were slightly unfocused, as though he had been smoking the bhang weed. 'The Mede has penetrated your armour,' he said, and placed the Periapt on Bay's forehead. Bay blinked and opened his eyes wide. Taita could see him struggling to throw off the influence. He exerted his own will to help him.

At last Bay shivered and his gaze cleared. 'You are right,' he whispered. 'Ishtar had overlooked me. There is great danger in this place.'

They looked down the length of the narrow valley. It was a river of yellow sand with no beginning and no end in sight. The far bank was close, no more than three hundred cubits across at the narrowest places, but it might have been two hundred leagues, and Trok's regiments were close behind them.

'South or north?' Bay asked. 'I cannot see the way round.'

Taita closed his eyes and exerted all his powers. Suddenly there was a sound in the terrible silence. A faint high cry. They all looked up and saw the tiny shape of a royal falcon turning high in the furious yellow sky. It circled twice then sped south along the valley, and disappeared into the haze.

'South,' Taita said. 'We will follow the falcon.'

They had been so intent on these deliberations, that neither of them had noticed that Hilto had eased his own chariot up closer to where they stood. He and Meren were leaning over the dashboard and listening to this exchange. Hilto was frowning with impatience. Suddenly he exclaimed, 'Enough of this! The way is clear ahead. We cannot afford any delay. Will you dare to follow if Hilto leads the way?'

He whipped up his team, and the startled horses jumped forward. Meren was taken so completely by surprise that he was almost thrown backwards over the footplate but he grabbed a handhold and managed to stay on the racing vehicle.

Taita shouted at Hilto, 'Come back! You are bewitched. You do not know what you are doing.'

Bay jumped up to catch the harness of the off-side horse, but he was too late: the chariot sped past him and out on to the flat ground. It gathered speed and Hilto's laughter floated back to them. 'The way is open. 'Tis smooth and fast.'

Nefer snatched up the reins of the stationary vehicle, and shouted, 'I will stop him or turn him.'

'No!' Taita turned back to him, desperately raising his hand in a command to stop. 'Don't go out there. There is danger. Stop, Nefer!'

But Nefer ignored his cries. With Mintaka beside him he lashed up the team and the wheels sang over the smooth hard sand. He was catching up with Hilto rapidly.

'Oh, sweet Horus!' Taita groaned. 'Watch the wheels.'

A fine feather of silver sand began to rise from behind the spinning wheels of Hilto's chariot. Then, as they watched in horror, the feather became a thick plume of yellow slush, then slabs of loose mud. The horses slowed as they sank to their hocks in the soft footing and lumps of mud were thrown up so high from their driving hoofs that they flew over Hilto's head. He made no attempt to stop or turn back but drove them on deeper into the quagmire.

'The sinking sands!' Taita cried bitterly. 'This is the work of the Mede. He has hidden the true road from us and led us into this trap.'

Abruptly Hilto's team broke through the crust into the treacherous swamp beneath. As its wheels dropped in over the rims, the chariot came to such a sudden halt that both Hilto and Meren were catapulted over the dashboard. They rolled across the innocent-seeming surface, but when they came to a stop and tried to stand up their bodies were coated with sticky yellow mud, and immediately they sank in to their knees.

The horses were completed mired. Only their heads and front quarters were free, but as they whinnied and plunged they sank deeper and deeper still.

Nefer was bemused and reacted too slowly to the disaster taking place before his eyes. By the time he attempted to turn back it was too late. Within ten cubits his wheels were in over the hubs and both horses were bogged down to the shoulders. He jumped down to help them, to try to unharness them and lead them back, but immediately he was trapped in the slimy mud, sinking in to the knees and then to the waist.

'Don't try to stand,' Mintaka warned him frantically. 'It will swallow you under. Throw yourself flat and swim.'

She threw herself headlong from the sinking vehicle, and lay flat on the quaking mud. 'Like this, Nefer. Do as I do.'

He recovered his wits and stretched out flat on the surface. In an awkward swimming motion, like a child learning to doggy-paddle, he reached the chariot before it disappeared completely. With his dagger he cut the leather straps that held the floorboards in place and, in desperate haste, ripped them up and threw them clear. They floated on the surface of the deadly quicksands, but the heavy-laden chariot slid inexorably below the surface and drew the horses down with it. Within minutes there was only a lighter patch on the dun-coloured plain to mark their grave.

Hilto's chariot had also been drawn under and his horses with it. He and Meren were floundering about, yelling with terror, managing only to keep their mud-daubed heads and shoulders clear.

Nefer shoved one of the floorboards to Mintaka. 'Use this!' he ordered her, and she crawled on to it.

He did the same with another board, which supported his weight. Towing two more boards with him by their leather straps he propelled himself across the swamp until he was close enough to throw them to Hilto and Meren. They dragged themselves out of the glutinous clutches of the mud. All four started to swim laboriously back towards where Taita and Bay watched in horror from firm ground.

Taita waved his arms and shouted urgently, 'You are already halfway across. Don't return here. Go on. Cross to the other side.'

Nefer saw the sense in this immediately. They turned for the far bank. It was slow, hard work, for the mud clung tenaciously to their arms and legs and to the bottom of the boards. Mintaka's lighter weight soon told and she drew ahead of the others. She was first to reach firm ground and to drag herself from the clutches of the sinking sands. At last Nefer, Hilto and Meren followed her. They were almost exhausted. They threw themselves down at the foot of the eastern dunes.

While they crossed, there had been time for Taita to consider their predicament. It seemed hopeless. They were split into two groups, with a gulf between them two hundred cubits wide. They had lost all of their horses and vehicles, their weapons and equipment, but the worst loss of all was the precious waterskins.

Now Bay touched his arm and whispered, 'Listen!'

It was a susurration in the air, far off, sometimes fading away, then growing louder again, a distant echo reverberating from the enclosing dunes. Though faint, it was unmistakable: the sound of a column of chariot cavalry on the march.

The three mud-soaked figures on the far side of the valley heard it also, and came to their feet. All of them stared back into the dunes and listened to Trok and his men coming on apace.

Suddenly Mintaka ran back to the edge of quagmire where they had abandoned the boards that had carried them across. Nefer stared after her, trying to fathom out what she intended. She gathered up the boards and waded out knee-deep, dragging the boards after her by their leather straps.

Nefer realized suddenly what she was doing, but he was too late to stop her. She threw herself flat on one of the boards and began to skim out over the yellow mud. She was out of his reach when at last he was forced to stop waist-deep.

'Come back,' he shouted after her. 'I will go.'

'I am lighter and faster than you,' she called back, and though he went on pleading with her she ignored him and used all her breath and strength on skimming forward.

The sound of chariots grew louder, and spurred Mintaka on to greater effort. Watching her Nefer was torn with fear for her safety and anger for her intransigence, but even stronger was his pride in her courage. 'She has the heart of a warrior and a queen,' he whispered, as she drew closer to the far bank.

Now they could hear the voices of the pursuers and the rattle of wheels and the clank of weapons, magnified by the sounding board of the dunes.

Taita tucked his staff under his belt to leave his hands free, then he and Bay waded out to meet Mintaka. Each took a spare board from her and launched themselves out on the treacherous surface. All three started to swim back to the east bank.

From out of the dunes behind them debouched the head of the column of pursuing chariots. The unmistakable figure of Trok was in the leading vehicle, and his bull voice roared out triumphantly and echoed from the dune walls.

'Forward! Charge!'

The leading phalanx of chariots broke into full gallop and came tearing towards the edge of the sinking sands. The three fugitives sculled themselves frantically on to the yellow morass. Behind them the yells of the charioteers grew louder.

Trok's bulk forced his wheels to sink deeper into the loose sand than those of the other vehicles, and though his horses strained under the whip, he fell back behind the first rank of the charge.

The other three chariots of the leading file ran headlong into the sinking sands, and were sucked in as swiftly as the other vehicles had been engulfed. Thus, Trok was alerted to the danger. He managed to bring his own team under control and swerve away from the morass.

He seized his short recurved bow from the rack and leaped down. Behind him the other chariots broke the charge and drew up in a mass. 'Bows!' shouted Trok. 'Massed volleys. Don't let them get away. Shoot them down.'

The archers ran forward and formed into ranks four deep at the edge of the swamp, full quivers on their backs and bows strung taut.

Mintaka had once more pulled ahead of her companions. She had passed the halfway mark, and though they were sculling frantically Taita and Bay were lagging ever further behind her.

Trok strode down the ranks, giving his orders. 'Archers, nock your arrows!' A hundred and fifty men fitted arrow to bow string.

'Archers, draw and aim!' They lifted their weapons and drew to the lip, aiming into the lowering yellow sky.

'Loose!' Trok yelled, and they fired a massed volley. The arrows rose in a dark cloud. They reached the zenith of their trajectory and fell towards the three small figures out in the swamp.

Taita heard them coming and looked back into the sky. The deadly cloud dropped towards them, whistling softly as the wings of a flight of wild geese.

'Into the mud!' Taita called urgently, and all three slipped off the boards and were immersed in the thick mud until only their heads protruded. The arrows fell thick as hail around them. One pegged deeply into the board on which Mintaka had lain only seconds before.

'Onward!' Taita ordered, and they hauled themselves back on to the boards and sculled forward again, gaining only a few yards before the air was once more filled with the hum of falling arrows, and they threw themselves back into the protection of the yellow mud.

Three times more they were forced to dive off the boards, but each time the range was longer for the archers and the volleys less accurate. Mintaka pulled away even faster than before and was soon out of range.

Trok's bellows of rage and frustration followed them as he urged his men to shoot. The arrows plopped into the mud around them, but the fall of the volleys was less concentrated.

Taita turned his head to look across at Bay. His huge scarified head was shining with mud and sweat. His bloodshot eyes bulged from their sockets, and his mouth was wide open, his filed teeth sharp as those of a shark.

'Courage, Bay!' Taita called to him. 'We are almost across.' As he said it, he realized that the words were a direct challenge to the gods.

On the bank behind them Trok saw them slipping slowly from his grasp. His troopers were using the shorter and less powerful bows designed to be shot from a running chariot. Two hundred cubits was the limit of their effective range. Trok turned and glared back at his lance-bearer, who was managing the horses of his team.

'Bring my war bow,' he shouted. Trok was the only man in the regiment who carried the long bow in his chariot: he had decided that for the rest of his troops the war bow's awkward length did not compensate for the added strength and range.

However, Trok's massive strength and the reach of his long arms set him above the strictures placed on lesser men.

He used the short recurved bow in most situations. However, he had designed a special rack on the side of his chariot to accommodate the extra length of the more powerful but unwieldy weapon.

His lance-bearer ran to him and placed the great bow in his hands. He brought also the quiver holding the special arrows, emblazoned with the head of the leopard, that fitted the long weapon.

Trok shouldered his way into the front row of archers, and they made way for him. He nocked a long arrow and measured the range with half-closed eyes.

The heads of the two swimmers were tiny blobs on the yellow expanse. The men around him were still shooting rapidly, but their arrows fell short, dropping ineffectually into the mud. Mentally he calculated the angle of release and took his stance with his left foot leading. He sucked in a deep breath and drew with straight left arm, until the string touched the tip of his hooked nose. The bow challenged even his strength. The muscles in his bare arms stood proud, and his features contorted with the effort. He held it for a heartbeat, adjusting his aim fractionally. Then he released, and the great bow-stock flexed and pulsed in his hands like a living creature.

The long arrow blurred as it climbed, high above the clouds of lesser missiles, outstripping them effortlessly. It reached its noon and dropped like a stooping falcon.

In the mud Taita heard the sharper shriller sound of its flight and looked up. He saw it coming straight at him, and there was no time for him to fall off his primitive craft or even to duck to avoid it.

Involuntarily he closed his eyes. The arrow passed so close over his head that he felt his hair stirred by the wind of its passage. Then he heard the solid thump of the strike.

He opened his eyes and rolled his head towards the sound. The long arrow had taken Bay in the middle of his naked back. It had transfixed his body, and the flint head had buried itself in the board on which he lay, pinning him to the wood like a shiny black beetle.

Bay's face was only an arm's length from his own. Taita looked into the deep black eyes, and saw the agony of death flare in them. Bay opened his mouth to cry out or to speak, but the copious rush of bright blood through his lips drowned any sound. Painfully he reached up to the necklace around his neck, and pulled it loose. He reached out to Taita offering him, as his last gift, the priceless relic that was twisted around his clawed fingers.

Taita gently untangled it from the rigid fingers and dropped the string around his own neck. He felt the essence of the dying shaman flowing from it into his own body, reinforcing his powers.

Bay's head dropped forward, but the arrow prevented him rolling off the board. Taita recognized the leopard inlay on the shaft of the arrow, and knew who had fired it. He reached across, placed two fingers on Bay's throat and felt the moment of his passing. Bay was gone, and no effort on his part could save him. He left him and swam onwards to where Nefer and Mintaka stood on the far bank calling encouragement to him. Four more of the long arrows dropped close to him, but none touched him and he drew slowly out of their reach.

Nefer met him and helped him to his feet in the thick mud. Taita used his staff to help himself out on to firm ground. He sagged down, gasping for breath. After only a minute he sat up again, and stared across the sinking sands to where Trok stood on the far bank, arms akimbo, every line of his body and head betraying his rage and frustration. Then Trok cupped his hands around his mouth and shouted, 'Think not that you have escaped me, Warlock. I want you and I want my bitch back. I will have you both. I will run you down. I will never lose the scent.'

Mintaka walked forward as far as she could go. She knew exactly where he was most vulnerable, and how to humiliate him most painfully in front of his men. 'Dear husband, your threats are as flaccid and empty as your loins.' Her high sweet voice carried clearly and two hundred Hyksos warriors heard every word. There was a shocked silence, and then a great roar of mocking laughter went up from their ranks. Even his own men hated Trok enough to take pleasure in his humiliation.

Trok brandished his bow above his head and stamped with helpless rage. At last he turned, snarling, on his men and they fell silent, abashed by their own temerity.

In the silence Trok shouted, 'Ishtar! Ishtar the Mede, come forward!'

Ishtar stood at the edge of the sinking sands and faced the little party on the far bank. His face was covered by the patterns of tattoos. His eyes were surrounded by purple whorls; his one wall eye shone like a silver disc. A double row of red dots ran down his long nose. There were fern-like tracings across his chin and cheeks. His hair was set into long hard spikes with red shellac. Deliberately he loosened his robe and let it fall to the sand.

He stood stark naked, and his back and shoulders were covered with leopard rosettes. A huge star of red was tattooed on his belly and his pubic hair was shaven, which emphasized his enormous dangling penis. Tiny bells of gold and silver were hooked through his pierced foreskin. He stared at Taita, and the Magus stepped forward to confront him. The gap between them seemed to shrink as they stared at each other.

Slowly Ishtar's member swelled and the bells tinkled as it stiffened into a massive erection. He thrust his hips forward, pointing the angry red head at Taita's. It was a direct challenge, emphasizing Taita's eunuch status, and exerting Ishtar's masculinity over him.

Taita lifted his staff and pointed at the Mede's groin. Neither moved for a long while, projecting all their strength against each other like thrown javelins.

Suddenly Ishtar groaned and ejaculated, spurting all his seed into the sand. His penis shrivelled, becoming small, wrinkled and insignificant. Ishtar sank to his knees and hurriedly pulled on his robe to cover his humiliation. He had lost the first direct confrontation with the Warlock. He turned his back on Taita and shuffled back to where the two priests of Seueth and the Nubian shaman squatted. He joined their circle, and they linked hands and began to chant.

'What are they doing?' Nefer asked nervously.

'I think that they are trying to divine the way around the sinking sands,' Mintaka whispered.

'Taita will stop them,' Nefer said, with a confidence he did not feel.

Suddenly Ishtar sprang to his feet, with renewed vitality. He let out a cry like a raven's hoarse croak, and pointed south down the sand valley.

'He has chosen the route the falcon revealed to us,' Taita said quietly. 'We are not yet safe.'

Trok's regiments mounted. With Ishtar riding beside Trok in the leading chariot they trotted away southwards following the winding river of fatal mud. As they passed, the troopers shouted threats and defiance at the forlorn group on the opposite bank.

After the dust settled they saw that Trok had left a small force, five chariots, ten men, camped under the dunes on the far bank to keep them under observation. Soon the last chariot in the pursuit column was gone into the yellow heat haze, and was hidden by the bend in the valley walls.

'Before nightfall Trok will have found the way across to our side,' Taita predicted.

'What can we do?' Nefer asked.

Taita turned to him. 'You are Pharaoh. You are the Lord of Ten Thousand Chariots. Give us your orders, Majesty.'

Nefer stared at him, speechless at this taunt. Surely Taita was jeering at him. Then he stared into those ancient pale eyes and saw that there was no mockery in them. His anger rose in his throat with the bitter taste of bile.

He was about to protest, to point out that they had lost everything, all their vehicles and water, and that there was a burning desert ahead of them and a relentlessly pursuing army behind them but Mintaka touched his arm, which steadied him. He stared into Taita's eyes and the inspiration came to him.

He told them his plan, and before he was finished Hilto was grinning and nodding, and Meren laughed and rubbed his hands together. Mintaka stood closer to him, proud and straight.

When he had given his orders, Taita nodded. 'That is the battle plan of a true pharaoh,' he said. His voice was flat and without emotion, but in his eyes was a spark of approval. He knew at last that the task Lostris had set for him would soon be finished. Nefer was almost ready to take charge of his own destiny.

They had covered no more than a few leagues when Ishtar pointed forward. Trok halted the column and strained his eyes in the strange yellow light and the shimmering heat-haze. Ahead the valley of the sinking sands narrowed sharply.

'What is that?' Trok demanded. It seemed that some sinuous sea monster was swimming across the gap. The crest of its dorsal fin stuck up from the yellow mud, black and sharp-edged.

'It is our bridge,' Ishtar told him, 'a ridge of shale running from one bank to the other. This is our crossing.'

Trok sent two of his best men ahead on foot to scout the shale bridge. They ran lightly across and reached the far side with dry sandals. They shouted and waved to Trok and he whipped up his horses and followed them across. In single file the rest of the column crossed behind him.

As soon as they were all safely on the far bank, Trok turned towards the north following the valley back to where they had last seen Taita's fugitive party.

But they had covered less than half the distance before the overcast cloud turned to a yellow fog, a brooding miasma that brought on the night prematurely. Within minutes the last of the light had been snuffed out, and the utter darkness forced the column to halt.

'The horses are tired.' Trok tried to put a brave face on the decision to halt for the night when his commanders gathered around him in the darkness for their orders. 'Water them and let them and the men rest. We will go on at first light. Even the Warlock will not have gone far on foot and without water. We shall have them before noon tomorrow.'

Taita unwrapped Mintaka's feet and nodded with satisfaction. Then he dampened them in the strong alkali moisture of the sinking sands, and rebandaged them. Over her protests Nefer made her don his own sandals. They were too large for her by far, but the bandages made them fit closer.

They had nothing to carry, no water or food, no weapons or baggage, nothing except the floorboards from the sunken chariots. With the Hyksos troopers on the far bank watching them curiously, Nefer led them up the face of the high dune, heading east. Panting, they reached the crest. Already their thirst was a raging torment.

Nefer took one last look across the sinking sands. Trok's troopers on the far bank had removed their horses' harness, laagered their chariots and were lighting their watchfires. Nefer gave them an ironic salute, and followed the rest of the party down the far side of the dune. As soon as they were hidden from the watchers they rested awhile. 'Every effort will cost us dear,' Nefer warned them. 'We will have no water for many hours more.'

As they lay panting in the heat they listened anxiously for the sound of the men and chariots. Mintaka gave voice to their fears: 'Pray to all the gods that Trok does not find his crossing and come back to us before dark.'

When they had recovered Nefer led them, under cover of the intervening sand dune, parallel to the valley of the sinking sands. They went only a short distance, but in the heat the effort taxed them severely. Once again they settled down to rest in the enervating yellow fog. They did not have long to wait before the darkness descended on them.

Night brought little relief from the heat. They climbed back to the top of the dune and below them saw the watchfires of the men on the opposite side of the valley. The flames gave just sufficient light for them to make out the layout of the Hyksos camp.

The enemy chariots were drawn up in a hollow square with the horses' heads hitched to the wheels. Two sentries sat beside the fires, and the rest of the men were lying on their sleeping mats within the shelter of the laager.

'They have seen us set out towards the east. We must hope that they believe we are still heading in that direction, and that they are off their guard,' Nefer said, and led them slipping and sliding down the face of the dune. They reached the bottom a few hundred cubits down the valley from the camp. This was just far enough to hide their movements and muffle any sounds they might make.

Using the glow of the campfires for orientation, linking arms so that no one would lose the way in the dark, they groped their way to the edge of the sinking sands.

They launched the wooden boards and sculled across the quagmire. They had become practised at this form of travel and within a short time they reached the far side.

Keeping close together they crept towards the camp, and crouched down just beyond the circle of firelight. Except for the two sentries the enemy camp seemed asleep. The horses were quiet and the only sound was the soft crackle of the flames. Suddenly one of the sentries stood up and walked across to where his comrade sat. The two talked softly. Nefer fretted at the delay, and was about to ask Taita for help when the old man anticipated him. He pointed his staff at the two dark figures. Within minutes their voices sounded drowsy, and at last the one sentry stood up, stretched and yawned. He sauntered back to his own fire, and settled down with his sword across his lap.

Taita kept the staff pointed at him, and slowly the man's head sank forward, his chin resting on his chest. From the other fire came a soft snore. Both men were fast asleep.

Nefer touched Hilto and Meren. Each knew his job. They crept forward again leaving Taita and Mintaka at the edge of the firelight.

Nefer came up behind the nearest sentry. The sword had slipped from his lap and lay beside him in the sand. Nefer picked it up and in the same movement slammed the bronze pommel into the man's temple. Without a sound the sentry toppled over and lay stretched full-length beside his fire.

With the sword in his fist Nefer glanced across at the other fire. Hilto and Meren had dealt with the sentry, who lay curled up like a sleeping dog. Hilto had his sword. The three ran forward and reached the nearest chariot. The javelins were still in the side-bins.

Nefer grabbed one. It felt heavy and comforting in his

grip. Meren, too, had armed himself. Suddenly one of the horses whinnied softly and stamped its hoof. Nefer froze. For a moment he thought that they had remained undetected. Then a sleepy voice called from within the square of chariots.

'Noosa, is that you? Are you awake?'

A trooper staggered into the firelight, still more than half asleep, naked except for his loincloth. He held a sword in his right hand.

He stopped and gawked at Nefer. 'Who are you?' His voice rose in alarm.

Meren hurled the javelin. It struck in the centre of the man's chest. He threw up his hand and slumped to the sand. Meren jumped forward and picked up his fallen sword. Howling like maddened *djinns* the three of them leaped over the shafts and rushed into the square of vehicles. Their shrieks had thrown the awakening men into wild confusion. Some had not even drawn their weapons and the captured swords rose and fell to a murderous rhythm. The blades dulled with blood.

Only one of the enemy rallied and turned upon them. He was a big brute of a man, and he beat them back, roaring like a wounded lion. He aimed a full cut at Nefer's head, and although Nefer caught it with a high parry, the blow numbed his arm to the shoulder. The bronze blade snapped off at the guard.

Nefer was disarmed and his adversary swung up his sword and aimed at his head to finish it. Taita stepped out of the darkness behind him, and rapped him over the skull with his staff. The man collapsed, and Nefer snatched the sword from his nerveless fingers before it struck the ground.

The fight was over. Five of the survivors knelt with their hands on their heads, while Hilto and Meren stood over them. Mintaka and Taita built up the fires, and by the light of the flames they made out that three of the troopers were dead, and two others gravely wounded.

While Taita treated their injuries, the others used spare tackle from the chariots to pinion the hands and feet of the prisoners. Only then could they drink their fill from the waterskins, help themselves from the bread bag and cut slices of dried meat from the provisions they found.

By the time they had eaten and drunk the light of the new day was strengthening. It was another threatening scarlet dawn, and the heat was already suffocating. Nefer selected three chariots, and the best of the horses to draw them. They stripped the chosen vehicles of any unnecessary equipment, such as the troopers' personal baggage and spare weapons beyond their own requirements. Nefer turned the unwanted horses loose and sent them galloping into the wilderness by waving a blanket in their faces.

Every minute the ruddy light of that eerie dawn grew stronger, and they mounted in haste. When they were ready to leave Nefer went to the group of bound prisoners.

'You are Egyptians, as we are. It pains me deeply that we have killed and wounded some of your companions. This was neither our choice nor our pleasure. The usurper Trok forced this upon us.'

He squatted down next to the big man who had nearly killed him. 'You are a brave fellow. I wish that some day we could fight side by side against the common enemy.'

The skirt of Nefer's apron had drawn up as he sat, and the prisoner's eyes went down to the smooth muscles of his right thigh. His mouth fell open. 'Pharaoh Nefer Seti is dead. Why do you bear the royal cartouche?' he asked.

Nefer touched the tattoo that Taita had inscribed there so long ago. 'I bear it by right,' he said. 'I am Pharaoh Nefer Seti.'

'No! No!' The prisoner was agitated and afraid, as he had probably never been on a battlefield.

Mintaka jumped down from the chariot and came to them. She spoke to the man in a friendly tone. 'Do you know who I am?'

'You are Her Majesty Queen Mintaka. Your father was my god and commander. I loved him well. Therefore I love and respect you.'

Mintaka slipped her dagger from its sheath and cut away his bonds. 'Yes,' she said. 'I am Mintaka, and this is Pharaoh Nefer Seti who is my betrothed. One day we shall return to Egypt to claim our birthright, and to rule in peace and justice.'

Nefer and Mintaka stood up and she went on, 'Give this message to your comrades-in-arms. Tell the people that we are alive and that we shall return to this very Egypt.'

The man crept forward on his knees and kissed her feet, then he crawled to Nefer and picked up one of his feet. He placed it upon his own head.

'I am your man,' he said. 'I shall carry your message to the people. Return to us soon, divine Pharaoh.'

The other prisoners joined him with protestations of loyal love. 'Hail, Pharaoh! May you live and rule a thousand years!'

Nefer and Mintaka mounted their captured chariot, and the freed prisoners shouted, '*Bak-her! Bak-her!*'

The three vehicles pulled out of the wrecked camp. Taita rode alone in the van, because he was best able to resist the wiles of Ishtar the Mede, and to discover the true road that had been hidden from them. Nefer and Mintaka followed closely, and Hilto and Meren brought up the rearguard. They headed back the way they had come.

They had gone only a short way, the valley of the sinking sands and the camp still in sight, when Taita stopped and looked back. The other two vehicles halted behind him. 'What is it?' Nefer asked, and Taita held up his hand. In the silence they heard the distant sound of Trok's division coming on along the far bank. Then suddenly, through the lowering red dawn, they saw the head of his column appear from out of the far dunes.

In the leading chariot Trok reined in sharply and

shouted at Ishtar, 'By the blood and seed of Seueth, the Warlock has outwitted you again. Did you not foresee that they would cross back and seize the chariots of our picket?'

'Did you also not foresee it?' Ishtar snarled at him. 'You are the great general.'

Trok threw back his whip arm to lash him across his tattooed face for such insolence, but when he looked into the Mede's dark eyes he thought better of it and lowered the whip. 'What now, Ishtar? Will you let them get clear away?'

'There is only one road back for them and Zander is coming down it with two hundred chariots. You still have them between the grindstones,' Ishtar pointed out darkly. Trok's face lit in a savage smile. In his fury he had almost forgotten Zander.

'The sun has hardly risen. You have all this long day to recross the shale bridge and follow them up,' Ishtar went on. 'I have their scent in my nostrils. I will cast my web to ensnare them and, like a faithful hound, I will lead you to the kill.'

Trok lashed his horses forward and rode out on to the firm sand at the edge of the swamp, directly opposite the three chariots on the other bank. He managed to summon up a laugh and a wide smile that were almost convincing.

'I am enjoying this more than you are, my friends. Revenge is a meal best eaten cold! By Seueth, I will enjoy the taste of it.'

'You must catch your rabbit before you can cook it,' Mintaka called back.

'I will. Be sure that I still have some surprises to amuse you.'

His smile faded as the three chariots started forward into the dunes, Mintaka waving back at him gaily. Although he knew that it was her intention to anger him, it galled him so much that his guts felt hot and sour with rage.

'Back!' he shouted at his men. 'Back across the bridge.'

As they went on Taita looked to the sky more frequently, and his expression was sober and thoughtful as the brimstone clouds sank closer to the earth.

'I have never seen a sky like this,' Hilto said, when they stopped to water the horses in the middle of the forenoon. 'The gods are angry.'

It was strange how readily they found the true road. The fork where they had made the wrong turning was plain to see from far off. It seemed that they could not possibly have missed the tall cairn of stones that marked it, and the main road to the Red Sea, travelled by so many trading caravans, was more deeply trodden and apparent than the rudimentary track they had followed into the valley of the Sinking Sands.

'Ishtar blinded us,' Nefer murmured, as they rode towards the crossroads, 'but this time we will not be so easily duped.' Then he looked up uneasily at the sky and made the sign against evil. 'If the gods are kind.'

It was Hilto, with his warrior's eyes, who picked out the dustcloud ahead of them. The low, clouded sky had obscured it until now when it was close. Hilto galloped alongside Taita's chariot and shouted to him, 'Magus! Those are chariots ahead of us, and many of them.'

They reined in and stared ahead. The dustcloud was moving even as they studied it.

'How far ahead?' Taita asked.

'Half a league or less.'

'Do you think that Trok has a second division coming up behind him?'

'You know better than I do, Magus, that that is the common tactic of the Hyksos. Do you not recall the Battle of Dammen? How Apepi caught us there between his two divisions?'

'Can we reach the crossroads before they cut us off?' Taita asked, and Hilto narrowed his eyes.

'Maybe so. But it will be a close race for it.'

Taita turned and looked back. 'Trok will be on the road behind us already. We dare not turn back into his arms.'

'It would be certain disaster to leave the road and enter the sands. We would leave a clear sign for them to follow. The horses would fail before the end of the day.'

'No wonder Trok laughed at us,' said Mintaka bitterly.

'We are once again between the hammer and the anvil,' Meren agreed.

'We must run for it,' Nefer decided. 'We must try to reach the crossroads and get on to the main road ahead of them. It is our only escape.'

'At our best speed, then, even if we use up the horses in the effort,' Hilto agreed.

They surged forward three abreast. The chariots bumped and swerved as their wheels caught the ruts in the track, but the horses were going well. The dustcloud ahead became more menacing as they ran towards it. The cairns of stones seemed never to grow closer. They were still more than five hundred cubits from the turning when the first chariots of the approaching division hove into sight, half obscured by dust and the awful yellow light.

They stopped as though uncertain of the identity of the three racing vehicles they saw coming towards them, then suddenly started forward again, coming straight at the fugitives.

Taita tried to force a last turn of speed out of the horses, but felt the weariness overtaking them. They held on until the last possible moment, but the enemy was charging head-on at them, and it gradually became certain that they could not reach the crossroads before them. At last Taita held up his clenched fist in the command to halt. 'Enough!' he cried. 'We can never win this race.'

They halted across the track, the horses lathered and heaving for breath. The charioteers were pale under the dust that coated their features and despair bloomed in their eyes.

'Which way, Pharaoh?' Hilto shouted. They were already beginning to turn to Nefer for leadership.

'There is only one way open. Back the way we have come.' And then, so low that only Mintaka could hear him, 'Into Trok's arms. But at least it gives me a last chance to settle the score with him.'

Taita nodded agreement, and was the first to swing his chariot into a tight full turn. He led them back towards the sinking sands. The others wheeled around and followed in his dust. At first the dust covered their view of the pursuit, but then a puff of hot wind blew it aside momentarily and they saw that they had already lost ground.

They tore onwards, but Nefer felt his horses start to fail. Their gait was heavy and laboured, their legs flopping and their hoofs starting to throw out sideways. Nefer knew that it was nearly over. He placed one arm around Mintaka's waist. 'I loved you from the first moment I saw you. I shall love you through eternity.'

'If you truly love me, then you will never let me fall into Trok's hands again. At the end, it will be the way for you to prove your love.'

Nefer turned to look down at her, puzzled. 'I do not understand,' he said, and she touched the captured sword that hung at his side.

'No!' He almost screamed the word, and hugged her to him with all his strength.

'You must do it for me, my heart. You cannot give me back to Trok. I do not have the courage to do it myself so you must be strong for me.'

'I cannot,' he cried.

'It will be quick and painless. The other way . . .'

He was in such distress that he almost ran full tilt into the back of Taita's chariot as it came to an abrupt swerving halt across the track ahead of them. Taita pointed ahead.

Trok was there. Even at distance they could make out his bear-like form at the head of his moving column, coming straight towards them. They looked back and the other enemy was closing in as fast.

'One last fight!' Hilto loosened his blade in its scabbard. 'The first the worst. The second the same. The last the best of all the game.' It was one of the adages of the Red Road, and he quoted it with genuine anticipation.

Taita looked up at the bile-coloured sky as another sultry gust rippled his hair, like wind through a field of silver grass.

Mintaka tugged Nefer's arm. 'Promise me!' she whispered, and his eyes filled with tears.

'I promise you,' he said, and the words scalded his mouth and throat. 'And afterwards I shall kill Trok with my own hands. When I have done that I will follow close behind you on the dark journey.'

Taita did not raise his voice but it carried to all of them: 'This way. Mark well my wheel tracks and follow them faithfully.'

To their astonishment Taita turned his horses off into the sand heading at a right-angle from the track, north into the unmarked shifting dunes. Nefer expected him to sink to the hubs immediately, but somehow he must have found a hard crust under the soft surface. He went on at a steady trot and they followed him closely, although they knew that this was a last, doomed attempt.

Looking back Nefer could still make out both clouds of dust from the two enemy divisions converging on them from the east and the west. There was not the least chance that, when they reached it, they would not find the place where the three chariots had left the track. Unless, of course, Taita could weave a spell of concealment to outwit Ishtar, but that was a despairing chance. Ishtar had proved that he was not susceptible to such trivial witchcraft and Trok with his own eyes must have seen them turn aside from the track.

Yet when he looked ahead he saw that Taita had the golden Periapt of Lostris in his right hand and around his wrist he had wrapped the necklace that had been the gift of Bay. He was not looking back at the pursuit, but his face was raised to the menacing sky and his expression was rapt.

Their plight seemed hopeless, but Nefer felt an illogical and perverse glow of hope. He realized that, in some mysterious fashion, the gift of Bay had enhanced the old man's already formidable powers. 'Look at Taita,' he whispered to Mintaka. 'Perhaps it is not yet the end. Perhaps there will be one more move of the bao stones left to us before the game is decided.'

Trok galloped down the track until he reached the spot where he had seen the three chariots turn aside and head into the dunes. Their tracks were so deeply etched into the sand that they might have been made by a single pair of wheels. At that moment Zander rode up from the opposite direction at the head of the second column.

'Well done! You have turned the quarry. We have them now,' Trok shouted at him.

'It has been a good chase,' Zander roared back. 'What formation do you want me to keep?'

'Take the rearguard once again. In column of fours. Follow me.' As he turned off to follow the fugitives, his two divisions of chariots fell in behind him. He looked ahead. Taita and his tiny party had already disappeared into a funnel of high sandhills, whose tops were purple and blue. The depths between them were sombre and shaded under the lowering sky. He had not gone two hundred cubits when the outside chariots of the column were bogged down in the soft sand. He knew then why Taita had maintained such a tight formation. Only in the centre line was the earth hard enough to support a chariot.

'In single line ahead!' He altered his formation. 'Stay in my tracks.'

The two combined divisions stretched out over half a league as they followed Trok into the uncharted wilderness, and the troopers looked up with mounting trepidation at the towering sand walls and the ugly sky above. Trok could not press his horses at the same killing pace and they came down to a walk, but he could judge by the tracks Taita had left that he, too, was moving more slowly.

They kept on for almost another league until abruptly the land ahead changed character. From the soft sand waves rose a dark island of rock. It was like some small craft lost in the ocean of the dunes. Its sides were honeycombed and eaten away by the abrasive sand-laden winds of millennia, but the peak was as sharp as the fang of some fabulous monster.

On the peak, tiny with distance, stood an unmistakable figure, sparse and tall with a wild bush of silver hair that glinted like a helmet in the strange and awful light.

''Tis the Warlock,' Trok gloated to Ishtar. 'They have taken refuge in the rocks. I hope they try to fight us there.' Then to his trumpeter, 'Sound the battle call.'

When Nefer and Mintaka saw the rockpile looming ahead they were both astonished.

'Did Taita know it was here?' Mintaka asked.

'How could he have known?' Nefer replied.

'You told me once that he knows everything.' And Nefer was silenced. He looked back to cover his uncertainty, and saw the dust of the pursuit close behind, rising to mingle with the yellow glare of the sunless sky.

'It matters not at all. How can it avail us?' he asked. 'We might be able to defend those rocks for a very little while, but there are hundreds of Trok's men. This is almost the end.' He touched the waterskin that hung from the rail beside him. It was almost empty, not even enough left to keep the horses alive for another day.

'We must trust Taita,' Mintaka said, and he laughed bitterly.

'It seems the gods have deserted us. Who else is there to trust but Taita?'

They went forward, with the horses down to a hampered walk. Behind them they heard the faint sounds of the pursuit: the cries of the captains urging their troopers to keep the line, the jingle of loose equipment and the groan and whine of dry wheel hubs.

At last they came up under the hill of black and ochre-coloured rock. It was a hundred feet high and the accumulated heat radiated from it like a bonfire. Not a single plant had found a foothold on it, but the wind had carved fissures and cracks in its cliffs.

'Drive the chariots close in against the cliff,' Taita ordered, and they obeyed. 'Now free the horses and bring them this way.' Taita set the example by leading his own team around the angle of the rockface. Here there was a deep fissure with sheer sides cutting into the rock pile.

'This way.' He led them as far as they could go along the sandy floor of the deep, vertical crack. 'Now make the horses lie down.'

All cavalry horses were trained to perform this trick. At the urging of their handlers they lowered themselves to their knees and then, grunting and blowing, they went flat on their sides on the floor of the fissure.

'Like this!' Taita told them. He had brought a bedding roll from the chariot. With strips torn from it he blindfolded the horses to keep them quiet and submissive. Then he drove a javelin deep into the loose earth and used it as an anchor to tie down the horses' swathed heads and prevent them from rising again. The others followed his example.

'Now bring what remains of the water. 'Tis a pity there is not enough to give the horses a last drink, but we will need every drop for ourselves.'

Almost as if he knew of its existence, Taita led them to a shallow overhang in the cliff. The head room under the overhang was so low that anyone trying to enter would have to go down on hands and knees.

'Use the loose scree from the cliff to wall this in.'

'A *zareba* wall?' Nefer looked puzzled. 'We cannot defend this place. Once we are in the cave we could not even stand, let alone swing a sword.'

'There is no time to argue.' Taita glared at him. 'Do as I tell you.'

Nefer's nerves were raw with fear for Mintaka, and he was wearied by the hardships they had lived through these last days. He glared back at Taita. The others watched with interest: the young bull challenging the older one. The seconds drew out until abruptly Nefer realized his own foolishness. Only one person could save them now and he capitulated. He stooped and picked up a large rock from the scree pile and staggered with it to the shallow cave. He placed it in position and ran back for another. The others joined in the work. Even Mintaka carried her share of the rough lumps of schist. The skin of her hands was raw and torn before they had closed in a narrow space behind the wall.

'What do we do now?' Nefer asked stiffly, still smarting from his encounter with the Magus.

'Drink,' said Taita.

Nefer poured from the skin into a leather bucket and handed it to Mintaka. She took a few sips then offered it to Taita.

He shook his head. 'Drink, and drink deep.'

When they had all drunk as much as their stomachs would hold, Nefer turned on Taita again. 'What now?'

'Wait here,' Taita ordered and picked up his long staff. He began to climb the jagged side of the hillock.

'What about this *zareba*?' Nefer shouted after him. 'What purpose is it to serve?'

Taita paused on a narrow ledge thirty feet above them and looked down. 'Your Majesty will know when the time comes.' Taita began to climb again.

'A hiding-place? A tomb, perhaps?' Nefer called sarcastically after him, but Taita did not answer or look back.

He climbed without rest or pause until he reached the peak of the hillock. He stood there gazing back in the direction from which Trok would come.

The little party in the gully at the foot of the hillock watched him, some puzzled, some with hope and one angrily.

Nefer roused himself. 'Fetch the javelins and the rest of the weapons from the chariots. We must be ready to defend ourselves.' He ran to where they had left the chariots. He came back with an armful of javelins, and Meren and Hilto following behind him similarly laden.

'What is Taita doing?' he asked Mintaka. She pointed up at the crest.

'He has not moved.'

They stacked the weapons then settled down at the entrance to the rough shelter. All their eyes went up to Taita again.

He was outlined against that dreadful sulphur sky. Nobody spoke, nobody moved, until they heard that dreaded sound again. They turned their heads to listen to the faint rattle and squeal of chariot wheels, hundreds of them, the voices of men, sometimes muffled by the dunes, at others clear and menacing.

Slowly Taita raised both arms and pointed them to the

sky. All their eyes followed the movement. In his right hand he held his staff, in the left the Periapt of Lostris, and at his throat he wore the gift of Bay.

'What is he doing now?' Hilto asked, in an awed tone. Nobody answered him.

Taita stood as still as if he had been chiselled out of the living rock. His head was thrown back, his hair fluffed out silver on his shoulders. His robes were belted up, so that his thin shanks were exposed. He looked like an old bird at roost.

The heavens swirled with low, heavy cloud. The light was transient, fading as the hidden sun was covered more heavily, flaring as the clouds thinned and fumed.

Still Taita did not move, his staff aimed at the pregnant belly of the heavens. The sound of the approaching column became clearer still, and suddenly there was a distant blare of a ram's horn trumpet.

'That is the battle call. Trok has seen Taita,' Mintaka said quietly.

Trok shouted at his trumpeter, 'Sound the advance!' but the warlike sound seemed to be swallowed up by the empty desert and the low, angry heavens.

'Wait!' said Ishtar the Mede. He was watching Taita's tiny figure on the peak of the rock hill. 'Wait!'

'What is it?' Trok demanded.

'As yet I cannot fathom it,' Ishtar said, without taking his gaze off the Warlock, 'but it is pervasive and powerful.'

The column remained halted, every man in it staring at the figure on the peak with awe. A terrible silence fell on the desert. There was no sound at all. Even the horses were still – there was no rattle or jingle of equipment.

Only the sky moved. It formed a whirlpool over the head of the Magus, a great turning wheel of smouldering cloud. Then slowly the centre of the whirlpool opened like the single eye of an awakening monster. From the heavenly eye a shaft of dazzling sunlight burst forth.

'The eye of Horus!' Ishtar breathed. 'He has called up the god.' He made a sign of protection, and at his side Trok was silent and rigid with superstitious dread.

The brilliant shaft of light struck the peak, and lit the figure of the Warlock like a bolt of blinding lightning. Around his head it spun a nimbus of silver radiance.

He made a slow circular pass with his long staff, and the Hyksosian charioteers cringed like curs under the whip. The clouds opened wider, and the sky was clear. The sunlight danced on the dunes and was reflected like a sheet of polished bronze into their eyes, dazzling and blinding them. They lifted their shields or their hands to protect their eyes from the strange radiance, but they made no sound.

On the peak Taita described another deliberate circle with his staff, and there was a sound at last: soft as a lover's sigh, it seemed to issue from the very heavens. Men's heads turned questioningly as they sought the source.

Once again Taita gestured and the sigh became a soughing, a gentle whistling. It came from the east, and slowly all their heads turned towards it.

Out of that strange, cloudless brilliance, they saw it coming. It was a solid dun wall that reached from the earth to the highest heavens.

'*Khamsin!*' Trok whispered the dread word.

The wall of airborne sand marched towards them with a terrible deliberation. It undulated and pulsed like a living creature, and its voice changed. No longer a whisper, it became a rising howl, the voice of a demon.

'*Khamsin!*' The word was yelled from chariot to chariot. They were no longer warriors hot for war, but small terrified creatures in the face of this destroyer of men, cities and civilizations, this eater of worlds.

The column of chariots lost its formation and broke up

into fragments as the drivers wheeled their teams and tried to run from it.

As soon as they left the narrow path of harder ground the sand sucked down their wheels. Men leaped from the cockpits and abandoned their vehicles, leaving the horses in the traces. Instinctively the horses sensed the menace and reared and screamed, trying to escape by kicking themselves free of the traces.

The *khamsin* bore down upon them inexorably. Its voice changed from a howl to a bellow. Men ran before it in mindless panic. They slipped and fell in the loose sand, dragged themselves up and ran on. They looked back and saw the great storm come on apace roaring like a crazed monster, rolling and roiling upon itself, twisting curtains of sand, brazen where the sunlight struck them, dun and sombre where their own mountainous heights shaded them.

Taita stood with his arms and staff outstretched and watched the army below him engulfed. He saw Trok and Ishtar still frozen like a pair of statues in the sunlight, and then, as the front of the storm reached them, they were gone with magical swiftness, they and all their men, chariots and horses, gone in the rolling billows of the *khamsin*.

Taita lowered his arms, turned his back on the monster and, without haste, started down the hillock. His long legs spanned the difficult places and he leaned upon his staff as he stepped from ledge to ledge.

Nefer and Mintaka were standing hand in hand at the base of the cliff. They welcomed him with a bemused expression, and Mintaka's tone was subdued and incredulous as she asked, 'You called up the storm?'

'It has been brewing all these last days,' Taita said, his face neutral and his tone equivocal. 'You have all remarked the heat and the dolorous yellow mists.'

'No,' said Nefer. 'It was not in nature. It was you. You knew and understood all along. You called it up. And I doubted you.'

'Go into the shelter now,' said Taita. 'It is almost upon us.' His voice was lost in the shrieking cacophony of the *khamsin*. Mintaka led the way, crawling into the low narrow cave through the opening in the rude wall. The others followed her, crowding into the tiny space. Before he entered Hilto handed in the almost empty waterskins.

In the end, only Taita stood outside the shelter. Almost as though the storm was his creature, his face was intent as it loomed over him. It struck with a force that made the living rock around them seem to quiver and vibrate and Taita was gone, his tall figure obliterated. The first gust lasted only a few seconds, but when it passed Taita was still there, unmoved and serene. The storm gathered itself bellowing, like a berserk monster, and as it hurled down on them in all its terrible majesty Taita stooped through the opening and sat with his back to the inner wall.

'Close it up,' he said, and Meren and Hilto blocked the entrance with the rocks they had placed at hand.

'Cover your heads,' said Taita, and wound his headcloth over his face. 'Keep your eyes closed, or you will lose your sight. Breathe carefully through your mouth or you will drown in sand.'

The storm was so overwhelming that its first front picked up Trok's chariot and rolled it over with the horses screaming as the lashing shaft broke their backs.

Trok was thrown free. He fought his way to his feet, but the storm struck him down again. He managed to pull himself up, using all his brute strength, but he had lost all sense of direction. When he tried to open his eyes he was blinded by sand. He did not know in which direction he was facing, or where he should try to escape. The storm was swirling upon itself so that it seemed to be coming from every direction at once. He dared not open his eyes again. The *khamsin* ripped at his face, and its harsh rush abraded the skin from his cheeks and lips until he covered them with his headcloth.

In the turmoil of sand and wind Trok screamed, 'Save me! Save me, Ishtar, and I will reward you beyond your greediest dreams.'

It seemed impossible that anyone could have heard his cry in the deafening uproar. Then he felt Ishtar seize his hand and squeeze it hard to caution Trok to hold fast.

They stumbled on, at times sinking to the knees in the sand, which ran like water. Trok tripped over an obstacle and lost contact with Ishtar. When he groped for him in panic he touched the object that had tripped him, and realized that it was one of the abandoned chariots lying on its side.

He screamed for Ishtar, staggering in a circle and Ishtar's hand grabbed his beard and led him on. He was scorched by sand, blinded by sand, drowning in sand.

He fell to his knees and Ishtar hauled him up again, ripping out a handful of his beard. He tried to speak but when he opened his mouth the sand rushed in and he choked. He knew he was dying, that no man could survive this terrible thing that had them in its grip.

It seemed endless, their tormented journey to nowhere. Then, abruptly, he felt the force of the wind diminish. For a minute he thought that the storm had already passed them by, but the roar had not abated – to the contrary, it seemed still to be rising. They staggered onwards, reeling and bumping into each other like two drunkards trying to lead each other home from the tavern. Still the wind force dropped. In a vague and confused way Trok thought that somehow Ishtar had worked a spell to shield them, but then a sudden gust almost lifted him off his feet and broke the grip that Ishtar had on his beard. He crashed into a wall of rock with such force that he felt his collar-bone break.

He dropped to his knees and clung to the rock, like a child to its mother's breast. How Ishtar had brought them to it he neither knew nor cared. All that mattered was that the cliff above them was breaking the full force of the storm. He felt Ishtar kneel at his side and pull up his tunic until it covered his head. Then Ishtar pushed him down flat in the shelter of the cliff and lay down beside him.

In the tiny cave Nefer crawled close to Mintaka and took her in his arms. He tried to speak to her, to comfort and encourage her but both their heads were swathed with cloth, and the wind drowned out all sound. She laid her head on his shoulder and they clung to each other. They were entombed in the roaring darkness, dumb and blinded and half suffocated. Each hot breath they drew had to be strained through cloth and taken only a sip at a time to prevent a rush of talcum fine sand passing between their lips.

After a while the roar of the wind deafened them and dulled all their other senses. It went on and on, without ceasing or relenting. They had no way to judge the passage of time, except the tiniest awareness of light and darkness through their closed eyelids. To mark the arrival of the day there was a faint rosy aura; when night fell it faded into utter darkness. Nefer had never known such complete and endless dark. If it had not been for Mintaka's body pressed close to his, he thought that he would have gone mad.

Every once in a long while she stirred against him and answered the pressure of his arms with her own. He might have slept, but there were no dreams, just the roaring of the *khamsin* and the darkness.

After another long while he tried to move his legs, but he could not. In a blind panic he thought he had lost control of his body. That he was weak and dying. He tried again with all his strength, and managed to move his foot and toes. Then he knew that he was entrapped by the sand that was filtering into their shelter through the chinks in the *zareba* wall. It had already piled up as high as his waist. They were slowly being buried alive. The thought of that insidious death filled him with terror. With his bare hands he scraped away enough sand to be able to move his legs then did the same for Mintaka.

He felt the others working at the same task in the crowded cave, trying to fight back the sand, but it trickled in like water. It was deposited on them from the dense clouds of swirling dust.

And the storm raged on.

For two days and three nights the wind never relented. During this time Nefer managed to keep back the sand just enough to move his head and his arms, but his lower body was encased solidly. He could not begin to dig himself out, for there was nowhere to which he could move the sand.

He reached up one hand and touched the stone roof inches above his head. He ran his fingers across it, and realized it was slightly domed. Their heads were in this small space, but the sand had sealed off the cave entrance so that no more sand could penetrate. But he could still hear the storm bellow endlessly.

He waited. At times he felt Mintaka sobbing quietly beside him and tried to comfort her with a gentle pressure of his arms. The air trapped with them in the tiny head space became fetid and stale. He thought that soon it would no longer keep them alive, but some fresh air must have been filtering through the sand, for although each breath was a struggle they were still alive.

They drank most of the water that remained in the waterskins, leaving only a tiny amount in the bottom. Then the thirst came. Even though they were unable to move their bodies to use up moisture, the hot dry sand and air sucked it out of them. Nefer felt his tongue slowly cleave to the roof of his mouth. Then it began to swell so his breathing, already difficult, became almost impossible because of the huge spongy thing that filled his mouth.

With the fear and the thirst he lost track of time, and it seemed that years had passed. Nefer aroused himself from the stupor that was slowly overtaking him. He realized that something had changed. He tried to fathom what it was, but his mind was numb and unresponsive. Mintaka was very still beside him. He squeezed her fearfully. In reply he felt a tiny shudder of movement. She was still alive. Both of them were alive, but entombed, able only to move some small part of their bodies.

He felt himself drifting back into that dark stupor, into haunted dreams of water, of cool green expanses of the great river, of cascades and bright rivulets of water. He forced himself up from the darkness, and listened. He heard nothing. That was what had roused him. There was no sound. The roaring clamour of the *khamsin* had given way to a profound silence. The silence of a sealed tomb, he thought, and the horror returned full force.

He began to struggle again, to try to work his way out of the sand. He managed at last to free his right arm, reached out and found Mintaka's covered head. He stroked it and in the silence heard her whimper. He tried to speak, to reassure her, but his swollen tongue would let no word pass. Instead he reached out beyond her to see if he could touch Hilto, who had been sitting on the far side of her. Either Hilto was gone or was beyond the reach of his arm, for he touched nothing.

He rested a while then roused himself once more, and made an effort to clear the sand from around the entrance to the cave. But there was little space to store what he scraped away. A handful at a time he scooped it away and pushed it into a nook in their tiny cell. Soon he was working at the furthest reach of his right arm, scraping away a few grains at a time. It was a despairing attempt but he knew that he had to keep trying or give up hope.

Abruptly he felt the sand cascade out from under his fingers, and even through the folds of his headcloth fresh air that had not been breathed seeped into the cave. And he was aware of the faintest glimmer of light beyond his closed eyelids. Painfully he began to pull away the cloth from his face. The light grew stronger and the air was sweet in his dry mouth and aching lungs. When his face was free of the cloth he half opened one eye, and was almost dazzled by the light. When his vision had adjusted he saw that he had opened a hole to the outside that was no larger than the circle of his thumb and forefinger, but from beyond there was quiet. The storm had passed.

Excited and with new hope he tugged at the cloth that covered Mintaka's head and heard her breathe the fresh air. Again he tried to speak, but again his voice failed him. He tried to move, to escape from the deadly grip of the heavy sand, but his body was still encased to the armpits.

With all his remaining strength, he struggled silently to free himself, but the effort soon exhausted him and his throat burned and ached with thirst. He thought how cruel it would be to die here with the promise of air and light mocking him through that tiny cleft.

He closed his eyes again wearily, giving up. Then he was aware of another change in the light, and he opened his eye again. With a sense of disbelief he saw a hand reaching through the opening towards him. An ancient hand, with desiccated skin covered with the dark blotches of age.

'Nefer!' He heard a voice so strange, so hoarse and altered, that for a moment he doubted it was the Magus. 'Nefer, can you hear me?'

Nefer tried to reply but still could not speak. He reached out and touched Taita's fingers. Immediately the old man's fingers closed over his with surprising strength.

'Hold hard. We will dig you out.'

He heard other voices then, rough and faint with thirst and effort, and hands scraped away the sand that entrapped him until at last they could lay hold of him and pull him free of the soft, deadly grasp of the sand.

Nefer slithered out through the narrow cleft as though the rocky hillock was giving birth to him. Then Hilto and Meren reached in again and dragged Mintaka out of the soft dark womb into the brilliant sunlight.

They lifted the pair to their feet and held them from falling again, for their legs had no strength. Nefer shrugged off Meren's hands, lurched across to Mintaka and embraced her silently. She was shivering as though in the crisis of malaria. After a while he held her at arm's length and studied her face with horror and pity. Her hair was white with sand, which clung thickly in her eyebrows. Her eyes had receded into deep purple cavities, and her lips were swollen black, so that when she tried to speak they cracked open and a drop of blood, bright as a ruby, trickled down her chin.

'Water,' Nefer managed to articulate at last. 'She must have water.'

He dropped to his knees and began frantically to dig into the sand that still blocked the cave. Meren and Hilto were working beside him and they uncovered the waterskin. They pulled it out, and found that most of the water that had remained had evaporated or been squeezed from it. There remained only sufficient for a few mouthfuls each, but even that amount was enough to keep them alive a little longer. Nefer felt strength return to his dehydrated body, and for the first time looked about him.

It was the middle of the morning. He did not know what morning or for how many days they had been buried. There was still a haze of fine sand like gold-dust in the still air.

He shaded his eyes, looked out over the desert and did not recognize it. The landscape had changed completely:

the high dunes had marched away to be replaced by others, of different shape and alignment. There were valleys where there had been mountains, and vales where hills had stood. Even the colours had changed: the sullen purples and bruised blues had been replaced by reds and golden yellows.

He shook his head in wonder, and looked at Taita. The Magus was leaning on his staff, watching Nefer with those pale, ancient but ageless eyes.

'Trok?' Nefer managed to say. 'Where?'

'Buried,' Taita replied, and now Nefer could see that he also was dried out like a stick of firewood, and suffering the same agonies as they were.

'Water?' Nefer whispered, touching his swollen and bleeding mouth.

'Come,' said Taita.

Nefer took Mintaka's hand and slowly they followed the Magus out into the brazen sands. Now at last thirst and exposure had taken their toll on Taita and he moved slowly and stiffly. The others staggered along behind him.

Taita seemed to be wandering aimlessly through the new valleys of fine sand that ran beneath their feet. He held out his staff in front of him, making a sweeping motion with it. Once or twice he lowered himself to his knees and touched the earth with his forehead.

'What is he doing?' Mintaka whispered. The water they had drank had not been enough to sustain her and she was weakening again. 'Is he praying?'

Nefer only shook his head: he would not squander his own meagre reserves by speaking unnecessarily. Taita moved on slowly, and by the way he was sweeping with his staff Nefer was reminded of a water-diviner at work.

Once again Taita knelt and placed his face close to the earth. This time Nefer watched him with more attention, and saw that he was not praying but sniffing the air close to the surface of the sand. Then he knew what Taita was doing. 'He is searching for the buried chariots of Trok's division,' he whispered to Mintaka. 'His staff is his divining rod, and he is sniffing for the scent of putrescence below the sand.'

Taita stood up painfully and nodded at Hilto. 'Dig here,' he ordered.

They all crowded forward and began to scrape away the loose sand with cupped hands. They had not far to go. An arm's span deep they struck something hard, and redoubled their efforts. Quickly they exposed the wheel rim of a chariot that was lying on its side. Another few minutes of frantic digging and they pulled out a waterskin. They stared at it in despair for it had burst open, perhaps when the chariot had capsized. It was dry, and though they squeezed it frantically it yielded not a single drop of the precious fluid.

'There must be another.' Nefer spoke through dry swollen lips. 'Dig deeper.'

They clawed at the sand in a last despairing burst of strength, and as the excavation deepened the stench of the dead horses in the traces grew stronger and more nauseating. They had been lying in the heat all these days.

Suddenly Nefer reached deeper into the hole and felt something soft and yielding. He pressed it and they all heard the gurgle and slosh of water. He swept away more of the loose sand and between them they lifted out a bulging waterskin. They were mumbling and whimpering with thirst, as Taita opened the stopper and poured it into the leather bucket that had lain beside the waterskin in the bottom of the excavation.

The water was the temperature of blood, but when Taita held the bucket to Mintaka's lips she closed her eyes and drank in a quiet ecstasy.

'Not too much at first,' Taita warned her, took the bucket from her and passed it to Nefer. They drank in turn, then Mintaka drank again, and the bucket made another circuit.

In the meantime Taita left them to continue his search. In a short time he called them to dig again. This time they were lucky: not only was the chariot under less sand, but there were three waterskins, and none was damaged.

'The horses now,' Taita told them, and they looked at each other guiltily. In their desperate preoccupation they had forgotten them. Carrying the waterskins they trudged back through the sand to the base of the cliff.

The narrow gully in which they had pegged down the horses must have been well aligned to avoid the full force of the *khamsin*. When they began to dig, using the wooden spade they had found among the equipment of the buried chariot, they found the first horse almost at once. However, the stink warned them what to expect. The beast was dead and its stomach ballooned with gas. They left it and dug for the next animal.

This time they were more fortunate. It was a mare, the most willing and robust of the horses they had captured at the sinking sands. She was alive, but barely so. They cut the retaining halter that had held her down, but she was too weak to come to her feet unaided. The men lifted her between them. She stood weak and shivering, reeling and threatening to fall again, but she drank greedily from the bucket Mintaka held for her and seemed at once to improve.

In the meantime the men were digging for the other horses. They found two more dead of thirst or suffocation, but another two still alive. They also responded immediately they were given water.

They left Mintaka to care for the three pathetic beasts and went back to the chariots they had uncovered to find fodder. They brought back bags of grain and another waterskin.

'You are doing good work with them,' Nefer told Mintaka, as he stroked the mare's neck, 'but I fear they are too far gone ever to pull another chariot.'

She rounded on him fiercely: 'I will bring all of them through, I swear to the goddess. There must be hundreds more fodder bags and waterskins out there under the sand. We may have to stay here many more days, but when we leave, these gallant creatures will take us out.'

Nefer laughed at her through his cracked, scabbed lips. 'I am in deep awe of your passionate nature.'

'Then provoke me no further,' she warned him, 'or you will see more proof of it.' It was the first time she had smiled since the passing of the *khamsin*. 'Now go back to help the others. We cannot have too great a supply of water.'

He left her, and went down into the sands where Taita was divining further afield. Not all the Hyksos chariots were so lightly covered with sand as the ones they had first found. Many were hidden for ever beneath the high new dunes.

They moved further and further away from the rocky hillock as the search went on. Beneath the sands they found many corpses, swollen bellies stinking.

Soon they were out of earshot of where Mintaka was tending the horses like a syce.

The cessation of all sound roused Trok, and he groaned as he tried to move. The sand was a stifling weight upon him. It seemed to crush in his ribs and force the breath from his lungs. Nevertheless, he knew that the spot Ishtar had chosen for them to ride out the storm was, either by chance or design, a good one. In any other place they might have been buried for ever. Here he had been able to keep close to the surface of the earth. In the past days as the layers of blown sand had built up over him and the weight had become unbearable he had managed to wriggle free, leaving only enough covering him to protect him from the full abrasive force of the *khamsin*.

Now he struggled up towards the light and air like a diver coming up from the depths of a deep pool. As he swam up laboriously through the sand his damaged shoulder was a burning agony. He struggled on until his head, still swathed in folds of cloth, broke free. He unwrapped it and blinked about him in the dazzling light. The wind had passed but the air was luminous with fine particles of suspended dust. He rested like that for a while until the pain in his shoulder abated a little. Then he pushed aside the layer of sand that still covered his lower body and tried to call out, 'Ishtar! Where are you?' but his voice was a formless croak. He turned his head slowly and saw the Mede, sitting near him, his back to the rocky cliff face. He looked like an exhumed corpse that had been dead for days. Then Ishtar opened his one good eye.

'Water?' Trok's voice was only just intelligible, but the Mede shook his head.

'So we have survived the storm just to die in the same grave,' Trok tried to say, but no sound came out from his ravaged throat and mouth.

He lay for a while longer, and felt any instinct to survive being extinguished under the slow seep of exhaustion and resignation. It would be so much easier just to close his eyes and drift off to sleep, never to wake again. That thought spurred him and he forced open his crusted eyelids, felt the grit under the lids scraping at his eyeballs.

'Water,' he said. 'Find water.'

Using the cliff side as a support he lurched to his feet and stood there swaying, hugging his useless arm to his chest.

Ishtar watched him, his one blind eye like that of a reptile or a corpse. Trok started forward drunkenly, bumping into the cliff at every few paces he took, making his way along the base of the rock until he could look out over the desert. The dunes were pristine and unblemished, as voluptuously curved as the body of a lovely young girl.

There was no trace of men or vehicles. His fighting divisions, the finest in all Egypt, had vanished without trace. He tried to lick his lips, but there was no spittle in his chalky mouth. He felt his legs give way under him and knew that if he went down he would never rise again. Using the wall of stone as a support he tottered on, not knowing where he was going and with no thought in his head but to go on.

Then he heard human voices, and knew he was hallucinating. There was silence again. He went a few steps further, stopped and listened. The voices came again. This time they were closer and clearer. He felt unexpected strength flow back into his body, but when he tried to call out no sound came from his parched throat. There was silence once more. The voices had ceased.

He started forward again, then stopped suddenly. A woman's voice, no mistaking it. A sweet, clear voice.

Mintaka. The name formed silently on his swollen lips. Then another voice. This time a man's. He could not make out the words or recognize the speaker, but if he was with Mintaka he must be one of the fugitives Trok had been pursuing. The enemy.

Trok looked down at himself. His sword-belt was gone, and his weapons with it. He was unarmed, dressed only in his tunic, which had so much sand in the weave that it chafed his skin like a hair-shirt. He looked around him for a weapon, a stick or a stone, but there was nothing. The scree had been covered by sand.

He stood undecided, and the voices came again. Mintaka and the man were in a gully among the rocks. While he still hesitated he heard the sand crunching like salt crystals under someone's feet. That person was coming down the gully towards where Trok stood.

Trok shrank back against the stone wall and a man

emerged from the mouth of the gully, twenty paces from where Trok hid. The stranger set off with a determined stride into the dunes. He was strongly familiar, but recognition eluded Trok until the man turned and called back towards the gully, 'Do not tax yourself unduly, Mintaka. You have come through a trying ordeal.' Then he walked on.

Trok gaped after him. He is dead, he thought. It cannot be him. The message from Naja was clear . . . He considered the possibility that a *djinn* or some evil spirit was impersonating the young Pharaoh Nefer Seti as he watched the young man go out into the desert. Then, through eyes bleary with sand, he saw him join three others, among them the unmistakable figure of the Warlock, who, Trok realized, must be responsible, in some strange and miraculous way, for the resurrection of Nefer Seti. But now he had neither the time nor the inclination to ponder this further. There was only one thought in his mind and that was water.

As stealthily as he could he crept forward into the gully where he had heard Mintaka's voice and peered round the corner of the cliff. He did not recognize her at first: she was as bedraggled as a peasant. Her hair and her tattered tunic were stiff with sand, and her eyes were sunken and bloodshot. She was kneeling at the head of one of a small herd of horses, holding a water bucket for it to drink.

Water was the only thing Trok could think about. He could smell it and his whole body craved it. He staggered towards Mintaka. Her back was turned to him and the soft sand covered the sound of his approach. She was not aware of him until he seized her arm. She turned, saw him, and screamed. He snatched the bucket from her hands and knocked her down. As his arm was useless he knelt on the small of her back to pin her down, while he drank from the bucket.

He swallowed huge gulps, gurgled and belched, then

drank some more. Mintaka was wriggling under him and screaming, 'Nefer! Taita! Help me.'

He belched again, pushed her face into the sand to silence her, and swallowed the last drops from the bucket. He looked around him, still crouching over her like a lion on its kill. He saw the waterskin against the wall of the gully and the javelins and swords stacked beside it.

He stood up quickly and started towards them. Instantly Mintaka tried to jump to her feet, but he kicked her down again. 'None of that, you bitch,' he croaked, and seized a handful of her thick sand-drenched hair. He dragged her after him through the sand until he could reach the waterskin. Then he had to drop her. He placed one huge sandalled foot on her back again, reached for the waterskin and held it between his knees while he unfastened the wooden stopper. He lifted the nozzle to his lips and let the warm, brackish liquid flow down his throat.

Although she was face down in the sand Mintaka realized that Trok was engrossed in his craving for water. She must act before he had satisfied it and turned his full attention on her. She knew that he had suffered more humiliation than he could bear and that he would kill her now rather than let her escape him again.

Desperately she reached out to the bundle of weapons stacked against the rock. Her fingers closed around the shaft of a javelin. Trok was still drinking with his head thrown back, but he felt her movement and lowered the waterskin just as Mintaka twisted to stab up at his belly and groin with the short but deadly weapon. However, the blow was aimed from her prone position under him and lacked force.

Trok saw the bright bronze point flash and, with a startled exclamation, jumped back to avoid it. 'You treacherous little slut!' He dropped the waterskin and lunged for her, but the moment his weight was off her Mintaka jumped up. She tried to slip past him and run out of the gully into the open desert, but he cut her off and reached for her with his long arm. He caught the hem of her tunic, but she leaped aside. The linen tore in his fingers and she twisted away from him, but he still had her trapped in the gully.

He lumbered after her but she ran to the cliff wall and started to scale it, lithe and quick as a cat. Before he could catch her she was out of his reach. She went up swiftly and he could not hope to follow her. He picked up the javelin she had dropped and hurled it up at her, but he was using his left hand and there was little power in the throw.

Mintaka ducked as the javelin flew over her head and struck the rock in front of her face. She climbed faster, driven by fear. Trok staggered to where the other weapons were stacked, and grabbed another javelin. He threw again. It missed her by a hand's width.

Trok grunted with fury and frustration and snatched a third javelin, but at that moment Mintaka reached a ledge in the cliff and crawled over it out of his sight. She lay there pressing herself to the rock. She heard him raving and swearing at her. Even in her distress she was sickened by the filthy words he sent after her.

Then another javelin flashed over where she lay and clattered against the rock face above her. It dropped back on to the ledge and she grabbed it before it could fall back to the gully floor. She peered over the edge of the ledge, ready to duck back.

Trok was staring up at her uncertainly, his injured arm dangling at his side. When her head appeared his face contorted with rage and the pain of his injury, and he started forward as if to climb up to her.

She showed him the point of the javelin. 'Yes, come up,' she hissed at him, 'and let me stick this in your great hog belly!'

He stopped. He would have to climb and defend himself with only one arm. He saw that her threat was real. While he hesitated, Mintaka began to scream again. 'Nefer! Taita! Hilto! Help me!'

Her voice echoed off the cliff and rang down the gully. He looked about him nervously, as if expecting to see a rush of armed enemies coming at him. Suddenly he reached a decision. He picked up the waterskin and slung it over his shoulder. 'Do not think you can evade me for ever. One day I will sample all the delights of your body and afterwards I will give you as a plaything to my troopers,' he shouted up at her. Then he tried to mount the mare, but she was still too weak to support his bulk and collapsed under him.

Trok hauled himself to his feet and lumbered away down the gully.

Mintaka feared that his withdrawal might be a trick. She dared not descend from her perch on the cliff. She screamed wildly, 'Nefer! Help me.'

She was still screaming when Nefer came racing back to her down the rocky gully, a sword in his hand, Hilto and Meren close behind him.

'What is it?' Nefer demanded, as she slid down the cliff into his arms.

'Trok!' She sobbed with relief to feel him hold her safely. 'Trok is alive. He was here.'

She blurted out an account of what had happened, but before she had ended Nefer was giving orders to the others to arm themselves and prepare to go after Trok.

Taita had come back to join them. He stayed with Mintaka while the three men followed Trok's footprints in the sand as cautiously as if they were tracking a wounded lion. They moved along the base of the cliff until they reached the fissure where Trok had weathered the fury of the *khamsin*. Nefer examined the disturbed sand and interpreted the signs. 'Two of them,' he said. 'They were buried by the storm, as we were. They dug themselves out. One waited here.' He picked up a thread of wool that had adhered to the rock, and held it to the light. 'Black.' It was a colour seldom worn by Egyptians. 'Almost certainly the Mede.'

Hilto nodded agreement. 'Ishtar would have the witchcraft to survive the storm. 'Tis certain he saved Trok, just as Taita saved us.'

'Here.' Nefer stood up and pointed out the sign. 'Carrying the waterskin, Trok returned to find the Mede, and they went this way.'

They followed the footprints a short way out into the desert. 'They have gone west. Back towards Avaris and the Nile. Will they ever reach it?'

'Not if I catch up with him,' Nefer said grimly, and hefted the javelin he was carrying.

'Majesty.' Hilto was respectful but firm. 'They have the waterskin and a long start. They will be well away from here by now. You dare not follow without water.'

Nefer hesitated. Though he saw the sense in what Hilto said it galled him sorely to let Trok escape. From what Mintaka had told him, Trok was injured and would not be too dangerous an opponent, even though Nefer himself was still weak.

In the end he turned aside and ran to the top of the nearest dune. Shading his eyes he looked westward, along the string of footsteps on the pristine, windswept sands until in the distance, half a league or more away, he made out two tiny figures moving steadily towards the west. He watched them fiercely until they disappeared in the wavering heat mirage.

'There will be another time,' Nefer whispered. 'I will come for you. I swear it on the hundred sacred names of Horus.'

They found and uncovered another sixteen of the buried chariots. With such an abundant supply of water and food, horses and men recovered swiftly. In addition, they had uncovered many more corpses of Trok's troopers. From these they were able to dress themselves. Nefer altered a pair of sandals to fit Mintaka, whose injured feet were almost completely healed.

By the tenth day they were ready to move. The four remaining horses were not strong enough to drag the chariots back through the loose sand, so Nefer decided to use them as pack horses, and load them with as much water as they could carry.

At nightfall, leading the horses, they started out across the dunes. Although the mare could not carry Mintaka's weight as well as its load, Nefer rigged a leather strap around its shoulders and insisted that Mintaka hang on this to help herself through the soft footing.

The *khamsin* had altered the landscape so greatly that Taita had to navigate by the stars. They kept going steadily through the whole of that night, and the one that followed. Before dawn on the second day they reached the old caravan road. It had been obliterated in places by the *khamsin*, but before they had gone much further the light strengthened and they saw the cairn of stones that marked the crossroads ahead.

They discovered that, since the storm had ended, someone had been on the road before them. Two pairs of footprints led westwards along the road, heading back towards the Nile valley and Avaris. One pair was large, the other smaller. Taita and Nefer examined them carefully.

'This one is Trok. Nobody else has feet like that, the size of a Nile barge. Mintaka was correct. He is injured, on his right side. He favours it as he walks.' Taita read the sign.

'As yet I cannot be certain about the other. Let us see if he leaves some clue as to his identity.' They followed the tracks as far as the marked cairn.

'Ah! There!' Close by the cairn someone had recently arranged an intricate pattern of stones in the sand. 'No doubt now. It is Ishtar the Mede.' Angrily Taita scattered the stones. 'This is an invocation to his foul Marduk the Devourer.' He hurled one of the smaller stones down the road that Trok and Ishtar had taken. 'If Ishtar had an infant with him, he would likely have sacrificed it. Marduk thirsts for human blood.'

Here, at the marker cairn, Nefer had a difficult decision to make. 'If we are to make the long journey to the east, we will need supplies and gold. We should not arrive at the court of the Assyrian as indigent outcasts.'

Taita nodded. 'There are many powerful men in Egypt who would lend us full support if only they could be certain that their pharaoh was still alive.'

'Hilto and Meren must go back to Thebes,' Nefer said. 'I would go myself but all the world will be searching for Mintaka and me.' He removed one of his royal finger rings and handed it to Hilto. 'This will be your token of recognition. Show it to our friends. You must return bringing us men and gold, chariots and horses. When we go to King Sargon we must arrive in some state to show him the support we still command in Egypt.'

'I will do as you command, Majesty.'

'Almost as vital to us will be intelligence. You must gather news. We must be informed of every action of the false pharaohs.'

'I will leave at nightfall, Pharaoh,' Hilto agreed.

They spent that long hot day lying under the shade of an awning they had salvaged from one of the buried chariots, discussing their plans. When the sun sank towards the horizon and began to lose its heat they parted company,

Hilto and Meren to head back west towards Thebes, and Taita, Nefer and Mintaka to go eastwards.

'We will wait for you at the ruins of Gallala,' were Nefer's last words to Hilto. Then they watched him and Meren take the high road and disappear into the gathering dusk.

Taita, Mintaka and Nefer took the caravan road towards Gallala. Twelve days later, with only a few drops remaining in the waterskins, they reached the deserted ruins.

The weeks became months, and still they waited at Gallala.

Taita spent days at a time in the hills that surrounded the city. Nefer and Mintaka caught occasional glimpses of him from a distance as he prowled the valleys and harsh gullies. Often they saw him tapping and prodding the rocks with his staff. At other times he sat by the almost dried-up wells outside the city walls, staring down the deep shafts.

When Nefer questioned him obliquely, he was distant and evasive. 'An army needs water,' was all he would volunteer.

'There is hardly enough water for us,' Nefer pointed out, 'let alone an army.' Taita nodded, stood up and walked away into the hills with his staff tapping against the rocks.

Mintaka set up quarters for them among the ruins, and Nefer roofed them over with the tattered tent. As a royal Hyksosian princess, Mintaka had never been called upon to cook a meal or sweep out a chamber, so her first efforts were disastrous. As he chewed a charred mouthful Taita remarked, 'If we want to destroy Trok's army the most effective way would be to send you to them as a cook.'

'If you are so skilled, then perhaps you might honour us with your great culinary skills.'

'It is either that or starve,' Taita agreed, and took his place at the hearth.

Nefer resumed his old role of hunter, and after his first day out in the desert returned with a plump young gazelle and four marvellously patterned giant bustard eggs that were only slightly addled. Mintaka sniffed her share of the omelette Taita made and pushed it away. 'Is this the same man who complained of my cooking?' She looked across the fire at Nefer. 'You are as guilty as he is. Next time I will go with you to make sure that what you bring back is edible.'

They lay side by side in one of the shallow wadis that cut through the hills and watched a herd of gazelle feeding towards them.

'They are dainty as fairies,' Mintaka whispered. 'So beautiful.'

'I will shoot if you have qualms,' Nefer told her.

'No.' She shook her head. 'I did not say I would not do it.' Her tone was determined, and by now he knew her well enough not to query her decision.

The ram moved ahead of his herd. His back was a delicate cinnamon shade and his underbelly was the silvery white of one of the thunderheads that rose above the horizon. His horns were lyre-shaped and polished between his pricked, trumpet-shaped ears. He turned his head on the long curved neck and gazed back at his small herd. One of the lambs began to stot, bouncing on stiff legs with its nose almost touching its bunched hoofs. This was the alarm behaviour.

'The little creature is just practising and showing off.' Nefer smiled.

The ram lost interest in this juvenile display, and came on towards where they lay in ambush. He picked his way over the stony ground with studied grace, stopping every few paces to look about warily for danger.

'He has not seen us, but he soon will,' Nefer whispered. 'We do not have Taita to gull him.'

'He is out of range,' she whispered back.

'Fifty paces, no more. Shoot or he will be gone in an instant.'

Mintaka waited until the ram once more turned away his head. Then she rose slowly to her knees and drew the bow. It was one of the short recurved weapons they had salvaged from a buried chariot. She released the arrow and it rose in a gentle arc against the pale desert sky.

With those huge dark eyes, the gazelle had instantly picked out her small movement of rising. His head switched round and he stared at her, on the point of flight. At the twanging release of the bowstring he leaped forward while the arrow was still in the air. He skimmed away, tiny puffs of dust rising where his hoofs touched the earth. The arrow rattled against the stones, where moments before, he had been standing. Mintaka jumped to her feet and laughed to watch him go, showing no sign of chagrin at having missed the shot.

'Watch him run, like a swallow in flight.'

Taita had taught Nefer that the true hunter loves and honours his quarry. He admired Mintaka the more for her compassion towards the creatures she hunted. She turned to him, still laughing. 'I am sorry, my heart. You will go hungry to bed this night.'

'Not with Taita at the cooking fire. He will pluck a feast from the very air.'

They raced each other to retrieve her spent arrow. She had a head-start, and reached it ahead of him. She stooped to pick it up, and the back of her short tattered skirt flew up. Her thighs were smooth and brown and her buttocks perfect rounds, the skin pale and unblemished where the sun had never touched it, lustrous as precious Oriental silk.

She straightened and turned in a flash to catch the

expression in his eyes. Though she was virgin and unversed in sensuality, her feminine instincts were full blown. She could see what passion her innocent gesture had roused in him, and the knowledge stirred her too. Seeing how he desired her made her want him with an intensity that was painful. She felt her loins melt with love for him, overflowing sweet and viscous like a honeycomb left in the heat of the midday sun.

Timidly she swayed towards him, but Nefer felt hot shame at the carnal desire that had almost overwhelmed him again. He remembered his promise to her. 'I would rather die than break my oath, and bring dishonour upon you,' he had told her, and at the memory he forced himself to turn away. He found that his hands were shaking and his voice was gruff as he said, with his eyes averted, 'I know where there is another herd, but we must hurry if we are to find them before dark.' He set off without looking back at her, and she felt bereft. She had wanted more than anything on this earth to feel his arms around her and his hard young body pressed to hers.

She gathered herself quickly and followed him, trying to push away the strange feelings that had so nearly engulfed her, but they would not so easily be set aside. She caught up with him, and trotted a few paces behind him.

She studied his back. She watched how his thick dark curls bounced on his shoulders. She wondered at how wide his shoulders had grown since she had first met him. Then she looked further down, and felt her cheeks burn as she watched his buttocks moving under the thin stuff of his short apron. She enjoyed a delicious sense of shame at her own lascivious feelings.

Too soon they reached the rim of the long wadi that cleaved the mountains. He turned his head to look back at her and almost caught her studying his body. She raised her eyes to his just in time.

'There are hundreds of old tombs in the bottom of the cliff here. I first saw them when my father brought me this way, just before he was—' He broke off, saddened by the memory of the last day he had spent with Tamose.

'Whose tombs are they?' she asked, to distract him from something so painful.

'Taita says they are a thousand years old, from the time of Cheops and Chephren who built the great Pyramids at Giza.'

'Then they must be almost as old as the Magus himself.' She smiled and he laughed.

'Have you ever explored them?' she asked.

He shook his head. 'Since we first arrived here, I have thought of doing so often, but there has never been an opportunity.'

'Let us do it now,' she said.

He hesitated. 'We should have ropes and lamps.' But she was already scrambling down the cliff, and he was forced to follow her.

At its base, they soon found that most of the tombs were out of their reach, set high in the sheer cliff face with a deadly drop below them.

After a while Nefer picked out an opening he thought they might be able to reach. They climbed a section where the cliff face had collapsed, and reached a narrow ledge. They worked their way along it cautiously, Nefer leading. He reached the dark opening and stooped to peer into it. 'Of course, it will be guarded by the spirits of the dead.' He tried to make it sound like a joke, but she sensed his unease and was affected by it.

'Of course!' she joked back, but behind her back made the sign against evil.

'It's very dark in there,' Nefer said thoughtfully. 'We should return tomorrow with an oil lamp.'

Mintaka looked over his shoulder. A short passageway

led at a slight upward angle into the solid rock. Even after the passing of centuries, engravings were still clearly visible on the walls.

'Look.' Mintaka touched one. 'This is a picture of a giraffe, and this is a man.'

'Yes,' Nefer grinned, 'and a very friendly man, at that. There is no mistaking it.'

She pretended to bridle, but could not hide her smile. The ancient artist had endowed the figure with a huge erect member.

'Here.' She moved deeper into the passage. 'These are writings. I wonder what they mean.'

'Nobody will ever know,' Nefer said, and stepped past her. 'The key to that ancient script has long been lost. We should go back.'

The floor was covered with a layer of soft windblown sand. After a short distance the recesses of the shaft were obscured by sinister darkness.

'We can explore just a short way further,' Mintaka said stubbornly.

'I don't think that's a good idea.'

'Here.' She pushed past him. 'Let me go first.'

'Wait!' He tried to restrain her, but she laughed and pulled away. He placed one hand on the hilt of his dagger and followed her, shamed by her example and his own reluctance.

The gloom thickened with each step forward until even Mintaka stopped and peered uneasily ahead. He stooped to pick up a chip of flint from the sandy floor and threw it over her shoulder into the dark reaches of the shaft. It rattled on the stone walls. 'Nothing,' she said in the silence that followed, but before she could take another step forward something moved in the darkness ahead. They heard a rustling sound that was magnified in the narrow space. They froze in their tracks, and stared into the darkness. There was a high-pitched shriek, echoed immediately by a chorus, the rustle became a rushing roar, and out of the darkness straight into their faces hurled a squeaking, fluttering cloud of darting shapes, whose wings lashed their startled faces.

Mintaka screamed, whirled around, ran straight into Nefer and threw both her arms around his neck. He seized her and held her hard, drawing her down on to the sandy floor.

'Bats,' he told her. 'Only bats.'

'I know!' she said breathlessly.

'They can't hurt you.'

'I know.' Her voice was calmer, but she made no effort to unwind her arms from around his neck. He pressed his face into her thick, springy hair. It smelt rich and perfumed as new-mown grass.

She made a soft, murmuring sound of pleasure, buried her face against his throat, and moved softly against him.

'Mintaka,' he tried gently to push her away, 'I gave you my promise that this would not happen again.'

'I release you from that promise.' Her voice was so soft as to be barely audible. She lifted her face to his. Her breath was warm and sweet-smelling. Her lips were tender and full, and quivered as though she were on the point of tears. 'I want to be your wife more than I have ever wanted anything in my life.'

He reached down and took her mouth with his own. It was wet and so hot that it seemed to scald his. He lost himself in it. She felt that she belonged nowhere else but in his embrace. Still kissing her he explored the angles and curves and plains of her back with his fingertips. He traced the outline of her spine, like a string of pearls running down between the firm ridges of muscle.

He placed a hand on her hip, and felt the curve of her waist like the shape of a precious ceramic vase. He reached behind her and enclosed one buttock in each hand, astonished by their symmetry and elastic firmness.

She thrust her hips forward to meet his, and he pulled her even harder to him. He felt his loins swell and stiffen, and tried to arch his back to hide it from her. She made a small sound of remonstrance, forbidding him to avoid her. She moved against him, glorying in this proof of his arousal, of how much he wanted her.

She had a fleeting memory of Trok thrusting his monstrous blue-veined thing at her, but that horrid episode had no relevance to what was happening here. Without effort the memory was expunged from her mind.

She felt Nefer's fingers running slowly down the cleft between her buttocks, and she concentrated on the sensation, marvelling that she could feel it echoed in the swelling tips of her breasts and in her secret depths.

'Touch me.' She spoke into his mouth. 'Yes! Touch me. Hold me. Stroke me. Love me.'

The sensations blended so that they seemed to envelop her every fibre, every part of her mind and body. He broke the kiss at last, and she felt his lips nuzzling her bare shoulder. She knew instinctively what he needed, and opened the front of her tunic and took out one of her breasts. It felt heavy in her hand, the tip aching and swollen. She entwined the fingers of her other hand in the thick curling hair at the back of his head, and placed her nipple in his mouth. When he sucked it, like a hungry infant, she felt something spasm and contract deep in her belly, and realized with wonder that it was her own womb.

Gently she changed him from one breast to the other, and the sensation did not fade, but instead grew fiercer.

In a daze of pleasure she became aware of his fingers lifting the front of her skirts and fumbling with her loincloth. She moved her legs apart to allow him to reach her more easily, and then, with her free hand, she helped him untie the knot at her hip. The cloth fell away and the air of the tomb was cool on her naked bottom and belly.

She felt him stroke the crisp pelt of curls that covered her pudenda, then he found the swollen lips that bulged from her cleft and parted them gently with trembling fingers. She cried out as if in pain and, without conscious volition, pulled aside the skirts of his apron and reached in to find him. She was startled by its girth and encircled it with thumb and forefinger. It leaped like a living thing in her grasp, and she wanted to look at it. Without releasing her grip, she pushed him back so that she could see down between them.

'You are so beautiful,' she breathed, 'so smooth, so strong.'

Then she kissed him again, and holding her mouth to his she fell backwards dragging him down upon her belly, spreading her thighs to welcome him, sensing his lack of experience. It made her feel maternal and possessive. In her own ignorance, she was guiding him, feeling him sliding and slipping in her overflowing desire, probing at the entrance to her very self. She altered the angle of her hips and he flew deeply into her, his belly flat against hers, filling her until she felt he might cleave her apart, crying out triumphantly in the bittersweet pain of it.

He was riding her like a runaway horse, and she paced him, meeting the thrusting drive of his hips with her own, mounting with him higher and faster, until she knew that she had reached the limit. Then, unbelievably, they went on far past that limit. Breaking free of earth and its bonds, then at the ends of the heavens, feeling it burst out of him, and flood her with liquid heat, swelling up within her so that she matched and met him, their separate beings welding together, so that they became a single entity. Their voices a single jubilant cry.

Long afterwards, when they had returned together from those distant heights, they lay in each other's arms, their sweat and their breath mingling and cooling, still linked by his flesh deep within hers.

'I don't want this ever to end,' she whispered at last. 'I want to stay like this with you for ever.'

A long while later he sat up languidly and looked towards the opening of the shaft. 'It is becoming dark already,' he said, in a wondering tone. 'The day has passed so swiftly.'

She came up on her knees, smoothed down her skirts, and he touched the fresh stains upon the hem. 'Your maiden's blood,' he whispered in awe.

'My gift to you,' she answered. 'The proof of my love for you alone.'

He reached up and tore from the hem of her skirt an encarmined shred the size of her little fingernail.

'What are you doing?' she asked.

'I will keep this for ever as a memory of this wonderful day.' He opened the locket he wore at his throat and placed the fragment of cloth with the lock of her dark hair that it already contained.

'Do you really love me, Nefer?' she asked, as she watched him close the locket.

'With every drop of blood that flows through my veins. More than life eternal.'

When they came into the room in the ancient building that they had restored and made habitable, Taita was at the hearth stirring the contents of the pot upon the coals. He looked up at Mintaka as she stood in the open doorway with the last light of the day behind her. Her skirt was still damp where she had washed it in the scanty waters of the well and it clung to her thighs. 'I am sorry we are so late back, Taita,' she said shyly. 'We followed the gazelle out into the desert.'

She had never apologized for their late return before, and Taita looked up at the two of them. Nefer was hovering over her with a soft, dazed expression. The emanation of their love was so strong that it seemed to form a shimmering aura around them and Taita could almost smell it in the air, like the fragrance of a wild flower.

So what was inevitable has happened at last, he mused. The only wonder is that it took so long. He grunted, non-committal. 'It is evident that you did not catch up with them. Did they run too fast or were you distracted?' They stood awkwardly, covered with confusion and guilt, knowing that to him they were transparent.

Taita turned back to the cooking pot. 'At least there is one provider among us. I have been able to snare a brace of wild pigeon. We need not go hungry to bed.'

The days that followed passed for the two of them in a golden haze of delight. They thought they were being subtle and discreet in Taita's presence, trying to keep their eyes off each other, and touching only when they thought he was not looking.

Mintaka had made a boudoir for herself in a bare cell that led off the main living room of their quarters. Each night Nefer waited until Taita was snoring softly before he rose surreptitiously and crept to her sleeping mat in this little room. Each morning she would rouse him long before dawn and send him back to his own mat in the main room, when they thought Taita was still sleeping.

On the third morning Taita announced inscrutably, 'It seems that these rooms are inhabited by rats or other strange creatures for I am kept from sleep by their scurrying and whispering.' They both looked stricken, and he went on, 'I have found more tranquil accommodation.'

He moved his own sleeping mat and possessions to a small ruin across the square, and to these he retired each evening after they had eaten dinner together.

During the days the lovers wandered out into the desert, to pass their time in talking, making love, and forming a thousand plans for the future, deciding when and how they might marry, how many sons and how many daughters she would bear him and finding names for each.

They were so lost in each other that they forgot the world that lay beyond the lonely desert spaces, until one morning when they left the ruined city before dawn, carrying a coil of rope and two oil lamps, determined to explore the ancient tombs more thoroughly. By a circuitous route they reached the top of the cliff, where they sat down to catch their breath and watch the magnificent spectacle of the dawn breaking over the blue, secret hills.

'Look!' cried Mintaka suddenly, starting out of his arms and pointing back towards the west along the old trade route that led down into Egypt. Nefer jumped up, and they gazed down the valley at the strange caravan coming towards them. There were five ramshackle vehicles leading, followed by a straggling column of humanity.

'There must be a hundred men, at least,' Mintaka exclaimed. 'Who can they be?'

'I don't know,' Nefer admitted grimly, 'but I want you to run back and warn Taita of their approach while I go and spy on them.'

She did not argue, but set off immediately for Gallala, racing down the back slope of the hills, leaping from rock to rock with the agility of a wild ibex. Nefer cached the rope and the lamps, then restrung his bow and checked the arrows in his quiver, before creeping along the crest of the hills, keeping off the skyline and out of sight until he reached a point from where he could look down on the slow-moving caravan.

It was a sorry spectacle. As it came closer, Nefer saw that the first two vehicles were knocked-about fighting chariots drawn by thin, overworked horses. They were designed to carry two men, but each contained four or five. Behind them came an assortment of wagons and carts in no better case than the leading chariots. Nefer saw that they were laden with sick or wounded men, huddled miserably together or lying on makeshift litters. Behind the wagons straggled a long file of walking men, some hobbling along on crutches or leaning on staffs. Others carried litters on which lay other sick or wounded figures.

'In the name of Horus, they look like fugitives from a battlefield,' Nefer muttered, as he strained his eyes to make out the features of the men in the leading chariot.

Suddenly he stood up from behind the rock that had hidden him, and shouted with excitement. 'Meren!' He had at last recognized the tall figure who held the reins of the first chariot. Meren pulled up the horses and shaded his eyes to stare into the eye of the rising sun. Then he, too, shouted and waved as he saw Nefer on the skyline. Nefer ran down the slope, slipping and sliding in the loose scree, and he and Meren embraced, laughing and both speaking at once.

'Where have you been?'

'Where are Mintaka and Taita?'

Then Hilto was hurrying to Nefer, and making loyal salutations. Behind him crowded the host of exhausted and wounded men. Their faces were drawn and gaunt, and blood and pus had soaked through their dirty bandages and dried to a crust. Even the men in the wagons and on the litters, who were too far gone to stand, lifted themselves to stare in awe at Nefer.

With a quick appraisal Nefer could see that these were warriors, but warriors beaten in battle, their bodies and spirits broken.

After Hilto had greeted Nefer he turned back to them, and shouted, 'It is even as I promised you! Here before you stands your true Pharaoh, Nefer Seti. Pharaoh is not dead! Pharaoh lives!'

They were silent and apathetic, sick and demoralized. They stared at Nefer uncertainly.

'Your Majesty,' Hilto whispered to him, 'please stand on this rock so that they may have a clear view of you.'

Nefer sprang up on to it and surveyed them with interest. They stared back at him in silence. Most had never laid eyes on their king before. Even the few who had seen him in formal palace processions had done so from a distance. Then he had been a doll-like figure, covered from throat to foot in splendid robes and jewels, his face a white mask of makeup, sitting stiffly on the royal carriage drawn by the white bullocks. They could not reconcile that remote, unnatural figure with this strapping young man, virile and hard-looking, his face tanned by the sun and his expression alive and alert. He was not the child-pharaoh they had known by reputation alone.

While they still stared without comprehension, or exchanged dubious glances, another figure seemed to materialize out of the air. Like a *djinn* he appeared beside Nefer on the rock. This one they knew well, both by repute and by sight.

‘’Tis Taita the Warlock,’ they breathed with awe.

‘I know what you have suffered,’ Taita told them, in a voice that carried clearly to every ear, even to the sick and wounded on the wagons. ‘I know what price you have paid to resist the tyranny of the assassins and usurpers. I know that you have come here to find if your true king still lives.’

They murmured in agreement. and suddenly Nefer knew now who they were. These were some of the survivors from the rebellion against Naja and Trok. Where Hilto had found them was a mystery, but these shattered remnants had once been fighting troopers, élite charioteers and warriors.

‘This is where it begins,’ Taita said softly at his side. ‘Hilto has brought you the seeds of your future legions. Speak to them.’

Nefer surveyed them for a moment longer, standing proud and tall before them. He picked out a man in the ranks, who was older than the others, with the first snows in his hair. His eyes were sharp and his expression intelligent. Despite his rags and half-starved body he had the air of authority and command. 'Who are you, soldier? What is your rank and your regiment?'

The man lifted his head and squared his gaunt shoulders. 'I am Shabako. Best of Ten Thousand. Adept of the Red Road. Commander of the centre of the Mut regiment.'

A lion of a man! Nefer thought, but said only, 'I greet you, Shabako.' He lifted the skirt of his *chiton* and exposed the tattooed cartouche upon his thigh. 'I am Nefer Seti, the true Pharaoh of Upper and Lower Egypt.'

A sigh and a hum went through the scarecrow ranks when they recognized the royal cartouche. As one man they threw themselves to earth in obeisance.

'*Bak-her*, Divine One, beloved of the gods!'

'We are your loyal subjects, Pharaoh. Intercede for us with the gods.'

Mintaka had come with Taita and now stood below him. Nefer reached down and took her hand. He lifted her on to the rock beside him. 'I give you the Princess Royal, Mintaka of the House of Apepi. Mintaka, who will be my queen and your sovereign lady.'

They greeted her with another shout of acclamation.

'Hilto and Shabako will command you,' Nefer decreed. 'For the time being Gallala will be our base, until we return victoriously to Thebes and Avaris.'

They rose to their feet, even the gravely wounded attempting to climb from their litters, and they cheered him. Their voices were thin and almost lost in the great silences of the desert, but the sound filled Nefer with pride and renewed his determination and resolve. He climbed up into the leading chariot, took the reins from Meren and led his little raggle-taggle army down into his ruined capital city.

When they had set up their barracks among the ruins, Nefer sent for Shabako and Hilto and the other officers among them. Late into that first night, and for many nights that followed, he sat with them and listened to their accounts of the rebellion, the fighting, and their ultimate defeat by the combined forces of the two pharaohs. They told him of the terrible retribution that Trok and Naja had visited on those rebels who had fallen into their clutches.

At Nefer's orders they detailed the order of battle of the new Egyptian army, the names of the commanders, the numbers and names of their regiments and the total of men, chariots and horses that Naja and Trok had at their disposal. There were three army scribes among the fugitives and Nefer set them to work, writing down all these details and the lists of the enemy garrisons and fortifications on clay tablets.

In the meantime Taita, with Mintaka assisting him, set up an infirmary where all the wounded and the sick were housed. Hilto had brought a dozen or so women with him, wives of some of the fugitives, or merely camp-followers. Taita brought them in to act as nurses and cooks. Taita worked during all the daylight hours, setting broken bones, drawing barbed arrowheads from the flesh with his golden spoons, stitching sword-cuts and in one case even trepanning a cracked, depressed skull that had received a blow from a hardwood war club.

When the light faded and he could no longer work with the sick, he joined Nefer and his commanders as they pored over the maps drawn on tanned lambskins, planning and scheming by the light of the oil lamps. Although Nefer was nominally their supreme commander, in reality he was a student of the art of war and these experienced old soldiers were his instructors, the lessons he learned from them invaluable.

It was after midnight usually before Nefer could adjourn these grave councils, and sneak away to join Mintaka on the sheepskin mat where she patiently waited for him. Then they made love and whispered together. Although they were both exhausted by their labours, the dawn was often creeping over the silent desert before they fell asleep in each other's arms.

In total there were less than a hundred and fifty souls and fifty horses in Gallala, but within the first few days it became evident that the bitter wells of the city could not support even these meagre numbers. Each day they emptied them and each night it took longer for them to refill. Even the quality of the water began to deteriorate: it became more bitter and brackish every day, until it was only barely potable unless mixed with mare's milk.

They were forced to ration the water. The horses were distressed and the mares lost their milk. Still the trickle of underground water shrivelled.

At last Nefer called an emergency council of his commanders. At the end of an hour of solemn talk, Hilto summed up gloomily, 'Unless Horus works a miracle for us, the wells will dry completely, and we will be forced to abandon the city. Where then will we flee?'

They looked at Nefer, who turned expectantly to Taita. 'When the water dries up, where do we go, Magus?' he asked.

Taita opened his eyes. He had sat in silence through the long debate and they had thought he was dozing. 'Tomorrow, at first light, I want every man who can walk and wield a spade assembled before the gates of the city.'

'To what end?' Nefer asked, but Taita smiled enigmatically.

In the cool of the dawn fifty-six men were waiting before the ancient gates when Taita stepped through. He was wearing all his regalia, the Periapt and the gift of Bay, and his other necklaces, bracelets and amulets. He had washed his hair until it shone, and Mintaka had braided it for him. He carried his staff with the carved serpent's head. Nefer was beside him, a solemn expression covering his mystification. Taita looked over the assembled men. As he had ordered, they all carried digging tools – wooden spades and shovels, metal-tipped digging staves. He nodded with satisfaction then descended the steps and set off up the valley.

At a word from Nefer the men shouldered their tools and followed the old man, falling naturally into a military marching formation. However, they had not far to go, for Taita stopped at the foot of the hills and stared up at the heights.

Nefer recalled that this was the area where Taita had spent so much time over the last few months. Often he and Mintaka had seen him sitting here, drowsing in the sun with hooded eyes like a blue-headed lizard, or prodding and tapping among the rocks with his staff.

For the first time Nefer studied the rock formation of this section of the hills and realized that they were different. The rock was friable and veins of grey limestone had intruded into the schist. A profound fault ran diagonally through the face on the bare, burned hills, edged with strata of different colours. Then he noticed something else. Recently someone had placed marks on some of the stones, esoteric hieroglyphs painted with a white paste, probably made from crushed limestone mixed with well water. There were also cairns of stones placed in a pattern on the earth.

'Nefer, the men must be divided into the five teams,' Taita told him, and Nefer gave the orders. When they were ready, Taita ordered the first forward. 'Start driving an adit into the hillside here.' He pointed out the hieroglyphs that marked the opening to the horizontal shaft where he wanted them to begin digging.

The men looked at each other, puzzled and uncertain,

but when Taita glared at them wordlessly, Shabako took over quite naturally. 'You heard the Magus. Get on with it, now, and handsomely!'

It was hard work, even though the underlying rock was shattered along the line Taita had chosen. They had to prise out each lump, then dig out the loose earth that lay behind it. Clouds of dust rose around them, and soon their bodies were powdered with it. Even though their hands were toughened by use of club and sword, their palms blistered, tore and bled. They wrapped them with linen strips and worked on without complaint. The heat came up swiftly with the rising sun, and Shabako pulled the first team out of the excavation and sent in the next.

They rested for an hour at noon when the heat was at its height. Taita went into the shallow cave and inspected the rock face intently. He emerged into the sunlight without comment, and Shabako ordered the work to continue. It went on until it was too dark to see what they were doing, then Shabako released them and sent them down the hill to their frugal dinner. The supplies of *dhurra* millet were dwindling almost as swiftly as the well waters.

Taking advantage of the coolness, they started again before dawn. By nightfall they had driven the adit only twenty cubits into the hillside. There they struck a solid stratum of blue, crystalline rock. The bronze-tipped staves made no mark upon it, and the men began to mutter.

'Are we warriors or miners?' mumbled one old veteran, as he inspected his bruised and blistered palms.

'What are we supposed to be digging? Our own tombs?' asked another, as he bound up the deep cut in his shin inflicted by a carelessly wielded stave.

'How can we dig through solid rock?' Yet another wiped the running sweat and mingled dust from his bloodshot eyes.

Taita sent them down the valley to where a thick grove of dead acacia trees stood as a silent monument to the water that had long ago dried. They cut cords of the dried branches and carried the bundles back to the diggings. Under Taita's instructions they stacked the firewood on the adamantine rock, and lit it. They let the fire burn through the night, stoking it at intervals, and the next morning, when the rock glowed with the heat, they quenched it with skins filled from the failing wells. In clouds of hissing steam, the rock crackled, burst and exploded.

One man was hit by a sharp flying fragment, and lost his right eye. Taita removed its remains, and stitched the lids closed.

'The gods gave us two eyes for just such a mishap,' he assured his patient. 'You will see just as well with one as you did with two.'

They let the shattered rock cool then prised out great blackened chunks of it. Behind these the rock was still solid and impenetrable. They stacked fresh cords of firewood upon it and repeated the arduous, dangerous process, with the same result. They had gained a few cubits for the expenditure of days of heartbreaking labour.

Even Nefer was discouraged, and told Mintaka so when they lay together in the darkness that night.

'There are many things that we do not understand, my heart,' she cradled his head and whispered.

'We don't even know why he is making us dig this hole, and when I ask him he gives me that infuriating look of his, like an ancient tortoise. The men have almost had enough of it, and so have I.'

She giggled. 'Ancient tortoise! You had better make sure he doesn't hear that. He might turn you into a toad, and I should not like that at all.'

Early the following morning, the teams of weary, disgruntled men traipsed up the valley and assembled around the mouth of the tunnel to await the arrival of the Magus.

With his usual sense of the dramatic, Taita came up the slope with the first rays of the rising sun behind him, suffusing his silver bush of hair with light. He carried a roll of linen cloth over one shoulder. Nefer and the other officers stood to welcome him, but he ignored their salutations and gave instructions to Shabako to hang the linen over the mouth of the shaft like a curtain. When it was in place he entered the screened shaft alone, and a silence fell over the men gathered outside.

It seemed like a long wait but was in reality less than an hour, for the sun had risen only a hand's breadth above the horizon, when the linen curtain was jerked aside and Taita stood in the entrance of the cave. Either by chance or the Magus' design, the sunlight shone directly into the shaft. The blank face of the adit was brilliantly lit, and the ranks of men crowded forward expectantly. They saw that now a representation of the wounded eye of the great god Horus was painted on the blue rock.

Taita's expression was rapt as he began to chant the invocation to the Horus of Gold. The waiting congregation fell to their knees and came in with the chorus:

'Horus of Gold, mighty bull!
Invincible in strength!
Master of his foes!
Holy in his rising!
Wounded eye of the universe!
Attend our endeavours.'

After the last verse Taita turned and, with every eye fixed avidly upon him, strode back down the adit until he stood before the blue-grey wall of newly exposed rock at the end. Tiny crystals of feldspar were embedded in it and sparkled as the sun played on them.

'*Kydash!*' Taita cried, and struck the wall with his staff. The men at the entrance shrank back, for this was one of the words of power.

'*Mensaar!*'

They gasped with awe, and he struck again.

'*Ncube!*' He struck for the third and last time, then stepped back.

Nothing happened, and Nefer felt a sinking disappointment and anticlimax. Taita stood unmoving, and slowly the sun climbed higher and the shadow spread across the rock wall.

Abruptly Nefer felt a tingle of excitement, and the men around him stirred and whispered. In the centre of the rock face, under the painted eye, a dark damp spot appeared. It spread gradually, and a single drop of moisture oozed out, sparkling like a tiny gem in the sunlight. Then it trickled slowly down the wall and balled in the dust of the floor.

Taita turned and walked out of the shaft. Behind him there was a sharp sound, like the breaking of a dry branch, and a fine crack split the rock from top to bottom. Water dripped to the floor, drop after drop, the tempo accelerating into a rapid patter. Another sound, like a shard of pottery snapping in flames, and a chunk of rock fell out of the wall. A sluggish trickle of yellow mud oozed out of the opening it left. Then, with a roar, the entire rock face collapsed, there was a rush of mud and a gushing fountain of crystal-bright water. Knee-deep, it swept the length of the shaft, burst from the mouth and spilled down the hillside, bounding and rippling over the rocks.

There were shouts of amazement, praise and disbelief from the dusty ranks. Suddenly Meren ran forward and plunged headlong into the rushing torrent. He came up spluttering with his wet hair slicked down over his face. He scooped up a double handful and gulped it down. 'Sweet!' he shouted. 'It tastes sweet as honey.'

Men threw off their clothing and rushed naked into the stream, splashing sheets of spray, throwing handfuls of mud, ducking each other and shouting with laughter. Nefer could not long resist the temptation before he shed all dignity and jumped in on top of Meren and wrestled him beneath the surface.

Taita stood on the bank of the stream and looked down on the mayhem with a benign expression. Then he turned to Mintaka. 'Put the thought out of your mind,' he said.

'What thought?' She feigned innocence.

'It would be an outrage to have a princess of Egypt cavorting with a rabble of rough, naked soldiers.' He took her hand and led her away down the hill, but she looked back wistfully at the revels.

'How did you do it, Taita?' she asked. 'How did you make the fountain appear? What kind of magic was it?'

'The magic of common sense and observation. The water has been there for centuries, just waiting for us to dig down to it.'

'But what about the prayers and the words of power? Were those of no effect?'

'Sometimes men need encouragement.' He smiled and touched the side of his nose. 'A little magic is a sovereign tonic for flagging spirits.'

For months thereafter every man was employed in the digging of a channel to lead the sweet flood of water down the hillside and into the old wells. These now became storage cisterns for the settlement. When they brimmed over, Taita surveyed the old fields at the lower end of the valley that were now a stony desolation. However, the outlines of ancient irrigation ditches were still visible. Their levels had been set out by the old inhabitants, and it took small effort to clean out the contour lines and divert the overflowing waters into them.

The desert earth was fertile; the goodness had not been leached out of it by heavy rainfall. The continuous sunshine and abundant water had a miraculous effect. They planted the millet seed smuggled in from Egypt. All Egyptians were farmers and gardeners by nature and tradition, and they lavished their skills upon the land and the crops. Within months they had reaped their first harvest of *dhurra*. Then they planted grass fields for grazing, which flourished and provided far beyond their present needs. The women joined in the cutting, drying and stacking of fodder, and within the year they had sufficient to sustain an army of cavalry, though yet they lacked the horses.

Almost every day fugitives drifted into the city, having braved the desert crossing to escape the tyranny of the false pharaohs. They came singly or in small parties, weary and almost dying of thirst and starvation. The guards posted along the hills intercepted them, and sent them in to Hilto. He made them swear the oath of fealty to Pharaoh Nefer Seti, then issued them with rations and, depending on their suitability, sent them to the training regiments or put them to work in the fields or on restoring the dilapidated buildings of the old city. These waifs and foundlings were not the only recruits, however. A cohort of deserters from the armies of the false pharaohs marched in smartly with their javelins, shouting the praises of Nefer Seti as soon as they were in sight of the walls. Then a squadron of twenty chariots, driven by crack troopers of the Ankh regiment with a colonel named Timus at their head, came in under arms and joyously swore themselves in as the liegemen of Pharaoh Nefer Seti. Timus brought the momentous news that Naja and Trok were prepared at last to march on their combined offensive against King Sargon of Babylon and Assyria.

Over the last few months the two pharaohs had mustered their expeditionary force of three thousand chariots at Avaris, and now they had almost finished their preparations to cross the land bridge that linked Egypt with the eastern lands to the north of the Great Bitter Lake and Lake Timsah. First they had sent a column to drive in the Babylonian pickets along the border then, once the road was cleared, they had shipped in tens of thousands of water jars in carts and wagons and placed them at strategically located storage stations across the dry lands. The country beyond was fertile and well watered.

They planned to cross the land bridge in the full of the moon, using its light and the cool nights to sweep past Ismailiya and up over the Khatmia Pass and on to Beersheba, gathering up the forces of their vassal satraps as they went.

Nefer and Taita had been preparing the defences of Gallala against an imminent attack by the false pharaohs. They knew that their presence in the ancient city must by now be common knowledge throughout the two kingdoms. They had confidently expected Naja and Trok to move against them first, before starting on the Mesopotamian adventure. Therefore they were amazed to have this reprieve.

'They have not taken seriously the threat that our presence so close to their borders poses,' Nefer exulted. 'If they had attacked us now while we are still so weak, we would have had no choice but to fly.'

'Perhaps they took that possibility into their calculations,' Taita agreed. 'Perhaps they are intent on conquering Mesopotamia and cutting off any support that we might have attracted in the Orient. Then they would have us surrounded. I think they have miscalculated, for they leave us to grow stronger for at least another year.'

'Can we be certain that this is not a diversion?' Nefer asked thoughtfully. 'Is the eastern expedition a pretence? Perhaps their true offensive will be directed against us after they have lulled us into a sense of false security.'

'There is always that possibility. Trok is a bull, but Naja especially is cunning and devious. It is the type of bluff he might try.'

'We must keep the expeditionary army under observation,' Nefer decided. 'I will take a scouting party north to watch the road through Ismailiya, and make certain that they pass that way.'

'I will go with you,' Taita agreed.

'No, Magus,' Nefer demurred. 'You will best be employed here, to keep our defences alert, and ensure that if Naja leads three thousand chariots down upon us, the populace is poised for instant flight. Also, there is another service I require of you . . .' He hesitated. 'That is to care for Mintaka. I believe she might be discontented here with the other women, and may attempt something unwise.'

Taita smiled. 'Precipitous action on the part of the princess is always a distinct possibility. However, I know well enough where my first duty lies. I will go with you.' Though Nefer argued long and strenuously, Taita was adamant, and in the end Nefer was secretly relieved to know that the old man would be at his side, as always.

Even with the latest arrival of troops to their cause, they could muster only thirty-two battle-ready chariots, and less than a hundred horses fit enough to draw them.

They left half of the chariots under the command of Shabako to defend Gallala. Taking Hilto and Meren with them, they set out with sixteen fighting vehicles to drive around the eastern shore of the Great Bitter Lake and intercept the main route north of Ismailiya. The new moon was only days past full, the nights dark but pleasantly cool, so they made good progress, and completed the journey through the uncharted wilderness before the moon was into its second quarter.

At dawn on the fifteenth day after leaving Gallala they lay hidden on the hills to the east of Ismailiya, from where they could overlook the town. The main highway ran below their lookout post and the army of the two pharaohs would have to pass this way. Ismailiya was the Egyptian border fortress, and the natural starting point for the campaign.

'It seems that our intelligence is good enough,' Nefer called down to Taita. He had climbed one of the tall cedar trees on the front slope of the hill, and from there he had a fine uninterrupted view over many leagues of terrain. 'The town is swarming with activity. There are horse lines and a city of tents outside the walls of the fort.' He shaded his eyes. 'There are clouds of dust coming up the road from the delta. It looks like all the wagons and chariots of Egypt are on the march.'

He continued to call down his sightings to the Magus through the rest of that morning, until the heat had built up to the point where all activity around the city and upon the roads fell off into the somnolent noonday. Then he climbed down and went to find shade, like the rest of the squadron, to wait out the hot hours.

In the late afternoon as the air cooled, they roused themselves to feed and water the horses. Then Nefer climbed once more to his vantage-point.

It was at once apparent that they had arrived just in time. The road to the east was an artery pulsing with the life force of a mighty army. Squadron after squadron, fifty chariots strong, wound out through the gates of Ismailiya, each followed by wagons carrying their baggage and fodder, and streamed down the road towards their hiding-place. The vanguard passed so close to where Nefer sat in the high branches of the cedar tree that he could make out individuals among them.

The army flowed by like an endless river, glinting with the reflections of bronze weapons, and the dust rose in a dense cloud over it all until it threatened to obscure the sun.

Four cohorts made up the vanguard, and then came a gap. Obviously this was to let the dust settle a little and to alleviate the discomfort of the royal party that followed.

Next came two chariots riding abreast. Both vehicles were so massive, and covered with gold leaf, that each needed six horses to draw it. Nefer's hatred rose with the taste of gall into the back of his throat as he recognized the drivers.

Trok had the reins of the nearest chariot. There was no mistaking his broad shoulders nor the dark, beribboned bush of his beard. He wore a gold helmet shaped like a beehive, decorated with a crest of foaming white ostrich plumes. On his shoulder clanged the double shield, each leaf as thick as his thumb, so weighty that it was said that he alone of all his army could wield it, just like the great war bow in the rack at his right hand.

In the other great chariot rode Pharaoh Naja Kiafan. Like his namesake the cobra, he cut a slimmer, more graceful figure. He wore a pectoral of gold and precious stones that sparkled in the red sunlight that filtered through the dustclouds. On his head he wore the blue war crown of Egypt, and at his side, sheathed in silver and electrum, studded with turquoise and lapis lazuli, was the legendary blue sword, that he had plundered from the body of Nefer's father.

Strangely, though he lacked the physical stature of Trok, Naja was the more threatening of the two.

The golden chariots passed and were hidden by their own dustclouds, but Nefer remained stretched out on the main branch of the cedar tree as the warlike phalanxes rolled by below him.

The sun had slipped below the horizon, but there was still just enough light to make out the next section of the endless procession. Nefer straightened up with renewed interest and attention.

Swaying and rolling over the surface of the highway, which was already rutted by the passage of the hundreds of chariots and wagons that had preceded them, came two litters drawn by teams of bullocks. They were so capacious, the silk curtains decorated with golden stars and rosettes, that Nefer knew the passengers within must be women of the royal harem. Nefer could not imagine Trok taking his wives or concubines on campaign with him – he had heard that Trok relied for his pleasure on the prisoners he took from the captured enemy towns and that he enjoyed boys or girls with equal gusto. So if they did not belong to Trok, they must be Naja's women. Nefer wondered if Naja had tired of Heseret and taken other wives.

Then the curtain of the second litter jerked open, a girl jumped down into the dusty roadway and skipped along beside the bullocks. Though she had changed markedly since he had last seen her, he could not doubt that this lovely creature was Merykara, his younger sister. She no longer wore the side-lock of childhood, her hair was bobbed upon her shoulders and cut in a thick straight fringe at the level of her eyebrows. The loss of her side-lock was the token that she had seen her first red moon. Nefer felt a pang that his funny little monkey was a child no more. Then it occurred to him that there was no longer any impediment to Naja taking Merykara to the connubial bed. He had heard that Naja was a voluptuous satyr and the idea of him ravishing his little sister revolted Nefer so much that he could taste it in the back of his throat, like rotten fish.

He felt an overwhelming desire to speak to Merykara, to learn if she was happy, if there was aught he could do to make her lot easier. Then it ocurred to him to rescue her and take her back to Gallala. He knew that such thoughts were dangerous, and that his comrades would try to dissuade him from such suicidal fantasy.

Following close behind the litters he saw the carts carrying the war chests of the false pharaohs. Here was a motive that the others would understand. They were unornamented carts painted a dull, sombre blue, but sturdily built and with the trucks reinforced to withstand the great weight of their cargo. The metal-shod wheels cut deeply into the road surface. The doors at the rear of the truck bed were chained and locked, and armed men marched beside them. These were the standard conveyances of the treasures without which no army marched. Nefer knew that they contained gold bullion cast into bars and fingers, rings and beads. These would be used to pay the troops, and to buy the allegiance of minor kings and satraps, to subvert the allies of Babylon and Assyria, and to bribe spies and informers in the ranks of the enemy.

Nefer slid down the trunk of the cedar to the ground. Taita was dozing quietly there, but he opened his eyes before Nefer could touch his arm. 'The war chests of the false pharaohs,' Nefer whispered in his ear. 'Enough to pay an army or buy a throne.'

For many nights that followed Nefer and the Magus stalked the column from the moonlit shadows, moving parallel to the carts that carried the treasure, observing the routine and behaviour of the guards. From the first they realized that it would be impossible to seize the carts and carry away that mass of bullion without the entire army coming down upon them.

'At the speed those oxen are capable of maintaining, Naja's chariots would catch us before we had gone a league with them,' Nefer observed ruefully.

'We will need to be a little more subtle than that,' Taita agreed. 'The only time when we might be able to tamper with the chests would be when they go into laager during the day.'

'What about the guards?'

'Ah!' said Taita. 'The guards will present some small problem.'

Each day when the sun rose high and the heat became oppressive the entire army went into laager. The litters bearing the royal wives, and treasure carts were usually placed in a separate encampment a short distance from the main army. At first there was a great bustle as the animals were loosed from their harness, fed and watered, the sentries posted and the tents of the wives erected. Then the fires were lit and the midday meal was cooked and eaten, washed down with beer. After that Heseret, Merykara and their maids retired to their tents. The men who were not on sentry duty lay down under makeshift shelters to rest after the long night's journey. Gradually a languid silence fell over the huge muster of men and animals, and the camp slept.

Nefer and Taita left the rest of their party lying in a patch of dense thornbush up in the valley and crept to the camp. They were able to get within a few hundred paces of the sentries and lie there unobserved for an hour, whispering together, trying to find some manner of reaching the war chests without being discovered by the sentries.

'Is there no way we can distract them?' Nefer asked.

'For that we will need help from inside the camp,' Taita said.

'Merykara?' Nefer looked at him sharply.

'Merykara,' Taita agreed.

'How can we get a message to her?' Nefer looked puzzled, but Taita smiled, touched the Periapt of Lostris that hung on his necklace and closed his eyes. After a while Nefer thought he had fallen asleep. The old man knew exactly how to infuriate him.

His age is catching up with him at last, he thought irritably, and was about to shake him awake, when he heard voices from the camp, and looked up.

Merykara had come out of her tent. She had obviously been sleeping for her face was flushed and marked by the pillow. She stretched and yawned. She wore only a blue linen skirt, whose pleats hung below her knees. Her upper body was bare. Despite himself Nefer was astonished at the way her breasts had bloomed: they were pear-shaped and the nipples stood proud and rosy. Merykara was arguing with the guard at the entrance to her tent and her voice rose imperiously so that Nefer could hear every word. 'I cannot sleep, and I am going out to walk awhile.' The sentry was trying to restrain her, but she shook her head until her hair danced on her shoulders. 'No, I will not let you escort me. I want to be alone.' The sentry insisted and she flared at him, 'Stand aside, you insolent creature, or I will report your behaviour to my husband.' Reluctantly the sentry acceded to her orders and grounded his spear. He called after her anxiously, 'Please, Your Majesty, be not too long nor venture too far. It will be more than my miserable life is worth should Pharaoh find out about this.'

Merykara ignored him, ducked through the horses' lines, and came out through the gate of the thornbush fence that surrounded the camp. She looked back only once to make certain that she was not observed by any of the sentries. Then as though to an assignation, she came directly to where Nefer and Taita lay among the desert scrub.

Nefer saw that her green eyes were rapt and that there was an intent expression on her lovely face, as though she were listening to music that she alone could hear.

When she was close enough to touch, Nefer said softly, 'Merykara, don't be afraid. It's Nefer.'

She started like an awakening sleep-walker and stared down at him. Then her face lit with an expression of untrammelled joy and she sprang forward to embrace him.

'Wait!' Nefer ordered. 'Don't betray us to the guards.'

He was proud of her, for she obeyed him and stopped instantly. She had always been an intelligent child. She glanced around quickly and her voice trembled when she said softly, 'I was sound asleep, but suddenly I woke and knew that I had to come out into the desert. It was almost as though a voice in my head was calling to me.' She looked at Taita. 'Was it your voice, Magus?' Then her eyes went back to Nefer. 'Darling brother, you will never know how I have missed you. First I thought you were dead, and I mourned in your funeral procession with ashes on my head. Look, here are the scars where I cut my arms to bleed for you.'

'I am alive, Merykara. Believe me, this is no shade you are looking at.'

'I know, Nefer. All the world knows now how you took Mintaka away from Avaris into the desert, and I knew in my heart that you would come for me also, one day.' She smiled through happy tears. 'I knew you would come.'

'Yes,' Nefer said, 'we will take you away with us. But first there is something you must do to help us.'

'Anything for you and Taita,' she agreed readily.

Speaking swiftly and urgently, Taita told her what she had to do and then he made her repeat it. She did so faultlessly. 'You are a clever girl, my little one,' Taita said. 'That is exactly what we want you to do.' He handed her a small packet. 'Here is the powder. Remember, just enough to cover your fingernail in each jar.'

'First you call me clever, and then you treat me as though I were stupid,' she snapped.

'Forgive me, Your Majesty.' Taita made a gesture of penitence.

'Don't call me that either. I hate being married to that slimy serpent, and now I know what he is going to do to me, I hate it even more.'

'You are not easy to please, Merykara. Now, go back to the camp before the guards come looking for you.'

She stooped quickly and kissed Nefer on the lips. 'Until tomorrow then, my beloved brother.'

The following noon the mighty army of Egypt camped below the high plateau where the sandy desert and the dry lands ended. They had almost completed the crossing and tomorrow they would go up through the pass into the cooler lands where the oases were only a day's journey apart, where forests and fields and vineyards grew and mountain streams flowed all year round.

When the escort of the royal wives began to set up camp for the day, they found that the young Queen Merykara was fractious and overbearing, not at all her usual sweet and gracious self. She wanted her own tent set further apart from that of her sister, Queen Heseret, and when this was done she insisted that they move the carts that carried the army war chests down into a narrow wadi two hundred paces from the main encampment. In vain the commander of the guard pointed out that the bed of the wadi was soft and sandy and the wheels of the heavy vehicles would sink in deeply.

'I don't care if they disappear into the sand completely,' she told him. 'I am sick of looking at those ugly carts and listening to the mooing of the bullocks. Get them out of my sight.'

The commander thought of appealing to Pharaoh Naja Kiafan to ratify this unreasonable order from his youngest wife. Then he contemplated the fact that the column was spread out over almost four leagues of desert. It would take an hour of hard riding to reach Pharaoh at its head, and the return ride would be just as arduous. The day was even hotter than those that had preceded it and, besides, he had a tryst with one of Merykara's slave girls, an enchanting little black Nubian who knew more tricks than a performing monkey. He moved the carts into the wadi bottom and, as a sop to his conscience, doubled the guard upon them.

Having got her own way, Merykara became once again the endearing girl they all loved so well.

'I am so sorry I was hard on you, Moram. It must be this awful heat that affects us all,' she told the commander of the guard sweetly in front of his men. 'I am going to have Misha bring you five jars of the finest beer from my private stores to make it up to you. But be certain that you share it equally with all your men for I have given them extra work and trouble too.'

Misha, the statuesque Nubian maid with an imperious carriage and a legendary pair of buttocks, brought the beer jars to Moram's tent, and the men lined up to receive their share, calling down the gods' blessings on Queen Merykara and toasting her health as they swigged down the first draught of the frothing liquor.

Despite his promise to Merykara, the beer was of such surpassing excellence that Moram drank more than his share. As soon as they were alone in his tent he pounced on Misha who, squealing and resisting playfully, finally allowed him to lift her clothing and unveil her prodigious buttocks. They sprang out from under her short linen skirts, shining black as new mined anthracite, great quivering rounds, dark full moons that overflowed his clutching hands.

In a transport of lust he mounted her, but after less than a dozen mighty thrusts, he keeled over slowly, fast asleep before he reached the floor. Misha stared at him in astonishment. Nothing like this had ever happened to her in all her short but busy lifetime. Moram let out a snore that reverberated like distant thunder, and she sprang to her feet, pulled on her skirt, delivered one furious kick to his sleeping form and stormed out of the tent back to her mistress. The guard at the entrance to the royal tent was also sleeping like a dead man.

'All men are pigs,' Misha said, in her savage native

tongue, and kicked him with all the strength of her long and shapely right leg.

Nefer led a small party of his men down the dry riverbed. They kept close under the bank, and the soft sand muffled their footsteps.

The four treasure carts were drawn up side by side, and their wheels were chained together so that they could not be driven off in haste by bandits or robbers.

Eight armed men were posted around them as sentries, and every one was laid out on the soft sand like a corpse awaiting the embalmers. Taita went to each in turn, felt for the pulse in the throat then drew back a lid to examine the eye of the unconscious man. Finally he nodded to Nefer, and went to the rear door of the first cart.

He took a long bronze probe from his pouch and worked intently on the massive bronze lock. It fell open and the hasp snapped back. Taita swung open the heavy metal door to reveal the four small cases that were tied down to ringbolts in the wagon bed. The lids of the treasure chests were sealed with a clay tablet that carried the cartouche of Pharaoh Naja Kiafan.

Taita used his dagger blade to lift the seals, and dropped them into his pouch so that they would not be evidence of tampering when next the cart doors were opened. He used the point of the dagger to unscrew the fastenings that held down the lid, then lifted it. The chest was filled with small leather pouches. Taita weighed one in his hand, and smiled. He opened the mouth of the pouch to see the unmistakable glint of the precious metal within.

While he had been busy, Nefer and Meren had dug a shallow hole in the soft sand under the wagon truck. Taita passed down the leather pouch to Nefer, who laid it in the bottom of the hole. In all Taita selected fifty of the heaviest leather bags from the first chest. Then he screwed back the lid. Using a lump of fresh damp clay that he had brought with him he resealed the lid. With the engraved ruby ring that Naja had given him as a gift when he had left Thebes, he imprinted the clay seal with the royal cartouche. Then he went on to the next chest in the row of four.

'We are not taking enough,' Meren grumbled. 'We are leaving more than half of it for Naja and Trok.'

'Greed would be our undoing,' Taita grunted, as he prised up the lid of the last case. 'This way they will not know that any of the bullion is missing until the paymaster opens the cases again and counts it, which may not be for several more months.'

From each case in the four carts they lifted fifty leather bags and buried them in the loose sand of the wadi bed. Though they worked as swiftly as care would allow, the sun was low in the western sky when they resealed the final chest and locked the rear doors of the last cart. One of the sleeping guards stirred and mumbled, and tried to sit up. Taita went to him and laid a gentle hand on his brow. The man sighed and lay back. Taita pulled open his mouth and sprinkled a pinch of white powder under his tongue, and he lay quiet.

'We must hurry now. They are beginning to revive.'

They spread sand over the rows of bags in the bottom of the hole beneath the last wagon, and then roughed and dotted the surface with footprints so that the smooth sand would not be conspicuous.

'How much do you estimate we took?' Nefer asked.

'Impossible to tell until we weigh it,' Taita said, 'but I would guess we have at least three lakhs.'

'Enough to recruit and equip an army,' Nefer muttered, as he worked.

They made one last quick but thorough inspection of

the carts and the area around them, to make sure that they had overlooked nothing. Then leaving the guards still in heavy drugged sleep, they slipped away down the wadi.

They climbed into the foothills below the plateau, back to where they had left Hilto with the chariots. From this vantage-point they kept watch on where they had buried the plundered gold. They observed no evidence of any outcry or unusual activity in the wadi. Perhaps the guards felt too guilty when they woke to make any report on their dereliction of duty.

Just before dark they saw the straining teams of bullocks heave the four carts out of the sandy riverbed, and trudge away behind the royal litters as the host of the false pharaohs resumed the night march.

For five more days and nights the great army of Egypt streamed past this spot. There were successive squadrons of chariots, regiments of slingers, archers and spearmen. These were followed by marching columns of slaves who would be used for the heavy labour of building fortifications and sapping the walls of besieged cities. Then came the craftsmen, the chariot builders and carpenters, the armourers and arrow makers, and after them the camp-followers, the wives, sweethearts and whores with their slaves, servants and infants. They were followed by the merchants with wagon-loads of goods and luxuries of every possible description to sell to the troops when they were rich with loot and plunder.

Yet out of all this multitude the watchers on the hills saw nobody enter the dried wadi where the gold was buried, and though each day companies and regiments camped nearby no one approached the wadi to use it as a latrine or a camping site.

When the last vehicle in that mighty host had trundled past and climbed up through the rocky Khatmia Pass, and the last straggler had limped by, Nefer and Taita were certain that the short-weight of bullion in the treasure carts had not been discovered by the army paymasters, and they were almost certain that the cache in the riverbed had not been stumbled upon by chance.

When at last the eastern highway was deserted they came down from the hills during the night and left the chariots on the high bank of the wadi with the horses still in the traces, ready for instant flight. Nefer and Meren went down into the sandy bed, and in the moonlight the tracks left by the treasure carts and the oxen were still plain to see. After only a few thrusts with the wooden spade Meren whistled with glee and turned up the first pouch of gold. As they lifted each bag from the hole they counted them, making certain that they overlooked not a single one. Then they carried them up the wadi bank, staggering under their weight, and stacked them beside the waiting chariots. Eight hundred leather bags filled with fine gold made an impressive pile.

'Too much! We will not be able to carry away all of it,' Nefer said doubtfully.

'It is one of the natural laws of this wicked world.' Taita shook his head. 'Of gold there can never be too much.'

The light fighting chariots had not been designed as transport carts, but they loaded them until the axles sagged and the coachwork groaned. Still they had not taken half of it on board. Nursing the horses, leading them by the reins, they took the overloaded chariots up into the hills then came back for the next load. It required two more trips to carry it all away.

They divided the treasure into five equal parts and buried four in separate caches, well dispersed, taking great care to conceal them and leave no sign. Thus, if one hoard was discovered they would not lose all. The fifth part they loaded on to thirteen of the chariots and Nefer sent them back to Gallala under the command of Hilto. Once he reached the city Hilto would return with a convoy of heavy wagons to fetch in the remainder.

Nefer kept back the remaining three chariots. They would be driven by himself, Taita and Meren. The two squadrons parted company, Hilto taking his laden vehicles south again, and Nefer leading his smaller group eastwards, shadowing the army of the two pharaohs.

Nefer travelled by day, knowing that the army they were following would be resting in camp, and with a daylight view ahead they were unlikely to run into any surprises.

They went up through the pass on to the plateau where they found ample water, although much of it had been fouled by the thousands of animals and men who had been there ahead of them. The horses were well rested, and they travelled fast in the lightly laden chariots. They passed hundreds of abandoned campsites, marked by dead fires and sagging lean-to shelters, litter and scattered filth. There were also hastily dug graves, for an army on the march suffers constant attrition. Some had already been dug open by the hyena and the jackal, the corpses dragged out and partially consumed.

'We will need her,' Nefer said, as he dismounted and stood over the body of a young woman, probably one of the army whores. There was no way of telling how she had died for the vultures had almost completed what the hyena had begun. Her eyes and lips were missing and her skull grinned at them through blood blackened teeth.

'In all love of the gods,' Meren cried, 'have you lost your senses? That thing stinks to the skies.'

'Help me wrap her.' Nefer ignored his protest. He had found a length of discarded linen, so torn and dirty that even the Bedouin who scavenged behind the army had found no use for it. Between them they lifted the remains of the dead woman on to it and wrapped her neatly. Then, to his loudly expressed disgust, they tied the bundle to the back of Meren's chariot.

Though they had been travelling under the dust pall since dawn, it was mid-morning before they caught up with the rearguard of the army. The entire expeditionary force had already gone into laager for the day, and the smoke from the cooking fires marked the position of hundreds of separate encampments along the road ahead.

Nefer led them off the road, and they circled out to avoid the baggage train, keeping out of sight of the road. Scouting the terrain ahead, they went forward cautiously. Eventually they caught up with the convoy of treasure carts and the tall litters of the royal wives halted in a grove of olive trees. It was well past noon when Nefer crept up close to them, and climbed a tamarind tree from which he could spy over the thornbush *zareba* that surrounded the camp.

Queen Merykara's pavilion was set up at some distance from that of Heseret, but the two sisters were sitting under a linen awning, protected from the sun and picking at the lavish meal their serving maids had brought from the cooking fires.

Nefer was not close enough to overhear their conversation. Heseret sat facing him, chattering and laughing gaily. She was even more beautiful than Nefer remembered her. Even in these informal circumstances she was wearing carefully applied makeup, which was intended to make her resemble the statue of Hathor in Memphis. She was decked out in a suite of magnificent jewels, and her thick dark hair had been freshly oiled and crimped. Misha, the tall black slave girl with the legendary posterior, leaned over her shoulder to refill her golden bowl. A splash of the red wine spilled down the front of Heseret's dress. She sprang to her feet and thrashed Misha over the head with a heavy fan of silver and ostrich feathers. The girl fell to her knees and covered it with both hands but the blood sprang up between her fingers. Merykara tried to restrain her elder sister, but

Heseret rained blows on Misha's head until the shaft of the fan snapped in two, then hurled the broken end at Merykara and flounced away, yelling threats and abuse over her shoulder.

Merykara lifted the slave girl to her feet and led her away to her own pavilion. Nefer waited patiently, hidden in the top branches of the tamarind tree. Some time later, Misha left the tent with her head bandaged. Still weeping she disappeared among the trees. Nefer did not move, until Merykara appeared in the opening of her pavilion.

When they had last spoken, Nefer had warned her to keep alert and to wait for him to come to her. Now she looked around her carefully, spoke to the guard at the door of the tent, and began to wander, without any apparent purpose, around the periphery of the camp. Clearly she had taken Nefer's instructions seriously and was searching the surrounding countryside for a glimpse of her rescuers. She was the only person stirring: most of the others were sheltering from the sun and the heat, and even the sentries showed no interest in her.

Nefer took a small polished silver mirror from his pouch, picked up the sun's reflection and shot a ray of light into Merykara's face. She stopped instantly, shaded her eyes, and peered in his direction. He flashed thrice more, the agreed signal and, even from that distance, saw her smile become as radiant as the reflected sunbeam that danced over her lovely face.

Merykara lay in the swaying, jolting litter, on cushions and a mattress stuffed with swansdown. Misha was curled at her feet like a sleeping puppy, but Merykara was awake and alert. The curtains of the litter were drawn back to let in the cool night air and she could hear the sounds of the army on the march: the clatter of hoofs, the creak and rattle of the wagons, the lowing of the draught oxen, the cries of the wagoners and the tramp of the guards alongside the litter.

Suddenly there was a commotion ahead, the swish and crack of whips, the crash of wheels over rocks, the sound of running water and the splashing of animals and vehicles. Then Merykara heard her sister's querulous voice: 'Ho there! What is happening?'

'Your Majesty, we are fording a small stream. I must beg you to dismount, lest the litter capsize. The safety of your divine person is all our concern.'

She heard Heseret complain bitterly about the inconvenience, and Merykara took advantage of the diversion to whisper her final instructions to Misha. Then they climbed down from the litter. Slaves waited with lanterns to lead them down to the riverbank, where Heseret was already waiting.

'They woke me when I was sleeping,' she told Merykara. 'I shall report that oaf of a caravan master to my husband, the Pharaoh of Upper Egypt.'

'I am sure that it will be beneficial to your health to have the skin flogged from his back,' Merykara agreed, with sweet irony. Heseret tossed her head and turned away.

At that moment a nightingale called upstream from where they stood, and Merykara thrilled to the sound. As children Nefer had tried to teach her how to imitate that low, warbling note, but she had never mastered it. Three times the bird called, but only she took notice of it. The others were engrossed in getting the ungainly litters and the heavy treasure carts across the treacherous riverbed. The thousands of vehicles ahead of them had cut up the entrance to the ford, and churned the bottom to a morass. It was after midnight before the crossing was accomplished and the last treasure cart was dragged through with loud exhortations to the oxen to 'Heave away!' and the flourish and cracking of whips up the far bank.

Then the caravan master brought up sedan chairs for the royal wives. They were helped into the seats and carried over by teams of slaves. When they reached the far bank there was further consternation and confusion for one of the treasure carts had lost a wheel and was blocking the road ahead. Now, in addition to this mishap, the slaves who had carried Heseret across in the sedan chair had allowed the water to flow over her feet and ruin her sandals. Heseret insisted that they were punished on the spot, and the slash of the overseers' whips and the howls of the miscreants added to the uproar.

Over it all Merykara heard the nightingale call again, this time close at hand and on the same side of the stream. 'Do not fail me,' she said to Misha.

'My life is yours, mistress,' the girl replied, and Merykara kissed her.

'You have proved that often, and I shall never forget it.' She turned from Misha and walked calmly into the darkness.

Only Heseret paid her the least notice. 'Where are you going, Merykara?'

'To drown the bad fairies.' Merykara used their childhood euphemism. Heseret shrugged, climbed back into her own litter and drew the curtains.

As soon as she was hidden from the road, Merykara stopped and gave her own inept version of the bird call.

Almost at once a firm hand closed on her upper arm and her brother whispered in her ear, 'Pray desist, little one, you will terrify every nightingale from here to Beersheba.'

She spun round, threw her arms about his neck, and hugged him with all her strength, too overcome to speak. Gently he loosened her grip then took her hand and led her along the dark riverbank. He went swiftly and he seemed to have the night eyes of a leopard for he never stumbled or hesitated. He did not speak except to whisper a warning when there was a hole or an obstacle in the path. She followed him blindly. After what seemed half the night, he stopped to allow her to rest.

'Does Misha know what to do?' he asked.

'She will keep the curtains of the litter closed and tell anyone who asks that I am sleeping and will not be disturbed. No one will know that I am gone.'

'Until they halt tomorrow,' he qualified. 'We have only that much time to get away. Are you ready to go on? We must cross back over the river here.'

He picked her up easily and carried her across, and she was amazed at how strong he had grown. She was a doll in his arms. He set her down again on the opposite bank, and they went on.

After a while she tugged on his hand. 'What is that awful smell?' She gagged.

'It's you,' he told her. 'Or, at least, one who shall take your place.'

Before he finished speaking two dark figures stepped out into the starlight on the path ahead of them, and Merykara gave a small gasp of fright.

''Tis only Taita and Meren,' Nefer reassured her. They led her into a coppice in which they were screened by the dense growth of leafy branches, and Meren opened the shutter of the lantern he carried. Merykara gasped again as, by the feeble yellow light, she saw the gruesome object stretched on the ground. It was a corpse, but so dreadfully mutilated that it was difficult to tell that it was human and female.

'Quickly, now!' Nefer told her. 'Give me all your jewellery and your clothing.'

Merykara stripped herself naked, and handed everything to Nefer. Taita handed her a small bundle of spare clothing, tunic, skirt and sandals, to replace her own.

Nefer knelt beside the corpse and placed the strings of necklaces around the dead girl's neck, and the rings and bracelets on her skeletal fingers and wrists. He could not work Merykara's skirt and loincloth up over the rigid legs, so he ripped them to tatters and rubbed them in the dirt, then he stabbed his own thumb with the point of his dagger and dribbled fresh blood on the fine cloth. From near at hand there came the shrieking, whooping chorus of a pack of hungry hyenas.

Merykara shuddered. 'They have smelt the body.'

'They will leave only enough evidence to convince Naja that you were devoured by wild animals.' He stood up. 'Now we must go.'

The chariots were waiting a little further upstream. Nefer had not wanted to leave their tracks too close to the body of the dead girl. As he pulled his sister up on to the footplate beside him, he looked into the east. 'The morning star,' he said quietly. 'It will be light in an hour. We must make the most of the darkness that remains.'

When the dawn bloomed, like a bouquet of roses and mimosa blossom, across the sky behind them they were already halfway down the escarpment of the plateau, and the desert was spread out below them.

It was such a grand sight that involuntarily they reined in the horses and stared out across the ocean of golden sands in awe. All except Meren. With the air of a pilgrim who has travelled across half the world to reach the shrine of the goddess he worshipped, he stared at Merykara as she stood beside her brother in the leading chariot. Through the long night ride she had been hidden from him by the darkness, but now the early sun played upon her, and he stared. He had known her for most of his life as the saucy, impish little sister of his best friend, but this was the first time in two years that he had laid eyes upon her. Time had wrought a miracle of change. Now, every movement she made, each gesture and turn of her head, was perfect grace. Every angle and plane of her face, every curve and line of her slim body was exquisite. Her skin was cream and mother-of-pearl, her eyes greener and brighter than any emerald, her voice and laughter the most enchanting music he had ever heard.

Taita caught his expression and smiled inwardly. Even in the most dire situations, life struggles to renew itself, he thought, but aloud he said, 'Majesty, we must not linger here. The horses are in need of water.'

At the foot of the hills they left the highway and struck out in a southerly direction towards the Great Bitter Lake. They kept going until they reached the first cache of water jars they had left for their return journey, and found that Hilto had been there before them. From his tracks they could tell that his chariots, heavily laden with gold bullion, were moving only slowly, and that he was not far ahead.

They found with relief that he had not used up all the water but had left four jars untouched, enough to keep their horses going until they reached the next oasis at Zinalla.

Although Merykara had been sparkling and animated when she chatted and jested with Nefer and Taita, by some chance she had not acknowledged Meren or even glanced in his direction, except when she knew it was safe to do so. Although once not long ago he had treated her with lordly disdain, Meren was now too overcome to approach her directly. For she was a queen, albeit to a false pharaoh, and in his eyes at least a goddess.

For the hundredth time since they had halted he placed

himself artlessly in her direct line of vision as she rested in the scant shade of a flowering acacia tree. This time she lifted her eyes and inclined her head. He made a loyal obeisance. 'Greetings, Your Majesty. I am delighted to see you safe. I was infernally worried for your safety.'

She gave him a single long look, searching and calculating, to take in his increased height and the confident, powerful set of his shoulders. She saw how long and thick his hair had grown, and not for the first time that day she was aware of a strange congestion in her breathing. 'Meren Cambyses,' she said sternly, 'the last time I had any truck with you, you broke my favourite kite. Can I ever trust you again?'

'With your very life,' he said fervently.

When the horses were fed and rested and it was time to move on, Merykara told her brother casually, 'Your horses have borne my extra weight all night. I think I should relieve them now.'

'How will you do that?' He looked puzzled.

'I will ride in another chariot,' she said, and went to where Meren waited for her.

The following day they reached the oasis of Zinalla and found Hilto's squadron there before them. Now Nefer redistributed the weight of men and bullion equally between the fifteen chariots and they went on towards Gallala at a much better pace.

Mintaka was on the roof of the temple of Hathor, which she and some of the women and old men were making habitable for the goddess so that they might resume their worship in her presence. The building might have been a thousand years old, there was no way of telling, but many of the murals were in a marvellous state of preservation and needed only a little touching up. The roof was another matter. However, the elements were kindly and so consistent that the great holes mattered little. It was only necessary to remove the rotten rafters, which placed the worshippers below in mortal jeopardy. Mintaka was supervising this work. She was dressed like the other women in simple, well-worn clothing, and like them she was burnt brown by the sun. This life was so different from that closeted existence in the *zenana* of Avaris, and she revelled in her new freedom, the friendship and company of her common companions.

She straightened and stretched her aching back, balancing easily on the high wall. Then she shaded her eyes and looked out over the green fields of young *dhurra*, and the patterns of irrigation ditches filled with sparkling water from Taita's fountain. Herds of cattle and a flock of fat-tailed sheep were grazing in the lush paddocks, but very few horses. Like every other person in Gallala, she felt the lack of them keenly.

Then, as she had every hour over the past long and lonely days since Nefer had left the city, she raised her eyes and looked down the length of the valley, between the bare, forbidding hills that stood in such bleak contrast to the green fields clustered around the city. This was the direction from which Nefer would come. She searched the blue distance without real hope for she had been disappointed too often recently.

Suddenly she narrowed her eyes against the glare, and her heartbeat quickened. Something was there, tiny against the soaring immensity of the sky, insubstantial and ethereal as a feather blowing in the wind. A dust-devil, perhaps, one of the whirlwinds born of the heated desert airs.

She looked away and wiped the sweat from her thick dark brows, resting her eyes. When she looked again the dustcloud was closer, and she allowed herself to hope. At that moment a ram's horn sounded a single long blast. The lookouts on the crest of the hills had seen it also. Around her the others stopped work and peered down the valley. From the streets below came the excited shouts of the children, grooms ran to the stables, the charioteers to where their vehicles lay beyond the market-place. All was happy bustle.

Mintaka could restrain herself no longer. She went down the scaffolding that covered the outer wall of the temple with the alacrity of a vervet caught stealing fruit in an orchard. Shabako was driving his chariot across the forum, past the battle memorial of Tanus, heading for the gates.

'Shabako!' She ran to intercept him. He swerved to meet her, and as he pulled up the team she leaped on to the footplate behind him. They raced out through the gates and down the rutted track. Ahead, the dustcloud was coming on apace.

'Is it them, Shabako? Tell me it is.'

'I do believe it is, Majesty,' he shouted, above the rush of the wind.

'Then why do you drive so slowly?'

Over the rise ahead came a single vehicle, and she clung to the dashboard, trying to make out the charioteer, but he was still too far away.

'Look, mistress! He flies the blue pennant.' Shabako pointed to the scrap of dyed cloth that fluttered on the long bamboo rod above the chariot.

''Tis Nefer! Oh, all praise to the goddess, it is him!'

She ripped off her headcloth and waved it, while Nefer lashed up his team and came on at the charge.

'Let me off!' She beat on Shabako's shoulder to enforce the order and he slowed the horses to a trot. She jumped from the moving vehicle and landed gracefully in balance. Then she ran to meet the advancing chariot with her arms open wide.

Coming up behind, Taita thought that in his eagerness Nefer might run her down, but at the last moment he swerved and, as the chariot lost speed, he leaned far out over the side of the cockpit and reached down for her. Trustingly she threw herself into the circle of his arm. If she had hesitated or flinched she might have been dashed beneath the galloping team or crushed under the metal-shod wheels but he caught her up, swung her high and she laughed in his arms.

Nefer called his council to assemble in the old city forum and made a full report to them. He described in detail the lifting of the bullion out of the treasure carts and they listened agog. Then he presented Merykara to them and related how she had been rescued from under the very noses of Trok and Naja. They shouted, '*Bak-her!*' and stood to applaud him.

Then Nefer sent for the scribes, and they weighed the gold bullion in front of the members of the council. The final tally was well over half a lakh. 'My lords, this is only a fifth part of what we have won. Hilto will take a convoy of wagons back to retrieve the rest. He will leave tomorrow but he will need men to go with him.'

It seemed that every able-bodied man in Gallala was desperate to volunteer, but when Shabako and the most tried and experienced of his warriors were passed over, they protested bitterly. 'Will Pharaoh have us sit here in Gallala, dreaming at the hearth like old women?' Shabako asked.

Nefer smiled. 'I will have sterner work for you. But now the sun is well set, and a victory feast is prepared for us. We will meet again soon in war council, I give you my oath on it,' he assured them, and adjourned the assembly. They went away grumbling, but their mood revived after the first jars of freshly brewed beer had been disposed of.

Nefer had ordered the slaughter of two bullocks and a dozen fat sheep, and the women had spent every minute since his return preparing a celebratory feast. Every man and woman in the city was invited, and even the garrisons of hilltop forts and watchtowers were sent their share. Like the digging of the fountain, the winning of the gold was an achievement that had knit the community closer.

Taita had composed a heroic poem to honour the occasion and, like all his creative efforts, it was an instant, overwhelming success. They would not let him sit down when he had finished, but yelled and banged their bowls on the board until he had repeated all sixty verses. By then they had memorized the entire epic and the musicians had extemporized a musical score. The entire company joined with gusto in the third and final rendition.

Then Nefer called upon any citizen who felt an oratorical urge to stand up and speak out. Some of the speeches were incoherent but well received, others were hilarious or so poignant that most of the women and many men were reduced to tears. In this emotional atmosphere Merykara leaned across Mintaka to speak to her brother. The din around them was so great that she had to raise her voice to be heard. 'Royal and divine brother!' she teased him, for she had also sampled the contents of the beer pots. 'I have a boon to ask of you.'

'Little sister, who is little no more, ask what you wish and if it is in my power you shall have it.'

'It is very much in your power.' She broke off, looked down the table at Meren, caught his avid eye, lowered her gaze and blushed an appealing shade of pink. 'You know that as a child I was married without my consent and against my will. That marriage was never consummated. I want you to proclaim my divorce from Naja. I want you to set me free so that I can go to a husband of my own choice. This would be the most precious gift you could ever give me.'

'Is that possible?' Nefer sobered at once, and looked at Taita. 'Do I have it in my power to divorce a husband and wife in the sight of the gods?'

'You are Pharaoh,' Merykara cut in, before Taita could reply. 'Just as Trok divorced Mintaka, so you are able to divorce me from Naja.'

'Trok divorced Mintaka?' Nefer demanded, so sharply that all those within hearing fell silent.

'Did you not know?' Merykara asked. 'Forgive me for breaking it to you in such a tactless, thoughtless fashion. I thought that such momentous news would have reached even here.' Nefer took Mintaka's hand and shook his head, too overcome with emotion to speak. Merykara went on blithely. 'Oh, yes! On his own sacred holy-day, in his own new temple, Pharaoh Trok sacrificed a ram and proclaimed three times "I divorce her."' Merykara clapped her hands. 'And, poof! the dread deed was done.'

Nefer drew Mintaka a little closer to him, and looked at Taita. The old man knew the law better than any temple scribe in Egypt, and now, in answer to Nefer's silent enquiry, he nodded solemnly.

Merykara was rattling on. 'Of course, immediately after the divorce he sacrificed another ram and passed sentence of death upon Mintaka for adultery and sacrilege in dishonouring a god.'

Nefer turned his head and stared deeply into Mintaka's eyes. She stared back as they considered the implication of Merykara's revelations. Slowly a strange expression spread over Nefer's face, like that of a condemned man hearing of his reprieve. 'You are free, my one true love,' he said. 'And your freedom has set me free.'

Before dawn the following morning, while most of the city was still sleeping off the effects of the good strong beer, Nefer sought out Taita in his private quarters in one of the old buildings. Taita looked up from the papyrus scroll he was reading by the flickering yellow light of an oil lamp.

'Are you occupied with some important matter?' Nefer asked, with strange diffidence.

'You can see that I am,' said Taita, but resignedly he began to roll the scroll on to its wooden spine. For a while Nefer wandered aimlessly around the room, pausing to examine some articles that the old man had collected since they had been here in Gallala: preserved skins of colourful birds, skeletons of small mammals and reptiles, oddly shaped pieces of dried wood or plants, and other amorphous substances in bowls or bottles or bags that were piled on the benches or in odd recesses. Taita waited patiently for him to come to the reason for this visit, though he knew well enough what it must be.

Nefer picked up a fossil of some antediluvian crustacean and held it to the lamplight. 'Mintaka is no longer married to Trok,' he said, without looking up.

'Stone deaf as I may be in both ears, even I was able to make that out.'

Nefer replaced the fossil and took up a copper statuette of Isis with the infant Horus sitting on her lap and nursing at her breast that Taita had dug up from beneath the city walls. It was coated with a rich layer of green verdigris.

'What are the restrictions placed on the marriage of a king under the statutes of Chephren?' he enquired casually.

Taita picked his nose thoughtfully and examined what he had retrieved on the end of his forefinger. 'Like any other bride his wife should be free to marry, either a virgin or a widow,' he said.

'Or divorced by her husband.'

'Or divorced by her husband, or by the decree of the reigning Pharaoh.' Taita nodded. 'And before he is deified or married the king should be ordained in his sovereignty.'

'To be ordained, Pharaoh must have reached his majority, which I have not, or taken his godbird, which I have attempted but failed, or he must have become an adept of the Red Road.' Nefer paused then went on, 'Which I have not. Yet.' He emphasized the last word and Taita blinked, but did not reply.

Nefer set down the idol and looked at Taita with determination. 'I intend to run the Red Road.'

Taita studied him in silence. 'You are not yet at your full growth and strength.'

'I am grown enough and strong enough.'

'Who will ride with you?'

'Meren,' said Taita firmly.

'There are others stronger and more experienced who might be of greater help to you. There will be many who would dearly love to gather the hair braid of a pharaoh of the Tamosian line.'

'I have promised Meren,' said Nefer firmly.

Two puppies, tripping over their own paws in their enthusiasm and ignorance, Taita thought, but instead he said, 'There are no unbroken horses in Gallala – at least none that would answer the purpose.'

'I know where to find them. Naja and Trok have left all the remaining herds of Egypt unguarded.' Taita did not bother to point out the fallacy of that assertion. The false pharaohs had left more veteran troops to guard Egypt than ever they had taken with them on the adventure to Mesopotamia, but he knew that Nefer was not inclined to listen to any argument that ran contrary to his fixed intention.

'If you fail in the attempt you will lose much more than your hair. You will lose so much prestige that your claim to the throne might fail also.'

'I shall not fail,' Nefer said quietly. Taita had anticipated that exact reply.

'When do you intend to attempt the Red Road?' he asked.

'First I must have my horses.'

As soon as they had dug the fountain and it had become feasible to use Gallala as a permanent base Nefer, advised by Taita, had instituted a cleansing system for the city. The human waste, the manure from the cattle pens and horse lines were gathered up by the dung carts and spread on the fields as fertilizer, while the rest was carried out to dumps at the end of the valley, which soon became the home of a permanent population of crows and kites, vultures and the offal-eating marabou storks, with their obscenely naked heads. The baboons came down from the hills, and hundreds of jackals and pariah dogs picked over the heaps of rubbish.

At Nefer's orders traps were set each evening on the dumps, and the following morning the captured animals were taken away in cages.

In the meantime Shabako and his most trusted men were sent as scouts and spies back to the towns and villages of the Nile valley. They drank in the taverns and questioned the travellers they met on the road. They scouted each fort and garrison, and counted the troops they saw entering, leaving and drilling. When they returned weeks later the intelligence they brought back was detailed and accurate.

They reported that the false pharaohs had left at least half of their infantry, spearmen, slingers and archers, to counter any threat to their rear. All the border forts were fully manned and guarded, and the garrisons seemed alert and vigilant.

'What of the remount divisions?' Nefer asked, when Shabako had come to the end of his long report.

'Trok has taken most of his chariots with him to Mesopotamia. He has left less than two regiments in reserve in Egypt. However, all the army workshops are hard at work building more chariots.'

'Horses?' Nefer demanded.

'They have commandeered every animal in both kingdoms that they could lay their thieving hands on. They have even sent army dealers to Libya to buy what they could find. It seems that the remount depots at Thane and Manashi are at full strength. However, most of these animals appear young and untrained. The battle-hardened animals have been taken with the main army to the east.'

'Thane,' Nefer decided. 'It's much closer to the edge of the desert than Manashi.' He recalled that Thane was where Taita had used his requisition order from Naja to obtain fresh horses and chariots from Socco, Hilto's old comrade-in-arms, while they were on their way to rescue Mintaka from Avaris. He cast his mind back and tried to memorize the layout of the garrison and the surrounding terrain, but it had all been a long time ago.

'Tell me all you can about Thane. Is Socco still in command there?'

'We drank beer in the local brothel with a sergeant of the garrison. He told me that Socco has done such a good job there that Trok has promoted him to the rank of Best of Ten Thousand.'

Ten days later Nefer and Taita sat in the thick green grass and pretended to watch over the herd of goats that grazed around them. Although the land around the garrison of Thane was well irrigated and rich in grazing, it was also flat, treeless and featureless. There were no hills from which they could overlook the camp. The nearest high ground was along the edge of the desert, a league to the east.

The two of them were dressed in the ragged dusty black robes of the Bedouin. In this guise they were able to blend into the landscape as readily as a pair of hares or crows. At intervals they stood and herded the goats a little closer to the garrison, then squatted down again in the characteristic attitude of the Bedouin herdsman.

Not far from where they sat the herds of remounts were also grazing, tended by armed and uniformed herders. 'I would think there are upward of two thousand animals here,' Nefer guessed.

'Perhaps not as many as that.' Taita shook his head. 'Closer to fifteen hundred, but still more than we can handle.'

They watched and waited through the long, lazy afternoon. In the stockades alongside the cavalry lines the handlers were at work breaking the young animals to the chariot harness. Their shouted commands and the crack of the stock whips carried faintly to where Nefer and Taita sat. In the late afternoon the herds of horses were driven in from the fields and stockades to the long horse lines beyond the fort. From a distance they watched them tethered and bedded down for the night.

As the sun was setting Nefer and Taita rounded up their goats and drove them slowly back towards the desert. In the dusk a small detachment of four chariots came bowling down the road from Avaris. At the reins of the leading vehicle stood a burly officer wearing the silver pectoral plate of the Best of Ten Thousand. As he came closer they both recognized him.

'The curse of Seth on it,' Nefer murmured. ''Tis Socco, Hilto's old comrade-in-arms. Will he recognize us?'

They bowed their heads, slumped their shoulders in a submissive attitude, and shuffled along after the goats. Socco swerved off the road and drove directly at them. 'You stinking scum!' he shouted. 'How often must I warn you to keep your filthy, disease-ridden beasts off my grass and away from my horses?' He leaned out and struck Nefer across the shoulders. The whiplash hummed and cracked against his flesh, and red rage blinded Nefer. Before he could drag Socco out of the chariot, though, Taita made a restraining gesture that riveted him where he stood. It seemed to affect Socco too, for his tone moderated a little as he coiled his whip and said, 'If I catch you people here again, I'll lop off your balls and stick them up your bung-hole.' He steered the chariot back on to the road and trotted off towards the fort.

Six nights later in the dark of the new moon, they returned to Thane in force, every man from Gallala who could ride astride, forty horsemen with black-dyed robes and soot-daubed faces. Each rider carried a large bag slung behind him over his horse's haunches. The contents of the bags squirmed and writhed, emitting muffled yips and whimpers: for each contained two or three live jackals. Their legs were tied, and strips of flax twine were bound around their muzzles to gag them.

The horses' hoofs were muffled with leather boots so they made no sound as Nefer led them in single file in a wide circuit round to the westerly side of the fort, keeping well clear of the cavalry lines so that they did not alarm the sentries.

Every man knew what was expected of him for they had practised this manoeuvre many times, and they kept silently in their formation, a half-moon of dark horsemen between Thane and the river. They were spaced at intervals just close enough together that a quiet command could be passed down the line. Nefer was in the centre, Meren on the left wing and Shabako on the right.

When Nefer was satisfied that they were in position he gave the warbling call of a nightingale, three times repeated, and saw the red line of glowing spots in the darkness as his men opened the lids of the clay firepots they all carried and blew the tinder into flame. He did the same, and then he opened the mouth of one of the bags on his horse's rump and reached in. He brought out a fat vixen by the scruff of the neck. She writhed in his grip.

There was a harsh, tarry smell, strong enough to mask the natural odour of the animals. The fur and brush had been soaked in a black viscous liquid. Taita had gathered this sticky substance from a natural seep that he knew of in the wilderness. It oozed from the earth and Taita said that it came up from great depth. It was highly inflammable, but he had mixed it with another substance, a yellow crystalline powder, that made it even more so. Every one of the captured jackals had been treated with this mixture.

With his dagger Nefer cut the twine that secured the vixen's four paws together. When she sensed freedom, she kicked and thrashed in his grip. He touched the firepot to her furry brush, which burst into spluttering, smoking flame. She redoubled her efforts to escape, but before he released her he slipped the point of the dagger between her lips and cut the loop of twine that muzzled her. She opened her jaws wide and let loose a screech, unearthly and terrifying. Nefer dropped her to the ground and the little creature shot away, spreading a stream of fire and sparks behind her, howling and shrieking in a fashion that set even his nerves on edge and made the hair rise down the back of his neck.

He pulled another jackal out of the bag. All down the line balls of flame flared in the darkness and steamed out across the open fields and those terrible agonized howls made the night hideous. A few of the tormented creatures broke back towards the river valley but the rest headed instinctively for their home in the desert, with the garrison of Thane directly in their path. In a pack they bore down on the cavalry lines.

As Nefer released the last screaming jackal, he drew his sword and kicked his mount into a gallop. He raced after the burning animals, and on either hand his troopers rode with him. They were all yelling like demons, adding their voices to the uproar.

Some of the jackals dragged their flaming tails through the dry horse fodder and bedding, which burst into flame also. The scene was lit by an eerie flickering light that made the dark riders seem monstrous.

Ahead Nefer saw the nearest sentries hurl aside their weapons and flee, screaming as loudly as the burning animals.

'*Djinns!*' they howled.

'Save us! The dark legions of Seth are upon us!'

'The hordes of hell! Run! Run!'

The tethered horses were rearing and plunging. When a stake was pulled up from the earth, or one of the long lines snapped under the strain, twenty horses were freed at once and wheeled away before the line of yelling, shrieking riders that swept into the camp.

Nefer leaned from his horse's back and sabred one of the running guards, striking deeply between his shoulder-blades and letting the slack body slide off the blade. Then he swerved to where a bunch of terrified horses struggled against a line that resisted their combined efforts to break free. With a single slash he cut the rope and whooped to send them to join the panic-stricken horde, then rounded up another bunch of milling disorientated animals and pushed them out of the lines into the open fields. Shabako and his men rode with him, shouting and whipping the horses along, a racing tide of men and animals compressed into a single entity and lit only by the flames of the burning garrison behind them. The last of the jackals had burnt to death and their black, smouldering carcasses were left in the grass as the riders thundered towards the hills.

Shabako appeared out of the night and rode at Nefer's side. 'By the sweat and seed of Seth!' he shouted. 'That was fun!' Then he turned and looked back. 'No sign yet of any pursuit, more is the pity. A good hack and slash now would be the perfect ending to an entertaining evening.'

'I promise you much entertainment later,' Nefer laughed, 'but now, we must head off the herd, before they run their guts out.'

They pushed their mounts hard, moving through the galloping mass until they rode in the first rank, then cut across them flagging them down from the gallop into a trot and then a walk, turning them in the direction of the open desert and Gallala.

Dawn found the long herd of loose horses spread out down a gaunt, rocky defile, moving at an easy but steady pace with Nefer and Shabako pointing them while Meren and his drovers brought up the stragglers from behind.

Nefer squinted into the first rays of the sun, and called to Shabako, 'Keep them headed up and moving. I am going back to see if Socco and his men are after us yet.'

As he rode back, Nefer singled out Meren and three others, all skilled with javelin and sword. He signalled to them and they galloped up to join him. 'If they are after us, we should try to change their minds for them.'

Nefer led them along their back trail, and at a point where the rock defile narrowed they left the three troopers to hold their horses, and he and Meren climbed the steep rock-strewn slope.

By the time they reached the top the sun was clear of the horizon, but had not yet dissipated the cool of the night and the dust and heat-haze had not built up. The land glowed with that peculiar lambency of the desert dawn. Each distant detail of rock and dune, cliff and gnarled tree, was etched with breath-stopping beauty.

'There!' said Nefer. Meren's eyes were sharp, but his were more so.

'Ten riders.' Meren tried to hide his chagrin at not finding them first.

'Eleven,' Nefer corrected him, and he did not argue.

Instead he grinned delightedly. 'Fair odds to our five.'

'We will take them there.' Nefer pointed down into the gorge. 'There, where it narrows. We don't want them to carry back their news to Avaris. There must be no survivors.'

'That suits me above all things.' Meren laughed.

They waited among the boulders, standing by the heads of their horses, hands over their nostrils to prevent them whickering or snorting and springing the trap prematurely. In the middle of the gap, Nefer had placed a leather bag, that had earlier contained captured jackals. It was now stuffed with their cloaks, which were no longer needed in the rising morning warmth.

Their heads went up as, from lower down the gorge, they heard the click of hoof against stone and the rattle of a dislodged pebble. Nefer looked across the open ground to where Meren and one of the other men were hidden on the far side of the defile. He held up his left hand with fingers spread. The signal for silence and vigilance. His father had taught him that hand signals were always preferable to spoken commands, especially in the heat of battle when they might be lost and drowned in the tumult, or in situations when stealth was paramount.

Now he picked out other small sounds, loud in the great silence of the sands: the creak of tackle and the rattle of arrows in quivers. Nefer glanced around the boulder that hid him and two of his troopers. A scrubby growth of bottlebrush broke up the silhouette of his head.

A rider appeared in the mouth of the gorge, and halted his horse as he saw the leather bag lying in the path. He looked around carefully and the rest of his troop crowded up behind him. Even under the crocodile-skin helmet Nefer recognized Socco, and his back itched where the whip had raised a bloody welt.

Time to return a favour, he thought grimly. Socco took his time, an old soldier, wary and suspicious. Then he walked his horse forward and the others followed him. They halted in a tight group, all leaning out and staring down at the bag. Socco grunted an order, 'Steady now! Watch my back,' and swung down from his horse. He stooped over the bag, and Nefer gave the command, a chopping motion with his raised left hand.

The throwing thongs were wrapped around every one of their right wrists and the range was point-blank. They threw as one man, and because Hilto and Shabako had trained them to perfection no two picked the same target. Five javelins buzzed like enraged bees, and struck where no armour could deflect them, three in the throat and two in the back of the neck. Five men toppled from horseback, and fell under the hoofs of their startled steeds.

Nefer and his men burst from ambush at the gallop, swords drawn and screaming their war-cry, 'Horus and Seti!'

The survivors of that first murderous flight of javelins turned instinctively to meet them but did not have time to clear their swords from the scabbards before they crashed into them, their horses trained to charge in chest to chest. Two more of Socco's horses were taken off-balance and dashed off their feet, throwing their riders. Nefer picked the nearest man, who was still mounted, and killed him with a thrust to the throat. Now Socco cleared his sword and thrust up at Nefer's belly. Nefer turned the blow and his horse reared and lashed at Socco with both hoofs, one of which struck him a solid blow. He was thrown sprawling into the sand. Before Nefer could finish him another of the enemy rode at him, sword lifted high. Nefer rode in under the stroke and engaged him, cut and parry, as they milled and shouted, struggling at close quarters.

Socco's men had only just rallied from the first shock when Meren chose his moment perfectly and led the trooper with him in a furious charge into the mêlée. He sent a thrust to the heart and yelled in triumph. Then immediately he reversed his blade and killed again, a cut across the neck. His victim slid down on to the earth with his head half severed from the trembling jerking trunk.

Socco had lost his helmet and his sword and crawled desperately on his knees to try to retrieve the weapon. He was the only one of all his men still able to resist. Nefer leaned out from his horse's back and aimed at the opening where his breastplate of crocodile-skin armour was fastened between his shoulder-blades, but at the last moment could not bring himself to drive home. He changed his blow smoothly, rolling his wrist to present the flat of the sickle-shaped blade and cracked Socco across the back of his grizzled pate. The man dropped face down in the sand.

Nefer glanced round to make certain that Meren had everything in hand. Then slid off his horse to the ground just as Socco groaned, shook his head and tried to sit up. Nefer slammed his heel into his adversary's chest and thrust him back, then placed the point of his sword at his throat. 'Yield, Socco, or I will send the news of your passing to your mother and all the one hundred stinking goatherds who had a hand in fathering you.'

Socco's dazed expression cleared and became a defiant glare. 'Let me reach my sword, puppy, and I will teach you how to lift your leg when you piss.' He was about to add more to the insult, when suddenly the bellicose light in his eyes faded. He stammered wordlessly. He was gawking at the cartouche on Nefer's thigh.

'Majesty,' he gasped. 'Forgive me! Strike! Take my worthless life as forfeit for those gross and stupid words of mine. I heard the rumours that you still lived, but I had wept at your funeral and could not believe in such a miracle.'

Nefer smiled with relief. He had not wanted to kill him – he was an attractive old rogue, and Hilto said that he was one of the finest horse-handlers in all the armies of Egypt. Hilto should know. 'Will you swear the loyal oath to me as Pharaoh?' he demanded sternly.

'Gladly, for all the earth fears you in your name of Nefer Seti, beloved of all the gods, and light of this very Egypt. My heart beats only for you and my soul will sing my duty to you until the hour of my death.'

'Then, Socco, I promote you to Master of a Thousand Chariots, and Taita had best guard his title of Poet Laureate, for you turn a pretty phrase.'

'Let me kiss your foot, Pharaoh,' Socco pleaded.

'Give me your hand, rather,' Nefer said, seized his horny fist and pulled him to his feet. ''Tis a pity about your men.' Nefer glanced at the corpses. 'If they had shared your loyal sentiments, they need not have died.'

'They died at the hand of a god,' Socco pointed out. 'There is no greater honour. Besides, Taita the Warlock may be able to save the few who are still groaning and twitching.'

Three days later, when they rode into Gallala, they were droving nigh on four hundred horses, and Socco rode proudly at the right hand of his new pharaoh with his helmet sitting high on the bandages that were wound around his injured head.

Socco was not only quartermaster general of the armies of the false pharaohs with the rank of Best of Ten Thousand, but he was also an adept of the Red Road. He was able to give Nefer the exact tally of all the enemy fighting chariots and transport wagons, and where they were deployed. From memory he drew up a list of the numbers of horses and bullocks in depots of the delta, and the latest inventory of weapons stored in the armouries.

'Trok and Naja have taken almost the last serviceable fighting chariot with them on the expedition to the east. There are less than fifty left in Egypt, in either the Upper or Lower Kingdom. The military workshops at Avaris,

Thebes and Aswan are working day and night, but every chariot they turn out is sent immediately along the road to Beersheba and Mesopotamia.'

'Horses we now have, thanks to Pharaoh's bold stroke at Thane, even though most are young and unbroken, but we cannot fight a campaign without chariots,' said Hilto gloomily. 'We cannot seize what does not exist, and all the gold now in the royal treasury cannot buy a single squadron.'

While they had been away from Gallala on the great horse raid, Hilto had brought in the remaining gold from the caches along the eastern highway. There was over three lakhs of the precious metal in the ancient cisterns under the city of Gallala. He went on, 'Soon Trok must hear of our successes. He will realize that we have become a real threat. As soon as he has captured Babylon, he will divert part of his army to attack us here. If he sent only a hundred chariots, we could not stand against them in our present state.'

When all the others had had their say, Nefer stood to address the council. He did not speak long. 'Socco, you train the horses for me,' he said. 'Taita and I will find the chariots.'

'That, Majesty, will take a minor miracle,' said Socco gloomily.

'Be not so parsimonious, Master of a Thousand Chariots.' Nefer smiled at him. 'How can we make good your title with only a minor miracle? Let us put our faith in a major one.'

Taita stood on the black rock outcrop. Around him the sand dunes stretched away to the limit of the eye. From the base of the rock a hundred men watched him, puzzled but intrigued. The fame of the Magus was as boundless as the desert in which they found themselves. All of them were warriors who had come to Gallala of their own accord, forsaking the false pharaohs to offer their allegiance to Nefer Seti. That allegiance was wearing a little thin, for here they found themselves without weapons or chariots, and daily there were fresh rumours that either Trok or Naja or both were on the march to seek vengeance for their desertion.

Pharaoh Nefer Seti stood beside the Warlock on the pinnacle of rock. They were in deep discussion. Occasionally one or the other would gesticulate or point out towards the west, where there was nothing to see but sand, sand and more sand.

They waited patiently through the heat of the day. Not one expressed disenchantment or disbelief for they were all in awe of Taita. As the shadows in the hollows of the dunes deepened to purple, that ill-assorted pair, young monarch and ancient Magus, came down from the pinnacle and walked out into the dunes. Without any apparent purpose the Warlock wandered back and forth along one of the dune faces. He stopped at intervals and made strange, esoteric gestures with his long staff, then went on again with Pharaoh and his officers following him.

At last in the gathering dusk the Magus planted his staff in the soft sand and spoke quietly to Pharaoh Nefer Seti. Now, suddenly, they were all galvanized by the shouted orders of the officers.

Twenty men ran forward carrying the digging tools with which they had been issued. Under the direction of Hilto and Meren, and under the daunting eyes of their king and the Magus, they began to dig. When the hole was shoulder deep the loose sand ran back into it almost as fast as they shovelled it out, and they were forced to redouble their efforts to make any gains. The heads of the diggers sank slowly below the level of the surrounding earth, until abruptly there came an excited shout from the bottom of the excavation. Nefer strode forward and stood on the lip.

'There is something here, divine Majesty.' A man was kneeling in the bottom of the hole, and he looked up with sweat mixed with the grit that coated his face and body.

'Let me see.' Nefer jumped down and pushed the man out of the way. A patch of hide was exposed, still covered with hair but hard as cedarwood.

Nefer looked up at Taita. 'It is the body of a horse!' he called.

'What colour?' Taita asked. 'Is it black?'

'How did you know that?' Nefer was not really surprised.

'Does the halter carry the golden cartouche of Pharaoh Trok Uruk?' Taita answered his question with another.

'Dig it open!' Nefer ordered the sweating men around him. 'But gently now. Do no damage.'

They worked with great care, using their bare hands to sweep away the sand. Gradually they exposed the complete head of a black horse that wore on its forehead the cartouche of Trok, embossed on a gold disc, just as Taita had foreseen.

Then they went on to uncover the rest of the carcass. The animal had been wonderfully preserved by the hot dry sand. The embalmers in Thebes would have difficulty in matching what the desert had achieved. Beside it lay its harness mate, another stallion. Nefer recalled how he had last seen these magnificent animals as they drew Trok's chariot forward under the louring dustclouds of the *khamsin*.

By this time night had fallen and the workmen lit the oil lamps and placed them on the lip of the excavation.

They went on with the work through the night. The dead horses were unbuckled from the traces and lifted out. Their desiccated carcasses were so light that four men could carry them with ease.

Then they recovered the harness. It was in a perfect state of preservation, and Nefer set his grooms to work immediately, oiling the leather and polishing the gold and bronze parts.

Now they worked back to the chariot itself and a gasp went up from the diggers as the dashboard was cleared of the engulfing sand: it was covered with gold leaf, and gleamed in the lamplight, shooting out darts of light that pricked their eyes. The javelins and lances were still in their bins on either side of the cockpit, ready to the hand of the charioteer. Each weapon was a work of art in itself, the lance handles laminated for strength and the metal heads sharp as the scalpels of a surgeon. The arrows had been made by Grippa of Avaris, the shafts straight and true, the fletchings dyed crimson, yellow and green, the royal cartouche carved into the shaft.

Trok's great war bow was still in its rack, and only the bowstring needed to be replaced. Nefer flexed the shaft in his hands and wondered if he had the strength to wield it in battle.

When the entire chariot had been uncovered they passed ropes under the chassis and lifted it out of the excavation. The gold leaf had been beaten so thin that it added no more than two taels to the total weight of the vehicle, and to compensate for this the chassis had been carved from dark hard woods, hewn in the sinister rain-forests far to the south of Egypt's borders. These timbers were more resilient than the finest bronze, but light and tough. They could be fined down to save weight without sacrificing strength.

Now it was morning, and the sun was climbing above the horizon. Nefer and Taita circled the chariot as it gleamed in the light. It was so sleek and graceful that it seemed already in motion. Its single shaft seemed to pine like a lover for the touch of two proud horses. Nefer stroked the gold work. It was smooth as a lovely woman's skin and warm beneath his hand.

'It seems to be a living creature,' he breathed. 'Surely there was never a more magnificent weapon of war ever conceived.'

'Fifty years ago I built a chariot for Lord Tanus.' Taita sniffed and shook his head. 'You should have seen that one. But it rests with him in his tomb in far-off Ethiopia.'

Nefer hid a smile – the old man would never admit second best. 'Then I shall have to be content with this inferior work cart,' he said seriously. 'I need only the blue sword that Naja stole from my father to complete my armoury.'

Over the weeks and months that followed Taita pinpointed the other buried vehicles and their accoutrements. Teams of workmen dug them out and sent them to the chariot-makers who had set up a workshop in the lee of the rock pinnacle, roofed over with palm thatch. Here, fifty of them and nearly a hundred armourers laboured through the daylight hours, never letting up even in the furious heat of noon. The armourers polished and sharpened swords, javelins and lances. They rebound the shafts and reset the heads. Over slow fires they straightened the arrows that had warped. The chariot-makers stripped each vehicle as it came out from under the sand, checked each component, painted and lacquered the chassis and the panels, and balanced and lubricated the wheels to run true and sweetly. Then they reassembled them and sent them on to Gallala, loaded with the restored weapons, to equip the army that Hilto, Shabako and Socco were training.

Many of the vehicles were so deeply buried under the burning yellow dunes that they were lost for ever, or until the next great storm uncovered them, but in the end they salvaged a hundred and five. Enough to equip five squadrons.

When Nefer drove through the gates of Gallala in the royal chariot, Meren was on the footplate by his side.

Mintaka and Merykara stood together on the roof pediment of the temple of Hathor, and strewed oleander petals upon them as they passed below.

'He is so handsome.' Merykara's voice was husky with awe. 'So tall and handsome.'

'So tall and handsome and strong,' Mintaka agreed. 'He will be the greatest pharaoh in the history of this very Egypt.'

'I did not mean Nefer,' said Merykara.

By this time a thriving smuggling route existed between the city and Egypt, and other caravans came in regularly from the port of Safaga on the eastern sea. Since the capture of the treasure of Trok and Naja, Gallala had become a city rich with gold. Like hyenas the merchants sniffed the aroma of the yellow metal from afar and brought in their wares from the ends of the world. Nowadays there was no luxury or necessity that could not be obtained in the city's souks, so Mintaka was able to procure a wagonload of the finest red wine from the vineyards of the temple of Osiris at Busiris for the welcome banquet she had arranged for the evening that the charioteers returned.

At her orders, the butchers spitted and roasted ten whole oxen, and chickens and geese by the hundred. Fast relays of the new chariots brought up fresh fish, and baskets of lobsters in seaweed from the coast. Most of the long-whiskered crustaceans were still alive when they were dropped squeaking into the boiling pots. Hunters scoured the surrounding desert and came in with gazelle, oryx, and the flesh and eggs of the ostrich.

The banquet was a joyous celebration of their achievements and small victories over the false pharaohs. The wine had flowed to great effect when Nefer rose to welcome the guests and announce the recovery of the five squadrons of chariots from under the sands. 'With the horses that we freed from the tyranny of Trok . . .' there were hoots and guffaws at this '. . . and the weapons and chariots we now have, we are well able to defend ourselves against Trok and Naja. As you are aware, every day that passes sees fresh recruits to the blue banner. Soon it will not be merely a case of defending ourselves, but of taking back what was stolen from us and avenging the terrible deeds that those two monsters have perpetrated. They have the blood of true and noble kings upon their hands. They are the murderers of King Apepi, who was the father of the noble lady at my side, and they slew my own father, Pharaoh Tamose.'

The guests were silent and puzzled now, looking at each other for guidance. Then Hilto rose to his feet. Nefer had primed him, and placed the question on his lips. 'Divine Majesty, forgive my ignorance for I am just a simple man, but I do not understand. All the world knows that King Apepi died in an accident when his barge caught fire while anchored at Balasfura. Now you lay the guilt for his death on the pretenders. How can that be?'

'There is one among us who was a witness to the true events of that tragic night.' Nefer reached down and drew Mintaka to her feet. The company cheered her, for they had all come to love her for her beauty and her gracious spirit. When Nefer held up his hand they fell silent and listened to her with all their attention as she related the story of the murder of her father and brothers. She used simple words and spoke to them as friends and comrades, yet she was able to share with them her own horror and grief. When she had finished they were growling like a cage of hungry lions at feeding time.

Now Shabako rose and asked his prepared question: 'But, divine Pharaoh, you spoke also of the death of your own father, King Tamose of blessed memory. How was he murdered – and by whom?'

'For the answer to this question I must call upon the Magus, Lord Taita, from whom no secret, however devious and grisly, can be hidden.'

Taita faced them and spoke in a whisper that riveted their attention. His every word carried to the ears of even those on the outskirts of the gathering, and the softness of those words contrasted so effectively with the gruesome circumstances they described that men shuddered and women wept.

At the end Taita held up the broken arrow with its crimson, green and yellow feathers. 'This is the instrument of Pharaoh Tamose's death. The arrow that bears the signet of Trok, but which was loosed by Naja, the man whom Pharaoh loved and trusted as a brother.'

They howled their outrage and their craving for justice to the starlit skies above Gallala. Taita hurled the arrow on to the nearest fire over which one of the oxen was roasting. It would not have borne closer inspection, for it was not the arrow that had killed Pharaoh but one of those he had taken from the buried chariot. He sat down and closed his eyes, as if composing himself to sleep.

Nefer let the guests give full vent to their feelings and when they began to quieten a little he signalled for more wine flagons to be carried out.

There was one last proclamation he had to make, and he waited until the mood had mellowed further before he stood up again. All fell silent and watched him in anticipation heightened by the good wine from Busiris. The night had already held so many marvels and they wondered what was yet to come.

'Before a king leads his armies against the enemies of this sacred land of our forefathers, he should be a king indeed, a true and veritable king. I purpose to lead you against the usurpers, but I am not yet ordained as Pharaoh. I can achieve this confirmation if I wait until the year of my majority, but that is still far off, and I do not choose to wait that long. Nor will my enemies allow me that grace.' He paused and they watched him, fascinated – so young yet so tall and straight, as his father had been before him. Now he raised his right hand in the gesture of oath-taking.

'In the sight of my people and my gods, I will run the Red Road to prove to you that I am your king.'

Some sighed and shook their heads, others started to their feet and cried out, 'No! Pharaoh, we will not see you killed,' while others called, '*Bak-her!* If he fails then he fails as a brave man.'

That night Mintaka wept as she asked him, 'Why did you not tell me first?'

'Because you would have tried to stop me.'

'But why must you do it?'

'Because my gods and my duty require it.'

'Even if it kills you.'

'Even if it kills me.'

She stared long into his green eyes and saw how steadfast was his resolve. Then she kissed him and said, 'I am proud that I am to be wife to such a man as you.'

The astrologers among the priests of Horus, assisted by the Magus, consulted the calendars and set the date for the trial of the Red Road to be held on the day of the new moon of the god. Therefore, as Taita had remarked, Nefer had little time to prepare for the ordeal. He withdrew from all his other duties, leaving even the conduct of affairs of state to Taita and the council while he gave all his attention to the first task required of him. Before a novice could present himself for trial he must break and train his own team of horses to carry him on the Red Road.

Nefer had to pick out a team of horses from the herd they had captured at Thane, then train them to the shaft of the chariot. He would have liked to ask Socco to help him with the selection of his team: not only was he a famous horseman but he knew each of the captured animals. However, Socco was one of only five Red Road warriors in Gallala and was one of those who would examine Nefer. He could not assist him in his preparations for the ordeal.

There was another to whom Nefer could appeal: Taita's knowledge, understanding and experience of horsemanship and chariot tactics exceeded even Socco's. Yet Taita was not a Red Road warrior. His physical imperfections precluded him from the brotherhood, and added to that he had religious scruples. He would never forswear Horus and the other gods of the pantheon to pledge himself to the mysterious Red God of war, a god whose name was known only to his adepts.

The two spent the first day on the hillside above the green fields where the unbroken horses grazed. They sat together and watched the animals below them, discussing those that caught the eye. Nefer pointed out a handsome white colt, but Taita shook his head. 'A grey looks good in the traces, but I have always been wary of them. I have found they lack stamina and heart. Let us look for either black or bay, matched in colour.'

Nefer picked out a filly with a white blaze on her forehead, but again Taita shook his head. 'The Bedouin say that a white mark is the touch of a devil or a *djinn*. I want not a trace of white on the animals we choose.'

'Do you believe what they say?'

Taita shrugged. 'A blaze or a sock mars their symmetry.

You and your team should have the look of a pharaoh when you ride out.'

Taita and Nefer stayed on the hillside until nightfall, and went out again the next morning, as soon as it was light enough to see the path, with Meren and three grooms. They began to sort the horses, driving any imperfect animal into the adjacent field. By noon they had whittled down the herd to twenty-three animals, all clean-limbed and strong, no scars, no blemish, no obvious impediment in their gait. There was not a single white hair on any of them.

They let them settle down, and when the horses were grazing quietly they sat in the grass and watched them.

'I like that black colt,' Nefer said.

'He is lame. Almost certainly he has a cracked left front hoof.'

'He does not limp,' Nefer protested.

'Watch his left ear. He flicks it at every pace. Tell Meren to drive him out.'

A little later Nefer marked a black filly. 'She has a fine head and a bright eye.'

'She is too highly strung. The eye is more nervous than intelligent. She will wilt in the din of battle. Meren can let her go.'

'What of the black colt with the long tail and mane?'

'The tail disguises the fact that he is half a thumb's length short in the back.'

By late afternoon there were only six horses left in the field. In a pact of silence, they had avoided speaking of one particular colt. He was too obviously the choice they must make. He was a marvellous beast, not too tall or heavy, well proportioned, with strong legs and back. His neck was long and his head noble. They watched him a while longer.

At last Magus spoke. 'I can find no vice in him. There is a spark in his eyes that comes from the fire in his heart.'

'I will call him Krus,' Nefer decided. 'It is the Bedouin name for fire.'

'Yes, the name is important. I never knew a good horse with an ugly name. It's as if the gods are listening. Let Krus be your right-hander, but now you need a left-hander.'

'Another colt—' Nefer started, but Taita stopped him.

'No, we need a filly on the left. A feminine influence to keep Krus in check, and steady him in the heat of the fight. A great heart to pull with him when the road is hard.'

'You have chosen already, have you not?' Nefer asked.

'And so have you.' Taita nodded. 'We both know who she must be.'

Their eyes went back to the filly grazing placidly beside the main irrigation channel, a little separated from Krus and the rest of the herd. Almost as though she knew they were speaking about her, she raised her head and stared back at them, with large shining eyes behind thick lashes.

'She is beautiful,' Nefer murmured. 'I would love to take her without having to put a rope on her.' Taita was silent, and after another minute Nefer said impulsively, 'I am going to try.' He stood up and called to Meren. 'Take the others out of the field. Leave only the bay filly.'

When Nefer and the filly had the field to themselves, he left the fence, and moved casually in her direction, not going straight at her but strolling obliquely across her front. As soon as she showed the first sign of agitation he squatted down in the green grass and waited. She began feeding again but all the while she was watching him from the corner of her eye. Nefer began to sing the monkey song softly, and she raised her head and looked at him again. He took out a *dhurra* cake from the pouch on his belt, and without standing up offered it to her. She flared her nostrils and snuffled loudly.

'Come, my darling.'

She took an uncertain step towards him, then stopped and threw up her head.

'Sweetheart,' he crooned, 'my lovely darling.'

A step at a time she came in, then extended her neck to full stretch and sniffed noisily at the cake. Terrified by her own audacity she jerked back and galloped away, making a wide circuit of the field.

'She moves like the wind,' Meren called.

'Dov.' Nefer used the Bedouin word for the north wind, the soft cool wind of the winter season. 'Dov, that is her name.'

Having shown him her feminine capriciousness, Dov circled back flirtatiously and came to him from the other side. This time she accepted his offering readily and drooled saliva as she crunched it up. She ran her velvet muzzle over his open palm searching for crumbs, and when she found none she reached for his pouch and bumped it so demandingly that she knocked Nefer over backwards. He scrambled up and fished out another cake.

While she ate it he touched her neck with the other hand. As though flies were crawling over her, she made her dark mahogany-coloured hide dance, but did not pull away. There was a tick in her ear-hole, and Nefer plucked it off then crushed it between his fingernails and offered the bloody fragment for her to smell. She shuddered with disgust and rolled her eyes at the offensive odour, but allowed him to examine and fondle the other ear. When he left the field she followed him like a dog to the fence. Then she hung her head over the rail, and whickered after him.

'I am consumed with jealousy.' Mintaka had watched the encounter from the temple roof. 'Already she loves you almost as much as I do.'

The next morning Nefer came down to the field alone. Taita and Meren were watching from the roof of the temple. This was something between Nefer and Dov. No others should interfere.

Nefer whistled as he came down to the fence and Dov

threw up her head and galloped across the field to meet him. As soon as she reached him she pushed her muzzle into his pouch.

'You are a typical woman,' Nefer scolded her. 'You are interested only in the gifts I bring you.'

While she ate the cake he fondled and caressed her, until he could slip one arm around her neck. Then he walked her along the fence and back again, and she leaned her shoulder against him. He fed her one more cake and as she savoured it he moved back along her left flank, stroking her and telling her how beautiful she was. Then in one smooth movement he swung up and straddled her back. She started under him and he braced himself for her first wild plunge, but she stood trembling with her legs slightly splayed. Then she turned her head and stared at him in such comical astonishment that he could not help laughing. 'It's all right, my sweetling. This is what you were born to.'

She stamped her forefoot and snorted.

'Come now,' he said. 'Are you not going to try to throw me off? Let us get this question settled at once.' She reached back and sniffed his toe, as if she could not bring herself to believe the extraordinary solecism he had committed against her dignity. She shuddered and stamped her hoof again, but she stood firm.

'Come then!' he said. 'Let's try a canter.' He touched her flanks with his heels and she jumped with surprise, then walked forward. They went down the fence sedately, and he touched her again. She broke into a trot, then a gentle canter. Meren was whooping and shouting from the temple roof, and the men and women working in the fields straightened up and watched with interest.

'Now let's see you really move.' Nefer slapped her lightly on the neck and urged her forward with a thrust of his hips. She stretched out and floated away, her dainty hoofs seeming barely to touch the earth, like the gentle wind for which she had been named. She ran so that the wind stung his eyes and the tears streamed over his temples and wet the dense tresses of his hair.

Round and round the paddock they sped, while on the roof of the temple Mintaka clapped her hands and cried out with amazement.

Beside her, Taita smiled distantly. 'A royal pair,' he said. 'They will be hard to catch on the Red Road.'

The entire city had heard of the instant love affair between Pharaoh and his filly. Now the word spread rapidly through Gallala that Nefer was going to put the rope on Krus. Horsemen all, they knew that the colt would be a different proposition from the filly. They were in a ferment of excitement at the prospect of Nefer's first attempt to break him in. Nobody went out into the fields that morning and all work in the vehicle shops and on the buildings was suspended. Even the training regiments were given a day's holiday to watch the attempt. Thus, there was fierce competition for the best positions on the city walls and rooftops that overlooked the field below the fountain of Horus.

Nefer and Meren went out through the gates to ironical cheers and ribald advice shouted down from the walls by the wags among the crowd. Krus was in the centre of the herd. He stood out among the other animals, taller by a hand and his head was distinguished. All the horses had sensed the mood of the watchers, and were skittish and nervous as the two men paused at the gate and hung the coils of flax ropes over the fence.

'I will try him first with a cake,' Nefer said, and Meren laughed.

'Look in his eye. I think he would eat you before the cake.'

'Nevertheless, I will try. Wait here.'

Nefer went through the gate, and moved in slowly as he had with Dov. Krus disliked this attention. He arched that long neck and rolled his eyes. Nefer stopped and let him settle down to graze again. He took a *dhurra* cake from his pouch and held it out, but when he moved forward Krus tossed his head, kicked his heels to the sky and galloped furiously away down the fence line. Nefer chuckled ruefully. 'So much for my gifts. He will not make it easy.'

'Look at him run,' Meren called. 'Sweet Horus, if Dov is the north wind then this one is the *khamsin*.'

Krus was running with the other horses now, leading them. Nefer and Meren went into the field together and between them worked the herd gently down to the corner of the fence of heavy poles. There they milled around nervously in the dust as the men came up. Then they broke the wrong way, galloping back to the top end of the field before Nefer could cut them off. Twice more Krus led them out of the trap, but then Nefer sent Meren to cut him off on the far side of the field and Krus made his first mistake. He came thundering back towards Nefer.

Nefer shook out the loop on the end of the long flax rope he carried coiled over his shoulder, and waited for the colt to come through the narrow gap between him and the wooden slats of the fence. Nefer judged his moment and put the loop into flight, a spinning circle over his head, then as Krus galloped through with his neck stretched out, Nefer shot out the loop, which dropped neatly over his head and slipped back to the front of his shoulder. The coils of rope were whipped off Nefer's shoulder, one after the other, as Krus bore away. Nefer braced himself with legs spread wide, leaning back with the end of the rope wrapped half a dozen times around his wrist.

The rope came up hard with the running colt at the other end, and Nefer was yanked off his feet, and hauled face down on to his belly. The colt felt the grab of the rope and the weight, panicked and bolted. Nefer was dragged after him like a sledge, bouncing and rolling at the rope's end.

The crowds on the rooftops and the walls exploded into hysterical mirth and cheers. Mintaka stuffed her fingers into her mouth to stop herself screaming and Merykara covered her eyes and turned away. 'I cannot watch!' she cried.

The colt reached the fence at the end of the field and swung parallel to it. For a moment there was slack in the rope and Nefer used it to roll on to his feet. His belly and legs were grazed and covered with green grass stains, but the rope was tight around his wrist. It came up hard again and he was jerked forward brutally, but he kept on his feet. Using the impetus he went after Krus with long strides, dragged along on the rope's end.

After one circuit of the field Krus slowed to the heavy drag, and Nefer consolidated his gain by digging in the heels of his bronze-cleated sandals. Then as they slowed he swung himself out on the rope's end, catching the colt by surprise. The animal stumbled at the changed direction of the pull, and as soon as he steadied Nefer swung himself the other way. Twice more Nefer was pulled down, but each time he fought his way to his feet again and put pressure on the colt.

In the meantime Meren had opened the gate and driven the rest of the herd into the adjacent field, then he closed it so that man and horse had the empty field in which to fight it out.

Nefer dug in for a foothold and swung the colt's head towards the fence, forcing him to back up on the rope or crash into the heavy poles. He gathered up the slack in the rope then raced forward. Before Krus could recover he had taken three turns of rope around the heavy corner post of the fence and pinned him. Krus reared and plunged, shaking his head and rolling his eyes until the whites showed.

'I have you now,' Nefer gasped, and worked himself hand over hand down the rope towards him. Krus rose on his hind legs and struck out at the rope, whinnying shrilly. 'Gently, gently. Will you kill us both?'

Krus reared again and lifted Nefer off his feet. He came down foursquare and they confronted each other, the colt trembling wildly and sweating down his back and shoulders. Nefer was in no better case, the front of his body covered with scratches and grass burns, from which blood and pale lymph oozed. He, too, was running with sweat, and his face was contorted with the effort of holding down the colt.

They both rested for a space, then Nefer started creeping hand over hand down the rope towards Krus again. He reached the horse's head and flung one arm around his neck. Krus reared again and lifted Nefer high, but he kept his grip. Again and again Krus tried to break away, but Nefer hung on.

At last the colt stood trembling, and before he could recover Nefer had thrown a loop of the rope around his back leg and pulled it tight. When Krus tried to bolt again his nose was almost touching his right flank and he could only turn in a tight circle. Nefer secured the knots in the rope, so that they would not slip and strangle Krus, then staggered back.

He was so exhausted that he could barely keep his feet. Krus tried to run, but managed only to follow his nose in another tight circle. Round and round he went in a right-hand turn, slower and slower, until at last he stood confused and helpless, nose pointing at his rump.

Nefer left him and dragged his battered body to the gate.

The next morning the rooftops and walls were crowded once more with men and women, as Nefer made his way out of the gates and down to the field. He was trying not to limp. Despite the salves and unguents that Taita had mixed and that Mintaka had applied, his injuries had stiffened overnight. Krus was still standing in the same attitude in which Nefer had left him the previous evening, nose to tail.

Nefer began to sing softly as he came through the gate into the field. Krus did not move but laid his ears flat on his neck and bared his teeth in a vicious grin.

Nefer moved around him slowly, singing and whispering to him, and Krus fidgeted and tried to move away, but he was locked in that monotonous circle. Nefer seized the head rope and gently adjusted his knots so that they could be released and dropped with a single movement.

Then he moved quietly down Krus' left flank where he was hidden from the colt. He stroked his back and kept talking as he gathered himself. Then, in one easy movement, he swung up and straddled Krus' back. The colt's entire body convulsed then froze with terror and outrage. He tried to run but his head was held down. He made another uneasy circle. He tried to buck but the rope jerked up hard around his neck. He stood again, but with his ears laid back.

Nefer jerked the tag end of the slip-knot, first the one that secured his back leg and then the loop around his neck. The rope dropped away, and Krus lifted his head and arched his neck. For another moment nothing happened. Then he realized that he was free. Like a gull launching into flight, Krus seemed to rise straight up into the air on four stiff legs with his nose touching his front hoofs. He came down and jumped again spinning on his tail, switching from side to side. Nefer stuck to his back like a growth. Krus started to buck, kicking viciously at the sky with both back legs together. In a series of these wild running lunges he crossed from one side of the field to the other.

Then he rose high on his back legs and flung himself over, crashing down on his own spine with a thud that carried clearly to the watchers on the walls, attempting to crush his rider between himself and the earth.

Mintaka screamed, expecting to hear the crackle of breaking bone, but Nefer had jumped clear, landing like a cat, and crouched beside the colt as Krus lay on his back and thrashed his legs in the air.

'Only a clever and warlike horse will try like that to kill a man,' Taita remarked, without emotion.

Frustrated, Krus raised himself on his front legs, but before he could scramble back on to all four feet Nefer had vaulted firmly on to his back. The colt stood under him, trembling and shaking his head, then burst into a furious gallop. He tore across the field stretched in full stride, and aimed straight at the fence. Nefer lay stretched out on his neck and shouted at him, 'Yes! As fast as you like!'

Krus went at the high fence without a check, and Nefer shifted his weight to help him over. They rose together on a great wave of power, and sailed clear over the top bar, landing cleanly in balance.

Nefer laughed with exhilaration, and urged him forward with a thrust of his hips. 'Come on! Let's see your best speed.'

Krus went up the lower slopes of the bleak bare hills like a wild oryx, and disappeared over the skyline, headed out into the desert. The cheering and hubbub on the city walls died away, and a profound silence fell.

'We must send someone after them,' Mintaka cried in the silence. 'Nefer may be thrown. He could be lying out there in the wilderness with his back broken.'

Taita shook his head. 'It is between the two of them now. Nobody should intervene.'

They waited on the walls and rooftops while the sun made its noon then began to sink towards the horizon, but nobody left their position – they would not chance missing the climax of this trial of strength and nerve between man and beast.

'They have killed each other,' Mintaka fretted. 'That horse is a monster. If it has hurt Nefer I will have it destroyed,' she vowed furiously.

Another hour passed, slowly as dripping honey, and then a stir ran along the top of the wall. Men jumped to their feet and stared up at the crest of the hills, and a murmur rose slowly to an excited chorus of shouts and laughter.

On the skyline appeared a sorry pair. The colt's head was hanging, and his coat was dark with sweat, limed with the salt that had dried upon him. His utter exhaustion was evident in every halting pace he took. On his back Nefer drooped wearily, and as Krus picked his way down the slope they could see how Pharaoh's body had been bruised and battered.

Krus reached the foot of the hills. He was too far gone to jump the fence again, but he came submissively down the dusty road towards the city gates.

Mintaka shouted, '*Bak-her*! Well done, Your Majesty!' and immediately the cry was taken up and flung from man to man until it echoed from the hills above the fountain of Osiris.

'*Bak-her! Bak-her!*'

Nefer straightened on the colt's back and raised one fist high in a triumphant salute. The cheering redoubled.

Below the walls he showed his mastery by putting Krus through a series of turns, first one way then the other. Then he stopped him with a hand on his withers and made him back up. His commands were almost imperceptible, light pressure of his knees or a toe pressed behind Krus' elbow, or subtle shifts of his weight, but the horse responded submissively.

'I feared he had broken the colt's spirit,' Taita told Mintaka, 'but Krus is one of those rare creatures who needs firm treatment rather than kindness. Nefer had to establish his mastery and, Horus is my witness, I have never seen it done so swiftly and completely.'

Nefer rode in through the city gates and waved up at Mintaka, then went down the long avenue to the cavalry lines. He tethered Krus and held the leather bucket for him to drink. Once the colt had slaked his thirst he washed off the dust and dried sweat with hot water, then took him out of the stable to roll in the sand lot. He filled his nosebag with crushed *dhurra* sweetened with honey, and while Krus ate greedily, Nefer rubbed him down, telling him how brave he was, how they would run the Red Road together, and Krus switched his ears back and forth as he listened to him.

As the sun went down Nefer spread the straw bedding thickly on the stable floor. Krus sniffed at it, nibbled a mouthful then lowered himself wearily and stretched out upon his side. Nefer lay down in the straw beside him and pillowed his head on Krus' neck. They fell asleep together, and Mintaka lay alone that night.

The next day Nefer introduced Krus to Dov. The horses circled each other warily, sniffed each other's mouths and circled again. When Krus thrust his nose under Dov's tail she feigned outrage and lashed out at him with both back legs, then raced away flirtatiously with Krus prancing after her. Nefer let them graze together for the rest of the day, and the following morning showed them the chariot. This was not the magnificent royal vehicle, but an older, well-used one. He let them smell the shaft, which had been rubbed and polished smooth by contact with the flanks of many other horses. When they both lost interest in such a mundane object, Meren led Krus away while Nefer took Dov through the next step.

Stroking and caressing her, he placed the harness carefully over her shoulders and fastened the straps. She fidgeted unhappily but allowed him to place these unaccustomed restraints on her. He went up on her back and took her on two circuits of the field. When he brought her back, Meren had the shaft ready. It was not attached to the chariot, although it had the ring bolt at one end. Nefer hitched the harness to it, and Dov rolled her eyes nervously as she felt the weight hanging down her side. She turned her head to examine the shaft, and once she had satisfied her curiosity he took her head and led her forward.

She snorted and crabbed as the shaft followed her, but Nefer gentled and reassured her. After they had circled the field a few times she was no longer skittering sideways. Now came the crucial step. Nefer had borrowed Hilto's placid old mare and placed her in the right-hand traces. She stood there stolidly. He hitched Dov into the left-hand position. The calm nature of the old mare reassured Dov and she stood quietly. Nefer put their nosebags on them and fed them a ration of crushed *dhurra*. When she was relaxed and content, he padded Dov's back legs with strips of linen bandage so that she did not damage herself if she started kicking when she felt the full weight of the chariot behind her.

He need not have worried. He took her head and led her forward and she moved easily beside the old mare. Nefer touched her shoulder and she leaned into the harness and took her share of the weight like a veteran. Nefer broke into a run and Dov trotted at his side. Then he jumped up into the cockpit and gathered up the reins. He put the pair through a series of turns, each one tighter than the last, and though Dov had never felt the reins before she mimicked her right-hand partner faithfully. By the end of that first day she recognized the commands and responded to them instantly, rather than waiting for the old mare to show her the way. For another five days he ran the two mares together and Dov learned fast.

Now it was time to take Krus through the same routine. It was three days before he stopped bolting as soon as he felt the drag of the shaft. Nefer almost gave up on him, but Taita made him persevere. 'Give him your patience now and he will reward you a thousand times over,' he counselled. 'He has intelligence and heart. You will never find another to replace him.'

Eventually Krus resigned himself to the pole that slithered after him and aped his every move so alarmingly. Nefer was at last able to place him in the traces beside Dov. She turned her head and nuzzled his neck, like a mother with a fractious child. Krus calmed down and ate his *dhurra*. When Nefer led them forward he tried to turn sideways and balk but Nefer slapped him sternly across the haunch. He straightened up and fell in line with Dov, but he was shirking. Another slap and he put his shoulder into the traces and took his fair share. The sensation must have pleased him for soon he was hauling with a will. The only difficulty was to make him stop.

Meren threw open the gate of the paddock and jumped up on to the footplate as the chariot rolled past. They took the trade road and swept up the hills in a cloud of their own red dust.

It was the route they took at dawn every day over the months that followed. Each evening when they returned to Gallala the horses were quicker and ran truer, shoulder to shoulder like a single beast with two heads and eight legs. The two young warriors on the footplate were harder and tougher, burned dark by the desert sun.

Mintaka learned how it must feel to be a widow.

There were only five warriors of the Red Road in the fortress city of Gallala: Hilto, Shabako, Socco, Timus and Toran. Many others had tried but had lost their hair braids in the attempt.

Hilto and Shabako were adepts of the third and highest degree of the order, worshippers of the nameless god, the Bull of Heaven, the Sumerian god of war. Only his adepts knew his true name; from all others he was concealed behind the covert name of the Red God. He had no temple or shrine dedicated to him. He came when two or more of his adepts invoked his name upon any field where men had died in battle. Such a place was Gallala, for here Lord Tanus had vanquished the enemies of Egypt and piled their severed heads in the plaza of the city.

Secret catacombs honeycombed the limestone beneath the central square, making it a most suitable temple for the worship of the nameless one.

After midnight, while the rest of the city slept above, Hilto led a prime white bullock down the narrow tunnel that was the entrance to the catacombs, and he sacrificed it upon the stone altar they had built in the dark recesses of the main cistern. In the wavering torchlight the blood spurted and puddled on the paved floor. Then the five warriors of the order dipped their swords in the blood and prayed for the blessing of the secret god on their deliberations and implored him to help them choose wisely. Then they considered the ordeal to be set for Pharaoh Nefer Seti and his companion.

'There must be no concession made to Pharaoh. He must be tested as relentlessly as any other novice,' said Hilto.

'To do otherwise would be to give offence to the mighty and warlike one.' Even in this distinguished company he hesitated to use the god's true name. 'It would degrade the honour of those warriors who have ridden the Red Road before Nefer Seti,' Shabako agreed.

Their conclave lasted most of that night and, wrapped in their woollen cloaks, the two novices waited outside the entrance to the tunnel that led down to the catacombs. They spoke little for they were intensely aware that their very lives would be decided by the five warriors in the dark cave beneath where they sat. The light of the dawning day had not yet washed out the pinprick of the morning star from the eastern horizon when Shabako came to summon them before the conclave.

They followed him along the stone-lined tunnel. The torch he carried shone into the niches in which lay the painted mummy cases of men and women dead five hundred years and more. The air was dry and cool. It smelt of earth and mushrooms, decay and antiquity. Their footsteps echoed eerily, and there were faint whispers in the air, perhaps the voices of the dead or the rustle of bats' wings.

Then they smelt fresh blood, which splashed under their feet as they passed the carcass of the sacrificial bullock. There were torches in the brackets upon the walls of the echoing cavern where the warriors waited for them.

'Who approaches the mysteries?' called the voice of Hilto, but his face was hidden in the folds of his cloak.

'I am Nefer Seti.'

'And I am Meren Cambyses.'

'Do you wish to attempt the Red Road?'

'We do.'

'Are you both natural men, entire in body and mind?'

'We are.'

'Have you killed your first man in fair combat?'

'We have.'

'Is there a warrior who sponsors you, Nefer Seti?'

'I am the sponsor.' Shabako spoke up for him.

'Is there a warrior who sponsors you, Meren Cambyses?'

'I am the sponsor,' replied Socco.

When the catechism had been completed, Nefer and Meren were inducted into the first grade of the order. 'In the blood of the Bull, and the fire of his might, you are accepted by the god as his novices. You are not yet entitled to sit in conclave with the anointed warriors of the second and third grades, nor to worship the Red God, nor even to learn his hidden name. You have only the right to attempt the road that the god lays out for you. Knowing that it might mean death, do you accept this challenge?'

'We do.'

'Then know that there are five stages along the road and the first of these is . . .'

Each of the anointed warriors spoke in turn, explaining the ordeal Nefer and Meren faced and setting out the rules to which they must adhere. The five stages were designated as the javelin, the wrestler, the bow, the chariot and the sword. The two novices felt their spirits quail.

In the end Hilto spoke again. 'You have heard what the god has ordained. Are you determined to embark upon this endeavour?'

'We are.' Their voices were unnaturally loud, the tone cracked with false bravado, for now they knew the full extent of what lay ahead of them.

'Then from this point onwards there is no turning back,' said Hilto.

'The chariot is the main discipline,' Taita told them. 'Remember that it is a race. There will be ten chariots pursuing you. Speed is all. You must learn to get the very best out of your team.'

They worked relentlessly. By the time the new moon of Osiris was a sliver of bronze on the horizon, Dov and Krus had learned all that Nefer and Meren could teach them. They ran like one horse, leading with the same stride, aware of the balance and stability of the chariot behind them, using their weight and strength to hold true in the tightest turns, bringing it down from full gallop to dead stop in its own length, responding to the most subtle commands instantly.

Mintaka brought Merykara out into the desert, driving her own chariot, to watch them in training. At noon when they halted to water and rest the pair, Mintaka called out spontaneously, 'Perfection! Surely there is nothing more you can teach them. Nothing more for them to learn.'

Nefer gulped from the water jug then wiped his mouth on the back of his hand and looked up at the crest of the black rock hills.

'There is one who would not agree with you.'

The girls shaded their eyes and followed the direction of his gaze. They saw the figure perched up there, sitting so still that he might have been part of the rock.

'Taita. How long has he been watching?'

'Sometimes it seems that he has been watching for ever.'

'Is there something more he can show you?' Mintaka demanded. 'If there is, then why has he not already done so?'

'He is waiting for me to ask him,' Nefer said.

'Go to him at once,' Mintaka ordered. 'If you don't I will.'

Nefer climbed the hill and sat down beside Taita. They were silent for a while, and then Nefer said, 'I need you again, Old Father.'

Taita did not respond at once, except to blink like an owl caught out of his nest by the rising sun. He would never have a son, and no man had ever called him father before.

'You can help me. What must I still do?'

After a long pause Taita spoke softly. 'Krus senses when you are going to loose the javelin or shoot the arrow. He steps high at the moment, chopping with his right fore. Dov feels it and flinches.'

Nefer thought about it. 'Yes! I have felt the break in their stride at the moment of release.'

'It can throw your aim by a thumb's breadth.'

'What can I do?'

'You must teach them the fifth gait.'

'There are only four. Walk, trot, canter and gallop.'

'There is another. I call it the glide, but it must be taught. Most horses will never learn.'

'Help me teach them.'

They took the horses out of the harness, and Nefer went up on Dov's back. He took her for a short canter then brought her back to where Taita stood. The old man made her lift her right front hoof and tied a leather thong around her fetlock. Attached to the thong was a perfectly round, water-worn pebble wrapped in leather. Dov put her head down and sniffed it curiously. 'Take her round again,' said Taita.

Nefer prodded his toes behind her shoulder and she started forward. The pebble dangled on her leading foot, and instinctively she tried to rid herself of the nuisance, flipping her leading hoof with each pace. It changed her whole motion. Her back no longer came up to slap into his buttocks, there was no longer that rocking movement, that lunge. 'She flows like a river under me!' Nefer shouted with delight. 'Like the Nile herself!'

Within two days he was able to take off the bobber, and she would change from the canter or gallop into the glide at his command. The word of command was 'Nile'.

When they first brought it to him, Krus behaved as though the bobber was a venomous cobra. He reared and pawed the air. When he saw it coming in Nefer's hands, he rolled his eyes and quivered all over.

For three days he and Nefer pitted their wills against

each other, and then suddenly, on the fourth day, he flicked out his right hoof and glided away. The next day he was gliding on command as readily as Dov.

On the tenth day Taita watched from his hilltop as they came galloping down on the line of targets, Nefer with the javelin thong wrapped around his wrist. Krus was watching the painted wooden circles on their tripods, his ears pricked forward nervously, but before he could break and chop Nefer called, 'Nile!'

Dov and Krus changed gait simultaneously, the chariot steadied and glided forward like a fighting galley under sail. Nefer's first javelin slapped into the red central ring of the target.

Taita observed Nefer nock, draw and hold his aim. He was watching the yellow flag on its staff behind the row of targets that were set up two hundred paces in front of them. The flag stirred and flapped, filled for a moment then sagged limply as the hot breeze died away. Nefer loosed and the arrow rose on its lazy parabola of flight. It reached its zenith and as it started to drop the breeze puffed again on Taita's cheek.

The arrow felt the breeze also and veered perceptibly in flight. It dropped towards the target, and struck three hands' breadth to the leeward side of the red bullseye.

'Seth vomit on this treacherous wind!' Nefer swore.

'The light arrow feels it more,' Taita said, and walked back to the little cart that carried the spare bows and the quivers. He came back with a long bundle wrapped in a leather sheath.

'No!' Nefer said, as he unwrapped Trok's great war bow. 'It outdoes me!'

'When did you last attempt to draw it?' Taita asked.

'On the day we unearthed it,' Nefer replied. 'You should know. You were there.'

'That was six months ago.' Taita said, and glanced significantly at Nefer's bare chest and arms. The muscles had grown hard as carved cedarwood. He handed the bow to him.

Reluctantly Nefer took it and turned it in his hands. He saw that the stock had been rebound recently with fine electrum wire and lacquered. The bowstring was new – the sinews of a lion's forelegs, cured and twisted until they were hard and unyielding as bronze.

The refusal rose to his lips again but did not pass them for Taita was watching him. He lifted the bow and, without an arrow in place, raised it and tried to draw. It came back half a cubit, then his arms locked and although the muscles flattened and hardened across his chest it would move no further. Carefully Nefer released the pressure and the bow stock returned to rest.

'Let me have it back.' Taita reached out to take the weapon from him. 'You have neither the strength nor the determination.'

Nefer jerked it away from him, and his lips went thin and white, his eyes blazed.

'You don't know everything, old man, even though you think you do.'

He reached into the cart and snatched one of the long heavy arrows from the quiver that carried the cartouche of Trok embossed in the polished leather. Like the bow it had been salvaged from the buried chariot. He strode back to the firing-line and took his stance. He nocked the arrow. His chest swelled as he sucked in a full breath. His jaw clenched and he began the draw. It came back slowly at first and reached the median line. He grunted and his breath hissed out through his throat, the muscles in his arms stood proud and hard and he came back to the full draw, kissing the bowstring like a lover. In the same movement he loosed, and the heavy arrow leaped away, singing against the blue, made its noon and dropped, flying high over the line of targets, going on and on, twice the distance. Then the flint head struck a bright spur of sparks from a distant rock and the shaft snapped with the terrible power of the strike.

Nefer stared after the arrow in astonishment, and Taita murmured, 'Perhaps you are right.'

Nefer dropped the bow and embraced him. 'You know enough, Old Father,' he said. 'Enough for all of us.'

Taita took Nefer and Meren into the desert, three days' travel through the harsh and beautiful land. He led them to the hidden valley where the black liquid oozed to the surface through a deep cleft in the rock. This was the same thick, tarry substance that they had used to set alight the jackals' fur on the night raid at Thane.

They filled the clay pots they had brought with them and returned to the workshop at Gallala. Taita refined the black liquid, boiling it down over a slow fire until it felt slippery as fine silk between the fingers. 'It will lubricate the wheel hubs smoother and longer than clarified pig's lard, or any other concoction. It will give you an advantage of fifty paces in a thousand. Perhaps the difference between success or failure, or even life and death.'

Nefer was inclined to run the royal chariot on the Red Road, but Taita asked, 'Do you really want to ride in a golden sarcophagus?'

'The goldwork weighs only two taels. You weighed it yourself.'

'It might just as well be two hundred when you go out there.'

Taita went over every one of the one hundred and five

chariots they had exhumed from the sands, selected ten and stripped them down. He weighed the chassis and tested the strength of the joints in the carriagework. He spun the wheels on their hubs, judging by eye the slightest wobble in their rotation. At last he made his final choice.

He modified the hub assembly on the chosen vehicle so that the wheels were held by a single bronze pin that could be removed with a mallet blow. When he reassembled the chariot he discarded the dashboard and side panels, ridding it of every last tael of superfluous weight. Without the support of the struts and panels the riders would have to rely on their own sense of balance and a single loop of rope spliced to the footplate to steady themselves over the roughest ground. Finally he lubricated the wheel hubs with the black grease from the desert well.

Under Taita's supervision, they went over the harness an inch at a time, and Mintaka, Merykara and their maids sat up late into the night stitching and double stitching the joins and seams.

Then they chose the weapons they would carry, rolling the javelins and the arrows to detect any imperfection, suspending them on the special balance board Taita had designed, adding a bead of lead at haft or head until they were perfect. They sharpened the points so they would bite and hold in the targets. They resoled their sandals and filed the bronze cleats into spikes. They shaped new leather guards to protect their forearms from the whip of the bowstring and the javelin thong. They selected three swords each, for the bronze blades often snapped in the heat of combat. They sharpened the edges then burnished them with powdered pumice stone until they could shave the hair from their own forearms.

They cured and twisted spare bowstrings, to be carried as belts tied around their waists. Other than leather helmets and jerkins, they would wear no armour on the road, to lighten the load that Dov and Krus must draw. They worked behind the locked doors of the workshop, so that no others would learn of their preparations.

But above all else they trained and practised, built up their strength and stamina, and the trust of the horses.

For Dov and Krus the fire would be the worst of the ordeal. They built their own fires out in the desert, stacking faggots of wood and bundles of dry straw. They let the horses see the flames and smell the smoke, then blindfolded them. Though at first Krus balked and whinnied with terror, in the end he would run blind, trusting the man upon his back, so close to the crackling flames that they singed his mane.

Mintaka and Merykara spent long hours during the waiting days in the newly renovated temple of Hathor, sacrificing for their men and praying for the protection and intervention of the goddess on their behalf.

Thirty-five days before the full of the moon of Horus a strange caravan arrived in Gallala. It had come up from the coast, from the port of Safaga. It was led by a one-eyed and one-armed giant of a man named Aartla. The five warriors of the Red Road went out to meet him when he was still three leagues outside the city walls. They carried him back to Gallala in honour, for he was a brother warrior of the third degree who had run the Red Road almost thirty years before. Twenty years ago an arrow had pierced his eye during the Libyan campaign of Pharaoh Tamose, and five years later a Nubian axeman had sheared his arm with a single stroke below the elbow.

Aartla was a wealthy man now. He owned a travelling company of entertainers, men and women of special talents and skills. One of his troupe was reputed to be the strongest woman in the world. She could lift two horses into the air, one with each hand, and she could bite the end off a bronze rod and then bend the metal stump with the grip of her vagina. Another of his women was famed as the most beautiful in the world, though few had set eyes on her face. She came from a land so far to the north that at certain seasons of the year the rivers turned to white stone and ceased to flow. Aartla charged ten taels of silver for the privilege of seeing her face unveiled. They said she had golden hair that hung to the ground, and eyes of different colours, one golden and the other blue. The price that Aartla charged for viewing the rest of her charms was in proportion, and only a rich man might sample all her delights.

In addition Aartla possessed a black slave girl who ate fire, covered herself from head to foot with a cloak of live scorpions, and draped a great python around her neck. At the climax of her performance she enticed the serpent to crawl into the secret opening of her body until all its length had disappeared into her womb.

These wonders were intended merely to whet the appetite of the audience for the main attractions of Aartla's circus, which were his champions: a company of fighting men, wrestlers and swordsmen who stood to meet all contenders in combat. Aartla offered a purse of a hundred taels of pure gold to any man who could defeat one of his champions. The side wagers made on these contests were legendary and were the source of Aartla's immense wealth. Though nowadays he never fought, he was still a warrior at heart and a devotee of the Red God.

When word reached him that a pharaoh of the Tamosian dynasty was determined to run the Red Road, he brought his champions across half the world to oppose him. He loved the game so well that he made no charge for this service.

His brother warriors had prepared one of the ancient palaces of the city to house Aartla and his troupe. On the night after his arrival they held for him a great welcome banquet, to which only Nefer and Meren were not invited. 'We could not have accepted,' Nefer explained to Mintaka. 'We are not brothers of the order. Besides, to sit down with the men who will oppose us would be flying in the face of convention and tradition.'

The day after the welcoming banquet the champions resumed their never-ending practice and training, under the sharp eye of Aartla. They worked in the courtyard of the ancient palace, and all strangers were excluded. Aartla was too shrewd to let other gamblers assess the form and style of his champions without paying good gold for the privilege.

However, Taita was no stranger. When Aartla had lost his arm Taita had trimmed and sewn up the stump, and saved him from the gas gangrene that had infected the wound and threatened Aartla's life. Aartla welcomed him to the practice courtyard and sat him on a pile of cushions on the side of his good eye. The most beautiful woman in the world served him honey-flavoured sherbet in a golden bowl, and smiled at him with those haunting mismatched eyes from behind her veil.

First, Aartla gave Taita the latest news of the Egyptian campaign in Mesopotamia, whence he had come. It seemed that King Sargon, with his armies broken and scattered, had retreated behind the walls of Babylon, his capital city. The final outcome could not be in doubt. The armies of the false pharaohs would soon be free to return to Egypt and deal with the other threat posed to their monarchy by the little army of Gallala. When he said this his look was significant, a timely warning to an old friend.

While they sat on the cushions and discussed many other things, politics, power and war, medicine, magic and the gods, Taita seemed engrossed in their discussion, hardly glancing at the athletes who struggled and sweated in the sunlight. But his pale ancient eyes missed not a single throw or swordstroke.

The champions lived by their murderous skills. They

were devotees of the Red God, and their endeavours were a form of worship. When Taita returned to his cell that evening, where Nefer and Meren waited for him, he was grave. 'I have watched your adversaries at practice, and I warn you that there is still much work for us to do,' he said, 'and only days left to us.'

'Tell us, Old Father,' Nefer said.

'First there is Polios, the wrestler . . .' Taita began, and he outlined the character and strength of each champion, his style of combat and his particular strengths. Then he discussed any weakness he had discerned in them, and how that might best be exploited.

The five warriors of the order, assisted by Aartla, began to lay out the course to be run. They spent day after day in the wilderness, surveying a wide circular track that began in the central forum of Gallala, went up into the hills and the broken lands, then three leagues later came back down the long valley past the fountain of Taita, and through the city gates to finish back in the forum. Once they had laid out the course, they sent parties of workmen to build the obstacles along the way.

Ten days before the contest, Hilto and Shabako read out the proclamation to the populace of the city. They described the course in detail, and the rules governing the trial. Then they named the champions who would oppose the novices.

'In the ordeal of wrestling, Pharaoh Nefer Seti will be matched against Polios of Ur.' The crowd sighed for Polios was a famous fighter. His nickname was the Backbreaker. Recently he had killed a man in Damascus, his seventeenth victim in the ring.

'Meren Cambyses will be matched against Sigassa of Nubia.' They knew him almost as well. He was called the

Crocodile, for some strange disease had made his skin as hard, lumpy and black as that of one of the great reptiles.

'In the ordeal by sword, Pharaoh Nefer Seti will meet Khama of Taurine.'

'Meren Cambyses will meet Drossa of Indus.'

That night Mintaka and Merykara sacrificed a white lamb to the goddess, and wept as they pleaded for her protection over the men they loved.

For seven days before the running of the Red Road the five warriors held trials to select the chasers. There were no shortage of contenders for the honour. Any man who plucked the hair braid of a king could expect immortality. Hilto promised that there would be a carved stele five cubits high raised in the temple of his preferred god or goddess to commemorate his feat. He would receive a thousand taels of gold, sufficient to purchase a fine estate when at last they returned to the motherland. In addition he would take as trophies all the weapons and accoutrements of the novice he succeeded in running down.

The five warriors made the final selection by a process of elimination, and proclaimed it from the stone platform in the centre of the forum. 'They have chosen the ten best and most experienced men available, and given them their pick of chariots and horses. There will be great danger both behind and in front,' Taita warned the pair, as he went over the list again. 'Consider this one, Daimios. He is a captain of chariots. He knows how to get the best out of a pair of horses.'

'It will all depend on the start,' Nefer said.

'And that will be decided by the Red God alone.'

For a seven-night before the trial Mintaka denied Nefer her couch. 'My love will weaken your resolve, and drain your strength. But I will miss you a hundred times more than you will me,' she told him as together they braided Krus' long mane.

The day before the full moon of Horus, Taita ordered them all to rest. Dov and Krus grazed quietly together in the field below the fountain. Merykara made up a basket of figs and oranges and *dhurra* cakes, and she and Meren sat beside the fountainhead watching the horses on the green grass below them. When they had eaten the simple meal, Merykara knelt behind him and plaited his hair into a rope that hung halfway down his back. 'It is so thick and lustrous,' she murmured, and buried her face in it. 'It smells so good. Let no other take it from you, but bring your braid back to me.'

'How will you reward me if I do?' He turned his head to smile at her.

'I will give you such a reward as you have never dreamed of.' She blushed as she said it.

'I have dreamed of it,' he assured her fervently. 'I dream of it every night of my life.'

In the morning Taita came to wake Nefer. He found him asleep, with one arm thrown over his face. At Taita's touch he sat up, stretched and yawned. The thick braid of his hair, which Mintaka had plaited, hung down his back. As he looked at Taita his eyes focused and hardened, as he remembered what the day would bring forth.

While Nefer drank a bowl of sour milk and ate a handful

of figs, Taita went to the window and looked out over the rooftops to the grove of young palm trees they had planted above the wells. He saw the topmost fronds sway and nod to the breeze. They had all prayed for a still day, but this breeze carried with it the threat of failure. Now Nefer would have to rely more than ever on the great war bow to counter it.

Taita said nothing to Nefer of his misgivings. Instead, he turned and cast his eyes down the avenue. The sun was not yet risen, but it seemed that half the populace of Gallala was streaming out of the city gates.

'They are anxious to secure vantage-points along the course, and to watch as much of the run as possible,' he told Nefer. 'No one except the participants and the judges are allowed to ride. All others must follow the chase on foot. Some argue that it might be possible to watch the javelin and the wrestling, then cut across the hills to look down on the swordplay from close at hand. Those who are less fleet of foot will climb to the summit of Eagle Mount and watch the crossing of the chasm below them then run back here to see the finish.'

Despite the great exodus from the city many hundreds of others had chosen to watch the start and crowded into the forum. Others had climbed high above the square and were perched on the walls and balconies. Even so early in the day the air was festive and the mood feverishly excited. Some of those on the walls had brought their breakfast and chewed bones and scraps showered on to those below. Others shouted their wagers to Aartla and his scribes. Aartla was offering even money that Nefer and Meren would cross the chasm, two to one against them passing the swordsmen and four to one against them finishing the course without being overtaken by the pursuit.

As the sun rose above the walls the ten chariots of the pursuers filed into the forum. The gongs beat, the drums rolled and the sistrum rattled, women squealed and threw flowers, and children danced around them, but the charioteers were grim and intent as they lined up along the starting barrier.

There was an interval now of tense expectation and then the sound of cheering from the cavalry lines, swelling and coming closer. Then, to an explosion of '*Bak-her!*', the stripped-down chariot of the novices entered between the eroded columns at the entrance to the forum.

Dov and Krus had been groomed until their coats shone like burnished metal in the early sunlight. Their manes were plaited, coloured ribbons twisted into the strands, their tails were clubbed.

Nefer and Meren wore only light leather armour, and their bodies were oiled for the wrestling. They stepped down from the footplate of the chariot and went down on their knees, with their hands resting on the hilts of their swords. Taita came forward and stood over them. He recited a prayer to Horus and the Red God, asking for their blessing and protection. Finally, he took an amulet from around his own neck and placed it over Nefer's bowed head.

Nefer looked down at the object as it dangled on his chest and felt a tingle of shock, almost as though a strange current of power flowed from it. It was the golden Periapt of Lostris, the locket of his grandmother, which nobody but Taita had ever touched.

Then Hilto, wearing the red cape of the third degree of the order, mounted to the stone platform in the centre of the forum. He read aloud the rules. When he had finished he asked, in a stern voice, 'Do you understand and undertake to abide by the rules of the order of the Red Road?'

'In the name of the Red God!' Nefer affirmed.

'Who will cut the hair braids?' Hilto asked, and Mintaka and Merykara stepped up behind the kneeling warriors. Mintaka's eyes were heavily underscored with purple, for she had not slept the previous night. They were both pale and tense with anxiety. Nefer and Meren bowed their heads, and lovingly the women lifted the braids and sheared them away. They handed them to Hilto, who attached them to the tips of the tall pennant rods on each side of the footplate of their chariot. These were the trophies that the pursuers must attempt to snatch, and which Nefer and Meren must defend with their lives.

'Mount your chariot,' Hilto ordered, and Nefer and Meren climbed to the footplate. Nefer gathered up the reins. Dov and Krus arched their necks, stamped and backed up a single turn of the wheels.

'Bring on the birds!' Hilto ordered.

The handlers climbed into the circular sanded cockpit, each with a fighting cock under his arm. The wattles of both birds had been cut away so their heads were sleek, almost reptilian, with no dangling flesh or skin to give the enemy bird purchase. The sunlight gleamed on their plumage with the iridescence of oil spilled on water.

A tense, aching silence fell over the crowded forum. The handlers knelt, facing each other, in the centre of the sanded pit, and held their birds in front of them. The birds did not have artificial spurs strapped to their feet: the long metal spikes would make a kill too swift and certain, but their natural spurs had been sharpened and polished.

'Bait your birds!' Hilto called, and the handlers thrust them at each other, without allowing them to touch. The eyes of the two roosters gleamed with malice, their heads began to swell with rage and the naked skin of their heads and throats turned an angry crimson. They beat their wings, and tried to break from the handlers' grip to fly at each other.

With his drawn sword Hilto pointed across the forum at the ruined roof of the temple of Bes, the patron god of Gallala, where a blue flag flapped idly in the hot breeze. 'The novices will start when the birds are released. The flag will be lowered when one of the birds is killed, and only then will the chase begin. The Red God, in his infinite wisdom, will determine how long the birds will survive and how long the lead time will be. Now, hold yourselves in readiness.'

Every eye, even those of Nefer and Meren, turned to the challenging cock-birds. Hilto lifted his sword. The birds' hackles were raised, they were crimson with rage, fighting to be at each other.

'Now!' cried Hilto, and the handlers set them free. They flew across the sand in a flutter of bright wings, leaping high, thrusting with claws and spurs.

'Ha, Dov! Ha, Krus!' Nefer called and they sprang away, throwing gravel and dust from under their hoofs. A mighty shout went up from the crowd and the chariot raced once around the forum then out into the open avenue. Behind them the cheering faded as they tore through the gates and turned on to the track that led into the hills, its length marked every two hundred paces with white linen flags, which shook and flapped lazily in the early breeze that came in off the desert. 'Keep the flags to the right!' Meren reminded Nefer. If they missed a flag on the wrong side the judges would send them back to round it fairly.

While he drove, saving the horses, bringing them down to a trot as the slope rose steeply under them Nefer assessed that breeze by flag and dust, judging its strength and direction. It was coming harsh and hot from the west, strong enough to blow the dustcloud aside behind them. This was the worst possible wind. It would drain the horses, and confuse the range when they came to the trial of javelin and bow. He thrust the thought aside to concentrate first on the ascent of the hills.

The gradient tilted sharply upwards, and at a word of command from Nefer they sprang down from the footplate and ran beside the horses, to lighten the burden. Dov and Krus surged ahead so strongly that they had to take a grip on the harness to keep pace with them. As they reached the crest, Nefer halted them and let them rest for a measured three hundred beats of his own heart.

He looked back at the city walls below and heard the regular roar swelling and subsiding like the sound of distant surf on a coral reef, the characteristic sound of the cockfight as the crowd hailed each attack of the birds. But the flag still flew on the crumbling top of the temple of Bes to signal that the fight had not been decided. He turned away and looked down the length of the level plain that stretched ahead, and picked out the line of javelin butts, five of them spaced at intervals of two hundred paces. There was a low fence of thorn brush running parallel to them that would keep the chariot at a range of fifty paces.

Nefer jumped to the footplate, and called, 'Come away!' and the pair strode forward. He glanced back and the blue flag still flew on the tower of Bes.

As they raced in on the line of targets, Nefer wound the thong around his wrist and composed himself, seeing in his mind's eye the target, imagining the flight of the missile from his hand to the inner red circle, ignoring the yellow outer. He watched the wind moving the flags.

He saw Shabako standing on a low knoll near the centre of the line. He would show a red flag for an inner, and a yellow for a miss. They carried only five javelins, and they would be allowed only one yellow. If they failed on the first run they must turn back, retrieve the thrown javelins, and run again until they had scored the four reds.

Nefer handed the reins to Meren, who steered in close to the dividing fence to give Nefer the best shot. The first target came up fast, and Nefer braced himself on the bouncing swerving footplate.

'Nile!' He gave the command and instantly Dov and Krus changed their gait into that wonderful gliding motion. The chariot steadied under him and he rode the easy movement with his legs and he threw. There was never a doubt from the moment the javelin left his hand, its velocity accelerated by the whip of the thong – he had allowed for the wind. It flew fifty paces swinging across the wind into the heart of the red circle, and from the corner of his eye Nefer saw Shabako wave the red flag to acknowledge the strike. He snatched another javelin from the bin, and wound the thong. He felt a supreme almost godlike confidence: he knew that the next four darts would fly as true as the first. He watched the second target come up, and he threw again. It was another perfect throw. He did not even have to glance at the flag, and beside him Meren shouted, '*Bak-her*, brother!' and steered for the third.

They were running in close, and the thorn fence flew by the off-wheel in a blur. Nefer lined up and whipped his right arm into the throw, and at exactly that moment the wheel touched the fence and the chariot swerved violently and hung for a moment on the verge of capsizing. The horses pulled it straight with their combined weight, but the javelin was already in flight. With despair in his heart Nefer saw it fly wide, missing the target completely, and the yellow flag went up.

'It was me,' Meren gritted. 'I ran too fine.'

'Hold her true now,' Nefer snapped at him. 'We need two more reds.'

The fourth target came up but Nefer felt the altered motion under him. Krus was leading with the wrong foot, the collision with the fence had unbalanced him.

'Ho, Krus,' Meren called, and tried to steady him with the touch of reins. Then Dov leaned lightly against him and he felt her rhythm and picked up the step from her just as the fourth target came up.

Nefer threw and beside him Meren called, 'Red! A clean hit. You have done it.'

'Not yet,' Nefer told him, and snatched the last javelin from the bin. 'One more to go.'

They came down fast on the last target, and the men

were tense as drawn bow stocks, every muscle rigid and every nerve stretched tautly. Krus sensed it, felt it in the reins from Meren's right hand, with his right eye he saw the target come up, knew precisely the instant at which Nefer would throw and instinctively fell into his wicked old habit and broke step. The carriage lurched and swayed just as Nefer released. Even then it might have scored, were it not for the wind. A hot gust swept over them, strong enough to flog the heavy hair braids on the flag staffs. The javelin was already slightly off-line, but the wind aggravated the error. It drifted even further to the right and missed the red inner by the width of two fingers and quivered in the outer ring. Shabako held raised the black flag high above his head and waved it from side to side so that folds of cloth volleyed and flogged loudly, the signal of failure.

Their first run had been disqualified. They must retrieve the javelins and run the butts again.

Grimly silent, Nefer snatched the reins back from Meren and spun the chariot into a tight turn around the end of the thorn fence and they started back. He pushed the horses to the top of their speed – there was no thought of husbanding their strength now. For all Nefer knew, one of the fighting cocks was already slain and ten chariots had begun the chase.

They flew back along the line of targets, passing them so closely that Meren was able to pluck the javelins from the packed straw bodies without having to bring the chariot to a complete stop. The fourth javelin that had missed the target completely lay in the open, but even from a distance Nefer saw that the impact with the rocky ground had snapped the shaft in two. They were left with only four missiles to score four red flags. A single miss would mean that they would have to make their stand here, two against ten picked warriors: they would have to capitulate or fight to the death.

With only four javelins in the bin, they reached the

start of the line and Nefer halted the chariot and jumped down to the ground. He ran to Krus' head and stroked his forehead. 'Run true now, my darling. Don't fail me again.'

From a great distance came the sound of a long, sustained cheering. This time it did not fade away.

'One of the birds is dead!' Meren called. 'The chase has begun.'

Nefer knew it was true. One of the cocks had succumbed and the chasers were released to follow them. They had lost their starting advantage. The pursuing chariots did not have to run the test of the javelins. They would race past the butts without a check. Even if this time they managed a clean pass of the butts with four red flags, ahead of Nefer and Meren waited the wrestlers.

Mintaka and Merykara stood side by side, looking down into the cockpit. Though stools had been placed for them they could not sit for their blood was afire with anxiety as they watched the closing stages of the bloody conflict below them.

The two fighting cocks had been carefully matched, veterans of many epic battles, both had proved their courage and stamina. They were long-legged but their thighs were compact and balled with muscle. They could drive their wicked black spurs deeply through flesh to an adversary's bone. With serpentine necks and massive hooked beaks they could reach out to rip away feathers and flesh, and when they had bled and weakened their opponent, they would seize the death-hold, pinning him while they stabbed into his vitals.

The older bird had feathers of gold and copper, bright as the sunrise. His tail was a proud cascade shot with sapphire lights. The other bird was black, but lustrous sparkling black, and his bare head was purple red.

They circled each other now. They had fought hard and long, loose feathers strewed the sand and drifted in the hot puffs of the west wind. Both birds were bleeding, fat heavy drops that sparkled on their plumage. Their strength was draining away, and they were slightly unsteady on their feet. However, their eyes were bright and fierce as they had been at the beginning of the conflict.

'Please, adored and worshipful Hathor, give them both strength to survive,' whispered Merykara, as she clung tightly to Mintaka's hand. 'Let them fight until the setting of the sun.' Even she knew how vain was her appeal. 'And keep Meren and Nefer from harm.'

Suddenly the black bird flew up head high, and then with a powerful wingbeat shot forward with both legs fully extended. The red bird rose to meet him, but he was almost exhausted and his riposte lacked fire. He was slow to lift his legs to counter the thrust. They collided in a burst of feathers, rolled together and when they separated the red cock was dragging a wing. It was very close to the end now.

Merykara sobbed aloud, 'Oh, Hathor, do not let him die!' She seized Mintaka's arm and sank her fingernails into the flesh, leaving bright red half-moons on the skin, but Mintaka hardly felt it. She was watching with horror as the red bird staggered weakly and the crowd howled savagely.

The black bird knew he had won, and his strength revived. He went high again, springing on those long, hard legs, his wings wide and brightly glittering. He dropped and hit the red cock before he could recover his balance and knocked him flat and fluttering. He pecked murderously for the eye, caught a fold of the wattled cheek and hung on.

The red bird regained his feet, but the black was locked into him. The red bird ran painfully, carrying his opponent's weight, and the girls screamed in the uproar: 'Let him go, black shade of Seth. Let him live!'

A full circuit of the cockpit the red carried him, but

every stride was weaker, and at last he collapsed just below where they stood at the barrier.

'He is dead!' somebody yelled. 'The fight is over. Let the chasers go.'

'No! He lives yet,' screamed Mintaka fiercely.

The black bird released his grip on the other's head, and stood over him. With the last of his strength and courage the red bird forced himself to his feet and stood swaying, with both wings dragging in the sand and the blood pouring from the gash in his cheek.

The black bird seemed to be measuring the distance between them, then once more he leaped high and for a moment towered over his victim. Then he fell upon him and drove both spurs in to their full length, through heart and lungs. The red rooster crumpled under him and lay upon his back, his beak wide open in a silent death cry and his wings shivering convulsively.

The black rooster stood over the carcass, threw back his head and gave vent to a raucous crow of triumph that seemed to rip down Mintaka's spine, and made her shudder.

'The god has spoken! It is finished.' Hilto lifted the torn and bloody carcass by the neck, and the flag on the tower of Bes dropped. He turned to the charioteers, who crouched behind their teams of horses.

'You are free to take the Red Road!' he cried. 'Ride to death or glory!' The long whips cracked, the horses threw their heads, tossed their manes, and the ten fighting chariots swept together once around the forum, while the crowds scattered from under their wheels, women screamed and men cheered. Then they burst through the city gates and tore away into the hills, following the line of flags.

Nefer took a moment longer to pamper and reassure the horses; he stood with an arm around each of their necks and whispered to them. Then he ran back and jumped on to the footplate. He started them at a walk then brought them gently to a canter. Only when they were running in perfect unison, leading together, did he change their gait with the command, 'Nile!'

Smoothly they swept down on the targets for the second attempt and he passed the reins to Meren. He gave him no admonition, for he knew that Meren was still smarting from the first blundered attempt.

While he wrapped the thong around his wrist Nefer watched Krus' ears for any sign that he would break stride again, but he held them pricked forward and ran true. He held the line perfectly as they came level with the first target, and the javelin smacked into the red inner. It seemed that almost immediately the second target came up and he threw smoothly with just that final application of power in the stroke and the point sank deeply into the inner ring. Beside him Meren was silent, steering the team with his very breath and soul.

The third javelin twinkled like a beam of sunlight as it flew across the range and Shabako waved the red flag for another hit.

The last javelin was in Nefer's hand, the thong clinched firmly around his wrist, and he crooned to the horses, making his tone firm but reassuring. 'One more. Just one more for me!'

Krus seemed to gather himself and tuck in his chin and he held the line sweetly and as Nefer threw he knew it was going to strike in the very centre of the red. He shouted to them while it was still in flight.

'Ha! Ha! Come away.' And they surged forward, breaking from the glide into full gallop so strongly that Nefer had to brace his legs and clutch at the grab rope to prevent himself being thrown over backwards.

Shabako waved the red flag over his head and his voice carried clearly, '*Bak-her*, Majesty! You are through and clear!'

But Nefer knew they could never make up the ground they had lost, and the chasers were already coming up swift and hard behind them.

The line of flags led them in a wide circle to the north along the edge of a deep chasm with sheer sides, and on up a series of natural terraces where the bare earth was a soft peachy colour that belied its harsh and barren nature.

The step of the third and final terrace was lined with over fifty of the more hardy spectators who had climbed up from Gallala. As Nefer's chariot raced up towards them they cheered them onwards, and opened their ranks to let them through. The summit of the terrace was flat and level. In the centre of this open space the wrestlers waited.

Each stood in his own circle of white painted stones. Nefer steered down towards them, with the crowds running after them cheering and laughing with excitement. Just short of the stone rings, Nefer brought the horses to a halt, and two grooms who were standing ready ran forward to take their heads.

'See they drink only one bucket each,' Nefer ordered, as he jumped down. This was the first point at which they were permitted to water the horses, but Nefer did not want their bellies blown up with liquid.

Swiftly Nefer and Meren stripped off their leather armour and the short *chitons* beneath until they stood stark naked in the sunlight. The crowd hummed with admiration when their hard young bodies, trained to athletic perfection, were revealed, and some of the women of low status and dubious morality ululated and cavorted lewdly with excitement.

Now every second that passed brought the pursuing chariots closer. Nefer did not even glance at the dancing women but he and Meren strode forward, each towards the ring where his allotted opponent waited. Nefer paused outside the ring of white stones and looked at Polios of Ur who stood in the centre.

He was not exceptionally big or tall, no larger or heavier then Nefer, for the judges had matched them carefully and fairly. However, there was no fat or superfluous flesh on Polios. It was obvious that he had been limbering up, for he shone with sweat and oil and his muscles were engorged and flushed with blood. Everything about him was hard. His shoulders were in perfect proportion to his waist, his belly flat, his limbs long and supple. He stood with his arms folded over his chest and watched Nefer with a hard flat stare.

Nefer took one long breath and heard again Taita's words in his ear, as clearly as if he had spoken again in his ear, 'The left knee. That is his only weakness.'

He dropped his eyes to the limb but Polios' left knee seemed as sturdy as the right. Hard and impregnable as the main stem of an olive tree.

Nefer touched the golden charm at his throat, and stepped into the ring of stones. The crowd howled and yelped and shouted. Polios placed his hands on his knees and hunched his shoulders, and watched him with the flat implacable stare of a serpent. Nefer knew that he must make the first advance, for Polios was in no hurry. His task was to delay Nefer here until the pursuing chariots could catch up with him. Nefer circled him once, and Polios turned slowly to keep facing him.

'Yes,' Nefer told himself, 'there it is. He drags his left

toe.' But it was so tiny a flaw that he would never have picked it out without Taita's advice.

'An old injury,' Taita had told him. 'Here!' and he had pressed his thumb into Nefer's knee to mark the exact site of it. But then Taita had gone on, 'Even so, do not rate him lightly. He is a man-killer. This is his favourite throw, and it is well nigh irresistible.' Taita had demonstrated it.

Nefer circled back the other way and Polios turned with him. He saw it now, a faint unnatural hollow below the bulge of the kneecap. He could not afford another moment and he closed.

Each of them fell into the classical prelude, grabbing at each other with both hands, seeking the throwing grip, changing the holds, shifting weight, pushing and then giving, feeling the other man's balance. Then suddenly Polios leaped forward, coming in low, under Nefer's guard, and though Nefer had been expecting it he could not prevent one long arm whipping around his waist. Suddenly he was lifted high so only the tips of his toes touched the earth, and Polios spun with him in his arms, turning him backwards so that he could not keep his balance. Then suddenly Polios dropped on his right knee, and brought Nefer down with him. His other leg was braced solid, left thigh parallel to the ground like a carpenter's bench, Nefer came down across it and it caught him in the small of his back, at the level of his kidneys. It should have snapped his spine, but Nefer had practised the counter a hundred times with Meren. He arched his back to take the strain and at the same time slammed both his heels in the ground to break the force of it. Even so he felt his spine creak as his vertebrae were strained to the very limit.

Polios came down on him with the full weight of his upper torso, but Nefer reached under his back and clamped his right hand on Polios' knee. Taita had made him spend hours hardening his right thumb, squeezing a ball of leather until he could leave a deep indentation in the surface. Even then Taita had not been satisfied. He had made Nefer continue these exercises until he could crack a cowrie shell between thumb and forefinger. Then time and again Taita demonstrated the exact point under the kneecap where the injury lay, and the direction of pressure he must apply to sunder it. Nefer found it now, and drove his thumb into the hollow between the head of the tibia and the unattached kneecap.

Every muscle in Nefer's right arm stood out with the effort and his eyes seemed to bulge from their sockets. Then suddenly he felt something give under the point of his thumb, and he made one final effort. His thumb went in deeper, the weakened cartilage and sinew crackling and popping as they tore, the kneecap lifted in Nefer's grip, ripped from its seat.

Polios screamed, a sound of such extreme agony that it hushed the roar of the spectators that crowded the edge of the ring. Polios released his own hold and tried to push Nefer away from him, but Nefer rolled easily with the throw, never releasing his grip on the mangled kneecap, tearing it further open. Suddenly, rendered helpless as an infant, Polios sobbed and choked on the pain of it.

Nefer came up on top of him and forced his face into the earth. He twisted his left leg up behind him, and Polios could not resist. Nefer bent the shattered knee back until the heel touched Polios' buttocks, and put all his weight upon it. The terrible cry that Polios gave out sounded not human.

'Yield!' Nefer commanded, but Polios was dumb and paralysed with agony. The umpire ran forward to touch Nefer's shoulder and signal his victory.

Nefer sprang to his feet and left Polios writhing and blubbering in the dirt. The spectators parted silently in front of him, stunned by the swiftness and completeness of his victory.

Nefer heard someone in the crowd say, 'He will never

walk on that leg again,' but he never looked back as he ran to the other ring and pushed out of his way the men that surrounded it.

Meren and Sigassa, the Crocodile, were locked chest to chest. They rolled across the ring, first one on top then the other. Nefer saw at a glance that Meren was injured. Sigassa's diseased skin was thick and horny, impervious to pain, and he used it now like a weapon, rubbing himself against him, tearing Meren's flesh so the blood oozed up from the shallow lacerations across his chest and arms. Taita had warned them of that, but it was impossible to avoid his loathsome embrace, and Meren was being overpowered. Nefer had arrived only just in time.

The rules of the Red Road were deliberately stacked against the novices. However, they allowed one novice to come to the aid of the other, but only after he had defeated his own opponent. This was one of the few concessions they were granted. Nefer took full advantage of it.

The moment he was into the ring Nefer stooped and picked up a white pebble the size and shape of a dove's egg. As he ran to Meren's aid, he placed the stone in the centre of his palm, wrapped his fingers and thumb around it and clasped it so firmly that his knuckles whitened with the pressure. He had turned his fist into a weapon as effective as a carpenter's mallet.

The crowd shouted a warning to the Crocodile, and he released Meren and came to his feet in one swift movement. Head down he charged at Nefer. Taita had warned them that his bald and knobbly skull was a deadly battering ram. Sigassa had already cracked two of Meren's ribs with his first charge, and now he strove to do the same to Nefer.

Nefer let him come on, judging his moment, placing his feet firmly and then he swung his clenched right fist into the side of Sigassa's jaw, at the precise point that Taita had shown him. The weight and speed of Sigassa's own rush met the full power of Nefer's shoulders behind the blow.

The great scaly head snapped back and Sigassa's legs turned soft as porridge under him. But his momentum carried him on, he sprawled full length over the line of marker stones.

No one in the crowd had ever seen a bare fist used as a weapon. They gaped in amazement. Even Nefer was startled by the result, for Sigassa lay without twitching. Nefer recovered in a moment and yelled at the umpire, 'Sigassa has left the ring! He must forfeit!'

The umpire shouted his agreement, 'Nefer Seti is the victor. Sigassa forfeits the bout. You are through and clear, Nefer Seti!'

Nefer ran to Meren and hauled him to his feet. 'Are you hurt?'

'My ribs! The swine butted like a bull,' he gasped.

'We must go on.'

'Of course.' Meren straightened and squared his shoulders. His face was grey as ashes with the pain. 'It is nothing.' But he clutched the side of his chest as they ran back to the chariot. Hastily they pulled on their discarded *chitons* and strapped on the leather armour.

'That took too long. We are losing ground every second.' As they scrambled up on to the footplate of the chariot they both looked back down the terraced slope of the hills towards the javelin butts on the plain below.

'There they are,' Meren grunted, and they saw the dustcloud boiling up pale and ethereal in the sunlight. The pursuing vehicles were still only dark specks beneath the hovering dust, but seemed to grow in size even as they watched them.

There was nothing to say. The pursuers would not be tested by the wrestlers. They would ride straight past the rings of stones. Nefer and Meren knew how meagre was their lead, and how swiftly they could lose even that small advantage. It needed only one more wrong step or miscalculation on their part.

Nefer shook out the reins and called to the team. Dov

and Krus had rested while they had been wrestling. Now they were refreshed, they leaned their full weight into the harness and sped away. Ahead, the line of flags marking the course began the wide turn back into the south, in the direction from which they had come.

'Halfway through!' Meren tried to sound gay, but his voice was tight with the pain of his cracked ribs, and each breath he drew was agony. They crossed the plateau and reached the far side where the terraces dropped in a series of giant steps to the rim of the chasm. They looked down towards the paddocks and pastures of the irrigated lands, startlingly green against the ochre and dun hues of the surrounding landscape, and the towers and rooftops of Gallala, so tumbled and earth-coloured that from this distance they seemed not man-made but natural features of the desert.

They looked ahead and the chasm gaped at them like the maw of a monster. Its sides were sheer and unscaleable, falling to shaded purple depths. There were small groups of people on the path that skirted the top of the cliffs. These were the spectators who had watched the trial of the javelins and who had taken the short-cut and were hurrying to watch the archery trial.

Nefer drove hard down the terrace, pushing the horses to their best speed, trying to win back even a few yards from the pursuit. This was where Krus made up in full measure for his mistakes at the javelin butts: his great strength bore them on and gave new heart to Dov at his side. They reached the lip of the chasm and raced along the edge, so close to it that the small pebbles thrown up by the wheels were flung out over the void. Though Krus was on the side closest to it he never broke his stride but leaned into the traces and ran with all his heart and will. Nefer felt his spirits soar on high.

'We can still beat them to the bridge,' he shouted in the wind. 'Come away, Krus! Come away, Dov.'

Nefer looked ahead and saw the tall, unmistakable figure of Taita standing on the lip of the precipice. He was staring across the chasm at the archery targets on the far side, and he did not look round as they pulled up behind him and jumped down from the chariot.

The previous evening Taita had predicted, 'With the west wind blowing, the archery and the crossing of the chasm will determine the final outcome. I will wait for you there.'

They took down the bows and arrow quivers from the racks, and left the horse, in the care of the waiting grooms as they hurried to join Taita at the edge of the cliff.

'We lost time at the javelin butts,' Nefer told him grimly, as he strung the great war bow, one end anchored on the ground between his feet as he exerted all his strength and weight on the other end to flex the stock.

'Krus was too eager,' Taita said, 'and so were you. But there is no profit in looking back. Look ahead!' He pointed across the deep void to where the targets were suspended on a light bamboo scaffolding.

As at the javelin butts, there were five targets. They were inflated pigs' bladders, each suspended on the cross-piece of the scaffold by a length of flax twine. They were well separated so that an arrow intended for one would not strike another by chance. The twine that held them was two cubits long, so that they had freedom of movement. Light as air they danced on the west wind, bobbing and ducking unpredictably.

The great open void between them made it almost impossible to judge the range accurately, and the west wind swirled and eddied along the cliffs. The force and direction of the wind that they felt on this side of the chasm would be different from that on the far bank. However, it would affect the arrows almost as much as the targets.

'What is the range, Old Father?' Nefer asked, as he chose

a long arrow from the quiver. Earlier that morning Taita had paced out one side of a right-angled triangle along this lip of the chasm. Then he had gauged the angle subtended by the targets on the far side with a weird arrangement of pegs and strings on a board. He had used these measurements, in a manner that was unfathomable to Nefer, to calculate the range across the chasm.

'One hundred and twenty-seven cubits,' Taita told him now. Nefer added this information to his own calculations of wind speed and direction, as he took his stance on the crumbling edge of the cliff. Meren stepped up beside him with the lighter cavalry bow in his hand.

'In the name of Horus and the goddess,' Nefer prayed, 'let us begin!' They shot at the same time.

Nefer's arrow dropped over the crosspiece of the scaffold, too long and high. Meren's arrow rose at a steeper angle aimed wide into the wind. As it slowed at the top of its trajectory the wind took hold of it, and it veered to the left; almost at the limit of its range it dropped towards the dangling bobbing line of pigs' bladders. It struck the middle target cleanly and they heard the pop as it burst, and disappeared like a stroke of magic.

A joyous shout went up from the watchers, and the umpire called the hit in a loud voice, but Meren muttered as he nocked another arrow, 'That was a fluke.'

'I'll take any more flukes that you have in your quiver,' Nefer told him. '*Bak-her*, brother, *Bak-her*.'

They drew and fired again, this time Meren's arrow fell short, rattling against the rocks of the cliff. Nefer missed the bladder on the right-hand end by half a cubit, and cursed Seth for the wind he had sent.

Unlike the javelins, the rules of the Red Road placed no limit on the number of arrows they were allowed. The only stipulation was that they must carry them all on the chariot from the start, so it was a trade-off between weight and numbers. They had each brought fifty missiles, but one of Nefer's long arrows weighed half again as much as one of Meren's.

They shot and missed, and shot again and missed again.

Taita had watched the wind and the flight of each arrow. He had gathered all his powers around him to feel the strength and impetus of the treacherous wind. He could almost see it, the flow and the strength of it, like the currents in a clear stream of water.

'Hold the same point of aim!' he ordered Nefer. 'But wait for my command.'

Nefer drew to full strength and though every muscle in his right arm quivered with the strain he held it.

Taita read the wind, became part of it, felt it in the depths of his being. 'Now!' he whispered, and the arrow leaped out high over the void and wavered on the capricious airs. Then like a towering falcon it seemed to gather itself and stoop to the target. The bladder popped as it struck, and the crowd howled.

'The next one!' Taita ordered, and Nefer drew, held his aim high and to the right of the second bladder.

'Now!' Taita whispered. The old man seemed to control the flight of the arrow by the force of his mind. At the very last instant before it struck the west wind tried spitefully to turn it aside, but it held the line and the bladder burst with a sharp crack.

'The next one. Draw!' whispered Taita. 'Hold!' and a heartbeat later, 'Now!' This time the arrow almost touched the bladder, but at the last moment the ball bounced aside.

Nefer shot again on Taita's command and he missed by a full arrow length, high and left. The strain of working the great bow was too much, his right arm ached and his muscles cramped and jumped involuntarily.

'Rest!' Taita ordered. 'Take the Periapt of Lostris in your right hand, and rest.'

Nefer laid aside the bow and stood with his head bowed

in an attitude of prayer, with the golden amulet in his right hand. He felt the strength begin to flow back into his bow arm. Meren was still trying with the smaller bow, but the pain of his cracked ribs almost doubled him over and the sweat of agony ran down his pale face.

At that moment the crowd along the top of the cliff stirred and turned and looked back up the terrace. Someone shouted, 'They come!' and the cry was taken up, until the shouting was deafening.

Nefer lifted his head and saw the first chariot come whirling over the skyline. It was close enough for him to recognize Daimios at the reins, his golden hair streaming back on the wind. Behind him came the other chariots of the pursuers strung out in a line. Faintly he heard the drivers shouting to the horses and the rumble of the wheels over the rough ground.

'Do not look at them,' Taita ordered him. 'Do not think about them. Think only of the target.'

Nefer turned his back on the approaching line of vehicles and lifted the bow.

'Draw and hold!' Taita said. The wind spurted and dropped. 'Now!' The arrow sped unerringly across the chasm and the fourth bladder burst.

Nefer slid another arrow from the quiver, then he paused with the shaft in his hand and felt despair in his heart. A dust-devil came spinning down out of the desert on to the line of targets. The dun-coloured curtains of dust and sand and debris obscured the range, and the single remaining bladder disappeared in its depths.

High on the hill behind them the pursuing charioteers shouted with triumph, and Nefer heard Daimios' voice above the roar of the whirlwind, 'Now you must stand and fight me, Nefer Seti.'

'One more target before you are clear,' Socco, the umpire, shouted sternly. 'Stand your ground.'

'There is no target,' Nefer protested.

'The will of the Nameless God,' Socco told him. 'You must submit to it.'

'There!' shouted Taita. 'There is the manifest will of a greater and more powerful goddess.' He pointed across the deep ravine at the impenetrable cloud of yellow dust.

Like a cork floating up from the depths of a turbid lake, the bladder with its broken string trailing under it rose to the top of the dustcloud, and skittered in the heated air.

'Now, in the name of the goddess Lostris!' Taita urged Nefer. 'She is the only one who can help you now.'

'In the name of the goddess!' Nefer shouted, threw up the great bow and shot at the tiny balloon in the wild embrace of the storm. Up and up climbed the arrow, and it seemed that it must miss to the left, but abruptly the bladder ducked and dived to meet it. The razor-sharp flint arrowhead slashed it open, it burst and whipped away like a rag on the wind.

'You are through and clear!' Socco released them with a shout. Nefer dropped the bow and ran to the chariot. Meren ran after him, favouring his injured ribs, and the crowd urged them on as Dov and Krus jumped away together. Behind them the cries of the pursuit were frustrated and angry, but Nefer did not look back.

A thousand paces ahead the suspension bridge spanned the gorge from cliff to cliff, with the terrible drop below, but before they reached it they must run the fire.

Shabako was the umpire of the bridge crossing. On horseback, he had galloped across from his post at the javelin butts as soon as Nefer and Meren had cleared them. Now he had taken his next station at the bridge. This was the most crucial stage of the entire Red Road.

The novices had a choice here. They could decline to

breach the wall of fire to reach the bridge. Instead they might take the long route and cross further down the valley where the cliffs fell gently away. However, this added almost two leagues to the course.

Shabako stood at the head of the bridge and watched Nefer's chariot leave the archery butt and, with the pursuit close behind, come racing towards him along the lip of the precipice.

Shabako's sympathies were with his pharaoh. However, his loyalty to the Red God was even more compelling. Though he longed with all his heart to see Nefer succeed, he dared not show him favour. That would go against his sacred oath, and place his immortal soul in peril.

He considered the fence. Along the length of it his men crouched with burning torches. The fence was twice the height of a man and made of bundles of dried grass that would burn like tinder on this hot, dry wind. The fence was built in a semi-circle with each end anchored on the edge of the cliff. It held the head of the bridge in its arms. There was no way round it. To reach the bridgehead the novices must break through it.

Reluctantly Shabako shouted the order to set the fire. The torchbearers ran down its length, dragging the flames along the bottom of the fence. They caught instantly, rising in a towering wall of awful crimson flame and dark smoke.

Nefer saw the wall of flame rise ahead of them, and though he had anticipated it, still his spirits quailed and he feared for the horses, for they had already endured so much. He watched Krus' ears and saw them switching back and forth with alarm as he smelt the smoke and watched the flames leap and tumble on the wind.

Not far behind them he heard Daimios' derisive jeers: 'Take the long road, Nefer Seti. The fire is too hot for your tender skin.'

Nefer ignored him and studied the wall of fire as they bore down on it. There was no weak place that he could see, but the nearest end had been lit first and the flames burned faster and more furiously. As he watched, a heavy bundle of the dried grass fell out of the wall and left a narrow gap through which he could make out the wavering heat-obscured outline of the bridgehead beyond.

He steered for the gap and told Meren beside him, 'Cover your head!' They wound headcloths over their heads and splashed water from the skin over themselves, drenching their head clothes and *chitons*.

'Have the blindfolds ready,' Nefer told Meren.

They were so close now that they felt the heat blazing out to meet them, and Krus broke step and began to balk at the barrier of leaping flame that confronted him.

'Mount up!' Nefer ordered, and still at the gallop they ran out along the shaft between the horses and swung up on to their backs, riding astride. Nefer stretched out along Krus' neck and spoke to him calmly. 'It's all right, my darling. You know the blindfold. You know I will not hurt you. Trust me, Krus! Trust me!' And he covered his eyes with the thick woollen cloth, and steered him with his knees at the narrow gap in the burning wall. The heat poured over them in a wave. Their wet clothing steamed and Nefer felt the skin on the back of his hands blistering. The tips of Krus' mane blackened and crisped. But both horses ran on strongly.

They struck the wall of blazing grass, and it exploded around them. Nefer felt his eyes frying in his head and he closed them tightly and urged Krus on. They burst out of the far side, trailing sparks and fire.

Nefer looked back under his arm and saw Daimios aiming his chariot at the gap they had broached in the burning wall. Daimios' horses were not blindfolded, and they saw the flames and shied off the line and began to rear and plunge, fighting to avoid the horror they saw ahead of them.

'Daimios' horses have refused!' Nefer shouted across at Meren on Dov's back. 'We have a chance now.'

They charged up to the bridgehead, reined the horses down and halted them just short.

'Keep them blindfolded!' Nefer ordered. 'Don't let them see the drop.'

The catwalk of the bridge had been built deliberately too narrow for a chariot to drive across, and it would not carry the weight. They would have to break the vehicle down and carry it across piecemeal. While Meren unbuckled the harness and hobbled the horses, Nefer seized the mallet and knocked the bronze retaining pins out of the hubs. Then he pulled off the wheels. He picked up one of them and Meren took the other. They ran to the head of the bridge.

The bridge swung gently and undulated to the impulse of the wind. It was not wide enough for the two of them to cross shoulder to shoulder. Nefer did not hesitate but ran out on to the narrow way, and Meren followed close behind him. The bridge moved under their feet like the deck of a ship at sea, but they balanced the motion and fixed their eyes on the far bank, never looked down at the terrible void beneath them and the gut of the gorge lined with jagged rock.

They reached the far side, dropped the wheels and ran back. At the burning fence, the flames were still too high and fierce to let Daimios pass, though they saw him flogging his team and screaming abuse at them.

They discarded the waterskin, the last of the arrows and every other piece of redundant equipment, and picked up the chassis of the chariot between them. They carried it out on to the bridge, where the wind caught their hair braids on the ends of the long staffs and whipped them jubilantly. Each careful step they took seemed to take a lifetime, but at last they reached the far side, dropped the chassis and ran back. Nefer picked up the shaft and balanced its weight across his shoulders. Meren carried the harness and the swords and they crossed again. Now only the horses remained to bring over.

When they started back they saw that the flames were dying, but where the fence had collapsed it had formed a thick bed of ash that still glowed with oven-like heat. Rastafa, one of the pursuers, forced his horses into it with whip and threatening shouts, but within a few paces the hide was burned from their legs and the raw red flesh showed through. They turned back despite their driver, screaming and kicking at the pain.

Nefer led Meren back at a run with the bridge swaying under them. They reached the horses. Dov and Krus stood patiently, hobbled and blindfolded. They unbuckled the knee hobbles.

'Take Dov across first,' Nefer ordered. 'She is the steady one.'

While Nefer waited on the near side, with his arm around Krus' neck, Meren led Dov out on to the catwalk of the bridge. She felt it move under her, lifted her head and snorted with alarm. Meren talked softly to her. Gingerly she took another pace and stopped again.

'Don't rush her,' Nefer called. 'Let her set her own pace.' A step at a time Dov moved out on to the high bridge. When she reached the middle she froze, and stood with all four legs splayed and trembling. Meren stroked her forehead and whispered to her and she went on. She reached the far side, stepped off the catwalk, felt the solid earth under her hoofs, whinnied and shook her head with relief.

Still blocked by the burning barrier Daimios shouted, 'They have got one of their team across. We have to stop them now. Rastafa, give me your horses. They are crippled already. I will ride them through, even if it kills them.'

Nefer glanced back and saw Daimios ride into the

glowing bed of ash. It reached as high as his mount's knees, and the maimed animal stumbled and almost fell but Daimios drove it on in a torrent of sparks and the stench of burning hair and flesh. The terribly injured creature carried him through then collapsed as soon as it reached open ground. Daimios jumped from its back, drew his sword and rushed towards Nefer.

Nefer drew his own sword, and called to Meren across the chasm, 'Come back and take Krus over. I will hold this bastard in play.' He stepped forward to meet Daimios as he charged in. He met his cut high in the natural line, and the blades jarred and scraped their full length. Daimios reversed and cut again at his head. Nefer caught the stroke, then riposted, forcing him to jump back.

Nefer had one moment to glance back and saw that Meren was already leading Krus out on to the swaying catwalk. Krus felt it move under his hoofs, tossed his head and tried to back away.

'Come away, Krus!' Nefer shouted at him sternly, and at the sound of his voice the colt steadied and stepped gingerly on to the planking.

Daimios came in again and Nefer had to concentrate everything on him. He aimed a rapid series of thrusts at Nefer's throat and chest and when Nefer blocked and parried he reversed and cut low at his ankles. Nefer jumped over the glittering circle of the blade and went for his exposed shoulder. He touched him and saw the blood spring brightly on the tanned and oiled muscles.

But Daimios seemed not to feel the shallow wound. He came on as strongly as before. They exchanged parry for thrust and block for cut, then Daimios stepped back and circled to the left, trying to move in behind him and cut him off from the bridgehead, but Nefer went at him again and forced him to give ground.

A moment's respite and Nefer saw that the flames had

died down, the grass fence burned almost entirely away. The other chasers had left their chariots and were jumping over the bed of glowing ash and running to join the fight.

'Form a ring around him, and cut him down!' Daimios shouted to them as they ran up.

Nefer glanced back and saw that Meren had led Krus far out on the catwalk. The colt was trembling and sweating at the sensation of the moving deck under his hoofs, but he could not see the terrible aching void below him.

Just then the other chasers ran up, brandishing their blades and jeering at Nefer: 'Now, we will ram your hair braid up your right royal arse.'

Nefer retreated quickly on to the head of the bridge. Now they could come at him only one at a time, and the jeers died away. They paused in a group at the head of the catwalk.

'He has nicked me,' said Daimios. 'Do you go after him, Rastafa, while I bind it up.' With his teeth he tore a strip off the hem of his tunic, and tied it over the shallow flesh wound. While he was doing this Rastafa ran out on to the bridge. He was bearded and swarthy with a dark and angry gaze, a big man but quick as a ferret. He balanced easily on the moving deck and thrust at Nefer's throat, coming on so strongly that Nefer had to fall back again.

Krus heard the clash of blades and the shouting close behind him and he reared up in protest. The bridge jumped and wobbled under him, and for a terrible moment it seemed that the colt might lose his balance and go over the side, but by some miraculous chance he came down on all four legs, and stood quivering on the wildly swinging catwalk.

It was Rastafa who stumbled and teetered on the edge. He windmilled his arms as he fought to regain his balance. Nefer took one quick step towards him and stabbed him under his lifted arm. The bronze blade slipped in between the ribs and went in deeply. Rastafa looked at him with mild surprise, and said, 'It hurts. In the name of Seth, it hurts!'

Nefer jerked the blade out and Rastafa's heart-blood fountained after it. Spouting crimson, he toppled backwards, and went spinning into the abyss, arms and legs spread like the spokes of a wheel. His voice was a wild screech, fading in volume as he fell away, and the sound was cut off abruptly as his armour clattered on the rocks in the gut of the gorge.

His comrades hesitated at the bridgehead, appalled by the horror of that death plunge, suddenly reluctant to step out on to the narrow way.

Nefer seized that moment to turn back and stroke Krus' trembling haunches, 'Steady, Krus. I am here, my darling. Walk on!' Krus calmed to his voice, and then, as the wild gyrations of the bridge eased, he took a step forward and another.

'Walk on, Krus, walk on.'

They were almost halfway across when Meren shouted a warning: 'Behind you, brother!'

Nefer whirled around just in time to meet another opponent. Nefer knew him by reputation. He was a Libyan slave, and was fighting for his freedom. Fearlessly, he ran down the narrow deck, straight at Nefer. He used the full impetus of his charge and Nefer was only just able to turn aside that first stroke. They locked blades and came chest to chest, clamping each other in a murderous embrace with their free arms. They heaved and wrestled, shifting and shoving for the advantage.

Krus heard the struggle behind him and it spurred him on. He lunged forward again, covering another few paces towards the safety of the far bank.

Nefer was face to face with his man. His teeth were black and jagged and his breath stank like rotten fish. He tried to sink those filthy fangs into Nefer's face, snapping at him like a dog, but Nefer pulled back then butted with his forehead, slamming the peak of his leather helmet into the bridge of the man's nose. He felt the bone and gristle break, and the man released his grip and reeled back. He lost his footing and grabbed the side rope of the bridge to steady himself, hanging on desperately, his back arched out over the drop. Nefer chopped off his grasping fingers, and the rope slipped from the bloody severed stubs. He went over backwards, screaming and twisting in the air. He seemed to fall for a long time before he struck the rocks far below with a meaty thump.

There were three men on the catwalk behind him, led by Daimios. He had bound up his wound, and seemed unhurt. But he had seen what had happened to his two comrades and now he was more wary. Nefer engaged him, keeping him off a full blade's length, giving him ground only as Krus moved forward slowly and hesitantly towards the far bank.

Suddenly Meren shouted triumphantly, 'We are across, Nefer.' And he heard Krus' hoofs clatter on the rock bank. 'Krus has come over.'

Nefer could not look round for Daimios' blade flashed and gleamed before his eyes, but he shouted, 'Cut down the bridge, Meren, cut away the mainstays, and let her fall.'

Daimios heard the command and jumped back with alarm. He glanced over his shoulder and saw how far he had come out on to the catwalk, how far it was back to the other bank.

Meren stood over the two thick ropes that carried the full weight of the catwalk. He hacked at one, and his first stroke cut halfway through, the strands parted with a sharp popping sound and began to unravel like mating serpents.

Pale horror washed over Daimios' sweaty face and he turned and fled, his comrades with him, back along the narrow way. Nefer whirled and ran towards where Meren stood over the ropes. He reached the end of the bridge and jumped to safety. Immediately he attacked the other mainstay, chopping at it with full overhead blows. One of the stays parted and the entire bridge shivered then tilted violently to one side. Daimios flung himself forward and dragged himself on to firm ground just as the second stay gave way, and the bridge sagged and fell into the abyss.

Daimios recovered and stood on the edge of the precipice, glaring at them across the void. Nefer sheathed his sword and gave him a taunting wave. 'You have a long ride ahead of you.'

Then he ran to help Meren reassemble the chariot. They had practised this a dozen times under Taita's watchful eye. While Meren lifted one side of the chassis Nefer eased the wheels on to the hubs and drove the bronze locking pins home with the mallet. Then they lifted the shaft and fastened it to the ringbolt in the footplate.

Nefer wasted a few seconds to look back across the gorge. He saw that Daimios and the surviving chasers were already mounting their chariots, and through the last wisps of smoke from the smouldering grass fence, he saw them speed away in a line ahead, following the track along the edge of the gorge that would lead them eventually to where the cliffs flattened out, so that they would be able to bring their vehicles and horses across, and renew the pursuit.

'We have won enough time.' Meren tried to sound confident, but the effort of bringing the nervous horses across the bridge had taxed him severely, and he pressed a hand to his injured side.

Nefer feared for him. 'Perhaps, but that will depend on the Red God,' he said and touched the Periapt of Lostris at his throat.

They buckled the horses into the harness and hitched them to the long shaft. Then they scrambled up on to the footplate and started them along the line of marker flags. They could push the horses to the utmost on this stretch, for at the end of it waited Khama of Taurine and Drossa of Indus. The horses might have a long rest indeed while their drivers went into the ring with the two most notorious swordsmen in Aartla's troupe.

Nefer forced the pace, and the marker flags sped by in quick, regular succession. They crested the final rise and saw ahead of them, at the far end of the long, narrow valley, the city of Gallala with her gates standing wide open to welcome them.

But at the head of the valley, between them and the city, gathered in a shallow basin of hills, was a large crowd of many hundreds of persons. It seemed that every last citizen had come out from the city to watch the trial by swords.

They rode down fast, and heard the din of the crowd rise like the sound of storm surf to greet them.

There was a lane through the crowds demarcated by wooden railings that led them to the two rings of white stones in the centre. As they jumped down and the grooms ran forward to hold the horses, Nefer embraced Meren.

'You are sore hurt, brother,' he whispered to him. 'There is no shame in that, for it was a wound received with honour, but it will hamper you. You must not try to confront Drossa, and trade him blow for blow. He is fast and strong, and he wears full armour. Run from him and keep running until I can come to your aid.'

They parted then, each to the ring allotted to them by the umpires and Nefer halted at the line of white-painted stones, and looked at the warrior in the centre.

Khama of Taurine wore full armour, helm, breastplate and greaves. If Nefer and Meren had wanted the same protection they would have had to carry it in the chariot from the start, but the weight of the two suits would have drained even Krus' strength.

From the edge of the ring of stones Nefer studied his man. Khama's helmet was a hideous mask with spread wings above the ears, and the nosepiece was an eagle's beak. The eyes that glittered behind the sockets were inhuman and implacable. His chest was protected by a bronze cuirass. His gauntlets were covered with golden fish scales. He carried a small circular shield on his left shoulder.

'Throat, wrist, armpit, ankles and eyes,' Taita had instructed Nefer. 'All else is covered.'

Nefer lifted the Periapt of Lostris over his head and wound the long golden chain around his left wrist. Then he held the tiny golden figure to his lips and kissed it. He stepped over the white stones and went forward to meet Khama of Taurine.

They circled once to the right, then back, and suddenly Khama burst upon him with a blazing series of thrusts and cuts that were so rapid as almost to cheat the eye. Carrying that weight of armour, Nefer had not expected him to be so fast. He had to exert all of his skill and strength to hold him off, and still he received a cut through his leather body armour that scored his ribs. He felt the hot blood trickle down his flank as they disengaged and circled again.

The crowd was shouting and roaring like a storm sea all around them, but in the sudden quiet as they disengaged he heard a cry of pain from the other ring and he recognized Meren's voice. Meren had taken a hit, and by the sound of it a grievous one. He needed Nefer's help, probably his life depended upon it. But Nefer's own life was in terrible jeopardy, for he had never faced an opponent such as this Khama before.

Even Taita had not been able to divine any weakness in him, but as they came together again in the whirl and clangour of metal on metal, Nefer noticed a tiny flaw. When Khama made a low underhand cut, he opened his right side for an instant and thrust his head forward, an awkward gesture out of keeping with his otherwise fluid and graceful style.

Nefer knew that he could not hold out much longer. Khama was simply too skilful and powerful for him.

'Everything on one throw of the dice.' He took the

gamble, and offered his right hip unguarded and like a striking adder Khama went for it with the low cut, his front opened and his head thrust forward. Prepared for it, Nefer swayed his hip out of the shot and the blade slit the hem of his *chiton* without drawing blood.

The golden Periapt of Lostris twinkled as he spun it on the end of its chain then Nefer whipped it in like a slingshot, using the chain to speed the throw so it became a darting beam of light. It flashed into the eye socket of Khama's helmet and the sharp metal edge sliced deeply through his eyeball.

Khama reeled back with a mixture of eye jelly and blood pouring down his golden mask. He was blinded and disorientated with pain, trying to wrench off his helmet to reach his burst eyeball. As the rim of his helmet lifted and exposed his throat, Nefer drove his point in a thumb's width above the lump of his Adam's apple. The point angled up into the back of his brain, and Khama flung his arms wide and went down, dead before his armour clanged on the sun-baked earth.

Nefer placed his cleated sandal on his throat and had to wrench with all his strength to draw the point of his sword free from where it was trapped between the metal of the helmet and the bone of his skull.

Nefer left the corpse lying, and wrapping the chain of the amulet around his wrist again, ran from the ring. He tried to reach the other ring where he knew Meren was in mortal danger, but the crowds impeded him. He swung his sword to clear the way and the spectators fled screaming ahead of him. He broke through the press and saw that in the second ring Meren had lost his weapon and was bleeding profusely from a terrible gash in his right side, and a cut that had half severed his ear. It dangled down his cheek on a thread of flesh. Somehow he was managing to stay out of Drossa's reach, backing frantically away from him.

Drossa was laughing, bellowing like a bull with the joy of killing, the sound echoing eerily within the confines of his crested war-helmet. He was goading Meren into a position for the killing stroke, taking his time, enjoying it.

Drossa's back was turned to Nefer. Nefer sprang at him and aimed a thrust through the lacing of his cuirass. With the instincts of a wild animal, Drossa sensed the danger and spun to face him, Nefer's thrust struck the metal breastplate and glanced aside and Drossa aimed a full-blooded cut at his head. Nefer ducked and recoiled, and they circled each other.

Meren saw his chance and stooped to pick up the sword he had dropped, but Drossa leaped at him. Meren was so weak that he stumbled backwards and fell. Drossa kicked the fallen sword out of the ring and placed his foot between Meren's shoulders and pinned him down.

'Behold, mighty Pharaoh, feared by all the world, I have your bum-boy in my power.' He feigned the stroke of a headsman, but stopped his blade against the back of Meren's neck. 'Shall I give you his head? A gift fit for a king.'

Nefer felt red blind anger sweep over him, and he rushed at Drossa to drive him off Meren's prostrate form. He felt the sting of the blade across his thigh, which sobered him. He jumped back, and saw by Drossa's eyes in the helmet slits that he was toying with him, drawing the last drop of sadistic pleasure from the encounter. Drossa was an entertainer, and the crowd were loving his performance. They howled their approval.

Suddenly Meren reached up and grasped Drossa's ankle with both bloody hands, and tried to trip him. Drossa stumbled, swore and kicked his foot free, but for an instant he was off-balance and Nefer seized the opportunity and rushed in. He aimed for the throat, into the gap between the chinpiece of the helmet and the top of the breastplate. Drossa twisted away and the point of Nefer's sword rang on metal.

Nefer had missed his chance for a kill, but he had driven Drossa off his victim, and Meren scrambled to his feet and staggered behind Nefer, using him as a protective shield.

They circled again, and Nefer felt the first cold draught of despair lift the hairs on his forearms. He knew he could not expect a man like Drossa to give him another chance. In despair he tried again with the Periapt, swinging it on the length of gold chain and aiming for the eye slits in Drossa's helmet. Drossa dropped his chin and the golden charm glanced off the brow of his helm. If it had not been upon the chain Nefer would have lost it, but he recovered it and let the chain wind itself around his left wrist again.

'That is no weapon but a child's toy.' Drossa laughed scornfully.

They circled and feinted, Drossa moving easily, but Nefer was hampered by his need to guard Meren. He could not launch an attack, and leave Meren unprotected.

Drossa was working the two of them like a sheepdog with a flock of lambs, pushing them back against the line of white stones. He wanted to make a spectacular kill to please the crowd, and enhance his own reputation.

'The chasers!' someone in the crowd yelled, and every head swung and lifted to the crest of the rise at the head of the long valley.

Daimios' chariot raced over the skyline. Desperate to make up for his humiliation at the bridgehead, he was riding hard and outstripped the rest of his troop. He came tearing down towards them at the top of his speed.

'You belong to me, mighty Egypt!' Drossa mocked Nefer. 'I will not let an upstart like Daimios take your hair braid from me.'

He moved in menacingly, and Nefer could see the icy determination in the pale eyes that watched him through the helmet slits.

Nefer whispered to Meren, 'If I fall, save yourself. Step out of the ring.'

'No, Pharaoh, I will ride with you as your lance-bearer on the road to paradise,' Meren said softly, and his strength failed him. His legs gave way under him, and bleeding he sagged to earth. Drossa seized the moment, and came down upon Nefer like an avalanche. His sword clanged and rang on Nefer's desperate guard like a coppersmith's hammer on the anvil.

Each blow jarred and numbed Nefer's right arm to the shoulder, and he knew he could not last out much longer. Still he watched Drossa's eyes to read each blow, and saw them narrow and gleam as he gathered himself for the killing stroke.

It came from on high, like a thunderbolt from the sky and all Nefer could do was lift his own blade above his head to meet it. He knew he could not turn or stop it with one hand, it was too powerful. So he braced his sword hand, gripping the right wrist with his left hand, the hand that held the golden Periapt.

The two swords came together with force that bronze could not resist. Both blades snapped cleanly and spun away, glittering out of the circle of white stones.

At a stroke they were both disarmed, and for an instant they stared at each other in astonishment. Nefer recovered first and hurled the hilt of the sword at Drossa's head. Instinctively Drossa blinked and ducked. Nefer charged him and they came chest to chest.

Like a pair of temple dancers they whirled together, first one way then back again, trying to throw each other. Irresistibly Drossa worked his arms under Nefer's armpits and locked his armoured fists between his shoulder-blades. With wristlets of silver and gauntlets of gold he started to grind Nefer against his bronze cuirass. Nefer had no response as he was lifted off his feet. He had no weapon to defend himself, except the Periapt of Lostris.

With the last of his strength he managed to throw a loop of the gold chain over Drossa's helmet. He took a turn around each of his own wrists and pulled the chain downwards until suddenly it found the gap below the rim of the helmet and closed around Drossa's neck. Nefer strained and sawed the ends of the chain, and felt the golden links biting deeply in living flesh.

Drossa gasped, released his grip and reached up with both hands to try to break free. He seized Nefer's wrists and tried to pull them away from his throat, but this increased the cutting power of the links. Staring into the slits of the helmet, Nefer saw Drossa's eyes start from their sockets and swell with blood. He took another turn around his right wrist and sawed the chain back and forth. Drossa made a gargling sound and a vein popped in one of his eyes. It bulged crimson as a ripe berry from the socket, and still clutching Nefer's wrists Drossa sank to his knees. Nefer stood over him and rolled his wrists, tightening the chain until suddenly he felt it cut through something gristly and Drossa's breath burst explosively from his severed windpipe. Nefer took another wrap of the chain and pulled again, feeling it cut its way down to bone. Blood erupted in thick gouts from under the rim of the helmet, and Nefer gathered himself and exerted all his remaining strength. The chain found the joint between two vertebrae in Drossa's neck and cut through. Drossa's head sprang from his shoulders and, still clad in the heavy helmet, rolled across the ring.

As Nefer staggered backwards he heard the umpire shout, 'You are free and clear,' and he slipped the bloody golden chain back over his head. As he did so he looked over the heads of the maddened crowd, back up the slope of the hill. Daimios' chariot was already halfway down, and coming straight towards him at full gallop.

Nefer stooped over Meren. 'Can you stand?' he asked, but when Meren made the effort his legs collapsed under him and he sprawled on the trampled earth. Nefer pulled him up by one arm then swung the arm over the back of his neck. Taking the weight across his shoulders, he raised

Meren to his feet, grabbed him behind the knees and lifted his inert body off the ground, his head dangling down his back and his legs down his front.

Meren was a heavy man, and Nefer was almost exhausted, near the limit of his strength. He staggered with him to the waiting chariot and dropped him in a heap on the floorboards. For a moment he leaned panting against the near wheel, and looked back.

Daimios had reached the level ground at the bottom of the slope, and was less than four hundred paces away, coming on swiftly, so close that Nefer could see the triumphant expression on his face. Daimios leaned forward and cracked the long black lash over the backs of his team and the horses seemed to spring forward, coming on even faster. The chariots of the other chasers were following him down the slope, six of them all told. If he had any thought of standing to fight them, Nefer put it out of his mind at once. In his present state he could not even take on Daimios in a straight fight. He had to run.

Nefer took two turns of the grab rope around Meren's body, worked them up under his armpits and clinched the knot, strapping him to the floorboards. Then he dragged himself up on to the footplate and stood straddling Meren's body.

'Turn them loose!' he called to the grooms, who held the horses' heads, and they released them and jumped out of the way.

'Come away, Dov! Come away, Krus!' he called to them, and snapped the reins along their gleaming backs. They sprang forward together and the crowds scattered ahead of them. He pointed their heads down the valley towards the open gates of the city, and let them run.

Between his feet Meren groaned involuntarily as the chariot jolted and lurched, and Nefer tried to steer to miss the patches of rough ground. Behind him he heard the crack of the lash, he glanced back and saw Daimios bearing down on them. He was flogging on his team and shouting at them angrily, but Dov and Krus were holding them off despite Daimios' cruel work with the whip. Nefer looked ahead and judged the distance they still had to run.

It was less than half a league to the gates of Gallala. Already he could make out the wreaths of palm fronds that adorned the walls and decorated the red stone columns of the entrance.

At that moment he paid the price for his inattention. His off-wheel hit an outcrop of rock at the edge of the track, and the vehicle bounced high and slewed wildly under him. It almost capsized, but as he fought for control Krus leaned into the traces and helped him to pull it straight.

Now when Nefer looked back he saw that the mistake had cost them dear, for Daimios had gained a hundred paces on them. He was within javelin range, and Nefer saw him reach for the missiles in the bin at his side and wind the thong on to his wrist.

Nefer had no reply to him. He had used all his darts at the first stage. He had dropped his bow at the chasm, and his last sword had snapped in the bout with Drossa. He did not even have his whip. His only defence was speed.

He called to his horses, 'Come, Dov! Come away, Krus!' And their ears flicked back as they heard him call their names and their hoofs drummed on the hard earth and the wheel hubs squealed, for even Taita's black oil was running dry.

Then there was the sound of other hoofs, blending with those of Nefer's team, and this time when he looked back Daimios was closer still, his horses whipped and galled until their flanks and backs were bloody. Daimios had a javelin poised and now he hurled it. Nefer watched the dart leave his hand, and fly in like a poisonous insect. He flinched instinctively, as it slammed into the floorboards beside his right foot. It stood out quivering.

'Come away, my darlings.' His voice took on a strident note, and the horses heard it. 'Give me all you've got!' Krus found a little more in his great heart, and swept Dov along with him. They began to pull away from Daimios' scourged and bleeding pair.

'Pull, you swine!' Daimios screamed. 'Pull, or I'll take the hide off your backs.' And as his long lash sang, they raced together as though an invisible rope linked the two vehicles.

Daimios seized another javelin and wrapped the thong. As he swung his arm back for the throw, Nefer judged his moment skilfully and flicked the reins. With the javelin in the air, Dov leaned into Krus' shoulder and they swerved slightly, just enough for the dart to fly past Nefer's shoulder. But the turn had cost ground, and Daimios snatched his last javelin from the bin and wrapped the thong around his wrist. He was close now, very close.

Nefer watched him with a feeling of desperation, gathering his team with a firm rein so they could anticipate his command. The moment Daimios swivelled his right shoulder forward in the throw, Nefer turned his team back the other way, jinking their run at full gallop. But the javelin did not leave Daimios' hand: he had feinted. He raised the javelin again into the ready position, levelled and ready to throw.

Nefer was forced to swing back or leave the track and tear into the rough ground and scattered boulders. He changed the angle and this time Daimios aimed not at Nefer but at Dov, whose flank had been exposed by the turn.

The dart took her high in the shoulder. It cut through hide and bunched muscle, but then struck the bone and did not penetrate to her vitals. It was not a mortal blow, but a crippling one, for the javelin head was barbed and it dangled down her flank, hampering each stride she took.

She tried, she tried with all her heart, but she could no

longer keep pace with Krus, and the blood ran back along her flank and splattered on Nefer's legs. He could feel the chariot slowing under him, and though he called to Dov, the javelin slapped against her flank with each stride she took, and tangled in her forelegs.

Daimios sped forward and from the corner of his eye Nefer saw the heads of his racing horses draw level with his near wheel, and Daimios' voice hoarse with effort and triumph sounded almost in his ear.

'It is over, Nefer Seti. I have you now.'

Nefer turned his head and looked across at him. Daimios' lips were drawn back in a horrible rictus, like that of a corpse who had died of the lock-jaw. He had thrown his last javelin, and had discarded his whip, but he had drawn his sword.

How far to run to the gates? Nefer thought. Less than five hundred paces. So close, so very close! But still too far.

Instinctively he looked to the roof of the temple. It was lined with tiny human figures, and among them, just where he expected to see it, he picked out the scarlet of Mintaka's tunic, and saw that she was waving a green branch over her head, her long dark hair tossing like a pennant on the north wind.

A prize beyond all others, he thought, and his hand fell upon Daimios' javelin that was pegged into the floorboard beside his foot. The head was buried deeply into the woodwork, but he braced himself. Twisting and jerking, he pulled it free.

He did not have a throwing thong, but he held it like a spear, and looked across at his adversary. Daimios' eyes narrowed as he saw the weapon in Nefer's hand and he took the guard position with the sword. He drew up inexorably alongside Nefer and lunged. Nefer turned the blow with the stock of the javelin. The two vehicles swerved apart then came back together and struck so hard that Nefer was almost thrown over the side and had to clutch wildly at the reins to steady himself.

Daimios swung a cut at the long staff on which flew Nefer's hair braid, but did not sever the hard bamboo. Nefer recovered his balance and thrust at Daimios with the javelin, driving him off. Now the two vehicles were running wheel to wheel, and hub to hub.

Nefer and Daimios were leaning across, hacking and stabbing at each other. The bronze blade slashed across Nefer's chest, and though he threw himself back against the reins it cut through the leather of his breastplate and he felt the sting of the razor edge. But he thrust the point of the javelin at Daimios' face, and forced him to swerve away.

Dov was labouring hard, the barbs of the javelin still fixed in her skin, and the shaft banging her legs at each stride.

Nefer heard the sound of many voices, soft at first and almost drowned in the drumming of hoofs and the squeal and rumble of the wheels, but the sound was growing louder at each stride. He looked up and through the running sweat that stung his eyes saw the gates directly ahead. The city walls and the rooftops were lined with the crowds. Through the hubbub of their cheering, he thought he heard the sound of Mintaka's voice. 'For me, my heart, do this for me!' It may have been but a figment of his own exhaustion, but it steeled him, and he called to the horses and gathered them with the reins. But Dov was staggering and failing.

Daimios came in again, and this time when Nefer thrust at him, he swung a full blow not at the man but at the javelin. His blade sheared through the shaft inches from Nefer's fist, leaving him with a useless stump. Nefer hurled it at Daimios' head but he ducked under it, and struck at Nefer again, forcing him to dodge to the far side of the footplate to avoid the bright blade.

Daimios took instant advantage, and forced his way

ahead of Nefer. As he came past he reached across and seized the rod on which Nefer's hair braid danced and whipped in the wind. He tried to snap it off, but although it bent almost double it resisted his efforts. Still holding the staff in one hand Daimios reached up with the other hand for the thick dark hank of hair. It flicked and danced at his fingertips, but he was trying to keep a grip on the hilt of his sword at the same time, and he could not quite get a hold of the trophy. He dropped his sword, and this time caught hold of the braid and tried to tear it free, but the bamboo was resilient and tough, and the braid securely tied.

Krus and Daimios' off-side horse were galloping shoulder to shoulder. Daimios was completely absorbed with trying to wrest his trophy from the bamboo staff. He knew that Nefer was disarmed and no real danger, and he ignored the stone gates that loomed up ahead of them.

'Lean in!' Nefer shouted at Krus. 'Give him your shoulder!' Nefer sawed the reins. This was what they had trained for, all those months in the desert. With Taita driving the other team, Nefer had taught Krus to love this contest of strength, and now he bore in with his great right shoulder, tucking it in just behind the other horse, lifting him off-balance. The locked chariots veered to the right, and the gateway was coming up fast. The portals were columns of hewn red stone, and though the grit-laden winds of the centuries had polished and shaped them they were still massive and forbidding.

'Ride him off!' Nefer shouted to Krus, and encouraged him with a strong hand on the reins. Krus forced the other horse another yard over until he was headed straight for the solid red stone wall.

At the very last instant Daimios became aware of what was happening and, with a wild cry of alarm, he let go of the bamboo rod and tried to recover control of his racing chariot, but Krus dominated the other horse and drove him headlong towards the stone gateway.

Daimios realized that he could not stop the flying chariot and avoid the collision. He tried to jump from the hurtling cockpit, but he was too late. Both his horses ran full tilt into the stone column. It killed them instantly. Nefer heard their last terrified screams as they went in, the crash of the impact, the crackle of their breaking bones and the shattering and rending of timbers. One wheel was torn clean off and for a moment bounced along beside Nefer's vehicle. Daimios was hurled like one of his own javelins straight into the wall. He struck head first and his skull burst as though it were an overripe melon. His strong white teeth were embedded in the surface of the red stone, souvenirs to be prised out later by urchins, threaded on chains of gold and sold in the market-place.

Nefer steered Krus and Dov into the gateway, and though the hub of their near wheel scraped the red stone they tore through into the central avenue of the city, which was lined on both sides by the joyous crowds. They had strewn the paving with palm fronds and flowers and even with shawls and headcloths and other pieces of their own apparel.

Nefer's first concern was for Dov. He halted the horses, jumped down and ran to the wounded filly. The barbs of the javelin were buried deeply in her shoulder. He trusted only Taita to remove them, but he snapped off the shaft, so that it no longer dangled down her side. Then he climbed back to the footplate and took the reins again.

The crowds swarmed into the avenue and ran along beside the chariot as it moved on at a walking pace. They reached up to touch Nefer, using their headcloths to wipe up the blood that dribbled down his legs from his wounds. The blood of a god, a pharaoh and a Red Road warrior would transform the cloth into a sacred relic. Hysterically they screamed their praises.

'Pray for us, mighty Egypt. Pharaoh indeed!'

'Lead us, great Pharaoh. Let us share your glory.'

'Hail, divine brother of the Red God!'

'May you live a thousand and a thousand years, Nefer Seti, true Pharaoh!'

At the entrance to the forum the crowd was so dense that the city guards had to run ahead of the chariot and club them out of the way before Nefer could drive through into the forum.

In the centre of the forum on the raised stone dais Hilto and Shabako stood to welcome their new brother warriors.

Nefer halted the battered, dusty and blood-splattered chariot below the platform, and the two men came down and helped him lift Meren. Between them they carried him into the temple of Hathor where Taita waited to care for him. They laid Meren on the trestle Taita had prepared, and the old Magus began work on him immediately, first at tending to the deep sword thrust in his side. Merykara's tears fell upon Meren's broken and bleeding body, and anointed his wounds.

The warriors of the Red Road led Nefer back into the forum. Then Nefer went down the steps, lifted the two hair braids from the chariot, and carried them to the brazier that burned on its tripod in the centre of the raised stone dais. He knelt before the brazier, and declared, 'No enemy has laid hands upon these trophies of our honour and valour.' He held them high for all the world to witness, and then he spoke clear and proud: 'I dedicate them to the Red God.'

He flung the hair braids on to the fire. They burned up brightly. Nefer rose to his feet and, weakened by his wounds, swayed as he stood before them. 'I have run the Red Road! Though I lack the years, I have confirmed my right to the double crown of Egypt. I declare myself Pharaoh. The one true Pharaoh. Let any other pretend to the crown at his peril.'

They cheered him then while the warriors of the Red Road knelt before him, kissed his right hand and foot, and swore their allegiance unto death and beyond.

Nefer raised his right arm for silence, but his legs gave way under him and he might have fallen had not Mintaka rushed forward and steadied him. With one arm around her shoulders he looked into her eyes, and whispered, 'What I have done was for this very Egypt and for you, my love.'

His voice was so husky and low that only she heard him. She reached up and kissed him full on the lips, and the populace recognized this gesture as an open declaration of betrothal. They shouted until the echoes startled flocks of rock-pigeons from the cliffs beyond the walls.

Floating on the waters of the two great rivers, the city lay before them like a lotus flower, ready for plucking. Its walls were of burned brick. They were twenty-seven cubits thick and taller than the tallest palm trees of this fertile and well-watered land.

'What is their span?' Trok asked Ishtar the Mede. 'How far is it to ride around this city?'

'Ten leagues, Majesty,' Ishtar told him. 'Half a day's ride.'

Trok stood taller on the footplate of his chariot and shaded his eyes. 'Is that the Blue Gate of legend?' he demanded. He knew that Ishtar had lived in this royal city of Babylon for fifteen years, and had learned much of his magic here in the temple of Marduk.

Even at this distance the gateway glimmered like an enormous gemstone. The threshold was so wide that ten chariots could enter driving abreast, and the carved cedarwood gates were higher than ten men standing on each other's shoulders.

'It is truly blue in colour,' Trok marvelled. 'I have heard that it is covered with lapis lazuli.'

'Not so, Majesty.' Ishtar's face twisted in a condescending grimace. 'They are ceramic tiles. Each tile depicts one of the two thousand and ten gods of Babylon.'

Trok cast a general's eye along the miles of wall on each side of the Blue Gate. There were watchtowers at every two hundred paces, and at regular intervals the massive walls were heavily buttressed. Ishtar knew what he was thinking.

'There is a road along the top of the wall, wide enough for two chariots to ride abreast. Within an hour Sargon can move five thousand men along it to any point that is threatened by a besieging army.'

Trok grunted, to show that he was unimpressed. 'Still and all, any wall can be undermined and sapped. We need only one breach.'

'There is an inner wall, divine Pharaoh,' Ishtar murmured in a silky tone. 'It is almost as impregnable as the first.'

'If we cannot go through, we will find a way round.' Trok shrugged. 'Are those the gardens of Sargon's palace?' He jutted out his beribboned beard to indicate the terraces that rose in mighty tiers into the sky. They were so skilfully raised upon each other, a soaring inverted pyramid, that they seemed to float like a mighty eagle with spread wings, free of the bounds of earth.

Ishtar pointed with one sinewy, blue-tattooed arm. 'There are six terraces built around a vast courtyard, each wider than the one before. The *zenana* alone has five thousand rooms, one for each of Sargon's wives. His treasury is buried in a deep dungeon below the palace. It is packed with gold to the height of a man's head.'

'Have you seen these wonders with your own eyes?' Trok challenged him.

'Not the *zenana*,' Ishtar admitted, 'but I have entered the main vault of the treasury, and I tell you straight, King-who-is-a-god, that in all your army you do not have sufficient wagons to carry away such a treasure as lies before you.'

'And I tell you straight, Ishtar the Mede, that I can always build new wagons.' And Trok threw back his head and laughed with animal high spirits.

The march to Babylon had been one long triumph, an unbroken string of victories. They had met Ran, Sargon's eldest son, on the banks of the Bahr al Milh: between the chariots of Trok and Naja they had ground his army like *dhurra*, and swept the chaff into the lake until the waters ran red with blood, and the bloated corpses floated from one bank to the other.

They had sent Ran's severed head to his father, skewered on a spear. Maddened with grief, Sargon had charged into the trap they had prepared for him. While Naja retreated before him to lure him on, Trok had circled out to the south then come at him from the rear with a thousand chariots. When Sargon turned back to defend his baggage train, they had him in a glittering ring of bronze.

Sargon had managed to break out with fifty chariots but he had left two thousand chariots and eleven thousand men behind him. Trok emasculated the prisoners, an undertaking that took two days to accomplish. But he joined in the work in person, bloody to the elbows like a butcher, and with a ribald jest to each of his victims as he dangled their severed genitalia in front of their eyes. Afterwards he allowed his victims to bleed to death, their blood an offering to Seueth, the hungry god who loved such fare. Trok sent the severed trophies to Sargon, packed in salt, in a hundred cedarwood chests. A subtle warning as to what he might expect when Trok and Naja came to Babylon.

Babylon was built upon the narrow spit of land between the two rivers, the Euphrates to the west and the Tigris to the east. In his headlong retreat Sargon had not been able to destroy the bridges. In any case, it would have taken an army to tear down those massive piers of burned brick on which they were built. Sargon no longer had an army. He had left one depleted regiment of foot to defend the bridges, but they were demoralized and without chariots to support them. They had not lasted long against the two pharaohs.

Trok had bound the survivors hand and foot and dropped them from the central span of the bridge into the broad brown river, and the Egyptian troops had lined the parapet to delight in their antics as they drowned.

Now Babylon lay before them, little more than a year since they had marched from Avaris.

'You know the defences, Ishtar. You helped design some of them. How long before the city falls?' Trok demanded impatiently. 'How long will it take me to breach the walls?'

'The walls are impregnable, Majesty,' said Ishtar.

'We both know that is not true,' Trok told him. 'Given enough time, men and determination, there is no wall built that cannot be breached.'

'A year,' Ishtar murmured thoughtfully. 'Or two, maybe three.' But there was a sly look on his tattooed face, and his eyes were shifty.

Trok laughed and playfully seized a handful of Ishtar's lacquered spiky beard. He twisted it until his blue whorled face contorted with pain and his eyes watered. 'You want to play games with me, wizard. You know how I love a good game, don't you?'

'Mercy, mighty Egypt,' Ishtar whimpered. Trok pushed him away so hard that he almost fell from the footplate of the chariot and had to clutch at the side of the dashboard to steady himself.

'A year, you say? Two? Three? I have not that amount of time to sit here and look upon the beauties and wonders of Babylon. I am in a hurry, Ishtar the Mede, and you know what that means, don't you?'

'I know, god without peer. And I am but a man, fallible and poor.'

'Poor?' Trok shouted in his face. 'By Seueth, you slimy charlatan, you have milked me of a lakh of gold already, and what do I have to show for it?'

'You have a city and an empire. After Egypt itself, the richest in the world. I have laid it at your feet.' He knew Trok well by now, knew just how far he could go.

'I need the key to that city.' Trok watched his face, happy with what he saw there. He knew Ishtar almost as well as the magician knew him.

'It would have to be a key made of gold,' Ishtar mused. 'Perhaps three lakhs of gold?'

Trok let out a great burst of laughter and aimed a blow at his head with a mailed fist. It was not intended to do damage, and Ishtar ducked under it easily.

'With three lakhs I could buy another army.' Trok shook his head and the ribbons in his beard danced like a cloud of butterflies.

'Yonder, in the treasury of Sargon, lie a hundred lakhs. Three from a hundred is a small price to pay.'

'Give me the city, Ishtar. Give it to me within three full moons and you shall have two lakhs of gold from the treasure of Sargon,' he promised.

'If I give it to you before the next full moon?' Ishtar scrubbed his hands together like a carpet trader.

Trok's grin slid from his face at the prospect, and he said seriously, 'Then you shall have your three lakhs, and a convoy of wagons to carry them away.'

The army of the two pharaohs went into camp before the Blue Gate, and Trok sent an emissary to Sargon to demand the immediate surrender of the city – 'to save such a prodigy of architecture from the flames, and your person and family and populace from the sword', as Trok humorously phrased his demand. In reply Sargon, sanguine and defiant behind his walls, sent the messenger's decapitated head back to Trok. The preliminaries having been dealt with, Trok and Naja made a circuit of the walls to allow the Babylonians to view their full might and splendour.

They drove the golden chariots, Trok's drawn by six black stallions, Naja's by six white. Heseret rode beside Naja, glittering with jewels and wearing the golden *uraeus* on her high-piled curls. Behind the golden chariots marched fifty prisoners, Babylonian women captured from the outlying towns and villages between the two rivers. All were pregnant, some very near their time.

They were preceded by a vanguard of five hundred chariots and followed by a rearguard of another five hundred. The slow, stately circuit of the city took all that day, and at sunset they came back to the Blue Gate. Sargon and his war council were gathered on the parapets above the shining gateway.

Sargon was tall and thin, with a shock of silver hair. In his youth he had been a mighty warrior and had conquered the lands as far north as the Black Sea to add to his domains. He had suffered defeat only once in all his campaigns and that had been at the hands of Pharaoh Tamose, the father of Nefer Seti. Now another pair of Egyptians stood at his gates, and he did not delude himself into believing that these would be as merciful as the first.

To confirm him in this belief, Trok had the pregnant

women stripped naked and marched forward one at a time. Then, while all the city watched their swollen bellies were slit open, the unborn infants ripped out and the tiny bodies piled on the threshold of the Blue Gate.

'Add these to your army, Sargon,' Trok bellowed up at him. 'You will need every man you can get.'

It had been a long and exciting day for Heseret, and she retired to her tent with all her slave girls, leaving her husband and Trok to pore over a map of the city by lamplight. It was a work of art, drawn on a finely tanned sheepskin, the walls, roads and canals drawn to scale, each of the main buildings depicted in coloured detail.

'How came this into your possession?' Naja demanded.

'Twelve years ago, by the command of King Sargon, I surveyed the city and drew this map with my own hands,' Ishtar replied. 'No other could have achieved such accuracy and beauty.'

'If he commissioned it, why did you not deliver it to Sargon?'

'I did.' Ishtar nodded. 'I delivered the inferior draft to him, while secretly I kept the fair copy you see before you. I knew that one day someone would pay me more handsomely than Sargon ever did.'

For another hour they studied the map, muttering a comment now and then, but for the most part silent and absorbed. As fighting generals with a professional eye for the salient features of a battlefield, they were able to admire the depth and strength of the walls, towers and redoubts that had been built up layer upon layer over the centuries.

At last Trok stood back from the table. 'There is no weakness that I can divine, magician. You were right the first time. It will take three years of hard work to break through those walls. You will have to do better than this to earn your three lakhs.'

'The water,' whispered Ishtar. 'Look to the water.'

'I have looked to the water.' Naja smiled at him, but it

was a serpent's smile, cold and thin-lipped. 'There are canals supplying every quarter of the city, enough water to grow Sargon's six terraces of gardens that reach up into the sky, and to water and feed the city for a hundred years.'

'Pharaoh is all-seeing, all-wise.' Ishtar bowed to him, 'but where does the water come from?'

'From two mighty rivers. After the Nile itself, the mightiest rivers in the world. A supply of water that has not failed in this millennium.'

'But where does the water enter the city? How does it pass through, under or over those walls?' Ishtar insisted, and Naja and Trok exchanged a look of dawning comprehension.

Half a mile north of Babylon, outside the city walls, on the east bank of the Euphrates, at a point where the flood broadened and ran sluggishly, stood the temple of Ninurta, the lion-headed winged god of the Euphrates. It was built on stone piers that extended out into the river. The multiple images of the god were engraved on a frieze that ran around all four outer walls. In the Akkadian language, chiselled into the stone lintel over the entrance, was a warning to all who sought to invade the sanctuary, calling down the wrath of the god upon them.

Ishtar the Mede worked a charm on the threshold to nullify the curse, slitting the throats of two captives and splashing their blood on the portals. Once the way was cleared Trok, with twenty troopers at his back, strode through into the temple courtyard where all the purple-robed priests of Ninurta were gathered. They were chanting and gesticulating, waving their arms towards the intruder, splashing water from the Euphrates in his path, invoking Ninurta to build up an invisible wall of magical power to turn Trok back.

Trok strode through the wall without a check and killed the high priest with a single thrust through the old man's throat. Wailing at such sacrilege, the other priests prostrated themselves before him.

Trok sheathed his sword and nodded to the captain, who commanded the guard. 'Kill them all. Make certain no one escapes.'

The work was done swiftly, and when the courtyard was littered with purple-clad bodies Trok commanded, 'Do not throw them into the river. We do not want the city guards to see them float past and guess what we are about.'

Then he turned to watch Ishtar who, once all the priests had been disposed of, had entered the courtyard to work another charm to counteract the baleful influence of the god they had invoked. At the four corners he burned bundles of herbs, which emitted a thick, greasy smoke that was repugnant to Ninurta and, as Trok remarked jovially, to all gods and lesser mortals equally. Once Ishtar had completed the purification, he led the way into the holy places of the temple, and Trok and his troopers followed him, with blood-caked blades bared.

Their cleated sandals rang hollowly in the gloomy recesses of the high, cavernous hall, and even Trok felt a religious chill as they approached the image of the god on his plinth. The lion's head snarled silently and the wings of stone were spread wide. Ishtar declaimed another lengthy prayer to the god to placate him, then led Trok into the narrow space between the rear wall and the idol's back. Here he pointed out a heavily grilled gate built into the body of Ninurta. Trok seized the bars of the grille, and shook them with all his bear-like strength. They did not move.

'There is an easier way, all-wise Pharaoh,' Ishtar suggested sweetly. 'The key will be on the body of the high priest.'

'Fetch it!' Trok snapped at the captain of his guard, who

ran. When he returned there was blood on his hands, but he carried a bunch of heavy keys, some of them as long as his forearm. Trok tried two in the lock on the grille, and the second turned the ancient mechanism. The gate swung open on creaking hinges.

Trok peered down a descending spiral staircase into darkness. The air coming up the deep shaft was cold and dank, and he heard the sound of running water far below.

'Bring torches!' he ordered, and the captain sent four of his troopers to take down the burning torches from their brackets. With a torch held above his head, Trok started down the narrow, unprotected stairwell. He went gingerly, for the treads of the stone steps were slimy and slippery. The sound of running water grew louder as he went down.

Ishtar followed him closely. 'This temple and the tunnels beneath it were built almost five hundred years ago,' he told Trok. Now there was the gleam of water below them, and the sound of the torrent running swiftly in the darkness. At last Trok reached the bottom and stepped down on to a stone pier. By the wavering torchlight he saw that they stood in a wide tunnel with a curved roof, an aqueduct of impressive dimensions. The roof and walls were lined with ceramic tiles, laid in geometric patterns. Both ends of the tunnel shaded off into deep darkness.

Ishtar picked a fragment of fungus from the wall and tossed it into the flow. It was whisked away down the duct and disappeared from sight. 'It is deeper than a man's head,' he said, and Trok looked speculatively at the captain of the guard, as though he considered testing that statement. The captain shrank back into the shadows trying to appear insignificant.

'This footpath on which we stand runs the full length of the aqueduct,' Ishtar explained. 'The priests who repair and maintain the tunnel use it to gain access.'

'Where does it start and where does it end?' Trok demanded.

'There is a sump in the bed of the river, under the piers of the temple, into which the water flows. The far end of the aqueduct emerges in the other temple of Ninurta within the walls of Babylon, near the Blue Gate,' Ishtar explained. 'Only the priests know of the existence of this tunnel. All others believe that the water is a benevolent gift from the god. After it gushes from the fountain in the temple precinct, the water is lifted by *shadoof*, water wheels, to the gardens of the palace, or sent by canals to every quarter of the city.'

'I do believe, Ishtar the Mede, that you are close to earning your three lakhs.' Trok laughed with delight. 'It remains only for you to lead us down this rabbit-hole, and into the city of wonders and treasure, especially the treasure.'

Trok reasoned that the priests at the main temple of Ninurta within the city walls must regularly correspond with those in the river temple. Almost certainly they used this aqueduct as a thoroughfare between the two communities. It would not take long for them to discover that something untoward had happened to their brethren in the river temple. He had to make his plans swiftly.

Trok chose two hundred of his best and most reliable men, all members of his own leopard tribe. He divided them into two groups. Once they had fought their way through the aqueduct into the city, the first group were to secure the Blue Gate and keep it open until Pharaoh Naja Kiafan could lead the main force through it. The second, much smaller group were to make their way into the palace, and seize Sargon's treasury before he was able to dispose of the gold. 'Although it would take a thousand wagons to carry it all away,' Ishtar assured him.

The chosen two hundred were dressed in the uniforms of Sargon's army, taken from the prisoners and the dead men left on the battlefield. They wore the long ankle-length tunics of striped material, belted at the waist, and the tall beehive-shaped helmets. Ishtar showed them how to curl their beards and hair into the characteristic ringlets of the Mesopotamians. They wore only a red sash to distinguish them from the foe. Rough copies of the city map were hastily drawn by the army scribes and issued to the captains of both divisions so that they knew the lay-out of streets and buildings. By evening every man knew exactly what was expected of him once he entered the city.

As soon as it was dark Naja quietly moved his assault force up into position outside the Blue Gate, ready to dash through into the city as soon as Trok's men threw it open.

In the courtyard of the river temple of Ninurta, Trok mustered his division. While it was still daylight, he and Ishtar led them in single file down the spiral staircase to the level of the aqueduct. There was no hurry, for they had many hours in which to make the long subterranean journey. Their cleated sandals had been muffled with leather socks, so their heavy footsteps did not echo along the gloomy tunnel. They marched in silence, every tenth man carrying a torch, giving just sufficient light for the men who followed to make out their footing on the slimy stones of the pier. At their left hand the never-ending flow of water rustled darkly by. Every thousand paces Ishtar stopped to placate the god Ninurta with gifts and incantations, and to clear the way ahead of the magical obstacles and barriers placed by the dead priests.

Nevertheless, the silent march seemed endless to Trok, and it came as a surprise when abruptly Ishtar stopped and pointed ahead. The faint glimmer of light was reflected off the shiny ceramic walls. Trok signalled the men following him to halt, then went forward with Ishtar. Over their own garments they wore headdresses and purple robes taken from the bodies of the slaughtered priests.

As they went towards the source of the light, they saw another grille gate across the tunnel, and the distorted shadows of men thrown on the walls by the light of a torch set in a bracket above the gate. As they drew closer they saw that on the other side of the grille two robed priests were seated on stools, with the bao board between them, absorbed in their game. They looked up when Ishtar called softly to them. The fat one stood up and wobbled to the gate.

'Are you from Sinna?' he called.

'Yes!' Ishtar assured him.

'You are late. We have been waiting since nightfall. You should have been here hours ago. The high priest will be displeased.'

'I am sorry,' Ishtar sounded contrite, 'but you know Sinna.'

The fat priest chuckled. 'Yes, I know Sinna. He taught me my responses thirty years ago.'

His key jangled in the lock of the gate, and then he swung it open. 'You must hurry,' he said. Trok trotted forward with the hood over his face, holding his sword in the fold of his robe. The priest stood back against the wall to let him pass. Trok stopped in front of him, and whispered, 'Ninurta will reward you, brother,' and killed him with a thrust up under his chin into his brain.

With a shout of alarm, his companion leaped to his feet, knocking over the bao board and scattering the stones across the pier. With two long strides Trok reached him and chopped his head half off. Without another sound, the priest fell backwards into the dark stream and, with his robes ballooning about him buoying him up, he was carried away down the tunnel.

Trok gave a soft whistle and, with the muted tramp of

muffled feet, his men moved up into the torchlight with drawn swords. Ishtar led them forward until they reached the foot of another steep stone stairway. They went up it quickly until they came to a heavy curtain blocking their way. Ishtar peeped around its edge and nodded. 'The temple is empty.'

Trok stepped through, and looked about him. This temple was even larger and more impressive than the river temple. The ceiling was so high that the light from fifty torches was eaten up by the shadows. Below them the image of the god crouched over the mouth of the shaft from which the full force of the aqueduct spurted like a gigantic fountain into a deep pond with a white marble coping. The corpse of the priest that Trok had almost decapitated was floating in the pool, from which the water spilled over into the canal that carried it to the city. Although the smell of incense was thick in the air, the great hall of the temple was deserted.

Trok signalled his men to come forward. As soon as they emerged from the tunnel they formed up behind their captains in silence. Trok gave the hand signal and they went forward at a trot. Ishtar led the smaller band through a side door of the hall into a corridor that connected with the palace of Sargon. Trok led his men out into the narrow lane behind the temple and, working only from his memory of the map, turned at the second lane into the wide avenue that he knew led to the Blue Gate. It was still dark and the stars blazed above the sleeping city.

They met a number of cloaked figures on the way, one or two staggering drunk, but the others scurried out of their way and let the dark column of armed warriors pass. A woman with a child in her arms called after them, 'May Marduk smile upon you, brave warriors, and keep us safe from Trok, the barbarian of Egypt.' Trok understood just enough Akkadian to catch her meaning, and smiled into his beard.

Disguised in their plundered robes, they reached the end of the avenue without being challenged further, but as the gateway loomed ahead a voice sang out at them from the door of the guardhouse.

'Stand ho! Give the watchword for tonight.' The centurion of the gate, with five men at his back, stepped out into the torchlight. But they were ill-prepared, without helmets and body armour, their eyes puffy and their faces still crumpled with sleep.

'The honourable emissary of King Sargon to the pharaohs of Egypt,' Trok mumbled in execrable Akkadian, and gave the hand signal for his troops to charge. 'Open the gate and stand aside!' He ran straight at the centurion.

For a moment longer the man stood uncertainly. Then he saw the glint of swords and shouted urgently, 'Stand to arms. Turn out the guard.' But it was too late. Trok was on him, and dropped him in his tracks with a single blow. His men swarmed over the other guards before they could defend themselves, but the noise had alerted the sentinels on the parapets above the gate. They sounded the alarm with braying ram's horns, and hurled their javelins down into the attackers.

'Winkle them out of there!' Trok ordered, and half of his men rushed up the ramps on either side of the gateway to reach the parapet. They were at once locked in close and desperate fighting with the guards on the wall. Trok kept half of his men with him.

Ishtar had described the gate room that housed the complicated machinery, a system of heavy winches and pulleys, that operated the massive gates. Trok led his men to the entrance before the defenders within could close the doors, and after only a few minutes of furious fighting they had killed or wounded most of them. The survivors threw down their weapons, some fell to their knees and pleaded in vain for quarter. They were stabbed and clubbed as they knelt. The others fled out of the postern gate, and Trok led his men to the massive winches. With two men on each spoke of the capstans they began to open the gates.

But the ram's horns had aroused the city guards, who swarmed out of their barracks, some without armour and still half asleep, and rushed to defend the gateway.

Trok barred the heavy door to the winch room and placed men at the entrance to defend it. On the parapets above the gateway his men had killed the defenders or thrown them from the top of the wall, and now they fought on the ramps, holding off the attacking Babylonians.

The door to the winch room trembled and bulged as the Babylonians battered at it, trying desperately to break in, but the winches revolved slowly to the efforts of Trok's men, and the mighty gates rose from their seatings, the gap under them widening inexorably.

The avenue leading to the gates was by now crowded with Babylonian defenders, but they were hampered by their own numbers. Only four abreast could mount the ramps to the top of the walls, and Trok's men met them and hurled them back. Others were still trying to break into the room that housed the winches, but the doors were sturdy. When at last they smashed them down they found Trok and his men waiting for them on the threshold.

Outside the walls Naja's men had swarmed forward with crowbars and levers. They forced the heavy gates wider and wider, until at last a squadron of chariots could pass through. Then they stood aside, and Naja led a phalanx of fighting chariots in a brutal charge through the gateway, and swept the avenue from side to side. The army of Egypt poured through behind them. Trok took command of them and led them rampaging through the city towards the palace.

The sack of Babylon had begun.

The defence of the palace was stubborn, led by Sargon himself. However, by that evening Trok had opened a breach in the outer walls of the first terrace. He led a strong contingent through and the defence collapsed. When they burst into Sargon's bedchamber he was kneeling before the image of Marduk, the devouring god of Mesopotamia, with a bloody sword in his hands. Beside him lay the body of his favourite wife, a grey-haired woman who had been with him for thirty years. He had given her a merciful death, compared to what she might have expected from Trok's men. However, Sargon had not been able to steel himself to fall on his own sword. Trok knocked the weapon out of his grasp.

'We have much to discuss, Your Majesty,' he promised him. 'Was it not you who referred to me as the Black Beast of Seueth? I hope to convince you that you painted me the wrong colour.'

The women from the *zenana* were herded out of the palace, only five hundred of them, not the five thousand of which Ishtar had spoken. Trok selected twenty, the youngest and prettiest, for his personal entertainment, and the rest were given to his senior officers. After they had enjoyed them, they would be passed on to the common soldiery.

It took another two days to break into the treasury buried deep in the earth below the palace, for many ingenious constructions and devices guarded it. Without the expertise and first-hand knowledge of Ishtar the Mede, it might have taken even longer to penetrate to the main treasure chamber.

When the way was clear, Trok and Naja, Heseret following them, descended the stairway and entered the chamber. Ishtar had lit the interior with a hundred oil lamps, their rays cunningly reflected by burnished copper mirrors to show off the booty to full effect.

Even the two pharaohs and Heseret were stunned into silence by the splendour of the treasure. The silver had been cast into bars, the gold into conical ingots that fitted into each other to facilitate stacking. They were all stamped with the goldsmiths' marks and the royal cartouche of Sargon.

Heseret, for once speechless, had to shade her delicate eyes against the dazzle of the masses of precious metal. Naja walked forward slowly between the stacks, which were higher than his head, stopping every few paces to stroke the ingots. At last he regained his voice and whispered, 'They feel warm and smooth as the body of a virgin.'

Trok picked up a heavy bar in each hand and laughed with delight. 'How much?' he demanded of Ishtar.

'Alas, splendid and divine Majesty, we have not yet had the opportunity to count it. But we have consulted the scrolls of Sargon's scribes. They record the total weight of silver at fifty-five lakhs, the gold at thirty-three.' He spread his tattooed hands deprecatingly. 'But who would trust the count of a Babylonian?'

'Sargon is a greater robber than I gave him credit for.' Trok made it sound like a compliment.

'At least there is enough here to pay me the pittance you promised me?' Ishtar suggested smoothly.

'I think we should discuss that further.' Trok smiled at him genially. 'I am a kindly and generous man, Ishtar, as you know full well. However, over-generosity is a form of stupidity. Stupid I am not.'

Once he had finished gloating over the contents of the treasury, there was much else to see and marvel at within the city. Trok and Naja toured the palace, climbing to the top terrace with its fountains, gardens and groves. From this height they could look down on both the great rivers and the vista of fields, marshes and papyrus beds outside the city walls.

Next they visited all the temples, for these magnificent buildings were also stuffed with bullion, beautiful furniture, statuary, mosaics and other works of art. As they removed these Naja and Trok spoke to the incumbent god in conversational tones, as brother gods and equals. Trok explained that Babylon was no longer a capital city but merely a satrapy of Egypt. Therefore the god should remove his earthly seat to Avaris, where Trok undertook to provide him with suitable accommodation. The removal of the god's wealth should be considered in the nature of a loan which would later be repaid.

The greatest of these temples was that of Marduk the Devourer. Trok found this to be not only a mine of precious metal and jewellery but a place of endless fascination.

Ishtar was a disciple of Marduk, and as a young man had studied the mysteries in this same temple under the high priest. As he had not yet been paid his reward, he stuck as close to Trok as a tick to the belly of a lion. He instructed Trok in the worship of Marduk, and Trok remarked, 'Marduk has tastes very close to those of my own familiar, Seueth. They might well be brothers.'

'As always, Your Majesty is perspicacious. However, Marduk had a far greater appetite for human sacrifice than Seueth. And he is particular about how it is presented to him.'

He led Trok through the maze of passageways and corridors, through gardens, courtyards and echoing halls into the holy of holies deep in the heart of the temple, which was a small city in itself. They came at last to the furnace complex.

When they stood above the main sacrificial chamber, Trok gazed down into the gut of it in total fascination. He was amazed by the design and the construction. 'Describe it to me,' he ordered Ishtar.

'There are two furnaces, not a single one, one behind each of those walls.' Ishtar pointed down at the walls of shining copper. 'When the charcoal fires are lit they are fanned with great bellows, until the metal walls glow like the rising sun with the heat. The walls are movable. By means of pulleys the priests are able to roll them forward, or pull them apart . . .'

When Ishtar had finished his explanation, Trok thumped his mailed fist into the palm of his other hand. 'In the names of Seueth and Marduk, I have never heard the like. I must see it demonstrated. If it is as you describe, I will have the same contraption built in my own temple in Avaris. Order the priests to fire up their infernal furnaces. We will celebrate my victory with a sacrifice to Marduk.'

'It will take several days for the furnaces to reach the desired heat,' Ishtar warned him.

'I have several days,' Trok said. 'I have to supervise the consignment of the booty, and also I must see to the contentment and well-being of twenty of Sargon's young wives.' He rolled his eyes. 'A most arduous task. In any event, my ruffians are still busy sacking the city. It will be some time yet before I can bring them back to their senses.'

Three days later Trok held a victory banquet for his senior officers on the upper terrace of the great palace. The guests reclined among groves of orange trees growing in huge clay pots, all in full blossom so the air was filled with their sweet perfume. Around them the fountains tinkled and burbled. The banquet table was covered with silken carpets. The bowls and vessels were of silver and gold and set with precious stones – they had been taken from the temple offertories. The stools on which the guests sat were Sargon's wives, kneeling naked except for their golden chains. Later when the flagons of foaming beer and the sweet wine had taken effect, the living stools were used as pillows and mattresses.

In the midst of this revelry Ishtar crept to Trok's side,

and whispered in his ear, 'Pharaoh god, who swallows the seas and eats the stars, the furnaces are ready.'

Trok staggered to his feet and clapped his hands. 'Gentle brethren!' he addressed his officers, and they roared with laughter at the jest. 'I have an entertainment to offer you. Follow me!' And he made unsteadily for the staircase with his men crowding after him.

They lined the parapet of the gallery, and looked down into the sacrificial chamber. Smoke shimmered from the twin chimneys above their heads, and they began to sweat in the heat reflected from the glowing metal walls.

'We are gathered here today to make sacrifice to the great god Marduk, who has given us his city as a prize of war,' Trok told them, imitating the sing-song, sanctimonious tones of a high priest. They cheered him delightedly.

'What better sacrifice can we offer than a king and his royal family?' They cheered again.

Trok waved to Ishtar, who darted down the stairway to the chamber below where a hundred slaves stood at the windlasses ready to activate the mechanism. At a signal from the high priest they began to chant a hymn to Marduk.

The priest stepped out on to his pulpit above the open chamber with its glowing walls. With the chanting slaves as a background, he lifted both arms and began to sing a prayer to the god in a reedy falsetto voice.

At his signal a small door opened in the fixed stone wall of the furnace chamber, and another priest led in a file of human beings. They were clad in simple white tunics, and wore no adornment other than the halters around their necks.

They were of both sexes, and all ages. Some were mere infants carried in their mothers' arms; some were toddlers; others were on the verge of adolescence. But the tallest was a lean white-haired man with the carriage of a king and a warrior.

'Hail, Sargon, mighty ruler of heaven and the sacred

earth between the two great rivers,' Trok mocked him. 'I am about to do for you what you did not have the courage to do for yourself. I am sending you as a messenger into the loving arms of your god, Marduk the Devourer. Because I am a compassionate man and I do not want your wives, your little sons and daughters to mourn you, I am sending them with you to keep you company on the way.' He paused to let the laughter of his men subside. Then he went on, 'Give this message to Marduk, when you stand face to face with him. Tell him that Trok, his divine brother, greets him, and demands his good favour.'

Sargon gathered his sons around him and did not deign to look up at Trok or to reply to his words.

Trok looked across at the high priest. 'Now, priest, show us how this machine of yours works.'

The high priest began to sing again, but a different prayer, harsh and primitive. In the room behind him the slaves sang with him, and in unison took a step forward then brought their bare soles down on the stone slabs with a sound like a clap of thunder. One step at a time the windlass began to turn.

At first nothing appeared to change then Ishtar whispered, 'Observe the burning walls, mighty Trok, greatest of all hero kings. See how they begin to move towards each other, slowly. Oh, so slowly. Until they meet at last, and the sacrifices crisp and blacken like moths in the lamp flame.'

Trok leaned forward, his face bright with sweat and anticipation.

'Marduk is pleased,' Ishtar announced, looking up from the bowl. 'The sacrifice that you made to him in the furnace was most acceptable to him.'

Trok nodded. 'Tell my brother Marduk that I am pleased he is pleased.'

Trok knelt on a pile of leopardskins spread on the stone floor in the inner sanctum of the temple before the altar of Marduk the Devourer. The golden image of the god was of a comely youth, with a smiling countenance. The statue was three or four times life-sized. The only characteristics that distinguished the god from a mortal, other than his size, were tiny goatlike horns on each side of his curly head and cloven hoofs instead of feet.

'You told me that Marduk was a terrible god, crueller and fiercer than any other in the pantheon, more ferocious even than Seueth,' Trok had challenged Ishtar when first he had seen the image, 'yet this is a pretty boy.'

'Divine Pharaoh, be not deceived!' Ishtar had warned him. 'This is the face that Marduk shows the world of men. His true aspect is so hideous that any man who looks upon it is instantly rendered blind and slobbering twitching mad.'

Sobered by that thought Trok had knelt before the image and remained silent while the priests had brought in twin newborn infants, and offered them to the god. Ishtar had slit their throats so skilfully that they made hardly a cry as they bled into the golden divination bowl that he held beneath them.

When the small exsanguinated bodies were dropped into the marble chute that led to the furnace beneath the sanctum, Ishtar had placed the golden bowl before the altar and lit the incense braziers. Chanting and mumbling, he threw handfuls of herbs on the flames until the vault filled with wreaths of blue smoke and the air became fragrant and enervating. After a while Trok found it difficult to think clearly and his vision became distorted so that the shadows seemed to waver and dance, and he heard the sounds of distant, mocking laughter. He closed his eyes and pressed his fingers to the lids. When he opened them again he saw that the sweet smile on the face of the god had become a leer so obscene and frightening that his skin crawled as though poisonous insects were creeping upon it. He tried to look away but found he could not.

'The great god Marduk is pleased,' Ishtar repeated, reading the auguries reflected in the surface of the blood-filled bowl. 'He deigns to answer your questions.'

'Tell Marduk that I honour him as my peer. I shall send a thousand more sacrifices into his furnace.'

'Marduk hears you.' Ishtar picked up the bowl and peered into it. After a long silence he began to rock gently back and forth with the bowl in his lap. He looked up at last. 'Behold Marduk, the great god of Babylon! Speak to us, dreadful one, we entreat you!'

He opened his arms to the golden statue, and the god spoke in the voice of a child, lisping and mellifluous.

'I greet you, my brother Trok,' said this strange voice. 'You wish to know about the fledgling falcon that spreads its wings and sharpens its talons in the desert places.'

Trok was startled not only by the disembodied voice but also by the accuracy of this statement. Indeed, he had intended asking for counsel on his plans to attack and destroy Nefer Seti. He tried to reply, but his throat was closed and as dry as the wrappings of an ancient mummy.

The sweet, childlike voice went on, 'You have had good counsel from my loyal servant Ishtar the Mede. It was as well that you hearkened to him. If you had not done so, if you had marched on Gallala when you purposed to do so, you would have encountered a disaster even greater than the *khamsin* winds that destroyed and buried your legions.'

Trok recalled bitterly how Ishtar had dissuaded him from

leading another army into the eastern desert to attack Nefer Seti and to capture Mintaka, his runaway woman. Long ago his spies had reported to him the exact whereabouts of the pair at Gallala. He had assembled another force of chariots and foot soldiers for the expedition. He knew that if he did not rid himself of this challenge to his throne, if he did not crush the boy pharaoh before he attained his full strength, then soon the rebellions and insurrections would spread through his entire realm. Once that happened he knew that the dynasty he was founding would end in destruction and extinction. As much as he longed to rid himself of the challenge and the threat of Nefer Seti, he longed much more to recapture the only woman who had ever humiliated and defied him. His hatred for her surpassed any other of his emotions.

Ishtar had prevented him marching. With predictions of dire consequences, with warnings of disaster and death, Ishtar had persuaded him to divert his forces into this joint expedition with Naja to the fabled city of Babylon. Although, thus far, the expedition had turned out to be a triumph, although the booty and the slaughter had been beyond counting, still Trok felt himself unfulfilled.

He spoke as much to himself as to the golden god when he growled, 'I must have Nefer Seti. The double crown will sit uneasily on my head until I kill him and throw his body on the flames so that he will never know resurrection. Already I have expunged his name and the name of his sire from every edifice and monument in Egypt, but I must destroy him and his memory for ever.'

In his anger and hatred he sprang to his feet, and shouted at Ishtar and his god, 'You have cheated me of my destiny once before with your ill omens and baleful warnings. Now I address you as your peer, your equal, and not as a worshipper. I demand that you deliver the person and the soul of Nefer Seti to me, in justice and retribution. I will not accept another refusal from you and your minion here.'

In his fury and frustration Trok aimed a kick at Ishtar. The Mede saw it coming and rolled aside. Trok's bronze-cleated sandal caught the divining bowl and the blood of the babes splattered across the flags and down the front of the altar.

Even Trok was appalled by what he had done. He stood frozen before the image waiting for the reaction of the god.

'Sacrilege!' Ishtar wailed. 'Trok Uruk, now your enterprise is surely doomed.' Then he prostrated himself in the puddle of blood, so terror-stricken that he could not raise his eyes to the image.

A dreadful hush had fallen over the sanctum. The faint rumble of the flames of the sacrificial furnace under the stone floor on which they stood seemed to enhance it.

Then there was a sound, soft but unmistakable. It was the sound of breathing, like that of a sleeping child to begin with but then growing harsher and stronger. Now it was the breathing of a wild beast, then of some monster that echoed through the temple. At last it became the furious sound of an outraged god, roaring like all the storms of the heavens, thundering like the galeswept waves of the ocean. So terrible was it that even Ishtar the Mede whimpered like a child.

'The god will never allow you to succeed now. You dare not march against Taita and his protégé, not until the Warlock is dead,' Ishtar whispered.

Then a terrible voice spoke, so harsh and unearthly that it raked Trok's nerves and made him shudder. 'Hear me! Trok Uruk, you mortal man who claims to be part of the godhead!' The thunder echoed and rolled around the dark recess of the sanctum. 'You know that you are no god. Hear me, blasphemer! If you march against Gallala in defiance of me and my prophet, Ishtar the Mede, I shall destroy you and your army just as I buried your other army in the sands of the desert. This time you shall not escape my wrath.'

Even though he was befuddled by the poisonous smoke of the incense braziers, and fearful of the rage of Marduk that filled the temple, Trok was still cunning enough to sense some false note in Ishtar's protestations, something not convincing in the force of Marduk's fury.

He gathered his courage, which had been scattered by the supernatural manifestations of the god, and tried to identify exactly what had given him pause. He realized that the sound of the bestial breathing, and the thunderous voice issued from the belly of the golden statue. He stared at it hard and saw that the navel of the god was a dark slit. He took a step towards the statue and Ishtar raised his head in alarm and cried, 'Beware, Pharaoh! The god is angry. Do not approach him.'

Trok ignored him and took another step forward, staring at the god's belly button. He saw a faint gleam in the depths of the aperture, a shadowy movement. Often in battle he had sensed the exact moment when the fates had swung in his favour and he felt it now. He steeled himself and shouted, above the awful sound of the god's breathing, 'I defy you, Marduk the Devourer! Strike me down if you are able. Heap your temple fires upon me, if you can!'

Suspicion became certainty as that glimmer showed again in the slit in the god's belly, and the breathing faltered. Trok drew his sword and, with the flat of the blade, knocked Ishtar out of his way. Then he ran forward, darting behind the golden image. Quickly he examined the back, tapping the metal with the tip of his blade. It sounded hollow as a drum, and when he looked more closely he discovered a removable panel that fitted almost perfectly.

'A trap-door!' he growled. 'It seems that there is more in Marduk's belly than ever went in through his mouth.'

He ducked back and peered into the slit in the god's belly. A human eye looked back at him. The pupil widened with astonishment, and Trok gave a mighty shout: 'Come out of there, you slime of the great beast!' He placed his shoulder against the idol and heaved with all his strength. The statue wobbled on its stone base, and Trok heaved again. Slowly the image went down with a crash on to the stone flags. Ishtar screamed and leaped out of the way as it threatened to crush him.

The head of the god was bent at an angle by the fall, and in the silence after the shattering impact there was a scrabbling sound, like startled rats, from the interior of the fallen idol. The trap-door flew open and a small figure crawled out. Trok seized it by its thick head of curls. 'Mercy, great King Trok,' the girl pleaded, in that honey-sweet voice. 'It was not I who tried to deceive you. I was doing the bidding of others.' She was such a lovely child that, for a moment, Trok felt his rage subside. Then he snatched her up by the ankles and dangled her upside-down in one fist. She was weeping and writhing in his grip.

'Who ordered you to this?' Trok demanded.

'Ishtar the Mede,' she wept.

Trok swung her twice in a circle around his head, building up speed and momentum, then dashed the child against the temple column. Her screams were cut off instantly. Trok let her corpse drop in a crumpled heap on the altar.

He turned back to the golden idol and thrust his sword into the opening of the trapdoor, rummaging around in the belly of the God. There was another squeal and a grotesque creature shot out of the opening. At first Trok thought it was a huge bullfrog, and jumped back in alarm. Then he saw that it was a hunch-backed dwarf, even shorter and smaller than the girl he had just killed. The dwarf bellowed with a voice like a bull, the deafening roars out of keeping with his diminutive stature. He was the ugliest man Trok had ever laid eyes upon, with eyes out of kilter and of disparate sizes. Clumps of black hair bushed out of his ears and nostrils, and from the huge moles that hung from his face.

'Forgive me, that I tried to deceive you, mighty god and King of Egypt!' Trok slashed at him with the sword, but the creature ducked and dodged and leaped nimbly about the sanctum, roaring with terror in that outlandish voice. Trok found himself laughing at his antics. The dwarf shot behind the curtains at the back of the chamber and disappeared through a secret doorway.

Trok let him go and turned back to Ishtar, just in time to seize a handful of his stiff-lacquered hair as he tried to flee from the chamber. He flung him full length on the stone floor and kicked him in the ribs, belly and back. 'You have lied to me.' Trok was no longer laughing, and his face turned dark purple with rage. 'You have deliberately misled me. You have diverted me from my purpose.'

'Please, master,' Ishtar wailed, rolling across the floor to avoid the savage kicks, 'it was for your good alone.'

'Was it for my good that you allowed the spawn of Tamose to flourish in Gallala unchecked, and to spread rebellion and sedition throughout my realm?' Trok bellowed. 'Do you think I am mad, and so stupid that I should believe that?'

'It is true,' Ishtar blubbered, as Trok's toe caught him in the ribs and knocked him over on his back. 'How could we go against a Warlock who commands the storm to his will as though it were his pet dog?'

'You are afraid of Taita.' Trok stood back to regain his breath. 'The Warlock?' he demanded incredulously.

'He overlooks us. He can turn my own spells back upon me! I cannot prevail against him. I sought only to save you from him, great Pharaoh.'

'You sought only to save your own blue-tattooed skin,' Trok snarled, and rushed in again to slam kicks into Ishtar's doubled-up body.

'I beg of you, first of all the gods,' Ishtar covered his head with both arms, 'give me my reward and let me go. Taita has dissipated my powers. I cannot confront him again. I can be of no further use to you.'

Trok stood with one foot drawn back, frozen in the act

of delivering another kick. 'Your reward?' he demanded in astonishment. 'Surely you do not believe that I will reward your disloyalty with three lakhs of gold.'

Ishtar came up on his knees and tried to kiss Trok's foot. 'I have given you Babylon, great master. You cannot deny me what was promised.'

Trok laughed angrily. 'I can deny you anything I please to. Even life itself. If you wish to live another day then you will lead me to Gallala, and take your chances in a trial of magical strength with the Warlock.'

It seemed that all Egypt had heard that Nefer Seti had run the Red Road and was ordained in his kingship. Each day visitors from all over the country arrived in Gallala. Some were the colonels and captains of the regiments that Trok and Naja had left to guard Egypt in their absence. Others were emissaries of the elders of the great cities along the Nile – Avaris and Memphis, Thebes and Aswan – and the high priests from the temples in those cities. Sickened and saddened by the tyrannies and excesses of Naja and Trok, and emboldened by their absence in Babylon so far to the east, all had come to swear allegiance to Nefer Seti.

'The populace of Egypt is ready to welcome you,' the emissaries told him.

'Our regiments will declare for you as soon as you step again on to the sacred soil, and they see your face, and know that the rumours of your survival are true,' the captains assured him.

Nefer and Taita questioned them keenly, demanding to know the muster of their regiments and their state of readiness. It soon became apparent that Trok and Naja had skimmed the cream of the regiments for their Mesopotamian adventure, and left only the reserve battalions, made up mostly of new recruits, the very young and untried, or the elderly nearing the end of their military lives, tired and unfit, already looking forward to the retirement and their little plot of land near the river where they could sit in the sun and play with their grandchildren.

'What of the chariots and horses?' Nefer asked the crucial question. The captains shook their grey heads and looked grave. 'Trok and Naja stripped the regiments bare. Almost every vehicle went with them on the western road. They left hardly enough to patrol the eastern borders to discourage the Bedouin raiders from the desert.'

'What about the workshops in Memphis, Avaris and Thebes?' Nefer wanted to know. 'Each of them can turn out at least fifty chariots in a month.'

'As soon as horses are trained to pull them, they are sent to the east to join the army of the twin pharaohs in Babylon.'

Taita assessed this information. 'The false pharaohs are fully aware of the threat we pose to their rear. They want to ensure that if the regiments they have left in Egypt rebel against them and declare for the true Pharaoh, Nefer Seti, they will lack cavalry and chariots to be an effective force.'

'You must return to your regiments,' Nefer ordered the officers. 'We are too many in Gallala already, and we are near the limits of our food and water. Do not allow any more vehicles or horses to leave Egypt. Keep your men in training, and equip the best of them with the new chariots as they become available. I will come to you soon, very soon, to lead you against the tyrants.' They left, praising his name, and with renewed assurances of their loyalty.

'You dare not fulfil your promise to them prematurely. You can only return to Egypt with a powerful force under your command, well trained and well equipped,' Taita advised Nefer. 'These captains who have come over to you are good, loyal men, and I know you can count on them. However, there will be many others who remain true to

Trok and Naja, either in fear of the consequences when the false pharaohs return or because they believe in their divine right to rule. Also, there will be many who are undecided, but who will turn against you if they detect any weakness.'

'Then we have much to do.' Nefer accepted this advice. 'We must still break the last of the horses we took at Thane and complete the repairs to the chariots from the dunes. Then our men must finish their training so that they can stand up against Trok and Naja's veterans. When we have done these things, we will return to Egypt.'

So the little army of Gallala redoubled its efforts to build itself into a force to challenge the might of the false pharaohs. They were inspired by their young commander, for Nefer worked harder than any of them. He rode out with the first squadrons long before dawn, and with the other warriors of the Red Road at his side, and Taita to advise him, he gradually forged his divisions into a cohesive body. When he rode back into the city, weary and dusty, in the evening, he would go to the workshops where he cajoled and argued with the foremen armourers and chariot builders. Then, after he had eaten, he would sit up in the lamp-light with Taita, going over the battle plans and the dispositions of their forces. Usually it was after midnight when he stumbled to his bedchamber. Mintaka woke and rose from the bed without complaint to help him strip off his armour and sandals and to bathe his feet and massage aching muscles with sweet oils. Then she warmed a bowl of wine and honey to help him sleep. Often the bowl dropped from his hand before he had finished it, and his head flopped back on to the pillow. Then she would slip off her *chiton*, take his head on to her bosom and hold him until he woke to dawn's first promise.

Each day Meren sank a little lower from the wounds he had received on the Red Road. Taita had strapped his broken ribs and they had healed swiftly enough. He had sewn back the torn ear so neatly that now it was cocked only slightly awry, and Merykara thought that the half-moon scar down his cheek made him look older and more distinguished. However, the sword thrust under his arm worried even Taita: when he probed it he knew from its angle and depth that the weapon must have penetrated Meren's lung. Twice, when it seemed to have healed over, the wound broke open again and leaked foul-smelling pus and fluid. Sometimes Meren was lucid, able to sit up and eat without assistance. Then, when the morbid humours welled up again, he sank back into semi-consciousness and fever.

Merykara stayed at his bedside, changing his dressings and anointing the wound with the unguent Taita brewed for her. When Meren was stronger she sang to him and related all the news of the city and the army. She played bao with him, and made up rhymes and riddles to amuse him. When the wound turned again, she fed him and bathed him like a baby, stroking his sweat-soaked head until he calmed. At night she slept at the foot of his bed, coming awake immediately every time he stirred and muttered in delirium.

She came to know his body as intimately as if he had been her own child. She cleaned his teeth with the green twigs of the acacia tree, chewing the ends into a stiff brush with her own small white teeth. She dressed his hair, brushing it until it grew out long enough to plait again. She trimmed his nails, and came to know and love the shape of his fingers callused by the hilt of sword and chariot reins. She scraped the wax from his ears, and the dried mucus from his nostrils without the slightest revulsion. She used her own ivory comb on the soft dark hair that grew in thick clumps under his arms, curled on his chest and nestled at the base of his belly.

Each morning she washed every part of him, every crease, plane and bulge of hard muscle, and mourned as his flesh melted off him in the fevers and his bones began to show through.

At first she averted her eyes from his manly parts as she washed them, but soon this seemed prudish to her. Then she cupped them in the hollow of her hand and studied them closely. They invoked in her feelings of tenderness and compassion. They were so soft and warm, the skin so smooth and flawless. Then her emotions changed when she gently drew back the skin in the way that Mintaka had shown her, and the pink tip popped out, silky as an oleander petal. It stiffened and swelled in her hand until she could barely encompass its girth with her thumb and forefinger. When this happened she felt a strange, breathless sensation, and a warmth in the most unlikely parts of her own anatomy.

One night she woke with the moonlight from the window lying like a silver bar across the stone floor of the chamber. For a moment she thought she was in her own bedchamber in the river palace of Thebes, but then she heard Meren's painful breathing, the incoherent cries inspired by his nightmare, and it all came back to her with a rush of dread. She jumped up naked from her mattress at the foot of his couch and ran to him.

When she lit the lamp, she saw that his eyes were wide open but unseeing, and that his face was ashen and contorted, there was a white scum on his lips and his body was shining with running sweat. He was throwing himself about so violently on the crumpled linen sheets that she was terrified he would injure himself further. She knew that this was the crisis Taita had warned her to expect.

'Taita!' she screamed. 'Please, we need you now.' Taita's cell was across the courtyard from theirs, and he always slept with his door open so that he could hear her call.

'Taita!' she shrieked again, as she threw herself across Meren's chest to restrain him. Then she remembered that the Magus had gone into the desert with Nefer and a squadron of chariots on some mysterious expedition, and it was unlikely that they would return for many days. She thought of calling Mintaka, but her chamber was at the other end of the ancient palace, and she dared not leave Meren.

She was on her own. She knew that Meren's life was in her hands, and at that thought she felt her panic subside. A cool determination took its place. She lay against him and held him tightly, whispering encouragement and reassurance. After a while he calmed so that she could leave him for a moment. She went to the chest against the window wall, found the vial that Taita had left for her, mixed the pungent contents with wine and warmed it on the brazier as he had instructed her.

When she held the goblet to Meren's lips he tried to refuse, but she forced him to drink. When the bowl was empty she heated water and washed the sweat from his face, the scum from his lips. She was about to wash his body when a sudden seizure racked him, and he began to shake and groan. Her terror returned in full force. She flung herself on him and clung to him with all her strength. 'Do not die, my darling,' she pleaded with him, and then in a stronger voice, 'I will not let you die. O Hathor, help me. I will drag him back from the underworld with my own hands.' She knew she was in a battle, and she fought with him, extending all her strength and adding it to his. When she felt him go limp in her arms and his sweat-drenched body start to cool, she cried out, 'No, Meren, come back! Come back to me. You cannot go without me.'

She placed her mouth over his and tried to breathe her

own life into him. Suddenly he gave an explosive gasp, emptying his lungs, and she thought it was all over. She hugged him with both arms around his bony chest, and when she released the pressure he took another noisy breath, then another and another. The flutter of his heart became a strong, regular thumping that reverberated through her frame.

'You have come back,' she whispered. 'You have come back to me.'

He was still cold, and when he shivered, she held him with both her arms around his chest, and wrapped her legs around his hips, warming him with her own body. Slowly, his breathing became deep and regular, and she felt the warm blood flowing back into his veins. She lay with him and felt a deep sense of fulfilment, for she knew that she had saved him, and that from this night onwards he would belong to her alone.

In the dawn another miracle occurred. She felt his body awaken, and what she had once held soft and small in the palm of her hand now swelled against her once more, becoming enormous, hard as bone, pressing up between her spread thighs.

She looked into his face and saw that he was conscious, his eyes dark and sunken in the wasted sockets, but with an expression of such awe and tenderness in them that her heart swelled within her chest so that she felt she might suffocate with the strength of her own torrential emotions.

'Yes?' he asked.

'Yes,' she answered. 'It is what I want more than anything else in all the world.' She spread herself, and reached down to guide him, aching inside with her need for him, taking him in deeply to the core of her existence, rising with him as if on wings to a place she had never been before, then crying out as she felt him fill her with a hot flood, as though she had drawn out of him and into her own body all his fever and pain and suffering, sensing the deep peace in him as he slumped against her and slept.

She lay quietly beside him, careful not to disturb him, revelling in the sound of his breathing and the warmth of his thin, ravaged body, savouring the ache where he had been deep within her.

She felt him coming awake and kissed him gently on the lips to welcome him back. He opened his eyes and looked into hers, first with bewilderment and then with dawning joy as the events of the night came back to him.

'I want you to be my wife,' he said.

'I am your wife already,' she replied, 'and I will be your wife until the day I die.'

Nefer looked back along the column of chariots. They were at full gallop, four abreast. The platoon commanders were watching for his signal. He looked ahead and saw the line of enemy foot soldiers out in the plain, distorted by the heat mirage so that they seemed to be a wriggling serpent, swimming in a lake of shimmering water where there was no water. He steered for their centre. Under Taita's care, Dov had fully recovered from her wound and now she ran strongly, matching Krus' long stride.

As they raced in he saw the enemy formation change: like a giant hedgehog, the line rolled itself into a ball, a tight circle two ranks deep, facing outwards, the outer rank with their long lances levelled, and the second rank with their lances thrust through the gaps, so that they offered a glittering wall of bronze spearheads. Nefer raced straight at the centre of the double row of lances, and then, when they were only two hundred paces away, he gave the hand signal for the 'wings of Horus'.

The formation of chariots opened like a blossom in the sun, successive ranks wheeling alternately right and left, spreading the wings of Horus to envelop the hedgehog of crouching infantrymen. The chariots whirled around them like the rim of a wheel around the hub, and the arrows from the short recurved cavalry bows flew into them in a dark cloud.

Nefer gave the signal to break off the attack and withdraw. Smoothly the chariots re-formed into columns of four and wheeled away. Another signal, and they split down the centre and came racing back, their javelins poised and the throwing thongs wound around their wrists.

As he swept past the infantry circle, Nefer raised his right fist in a salute, and shouted, 'Well done! That was much better.'

The foot-soldiers raised their lances to acknowledge his praise and shouted, 'Nefer Seti and Horus!'

Nefer slowed the horses and turned them, trotting back to halt his squadron in front of the ranks of infantry. Taita stepped out of the defensive circle to greet him.

'Any injuries?' Nefer asked. Even though the tips of the practice arrows they had shot into the hedgehog were padded with leather, they could still knock out an eye or inflict other damage.

'A few bruises.' Taita shrugged.

'They have done well,' Nefer said, then shouted to the centurion commanding the infantry, 'Let your lads fall out. I want to speak to them. Afterwards they can eat and drink. Then we will practise the false retreat again.'

There was an outcrop of rock that formed a natural podium, and Nefer climbed to the top of it while all the men, infantry and charioteers, gathered below him.

Taita squatted at the base of the rock and watched and listened. Nefer reminded him strongly of Pharaoh Tamose, his father, at the same age. He had the easy manner, and spoke simply but effectively in the colloquial language that his men understood best. At times like these he became one of them, and the warmth and respect they felt for him was evident in the way they responded, grinning and crowding closer to catch every word, laughing at his jests, scowling with shame at his rebukes, and glowing at his compliments.

Nefer reviewed the morning's exercises, giving them the credit they deserved, but ruthlessly picking out every deficiency in their performance.

'I think you are almost ready to give Trok and Naja the surprise of their pretty lives,' he ended. 'Now, get something to eat. We have not finished for the day – in fact we have barely begun.' They laughed and began to disperse.

Nefer jumped down from the rock, and as he did so Taita sprang to his feet and said quietly but urgently, 'Stop, Nefer! Do not move!' Nefer froze where he stood.

The cobra must have had its nest in the rock pile, but the noise and the trampling of feet and hoofs had disturbed it. It came slithering out of the crack in the dark rock just as Nefer jumped down and landed almost on top of it. The serpent reared up behind him, almost as high as his waist. Its hood was flared open, and its feathery black tongue flickered between the thin grinning lips. Its eyes were beads of polished onyx, with sparks of light in the black centres, and they were fastened on Nefer's long bare legs within easy striking distance in front of it.

The nearest men had heard Taita's warning and they turned back. Now almost five hundred men were gathered around Nefer, but none dared move. They stared in horror at the mortal predicament of their pharaoh.

The cobra gaped wide, the preliminary to the attack, and the bony fangs came erect in the pale roof of its mouth. Drops of venom sparkled on the needle points.

Taita swung the Periapt of Lostris on its long chain like a pendulum, and it twinkled in the sunlight. He sent it swinging past the cobra's raised head. Distracted, the serpent swivelled its eyes away from Nefer to stare at the glittering charm. Taita had his staff in his other hand, and he edged closer. 'When I strike, jump clear,' he whispered, and Nefer nodded. Taita moved gradually out to one side and the cobra turned with him, fascinated by the golden charm.

'Now!' said Taita, and thrust at the cobra with his staff. At the same instant Nefer jumped clear, and the snake struck at the staff. Taita jerked away, so the cobra missed and for an instant it was stretched out along the bare earth. With a movement even faster than the strike, Taita pinned it behind the head with the curved end of the staff, and a shout of relief went up from the watchers.

The cobra writhed and coiled into a glittering scaly ball around the end of the staff. Taita reached down and worked his hand through the heaving coils until he could grip the snake behind its head. Then he lifted it up and showed it to the men, who gasped with fear and horror. They shrank back instinctively as it coiled around Taita's long, thin arm. They had expected him to kill it but, still carrying the writhing snake, Taita walked through their ranks, out into the open desert.

There he threw the serpent from him. As it struck the ground it uncoiled and slithered away across the rocky earth. Taita watched it, rapt.

Suddenly there was a shrill cry from the sky above. They had all been so intent on the capture of the cobra that no one had seen the falcon hovering high in the blue above them. Now it stooped towards the earth, dropping towards the cobra. At the last moment the snake became aware of the danger and reared up again, its hood spread wide. In full flight the falcon sank its talons into the flared hood, an inch behind the head, then rose on heavily flogging wings, carrying the cobra dangling and twisting below it.

Taita watched the bird as it bore away the snake. It dwindled in size in the distance and at last disappeared into the blue-grey heat-haze that shrouded the horizon. Taita stood a long time staring after it. When he turned and walked back to where Nefer stood his expression was grave, and he was silent for the rest of that day. In the evening he rode back to Gallala in the chariot beside Nefer, still silent.

'It was an omen,' Nefer said, and glanced at him. He saw by Taita's face that this was so. 'I have listened to the men,' Nefer went on quietly. 'They are disturbed. None of them has ever seen the like before. The cobra is not the natural prey of the royal falcon.'

'Yes,' said Taita. 'It was an omen, a warning and a promise from the god.'

'What does it mean?' Nefer studied his face.

'The cobra threatened you. That means great danger. The royal bird flew towards the east with the snake in its talons. It means great danger in the east. But in the end the falcon triumphed.'

They both looked towards the east. 'We will take out a scouting expedition tomorrow at the first light of dawn,' Nefer decided.

In the chill darkness before the dawn Nefer and Taita waited on the mountain-top. The rest of the scouting party were encamped on the back slope. All told they were twenty men. For the sake of stealth they had left the chariots in Gallala and they travelled on horseback. Wheels threw more dust than hoofs alone, and hoofs made accessible these high, precipitous places along the coast where wheels could not travel.

Hilto and Shabako had taken other scouting parties to cover the terrain to the south; between them they could sweep all the eastern approaches to Gallala.

Nefer had brought his party from the Gebel Ataqa down along the western shores of the Red Sea, looking in on every port and fishing village along the way. Apart from a few trading caravans and wandering bands of Bedouin they had found nothing, no sign of the danger foreshadowed by the omen. Now they were camped above the port of Safaga.

Taita and Nefer had woken in the darkness and left the camp to climb to the look-out peak. They sat close together in companionable silence. Nefer spoke at last.

'Could it have been a false omen?'

Taita grunted and spat. 'A falcon with a cobra in his talons? It is not in nature. It was an omen, without doubt, but false perhaps. Ishtar the Mede and others are capable of setting such snares. It is possible.'

'But you do not think it is?' Nefer insisted. 'You would not have driven us so hard if you believed it to be false.'

'The dawn comes on apace.' Taita avoided the question, and looked instead to the darkling eastern sky, where the morning star hung, like a lantern, low on the horizon. The sky softened like a ripening fruit, turning the colour of persimmon and ripe pomegranate. The mountains of the far shore were black and sharp and ragged as the fangs of an ancient crocodile against the lightening backdrop of the heavens.

Taita stood up suddenly and leaned on his staff. Nefer never failed to be amazed by the acuity of those pale old eyes. He knew Taita had seen something. Nefer stood up beside him.

'What is it, Old Father?'

Taita laid a hand on his arm. 'The omen was not false,' he said simply. 'The danger is here.'

The sea was turning the grey of a dove's belly, but as the light strengthened the surface was speckled with white.

'The wind has whipped the sea into white horses,' Nefer said.

'No.' Taita shook his head. 'Those are not breakers. They're sails. A fleet under sail.'

The sun pushed its upper rim above the tops of the far

mountains, and sparkled on the tiny triangles of white. Like a vast flock of egrets returning to the roost, a fleet of dhows was heading into the port of Safaga.

'If this is the army of Trok and Naja, why would they come by sea?' Nefer asked quietly.

'It is the direct and shortest route from Mesopotamia. The boat crossing will save the horses and the men from the hard road through the desert. Without the warning of the snake and the falcon, we would not have expected danger from this direction,' Taita answered. 'It is a cunning move.' He nodded approval. 'It seems that they have commandeered every trading vessel and fishing boat in the entire Red Sea to make the crossing.'

They scrambled back down the mountain to the camp in the gorge below. The troopers were awake and alert. Nefer called in the sentries and gave them their orders. Two would ride back with all speed to Gallala, carrying his orders to Socco, whom he had left in command of the city. Most of the other men he split into pairs and sent south to find the scouting parties under Hilto and Shabako and bring them in. He kept five troopers with him.

Nefer and Taita watched the men he had despatched ride away, then they mounted and rode down through the hills towards Safaga, with the five men Nefer had selected following them. They reached the high ground above the port in the middle of the morning. Taita led them to an abandoned watchtower that overlooked the port and the approaches. They left the horses in the care of the troopers and climbed the rickety ladder to the top platform of the tower.

'The first boats are entering the bay.' Nefer pointed them out. They were deeply laden but with the wind on the quarter they came in swiftly with the bow waves curling white as salt in the sunlight and the big lateen sails bulging.

They rounded up just off the beach and dropped the heavy coral anchors. From the top of the tower Nefer and

Taita had a fine view down on to the open decks, which were crowded with men and horses.

As soon as the dhows were anchored the men removed the wooden gunwales along the dhows' sides. Their faint cries carried up to the ruined watchtower as they urged the horses to leap out. They struck the water with tall splashes of spray. Then the men stripped down to loincloths and jumped in after them. They seized the horses' manes and swam alongside them to the beach. The animals came ashore shaking the water from their bodies in a fine mist that turned to rainbows in the sunlight.

Within an hour the beach was swarming with men and horses, and defensive pickets had been set up around the mud-daub buildings of the little port.

'If only we had a squadron of chariots,' Nefer lamented, 'this would be the time to strike. With only half their force ashore and their chariots broken down, we could cut them to pieces.' Taita made no reply to such wishful speculation.

By now the bay was filled with shipping. The boats carrying the chariots and the baggage had anchored close in, and as the tide ran out from under them they took the ground and listed over. Soon the water was only knee deep around their hulls. The men from the beach waded out to begin unloading. They carried the parts of the broken-down chariots ashore and reassembled them on the beach.

The sun was setting over the western mountains when the last dhow entered the bay. This was the largest of them all, and at the peak of her stubby mast she flew the snarling leopard head gonfalon and the gaudy colours of the House of Trok Uruk.

'There he is.' Nefer pointed to the unmistakable figure in the bows.

'And that is Ishtar beside Trok, the dog and its master.' Taita had a fierce gleam in his pale eyes that Nefer had seldom seen before. They watched the strange pair wade ashore.

There was a stone jetty running out across the beach. Trok mounted it. It gave him a vantage-point from which to watch the disembarkation of the rest of his army.

'Do you see Naja's standard on any of the other ships?' Nefer asked, and Taita shook his head.

'Trok alone leads the expedition. He must have left Naja to hold Babylon and Mesopotamia. He has come to take care of personal business.'

'How do you know that?' Nefer demanded.

'There is an aura around him. It is like a dark red cloud. I can sense it even from here,' Taita said softly. 'All that hatred is focused on one person alone. He would never let Naja or anyone else share in the lust for revenge that has brought him here.'

'I am the object of his hatred?' Nefer asked.

'No, not you.'

'Who, then?'

'Above all else he comes for Mintaka.'

When the sun set, Nefer and Taita left the five troopers to shadow Trok's advance and rode hard through the night, back towards Gallala.

The morning after his landing at Safaga, Trok captured two Bedouin leading a string of donkeys down the road to Safaga. Unsuspecting, they walked out of the desert straight into the arms of his pickets. Trok's reputation had penetrated even into these desert fastnesses, so as soon as they learned who was their captor the Bedouin were desperate to please. They gave Trok tantalizing accounts of the resurrection of the ancient city. They told him of the fountain of sweet water that now flowed from the cave in the hills, and of the pastures of lush grass that surrounded Gallala. They also gave him an estimate of the numbers of chariots that Nefer Seti commanded, and Trok realized that he outnumbered his enemies five to one. Most important of all, they gave him details of the route from Safaga to the ancient city. Up to now Trok had had only second-hand knowledge of the approach march to Gallala, and it seemed that he had been misinformed. He had been told that even travelling fast it was a journey of three or four days, and he had planned on carrying his own water and fodder wagons with him from the coast. This would have been a long and laborious process. This new intelligence changed everything. The Bedouin assured him he could reach Gallala in a day and a night of hard riding.

He weighed the risks and dangers, then decided on a dash through the desert to Gallala to take the city by surprise. It would mean, of course, that they would ride straight into battle with the horses exhausted by the long march and with their waterskins empty. However, with numbers and surprise on their side they could seize the fountainhead and the pastures that the Bedouin had described. Once they had those prizes victory was assured.

It took him two more days to disembark all his squadrons, and to assemble the chariots. On the second evening he was ready to begin the forced march on Gallala.

With the waterskins filled, the leading cohorts pulled out of Safaga as soon as the heat went out of the sinking sun. Each of the chariots had two spare teams behind it on lead reins. They would not stop during the night to rest the horses, but would change them as they tired. Any exhausted animals would be turned loose and left behind for the remount herds to bring up.

Trok led the vanguard, and set a killing pace, alternately walking up the inclines, then whipping the horses into a trot or a canter downhill and on level ground. Once the waterskins were empty there was no turning back. By midmorning the following day the heat had become fierce, and they had used up most of the spare horses.

The Bedouin guides kept assuring Trok that Gallala was

not far ahead, but each time they topped a rise the same daunting vista of rock and baked earth shimmered in the heat mirage ahead.

In the late afternoon the Bedouin guides deserted. With the grace of *djinns* they melted away into the heat mirage, and though Trok sent a brace of chariots after them they were never seen again.

'I warned you,' Ishtar the Mede told Trok smugly. 'You should have listened to my advice. Those godless creatures were probably in the pay of Taita the Warlock. Almost certainly he has masked the road, and led us astray. We do not know how far it is to this mythical Gallala, or for that matter if it really exists.' For this uninvited opinion, Trok lashed him across his tattooed face. This did nothing to alleviate the sense of doom and despondency that threatened to overwhelm Trok. He whipped up the horses once more and took them up the next long, stony incline that faced them. He wondered how many more lay ahead. They were almost at the end of their tether, and he doubted they could keep going through the night.

Somehow they kept struggling onwards, or at least most of his force did. Fifty or sixty chariots burned out their last teams of horses, and Trok left them scattered back along the road.

The sun came up on the second day, warm as a kiss after the chill of the night, but it was a treacherous kiss. Soon it stung and dazzled their bloodshot eyes. For the first time Trok faced the possibility of dying here on this dreadful road to nowhere.

'One more hill,' he called to his last team of horses, and tried to whip them into a trot, but they stumbled up the easy incline with their heads hanging, and the sweat long ago dried to white salt on their flanks. Just below the crest Trok looked back down the straggling column of his army. Even without counting them he saw that he had lost half of his chariots. Hundreds of dismounted troopers were staggering along behind the column, but even as he watched he saw two or three fall and lie beside the track like dead men. There were vultures in the sky following them, hundreds of dark specks turning in high circles against the blue. He saw some slant down to the feast he had prepared for them.

'There is only one way,' he told Ishtar, 'and that is forward.' He cracked the whip over the backs of his team, and they went on painfully.

They reached the top of the hill, and Trok gawked in astonishment. The scene in the valley below him was like nothing he had ever imagined. The ruins of the ancient city rose before him. Their outline seemed ghostly but eternal. As he had been promised, the city was surrounded by fields of cool green, and a network of sparkling water canals. His horses smelt the water and strained against the reins with renewed strength.

Even in his desperate haste, Trok took time to assess the tactical situation. He saw at once that the city was helpless and undefended. The gates stood wide open and from them poured the panic-stricken rabble of the escaping populace. Carrying their children and pathetic bundles of possessions they streamed away up the narrow but steep-sided valley to the west of Gallala. A few foot-soldiers mingled with the refugees, but they were obviously in rout and out of hand. There was no sign of cavalry or of fighting chariots. They were a flock of sheep before the wolf pack, but the wolves were parched and weak with thirst.

'Seueth has delivered them into our hands,' Trok shouted with triumph. 'Before the sun sets this day you will have more women and gold than you can use!'

The cry was taken up by the men who followed him over the ridge, and they rode down as fast as their exhausted horses could move to the first irrigation ditch. They spread out along the length of it, the horses sucking up the blessed liquid until their bellies swelled as though in pregnancy.

The men threw themselves full-length along the bank, plunging their faces under, or filling their helmets and pouring it over their heads and down their throats.

'You should have let me poison the irrigation canals,' Nefer said flatly, as they watched from the other side of the valley.

'You know better than that.' Taita shook his silver head. 'That would have been an offence that the gods would never forgive. In this bitter land only Seth or Seueth could contemplate such a foul deed.'

'On this day I could play Seth willingly enough.' Nefer smiled bleakly, but he said it merely to provoke the Magus. 'Your two rogues have done well.' He glanced at the two ragged Bedouin who knelt beside Taita. 'Pay them and let them go.'

'They place no value on gold,' Taita explained. 'When I lived at Gebel Nagara they brought their children to me, and I cured them of the Yellow Flowers.' He made a sign of blessing over the crouching men and said a few words to them in their dialect, thanking them for risking their lives to mislead Trok, and promising them his future protection. They kissed his feet then slipped away among the boulders.

Taita and Nefer gave their full attention to the unfolding battle in the valley below. Trok's men and horses had drunk until their bellies bulged and now they were mounting. Even though he had lost so many chariots on the approach march, Trok still outnumbered Nefer's forces at least three to one.

'We dare not meet him on open ground,' Nefer mused, and looked down upon the mass of refugees escaping up the valley below them. To begin with there had been very few women in the city – Nefer had deliberately kept their numbers down to eke out the reserves of food for his fighting men – and even they, including Mintaka and Merykara, together with all the children, the sick and wounded, had been evacuated from Gallala two days before. Meren had gone on one of the wagons carrying the contents of the treasury, the gold they had lifted from the false pharaohs. Nefer had sent them all to Gebel Nagara, where Trok would never find them, and the tiny spring of water would just support them until after the battle was decided.

Now Gallala was stripped of everything of value, every chariot, weapon and piece of armour. He gazed down on the refugees with satisfaction. Even from this close it was difficult to tell that they were not women and civilians, but disguised foot-soldiers. Many of these stalwarts were tripping and stumbling in their long skirts and shawls. The bundles they carried in their arms were not swaddled infants, but their bows and swords wrapped in shawls. Their long lances had been cached among the rocks higher up the valley where his main force was concealed.

All Trok's chariots had finished watering and they were coming on across the pastures in tight and ordered formations, wave after wave of fighting vehicles. The water had revived them miraculously, and before them lay the promise of plunder and rapine.

'Pray Horus that we can entice Trok to take up the pursuit and enter the valley,' Nefer whispered. 'If he does not take the bait and seizes the undefended city instead, then he denies us the water and grazing. We would be forced to come to battle on the open ground where he would have every advantage.'

Taita said nothing. He stood with the golden Periapt pressed to his lips and his eyes turned upwards in the attitude that Nefer had come to know so well.

The enemy were close enough now for Nefer to be able to pick out Trok's chariot among the moving mass of vehicles, as it wheeled into a position across the mouth of the valley crowded with the fleeing refugees. Trok was in the centre of the leading rank, ten of his chariots on each of his flanks, on a front wide enough to sweep the valley from side to side. Behind him the rest of his chariots were formed up. The dust settled around them and a terrible silence fell over them. The only sound was the faint babble and hubbub of the fleeing rabble in the gut of the narrow valley ahead of them.

'Come, Trok Uruk!' Nefer whispered. 'Order the charge! Ride into history!'

In the leading chariot in the front rank of the massed forces, Ishtar the Mede crouched beside Trok's massive armoured figure. He was so agitated that he reached up to tug at the ribbons of Trok's beard.

'The smell of the Warlock hangs in the air like the reek of a ten-day-old corpse.' His voice was shrill, and saliva frothed on his lips and flew in a cloud with the force of his emotion. 'He waits for you up there, like a man-eating beast. I can feel his presence. Look up, mighty Pharaoh!'

Trok was distracted enough to glance up at the sky. The vultures had dropped lower.

'Yes! Yes!' Ishtar pressed the small advantage. 'They are Taita's chickens. They wait for him to feed them with your flesh.'

Trok looked back up the valley at the prize that lay before him, but the shadows of the vultures flitted over the earth between them and he hesitated.

Hidden among the boulders on the steep side of the valley Nefer watched him. He was so close now that Nefer fancied that he could read his expression.

'Forward, Trok!' Nefer murmured. 'Sound the charge. Lead your army into the valley.' He could sense doubt in the manner that Trok fiddled with the reins in his hand, and turned his head to look down at the skinny figure of Ishtar beside him.

The Mede's blue-painted face was turned up to him earnestly, and he touched Trok and tugged at his armour with the force of his entreaties. 'It is a snare laid for you by the Warlock. If you never trust me again, you must trust me now. There is death in the air, and the stench of treachery. I can feel Taita's spells like bats' wings beating against my face.'

Trok scratched his beard, and glanced over his shoulder at the ranks of chariots parked wheel to wheel and his troopers leaning forward in cruel anticipation of his order.

'Turn aside, mighty Trok. Seize the city and the water fountain. Nefer Seti and the Warlock will perish out there in the desert, as we so nearly did. That way is certain. The other way is madness.'

On the hillside Nefer narrowed his eyes as he watched his disguised troopers scurrying away up the valley, and he knew that the moment was passing. 'What is holding Trok? Will he not commit to the charge?' Nefer cried aloud. 'If he does not charge now . . .'

'Look to the head of the valley.' Taita had not opened his eyes. Even in his agitation Nefer glanced up the valley, and stiffened with alarm. His fist tightened on the hilt of his sword until the knuckles turned white as bone.

'It is not possible!' he growled.

Near the top end of the valley, but fully visible from where Trok's chariots were drawn up, was a slab of rock. Square and ochre-coloured, it stood like a man-made monument beside the road. On top of this, above the stream of fleeing refugees, had appeared a single figure. It was a woman, young and slim, with long dark hair that hung to her waist. Her *chiton* was the crimson of the royal House of Apepi: it stood out brilliantly, a speck of colour in the bleakness of bare rock and sand.

'Mintaka!' Nefer breathed. 'I ordered her to go with Meren and Merykara to Gebel Nagara.'

'We know that she would never have disobeyed you.' Taita opened his eyes and smiled ironically. 'Therefore, it seems that she must have misheard you.'

'This is your doing,' Nefer said bitterly. 'You are using her as bait for Trok. You have placed her in mortal danger.'

'Perhaps I can control the *khamsin*,' Taita said, 'but not even I can control Mintaka Apepi. What she does, she does of her own free will.'

Below them Trok had turned to give the order for his chariots to wheel away, to let the rabble escape, and to seize the fountain and the city of Gallala as Ishtar was urging him. Before he could speak he felt Ishtar stiffen beside him, and heard him whisper, 'This is something that Taita has conjured.'

Trok jerked around and stared up the long rising valley. He saw the tiny figure in the crimson dress, standing high on the yellow rock platform. He recognized in an instant the object of all his hatred and rage. 'Mintaka Apepi,' he snarled, 'I have come for you, you adulterous little dog-bitch. I will make you plead for death.'

'It is an illusion, Pharaoh. Don't let the Warlock deceive you.'

'That is no illusion,' Trok said grimly. 'I will prove it to you when I bury my prong in her warm flesh, and prod her until she bleeds.'

'The Warlock has blinded you,' Ishtar howled. 'There is death all around us.'

He tried to leap down from the footplate and run, but Trok seized him by his lacquered locks and hauled him back. 'Nay, stay with me, Ishtar the Mede. I will let you have a taste of her sweet crevice before I throw her to my bully-boys to finish off.' He raised his clenched fist high above his head and shouted, 'Forward! March!'

The chariots on either hand rolled forward together, and the ranks behind followed Trok into the valley, the sun sparkling on the javelin heads, and the dust rose around them like smoke. The tail of the fleeing refugees was three hundred paces ahead when Trok gave his next order.

'Forward at the gallop! Charge!'

The horses leaped away, and in a rising thunder of hoofs and wheels they swept up the narrow valley.

'Trok has committed,' Nefer said softly. 'But at what cost? If he takes Mintaka . . .' He could not bring himself to go on, but he stared in anguish at her tall lithe figure standing serenely in the path of the storm.

'Now you have something to fight for,' Taita said gently.

Nefer felt all his love and deadly concern for Mintaka become battle rage, but it was a cold hard rage that sharpened every one of his senses and filled his being to the exclusion of all else.

As the phalanx of chariots swept by below where he stood on the side of the valley, he stepped out from behind the rock that had concealed him. The complete attention of Trok and his troopers was fixed on the helpless victims ahead of their racing chariots. They had no eyes for the tall figure that appeared suddenly high on their flank. But all Nefer's men could see him clearly. They were hidden among the boulders down both slopes of the valley. Nefer raised his sword above his head, and as the last chariot sped past he brought it down sharply.

The wagons were poised on the steep gradient, with their wheels chocked and lashed to hold them. They were screened from view with dried grass the exact colour of their surroundings, and they were so heavily laden with rocks that the axles sagged. At Nefer's signal his wagoners pulled out the wooden chocks and slashed away the lashings that held the wheels. From both sides of the valley the wagons rolled forward, gathering speed, bounding down on top of the massed chariots below.

When Ishtar screamed at his side, Trok tore his eyes from Mintaka's figure at the far end of the valley, and he saw the huge vehicles tearing down upon his squadrons. 'Back!' he shouted. 'Break away!' But even his bull voice was lost in the uproar. The charge once launched could not be stopped, and there was no space to manoeuvre in the narrow floor of the valley.

The first wagons crashed into the head of the charge. There was the rending of wood, the screams of crushed men and horses, the thunder of wagons overturning and capsizing, shedding their loads of rock.

Suddenly the way ahead of Trok was blocked by one of the cumbersome carts, and his horses swerved into the chariot running beside him. In an instant the magnificent charge was transformed into a shambles of shattered and overturned vehicles, and crippled horses.

The wagons had sealed off the valley at both ends. Even the chariots that had not been smashed and capsized were now bottled up in a struggling mass. The whole purpose of the chariot, its strength and threat, was its ability to run and turn, to charge and pull back at speed. Now they were immobilized, held by walls of stone, and Nefer's archers were on the slopes above them. The first volleys decimated the unprotected charioteers. Within minutes the valley was transformed into a slaughterhouse.

Some of Trok's men jumped down from their trapped vehicles and charged up the sides of the valley on foot. But they were exhausted by the gruelling approach march, and burdened with their armour. The ground was steep and rugged and they moved only slowly. From the cover of the boulders and walls of hastily erected stone *zarebas*, Nefer's men met them with long lances and hails of javelins. Most were cut down before they had reached the first rank of defenders.

Trok looked around him wildly, seeking some way out of the trap, but one of his horses was dead, crushed by the spilled load of rocks from the wagon that blocked his way forward. Behind him the other vehicles were so crowded that there was no room for him to turn or back up. Arrows and javelins were singing around him, clattering against the sides of the chariot, clanging off his helmet and breastplate.

Before Trok could restrain him, Ishtar took advantage of the confusion to spring down from the footplate and scuttle away between the wrecked chariots and plunging, shrilling horses. Then Trok looked ahead again, and incredulously he saw Mintaka still standing unmoved on the top of the ochre rock pile just ahead of him. She was staring at him with a cold look of revulsion on her lovely face that turned his rage to madness.

He snatched up his war bow from the rack at his side and reached for an arrow from the quiver, but then he changed his mind, threw the weapon aside and shouted at her over the heads of his rearing and plunging horses. 'No! An arrow is too good for a bitch in heat. I am coming to get you with my bare hands, I want to feel you struggling as I squeeze the last breath out of you, you filthy little harlot.'

He drew his sword and sprang down to the ground. He ran forward under the hoofs of his rearing horse, and scrambled over the overturned body of the wagon. Two of Nefer's men jumped out from behind the rocks to oppose him but he hacked them down and ran over their twitching corpses. His eyes were fastened hungrily on the girl in the crimson dress standing tall and proud ahead of him, the flame to the moth.

Nefer saw Trok break out of the trap, and he ran down the slope, springing from rock to rock. 'Run, Mintaka! Get away from him,' he shouted urgently, but either she did not hear him or she would not listen.

Trok did hear him, and he stopped and looked up. 'Come on, then, my pretty boy, I have enough blade for both you and your whore.'

Without breaking his run, Nefer hurled the javelin in his hand, but Trok caught it neatly in the centre of the light targe he carried on his shoulder, and the weapon spun away, clattering on the rock, and landed at Mintaka's feet. She ignored it.

The throw had been enough to divert Trok for the

moment, and Nefer sprang down on to the level ground in front of him. Trok went on guard as Nefer confronted him and then his face twisted into a ferocious grin. He crouched behind the bronze shield and waved the sword in his right hand. 'Come, puppy,' he said. 'Let us test your claim to the double crown.'

Nefer used the impetus of his run down the slope and came at him without a pause. Trok caught the first blow on the circle of bronze. Nefer jumped back just as Trok cut at him over the top of the targe. Nefer closed in again, trading thrust for cut.

Nefer's men had seen him charge down the hillside. They followed his example, left the cover of the rocks and came bounding down in waves. Within seconds the full length of the valley was choked from side to side with struggling, hacking, thrusting men.

Nefer feinted at Trok's hip, aiming at the joint of his armour. When Trok covered, he swung backhanded at his face. Trok was surprised by the change of direction and by the speed of the stroke. Though he jerked his head back the point of Nefer's blade split his cheek open and the blood gushed into his beard. The wound galvanized him, and Trok roared and rushed at Nefer. He swung blows from every angle with such rapidity that his sword seemed to form an impenetrable wall of shining bronze around him. Nefer was forced to fall back before the attack until he felt the stone slab on which Mintaka stood pressing into his back.

He could no longer retreat or manoeuvre, and he was forced to pit himself against all Trok's bull-like strength, and trade him blow for blow. In a contest of this nature, there were few men who could stand against Trok, who never seemed to flag, and he laughed as Nefer managed to turn some of his blows. 'Let us see how long you can stem the tide, boy. I can go on like this all day, can you?' he asked, without missing a stroke. Metal clanged and rang on metal, while Trok moved gradually to the right blocking the only way that Nefer might slip out of his clutches.

Trok's strength was like some malignant force of nature. Nefer felt that he was caught in a great storm wind, as helpless as if he were carried away on a rip-tide of the ocean. As much as the years of battle training had hardened him, they had not prepared him for this. He felt his right arm tiring and slowing as he tried to match Trok.

Trok nicked the side of his neck, and then seconds later sliced open his leather corselet and scored him along the ribs. Nefer knew that his only chance of surviving the storm was to trade his speed and agility against Trok's brute strength, but he was pinned against the rock. He had to break away.

He caught the next cut high on his blade and deflected it just sufficiently to make an opening through which he could escape, but as he leaped into it he exposed his left flank. Trok recovered and drove in a low thrust that laid open his thigh just above the tattooed cartouche. The blood ran down into his sandal and squelched at every pace he took.

The last of Nefer's strength was ebbing away, and Trok swept up his blade and locked it with his own, forcing his guard higher and higher. Nefer knew that if he attempted to break away he would expose his chest for the killing thrust. Yet the cut in his thigh had weakened and slowed him still further. The grin on Trok's face was triumphant. 'Courage, boy! It is nearly over. Then you can rest – for ever,' he gloated.

Nefer heard Mintaka shout something, but it made no sense, and he could not afford the distraction. Gradually Trok forced aside his blade and towered over him, so they came chest to chest, then suddenly he shifted his weight to the left, towards Nefer's wounded leg. Nefer tried to counter, but his leg gave way under him. Trok hooked his foot behind Nefer's heel and threw him over backwards.

The sword flew from Nefer's weakened grip, and as he sprawled on the sunbaked earth, Trok lifted his blade above his head with both hands for the killing stroke. He was poised like that when suddenly his expression changed to one of surprise and bewilderment. Without completing the blow he reached up behind his own neck with one hand. He brought the hand back and held it before his face. It was wet with his blood. He opened his mouth to say something, but a double stream of bright blood trickled from the corners of his mouth and he turned slowly away from Nefer. Trok stared up at Mintaka who stood on the pinnacle of the rock above him. With a detached feeling of disbelief, Nefer saw the shaft of the javelin sticking out of the back of Trok's neck.

As she saw Nefer go down, Mintaka had snatched up the javelin that lay at her feet, the weapon that Nefer had thrown at the start of the engagement. She hurled it at Trok's back. The point took Trok beneath the rim of his bronze helmet and went in deeply, just missing the spinal column, but opening the carotid artery.

Standing like a gargoyle with his mouth wide open, blood spewing out in a fountain, Trok dropped his sword and reached up. He seized Mintaka around the waist and dragged her screaming from her perch above him. He was trying to say something, but the sheets of blood pouring from his mouth drowned his voice.

Mintaka screamed as he crushed her to his chest, and Nefer scrambled to his feet. He picked up Trok's sword from where he had dropped it, and limped up behind him.

Mintaka's cries had given renewed strength to his sword arm. He sent his first thrust through the lacings of Trok's corselet, deeply into his back. Trok stiffened, and dropped Mintaka. She scrambled away, and Nefer pulled out the blade and stabbed again. Swaying on his feet, Trok turned slowly to face him. He took a step towards Nefer, reaching out for him with bloody mailed hands. Nefer stabbed him in the throat, and Trok dropped to his knees, clutching at the blade. Nefer pulled it away, slicing deeply into Trok's fingers and palms, severing the sinews and nerves.

Trok toppled forward on his face, and Nefer stabbed him through the lacing, between his shoulder-blades to his heart. He left the blade in him, and turned to Mintaka who crouched in the shelter of the rock. She flew to him, and clung to him with all her strength. Now that the danger was past, Mintaka lost all her icy control and she was sobbing, barely coherently, 'I thought he was going to kill you, my love.'

'He almost did, but for you,' Nefer gasped. 'I owe you a life.'

'It was terrible.' Mintaka's voice quavered. 'I thought he would never die.'

'He was a god.' Nefer tried to laugh but it came out wrongly. 'They take a little killing.'

He became aware that the sounds of battle from further down the valley had changed. With his arm still around her, he turned to look back. Trok's men had seen their pharaoh cut down, and the fight had gone out of them. They were throwing down their weapons, and wailing, 'Enough! Enough! We yield. All praise to Pharaoh Nefer Seti, the one true king.'

With the realization of victory, Nefer felt the last vestiges of strength flow out of his battered and bleeding body. He had just enough left to raise his voice, and shout, 'Give them quarter. They are our brother Egyptians. Give them quarter!'

As Nefer slumped down, Taita materialized at his side and helped Mintaka lower him to the ground. While the two of them dressed his wounds, and staunched the bleeding from the deep cut in his thigh, his officers came to report to Nefer.

Nefer discounted his own injuries as he demanded to know who had survived the battle and who had been wounded and killed. With joy, and thanks to Horus and the Red God, Nefer saw that his trusted captains, Hilto, Shabako and Socco, were among the men who crowded around him, exulting in the victory, proud of themselves and their men, filled with joy to see him alive.

They made a litter of lances and carried him back down the valley to Gallala, but it was a long journey for Trok's captured officers, and men crowded the roadside, kneeling unarmed and bare-headed to plead for his mercy, shouting repentance and remorse that they had ever taken up arms against the true Pharaoh.

Three times before they reached the gates of the city, Nefer signalled for his litter to be lowered and allowed the captured centurions and captains to come forward and kiss his feet. 'I spare you from the traitor's death you so richly deserve,' he told them sternly, 'but you are all reduced to the rank of sergeants of the Blue, and you must prove once more your duty and loyalty to the House of Tamose.'

They praised him for his mercy, but Nefer frowned and shook his head when they addressed him as a god. 'I am not one of the pantheon, as the blasphemers Trok and Naja claim they are.' But they would not be dissuaded, and renewed their praises and entreaties, and his own men, led by his brother warriors of the Red Road, joined their voices to those of the defeated, begging him to declare his divinity.

To distract them Nefer issued his orders with a frowning mien. 'The corpse of Trok Uruk, the false claimant to the double crown of this very Egypt, shall be burned without ceremony, here upon the battlefield, so that his soul shall wander through all eternity seeking but never finding a home.'

They murmured with awe for this was the most dreadful punishment that could be devised.

'The other enemy dead are to be treated with all respect, and allowed embalmment and a decent burial. The name of Trok Uruk shall be erased from every monument and building in the land, and the temple that he erected to himself in Avaris shall in his stead be dedicated to the winged Horus in memory of the victory that he gave us this day before the city of Gallala.'

They shouted their approbation at this decree, and Nefer went on, 'All the possessions of Trok Uruk, all his treasure and estates, his slaves and buildings, his warehouses and goods of whatsoever nature shall be forfeited to the state. Send water wagons back along the road to Safaga, with grooms and surgeons to bring in all the horses, chariots and men that Trok Uruk left along the way during his arrogant march on our capital here in Gallala. If they repudiate the false pharaohs and swear allegiance to the House of Tamose the prisoners shall be pardoned and recruited into our armies.'

By the time Nefer had given his last order, and issued his last decree for that day, his voice was hoarse, he was pale and almost exhausted. As they carried him through the city gates he asked Mintaka quietly, 'Where is Taita? Has anybody seen the Magus?' But Taita had disappeared.

Taita watched from the hillside above the battlefield as the jaws of the trap closed on Trok's army and his chariots were smashed by the rock-filled wagons, the arrows and the javelins falling like flights of locusts upon the survivors, when a single bizarre figure caught his eye in the chaos.

Ishtar the Mede scampered between the rocks. Like a running hare he disappeared from sight only to reappear further up the slope, ducking and dodging. By some chance or magical charm he avoided the arrows and javelins of Nefer's troops and at last dived over the crest and disappeared from sight.

Taita let him go. There would be time for him later. He

watched the climax of the battle, extending all his powers to act as a shield over Nefer during his single combat with Trok at the base of the rock. Even at this distance he managed to deflect many of Trok's blows that should have been fatal, and when Trok went for the final thrust into Nefer's thigh his blade might have found the great femoral artery if Taita had not used all his influence to turn the point aside.

Since that time long ago when Taita had saved Mintaka from harm during the encounter with the cobra of the goddess, she had become a subject who responded readily to his influence. She had the intelligence and imagination that opened her mind to him. It was impossible to influence a fool. He had summoned her back to Gallala to show herself to Trok at the head of the valley, and to lure him into the trap. Then, when she had stood frozen with horror on the rock above the fighting pair, Taita had bent her to his will once again and put into her mind the impulse to reach down for the javelin that lay at her feet. He had bolstered her right arm as she steadied her aim and threw. Then, as the life went out of Trok, he had rushed down the slope to minister to Nefer and to bind up the wound that had cut so perilously close to the pulsing artery in his thigh.

When his brother warriors of the Red Road lifted the young pharaoh on to the litter of spears, Taita with his duty done for the present drifted away into the throng. Nobody paid him any heed as he went.

He picked up the tracks that Ishtar had left as he escaped out of the narrow valley and followed them until they were impossible to discern on the earth on the top of the hills, which was baked hard as mosaic tiles by the sun.

Taita stopped and crouched down. From his pouch he took out a sliver of dried root and slipped it into his mouth. As he chewed on it, he opened his mind and reached out to detect the Mede's aura, the trace he had left as he passed. As the root sharpened his senses Taita saw the aura in the corner of his vision. It was a shadow, dirty grey and ephemeral, that vanished when he looked directly at it. Each person had his own aura. Nefer Seti, on account of his noble and divine inner being, threw a rosy essence that to Taita was readily detectable. Taita had followed that faint rosy emanation to find Nefer after he had been mauled by the lion and he and Mintaka were lost in the desert beyond Dabba.

Ishtar the Mede's aura was dark and tainted. Taita stood up and went on again after it, striding out on his long legs with his staff tapping on the stones. Every so often he saw physical confirmation that he was on the right track, by a smudged footprint in a softer patch of earth or by a recently dislodged pebble.

Ishtar had circled round to the south then come back towards Gallala. Taita was alarmed and lengthened his stride. If Ishtar was trying to get close to Nefer again to work some mischief, Taita must intercept him. However, the pursuit led him to one of the chariots Trok had abandoned on his march up from the coast. From the wreck Ishtar had salvaged something, and Taita closed his eyes and worked out what it was.

'A waterskin,' he murmured, and Taita saw where he had scraped away the earth to drag the skin out from under the side of the capsized chariot. Another dry and empty skin was still hanging there. Ishtar had left it, probably because he knew he could carry the weight of only one full skin. Taita picked up the empty skin and slung it over his shoulder. He left the chariot, with the dead horses in the traces already beginning to stink, and followed Ishtar onwards.

Carrying the waterskin with him, Ishtar had gone back towards Gallala. When he topped the ridge above the city he had crept down to the bank of the closest irrigation canal. The imprint of his knees was clear in the wet clay where he had knelt to drink and then to fill the skin he carried. Taita drank himself. After that he filled his own waterskin. Then he rose and followed the traces Ishtar had left as he started back eastwards along the road towards Safaga and the coast. Taita strode after him.

Night fell and Taita kept on. Sometimes the aura of the Mede faded away completely, but Taita followed the road. At other times it grew stronger, until Taita smelt it, a faint, musty, unpleasant odour. When it was this strong he could fathom the essence of the Mede. He could detect his vindictive and vengeful nature. He divined that Ishtar was frightened and demoralized by the turn that the fates had taken against him, but his powers were still formidable. He constituted a great and real danger, not only to Nefer and Mintaka but to Taita himself. If he were allowed to escape and regenerate his scattered powers, he might threaten the future of the House of Tamose and Apepi. Ishtar was one of the higher adepts, an evil one, which made him all the more dangerous. He could certainly overlook his selected victims, and conjure up all manner of profanities to bring down disaster on Nefer and Mintaka. He could sicken and sour their love for each other, bring down suffering, miscarriage and plague, pains and disease with no focus or reason, mental aberrations, madness and eventually death.

Even Taita was not immune to his baleful spirit. If he were allowed to escape, Ishtar might gradually erode Taita's powers and frustrate his work. Unless Taita acted now, while he had the opportunity, to destroy him utterly.

The gibbous moon rose over the stark hills and lit Taita's way. He was in that long swinging stride with which he could cover the ground as swiftly as a mounted man. He could sense that ahead of him Ishtar was unaware that he was being followed and his pace was much slower. Every hour that passed Taita felt his aura stronger and nearer. I will be up to him before sunrise, he thought, and at that moment he doubled over and vomited in a projectile stream on to the stony track. Overwhelmed with a sudden, terrible nausea, Taita almost collapsed but regained his balance, and staggered back, wiping the bitter taste of bile from his mouth.

'Careless!' he rebuked himself angrily. 'So close to the quarry I should have taken greater care. The Mede has detected me.'

He drank a little water from the skin, then went forward cautiously. He pointed his staff ahead and swung it slowly from side to side. Suddenly it grew heavy in his hand. He followed that direction and saw ahead of him, glinting in the moonlight, the circle of pale pebbles laid out on the side of the track.

'A gift from the Mede,' he said aloud.

Nausea seized him once more, but he choked it back, struck the earth with the staff and spoke one of the words of power.

'*Ncube!*' His nausea receded, and he could approach the circle closer.

It is not enough that I should break his spell, he thought grimly. I must turn it back upon the Mede.

He used the tip of his staff to move one of the pebbles out of the circle, disrupting its power. Now he could squat beside the pattern without experiencing any harm. Without touching any of the pebbles he leaned close and sniffed at them. The smell of the Mede was strong upon them and he smiled with cold satisfaction.

'He touched them with his bare hands,' Taita whispered. Ishtar had left traces of his sweat on them. Taita could use that faint effluent. Careful not to make the same mistake, he moved the pebbles with the tip of his staff, forming them into a different pattern, an arrowhead pointing in the direction that Ishtar had taken. He took a mouthful of water from the skin and spat it on the pebbles, which shone wetly in the moonlight. Then he pointed his staff like a javelin along the same line as the arrowhead of pebbles.

'*Kydash!*' he shouted, and felt pressure build up in his

eardrums as though he had plunged deeply below the surface of the ocean. Before it became unbearable, it began slowly to abate, and he felt a sense of well-being and pleasure. It was done. He had turned it back upon the Mede.

A league ahead Ishtar the Mede was hurrying along the track. He was by now fully aware of the pursuit. He was confident that the barrier he had placed across the track would stop most men, but he knew it would not long deter the one he feared most.

Suddenly he staggered in mid-stride and clutched his ears with both hands. The pain was blinding, as though a red hot dagger had been thrust deep into each of his eardrums. He groaned and dropped to his knees. 'It is the Warlock.' He sobbed. The pain was so intense that he could not think clearly. 'He has turned it back on me.'

With shaking hands he reached into the pouch on his belt and brought out his most potent talisman, the dry embalmed hand of one of Pharaoh Tamose's infants who had died soon after birth during the plague of the Yellow Flowers. Ishtar had robbed the little prince's tomb to obtain it. The hand was dark and clawed like a monkey's paw.

He held it to his pounding head, and felt the pain start to abate. He came unsteadily to his feet, and broke into a shuffling dance, chanting and wailing. The pain in his ears cleared. He gave one final leap in the air and stood facing back along the way he had come. He could feel the presence of the Warlock close, like the threat of thunder on a close summer's day.

He thought of laying another snare, but knew that Taita would send it back to him. I must turn aside and conceal my path, he decided. He ran on along the road seeking the place where he could turn. He found where the track crossed an intrusion of grey schist, so hard that even the passing of Trok's legions had left no mark upon it.

With his left forefinger he traced out lightly the sacred symbol of Marduk on the rock, spat on it and uttered the three hidden names of the god that would summon him.

'Hide me from my enemies, mighty Marduk. Bring me safely back to your temple in Babylon, and I will make for you the sacrifice you love so well,' he promised. Best of all Marduk loved little girls sent into his furnace.

Ishtar stood on one leg and hopped backwards five and fifty paces, the esoteric number of Marduk known only to the adepts. Then he turned sharply off the road and set out at right angles to it, heading into the northern wilderness. He went swiftly, trying to open the distance between him and the man who pursued him.

Taita reached the point where the ridge of grey schist crossed the road, and stopped abruptly. The aura that had been so strong only moments before had disappeared like mist in the warmth of the rising sun. There was neither taste nor smell nor a glimpse of the Mede remaining. He went on down the road a short way, but found that the trail was dead and cold. Quickly he retraced his steps until he reached the point where he had lost it. Ishtar would not have wasted his time with a simple spell of concealment. He knows that the Ashes or the Water and Blood would hardly give me pause, he thought.

He looked up at the sky, and from the starry firmament picked out the single red star low on the horizon, the star of the goddess Lostris. He held up her Periapt and began to chant the Praise to the Goddess. He had barely completed the first stanza when he felt an angry, alien presence. Another god had been invoked on this spot, and knowing Ishtar he could guess well enough who that was. He started on the second stanza of praise and on the bare rock ahead of him appeared a glow, like that of the copper walls of the furnace in the temple of Marduk when the sacrificial fires were burning.

Marduk is affronted, and shows his anger, he thought, with satisfaction. He went to stand over the faintly glowing spot and intoned. 'You are far from your own land and your temple, Marduk of the furnace. Few worship you in this very Egypt. Your powers are dissipated. I invoke the name of the goddess Lostris, and you cannot stand against it.'

He lifted the skirt of his *chiton*. 'I quench your fires, Marduk,' he said, and squatting like a woman, he urinated on the rock. It sizzled and steamed like a bar of metal from the forge of the coppersmith drenched in the trough. 'In the name of the goddess Lostris, Marduk the Devourer, stand aside and let me pass.'

The rock cooled quickly, and as the steam dispersed he could make out once more the shadowy traces of the Mede beyond as they turned off the track towards the north. The veil that Ishtar had laid was pierced and torn. Taita stepped through it and set off again after him.

The horizon paled and the light increased to a golden radiance in the east. Taita knew that he was gaining steadily, and he strained his eyes ahead in the gathering light for the first glimpse of his quarry. Instead he came to an abrupt halt. At his feet gaped a terrible abyss, whose sheer sides dropped into darkness far below. No man could scale those depths, and there was no way around this obstacle.

Taita looked across at the far side. It was at the very least a thousand paces across, and the precipice was even more daunting when seen from this angle. There were vultures soaring over the bottomless gulf. One of the grotesque birds circled in to alight on its shaggy nest of sticks and twigs built on a ledge high in the opposite cliff face.

Taita shook his head with admiration. 'Wonderful, Ishtar!' he murmured. 'Even the vultures. That was a masterful touch. I could not have improved upon it, but such an effort called for a great expenditure of strength. It must have cost you dearly.'

Taita stepped out over the edge of the cliff, and instead of plunging down into airy space, there was firm ground under his feet. The vista of cliffs and gorges, even the circling vultures, wavered and broke up as a mirage does when you walk towards it.

The abyss was gone and in its place was a gentle plain of stony ground, with low hills still blue with shadows at the far end. In the middle of this plain, not five hundred paces away, stood Ishtar the Mede. He was facing Taita with both arms held above his head, trying desperately to preserve the illusion that he had created. When he saw that he had failed and that Taita was striding towards him like an avenging *djinn*, he dropped his arms with a hopeless, resigned gesture and turned towards the limestone hills at the far end of the stony plain. He broke into a shambling run, his black robes swirling around his legs.

Taita followed him with his long indefatigable strides, and when Ishtar looked back there was desperation on his blue-whorled face. For a moment he stared in terror at the tall silver-haired figure, then he turned and ran faster. For a while he pulled away, opening the gap, then his run faltered, and Taita gained upon him inexorably.

Ishtar dropped the waterskin from his shoulder, and ran with a lighter step, but he was only a few hundred paces ahead of Taita when he reached the low hills that were grey blue with limestone outcrops in the early light. He disappeared into one of the gullies.

When Taita reached the mouth of the gully he saw Ishtar's footprints strung along the sandy floor ahead of him, but they disappeared round the corner where the gully turned sharply to the right. Taita followed him, but as he reached the corner of pale limestone pillars, he heard the thunderous grunting and roaring of a wild beast. As he stepped round he saw that the gully narrowed ahead of him, and standing foursquare in the way, its tail lashing from side to side, was a huge male lion.

The lion's black mane was erect, a great bush that shook like grass in a high wind at each roar that erupted from the gaping jaws. Its eyes were golden and the pupils were implacable black slits. The rank, bestial scent of the animal was thick in the hot air, the stench of the rotting carcasses on which it had feasted with those long yellow fangs.

Taita looked down at the sandy earth on which the massive paws were planted with all the claws unsheathed. He could still see Ishtar's footprints in the sand, but the paws of the lion had left no mark.

Taita never broke his stride. He raised the Periapt on its chain, and walked straight at the slavering animal. Instead of rising in pitch the roaring became muted, the outline of its head turned transparent so that he could see the rock walls of the gully through it. Then, like river mist, the animal faded and was gone.

Taita walked through the space where it had stood and rounded the corner. Ahead of him the gully became narrower still and the sides were steeper. It ended abruptly against a wall of rock.

Ishtar stood with his back against the rock, staring at Taita with mad eyes. The whites were yellowed and bloodshot, the pupils black and dilated. The smell of his terror was more rank than the odour of the phantom lion had been. He raised his right hand and pointed a long bony finger at Taita. 'Back, Warlock!' he screamed. 'I warn you!'

Taita walked towards him and he screamed again, this time in a guttural language, and made the gesture of hurling some unseen missile at Taita's head. Quickly Taita held the Periapt of Lostris before his eyes, and felt something fly close past his head, with the sound of a flighting arrow.

Ishtar turned and bolted into a narrow opening in the rock wall behind him, that had been screened from Taita by his body. Taita paused before the entrance, and tapped the stony portals with his staff. The rock rang true, and he heard Ishtar's blundering footsteps echoing out of the dark entrance. Taita was almost certain that this was no illusion, but the real entrance to a cavern in the limestone cliff.

Taita stepped through after him, and found that he was in a low, rocky passage, dimly lit by the sunlight through the entrance behind him. The floor of the cave sloped away in front of him, and he went on, stepping more cautiously. Now he was certain that the passage was real in time and dimension, not something conjured up by the Mede to thwart him and turn him aside.

He could hear the echoes of Ishtar's footsteps, distorted and magnified in the tunnel ahead. Taita counted his paces as he went forward into darkness. After a hundred and twenty the light strengthened again, a strong emanation from some source deeper in the hillside.

Suddenly the tunnel took a sharp bend, and as he stepped round it Taita found himself in a large cavern with a high roof. In the centre of the roof was an aperture which must lead to the outside world and open air for a beam of bright sunlight fell from it to the floor of the cavern.

From the floor rose sharp-pointed stalagmites, the crystals glimmering like the fangs of a man-eating shark. From the high roof hung down matching stalactites, some shaped like spearheads and others like the shining wings of the gods.

Across the cavern Ishtar crouched against the far wall. There was no escape that way. When he saw Taita appear in the mouth of the tunnel he began to shriek and blubber. 'Mercy, mighty Magus! There is a bond between us. We are brothers. Spare me and I will show you such mysteries as even you have never dreamed of. I will place all my powers at your disposal. I will be your faithful dog. I will devote my life to your service.'

So abject were his entreaties and his promises that, despite himself, Taita felt his resolve waver. It was just the mere flicker of doubt in his mind, but Ishtar picked up the tiny chink in his armour, and exploited it instantly. He flung out one hand with the thumb and forefinger forming a circle, the sign of Marduk, and shouted something in that strange guttural tongue.

From behind him Taita felt an insupportable physical weight bear down upon his shoulder, and something like the invisible tentacles of a giant octopus envelop his body, trapping his arms to his sides, wrapping around his throat in a strangler's grip. He smelt scorching human flesh, the aura of the Devourer, suffocating him. He could not move.

On the far side of the cavern Ishtar danced and capered, his tattooed face contorted in a grotesque mask, his tongue sticking out between his blue lips and lapping at the air like that of a cat. He lifted his skirts and thrust his hips out at Taita. His penis was in full erection, the skin peeled back from the swollen purple head like an obscene fruit. 'Your frail goddess cannot protect you here deep in the earth, Taita. You can no longer prevail against Marduk the Devourer and Ishtar, his minion,' he shrieked. 'Our contest is over. I have defeated you and all your wiles, Warlock! Now you will die.'

Taita turned his eyes up towards the high dim roof of the cavern and fixed all his attention on one of the long gleaming stalactites that hung down from it like a great shimmering dagger. He gathered all his reserves, lifted the staff in his right hand and pointed it upwards. With the last breath in his lungs he shouted, '*Kydash!*' the word of power.

There was a crack like the ice shattering in the depths of a glacier, the stalactite broke from the roof and plunged downwards. Driven by its own immense weight, the point struck Ishtar on the top of his shoulder, close to its juncture with his neck. It transfixed him through chest and belly and tore out through his anus. The long stone spike pegged him down on the cavern floor like a gutted fish on the drying rack.

As Ishtar twitched and shuddered and kicked convulsively in his death throes, Taita felt the weight lifted from his shoulders and the pressure on his throat relax. Marduk had retreated and Taita could breathe again. The smell of burnt flesh was gone. The air was ancient and sterile once again, cool and tainted only with the faint odour of fungus.

He picked up his staff, turned and walked back along the tunnel into the open air and the sunlight. At the entrance he turned back and with his staff struck the limestone portals of the tunnel, once, twice, three times.

Deep in the earth there was a rumble of collapsing rock, and a gust of air and dust blew from the tunnel mouth as, deep in the earth, the roof of the cavern caved in.

'With the stone spike driven through your heart, not even your foul god can free you from your tomb. Lie in it through all eternity, Ishtar the Mede,' Taita said, and turned away. With his staff tapping on the stones, he struck out along the road back to Gallala.

The three messengers reached Babylon in the spring when the snows were still thick upon the distant mountain-tops in the north where the two great rivers rise.

Pharaoh Naja Kiafan gave them audience on the uppermost terrace garden of the palace of Babylon. Queen Heseret sat beside his throne. She wore the most magnificent jewels that the treasury of King Sargon had yielded. Her high-piled dark hair was covered by a silken net on which gemstones sparkled like all the stars of the firmament. Her arms were laden with bracelets and her fingers with rings so heavy with emeralds and rubies and sapphires that she could barely lift them. Around her throat was a stone the size of an unripe fig, as clear as water from a mountain spring and so adamantine that it could cut through glass or obsidian. This marvellous gem came from the land beyond the Indus river, and when the sun caught it, the shafts of light it threw out pained the eye.

The messengers were all high officers from the army that Pharaoh Trok had taken westward four months before. They came in great fear of their lives, for they bore evil tidings. They had ridden so far and so fast that they were thin and burned dark by the suns of the desert and the high mountains. They threw themselves at the foot of the throne on which Naja sat in glory and splendour to overshadow even that of his wife. 'All hail to you, Pharaoh Naja, mightiest of the gods of Egypt,' they greeted him. 'We are bearers of terrible tidings. Have mercy upon us. Though what we have to tell you will displease you, be merciful and turn away your wrath from us.'

'Speak!' Naja commanded sternly. 'I alone shall judge if you are to be spared.'

'The news we bring is of Pharaoh Trok Uruk, your brother god and the co-ruler of Egypt,' said the officer who was a Commander of the Vanguard, bore the rank of Best of Ten Thousand and wore the Gold of Valour upon his chest.

'Speak!' Naja ordered again, for the man had faltered.

'In the desert that surrounds the ancient city of Gallala there took place a mighty battle between the armies of Pharaoh Trok Uruk and those of the usurper Nefer Seti.' He fell silent again.

'Continue!' Naja rose to his feet, and pointed the royal flail at the man's face, a gesture that threatened torture and death.

The messenger went on hurriedly, 'By the means of

cowardly deceit and wicked witchcraft the army of your brother and our Pharaoh Trok Uruk was lured to destruction. He is slain and his army decimated. Those of his men who survived have gone over to the enemy, and have rallied to the standard of the false pharaoh Nefer Seti, may Seth visit him with a terrible vengeance and eradicate his name and all his works. This same wicked usurper with all his force marches on Avaris and both kingdoms of this very Egypt!'

Naja sank back on his throne and stared at him in astonishment. At his side Heseret smiled. When she did so, the cruel lines at the corners of her mouth vanished and she was transformed, becoming once more ineffably beautiful. She touched Naja's arm with a bejewelled finger, and when he leaned towards her she whispered in his ear, 'Praise to the gods, and all hail to the one and only Pharaoh of the Upper and Lower Kingdoms, the mighty Naja Kiafan!'

Naja tried to remain stern and expressionless but a tiny smile played for an instant over his lean and handsome features. It took him a moment to suppress it then he rose again. His voice was sibilant and soft, but menacing as the sound of a sword blade being swiped across the face of the whetstone. 'You bring the news of the death of a pharaoh and a god. Woe upon you for you are now contaminated and steeped in misery and misfortune.' He made a gesture to his bodyguard who stood around the throne. 'Take them away and give them over to the priests of the god Marduk that they be sacrificed in the furnace to appease the wrath of the god.'

When they were bound and led away to the sacrifice, Naja stood again and announced, 'The god and Pharaoh Trok Uruk is dead. We commend his soul to the gods. I declare before you all that there is now only one ruler over both kingdoms, and over all the territories and all the conquered lands and possessions of Egypt. I declare further that ruler to be myself, Pharaoh Naja Kiafan.'

'*Bak-her!*' cried all the courtiers and captains, who stood around his throne, and they drew their swords and beat them on their shields. '*Bak-her!* Exalted be the king-god Naja Kiafan!'

'Send word to all my commanders and the generals of all my armies. We will meet in war council at the noon hour this same day.'

For eleven days that followed, from dawn to dusk, Pharaoh Naja sat at the head of his council in the throne room of the palace of Sargon. With sentries at the doors to bar interlopers or spies they drew up their plans and their order of battle. On the twelfth day Naja commanded the muster of his armies in Mesopotamia, and sent ambassadors to the subservient kings and satraps in all the conquered territories between Babylon and the borders of Egypt. He ordered them to prepare all their forces for war, and place themselves under his command for the campaign against Nefer Seti.

In the full of the following moon, when the army mustered before the Blue Gate of the city of Babylon they were forty thousand strong, all veteran and blooded troops, well equipped with horse and chariot, bow and sword.

Heseret stood with her husband, the one and only true Pharaoh of Egypt, on the ramparts of the city to review the array.

'What a glorious sight,' she told him. 'Surely there was never such a muster as this in all the annals of war.'

'As we march westwards, back towards the motherland, our numbers will be swollen by the Sumerians and the Hittites, the Hurrians and all the armies of the conquered lands through which we pass. We will return to Egypt with two thousand chariots. The puppy dare not stand against us.' He looked down at her. 'Do you feel no pity for your brother Nefer?'

'None!' She shook her head so her jewellery glinted and sparkled in the sunlight. 'You are my pharaoh and my husband. Whosoever rises against you is a traitor, and deserves death.'

'Death he shall have, and the treacherous Warlock will share his funeral pyre and burn beside him,' Naja promised grimly.

They smelt the river from afar, the perfume of the sweet cool waters on the desert air. The horses lifted their heads and whickered. The infantry quickened their step and gazed ahead, eager for the first glimpse of the waters that, at this season of the year, would be swollen and dark with rich silts, the flesh and blood of the motherland.

Nefer and Mintaka rode together in his chariot at the head of the long cavalcade that wound down the caravan road from Gallala. Meren and Merykara rode at his right hand in the second chariot of the column. Over the protests of Merykara, who thought him still too weak and sick, Meren had insisted on being in the van. 'I missed the battle at Gallala, but I vow I will never miss another. As long as there is breath in my body I will ride with my king and my dearest friend.' Though he was thin and pale as an egret he stood proud on the footplate, with the reins in his hands.

The leading chariots topped the escarpment, and below them stretched the green valley of the Nile, with the mighty river itself gleaming like a spill of molten copper from the furnace, glowing red in the early sunlight. Nefer turned and smiled at Meren in the chariot alongside. 'We are coming home!'

Mintaka began singing, softly at first then more strongly as Nefer added his voice to hers.

'Temple of the Gods,
Seat of ten thousand heroes,
Greenest in all the earth,
Our dearest love. Our sweetest home.
Our very Egypt!'

Then Meren and Merykara were singing with them, and the singing spread back down the column. Squadron after squadron picked up the joyous chorus as they wound down the escarpment.

Another army came to meet them, armed charioteers in the van, generals and captains leading their regiments, and legions of foot-soldiers following them. Behind them followed the elders, the priests and the governors of every nome, all dressed in their robes, chains and decorations of office, some in carriages and others in litters borne by slaves, and still others riding astride or on foot. After them came the dense masses of citizenry, laughing and dancing. Some of the women were carrying their infants and weeping for joy, as they picked out their husbands, lovers, brothers and sons in the ranks of the army of exile coming home.

The two cavalcades came together and mingled, and elders and generals prostrated themselves before Pharaoh's chariot. Nefer dismounted, raised up those he recognized and embraced the mightiest and most powerful of them, calling down the blessings of the gods on all his people.

When he mounted again they fell in behind him, and followed him to the banks of the Nile. There Nefer dismounted again and, fully dressed, plunged into the waters. While they lined the bank and cheered and sang, he bathed ritually and drank of the muddy brown waters.

Mounted once again and dressed in fresh linen robes, with the blue war crown on his head, Nefer led the vast concourse along the riverbank towards the city of Avaris. For a league outside the city the road was lined with the welcoming crowds. They had allayed the dust by sprinkling the road with Nile water, and had spread palm fronds and flowers in his way.

When they reached the city the gates stood wide open and the populace lined the walls. They had hung banners and bunches of sweet flowers and fruits from the ramparts. They sang anthems of loyalty, praise and welcome as Nefer, with Mintaka beside him, drove under the arch of the gateway.

Beautiful as a young god and goddess, they drove first to the magnificent temple on the riverbank that Trok Uruk had built to celebrate his own divinity. Nefer had sent instructions ahead of him, and the stonemasons had already been at work for weeks. They had chiselled away every portrait of the false pharaoh and expunged his name from the walls and tall hypostyle columns. They were still busy engraving the portraits and titles of the winged Horus, and of Pharaoh Nefer Seti, together with descriptions of his victory at the battle of Gallala.

Nefer drove there as his first duty to give thanks to the god and to sacrifice a pair of perfect black bulls before the stone altar. After the religious service he declared a week of holiday, festivity and feasting, with free millet bread, beef, wine and beer for every citizen, and games and theatre to amuse them.

'You are a sly one, my heart,' Mintaka told him admiringly. 'They loved you before, but now they will adore you.'

For how long? Nefer wondered. As soon as the news of our ascension to the throne reaches Naja, in far off Babylon, he will be on the march, if he is not already. The common people will love me until he knocks upon the gates.

Pharaoh Naja Kiafan anointed his trusted general Asmor as King of Babylon, a satrap of his own throne. He left him five hundred chariots, two thousand archers and infantry to hold and secure his conquests. Then, with the bulk of his army, he began the march on Egypt to recover his crown and throne from the man who had seized it.

Like a snowball rolling down a mountainside, the army of Pharaoh Naja Kiafan gathered weight and impetus as it advanced westwards over plain and mountain pass towards the frontier of Egypt. As he went, the vassal kings flocked to his standard, and by the time he stood on the heights of the Khatmia Pass his army had almost trebled in size.

Naja looked westwards, across the wide sand desert towards the city of Ismailiya at the head of the Great Bitter Lake, and to the borders of his homeland. He had known all along that at this point on the march he would be hampered by the size of his host, embarrassed by multitudes.

Ahead of him lay a great expanse of desert, with neither a single spring nor an oasis to sustain his army until he reached Ismailiya. Once again he was reduced to laying down water points along the route ahead. When he strained his eyes against the glare he could make out the lines of water carts, loaded with clay pots, strung out along the rutted road below the escarpment, like dark worms wriggling through the dun and ochre landscape. For months they had been at work building up water dumps in the desert, burying the filled pots in the sand, then leaving detachments of infantry to guard them while they returned for the next load.

It would take his army almost ten days and nights to make the crossing. During that time they would be strictly rationed, allowed just enough water to sustain the long night marches, and to eke out the burning days when they lay up to rest, enduring the heat in any scrap of shade afforded by linen tents or shelters made from thorn branches and grass.

'I will ride with you in the vanguard.' Heseret spoke at his elbow, breaking into his train of thought.

He glanced at her. 'We have discussed this before.' He frowned. After years of marriage her charms and beauty had begun to pall, overshadowed by her petulance, jealousy and demanding tempers. These days, Naja spent more and more time among his concubines, enduring her jealous tirades when he returned to her bed.

'You will come up with the other women in the baggage train, under the wing of Prenn, the centurion of the rearguard.'

Heseret pouted. Once, that had been appealing but now it was merely irritating. 'So that you can put Lassa with child, just as you have her sister,' she complained. She was referring to the two princesses given to Naja as hostages by the satrap of Sumeria as evidence of his loyalty to the crown of Egypt. The princesses were both young, slim and nubile, with large breasts. They painted their nipples and, in the shameless Sumerian fashion, walked abroad with them naked and uncovered.

'You become tiresome, wife.' Naja lifted his upper lip in a smile that was more a snarl. 'You know that it is political expediency. I needed a son from at least one of the wenches to place upon the throne when the old man dies.'

'Swear on the breath and heart of Seueth that you are not taking Lassa with you in the vanguard,' Heseret insisted.

'I swear it readily.' Naja smiled that deadly smile again. 'I am taking Sinnal of Hurria.' She was another hostage, younger even than the Sumerians, barely fourteen years of age but with bright copper-coloured hair and green eyes. Her buttocks were large and rounded. Heseret knew from experience that Naja would enter through the back gate to the citadel, as readily as through the front.

'I need a son from her as well,' Naja explained, reasonably, 'to place on the throne of Assyria.' He laughed then, a soft, mocking snigger. 'The duties of royalty are onerous indeed.'

She gave him a furious glare, and called for her litter with its screens and cushions of silk to take her back down the column, to where Prenn was bringing up the rearguard.

On Taita's advice, Nefer had established a screen of scouts along the shores of the Red Sea to report any invasion by dhows, yet Taita was certain that Naja's main invasion force must come through the Great Sand Desert. Naja and Trok had passed this way on their Mesopotamian adventure. Naja knew the route well, and his army was too large to bring across the Red Sea in boats as Trok had done with his much smaller force.

Thanks to a marvellous innovation by the Magus, Nefer and his staff knew the exact numbers and composition of Naja's muster. One of the centurions, high in the chain of Naja's command, who was an old associate of Taita and who owed him a debt of gratitude, had sent a message to Taita declaring his loyalty to the Pharaoh Nefer Seti and his intention of defecting and coming to join Nefer's army. Through another of his minions, a trader in fine carpets, who was leading a caravan to Beersheba, Taita had sent the centurion a reply, instructing him to remain at the head of his division. 'You are more valuable to us as a source of intelligence than as a warrior,' he had told him, and through the carpet trader had sent him two unusual gifts: a basket of live pigeons and a papyrus scroll on which was set out a secret code.

When the pigeons were released by the centurion, they returned immediately to the coop in Avaris in which they had been hatched, and they carried with them, tied to one leg with a silken thread, a coded message written on a tiny roll of the finest and lightest papyrus sheet. Through these messages, Nefer had in his possession the precise numbers and disposition of the troops Naja commanded. He knew the exact day on which Naja had marched from Babylon, and how many troops he had left there under Asmor. Nefer was able to follow his advance westward, through Damascus and Beersheba and all the other towns and garrisons along his line of march.

Very soon it became apparent that Taita had assessed the situation correctly, and that Naja would not attempt a surprise crossing of the Red Sea. He was indeed intent on a frontal assault through the Great Sand Desert.

Nefer pulled in his pickets from along the Red Sea coast, and immediately moved his headquarters and most of his army forward to the frontier garrison of Ismailiya on the edge of the desert. Here there were bountiful sweet-water wells, and ample grazing for the horses.

While they waited in Ismailiya, reports continued to be carried in by the returning pigeons. Not only did Nefer know Naja's strength, he knew also who commanded each of his divisions.

Mintaka sat on his war council in the fort of Ismailiya. Her contributions were invaluable: she was Hyksos born, and she knew well those officers on Naja's staff who had once been on her own father's staff. As a child she had listened to her father's assessment of each of them, and she had a formidable memory, trained and sharpened over the bao board. She was able to advise Nefer on the strengths, weaknesses and personal peculiarities of each of these men. She went over the lists they had received.

'Now this one, Centurion Prenn who commands Naja's rearguard, is related to me, for he was one of my father's cousins. I know him well. He taught me to ride. I used to call him Uncle Tonka, which means "Bear" in my language.' She smiled at the memory. 'My father said of him that he was loyal as a hound, cautious and slow, but once he had sunk his teeth into the throat of an enemy he would hang on to the death.'

By this time Meren had almost fully recovered his health and strength. He begged Nefer for employment in some useful role, so Nefer sent him forward with a division of chariots to cover Naja's further advance, once he came down from the heights into the desert.

Meren's scouts watched Naja's water carts carrying their loads of clay jars forward and building up the dumps in the arid land through which Naja must pass to reach the frontier of Egypt. Meren asked to be allowed to attack and disperse the convoys of water carts, but Nefer sent orders to him not to interfere with them, merely to keep them under observation and to note carefully where they placed the water stores.

Then Nefer ordered the last reserves that he had been holding on the river to be brought up, and when these were encamped around Ismailiya he called a council of all their commanders. 'Even with Trok's vehicles that we captured at Gallala, Naja outnumbers us by almost three to one,' he told them. 'All his men are battle-hardened, and his horses trained and in fine condition. We cannot afford to let him cross the frontier and reach the river. We must meet him and fight him here in the desert.'

All that night they sat in council, and Nefer laid out his battle plan and issued his orders. They were to let Naja advance unopposed for the first five days. Then, once he was deeply committed, they would raid and destroy his water stores, both in front and to the rear of his advance. This would trap him in the midst of the sands.

'I know Naja well enough to stake the battle on his arrogance and his overbearing confidence in his own fighting skills. I am certain that even once we cut off his water supply he will not turn back, but will thrust onwards. His forces will reach Ismailiya after a forced dry march of many days through the desert. We will be able to meet them with our horses and troops well rested and watered on a battleground of our own choosing. This will make up some of the deficit in our opposing strengths.'

During the long council, Taita sat silently in the shadows behind Nefer's campaign stool. It seemed that he was dozing, but once in a while he opened his eyes then, blinking like a sleepy owl, closed them again and let his chin droop back on to his chest.

'Our greatest lack is in the number and condition of our chariots,' Nefer went on, 'but we can almost match Naja in archers, slingers and spearmen. I am certain that once he realizes his shortage of water, Naja will drive ahead of his foot-soldiers with all his chariots. Taita and I have devised a plan to lead his vehicles into a trap in which we can exploit the small advantage that we have.

'In front of the town and the wells we will throw up a series of low stone walls behind which our archers and infantry can conceal themselves. These works will be just high enough to block the advance of a chariot.' With a charcoal stick Nefer sketched out a design on the sheet of papyrus spread on the table-top in front of him. Hilto, Shabako, Socco and the rest of his staff craned forward to watch.

'The walls will be laid out in the design of a fish trap.' He drew the inverted funnel shapes, with the apex aimed back towards the fort of Ismailiya.

'How will you lead him into the funnel?' Shabako asked.

'With a charge of our own chariots and the mock retreat you have practised so often,' Nefer explained. 'Our archers and slingers will remain concealed behind the walls until Naja follows us into the funnel. The deeper they penetrate, the more tightly his squadrons will be compressed between the walls. They will offer a fine target for our slingers and archers as they pass at close range.'

Even Shabako looked impressed. 'You intend to shut them up in a stockade like cattle, just as you did with Trok.'

They discussed the plan with enthusiasm, offering suggestions and refinements. In the end Nefer put Shabako in charge of building the walls. Taita had spent the last five days surveying and marking them out for him, so the work could begin as soon as it was light the next day.

'We have little time left to us,' Nefer warned them. 'We know that Naja's forces are already drawn up on the heights of the Khatmia. His water wagons have almost finished laying down the dumps. I expect he will begin his descent of the escarpment within days.'

The council broke up at last and the officers hurried away to take up the tasks that Nefer had allocated to them. At last only three remained in the tower room of the old fort at Ismailiya, Nefer, Taita and Mintaka.

Mintaka spoke up for the first time. 'We have discussed already Prenn, my uncle Tonka,' she said, and Nefer nodded, but gave her a quizzical look. 'If I could meet him, if I could speak to him face to face, I am sure I could convince him to turn against Naja and throw in his lot with us.'

'What do you mean?' Nefer's voice was harsh and his expression stern.

'Dressed as a boy, with a small detachment of good men and fast horses, I could circle around Naja's main army and get through to Uncle Tonka in the rear. There would be little risk.'

Nefer's face blanched with anger. 'Madness!' he said quietly. 'Stark raving madness of the kind you exhibited at Gallala when you showed yourself as bait to Trok. I will not hear another word of it. Can you imagine what Naja would do to you if you fell into his hands?'

'Can you imagine what Naja would do if, in the critical moment of the battle, Uncle Tonka and his legions fell upon him from his own rear?' she flashed back at Nefer.

'We will not speak of it again.' Nefer came to his feet and slammed his fists down on the table-top. 'You will stay with Merykara here in the fort during the rest of the campaign. If you do not give me your word to put such stupidity out of you mind, I will have the door to your chamber barred and guarded.'

'You cannot treat me as a chattel.' Her voice crackled with fury. 'I am not even your wife. I will take no orders from you.'

'I am your king, and I demand your solemn word not to place yourself in jeopardy with this wild scheme of yours.'

'It is not a wild scheme, and I will not give you my word.'

Taita looked on, expressionless. This was their first serious argument, and he knew it would be all the more bitter because of the depth of their feelings for each other. He waited with interest to see how it would be resolved.

'You deliberately disobeyed my orders at Gallala. I cannot trust you not to do the same now. You leave me no alternative,' Nefer told her grimly, and shouted to the sentry outside the door to send for Zugga, the head eunuch of the royal harem.

'I can't trust Merykara either.' He turned back to Mintaka. 'She is completely under your influence, and if you put your mind to it you will turn her to this lunatic enterprise of yours. I am sending both of you back to the *zenana* in the Avaris palace. You are to remain there in the care of Zugga. You can amuse each other by playing bao until the battle is fought and the war is won.' And Zugga led Mintaka away. At the door she looked back over her shoulder at Nefer, and Taita smiled as he read her expression. Nefer had taken on a more stubborn adversary than both the false pharaohs combined.

That evening Taita went to visit her in the new accommodation that Mintaka now shared with Merykara in what had once been the commander's suite of the fort. A pair of large, placid eunuchs were at the door and another outside the barred window.

Mintaka was still seething with anger, and Merykara was every bit as outraged by her brother's treatment of herself and her dear Mintaka, and especially this humiliating incarceration.

'At least you have learned from this that it does not pay to confront a king, even if he loves you,' Taita told them gently.

'I don't love him,' Mintaka replied, with tears of anger and frustration in her eyes. 'He treats me like a child, and I hate him.'

'I hate him even more,' Merykara declared, not to be outdone. 'If only Meren were here!'

'Has it occurred to you that what Nefer is doing to you is evidence of his love and concern for your safety?' Taita suggested. 'He knows how dire will be your fate if you fall into the hands of Naja Kiafan and Heseret.' They turned upon him so roundly that he held up both hands to deflect their wrath and withdrew tactfully, their denials and recriminations still ringing in his ears.

The next morning both Nefer and Taita watched from the ramparts of the fort as the little caravan left Ismailiya, escorted by the eunuchs and a contingent of chariots, and headed back towards Avaris. Mintaka and Merykara were closeted together behind the silk curtains of the litter in the centre of the column. They did not show themselves or take their farewells of Nefer and Taita.

'Personally, I would have preferred to stir up a beehive with a short stick,' Taita murmured. 'It may have made for a more restful climate to have shown a little more tact.'

'They must learn that I am pharaoh, and that my word is law even to them. Besides, at the moment I have other concerns than female tantrums,' Nefer said, 'They will get over it.' But he stayed on the wall and watched until the swaying litter and the caravan disappeared in the hazy distance.

Taita and Nefer rode out and inspected the stone walls that Shabako had hastily thrown up along the eastern approaches to the oasis of Ismailiya.

'Shabako's efforts will not rank among the great architectural achievements of the age,' Taita gave his opinion, 'but that is all to the good. From the direction in which Naja will come, they appear to be natural features and will excite no suspicion until he enters the funnel and finds his front progressively narrowed.'

'Your plan has the towering virtue of allowing us to choose our own battleground.' Nefer nodded. 'With the help of Horus, we will turn it into a slaughter-ground.' Then he laid his hand upon Taita's skinny arm. 'Once again I find myself deeply in your debt, Old Father. This is all your work.'

'No.' Taita shook his head. 'It was a gentle nudge I gave to you. The rest of it is yours. You have inherited the military instincts of your father, Pharaoh Tamose. You will achieve the greatness that might have been his, had he not died so cruelly at the hands of the enemy who faces us now.'

'It is time for me to avenge that death,' Nefer said. 'Let us ensure that we do not let the cobra slither away again.'

Over the days that followed Nefer exercised his forces, and rehearsed in detail the plans and tactics of his defence. The battalions of archers and slingers marched out each morning and took up their positions behind the rough, ungainly walls. They placed small cairns of stones in front of the walls to mark the range, so that they would be able to judge precisely the moment to spring the trap. They concealed bundles of spare arrows close at hand so that they would not run short of missiles during the battle. The slingers moulded their clay balls and baked them in the fire until they were rock hard. Then they laid up mounds of these deadly missiles behind the walls, close at hand.

During the exercises, Nefer and his commanders played the role of Naja's troops and rode in from the desert, viewing their dispositions with a critical eye, making certain that they were completely concealed by the breastworks.

Then, while they waited, Nefer rehearsed his tactics before the walls, charging, wheeling and retreating, covering the ground so that his men came to know every fold, plain and gully, even the location of the aardvark holes and other small obstacles across the field. He chose carefully the secure points behind the walls where he could water the horses during the battle, and where his reserves would be held until they were needed. 'I doubt that there was ever a commander able to learn the board on which the game will be played as intimately as I,' Nefer told Taita, and ordered his squadrons out again to go through the same evolutions.

In the evening he rode back into the fort at the head of his squadron. The dust had mingled with his sweat and caked his face and body. He was weary to the bone, but content in the knowledge that he had done all in his power to ready his legions for what lay ahead.

When he pulled up Krus and Dov, threw the rein to the grooms and jumped down on to the hard-baked parade-ground, his sense of well-being evaporated. Zugga, the head eunuch of the royal *zenana*, was waiting for him, wringing his fat hands, his eyes red with weeping and his reedy voice whining with fear. 'Great Pharaoh, forgive me. I did my best but she is wily as a vixen. She has outwitted me.'

'Who is this vixen?' Nefer demanded, although he knew who it must be.

'The Princess Mintaka.'

'What has happened to her?' Nefer's voice was harsh with alarm.

'She has run away, and taken the Princess Merykara with her,' blubbered Zugga, in sure expectation of the strangling garotte.

Mintaka and Merykara spent much of the journey back to Avaris huddled together in the screened litter, whispering as they planned their escape. They soon discarded the notion of seizing one of the chariots from their escort and riding away in it. In the unlikely event that they were able to trick or overpower one of the charioteers, they knew that within an hour they would have the entire army of Egypt on their heels, led by a wrathful pharaoh. Gradually a better plan emerged from their deliberations.

Mintaka's first endeavour was to make herself agreeable to Zugga, their guardian and gaoler, and to impress him with her submissive resignation to his authority. By the time they reached the palace in Avaris four days later, she had him completely gulled, believing only the best of her gentle, innocent nature. There, in the most pretty and convincing manner, she appealed to Zugga to allow her and Merykara to visit the temple of Hathor to pray for the safety of Nefer and his victory in the looming battle. With some misgivings, Zugga acquiesced and the two women were able to spend almost an hour alone with the high priestess in the sanctuary of the temple. Zugga waited anxiously at the door, for no man, not even a eunuch, was allowed to enter the sanctum.

Great was Zugga's relief, and all his suspicions set at rest, when Mintaka and Merykara at last re-emerged, both as beautiful, demure and innocent as any of the temple virgins. A few days later when they asked to be allowed to pray again in the temple, and to make sacrifice to the goddess, Zugga was amenable to the request and waddled beside their litter chatting blithely through the curtain, and relating to the princesses the most juicy items of scandal in the life of the palace.

Once again the high priestess was waiting in the forecourt of the temple to greet Mintaka and Merykara and lead them into the sanctum. Without misgivings Zugga settled down to await the return of the lovely royal pair. The high priestess sent out two of her acolytes to serve him an overflowing platter of grilled chicken and fish, together with a large jar of excellent wine. Zugga ate it all and polished off the contents of the jug, then fell asleep in the shadow of the cow effigy of the goddess. When he woke the sun had set and he was alone. He saw that the litter bearers had gone. He heaved his vast bulk upright and experienced twinges in his belly that were not caused by dyspepsia but by a pressing sense of alarm. He shouted for attention and beat on the temple door with his staff. It was a long time before a priestess came to him with a message: 'The two princesses have pleaded for sanctuary within the temple. The holy mother has granted their plea, and taken them under her protection.'

Zugga was thrown into turmoil. The sanctuary of the temple was inviolate. He could not demand the return of his charges, not even under the authority of Pharaoh. The only course open to him was to return to Ismailiya and confess his failure, but that was risky. The young pharaoh had not yet revealed his true nature, and his rage might well be fatal.

The moment the temple doors closed behind them Mintaka and Merykara dropped their pretence of resigned innocence.

'Have you made the arrangements, Holy Mother?' Mintaka demanded eagerly.

'Have no fear, daughter. All is in readiness.' The priestess's brown eyes sparkled with amusement. Clearly she was enjoying this escapade, a break from the tranquil routine of temple life. 'I took the liberty of slipping a mild sleeping draught into the eunuch's wine.' She giggled. 'I hope you will not think I have overstepped myself, and that you will forgive me.'

Mintaka kissed her smooth pale cheek. 'I am sure Hathor will be as proud of you as I am.'

The priestess led them to a cell where all the items that Mintaka had requested were laid out for them. They dressed hastily in the rough peasant garments, and covered their heads with woollen shawls. Then, carrying the leather pouches slung across their shoulders, they followed the high priestess through the maze of corridors. The temple backed on to the Nile, and they became aware of the gentle swish of the river current against the outer walls growing louder ahead of them. At last they stepped out through a low doorway into the sunshine, and on to the jetty where a large dhow was moored. 'The captain has been paid with the gold you gave me, and he knows where to go. All the other items you asked for are stowed in your cabin on board,' she said.

'You know what to tell Zugga,' Mintaka said, and the old woman giggled again.

'I am sure that Hathor will forgive me such an insignificant falsehood. It is in such a good cause.'

As the pair jumped down on to the deck of the dhow,

the crew, who had been dozing in the shade, scrambled to their feet and rushed to set the lateen sail. Without waiting for orders, the captain steered out into the main flow of the current and turned the bows downstream, heading for the delta. For the rest of that day Mintaka and Merykara stayed in the tiny cabin, taking no chance that they might be recognized from the shore, or from a passing riverboat. In the late afternoon the dhow moored briefly against the east bank and two armed men came aboard, carrying heavy sacks. Immediately the dhow captain hoisted the sail again and they pressed on with all speed downriver. The two men came to the cabin and prostrated themselves before Mintaka.

'May all the gods love you, Majesty,' said the bigger of the two, a bearded Hyksos with large nose and strong features. 'We are your dogs. We came as soon as we received your summons.'

'Lok!' Mintaka smiled with pleasure to see his well-remembered face, and then turned to the other man. 'And surely this is your son, Lokka.' He seemed as big and doughty as his father. 'You are both well met and welcome. You, Lok, served my father well. Will you and your son do the same for me?' She spoke in the Hyksosian language.

'With our lives, mistress!' they told her.

'I will have hard employment for you once we go ashore, but until then rest and prepare your weapons.'

The dhow captain selected one of the many mouths of the delta where the current slowed and meandered through swamps and lagoons over which hovered clouds of water-fowl. Darkness fell before they reached the open sea, but the dhow captain steered his craft unerringly through the shallows and the hidden sandbars, until at last the miasma of the swamps was blown away on the clean salt airs of the Mediterranean. The two girls came up on deck.

'Just about now, Zugga will realize that we have flown.' Mintaka smiled at Merykara. 'I wonder what he will tell

Nefer. That we are safely locked up in the temple under the wing of the high priestess? I hope so.'

With half a moon in the sky they sailed out of the confined waterways and felt the scend of the open sea lift the deck beneath their feet. As soon as he had made his offing and there was deep water under his hull, the captain turned eastwards and hugged the coast throughout the night.

In the dawn Mintaka and Merykara stood in the bows, huddled in their shawls for warmth. They stared south at the low bleak desert shore to their right.

'To think that Nefer is only a few leagues out there,' Mintaka whispered. 'I feel as though I could reach out my hand to touch him.'

'Meren is there too, only a little further to the east. What a surprise they would have to know that we are so close.'

'My heart yearns for Nefer. I pray every hour to Horus and Hathor to keep him safe.'

'You no longer hate him, then?' Merykara asked.

'I never did,' Mintaka denied hotly, then hesitated. 'Well, perhaps for a moment and only a very little.'

'I know just how you feel,' Merykara assured her. 'At times, they can be so stubborn and bull-headed and . . .' she sought for a word to describe it '. . . and so male.'

'Yes!' Mintaka agreed. 'That's it exactly. Like children. I suppose we must forgive them, for they cannot help themselves.'

During the rest of that day and the following night they sailed eastwards along the coast, through the Khalig el Tina and along the string of islands and sandbars that enclosed the vast lagoon of the Sabkhet el Bardawill. The next morning the dhow edged in towards the beach at El Arish, and as soon as the water was waist deep the two bodyguards, Lok and Lokka, carried the women ashore then waded back to the boat to fetch the baggage. The small party stood and watched the crew of the dhow row off, then set the sail and head back out to sea for the return to Egypt and the delta.

'Well, we have done it,' said Merykara uncertainly. Despite Mintaka's company, she was feeling vulnerable and alone. 'But what do we do now?' She sounded close to tears.

'I will send Lok to find transport for us,' said Mintaka, and then to give her comfort and a little more confidence she went on to explain to Merykara, 'Nefer might have stopped us going southwards through the desert to find my uncle Tonka, but we have outwitted him.' She smiled more gaily than her spirits dictated, for she was even more aware than Merykara of their invidious position. 'Just think how furious Nefer and Meren would be if they only knew!' They laughed together, and Mintaka went on, 'Here we are in the rear of Naja's advancing army, and the road between Beersheba and Ismailiya lies a very few leagues south of us. When Lok finds a cart or wagon for us we can lose ourselves in the baggage train of Naja's army, hide among the camp-followers until we can reach the headquarters of Uncle Tonka.'

It was not quite as easy to find transport as Mintaka had made it sound. The quartermasters of Naja's army had been ahead of them, and had seized wagons and horses, as well as food and provisions from the local populace. In the end they had to settle for a string of five decrepit donkeys, and they had to pay dearly for these, with two heavy gold rings and two of silver. The animals were barely able to support the weight of even the two women, let alone their body-guards, so they walked most of the rugged path southwards, until on the third day after landing they topped a rise and saw in the valley below them the tail of the army of Pharaoh Naja. This great host filled the main east-to-west road in both directions as far as the eye could see, and the dust it raised sullied the sky like the smoke from a forest fire.

They went down to join it, and found themselves in the

baggage train. They fell in with the long caravan of wagons and pack animals. Mintaka and Merykara kept their heads and faces covered, and in their dusty, bedraggled clothing excited little notice. Lok and Lokka chaperoned them closely, and discouraged the attentions of any other travellers. The rate of march was of the slowest, so even on the poor donkeys they were moving a little faster than the rest of the cavalcade and, like a scrap of flotsam in the mighty river, they drifted forward towards the head. As they went they passed every type and condition of humanity, beggars and bawds, merchants and water-carriers, barbers, coppersmiths and carpenters, troubadours and jugglers. There were captains splendid in the Gold of Valour, driving their chariots furiously through the throng, lashing out of their path the limping cripples on their crutches, and the army women with their bastards at the breast, feeding on the march, toddlers whining at their skirts.

Mintaka and Merykara kept up the best speed the wretched donkeys could manage, and they camped that first night under the stars, surrounded by the campfires, the hubbub and stench of this immense agglomeration of humanity.

In the dawn, as soon as it was light enough to see the road underfoot, they set off again. Before noon they had caught up with the rearguard of the main army: the marching companies of spearmen, and the ranks of archers with bows unstrung, the battalions of slingers singing their marching songs in the barbaric language of the western islands. Next they passed the long lines of the horses of the remount division, twenty to a string, being led behind the fodder wagons and the water carts. Mintaka marvelled at the numbers: it did not seem possible that there were so many animals in all Egypt.

The soldiers looked at the two women, and not even their shoddy dress or the voluminous shawls wound around their heads could hide their youth and grace from such discerning eyes. They called suggestive compliments and lewd invitations as they passed, but the discipline of their officers and the stern presence of Lok and Lokka kept them from any further advances.

That evening they kept on travelling after the main army had encamped and after sunset they came upon a large *zareba* of poles and thornbushes just off the road. This had been set up in an easily defended defile of low hills. The entrance was heavily guarded, and there was much activity around it, the marching and counter-marching of the sentries, the scurrying of servants and orderlies, and the coming and going of chariots driven by officers of the Red. Above the gate of the stockade flew the gonfalon that Mintaka recognized at once: on it was depicted the severed head of a wild boar with its tongue lolling from the corner of its tusked jaws.

'This is the man we are looking for,' Mintaka whispered to Merykara.

'But how do we get in to see him?' Merykara asked doubtfully, eyeing the sentries.

They made their own rudimentary camp a little further down the road, but within sight of the gates of the regimental headquarters of General Prenn, centurion of the Red, and the commander of the rearguard of the pharaonic army.

From one of the leather saddlebags Mintaka brought out the precious oil lamp that had so far survived the journey, and by its light she wrote a short message on a scrap of papyrus parchment. It was addressed to 'Uncle Bear' and signed 'from your little cricket'.

The two women washed the dust from their faces, dressed each other's hair, and shook out their *chitons*. Then, hand in hand to give each other courage, they approached the gate of the stockade. The sergeant of the guard saw them coming and stepped out in front of them to head them off. 'Come now, you two juicy pieces of prong bait. You know better than to come flaunting your joy-clefts hereabouts. Get away with you.'

'You look like a kind and good man,' Mintaka told him primly. 'Would you allow any ruffian to talk to your own daughters in that coarse fashion?'

The sergeant checked, and gawked at her. She spoke the Hyksos language in the cultured tones and accent of the aristocracy. He lifted his lantern and shone the light upon them. Their dress was common, but their features made him draw breath sharply. These were clearly young women of high rank. In fact their faces were disturbingly familiar, even though he could not immediately place them.

'Forgive me, ladies,' he mumbled. 'Mistook you for—' He broke off, and Mintaka smiled graciously.

'Of course, you are forgiven. Will you deliver a message for us to Centurion Prenn?' She proffered the rolled parchment.

The sergeant hesitated a moment before he took it. 'I am sorry but I will have to ask you to wait here until I have an instruction from him.'

He came hurrying back within a very short time. 'My ladies! I am desolated to have kept you waiting. Please follow me.'

He led them to a pavilion of coloured linen in the centre of the stockade, and there was another short delay as he whispered to the junior officer in charge of the entrance. Then they were led through into the tent. The interior was sparsely furnished and the floor was covered by animal skins, oryx, zebra and leopard. On these a man was sitting cross-legged with maps and scrolls spread about him, and a wooden platter on his lap containing grilled ribs and a lump of *dhurra* bread. He looked up as the girls entered. His face was gaunt, his cheeks sunken, and even the ribbons in his beard could not disguise the fact that it was more grey than black. A leather patch covered one eye. He scowled at them.

'Uncle Tonka!' Mintaka stepped into the lamplight and threw back her head shawl. The man came to his feet slowly and stared at her. Then suddenly he grinned, and his single eye gleamed. 'I did not think it possible!' He embraced her and lifted her off her feet. 'I heard that you had deserted us and gone over to the enemy.'

When he put her down again and she had partially recovered from this display of affection, she gasped, 'That's what I have come to speak to you about, Uncle Tonka.'

'Who is this with you?' He glanced at Merykara, then blinked his one good eye. 'By Seth's foul breath, I know you.'

'It's the Princess Merykara,' Mintaka told him.

'Naja's runaway wife. He will be pleased to have you back.' Prenn chuckled. 'Have the two of you eaten?' Then, without waiting for a reply, he shouted to his servants to bring more meat and bread and wine. The two girls covered their faces again while they were served, but once the servants had gone Mintaka sat close to Prenn, on the side of his good ear, and dropped her voice so that they could not be overheard by a listener outside the tent walls.

He heard her out silently, but his expression changed as she described to him in detail the events of that terrible night when her father and all her brothers had died in the burning galley on the river at Balasfura. Mintaka thought she saw a tear gleam in the corner of his eye as she went on, but she knew that such a show of weakness was not possible in a centurion of the Red. Prenn turned away his face and when he looked back at her the tear was gone and she knew she had been mistaken.

When at last she finished speaking Prenn said simply, 'I loved your father, almost as much as I love you, little cricket, but what you are proposing is treason.' He was silent a while longer and then he sighed. 'All this I will have to think on. But in the meantime, you can't return whence you came. It is much too risky. You must stay under my care, both of you, until this affair is resolved.'

When they protested, he overrode them brusquely. 'It is not a request. It is an order.' He thought a moment. 'I will have you disguised as a pair of my pretty boys. That will cause little comment, for all my men know that I enjoy a slice of rump almost as much as a cut of breast.'

'Can I at least send a message to Nefer Seti?' Mintaka pleaded.

'That also is too great a risk. Have patience. It will not be for long. Naja is poised on the heights of the Khatmia. Within days he will begin the march on Ismailiya. The battle will be decided before the full moon of Osiris begins to wane.' His voice dropped to a growl. 'And I will be forced to a decision.'

From a distance Meren watched the great host of Pharaoh Naja come down the escarpment from the Khatmia Pass into the arid lands, and he released a pair of the pigeons that Taita had given to him. Two birds, so that if one was taken by a falcon or another predator the other might still win through. Both birds had a single strand of red thread looped around a leg, the signal that the advance had begun.

Meren shadowed the stately progress of the enemy legions across the desert, and at night crept closer to the camps to watch them watering from the stored jars and to eavesdrop on any of the loud conversations around the campfires.

By the fifth night Naja's full army was committed to the crossing, and the leading elements had passed the halfway mark between Khatmia and Ismailiya. Meren was able to cut in behind the rearguard and examine the now deserted water stores they had left behind them. He discovered that they were almost entirely used up, or had been carried away. Naja was so confident of his victory that he had left no contingency reserves for a possible retreat. From the unused jars that he did find Meren replenished his own waterskins, which were almost exhausted, and he smashed the few jars that remained.

Now he rode back parallel to Naja's line of march, but well out to the south and beyond the range of vision of his scouts, and circled out in front of the heavily encumbered, slowly moving host. He came back to where he had left the bulk of his force concealed. They were fifty chariots manned by crack troops and drawn by some of the finest horses in all Nefer's army. He paused only to water, and to change the pennants his chariots flew from the blue to the red of Naja's army. He consoled himself that this was a legitimate ruse of war. Then, at the head of his squadron, he cut back in front of Naja's vanguard and drove furiously along his intended line of march.

The men who had been left to guard the water dumps saw the approaching chariots coming from where they expected their comrades to arrive. When they recognized the false colours flying above them they were lulled. Meren gave them no time for second thoughts, but raced in upon them, and cut down any who tried to resist. The survivors were given a choice: death or defection. Most came over to Nefer Seti. A single mallet blow was sufficient for each of the clay jars, and the precious fluid poured out into the sand. Meren's squadron mounted again and went on to the next dump.

When at last they came in sight of Ismailiya Nefer rode out to greet them, and embraced Meren when he heard that he had fulfilled the task he had been set: Naja was now waterless in the wilderness. 'You have just earned your first Gold of Valour,' he told Meren, 'and you are promoted to the rank of Best of Ten Thousand.' He was relieved to see that Meren seemed to have recovered from his wound, and was now lean, eager and burned dark by the desert sun. 'In the battle that lies ahead, I am giving you command of the right wing.'

'Pharaoh, if I have pleased you, I beg a boon.'

'Of course, old friend. If it is in my power, you shall have it.'

'My rightful place is at your side. We rode the Red Road together, let us see this battle out together. Let me ride with you once again as your lance-bearer. That is all the honour I seek.'

Nefer gripped his arm, and squeezed hard. 'You shall ride in my chariot one more time. And it is I who will be honoured.' He dropped his hand. 'But we have no more time to chatter. Naja will not be far behind you. As soon as he discovers what you have done to his water supplies, he will be forced to come on at all speed.'

Instinctively they both looked back into the wilderness whence the enemy must come, but the heat-haze was grey and turbid and there was little to be seen across that grisly plain. However, they had not long to wait.

Pharaoh Naja reined in his chariot and gazed out over the remains of his water dump. Although the scouts had warned him, he was still appalled by the extent of the destruction. Slowly he dismounted and strode out into the littered field. Shards of shattered pottery crunched under his sandals, and suddenly his usual icy control snapped. He kicked one of the broken jars in fury and frustration, then stood with his hands clenched into fists at his sides and glared towards the west. Slowly he regained control of himself and his breathing slowed. He turned and walked back to where his staff waited.

'Will you give the order to turn back?' asked one of his captains diffidently.

Naja turned on him coldly. 'The next coward who suggests such a thing I will have stripped naked and tied feet first behind my chariot. I will drag him back to Egypt.' They dropped their eyes and shuffled their feet in the sand.

Naja lifted the blue war crown from his head, and when his lance-bearer handed him a square of linen cloth, he wiped the sweat from his shaven head. With the crown tucked under his arm he gave new orders. 'Collect all the waterskins from the entire army. From now on the water supply is under my direct control. No man or animal drinks without my permission. There is no turning back, no retreat. All the fighting chariots will move to the front of the column, even those of Prenn from the rearguard. The other vehicles and the foot must take their chances, and follow as best they can. I will take the cavalry ahead and seize the wells at Ismailiya . . .'

Heseret thrust her head out of the opening of her tent, and called to the captain of her bodyguard, 'What is the trouble, fellow? This is a royal and sacred enclosure, so what are those rogues doing in my stockade?' She pointed at the men who were taking the waterskins from one of her personal baggage carts parked alongside her tent. 'What do they think they are up to? How dare they remove our water? I have not yet bathed. Tell them to replace those skins at once.'

''Tis Pharaoh, your divine husband's order, Majesty,' the captain explained, although he was also agitated and alarmed at the prospect of being stranded waterless in this terrible desert. 'They say all the water is needed for the forward squadrons of cavalry.'

'Such orders cannot apply to me, the divine Queen of Egypt!' Heseret screamed. 'Put those waterskins back.'

The soldiers hesitated, but the sergeant touched the peak of his leather helmet with his sword. 'Forgive me, Your Majesty. My orders are to take all the water.'

'You dare defy me?' Heseret shouted in his face.

'Please forgive and understand my predicament, Your Majesty, but I have my orders.' The man stood his ground.

'By the sweet name of Isis, I shall have you strangled and your body burned, if you defy me.'

'My orders—'

'A plague on you and your orders. I shall go at once to General Prenn. I shall have new orders for you when I return.' Then she turned to the officer of her bodyguard. 'Ready my chariot and an escort of ten men.'

Across the flat and open plain, General Prenn's headquarters camp was in clear view of Heseret's tent. It took only minutes for her chariot to carry her there, but the guard at the gate of the stockade barred her way. 'Your Divine Majesty, General Prenn is not here,' he told her.

'I do not believe that,' Heseret flared at him. 'That is his standard flying there.' She pointed at the boar's head gonfalon.

'Your Majesty, the general left an hour ago with all his cavalry. He had orders from Pharaoh to join the vanguard.'

'I have to see him. It is a matter of extreme urgency. I know he would not have left without informing me. Stand aside and I will see for myself if he is here.' She drove the chariot straight at him and he jumped hurriedly out of her way. Her escort clattered after her.

Heseret went straight to the yellow- and green-striped command tent and tossed the reins to a groom. In her agitation she did not stand on ceremony, but jumped down and ran to the entrance of the tent. It was unguarded, and she began to believe that she had been told the truth, that

Prenn had indeed left. Nevertheless, she stooped through the doorway, and stopped dead in the threshold.

Two boys were sitting on the piles of animal skins in the centre of the floor. They were eating with their fingers from wooden platters, but they looked up at her startled.

'Who are you?' Heseret demanded, though she knew from Prenn's reputation who and what they were. 'Where is the general?'

Neither replied, but they continued to stare wordlessly at her. Suddenly Heseret's eyes narrowed and she took a step towards them. 'You!' she screamed. 'You treacherous, poisonous bitches!' She pointed a quivering finger at the girls. 'Guards!' Heseret shrieked at the top of her voice. 'Guards, here, at once!'

Mintaka came to her senses, seized Merykara's hand and pulled her to her feet. The two darted across the tent and out through the rear opening.

'Guards!' Heseret yelled again. 'This way!' Her bodyguard burst in through the doorway behind her.

'Follow them!' She raced after the fleeing pair, with her bodyguard hard after her. When they ran out into the open, Mintaka and Merykara were halfway to the stockade gate.

'Stop them!' Heseret shouted. 'Don't let them escape. They are spies and traitors.'

Her bodyguard charged after them, shouting to the guards at the gate, 'Stop them. Seize them. Don't let them escape.' And the sentries drew their swords and ran to block the gate.

Mintaka stopped as soon as she saw that they were cut off. She looked around her wildly, then still pulling Merykara by the hand ran to the thorn fence of the stockade and tried to scale it. But the bodyguard came up under them, seized their ankles and pulled them down from the wall. The thorns had ripped their arms and legs, and they were both bleeding, but they fought desperately, kicking, scratching and biting. The soldiers overwhelmed them at last and dragged them back to the command tent to face Heseret. She was smiling vindictively. 'Bind them securely. I am sure that my husband, the sole ruler of this very Egypt, will devise a suitable punishment for their crimes when he returns. I shall delight in their screams as they are forced to pay the ultimate penalty. Until that time they are to be caged like wild animals, and kept at the door of my tent where I can keep them under my eye.'

The bodyguard lifted Mintaka and Merykara, bound at wrists and ankles, into a chariot and carried them back to Heseret's encampment. One of the carts of Heseret's baggage train carried her stock of livestock in cages, chickens, pigs and young goats for her kitchen. The cage that had contained the sucking pigs was now empty – they had been slaughtered and eaten. The cage was made from lengths of bamboo lashed together with rawhide strips, and stank of the pig dung that coated the floor. The guards shoved the two girls through the narrow door. The interior was not high enough to allow them to stand upright. They were forced to sit with their backs to the bamboo wall, and their wrists were lashed behind them with rawhide strips to one of the struts. There was no protection from the sun.

'There will be guards standing over your cage day and night,' Heseret warned them. 'Should you try to escape I will have one of your feet cut off, to discourage further attempts.'

From the look on her face they knew that Heseret meant every word of the threat. Merykara began to weep, but Mintaka whispered to her, 'No, my darling. Be brave. Do not give her the satisfaction of watching you break down.'

From the watchtower above the fort at Ismailiya the sentry shouted the warning, 'Pharaoh! The pickets are coming in!'

Nefer sprang up from the table under the awning in the courtyard where he and Taita were eating the midday meal and going over the details of the defence yet again. He climbed swiftly up the ladder to the platform and shaded his eyes to look towards the east. Through the yellow glare he made out the chariots of his forward pickets coming in. As they drove down the bank of the wadi, the guards threw open the gates and allowed them to enter the fort.

'The enemy comes on apace!' the sergeant of the pickets shouted up to Nefer on the high platform.

'Well done, sergeant,' Nefer called back to him, and then to the trumpeter on the wall above the gate, 'Sound the call to arms!'

The ram's horn blared out across the plain, and the entire army that was encamped down the length of the broad wadi began to stir. The trumpet call was picked up and repeated, flung from legion to legion and from squadron to squadron. From the tents and sun-shelters men poured out, seized their arms and hurried to join their formations. Soon lines of marching men and columns of chariots were moving forward to their prepared positions.

Taita clambered up on to the high platform, and Nefer smiled at him. 'So, even deprived of his water, Naja has not turned back.'

'We never thought he would,' Taita said softly.

In the east the horizon started to darken, as though night had come on prematurely. On a wide front the dustcloud of the advancing enemy army boiled like a brewing thunderstorm.

'It still lacks many hours of noon.' Nefer looked up at

the pitiless sun. 'There is time to decide this battle before the close of day.'

'Naja's horses have drunk little in three days, and they must have been driven hard to reach us so soon. He knows he must win and reach the wells this day, or for him there will not be another.'

'Will you ride out to meet him with me, Old Father?' Nefer asked, as he strapped on the sword-belt that his orderly handed to him.

'No!' Taita lifted his left hand. On the second finger he wore a gold ring, set with a huge pigeon's-blood ruby. When it caught the sunlight and sparkled, Nefer recognized it as the token Naja had taken from his own finger and given to Taita in Thebes all those years ago, when he believed that the Magus had murdered the young pharaoh for him. Nefer understood that it was a talisman almost as powerful as would have been a lock of Naja's hair, a pellet of his dried excrement or the clippings of his nails. 'I will overlook the battle from here. Perhaps in my own feeble way I might be of more help to you than if I wielded a javelin or drew a bow.'

Nefer smiled. 'Your weapons are sharper and fly more truly than any I have ever held in my hand. Horus love and protect you, Old Father.'

They watched as the battalions of archers and slingers marched out of the wadi to take up their positions behind the breastworks. The ranks moved with purpose and swiftly, for every man among them knew what was expected of him, and had rehearsed this manoeuvre many times. As the last of them disappeared into the ambuscade, the field seemed deserted.

The dustcloud of Naja's advance was less than a league off when at last Nefer embraced Taita, and climbed down the ladder. When he strode out through the gates of the fort a roar went up from the massed squadrons of chariots. As he went down their ranks he picked out his captains and centurions among them, and called to them, 'Courage, Hilto! One more time for me, Shabako! Tonight we will drink a victory cup together, Socco.'

Meren had Dov and Krus in hand as he leaped up on to the footplate. Nefer took the reins from him and Dov recognized his touch and nickered, looking back at him with her great luminous eyes, with their long dark lashes. Krus arched his neck, and pawed at the ground with one front hoof.

Nefer lifted his right fist high and gave the command: 'March! Forward!'

The ram's horn sounded the advance and he led the van out, rank upon rank. They moved in majestic progress, down between the low breastworks from behind which not a single archer showed himself, out on to the open plain.

Nefer gave another hand signal, and the formations opened. Wheel to wheel the front rank moved forward to meet the great dustcloud that rolled towards them. On the markers he had laid out weeks before, Nefer halted his leading squadron, and let the horses rest while he studied the enemy advance.

Now where the dun dustclouds made a tenuous contact with the grey desert he saw the line of dark spots, and myriad flashes of metal wavering in the heated air. On they came and in the mirage the outlines of the chariots in the front rank of Naja's advance wriggled and changed shape like tadpoles in the depths of a pond.

Then they hardened and took on firm shape, and he could make out the horses and the armoured men on the vehicles behind them.

Meren murmured, 'Sweet Horus be praised. It seems he has committed all his vehicles. He holds no depth of chariots in reserve.'

'They must be desperate for water. His only chance of survival is to break our ranks with a frontal charge and win through to the wells.'

Closer and closer rolled the enemy, and now they could make out the features of the warriors in the front rank, and from their colours and pennants they identified each regiment, and recognized the captains who commanded them.

Two hundred paces away the mighty host rolled to a halt. A vast silence settled over the brooding landscape, broken only by the fretting susurration of the wind. The dust settled like a falling curtain and every detail of both armies was starkly revealed.

From the enemy centre a single chariot pulled forward. Even though dust coated the coachwork the gold leaf gleamed through, and the royal pennant flew above the driver's head. Naja halted less than a hundred paces to the front, so that Nefer recognized the cold, handsome face under the blue war crown.

'Hail, Nefer Seti, puppy of the dog I slew with my own hand!' Naja called in that sonorous voice. Nefer stiffened to hear him confess so openly to regicide. 'Upon my head I wear the crown I took from Tamose as he was dying. In my hand,' he raised the mighty blue sword, 'I carry the brand I took from his craven fist. Will you claim it from me, puppy?'

Nefer felt his hands begin to shake upon the reins and anger rose in a red cloud that obscured his vision.

'Steady!' Meren whispered at his side. 'Do not let him provoke you.'

With a huge effort Nefer forced aside the curtains of rage. He managed to keep his face expressionless, but his voice rang like metal on stone. 'Make ready!' and he lifted his own sword high.

Naja laughed soundlessly, wheeled his own chariot and drove back to his place in the centre of the opposing line.

'March! Forward!' Naja raised the blue sword. His front ranks gathered momentum, rolling towards Nefer's line. 'At the gallop! Charge!' They surged forward in a solid mass.

Nefer stood his ground and let them come on. Naja's

taunts rang in his ears still, and he felt a terrible temptation to abandon his well-laid-out plan, and rush forward to meet Naja head to head and pierce his traitor heart. With a violent effort he put aside the temptation, and lifted his sword. He described three flashing arcs with the blade above his head. His legions responded instantly. Like a flock of birds swerving in full flight or a shoal of fish avoiding the attacking barracuda, they turned as though possessed of a single controlling mind, and raced away over the plain, back the way they had come.

Naja's front rank had braced itself for the impact, but they met no resistance and, like a man stumbling over a step that did not exist, they lost impetus. By the time they had recovered, Nefer had pulled away another hundred paces. Now his squadrons smoothly changed their formation and drew together from extended order into a column of fours.

Naja tore after him, but within three hundred paces his flanks came upon a low stone breastwork that slanted across their front. They could not stop now, so they veered left and right towards their own centre. Like the current of a wide river forced suddenly into the mouth of a narrow rocky gorge they were squeezed together. Wheel snagged wheel, and horse teams were forced to give way to each other. The charge wavered and slowed as chariots and horses jammed into a solid mass.

At that fatal moment, the ram's horns brayed across the field, and at the signal the heads and shoulders of the archers and slingers rose from behind the breastworks on either hand. The arrows were already nocked and now the archers drew and flexed their short recurved bows. They held their aim a moment, choosing their targets with care. The first volley was always the most telling.

The slingers whirled their weapons on high, double-handed to counter the weight of the hard-baked clay balls in the leather pouches at the end of the long straps. They buzzed through the air as they built up a dreadful momentum.

Naja's leading squadrons were deep in the funnel between the breastworks, when the trumpets sang out again and the archers loosed, in a single concerted volley. They had been ordered to aim for the horses, and to pick out the enemy captains. The arrows flew in almost silently, with just the soft whisper of the fletchings through the air, but the range was short, and the strike of the arrowheads into living flesh sounded like a handful of gravel thrown into a mud-bank. The first rank of Naja's charge was shot down, and as the horses fell the chariots piled up over their carcasses, swerving out of control into the stone walls on either hand, or capsizing and rolling.

Then the slingers loosed their missiles with uncanny accuracy. The solid balls of burnt clay were the size of a ripe pomegranate but heavy as ivory. They could crack the skull of man or horse, snap a leg or shatter ribs as though they were dry twigs. They thudded into the next rank of charging chariots, and the havoc they wrought was terrible.

The vehicles that followed were unable to stop the charge, and crashed into the wreckage of those in front. The coachwork crackled and tore with the sound of green branches in a raging bushfire. Some of the long drive-shafts shattered and deadly splinters speared the horses that pulled them. Wheels burst and were torn from their axles. Men were hurled from the cockpits and trampled under the frantic hoofs of the rearing, milling horses.

At the head of his squadron, Nefer gave the hand signal that the men following him were expecting, and a swarm of foot-soldiers leaped out of hiding and dragged away the thornbushes that concealed the openings that had been deliberately left in the stone walls on either hand. In quick succession Nefer's chariots swerved through them and out into the open ground beyond the walls. No longer constricted, they were free to manoeuvre across the plain. They doubled back, circling in behind Naja's trapped squadrons, and falling on their rear echelons.

Now both armies were locked together, like fighting bulls, horn to horn. Not all of Naja's vehicles had been lured into the trap between the walls. There had simply not been enough space for them all to enter at one time. These loose chariots now came rushing forward to engage Nefer, and a traditional chariot battle swiftly developed. Running chariots circled, charged and withdrew, then charged again. The squadrons broke up into smaller units, and across the plain single vehicles viciously engaged each other, wheel to wheel, and man to man.

Despite the frightful losses he had inflicted on the enemy in the opening phase, Nefer was still heavily outnumbered. As the advantage swung back and forth, Nefer was forced to call in more and more of the reserves he had been holding concealed in the wadi behind the fort. Now he signalled in the last of them. He was fully committed. He had brought up every last chariot. But they were not enough. Slowly his horses and his men were being ground down by the sheer numbers of his enemy.

In the dust and clamour and turmoil, Nefer desperately searched the plain for Naja's golden chariot and the royal red pennant. He knew that if he could force Naja to single combat and kill him, he could still carry the day. But there was no sign of him. Perhaps he had been cut down in the defile between the walls, perhaps he was lying wounded or dead somewhere in the confusion of the battle.

Close by Nefer saw Hilto's chariot hemmed in by two of the enemy, and the old warrior wounded and thrown to earth. Hilto's squadron saw him go down, and broke up in confusion. Nefer felt the cold hand of despair squeeze his heart. They were losing the battle.

He saw a line of Red chariots circle out then sweep around behind the backs of his archers and slingers along the breastworks, and cut them down with arrows and javelins. The foot-soldiers scattered and fled, a screaming rabble, and their despair was infectious. Grimly Nefer remembered that Taita called it the 'little bird effect – when one flies they all fly.'

Nefer knew that his army would soon be in rout, and he shouted encouragement to the charioteers close enough to hear him, and tried to rally them by running down another enemy chariot and slaying the crew with a dozen strokes of the sword. Then he wheeled away in pursuit of another Red chariot, but by now Dov and Krus were almost worn out, and the enemy pulled away from them.

Then beside him Meren shouted, 'Look, Pharaoh!' and he pointed to the east out into the desert. With the back of his hand Nefer wiped his own sweat and splashes of enemy blood from his face, and stared out into the glare.

He knew then beyond all doubt that it was over, and that they had lost the battle. A fresh mass of enemy chariots was tearing in towards them. Where they had suddenly come from Nefer could not fathom. He had thought that Naja had committed all his vehicles. That did not matter now, for the battle was lost.

'How many?' Nefer wondered, with black desolation filling his soul.

'Two hundred,' Meren guessed. 'Maybe more.' His voice was resigned. 'It is all over, Pharaoh. We will die fighting.'

'One last charge.' Nefer shouted to the chariots nearest to him, 'On me the Blues! Death with glory.'

They cheered him hoarsely and wheeled in on either side of him. Even Dov and Krus seemed imbued with new strength, and the thin line of Blue chariots tore in at the new foe, going to meet them head to head. As they closed they saw that the leading enemy chariot flew the pennant of a general, a centurion.

'By Horus, I know him,' Meren cried. 'It's Prenn, the old sodomite.'

So close were they now that Nefer also recognized the gaunt figure, with the black patch over one eye. He had seen him on the staff of King Apepi, in the temple at Perra when they had met to negotiate the treaty of Hathor. The same wondrous day that he had first laid eyes on Mintaka.

'His arrival is untimely,' Nefer said grimly, 'but perhaps we can save the next generation of young boys from his amorous attentions.'

He steered Dov and Krus straight at Prenn, trying to force him to swerve and offer a flank shot for his javelin throw. But as they came closer together, Meren shouted, startled, 'He flies the Blue!' Prenn's pennant was streaming back, directly away from them, which was why Nefer had not noticed it until this moment, but Meren was right: Prenn was flying the Blue of the House of Tamose, and all his chariots with him.

Now Prenn slowed and held his right arm across his chest in salute to Nefer, and he shouted in a great voice that carried above the rumble of the chariot wheels, 'Hail, Pharaoh! May you live ten thousand years, Nefer Seti.'

In amazement Nefer lowered the javelin he had been about to hurl, and checked his horses.

'What are your orders, Pharaoh?' Prenn shouted.

'What strange business is this, General Prenn? Why do you call on me for orders?' Nefer called back.

'The Princess Mintaka delivered to me your message, and I have come to place myself under your command and to help you avenge the murders of King Apepi and Pharaoh Tamose.'

'Mintaka?' Nefer was confused, for surely she was still closeted in the sanctuary of the temple in Avaris. But then his warrior instincts took over, and he thrust aside those thoughts. There would be time for such musing later. 'Well met, General Prenn. You arrive none too soon. Lay your chariot alongside mine and we will sweep this field from end to end.'

They charged side by side, and Nefer's broken and scattered legions saw the blue pennants coming and heard the war-cry, 'Horus and Nefer Seti!' and the blaring of the ram's horn trumpets, and they took new heart. The Red squadrons of Naja Kiafan were in hardly better case and could offer only scant resistance as Prenn's fresh troops charged into them. They fought on for a while, but the heart was torn out of them. Some scrambled out of their chariots to kneel in the dust, hands raised in surrender, begging for quarter and shouting the praises of Nefer Seti. Their behaviour was infectious and spread across the battlefield, as the Red charioteers threw down their swords and knelt.

Nefer quartered across the field, searching for Naja. In his heart he knew that the victory would not be complete until he had avenged his father's murder. He came back towards the stone breastworks where last he had seen Naja at the head of his charge. He rode through the debris and detritus of battle, the shattered and overturned vehicles, the wounded and dying men and horses, the scattered corpses. Although most of the enemy were killed or had surrendered, there were still small isolated groups fighting on. Nefer's men had no mercy on these and cut them down, even when they tried to surrender. Nefer intervened where he could to halt the slaughter, and to protect the prisoners, but his men were mad with battle rage, and scores more died before he could save them.

He reached the stone breastworks and reined in Krus and Dov. From his height on the footplate he could see over the low wall into the narrow defile where he had trapped the forward legions of Naja's army. The smashed chariots were piled upon each other like the wreckage of a fleet thrown upon the rocks by a mighty storm at sea. Some of the horses had struggled to their feet and stood still tethered by the harness to their shattered vehicles. He saw a lovely bay mare standing on three legs with her off-fore broken by a slinger's clay ball, and near her a black stallion with its entrails dangling to the ground from a rent in its belly. Around each chariot lay the dead and the wounded. Some were still moving and weeping, calling to the gods and to their mothers for water and succour. Others sat dazed and slack-jawed with the agony of their wounds. One was trying feebly to pull out the arrow that was lodged deep in his stomach. Nefer looked for Naja's body among the dead, but all was confusion and many were buried in the wreckage. Then he picked out a flash of gold leaf, and the royal standard of Naja Kiafan lying in the dust and the puddles of congealing blood.

'I must find him,' Nefer told Meren. 'I must know he is dead.' He jumped down from the chariot.

'I will help you search.' Meren went to the horses' heads and tethered them to the wall. Nefer vaulted over the breastworks and scrambled over the other wreckage until he reached the golden chariot. It lay on its side, but the cockpit was empty. One of the horses was still alive, but both its front legs were broken, and it lifted its head and looked up at Nefer piteously. He took one of the javelins from the bin on the chassis, and killed the animal with a thrust behind the ear. Suddenly Meren shouted and stooped to pick up something from among the debris. He lifted his trophy high, and Nefer saw that he had found Naja's blue war crown.

'The swine's body must be close,' Nefer called to him. 'He would not have discarded that. It means too much to him.'

'Search beneath his chariot,' Meren called back to him. 'He might be trapped under it. I will help you lift it.' He came towards Nefer, scrambling over the wreckage, and at that moment Nefer caught a flash of movement from the corner of his eye. At the same instant Meren shouted an urgent warning: 'Look out! Behind you!'

Nefer ducked and whirled about. Naja had risen from

where he had been crouching behind the dashboard of the chariot. His shaven head was pale and shiny as an ostrich egg, and his eyes were wild. He still carried the blue sword of Tamose and he launched a double-handed blow at Nefer's head, but Meren's warning had saved him and Nefer ducked under the hissing blade. His own sword was still in the scabbard at his hip, but he carried the javelin with which he had delivered the *coup de grâce* to the maimed horse. Instinctively he thrust at Naja's throat, but Naja was quick as the cobra that was his namesake and twisted aside. This gave Nefer a moment to reach for his own sword, but Naja stepped back and looked about him. He saw Meren coming to Nefer's aid with bared sword, and he saw the empty chariot hitched to the wall with Dov and Krus in the traces. He drove Nefer back with another thrust of the blue blade, then whirled and sprinted away. Nefer hurled the javelin after him, but the thong was not wound on and the throw was wide. Naja reached the wall. As he jumped over it he cut the horses free with a slash of the blue sword and leaped up on to the footplate. He did not have hold of the reins, but he seized the whip from the bin and lashed Krus and Dov across the haunches. Startled, the pair leaped forward together and within half a dozen strides they were both at full gallop.

Behind them Nefer jumped to the top of the wall and saw Naja being carried away across the plain. He drew a long breath and whistled, the high piercing blast that Dov and Krus knew so well. He saw their heads go up, their ears prick and swivel towards him. Then Krus changed gait and swung into a tight turn, and Dov came smoothly round with him. The chariot was flung hard over in the turn and Naja had to clutch at the dashboard to prevent himself being hurled overboard. The pair of horses came pounding back towards where Nefer stood poised on the wall. Naja recovered his balance and held the blue sword at guard, ready to strike out at Nefer as soon as he came within reach. Nefer knew that his own bronze could never stand against that terrible blade. It would be certain death to throw himself on top of a swordsman of Naja's calibre armed with that weapon.

As the horses swept by below him, Nefer leaped lightly on to Krus' back and with his knees steered him out on to the open plain still at full gallop. He glanced back and saw Naja climbing out of the cockpit. He edged out along the drive-shaft to get at Nefer.

Nefer leaned down from Krus' back and with his own blade sliced the knot in the plaited leather rope that hitched the horses to the drive-shaft. The chariot was running free and veered off to one side. Naja's weight drove down the drive-shaft and the end of it dug into the soft earth. The racing vehicle was flicked end over end, and Naja was thrown clear. He struck the ground with his shoulder and even above the sound of hoofs and the shattering woodwork of the chariot, Nefer heard the bone break.

Nefer turned Krus back, and they charged at Naja. He had climbed painfully to his feet and stood swaying, and clutching his damaged right arm across his chest. In his fall he had lost his grip on the hilt of the blue sword. It had spun out of his hand, and ten paces away from where he stood the point had pegged into the earth. The blade still quivered from the impact, and the wondrous blue metal threw slivers of blue light, and the jewelled hilt whipped from side to side.

Naja staggered towards the weapon, but then he saw Krus bearing down on him, and an expression of utter terror turned his face the colour of cold ashes. He turned and started to run.

Nefer leaned from Krus' back, plucked the sword out of the sand, and turned Krus in pursuit of Naja. Naja heard the rising crescendo of hoofbeats behind him, and looked back. The mascara had run down his cheeks like black tears, and terror distorted his features. He knew then that he could not escape the terrible vengeance that was bearing down upon him. He fell to his knees and lifted both hands in supplication. With a slap across the withers and a sharp whistle Nefer brought Krus to a plunging halt before the kneeling figure, jumped down and stood over Naja.

'Mercy!' Naja sobbed. 'I yield to you the double crown and all the kingdom.' He crawled pitifully to Nefer's feet.

'I already have that. I lack only one thing. Vengeance!'

'Mercy, Nefer Seti, in the name of the gods and for the sake of your sister, the goddess Heseret, and the infant she carries in her womb.' Suddenly there was a dagger in his right hand, and he stabbed up viciously at Nefer's groin. Nefer was almost taken in, but he twisted away only just in time, and the point of the dagger snagged in the skirt of his *chiton*. Nefer struck the weapon out of his grasp with a flick of the blue blade.

'I admire your constancy. To the very end you are true to your base nature.' Nefer smiled down on him coldly. 'I grant you the same mercy that you showed my father, Pharaoh Tamose.' He drove the point of the blue sword into the centre of Naja's chest, and it came out between his shoulder-blades. An expression of agonized disbelief played over Naja's face.

'You have defiled this sacred blade. Now I will wash it in your blood,' said Nefer, jerked it free, then drove it in again deeply.

Naja toppled face first into the dust, and drew one more ragged breath, but the air from his lungs bubbled out of the wound between his shoulder-blades and he shuddered and died.

Nefer hitched the body by its heels to the traces that dangled from Krus' harness, then mounted and dragged it back across the field. The cheering followed him, wave upon wave, as he rode up to the gates of the fort. He cut the rope and left Naja's bloody corpse lying in the dust.

'Have the usurper cut into separate parts and send them to be displayed in every nome in this land. Let every citizen of this very Egypt look upon the fruits of regicide and treachery.'

Then he looked up to the figure who stood high upon the watch-tower of the fort, and raised the blood-smeared blue blade to him in salute. Taita lifted his right hand in acknowledgement and there was a flash of dark crimson light from the gemstone upon his finger, Naja's ruby ring.

He was on the tower through the whole day. What part did the Magus play in the battle? Nefer asked himself. Would we have triumphed without his influence? There was no answer, and he put the thought aside. He mounted the ladder to the top of the tower and stood beside Taita. From there he spoke to his men. He thanked them for their duty and their bravery. He promised them their rewards, a share of the plunder to all, and the honours of rank and chains of gold and titles of valour to the captains and centurions.

By the time he had named them all the sun was sinking through a low bank of purple thunderclouds towards the horizon. He ended his speech with a call to prayer: 'I dedicate this victory to the golden Horus, the falcon of the gods,' he cried, and as he prayed there was a strange omen. A fleeting ray of the last sunlight broke through the cloud bank and lit the tower of the fort. It glinted on the blue war crown on Nefer's head and on the blue sword in his hand.

At that same moment there was a wild cry from above: every head lifted and every eye turned towards the sky. A great murmur and sigh went up from the multitude. A royal falcon hovered in the air above the head of Pharaoh, and as they stared in wonder it uttered that strange, haunting sound again, then circled three times, and at last shot away in a straight line on rapid, incisive wingbeats into the darkling eastern sky and was gone in the gloom.

'A blessing from the god,' the soldiers chanted. 'Hail, Pharaoh! Even the gods salute you.'

But as soon as they were alone Taita spoke softly, so no one else outside the room could hear his words. 'The falcon brought a warning and not a blessing.'

'What is the warning?' Nefer demanded quietly, but with deep concern.

'When the bird called, I heard Mintaka cry out,' Taita whispered.

'Mintaka!' Nefer had forgotten her in the exigencies of the battle. 'What did Prenn tell me about her?' He turned to the entrance of the tent and shouted to the guards. 'Prenn! Where is the centurion Prenn?'

Prenn came at once, and knelt before Pharaoh. 'You have earned our deepest gratitude,' Nefer told him. 'Without you we could not have prevailed. Your reward will surpass that of all my other captains.'

'Pharaoh is gracious,'

'At the start of the battle, you spoke of the Princess Mintaka. I thought that she was safe in the temple of Hathor in Avaris. Where did you last see her and when?'

'Pharaoh, you are mistaken. Princess Mintaka is not in the temple. She came to me to bring your message. I could not bring her into battle with me, so I left her two days ago in my camp in the desert, on the road between here and the Khatmia.'

A terrible foreboding seized Nefer. 'Who else did you leave in the same encampment?'

'Some of the other royal women, the Princess Merykara, who had accompanied Mintaka, and Her Majesty Queen Heseret—'

'Heseret!' Nefer sprang to his feet. 'Heseret! If Mintaka and Merykara are in her power, what will she do to them when she hears that I have slain her husband?' He strode to the door of the tent and shouted for Meren. 'Mintaka and Merykara are in terrible jeopardy,' he told him.

'How do you know this?' Meren looked distraught.

'From Prenn. And Taita has read a warning in the cry of the falcon. We must ride at once.'

Heseret awoke in the darkness and chill of that dread time before the dawn when all the world is at its darkest and the human spirit at its lowest ebb. At first she was uncertain of what had interrupted her sleep, but then she became aware of the faint sound of many voices, still far off but growing stronger. She sat up, letting the fur blankets drop to her waist, and tried to make sense of the distant hubbub. She was able to make out words now: 'defeated' and 'slain' and 'flee at once'.

She screamed for her maids and two stumbled in to her, half awake and naked, carrying small oil lamps.

'What is going on?' Heseret demanded, and the eyes of the women were wide and dark with incomprehension.

'We know not, mistress. We were asleep.'

'You stupid girls! Go and find out at once,' Heseret ordered angrily. 'And make certain the prisoners are still in their cage, that they have not escaped.' They fled.

Heseret leapt from her bed. She lit all the lamps, then bound up her hair, pulled on a *chiton* and threw a shawl over her shoulders. All the time the din outside her stockade was growing louder, and now she could hear shouting, and carriages trundling past on the road, but still she made no sense of what was happening.

The two maids came scampering back into the tent. The eldest was breathless and almost incoherent: 'They say there has been a great battle at a place called Ismailiya, Majesty.'

Heseret felt a great surge of joy. Naja had triumphed: in her heart she was certain of it. 'What was the outcome of the battle?'

'We don't know, mistress. We did not ask.'

Heseret seized the girl nearest to her by the hair, and shook her so violently that clumps came away in her hands. 'Have you not a speck of brain in your thick skull?' She slapped her across the face, and left her lying on the floor of the tent. She grabbed a lamp and hurried to the door.

The guards were gone, and she felt the first pangs of fear. She ran to the cart and held up the lamp, peering into the pig cage. Part of her anxiety was allayed as she saw that the two bedraggled figures were still pinioned and tied to the struts at the back of the cage. They looked up at her with pale, dirt-streaked faces.

Heseret left them and ran to the gate of the stockade. In the starlight she made out a dark cavalcade streaming past. She saw the loom of carts and wagons being drawn by teams of oxen. Some were piled high with bales and boxes, others were crowded with women clutching their children. Hundreds of soldiers hurried past on foot and Heseret saw that most had thrown away their weapons.

'Where are you going?' she called to them. 'What is happening?' No one answered her, or even seemed aware of her presence. Heseret ran out into the road and seized the arm of one of the soldiers. 'I am Queen Heseret, wife of the Pharaoh of all Egypt.' She shook his arm. 'Hearken to me, knave!'

The soldier gave a strange barking laugh, and tried to shrug her off. But Heseret held on to his arm with desperate strength, until he struck her a heavy blow and left her lying in the dust of the roadway.

She dragged herself to her feet and picked out another soldier in the passing throng, who wore the collar of a sergeant. She ran to him, with blood dribbling from her nose. 'What news of the battle? Tell me. Oh, please tell me,' she begged. He peered into her face and there was just light enough for him to recognize her.

'The most dire news, Majesty.' His voice was gruff. 'There has been a terrible battle and the enemy has prevailed. Our army has been defeated, and all the chariots destroyed. The enemy comes on apace and will be upon us soon. You must flee at once.'

'What of Pharaoh? What has happened to my husband?'

'They say that the battle is lost and that Pharaoh is slain.'

Heseret stared at him, unable to move or speak.

'Will you come away, Your Majesty?' The sergeant asked. 'Before it is too late. Before the victors arrive, and the plundering and the rapine begin. I will protect you.'

But Heseret shook her head. 'It cannot be true. Naja cannot be dead.' She turned away. She stood alone on the roadside as the sun came up and the routed army still poured past her. This confused and disordered rabble bore no resemblance to the proud host that had assembled before the Blue Gate of Babylon only months before.

There were a few officers among them, and Heseret called to one, 'Where is Pharaoh? What has happened?'

The officer did not recognize her with blood on her face and in her dishevelled garments covered with dust. He shouted back, 'Naja Kiafan was cut down in single combat by Nefer Seti himself, and his corpse hacked into pieces and sent to be displayed publicly in all the nomes of Egypt. The enemy forces are coming on swiftly and will likely be here before noon.'

Heseret let out a keening wail. These details were too vivid for her to doubt longer. She gathered up a double handful of dust and poured it over her head. Still wailing she clawed her face with her own fingernails until fresh blood started and dribbled down her cheeks on to her *chiton*.

Her handmaidens and the captain of her own bodyguard came out of the stockade to fetch her in, but she was maddened with grief and screamed incoherent obscenities at them. She turned her face to the heavens and shouted blasphemy at the gods, blaming them for not protecting her husband who was a far greater god than any other in the pantheon.

Her sobs and screams grew louder, her behaviour wilder and madder. She ripped her own breast with the tiny jewelled dagger she always carried, urinated down her legs, and rolled in the mud she had created. Then suddenly she sprang up and rushed into the stockade. She ran to the pig cage on the cart, and screeched at Merykara through the bars: 'Our husband is dead. Slain by our own monstrous brother.'

'Praise be to Hathor and all the gods,' Merykara cried.

'You blaspheme!' Heseret raved at her. 'Naja Kiafan was a god, and you were his wife.' She was goading herself into deeper madness. 'You should have been a dutiful wife but you deserted him. You brought shame and humiliation upon him.'

'Meren is my husband,' Merykara told her. 'I despise that creature whom you call husband. He murdered our father, and he richly deserves the punishment that Nefer has given him.'

'Meren is a common soldier, and Naja is and was a god.'

Although Merykara's lips were swollen with thirst and sunburn, she forced herself to smile. 'Meren is more a god than Naja ever was. And I love him. He will be here very soon, and you had best set Mintaka and me free before he arrives, or he and Nefer will make you pay dearly for it.'

'Gently, sweet friend,' Mintaka whispered. 'She is mad. Look at her eyes. Do not provoke her. She is capable of any evil now.'

Heseret was far past reason or restraint. 'You love a common soldier?' she demanded. 'You dare compare him to my husband, the Pharaoh of this very Egypt? Then you shall have your fill of soldiers!'

She turned to the captain of her guards. 'Drag the sow from her filthy cage.' The captain hesitated. Merykara's warning haunted him: Nefer and his captains would be here soon.

Heseret gained a semblance of control over her emotions and sanity. 'I order you, Captain, obey me or face the consequences.' Reluctantly he gave the order to his men and they cut the leather thongs that bound Merykara's wrists to the strut, then reached into the door and dragged her out by her feet.

Merykara's hands and feet were blue and swollen where the ropes had restricted the blood-flow, and she could barely support her weight. The exposed skin of her face and limbs had been burned livid by the sun, and her hair hung down over her face in a tangle of knotted curls.

Heseret looked about her quickly and her attention fixed on a loose wheel that had been removed from one of the other wagons for repair. It was propped against the wall of the stockade.

'Bring that wheel here!' she ordered, and two men rolled it to where she indicated. 'Tie the bitch to it. No, not that way. Spreadeagled! With her arms and legs wide open to welcome her soldier lovers.'

They obeyed her, and strapped Merykara's wrist and ankles to the rim of the wheel, like a star fish. Heseret stood in front of her and spat in her face. Merykara laughed at her through cracked lips. 'You are mad, sister. Grief has addled your mind. I pity you, but nothing can bring Naja back to you. When his foul crimes are weighed in the scales of justice the monster at the gates of paradise will devour his black heart and he will pass into oblivion.'

Heseret slashed her across both her cheeks with the point of the dagger, superficial shallow wounds that nevertheless bled copiously. The blood dripped down the front of Merykara's *chiton*. Heseret used the dagger to split the linen cloth. Then with both hands she ripped it open from neck to hem. Merykara was naked under it.

Her body, untouched by the sun, was white and tender. Her breasts were small and tipped with clear pink, her belly was flat and white, and the hair at the base was a silky nest.

Heseret stood back and looked at her guards. 'Which of you will be the first?'

They gaped at the slender naked body on the wheel.

Mintaka called from the cage, 'Be careful what you do! Nefer Seti will be here very soon, and this is his sister.'

Heseret rounded on her. 'Shut your poisonous mouth. You will be next. Ten thousand men are out there, and you will pleasure most of them before this day is through.' She turned back to the men. 'Come, look at this sweet flesh. Will you not have a little taste of it? I can see your prongs growing stiff under your robes.'

'This is madness,' the captain whispered, but he could not tear his eyes from her pale body. 'She is a princess of the royal House of Tamose.'

Heseret grabbed the long spear out of the hand of the nearest soldier and struck him across the back with the shaft. 'Come, corporal, have you no balls? Let us see you plunge deep into this honey-filled hole.'

The man backed away, rubbing the welt across his back. 'You are mad. What punishment would Nefer Seti heap upon my head?' He turned suddenly and bolted from the stockade to join the flood of fleeing refugees in the roadway. His companions hesitated only a moment longer, then one muttered, 'She is mad! I am not waiting for Nefer Seti to arrive and find his sister like this,' and rushed to the gate with his companions hard after him.

Heseret ran after them. 'Come back! I order you!' But they mingled with the crowds and were gone. Heseret ran to a tall Nubian archer who was hurrying past, grabbed his arm and tried to lead him into the stockade. 'Come with me. I know you black animals, you have prongs big as that of a bull elephant and you love to give them employment. I have something that will please you.'

The archer shoved her away violently. 'Leave me, whore! I have no time for your trade now.'

She stared after him as he strode away up the long, congested road, and yelled after him, 'Not me, beast. How dare you insult the Queen of Egypt?'

Weeping and raving she ran back into the stockade. Mintaka called to her from the cage, 'It is over now, Heseret. Calm yourself. Free Merykara, and we will protect you.' She made her voice low and soothing for she knew that Heseret had crossed the borders of sanity and lost herself in the wilderness of dementia.

'I am the Queen of Egypt, and my husband is an immortal god,' Heseret screamed. 'Look at me and fear my beauty and my majesty.' She was covered in blood and filth, and she brandished the spear wildly.

'Please, Heseret,' Merykara added her entreaty, 'Nefer and Meren will be here very soon. They will care for you and protect you.'

Heseret glared at her. 'I need no protection. Don't you understand what I am telling you? I am a goddess, and you are a soldier's whore.'

'Darling sister, you are deranged with grief. Set me free so that I can help you.'

A cunning expression passed over Heseret's face. 'You think I cannot find a male prong to do for you? Well, you are wrong. I have one of my own.' She lifted the long spear and reversed the shaft, so that the blunt end pointed at Merykara. 'Here is your soldier lover, come to claim you.' She advanced on Merykara menacingly.

'No, Heseret!' Mintaka called urgently. 'Leave her be.'

'You will be next, you treacherous bitch. I will deal with you after I have serviced this one.'

'Heseret, no!' Merykara pleaded with her and writhed against her bonds. But Heseret seemed not to hear her, as she placed the shaft of the spear between her spread thighs.

'Sister, you cannot do this. Don't you remember—'

Merykara broke off and her eyes flew wide open with shock and pain.

'There!' said Heseret, she thrust the end of the shaft deeply into her.

'There!' she screamed. 'And there!' Deeper with each thrust, until it slid almost arm's length into her belly and came out smeared with Merykara's blood.

Now both girls were screaming at her, 'Stop! Oh, please stop!' But Heseret kept shoving the shaft into her sister.

'There! Does this satisfy your lust?'

Merykara was pouring blood, but Heseret leaned all her weight on the weapon and thrust it full-length into her. Merykara shrieked for the last time then sagged against her bonds. Her chin dropped forward on to her naked chest.

Heseret left the shaft buried in her slim pale body, and stepped back. She stared at what she had done with a bemused expression. 'It was your fault. Don't blame me. It was my duty. You behaved like a whore. I treated you like a whore.' She began to weep again and wring her hands. 'It doesn't matter. Nothing matters any more. Naja is dead. Our dearly beloved husband is dead . . .'

Dazed as a sleep-walker she went to her tent and into the luxuriously appointed but deserted interior. She pulled off the blood- and urine-soaked *chiton* and dropped in the centre of the floor, then she picked another robe at random from the pile in the corner, and pulled sandals on to her feet.

'I am going to find Naja,' she said, with sudden resolve. Quickly she gathered a few items and stuffed them into a leather satchel. Then with new determination she headed for the door.

As she stepped out into the early sunlight, Mintaka called to her from the cage. 'Please release me, Heseret. I must tend your little sister. She is badly wounded. In all charity, let me go to her.'

'You don't understand.' Heseret shook her head wildly. 'I have to go to my husband, the Pharaoh of all Egypt. He needs me. He has sent for me.'

She did not glance at Mintaka again but hurried out of the stockade, shaking her head and muttering incoherently to herself. She turned towards the west, in the opposite direction from the flood of terrified humanity, and started to run back towards Ismailiya and Egypt.

Mintaka heard her scream once more, 'Wait for me, Naja, my one true love. I am coming. Wait for me!' and then her ravings faded with distance.

Mintaka struggled against her bonds, twisting and tugging, bracing her bare feet against the struts of the cage to give herself better purchase. She felt the skin smearing from her wrists, and warm blood dripping down her hands and her fingers, but the leather thongs were tight and strong and she could neither stretch nor snap them. She felt her hands becoming numb from lack of blood. Whenever she rested from her struggle her eyes went to Merykara's limp body on the wheel. She called to her, 'I love you, my darling. Meren loves you. Don't die. For our sakes, please don't die.' But Merykara's eyes were wide open and her stare was fixed. Soon her eyeballs began to dry out and glaze over with a thin film of dust, and the flies swarmed busily over them and drank from the puddle of blood between her legs.

Once Mintaka heard a stealthy scuffle at the entrance to the tent and when she twisted her head she saw Heseret's two maids creeping out of the tent. They were each carrying a large bag crammed with valuables they had looted. Mintaka called to them, 'Please set me free. You shall have your freedom and a great reward.' But they glanced at her with startled, guilty expressions, scurried from the stockade and out into the road to join the retreating rabble of the defeated army passing eastwards.

Later there were voices at the gate and Mintaka was on the point of crying out. In time she recognized the coarse accents, and managed to check herself. Four men crept cautiously into the stockade. By their features, dress and talk, she knew they were ruffians of the lowest sort, probably members of those gangs of jackals and scavengers that followed every army for loot and pickings. She let her head sag, and feigned death.

The men stopped to examine Merykara's body. One laughed and made such an obscene remark that Mintaka squeezed her eyelids closed, and forced herself to hold her tongue with the greatest difficulty.

Then they came to her cage and peered in at her. She lay completely still and held her breath. She knew what a dreadful appearance she must have, and she tried to play dead.

'This one stinks like a sow,' one remarked. 'I would rather have it with Mistress Palm and her five daughters.' They all guffawed at the jest, then scattered to ransack the camp for loot. After they had crept away, carrying what they could, Mintaka watched the shadows lengthen across the beaten earth of the stockade floor, while outside the sounds of passing wagons and carts and people on foot slowly diminished. Just before sunset the last of them passed, and the silence of the desert and the dead settled over the camp.

During the night Mintaka dozed at times, overtaken by exhaustion and pervading despair. Whenever she started awake she saw Merykara's pale body stretched out in the silver moonlight and the terrible cycle of her grief began again.

The dawn came and the sun rose, but the only sound was the soughing of the desert wind through the branches of the scrawny thorn tree at the gate, and at times her own sobs. But these grew softer and weaker as another day passed without water.

Then she heard something else, a distant murmur that grew into a soft rumble, and she knew it was the sound of wheels coming on at speed – chariots, for she could hear the hoofbeats now and the sound of men's voices growing stronger, and stronger still, until she could recognize one. 'Nefer!' She tried to scream his name, but her voice was a draughty whisper. 'Nefer!'

Then she heard shouts of horror and dismay, and she twisted her head slowly and saw Nefer storm through the gateway, Meren and Taita close behind him.

Nefer saw her at once, and ran to the cage. He tore the gate off its hinges with his bare hand then pulled his dagger from its sheath to slash loose the leather thongs from her wrists. Gently he drew her out of the stinking cage and held her to his chest. He was weeping as he carried her into the tent.

'Merykara!' she whispered, through cracked and swollen lips.

'Taita will see to her, but I fear it is too late.' Mintaka looked back over his shoulder and saw that Taita and Meren between them had cut Merykara free from the wheel and drawn the blood-clotted weapon from her body. Now they were spreading a clean white linen sheet over her body, covering the terrible mutilations.

Mintaka shut her eyes. 'I am exhausted by sorrow and grief but, my darling, your face is the most beautiful and welcome sight I have ever beheld. Now I will rest awhile.' And she slumped into unconsciousness.

Mintaka came awake slowly as though she were rising up from the depths of that dark and terrible pit where demons live.

When she opened her eyes the demons that had haunted her dreams fled away, and she saw with immense relief the two most beloved faces in her world. Taita sat at one side of her couch and Nefer at the other.

'How long?' she asked. 'How long was I gone?'

'A day and a night,' Taita answered her. 'I gave you of the Red Shepenn flower.' She raised her hand to her face and found a thick coating of salve upon it. She rolled her head towards Nefer, and whispered, 'I am ugly.'

'No!' he replied. 'You are the most beautiful woman I have ever laid eyes upon, and I love you past the counting of it.'

'You are not angry with me for disobeying you.'

'You have given me a crown and a land.' He shook his head and one of his tears fell upon her face. 'Above that you have given me your love, which is more precious to me than all of that. How could I ever be angry with you?'

Taita rose softly and left the tent, and they stayed together all the rest of that day, speaking softly to each other.

In the evening Nefer sent for the others. When they had gathered around Mintaka's couch, Nefer looked at their faces gravely and saw that all of them were there: Taita and Meren, Prenn, Socco and Shabako moving stiffly from the pain of his wounds garnered on the battlefield of Ismailiya.

'You have come to see justice done,' he told them, then turned to the guards at the door.

'Bring in the woman named Heseret,' he ordered.

Mintaka started and tried to sit up, but he pushed her gently back upon the bolster.

'Where? How did you find her?'

'Our pickets found her wandering in the desert on the road back to Ismailiya,' Nefer explained. 'At first they did not recognize her or believe her claims to be a queen. They thought her a mad woman.'

Heseret came into the tent. Nefer had allowed her to bathe and provided her with fresh raiment, and Taita had treated the cuts and grazes on her face and body. Now she shrugged off the hands of her guards and looked around her with a regal lift of her chin. 'Prostrate yourselves before me,' she ordered the men who faced her. 'I am a queen.'

No one moved, and Nefer said, 'Bring her a stool.'

When she was seated upon it, he stared at her so coldly that Heseret covered her face and started to weep. 'You hate me,' she blubbered. 'Why do you hate me?'

'Mintaka shall tell you why,' he answered, and turned to the girl on the couch. 'Please describe to us the manner of the death of Princess Merykara.'

Mintaka spoke for almost an hour, and during all that time no one in the tent moved or uttered a sound, except to gasp and exclaim in horror at the most dreadful parts of what they were hearing. At the end Nefer looked at Heseret. 'Do you deny any part of this testimony?'

Heseret returned his cold stare. 'She was a whore, and she brought shame on my husband, the Pharaoh of Egypt. She deserved death. I am pleased and proud that I was able to be the instrument of justice.'

'Even now I might have forgiven you,' Nefer said softly, 'if you had shown a grain of remorse.'

'I am a queen. I am above your petty laws.'

'You are a queen no longer,' Nefer replied, and she looked confused.

'I am your own sister. You would not harm me.'

'Merykara was your sister also. Did you spare her?'

'I know you well, Nefer Seti. You will not harm me.'

'You are right, Heseret. I will not harm you. But there is

one who will not scruple.' He turned to his assembled captains. 'It is the ancient law of the rights of the one most injured. Stand forth, Meren Cambyses.'

Meren rose and stepped forward. 'Pharaoh, I am your man.'

'You were betrothed to the Princess Merykara. Yours is the greatest injury. I give into your keeping the body and the life of Heseret Tamose, who was a princess of the royal house of Egypt.'

Heseret began to scream as Meren placed a golden chain around her neck: 'I am a queen and a goddess, you dare not harm me.'

No one took notice of her cries, and Meren looked at Nefer. 'Your Majesty, do you place any restriction upon me? Do you urge or order me to show mercy and compassion?'

'I give her to you without reservation. Her life is yours.'

Meren loosened the sword in its sheath on his hip, and pulled Heseret to her feet with the chain. He dragged her blubbering and wailing from the tent. Nobody followed them.

They sat in silence, and through the linen walls listened to Heseret's wailing, entreaties and blandishments. Then there was a sudden silence and they steeled themselves. They heard a high, piercing shriek that ended as abruptly as it had started.

Mintaka covered her face with both hands and Nefer made the sign against evil with his right hand. The others coughed, and moved restlessly.

Then the curtains at the entrance parted and Meren stepped back into the tent. In his right hand he carried the naked sword and in the other a dreadful object. 'Your Majesty,' he said, 'justice has been done.' By its dense hair-tresses he held high the severed head of Heseret, the wife of Naja Kiafan, the false pharaoh.

It was five more days before Mintaka had recovered sufficiently to begin the long journey back to Avaris. Even then Taita and Nefer insisted that she be carried in a litter to ease the jolting and lurching over the rough road that lay ahead. They travelled slowly, and it was fifteen days later that they reached the escarpment and looked down from the arid wastes upon the wide green valley of the Nile.

Nefer helped Mintaka from the litter, and together they walked a short way from the road, so that they could be alone and savour to the full this joyous moment of homecoming. They had not been there long when Nefer stood up and shaded his eyes.

'What is it, my heart?' Mintaka asked.

'We have visitors,' he said, but when she exclaimed with annoyance at the intrusion he went on, 'These visitors are always welcome.'

She smiled then as she recognized the two mismatched figures approaching them. 'Taita. And Meren! But what strange attire is this?'

They were both dressed in simple robes and sandals, and slung on their backs they carried the leather satchels of holy men on a pilgrimage.

'We have come to say our farewells, and to take our leave of you,' Taita explained.

'You will not leave me now.' Nefer was dismayed. 'Will you not attend my coronation?'

'You were crowned upon the field of Ismailiya,' Taita told him gently.

'Our wedding!' Mintaka cried. 'You must stay for our wedding.'

'You were married long since,' Taita smiled, 'perhaps on the day of your birth, for the gods intended you for each other.'

'But you, my brother of the Red Road and my dearest friend,' Nefer turned to Meren, 'what about you?'

'There is nothing more for me here, now that Merykara is gone. I must go with Taita.'

Nefer knew that there was nothing further to say, that more words would degrade this moment. He did not even ask where they were going. Perhaps they did not know themselves.

He embraced them and kissed them, and he and Mintaka stood and watched them walk away, and their distant shapes slowly dwindle in size in the shimmering wastes of the desert wilderness, and they shared the same deep ache of regret and bereavement.

'They have not really gone,' Mintaka whispered, when at last they had disappeared from view.

'No,' Nefer agreed. 'They will always be with us.'

With the high priestess and fifty acolytes from the temple of Hathor preceding her, the Princess Mintaka Apepi came for her marriage to Pharaoh Nefer Seti.

They stood together on the terrace of the palace of Thebes that overlooked the broad brown flow of the Nile in flood, in the season most propitious to all living things in the land of this very Egypt.

Mintaka had long since recovered from her injuries and her ordeal. Her beauty was fully restored, and in this joyous moment seemed to be enhanced ten-fold.

It seemed that all of Egypt had come to bear witness to the nuptials. The crowds stretched back along both banks of the river as far as the eye could see. When the couple embraced and broke the jars of Nile water, the shout that went up to heaven must have startled the gods themselves. Then Nefer Seti led his new queen out by the hand and showed her beauty to the populace, who fell to their knees, and wept and cried aloud their loyalty and their love.

Suddenly a silence fell over this vast congregation and slowly every eye turned upwards to the tiny speck in the vaulted sky above the palace.

In the silence there was the wild lonely cry of a royal falcon and the bird began its stoop out of the high blue. In the end, just as it seemed it must come into violent collision, the falcon flared its wings wide and hovered over the tall figure of Pharaoh. Nefer lifted his right arm and held it out, and softly as a feather the magnificent bird alighted upon his fist.

A sound like the sea on a stormy day rose from ten thousand throats as they greeted the miracle. But Nefer's eyes fell on the thin loop of pure gold that was fastened about the bird's right foot above the great hooked talons. Engraved into the precious metal was a symbol that made Nefer's heart race as he recognized it.

'The royal cartouche!' he whispered. 'This was never a wild bird. This is Nefertem, my father's falcon. That is why it came to me so often in times of greatest danger, to warn and guide me. It was always my father's spirit.'

'And now Nefertem has come to affirm before all the world that you are king indeed.' Mintaka stood closer to him and gazed into his face with eyes that glowed with pride and love.

AUTHOR'S NOTE

I ask my readers to remember that *Warlock* is a work of fiction. Many of the places that I have written about do exist, but the others never did – or at least those like Avaris have long ago been lost and forgotten. Gallala is another case in point. Taita's spring dried up a thousand years ago and another earthquake destroyed the city and buried the ruins.

Likewise, most of my characters are fictitious – even Taita lives on only in my imagination.

Wilbur Smith